MARK DONOHUE

MARK DONOHUE
TECHNICAL EXCELLENCE AT SPEED

MICHAEL ARGETSINGER

FOREWORD BY ROGER PENSKE / DESIGN BY TOM MORGAN

DAVID BULL PUBLISHING

We recognize that some words, model names, and
designations mentioned in this book are the property of
the trademark holder. We use them only for identification
purposes.

Library of Congress Control Number: 2009920752

ISBN: 978 1 935007 02 9

David Bull Publishing, logo, and colophon are trademarks of
David Bull Publishing, Inc.

Book and cover design: Tom Morgan, Blue Design, Portland,
Maine (www.bluedes.com)

Printed in the United States

10 9 8 7 6 5 4 3 2 1

David Bull Publishing
4250 East Camelback Road
Suite K150
Phoenix, AZ 85018

602-852-9500
602-852-9503 (fax)

www.bullpublishing.com

Return

Foreword

BY ROGER PENSKE

Mark Donohue was the catalyst for all that we have achieved at Penske Racing. When I look at the 300-plus victories and what we've been able to accomplish, I remember that it was Mark who set the standard.

The first time I remember being aware of Mark was a day in 1960 at Lime Rock, in Connecticut, when Jay Signore told me I should watch this guy run in his Courier. Mark made an immediate impression and I started to follow his career closely. Walt Hansgen, who was a great friend and a driver I admired enormously, had taken an interest in Mark and was a strong advocate for him. When Walt died, it happened to be a time when I was putting a team together to run a Group 7 Lola in the USRRC and Can-Am. At Walt's funeral I talked to Mark and invited him to come see me at my Chevrolet dealership in Philadelphia, to discuss my plans. We clicked immediately; without him, it would have been very difficult to get my racing program off the ground.

Mark was my partner and best friend through that time. I was trying to work and keep my business going and we kind of grew together. I would be at the shop when I could, but he'd be there all the time. I remember when he lived above the offices at the Newtown Square race shop. He would work day and night to be certain the car was completely prepared for a race. He was so committed.

Mark and I had a similar vision of what we wanted the team to be, and Penske Racing never strayed from that original mission. "Let's hire the best people and treat them like we're all one organization"—that was the core of our mutual view. Mark saw himself as being as low on the totem pole as the guy who drove the truck; that was the way he wanted it to be, a very flat organization. There was nothing too large or too small for Mark to undertake. He personified the attitude of "whatever it takes" when approaching a goal. He was personally involved with and cared about each individual on the team. If you needed anything he would come to your home and help you. We would all sit together and talk, and ask, "What can we do to be better?"

As an engineer he brought technical expertise to the team, and he had tremendous versatility in developing cars—from a sophisticated Formula or Can-Am car to a Trans-Am sedan. And with his intensity and willingness to commit, he could drive them as fast as anyone.

It was Mark who cultivated that egalitarian attitude and team spirit. There have never been any big shots at Penske Racing. "I'll drive the truck"—"I'll do whatever is needed"—we are all that way. Everyone here has that kind of commitment to the organization. We don't have a lot of turnover; we still have many long-term employees who have been here 10, 20, 30 years. Mark set the tone for that. He was entirely dedicated, and others responded in kind.

Mark was understated when he won—he would have preferred not to go to the winner's circle if he didn't have to. His attitude was, "We were competitive today: we won the race." But I think he was already getting ready for the next race on his cool-off lap.

I believe Mark was the prototype for the new breed of what I call the American race driver of today. The best driver isn't the one who can lift the most in the weight room—although Mark understood the importance of physical fitness and pursued it with characteristic discipline—it's the one who understands what is needed technically. There is no question in my mind that he was underrated as a driver, but then you need only look at his record to see that. It was tremendous.

I couldn't be happier that this book has been written to celebrate my friend and colleague's life. For those who remember Mark, this book will revive fond memories of his performances and his sense of humor, while offering a great deal of insight into the driver they thought they knew. For a new generation of race fans, this book presents the opportunity to be introduced to a remarkable man.

Roger Penske
November, 2008

Introduction

Blessed is he whose fame does not outshine his truth.
—Rabindranath Tagore

Automobile racing in the 1960s and 1970s produced many legendary drivers remembered for their skill and bravery. Among these great figures the name Mark Donohue resonates deeply. Donohue was a new breed of race driver, one whose speed and versatility were matched by an inquisitive, analytical mind and a relentless work ethic. Handsome, the product of a loving family, private schools, and an Ivy League college, Donohue was also a master of the practical joke, with a friendly demeanor and perfect manners. Together, these qualities made him a favorite with fans and the media, and a role model for countless other drivers.

Mark Donohue's record was exceptional: He won a remarkable 38 percent of all the races he entered. Though best known as a road racer, his versatility also made him competitive on ovals, with his most famous victory coming at the Indianapolis 500 in 1972. He won national championships during his amateur sports-car days, and later dominated the popular Trans-Am sedan series from the late 1960s to the early 1970s, winning championships driving Chevrolet Camaros and AMC Javelins. His limited appearances in NASCAR included a win in a Cup race. In 1973 he won the Canadian-American Challenge Cup (Can-Am) title at the wheel of the iconic Porsche 917-30, and after winning the inaugural International Race of Champions (IROC) in early 1974, he retired at the pinnacle of his sport. Donohue's career had also included a one-race foray into Formula One in 1971, where he debuted with an impressive podium finish. He came out of retirement to pursue the Formula One World Championship in 1975. His death that year at the Austrian Grand Prix left the world of sports in shock and mourning.

Mark displayed great skill and maturity from his earliest days in racing, but 1966 was the year when his talent came to the fore driving the factory Ford GT40 and a Lola T70 for Roger Penske's new team in the Can-Am. He arrived on the public stage at the precise time that racing was turning a fresh page, gaining popular recognition that went beyond the hard-core enthusiast level.

Mark rapidly achieved superstar status within the racing world, and soon his name was known even by the average man on the street. If he was aware of this, he did a great job of not letting it show. He was what everyone wanted to be. Men not only admired his talent, but also his cool demeanor and self-control. Women loved his "sweet smile" and boyish good looks. With impeccable manners and a quick wit, he attracted loyal friends and supporters effortlessly. His appeal was strongest on a one-to-one basis, as Mark always seemed genuinely interested in the person he was talking to. That impression was correct; Mark liked people and gave each personal encounter his full attention.

I became interested in writing about Mark while completing my first book, a biography of Walter Hansgen (*Walt Hansgen: His Life and the History of Post-War American Road Racing*). Hansgen was an influential figure in Donohue's life, both encouraging his younger friend and using his influence to open opportunities for career advancement.

My personal connection to Mark, while slight, was sufficient to impress me with his character and unique qualities. In my research I discovered that over the years his story had largely been reduced to myth and misunderstanding. It was clear that an independent book was needed on this great figure from American racing history. His own book, *The Unfair Advantage*—co-authored by Paul Van Valkenburgh from tapes dictated by Mark—was originally published in 1975 and quickly sold out, soon becoming very hard to find. Twenty-five years later his sons, Michael and David, made the story available to a new generation of enthusiasts with a second edition from Bentley Publishing. Although not an autobiography, *The Unfair Advantage* stands on its own as a valuable piece of motorsports history. Van Valkenburgh told me that he and Mark considered it a technical autobiography. I think that is an excellent description.

This new book is the product of more than three years' research and relates Mark's story with a perspective and insight only possible with the passage of more than a third of a century since his death. The diverse voices that inform this biography come from those who knew Mark, including his loving family and friends, insider members of his race teams, professional journalists, fellow drivers who raced and competed alongside him, as well as race fans. The story recounts the earliest influences that shaped his character and places in context the importance of his achievements and contributions. His own book, organized on a chassis-to-chassis basis, recounts his experiences developing each car. While fascinating for its technical detail, the book makes little attempt to place in play the people and events that formed the backdrop and provided the stage for his accomplishments. Nor does it convey the hectic pace Mark kept as he competed in different series that often had race meetings scheduled on the same weekend and required extensive travel in North America and Europe.

For this book I have chosen a traditional linear biographical model that allows me to tell Mark's story as it progressed. I have also attempted to reconcile many of the errors of fact, time, and place inherent to a firsthand oral record. In *The Unfair Advantage* Mark was speaking into a tape recorder and in most cases recalling events of years before. It was inevitable that some confusion resulted from overlapping memories of races, cars, people, and places.

The Donohue family made the unedited original tapes that were used to create *The Unfair Advantage* available to me for my research. Hearing the story in Mark's own words is a powerful experience, and the quantity of previously unpublished material from these tapes was an exciting discovery for this biographer. The quotations from Mark in this book are drawn from the tapes unless otherwise indicated.

During Mark Donohue's time, racing was enjoying an era when increasingly powerful engines and rapid technical advances converged to make the driver the dominant factor in what made a car fast. This was particularly true for the type of driver-engineer epitomized by Mark. The "black arts" of car setup and chassis tuning were still evolving, and Mark was among the select few who were making the discoveries.

Don Cox, one of many outstanding engineers who worked with Mark, provides an insight into the unique talents Donohue brought to Penske Racing. "Mark was tenacious—he would do whatever it took to make the cars work," Cox says. "He could tell the engineers what the car was or wasn't doing, and we had a place to begin to look. He was totally involved—he was involved in the lives of the people in the shop, in team logistics, in equipment, and most importantly in every aspect of the race car itself. This was not the norm for other top drivers. Even though it did set the tone for later drivers, none ever had the day-to-day involvement in the total workings from the shop management on through as did Mark."

But Mark's well-earned reputation for testing and development has left him underrated today as a driver. He was blazingly fast, and the speed was there from his earliest days. When he began racing in SCCA he was immediately successful in the highly competitive production-car classes. Having attracted the attention of racing's elite, he broke into professional racing with the support of his mentor, Walt Hansgen, and became a full-time professional with Roger Penske's team. Fellow race drivers knew that Mark's success came more from his driving skill than from his much-touted engineering ability.

"Mark was a better race driver than people ever gave him credit for," says Bobby Unser. "Everybody thinks today that the engineering he did and the Penske money was the answer, but I'm going to tell you something—the cat could drive. I mean, he was fast. And he would do it lap after lap after lap. He was quicker than bejeezus."

Hurley Haywood puts Mark's talent in perspective. "Mark never gave himself very much credit as a driver," says Haywood. "He was a great talent, but he always liked to say he wasn't much as a driver and that it was engineering skill that made him quick. He was masterful in that and many people have emulated him. Many people wanted to adapt to that mold of the driver-engineer approach that Mark perfected.

"Mark understood the need to have a good car under him in order to showcase his talent," continues Haywood. "The best driver is not going to shine in a bad car. That's why he was so intent on the engineering side. Because he found the way to have a really good car most of the time should not detract from the fact that he was also a great driver."

Mark was the accessible hero who, even at the height of his popularity, would make himself available to people—and not just with a "Hello, nice to meet you." The superstar never behaved like one. At Nassau, after one of his earliest major victories, Mark was so busy satisfying every person eager for his autograph and a friendly word that at the end of the day, he was quite literally the last person at the track, hitchhiking back to town on a garbage truck. He engendered fervent loyalty among flaggers and other track workers. He spent time with them at post-race worker parties where he made genuine friends. He never patronized—he was, in spirit, one with them. When it all happened for Mark it happened fast, and he never lost his sense of wonder in it all.

His public persona was restrained, projecting a serious nature with an emphasis on matters technical. Those closest to him knew a different man. Associated Press motorsports editor Jerry Garrett was among the insiders, and described

Mark this way: "He was endlessly charming, charismatic, hilariously profane, mischievous to an almost unthinkable degree, a world-class practical joker, and (once the crew cut was gone) dangerously attractive to the opposite sex."

The media dubbed him "Captain Nice," but there was a great deal more to Mark Donohue. He was a complicated man with passions and life influences that gave him far greater depth than the word "nice" allows. He was extremely smart, and while comfortable in public, he was essentially shy and reserved. He could display extreme competitiveness and self-absorption, and was capable of selfishness in pursuit of a goal. Mark was a tireless worker and would literally do whatever it took to make a given project work. This demanding nature created tremendous pressure, both for himself and for those nearest to him, and he paid an extreme price in his personal life for his single-mindedness.

One cannot overstate the impact Donohue had on an entire generation. He captured the imagination of the average race fan and the dedicated racer alike, and opened up a new approach to the sport. If you worked hard enough at it, prepared well, and "did it like Mark," you just knew it could happen for you. That's why Mark Donohue's incredible legacy lives on: His talent and drive continue to inspire.

MICHAEL ARGETSINGER

It Was a Sport

Do not despise the bottom rungs in the ascent to greatness.

—PUBLILIUS SYRUS

CHAPTER 1:

An Exceptional Family

The remarkable impact Mark Donohue had on people—even those who never met him personally—came from a very genuine source. He was, at his core, the kind person he seemed. But how did it begin? Where did his intensity and competitiveness, allied with an essential goodness and generosity—even in the face of life-changing success—come from? There's no doubt that Mark's supportive and loving family played a huge role in making him the man he became.

"Mark's father was the finest man I have ever known," says Mark's brother-in-law, Dan Wulff. "It is no surprise that his son grew up to be the caliber of man he was." When Mark was born on March 18, 1937, the first child of Mark and Hazel Donohue, Mark Sr. was a successful patent attorney in Manhattan. A partner in the law firm of Brumbaugh, Graves, Donohue & Raymond, representing the cream of Fortune 500 companies, his clients were said to adore him. Mr. Donohue enjoyed great respect within his profession and was an influential figure in the New York State Bar Association.

Although Mark Sr. possessed natural charm and grace and was widely admired, success hadn't just fallen into his lap. He worked as a railroad conductor to put himself through school, graduating from the University of Delaware and Harvard Law School. "To embellish on this man's character would be to steal from him," says Wulff. Mark Neary Donohue Sr. was born on January 18, 1905, in Delaware, the son of Mike Donohue, an Irish immigrant who became a success in road construction and waste reclaiming businesses. Mike Donohue made his start collecting garbage with horses in the city of Wilmington. Later he established a construction company specializing in driving pilings for roads through the marshes.

Mark's mother, Hazel—known to all as Zilly—was a remarkable woman. Born December 1, 1903, in Choptank, on Maryland's eastern shore, Hazel Wright graduated in 1923 from Maryland State Normal School in Towson, Maryland, and was a teacher when she met Mark Neary Donohue. She went into school administration, and as the supervisor of schools for Prince George County, Maryland, was the first woman in the state to be a superintendent of schools.

Family lore had it that Zilly and Mark Sr. met at a dance and were immediately smitten. The romance was initially complicated, as Mark and a friend had switched names as a joke; when he phoned Zilly she initially refused to go out with him, thinking it was the other fellow. The story continues that later Mark deliberately drove his car into a ditch, declaring he would not budge until she agreed to marry him.

After their marriage, the couple moved to Summit, New Jersey, and Hazel taught elementary school in Maplewood for many years. She had a genuine love of children and a passion for teaching. "Hazel was the greatest—the most outgoing lady," remembers her son-in-law Dan Wulff. "She had so many talents—she could write, she could tell a story; she wrote a children's book of stories she remembered from her childhood."

Mark Neary Donohue Jr. was named for his father. When his sisters Nancy and Mary Ellen were born November 2, 1939, and on February 6, 1945, respectively, Mark soon became the much loved and admired big brother in the Donohue household at 68 Valley View Avenue in Summit.

Mary Ellen's husband Dan Wulff believes that the Donohue family was exceptional for combining great fun and spirit with exemplary values. "The thing is that they were all so bright, so vital, and each possessed unique insight into people's character. I was just a young kid, and a pretty wild one at that, when Mary Ellen introduced me to the family. Mr. Donohue could have thrown me out. He seemed to have an intuitive sense of the man I would become." Dan Wulff has never forgotten Mark Sr. telling him, "I don't think you'll ever let us down."

St. Theresa's Church in Summit helped shape Mark's life. He was baptized there, and at age seven received his First Holy Communion. Harold A. Murray, a priest who taught Mark in the parish school, remembered Mark as "a very human person," and recalled serious conversations between the two about a religious vocation. Though it would not be the direction Mark chose, the men remained friends throughout Mark's life.

The Donohues were devout Catholics and never missed Mass. They lived their religion but were not hesitant to challenge the priests' secular views. At the height of the Vietnam War, Father McGovern, delivering his Sunday sermon at St. Theresa's—the church the Donohues had been married in—was railing against the war. Dan Wulff recalls the dignified Mr. Donohue, a man well over six feet tall, standing up and interrupting the priest to state clearly, "The pulpit is no place to discuss politics." It was seemingly totally out of character for this consummate gentleman, but Mr. Donohue had heard enough.

Beth Boyle, a close friend of Mary Ellen's, remembers the Donohue family qualities as well. "They were extremely intelligent. Mary Ellen could see through to the heart of things that would take a year for most people to grasp."

Dan Wulff believes that they were just an exceptional family. "They were all so smart—they took people just as they were; they cared not about who you were or your background, just the quality of the person."

CHAPTER 2:
Stoicism

It isn't clear whether Mark had an unusually high tolerance for pain or if he simply summoned his considerable willpower to ignore it. His early years saw more than the average number of childhood illnesses, including scarlet fever, a tonsillectomy, and vein cauterizations. The biggest scare was still to come.

Seven-year-old Mark became violently ill on November 2, 1944, a day well remembered by his sister Nancy because it was her fifth birthday. His temperature ranged as high as 105 to 106 degrees, and his parents tended to his uncontrolled vomiting and extreme discomfort with ice packs and loving care. The next day they took him to the hospital where he was diagnosed with polio.

Polio was a much-feared childhood disease in the middle of the 20th century. Although the disease also affected adults, the most dramatic epidemics crippled thousands of young children every year. Little remembered today, the terror that parents experienced at the prospect of their children becoming infected was very real. Children were kept away from public places where large numbers of people congregated.

The disease raged from the early 1920s, reaching its peak in the 1950s before the Salk vaccine was introduced in 1955. At the time Mark was stricken in 1944, there was great controversy over the most appropriate treatment.

Hospitals did not keep polio patients on-site for fear of contagion, so Mark was brought home the same day as his diagnosis. While the family remembered that they feared for Mark's life only at the very beginning, the period that followed was one of great anxiety. Zilly and Mark Sr. wondered when,

and if, the muscle spasms typical to polio would come, and what part of their son's body would be stricken. Most frightening of all was the prospect that he could be left crippled. The spasms came for Mark two weeks after the diagnosis, and the pain in his legs was intense.

The Donohues chose a course of treatment for Mark known as the "Sister Kenny Treatment." Elizabeth Kenny was an Australian nurse whose title "Sister" referred to her former rank as chief nurse in the Australian Army. She developed a treatment of hot-packing, stretching, and passive manipulation as an alternative to the traditional approach of prolonged immobilization of polio-affected limbs through splinting and casting. Despite being controversial within the medical community, the Sister Kenny treatment had by the mid-1940s become the accepted standard of care in America. Nancy remembered her parents tearing up an old red blanket, soaking the strips in boiling hot water, and wrapping them around Mark's legs to prevent the muscles from atrophying during the spasms. Nancy was frightened: It was the only time she had ever witnessed her stoic big brother cry.

The treatment, along with constant family attention and care, worked. By late spring of 1945 Mark was fully recovered and walking. His limbs had not withered and he suffered no apparent aftereffect, although his legs remained weak for a long time.

Mark's experience was not unique among his generation of drivers. Two years later in New Zealand, his future teammate, rival, and friend, Bruce McLaren, was stricken at age ten by what was first thought to be polio, but was later diagnosed as Legg-Perthes disease. Bruce's course of treatment was more severe, involving lengthy immobilization. It was more than two years before he walked again, and he was left with a permanent limp, while Mark was fortunate to regain full strength, with no residual effects from the polio.

CHAPTER 3:
Finagle's Variable Constant

Mark had wonderful sisters. He was crazy about them and they were equally devoted to him. Mark did like to play tricks, however. As a teenager he loved nothing better than to take Mary Ellen for a ride in his Ford convertible and, while steering with his knees, pull his sweater up over his head. His 12-year-old sister would be terrified—the desired effect—and beg him to stop. He also taught Mary Ellen to drive, insisting she learn on a stick shift. One memorable day, recalls her friend, Beth Boyle, she engaged reverse gear at about thirty miles an hour and destroyed the transmission.

Driving on Summit's Kennedy Boulevard, Mark enjoyed his favorite sport of easing up on a car ahead, gently laying his front bumper on its rear bumper, and pushing it along the boulevard. The fun ended abruptly when proud little sister Mary Ellen announced at the family dinner table, "Dad, Dad, you won't believe the coolest thing that Mark can do in the car!"

The Donohues created an atmosphere of learning in their home. They loved to play with language, and at dinner would go around the table finding fifty different ways to say the same thing. Along with his sisters, Mark was subjected to piano lessons. According to Nancy—a talented musician who also played the harp—Mark practiced "honestly and ruthlessly," adding that he approached the piano the same way he ate sweet potatoes, "without complaint, but with a look of pain and distaste on his face." A Saturday-morning reward for completing music practice was to listen to *The Lone Ranger* on the radio, a particular favorite of Mark's. Later, with the advent of television in the Donohue household, his favorite became *I Love Lucy*.

If Mark wasn't challenged or interested in a school subject, he wasn't above taking advantage of the answers that were printed at the back of the book. One day a teacher remonstrated with him for not making an effort. Mark replied that it wasn't so—he was using a valid method. When asked to be more specific, he invented a new term, citing "Finagle's Variable Constant" as his reliable corollary. He added that if necessary, he resorted to the Max Factor. He was thrown out of class but laughed all the way to the principal's office. As an adult, it would sometimes give Mark pleasure to cite Finagle's Variable Constant in the appropriate situation. He was even more pleased when some people would nod knowingly.

The barn at the end of the Donohue driveway was the scene of great fun and games that often included the entire neighborhood. Cowboys and Indians was the game of preference. Later the barn became Mark's "garage," and even in his preteen years it was the place where he most likely could be found. Mark Sr. purchased a 1937 Ford convertible that remained unregistered, and at various times Mark had

every bit of it apart and back together again.

The driveway to the big brown and white house was long and curving. It ended in a loop, as described by Nancy Donohue, "around a narrow island with a sandbox in it and two big trees between which hung a hammock that was likely to be full of red ants." It was here that Mark, at age nine, began driving the family car. Backing down the awkward, tree-lined driveway was difficult, making it imperative to park the car facing forward in the barn. It was a trick to reverse the car into the barn with a minimum of turns and maneuvers. For Mark it was a competitive challenge he mastered before the age of 10. He immediately began practicing his now-patented technique, going ever faster. "I kept working at it until I mastered it," Mark later recalled. "Then I just kept on doing it at increasing speeds." Nancy remembered that Mark displayed dexterity and style in his driveway practice and believed that he never had an accident, although she suspected he "squashed the pachysandra on the banks of the driveway from time to time."

A frequent refrain from Mark Sr. was, "Now Mark, I don't want you fooling around with that car in the driveway and taking any chances." Mark would invariably reply: "When I'm doing something I don't fool around. I'm not taking any chances. I try to do it right and not take any chances."

Mark did admit taking a chance the day the barn caught fire while he was working on the '37 Ford. "My mother and two sisters, Nancy and Emmie, were in the kitchen," Mark wrote in a profile for *The Boys of Indy* by Phil Berger and Larry Bortstein. "I ran toward the house screaming for them to call the fire department. Then I ran back into the fire. See, the fire had started under the car and I knew where the fire extinguisher was." Mark extinguished the blaze before the fire department arrived, but Zilly was upset because she believed he had taken an unnecessary risk by returning to the barn. "I told her then, and my father when he got home that evening, that it had been a calculated risk, that I had known just what I was doing."

Burge (Burgess) Hulett lived just three doors down the street. The two boys shared adventures from their earliest years, and their friendship endured through Mark's lifetime. Burge's father, Carls Hulett, owned several weekly newspapers in northern New Jersey, and was a serious man. While the father and son had a difficult relationship, Burge's mother was always a friend to the boys, and her son's greatest champion.

By Mark's early teenage years the challenge was to drive the family's Willys Jeep station wagon down the driveway as fast as it would go. The game was heightened by the goal of coming close enough to a tree to knock the side mirror off the car. Burge was a frequent passenger on these drives and remembered that Mark "never creased a fender, but bought a lot of side mirrors."

Zilly treasured a story written by 13-year-old Nancy that provided a sister's perspective on her big brother. "He's fifteen years old and very handsome. But girls are simply not on his list. His interests go for two things; namely, the receiving of good marks in school and the working on his jalopy—oh! pardon me!—his car. The sounds that issue from the garage when he and the car are in there together will never be heard again—either in this life or the next."

CHAPTER 4:

Martha's Vineyard

Martha's Vineyard, the famous island off the south Cape Cod coast, is an idyllic place to live or vacation. In the 1950s it was pure magic. Mark Sr. and Zilly first rented a summer cottage there in 1950 in the East Chop area of Oak Bluffs. Before his family arrived in August, 13-year-old Mark spent the month of July on the island with Burge Hulett and his family. Burge knew Dave Lawton, just a year older, and the three boys became inseparable. The friendship with Dave was a constant throughout Mark's life, and an important influence on his racing career.

The Donohues returned every year after that first summer, and the Mark-Dave-Burge threesome went from one adventure to another. Boating was one fascination, and their outboard motorboats kept them busy. Aided and encouraged by their friend John Smith, who possessed some mechanical skills, they were constantly taking apart the Mercury outboard engines in an attempt to extract that little bit of extra power. Dave had an artistic streak and painted the bow of Mark's boat with a shark's mouth and eyes, just like the famous Flying Tigers symbol on the squadron's World War II P-40 fighter planes.

Nothing, however, matched the boys' fascination with cars—and speed. Dave Lawton remembers that it often got them into crazy situations and brought out their naturally competitive spirit. "Racing against one another was a common everyday activity no matter what the cars were," he says. "The trips from New Jersey to Providence or the Vineyard became legendary for their low elapsed times and the number of cars passed in the center lane of the then-common three-lane highways. I wish I could remember Mark's record for cars passed without pulling back into the right lane. I think it was in the seventies—maybe a hundred and seventy. Looking back, we lived the 1950s much like it is now portrayed in the movies or on television. It was a fun time."

Another lifetime friendship first developed on Martha's Vineyard. Rob McCullough—later nicknamed "Flint" by Mark because of the popular television character of the same last name—was three years older than Mark, but they shared a love of all things mechanical, and he played an influential role in Mark's early racing days.

Mark's first summer job was working as a "grease boy" at Val Bergeron's garage on the Vineyard during the summer of 1952. Bergeron was a Volkswagen dealer, and Mark continued to work for him as a summer employee all through high school and college. It was here that Mark learned to be a practical mechanic; all car problems had to be solved locally, since the Vineyard is an island. (Rob McCullough points out that Mark probably would have worked for Val for free just to be in the proximity of the beautiful Bergeron daughter!) Despite Mark's summer job, he and Dave and Burge continued their adventures. Dave Lawton remembers further modification to the boat with the Flying Tigers bow: "Mark modified his outboard engine that summer with straight pipes on the exhaust, direct from the exhaust ports. The exhaust was thus no longer muffled through the original underwater exhaust. It was loud! The police were not happy as there were numerous complaints about the noise. Since they knew him through his place of work, he always seemed to get out of trouble by giving them one of his big smiles and a laugh."

Burge's mother was his great supporter and encouraged Mark and Burge in their competitive spirit and adventures. She owned a 1949 Chevrolet and would allow them to drive her around the island when they were still only fourteen and fifteen years old. She would sit between them in the Chevy and time them on her wristwatch to see who could reach the fastest speed in a given number of seconds.

By the summer of 1953 Mark had a driver's license, although he wouldn't have his own car until he went back to school in the fall. The happy summer days on the Vineyard focused on girls, dancing, movies, and driving around. Dave Lawton remembers the social life he and Mark were living as something like "an episode from *Happy Days*." One day Mark loaded as many boys and girls as would fit into the family Jeep station wagon, and Dave did the same in the '49 Packard his father had let him rebuild. They were off for a great day at Katama Beach on the south side of the island. On the return drive Mark got a good run on Dave and caught him by surprise, passing the Packard on the run up to a favorite banked bend the boys called "Indianapolis." The extra weight in the Jeep, combined with the sand on the exit of the fast left-hand bend, caught Mark out and he spun. Dave dove to the inside and passed him to the cheers of all. It was summer fun at its best.

The boys formed a 100-mile-an-hour club, and the place to earn entry was on the island's airport road. By 1954 Mark had a 1953 Ford flathead convertible, but soon the car of choice was Mark Sr.'s new Chrysler 300 Hemi. Mark declared that the 100-mile-an-hour club was now a 120-mph club. The major event of that summer is remembered as the six-car race from Edgartown through Oak Bluffs to East Chop. Burge won in his MG TD, with Mark second in the Ford and Dave in third. The police came to see Mark the next morning at work and informed him that they would all be arrested on sight if they were seen driving on island roads.

No one considered the possibility of getting hurt. Once Dave was visiting a girl in Summit who Burge had introduced him to. Her mother woke him in the morning with the news that Mark and Burge had had an accident during the night. "She was appalled when I asked, 'How's the car?' It just never occurred to me that anything would happen to them," Dave recalls.

It may have been the same accident that Carls Hulett found particularly trying, as it destroyed his pretty yellow and black 1950 Chevy 2-door hardtop. Rob McCullough remembers, "Mark and Burge were arguing about how fast a particular right hand corner at the bottom of a hill could be taken. Burge, with Mark seated alongside, took his dad's car out to find out for sure. They were both thrown out of the car in the crash."

CHAPTER 5:

Pingry School Days and Blue Coral Wax

Mark was enrolled in the Pingry School in nearby Hillside, New Jersey. It was a small private day school for boys and young men where jackets and ties were worn every day. Most of Pingry's students were from affluent families. Mark's friend and classmate John Holman recalls that the school attracted fine teachers and enjoyed an excellent scholastic reputation that has continued to the present day. The student body was small, and many Pingry graduates number their school companions among their closest friends today. After graduation the young men went off to college, but would remain in touch with each other, partying together on holidays and during the summer. Most of the socializing happened at one or another's home, and many of the parties were at Chuck Wynn's house. Chuck recalls that Mark never displayed a competitive nature except behind the wheel of a car. "He was lots of fun to be with and, despite not being a star athlete, very much looked up to for his ability to handle a car."

Phil Burrows and Mark met at Pingry in the seventh grade and became constant companions. Phil was the star of the football team and Mark participated as team manager. Among the things holding Mark back in sports were severe allergies and frequent and persistent nosebleeds that would last for hours. Mark wasn't a fighter either, letting Phil fight the schoolboy scrimmages on his behalf. But Mark was active in school swimming, tennis, and track, and in his senior year was manager of the soccer team.

While Mark wasn't considered a gifted sports figure by the generally accepted schoolboy standards, he was, in fact, a natural athlete. This athleticism was apparent long before it found its ultimate expression in a race car. According to his sister Mary Ellen, a serious horseback rider who later ran a riding academy, "Mark was a natural jumper." On snowy or icy days when even she was afraid to exercise the animals, Mark would ride every horse in the stable. Later reports from racing contemporaries confirm his strength and coordination. Sam Posey recalls that Mark was immensely strong and capable of exceptional endurance in and out of a race car. Oscar Kovaleski noted Mark's tremendous upper-body strength when he observed him effortlessly picking up loaded fuel churns weighing more than 100 pounds in his pit space. Mark once made a personal assessment of his schoolboy athletic skills when a newspaper article claimed he had been a failure in other sports. "I wasn't really a failure," Mark said. "I just wasn't a star. I was average."

The Summit/Pingry crowd was made up of car guys who took great pride in their automobiles and in keeping them spotless. Mark's identity was as a very fast driver. Although not a Pingry student, Burge Hulett was a member of the group, and he and Phil Burrows had MG TDs. Mark's high school car was a red 1953 Ford Sunliner convertible. Mark Sr. bought it for Mark at the beginning of his junior year in the autumn of 1953. Mr. Donohue was unimpressed with Phil's MG TD, but Mark loved to drive it. He wanted a sports car, and by the following summer, the Ford's continental kit rear spare tire and bright red paint inspired Burge and Dave Lawton to call it Mark's "Guatemalan sports car." The name stuck.

Swapping cars was a custom between Mark and his friends. Dave Lawton came to Summit to visit Mark and Burge at Christmas in his '53 Studebaker Commander V8 Starlight hardtop. They all took pride in their cornering ability, and their favorite sports were racing through neighborhoods and staging point-to-point races, rather than drag racing. Mark was the acknowledged ace, as remembered by all the guys.

Linda Groves rode with the entire crowd and remembers Burge—a fearless motorcycle rider who taught Linda how to ride—as the wild one in the group. Mark was more interested in what made the car fast. Linda was one of Mark's closest friends and often drove his car even before she was old enough to have a license. Mark and Burge had a part-time job doing some street work for the town of Summit, and one day, Linda—still illegal—repeatedly drove by them in Mark's car, each time shutting off the ignition to create a backfire. "Mark really did want a sports car, but he would grin and tell me that the Blue Coral wax he had on the Ford made it faster than the other guys' cars."

Mark was an All-American type of guy—mild-mannered, sporting a crew cut—not an aggressive personality, but still very popular. He was outgoing, friendly, and always a lot of fun as remembered by those who knew him as a young person and as an adult. He dated many young women as a high school junior and senior but never had a steady girlfriend. "Mark and I were very close and went out a lot together with the group," says Linda Groves. "He would confide in me in his straightforward, almost naive way. He seldom dated

anyone more than a few times because he wasn't interested in shallow relationships. No one ever existed who didn't like him; he was just a sweet huggy-bear."

Mark was clear-minded and very smart. He brought a complete dedication to accomplishing his goals. At Pingry, and later at Brown, he was a brilliant student with excellent grades. He did it, in part, through devoting himself to study and putting in the necessary hours to accomplish his goals. Despite this serious side, he liked to kid around and was typically the leader in pranks.

"When Mark gave you directions how to get somewhere, you knew you were in for a treat," says Rob McCullough. "He was explicit and the directions were complex. After all of that he would say, 'Of course, that's if you drive out the driveway—if you back out it's all the opposite.' That was Mark."

He continued to display his competitive nature with boats. While visiting Phil Burrows at the family's summer home in Bayhead on the Jersey shore, Mark was invited to take their new speedboat out for a spin on the lake. He disappeared for the entire afternoon and returned quite unaware that his extended absence had caused concern. Mark had raced every boat on the lake.

CHAPTER 6:

Brown University and Professors Taruffi and O'Shea

Dave Lawton was a major influence on Mark's choice to attend Brown University in Providence, Rhode Island. Dave was a sophomore there when Mark began his studies in the fall of 1955. Brown, a prestigious Ivy League university with a fine engineering school, is the seventh-oldest college in America, having received its charter in 1764. Mark observed one of the university's most cherished traditions when he walked through the Van Wickle memorial gates with other members of his freshman class.

While Dave still lived in his family home in nearby Pawtucket, Mark moved into a dorm on campus (although he would later live in the Theta Delta Chi fraternity house). As a freshman at Brown, Mark was not permitted to have a car on campus. On weekends Dave would drive him from campus to pick up his '53 Ford. Dave's father owned a rental property in nearby Central Falls that included a barn, and he allowed Mark to park his car there. Mark would often have dinner with the Lawtons before heading off for his weekend visits to young women he knew at colleges throughout New England. It was during the autumn of 1955 that Dave and Mark drove to Watkins Glen, New York, to see the annual Sports Car Grand Prix.

They drove to Watkins Glen on Friday—Dave's Studebaker had been replaced by a red Jaguar XK120M roadster—arriving after practice but in time to experience the downtown Watkins Glen atmosphere. It was a colorful and exciting mix of race fans from all over the country, walking and driving up and down the main street of town. Local garages were booked by race teams and a great deal of the fun was wandering from one shop to another to observe the race preparations. Dave and Mark slept in the Jaguar with the top up—an experience one only wants to have once. After a full day at the track on Saturday—Sherwood Johnston won the feature Grand Prix in Briggs Cunningham's D-type Jaguar—Dave was exhausted, and asked Mark to take the wheel for the drive back on the New York State Thruway. Dave woke up once or twice thinking the wind was exceptionally strong, but went right back to sleep. Later Mark told him that he had kept the Jaguar at a steady 120 mph, but confessed that a couple of Ferraris had passed them.

There was a room in the Lawton house that Dave's mother referred to as "Mark's room." Dave's sisters were older and married, providing extra space for guests. Mark was to be in and out of the Lawton home in many different circumstances, extending long after college days.

Dave Lawton drove his Jaguar in gymkhanas and hillclimbs, often taking Mark along as his pit crew. They began to study different driving styles and to concentrate on the technical nuances of what made a car fast around a corner. Dave bought both the Piero Taruffi and Paul O'Shea books on competition driving, and he and Mark discussed them at length.

After Mark's second year at Brown, his father bought him a new 1957 Corvette. It had a 283ci engine with two four-barrel carburetors—fellow Brown man Link Eveleth recalls that Mark removed the progressive linkage on the twin carburetors, allowing both to open at once—and was rated at 245 horsepower. It was red and fitted with a three-speed manual transmission. Mark soon perfected the downshift into the non-synchronized first gear. Now Mark had a car with sufficient power to apply the techniques described by O'Shea and Taruffi. Dave recalls:

"We would go out at night to practice. The Corvette had enough power where one could get into a true 'drift' in a high speed corner where the front and rear wheels were lined up, the car was traveling at an inward angle to the path of travel, and one could steer with the accelerator. Taruffi explained the technique in his book in engineering terms and Mark caught on right away to the physics involved, as he was studying force vectors at the time."

When Mark would take his Corvette out for a drive during afternoon study breaks, he was constantly seeking an ideal corner to practice the four-wheel drift. He found one that was just right in a housing development in Seekonk, Massachusetts, just over the Rhode Island border. There were always two little boys playing in the front yard of the home on the corner. Mark told Dave that he found that if on the approach he took his hands off the wheel just long enough to wave to the boys, they would wave back rather than run to their mother. This technique made it possible to use that corner about twice a day.

That summer of 1957, Mark had his first job away from the Vineyard, at the Diamond Match Company in Cloquet, Minnesota. Mark didn't know anyone there, but with his red Corvette and his endearing smile, he had a fine summer. He made a trip to Elkhart Lake, Wisconsin, for the Road America 500—only the second full-fledged race he had ever seen. He was impressed with the D-type Jaguar Walt Hansgen was driving for Briggs Cunningham, and the Mercedes-Benz 300SLS roadster driven by Paul O'Shea. Mark also greatly admired the 3.8-liter V12 Ferrari 315 S that Phil Hill drove to victory. His greatest enthusiasm that day was for the Corvettes raced by Fred Windridge and Dick Thompson. Mark was exhilarated by the idea of developing his stock Corvette into a competitive race car, but discouraged at the financial reality of such a venture.

CHAPTER 7:

Triad of Ivyism

Mark and Dave Lawton were members of the University Sports Car Club. The club originally met on the Brown campus, but when Mark and others insisted on including non-university people as members, the administration dropped its charter as a university-sponsored activity. Meetings were subsequently held at The Auto Show, a foreign car dealership in Seekonk, Massachusetts, owned by sports-car racer Teddy Leonard.

The club's choice venue for competitive speed trials was at Jamestown Island's Fort Getty on the south coast of Rhode Island. The club regularly ran time trials on their slightly more than a half-mile course that featured at least one very challenging corner. Dave Belden, a year behind Mark at Brown, remembers that Mark was usually the quickest at these events. "He seemed to have a natural pace from the first time I saw him drive—and that pace was fast."

In the spring of 1958, Mark's junior year at Brown, the club participated in a hillclimb at Belknap, New Hampshire, conducted by the Narragansett Sports Car Club, a Rhode Island club open to all ages. Dave Belden was a sophomore, and although he didn't own a sports car, he served as a corner worker. Dave Lawton, by now a senior, had replaced his Jaguar XK120M with an Alfa Romeo Giulietta Spider Veloce. It was the ex-Rainville-Kaplan Veloce that had finished second in class that year at Sebring after winning in 1957. Mark's Corvette was among the eclectic range of cars present; the field also included such hybrids as a 1932 Ford roadster fitted with a small-block Chevy engine.

Another fast runner was Charlie Rainville. Charlie was a service manager at Jake Kaplan's Foreign Motors, Ltd., in Providence, and Mark spent a great deal of time there. Dave Belden remembers that Mark was greatly influenced by Rainville. "Mark was analytical about cars and a very good listener. Charlie Rainville was a good man to listen to." Rainville, in his highly modified Jaguar XK120 Silverstone—Borrani wire wheels, aluminum body, and a heavily modified engine that included C-type specs—seemed to be the man to beat. A fast time was put up by local real estate man Dick Jalbert in a Corvette that was loaded with every high-performance option available at the time. Mark's red Corvette was still very stock, and he did well to slightly better Jalbert's time. Rainville was the last of the favored drivers to make his run up the hill, and, trying perhaps a little too hard, he bent the Jaguar on a tight left-hand turn. Mark was an excited and happy winner with the Fastest Time of the Day (FTD) in his first sanctioned speed event. However, the handsome winner's trophy could only be awarded to a member of the sponsoring club. Jamie Weissenborn recalls that when informed he could be a member for a $5 fee, Mark declared that the price was too steep. The trophy went unclaimed.

The experience at the hillclimb convinced Mark that he needed a four-speed gearbox for the Corvette. He paid $300 for the transmission, and installed it with Dave Lawton's help. The shift gate was an extra expense and Mark was short of cash, but Dave had an idea. "I suggested that he use the three-speed shift gate, and I installed a choke cable set up to access reverse when needed. One had to select neutral before trying for reverse. Needless to say, you had to be on your toes when you drove this car."

Car control was an endless fascination. The Corvette was a powerful car and ideal for perfecting technique. Rob McCullough recalls that Mark sought out every potential venue to hone his skill. "Anytime there was an open body of ice, Mark would drive on it for hours, practicing slides. He would also bring the car to the auxiliary Naval Air Station in Charlestown, Rhode Island, for the Southern New England Timers Association–sanctioned drag races. He would make a run just to check his time, but never pursued drag racing seriously."

Brown University is built on a steep hill on the east side of Providence. When the roads would become icy or snow-packed, the city police would set up barriers to close the particularly dangerous South Angel Street, which ran alongside the college library, past the Rhode Island School of Design, and down into the heart of the city. Mark reveled in these conditions. After lowering the Corvette's tire pressures, he would drive around the barriers and charge up and down the hill with power on and fully sideways. Link Eveleth recalls that Mark always managed to conclude his runs just minutes before the police would arrive. "He was a lot of fun and had great spirit," he says.

Eveleth was also present the day Mark set the record for the fastest time around the college quad. It was in his sophomore year, before he acquired the Corvette. Mark drove his Ford convertible a full, flat-out lap on the sidewalks inside the enclosed quadrangle of dormitories and classrooms, with the glass-pack twin-pipe mufflers roaring even louder than the cheers of the encouraging crowd. "We all knew Mark was going to go for the record—it was just the kind of thing that appealed to his sense of fun and mischief. I'm pretty sure no one has bettered the time since," Eveleth says.

Mark did run two other hillclimbs with the Corvette without particular distinction. His most useful exploits in the car came when, at the suggestion of Charlie Rainville, he went to Thompson Raceway in Connecticut for practice laps. Thompson was a regular Sports Car Club of America (SCCA) race venue. Owner and promoter George B. Weaver Jr. made the 2.5-mile track available for testing and practice at reasonable rates. Weaver was a pioneer sports-car enthusiast, passionately imbued with the ideals of amateur racing. Though best remembered today for establishing Thompson Raceway, he was also a fine driver, known for his wins at Watkins Glen in the early years of the original street circuit, and for his prewar racing exploits as a member of the Automobile Racing Club of America (ARCA).

Mark learned a great deal from his relationship with Charlie Rainville, an outstanding driver with a strong technical grounding. Later Rainville became a key member of John Bishop's team, responsible for establishing the International Motor Sports Association (IMSA), which became the leading sanctioning body for professional American sports-car racing. Mark ran with Rainville several times at Thompson, along with other early racing friends, Fred Darling and Ralph DeCiantis. He picked up as much knowledge back in the shop with Rainville as he did following Charlie's rapid Alfa Romeo Veloce around Thompson. It was Rainville who recommended and tracked down the latest cerra metallic brake linings for Mark's Corvette. Dave Lawton also participated in many of these lapping sessions in his ex-Rainville Alfa. The two friends continued their practice of evaluating and analyzing everything from driving technique to car setup. They remained together on a fast learning curve.

A window on the collegiate Mark Donohue appears in *Liber Brunensis*, Brown's yearbook for 1958, when Mark was finishing his junior year. A photo showing Mark with an attractive young woman is captioned: "At left is 'Cherub' Donohue with beer can, tennis shoe, and charming companion: triad of Ivyism."

Dave graduated from Brown the year before Mark and went on a six-month tour of active duty in the U.S. Army Reserves. Like all young men in America, Mark had reported to the Selective Service Local Board on his 18th birthday to register for the draft. His severe asthma and general health history immediately resulted in the military physicians' classification of 4F. He was never called to serve.

CHAPTER 8:
Pink Ice Cream

In May 1959 Mark joined his fellow Brown University graduates as they ceremonially passed through the Van Wickle Gates—in the opposite direction they had taken four years earlier as incoming freshmen. Before graduating Mark had interviewed for engineering trainee positions at a number of large corporations, but none seemed to offer quite the right fit. He was reluctant to become a number in a big company, and job openings did not present themselves at the smaller concerns that may have been of interest to him.

Mark decided on another summer on Martha's Vineyard. He accepted a job helping to open a lunchroom at a bus stop and delicatessen Val Bergeron had acquired. He persuaded Burge Hulett to join him, and soon they were managing and operating "The Pit Stop." One day Mark cut his hand while setting up the soft-serve ice cream machine. The first half-dozen or so customers received the added treat of pink ice cream. Mark remembered it as a last summer of freedom, enjoying the pleasures of Martha's Vineyard. He was 22, he had his Corvette, and the days were easy and sunny.

He was dating 17-year-old Simone Bergeron, who remembers him as, at heart, a serious young man with strong family ties. She compares the two friends as she knew them: Mark as mischievous and fun, Burge as wild and unpredictable.

It was that summer that the *Vineyard Gazette* ran a series of articles on the nuisance created by motorcyclists who were apparently skidding their tires and leaving ugly black marks on the pavement. Rob McCullough read the stories with particular amusement. "Flint" knew that Mark's Corvette lacked positraction (so only one wheel could maintain traction), and that Mark and Burge enjoyed nothing better than practicing figure eights with the powerful car in the early-morning hours.

The young men lived in an apartment, remembered by Rob McCullough as being "pretty ragtag." It was above the store, and all summer Burge, Mark, and their friends had stacked empty beer cans and bottles on the roughly enclosed outdoor staircase. By summer's end they had created a wall on both sides. As they departed the island on the last day of the summer, Burge removed the bottom can from one side and Mark did the same from the other. They closed the door behind them as the entire staircase filled with the cascading empties.

The season on Martha's Vineyard ends right after Labor Day. Mark headed home to his parents in Summit, and decided to pursue a graduate degree in business administration at New York University to complement his credentials as an engineering graduate. Later he accepted a job at Raybestos-Manhattan in Passaic, New Jersey. The plant in Passaic manufactured conveyor belts, and, as a junior engineer, Mark found little to challenge him.

Over that winter—in the early days of 1960—Mark discovered ice racing. The sport, run much like regular road racing, had its own special atmosphere and typically brought out unusual cars and drivers. "There is nothing to match lying on your back on the ice with the wind howling and snow swirling while you reattach your red-hot exhaust system," remembers Joe Foering, a regular on the Lake Naomi ice. The popular Lake Naomi venue in Pocono Pines, Pennsylvania, is located just a few miles from the present site of Pocono Raceway. Mark ran his Corvette there on several occasions, and inevitably incurred body damage. Mark Sr. was in attendance the day his son hit a Porsche, knocking a fender off the red Corvette. To save money, Mark took on the repairs himself in his parents' basement, only to discover that he had a severe allergy to fiberglass. His arms swelled, sores opened, and he was confined to bed, curtailing further adventures on ice. Mark remembered it as "a grim time," but the ice racing had rekindled his desire to drive competitively. He and Burge were soon talking about going SCCA racing.

Burge introduced Mark to Lou Schulz, proprietor with Dave Ruggles of S&R Motors in Hanover, New Jersey, an importer of foreign cars, including Elvas. Elva was an English chassis constructor that had hit upon a very successful combination in the popular Elva Courier. The Courier used a standard 1500cc engine from the MG Car Company, while other components were borrowed from European sedans and sports cars. The relatively sophisticated light chassis and fiberglass body made the car much quicker than the popular MGA from which it derived its drivetrain. To purchase the Courier Mark had to part with the Corvette. It wasn't a difficult decision, as he well knew that preparing the Corvette as a race car was beyond his means. The $2,700 he received for the Corvette was just about enough to purchase the Elva.

Mark took delivery of the Courier in February of 1960. It had been in his hands just a few days when Dave Lawton came to visit on leave from his post at Fort Dix, New Jersey. Late one night they went out for a drive and Dave took the wheel.

"We were in a twisty, residential area and I really began to get into it. The car handled beautifully, very evenly balanced, neither oversteering nor understeering. Mark got a little upset as he hadn't driven it that hard himself as he was still breaking it in." The upset quickly forgotten, Mark was delighted that Dave had given the car his seal of approval. Dave's evaluation proved to be spot-on, as everyone who ever raced a Courier was to praise the car's handling characteristics.

CHAPTER 9:

Always Go First-Class

By this time Mark and Burge were beginning to outline their strategy to go racing. Burge had purchased a Bandini sports car. The first goal was to enroll in a drivers' school in Marlboro, Maryland, in March 1960. The SCCA had just begun to require completion of a drivers' school course in order to be licensed. Through the 1950s a driver had earned his novice permit by driving on the road with a designated observer who was empowered to provisionally qualify the applicant to participate in an SCCA road race.

Before attending the school, Mark and Burge needed to be accepted into the SCCA. In 1960 the group was still quite exclusive, and thought of itself as sort of an elite country club for just the "right sort" of person. Then, as now, it was peopled mostly by enthusiastic individuals, but pretension remained at certain levels. Mark and Burge came from the appropriate social circles, so they were accepted with relative ease, becoming members just three days before starting the Marlboro school.

The SCCA was, in 1960, still a purely amateur organization by design and regulation. Drivers were forbidden to participate in professional races under pain of losing their licenses. In cases where the group authorized such participation—and approval was required in advance—the SCCA member had to sign an agreement to waive any prize money or other remuneration. A slight softening in the rules had been approved that year, permitting a driver to accept some expense money under prescribed circumstances.

The all-amateur policy created a tremendous struggle between the members who wanted to see professional racing embraced and those who were determined to hold the line as a purely amateur organization. It had also become obvious that the SCCA's ideal did not match the reality. For many years drivers had received direct or indirect compensation to drive for manufacturers and other major interests who saw road racing as an excellent marketing tool to influence an upscale audience. While some members were suspended for merely racing in an unsanctioned event, a blind eye was turned to the essentially professional status of the club's stars, including Carroll Shelby, Walt Hansgen, Ken Miles, Jack McAfee, Paul O'Shea, and many others.

The issue was of vital importance to anyone who wished to pursue road racing at any level, because the SCCA was a large and powerful organization. Certainly there were independent regional sports-car clubs sanctioning races, but with the exception of the California Sports Car Club (Cal Club) in southern California, if you wanted to go road racing on a serious basis, your only option was the SCCA. The SCCA was divided into regions that organized and administered club business and activities, including racing, on a local level. It was a natural for Mark and Burge to join the Northern New Jersey Region.

When Mark drove the Elva Courier from Summit, New Jersey, to Upper Marlboro, Maryland, for the drivers' school, it was completely street-legal. Lou Schulz had only fitted the minimally required rollbar and competition seat belt. Burge, meanwhile, trailered his modified Bandini.

The typical SCCA drivers' school of the time opened with a classroom session on Friday evening that covered rules of the road, flags, and some rudimentary discussion of driving techniques. On Saturday morning, the chief steward held a drivers' meeting, and students were assigned to instructors. Mark's instructor was Pierre Mion, a respected SCCA driver who had won the national championship in the E Production class the previous year. Mion drove the Courier, with Mark as passenger, and pointed out braking and turn-in points. Mark was impressed with Mion's smoothness. "Pierre drove my Courier for ten laps, got out and said, 'go ahead,'" Mark later told Berger and Bortstein. "I never saw him again. Not that day anyway. But that was all the instruction I ever did get from him."

The remainder of Saturday, and the early sessions on Sunday, involved group lapping and practice starts. The school capped off with a practice race. Although no record remains of Mark's finishing position in the mixed bag of cars, he impressed the SCCA enough to come away with a Regional license.

A new driver could become eligible to enter National Championship races with as few as three races at the Regional level, assuming his competence was noted in the logbook and signed by the chief steward. Not all drivers necessarily had a burning desire to advance to National racing and leave Regionals entirely behind. This was certainly true for Mark, who simply wanted to race wherever there was an event he could easily get to. In fact, some of the best competition was often found at the Regional level.

April 10, 1960, marked a major milestone in Mark Donohue's life: It was the day of his first race. Dave Lawton joined Mark at Vineland Speedway in southern New Jersey and was possibly as excited as Mark when the result was a win. It was a small field of relatively inexperienced drivers, but the excitement before a driver's first race start and the thrill of victory must be experienced to be understood.

Years later, in his book *The Unfair Advantage*, Mark told co-author Paul Van Valkenburgh that his first race was at Lime Rock, Connecticut. If this is correct, the evidence is lost—or Mark was recalling the race at Lime Rock that took place two weeks after Vineland. There, the competition was stiffer. Lime Rock is a fast 1.5-mile circuit, and the still near-standard Courier was outclassed. Finishing fourth was an eye-opener for the always-competitive Mark. He could see that it would take a better-prepared car to win against the best.

Mark needed advice. His boyhood friend Jim Haas was great friends with Roger Penske from their days at Lehigh University. Roger, already big news in SCCA racing, was staying overnight at Jim's home in New Providence, New Jersey, on his way to a race at Cumberland, Maryland. Mark knew who he was—he had met him casually during his college years, through mutual friends—and wanted the chance to talk with him.

The two were the same age, and like Mark, Roger had been heavily involved in racing and sports cars in college at Lehigh in Bethlehem, Pennsylvania. Bob Rost—who would become Mark's brother-in-law—was just a year behind Roger and Jim at Lehigh, which he remembers as "the foundation college for sports car racing and enthusiasts. Jim Haas had a 1955 Porsche Speedster, someone had a Fiat-Abarth, and there were a number of XK120 Jaguars. Roger Penske and I both had XK120Ms. Roger later replaced his with a Corvette." Roger had launched his racing career early in 1959 with a Porsche RS he had purchased from racing legend Bob Holbert. Now in his second year, he was on his way to winning his first National Championship in his new Porsche RSK.

Mark met Roger over dinner at Jim's. He and Burge soaked up everything they could from him. Mark asked direct questions about what it would take to make his Courier competitive; Roger was candid. Jim recalls that Roger told Mark that he needed to do everything he could possibly do to the car that was legal. Penske said that if you want to race and win, you need to make a complete commitment. You had to always go first-class, he told the novice.

CHAPTER 10:
The Scaglietti Smoker

Mark took Roger's words to heart. He had little money, but managed to have Lou Schulz make the modifications necessary to turn the Courier into a competitive proposition. First, Schulz installed larger SU carburetors and a close-ratio transmission. (Mark had already replaced the windshield with a competition windscreen and converted the exhaust system to a straight pipe.) Mark enjoyed working with Lou, who he called "The Coach." Lou's top shop mechanic was a gregarious young Englishman named Jimmy Carter who became an important part of the close-knit group of racers from northern New Jersey.

The car was no longer practical to drive on the street; Mark had already fallen afoul of the law for the loud exhaust on his way to his first race. He found the perfect tow car, a 1954 Chevrolet station wagon—perfect because the $175 asking price was just about all he could afford. Actually, the '54 Chevy was well known for its robustness, and the car came to be a much-loved element of the first Mark Donohue race *equipe*. To provide additional panache, Mark and friends dubbed the vehicle the "Scaglietti"—after the elegant Italian coachbuilder—as unlikely a moniker as they could imagine.

Burge and Mark soon rigged the "Scag" with a special disincentive for tailgaters who used their bright lights. Under the hood, they mounted a reservoir of diesel fuel that could be put through the exhaust system with a flick of the windshield wiper control. The immediate result was a dense black cloud of oily fog that was so impressive, it once shut down a busy highway for five minutes or more. Sometimes Mark would trigger the device just for the pure joy of it while exiting a tollbooth or in some other unlikely situation.

Mark had accepted a new job with a company right in Summit. The Pulverizing Machinery Company was a subsidiary of the Martin Marietta Company, and, as its name implied, manufactured machinery that liquefied various materials, particularly for the food industry. Mark worked in the field with food clients including Dupont, Hershey, General Mills, Pillsbury, and Sara Lee, as well as large cosmetics companies that processed talc. His job was to ensure the equipment was working correctly and to train people on its use and maintenance.

Jill Stiles was secretary to the laboratory manager, and recalls Mark's sense of fun. "After Mark was finished with his testing he would come back to my office to deliver all his test results," Stiles says. "He would hand over his report, and with a mischievous look in his eye, say, 'See if you can type this up without any mistakes.' He would delight in finding typing errors if he could. If he could find no errors, he would see how many places had white-out marks. I would always come back at him and accuse him of having chicken scratch for handwriting. He would then giggle and walk out of the office, calling back, 'See you later, Straight Arrow.' That was his nickname for me, since I did not drink, smoke, or cuss. His nickname was Giggles, given to him for obvious reasons."

Mark loved to tell a good story. "After visiting one of the chocolate companies, Mark told me of the hordes of bees that had gathered in the train car that housed the sugar, and how they were caught up with the sugar and ground up with the cocoa powder and then used in the products," Stiles recalls. "I never knew what was truth or what was fiction, I just knew he loved to gross me out. . . . I guess you could say that he could be silly at times. The other employees of the company liked him a lot, and no one ever had a negative word about him. I found him to be a person that always had a smile and hello for everyone."

Mark had a lifetime reputation as a prankster with an offbeat sense of humor. A favorite trick was to reach out as if to shake your hand, and then quickly withdraw it with a move as if to indicate that he merely intended to arrange his hair. Although sophomoric, the trick amused Mark greatly. He was too kind and polite to pull it on anyone outside of his closest circle. His friends loved him enough to forgive him just about anything.

These were fun and carefree days. Mark drove the Scaglietti with the enthusiastic abandon he brought to every vehicle. Jim Haas and Mark were in Newark one day when Mark mentioned that he needed a certain Michelin tire for the Courier. Jim knew a place a few towns west where he could get a 25 percent discount. Mark said, "Let's go!" They piled into the Scag and a friend of Jim's came along for the ride. "Mark drove the Scag flat out through Newark traffic, really threading the needle all the way. When we got to where we were going my friend was practically limp. We almost needed to hose him down."

After the modifications were complete, Mark took the Courier to race at Marlboro on June 5. Both he and his car were now far more race-savvy and prepared than they had been three months before on the same track for drivers' school. Rob McCullough and Dave Lawton were along to witness Mark's victory against a strong regional field.

The success continued the next weekend, when Mark won at Vineland. Located in Cumberland County, close to Delaware Bay in the very southern part of New Jersey, Vineland Speedway was 120 miles from Mark's home in Summit. The Speedway, on the site of what is now Cumberland County College, had opened in 1955 as a half-mile dirt oval track, and first hosted sports-car races in 1958 when the 1.5-mile road circuit was added through the sand dunes. The main straightaway utilized the quarter-mile drag strip built the same year. After the straight there were four uphill right-hand turns followed by a downhill back straight. Finally an esses and a fast right-hand bend returned the cars to the main straight.

Mark learned an important lesson in race-car preparation that weekend. During practice, a transmission seal failed but Lawton and McCullough repaired it on the spot, allowing Mark to win the next day. The failure still troubled Mark who later complained to Lou Schulz. In a fatherly manner, Schulz explained the facts of life regarding racing: It was an unpredictable sport, and while Schulz could do his best to prepare the car, there were no guarantees on reliability. It was a critical realization for Mark, who began to understand that he would have to step up his personal commitment to the mechanical presentation of the car.

Lou Schulz was an important influence on Mark's career. He had an extensive background in racing, having driven in American Automobile Association (AAA) races both before and after World War II. He was instrumental in organizing and promoting many of the early road races in the Northeast, including Linden, New Jersey, and had helped Sherman "Red" Crise bring racing to Nassau in the Bahamas. Veteran race organizer and broadcaster Bill Claren believes that there may have been no one more important to Mark's success: "The record of wins from race starts that Mark achieved in

the Elva Courier is virtually unprecedented. It was Lou who prepared the car and showed Mark what he needed to know on the mechanical side. Great a talent as Mark was, if it had not been for Lou, he would never have achieved what he did in racing."

Oscar Weissenborn, the father of Mark's friend Jamie, was an ex-racer and had driven to Vineland for a day at the races. The next day he related to Jamie in a concerned tone that Mark needed to have the Chevrolet fixed. On his drive home Mark had come flying by with the Courier in tow, and Mr. Weissenborn had been smoked by the "Scag."

On the June 18–19 weekend, the New York Region of the SCCA made a brave attempt to revive the glory of the Vanderbilt Cup, and Mark desperately wanted to be part of the action. The famous race had last been contested in 1937 on a circuit created as part of Roosevelt Raceway, the thoroughbred track on Long Island, and had been won by Tazio Nuvolari in an Auto Union Grand Prix car. The 1960 race was run on an 11-turn circuit created in the parking lot of the famous track and delineated by white paint, hay bales, and pylons. The program included a full schedule of regional races for all classes, but the race for the Vanderbilt Cup featured the hugely popular and fast-growing Formula Junior class. The race's "special event" status allowed professional drivers to enter, although no prize money would be paid. Other inducements by the teams and constructors persuaded an impressive list of international race stars to participate. They included Pedro and Ricardo Rodríguez, Lorenzo Bandini, Carroll Shelby, and USAC stars Rodger Ward and Jim Rathmann, winners of the Indianapolis 500 in 1959 and 1960, respectively. Virtually all of the top SCCA Formula Junior drivers were there, including Walt Hansgen, Charlie Kolb, Jim Hall, Ed Hugus, Charley Wallace, and Harry Carter.

Mark tried to enter the support race for his class on Saturday, but he was too late—the field was full. He was given "first reserve" status, and his perseverance paid off. Fellow New Jersey driver Dick Webster crashed his MGA in practice and Mark was given a spot at the back of the 30-car field. Charlie Kolb, also in a Courier, started 28th, and the two tore through the field. Kolb got as far as third before suffering engine trouble, but Mark charged on to win the race, with John Heyer second. John remembers Mark being amused that Dick Webster, who wasn't even in the race, was mistakenly credited with the win in all the official results and post-race publicity. Mark just smiled and said, "I've got the trophy."

The month ended at Watkins Glen, New York, on June 25 for the Glen Classic. It was Mark's first time back at Watkins Glen since his visit there with Dave Lawton early in his freshman year at Brown. The 2.3-mile road course was fast and demanding, and its rolling terrain stood in distinct contrast to Vanderbilt's artificial circuit. Still, the result was the same. Mark won the race for a perfect month of June: He had raced every weekend and won each time.

CHAPTER 11:
First National Victory

Mark's debut at the National level of SCCA racing was a sensation. The annual Fourth of July National at Lime Rock was one of the most popular SCCA events in the Northeast. Prior to Mark's arrival as a competitor at the National level, the big names in F Production were Doug Diffenderfer and Charlie Kolb. Like Mark, Kolb drove a Courier and also frequently raced an Elva Mk 5 in G Modified. But he was best known for his exploits in Formula Junior, where he had run off a remarkable string of consecutive wins. Kolb won the Junior race that day at Lime Rock. He was an experienced and quick driver, and his Courier was considered the best-prepared example in the country. Kolb was a friend of Lou Schulz, who had told him about this promising young driver. Kolb remembers being immediately impressed with Mark's seriousness, and even more with how fast he was. He was happy to share setup tips with Mark and Lou. Diffenderfer, from Bethesda, Maryland, drove a Siata 208 S, and the 36 points he had earned by June 1 had him pointed toward the National Championship.

At the start of the race Mark quickly slotted into second behind Kolb. As the laps went by, the more-experienced driver pulled steadily away, and Mark soon realized he had no chance of catching him. Halfway through the race, Kolb's Elva broke and Mark found himself in the lead. He brought the Courier home for the win in his first National race, earning the 10 points that went with it. Diffenderfer was second, however, and his 8 points increased his total to 44. Third and fourth were Howard Hanna in a D.B.-Panhard and John Heyer in his Elva Courier.

Some of the joy of the occasion was diluted when Diffenderfer protested the legality of Mark's engine. This was

Mark's first experience with being protested. He was nervous and sought reassurance from Lou that he was, in fact, legal. The Coach told Mark not to worry. Sure enough, after being totally disassembled and inspected, the engine was found legal in all respects. It was returned to Mark in pieces, and his bill from S&R Motors for reassembly was $300. The SCCA compensated Mark with a check for $125, which left him less than impressed with the entire experience.

John Heyer from nearby Montclair, New Jersey, was a top competitor in the class. He too had purchased his Courier from Lou Schulz, and the two young men saw a great deal of one another working on their cars between races in the S&R shop. They had both obtained their National licenses at the same time, and Lime Rock had been their first National race. John and his wife Martha became two of Mark's closest friends. The Heyers were witty and warm and meshed happily with Mark.

Renee Warren and Bob Rost—a couple who would play an important role in Mark's life—had married while Bob was at Lehigh University. When Bob started racing, Renee found a world of new friends, including Lisa and Roger Penske. Renee was very social, and while Bob worked on his race car she made her way around the paddock, establishing new friendships. Martha and John Heyer were among the new acquaintances, and they in turn were friends of Mark's. "It was a joy being around the Heyers—they were outrageously fun," says Renee. "And Mark, who was close to the Heyers, was part of it."

Renee had first noticed Mark on the track when he was driving the Courier. "He had a style—he could make a car go. He got through those corners like nobody else. He was already a very, very good driver." Renee knew what to look for. Bob remembers that Renee could handle a sports car very well and outdrive most guys at the time.

Skip Barber, who was then one of the fastest production car drivers in the Northeast, says Mark was the only driver who truly impressed him. "The first time I ever saw him drive was at Marlboro, and the memory is still clear of him going through the first series of turns and using so much of the road—back then you really drifted cars," remembers Skip. "Nobody had any clue who this guy was, and he was visibly wonderful in the car—you couldn't miss it."

The Rosts invited Mark to stay with them at their home in Pittsburgh, where Renee would fix him up with dates for the weekend. "I introduced him to a couple of gals from Chatham College who would baby-sit for us. On at least one occasion one of the girls came along to a race at Marlboro and got to go on the victory lap with Mark." Mark dated a variety of attractive young women, including John Heyer's sister Elizabeth, but continued to resist becoming exclusively involved. His commitment to racing exceeded that of most of his fellow competitors. "Mark was a lot of fun to be with and liked a good joke; you could kid him and the kidding went both ways. But underneath it he was very serious. The racing was a great deal more than just a hobby to Mark, even at this early time," John says. Heyer remembers coming to terms with Mark's commitment at a Regional at Vineland where Mark experienced clutch trouble. "Most people would have gone home to come back another day. Mark was at the track Sunday morning at daybreak with the car jacked up, and he did the repair himself."

Bob Rost thought Mark was a different person at the track, and he personally liked the non-race Mark a lot better than the highly focused driver who would accept nothing short of perfection. "I was racing on a shoestring," recalls Rost. "I would recondition parts to make them go another race. Mark was disdainful of this and he chided me for racing with less than an ideal setup. For me there was no option and it was more important to race than to necessarily have the ideal setup. Mark saw it differently. We left each other pretty much alone when it came to racing."

Mark was becoming noticed, and at Vineland on July 24 he had the crowd on its feet. John Bornholdt for *Competition Press* said, "The biggest ovation of the day from the crowd was reserved for Mark Donohue in an Elva Courier." Mark had spun on the third lap while trying to take the lead from Sam Perry's Courier. He was in 19th place when he regained the track and was up to 15th by the end of the next lap. He passed four more cars on the following lap and was up to seventh place by the end of lap 10. On the 13th lap he caught and passed Jay Signore to take third place, and on the last lap of the race passed John Heyer to finish second.

On August 6 at the National on the airport circuit at Montgomery, New York, Diffenderfer's Siata had the legs on the Couriers, and he won ahead of Mark and John Heyer. The young Courier drivers were running on limited budgets. Mark had pursued the idea of running recapped tires to save money, only to learn that SCCA regulations prohibited the practice. When Mark learned that Diffenderfer was running

recaps he was outraged, and—the memory of Diffenderfer's protest of his engine still fresh in mind—lodged a protest of his own. The next day Mark was informed that his protest was valid and that Diffenderfer would be disqualified. Overnight Mark had thought the matter through and, taking the advice of Ed Brown, who had sponsored him for SCCA membership, he now withdrew his protest, allowing Diffenderfer's win to stand. Mark had made his point, and now chose sportsmanship over accepting a victory through the protest channel.

The Southern New Jersey region of the SCCA organized a "Triple Crown" regional race on August 21 at Vineland. It was a busy day for Mark, as the triple-crown format embraced three races in one day: a 10-lap preliminary race, a 15-lap final, and a four-hour enduro that was scored on an index of performance formula. F Production turned out an excellent starting field of 33 cars for the 10-lap prelim, and Mark finished second to fellow Courier driver Henry Klay. But when it counted most in the 15-lap feature race, Mark prevailed for the win. In the four-hour enduro he and co-driver John Heyer put 178 laps on the Courier. The 25 race laps logged earlier in the day hurt the effort as the brakes failed just past two hours. By the time Mark pitted and Lou removed all four wheels to make the necessary adjustments, a great deal of time had been lost. The index of performance wasn't kind to the Elva. Mark and John were classified 14th despite running seventh on the road in a field of 39 cars, including Corvettes and modified sports racers. But it was still valuable experience, and part of honing the craft of racing.

The Labor Day National at Thompson, Connecticut, was one of the SCCA's longest-running traditional dates and attracted a large entry. Thompson was just a 35-mile drive from Dave Lawton's home in Providence, Rhode Island, and Mark was able to enjoy the comfort of "his room" in the Lawton household. The 32-car field of F, G, and H Production cars included seven Elva Couriers alongside Alfa Romeo Giuliettas, Sunbeam Alpines, MGAs, Sprites, and Fiat-Abarths. It was a circuit Mark knew well, and he won the preliminary race on Sunday. On the holiday Monday he emerged in the lead by the second lap and stayed ahead the rest of the race for his second National win.

CHAPTER 12:

Jay and Barb

Mark's final National of the season was at Watkins Glen, the home of American road racing. SCCA racing traced its origins to the first Watkins Glen Grand Prix in October 1948—the first road race in America after World War II. That year, and through 1952, the race ran on a 6.6-mile road circuit that started in the village and traversed town, county, and state roads. From 1953 through 1955 it ran on a 4.6-mile public road circuit on the hill overlooking the town and Seneca Lake; it was this circuit that Mark and Dave Lawton had first visited in 1955 as spectators. Encompassing that site, a new purpose-built track was created on private land in 1956. Mark's first look at the new Glen circuit had been earlier in the year when he won the Glen Classic regional race in June.

Mark had just begun to develop a friendship with his close competitor and fellow Courier driver, Jay Signore. Signore had started out racing stock cars at the local New Jersey tracks. He was dating his future wife Barb, who had an Alfa Romeo Giulietta. Since women were not permitted in the pits at the stock-car races, the couple decided to try the more-congenial road-racing scene. After a few races in an Alfa, and then an MGA, Jay had obtained the Elva Courier—like Mark, he also bought it from Lou Schulz—and quickly established himself as one of the top drivers. Jay recalls, "The Courier was as close to a race car as you were going to get—they handled almost like a formula car." The Watkins Glen weekend helped cement what became one of the closest relationships in Mark's life.

"Right at the very beginning we became good friends," recalls Barb. "I think the really close part of the friendship began one day at Watkins Glen when Mark had a problem with his car. Jay went over and helped him. That really glued the whole thing together. Mark said, 'I can't believe you're helping me.'"

Mark was struggling that weekend. The traditional event always drew the largest and most competitive fields, and Mark felt he had slipped behind on the technical side. Unable to obtain the latest hot pistons that foreign car importer Hank Thorpe had supplied to Jay Signore, Mark and Lou Schulz had attempted to make up the lost power by raising the compression ratio. Jay explains the process: "We were so competitive with one another—and Hank Thorpe was kind of helping me out. Mark always seemed to be an inch ahead of you with the latest mods. Then through Hank I got some special pistons and we became equal again. Then Lou and Mark went the next step and they tried to put the engine together without a head gasket to increase the compression ratio. Mark was having trouble with the car overheating—it wouldn't seal the water. Mark and I took his car down to Smalley's Garage that night and I took the head off, fixed it all up—gave him the head gasket. Put the whole thing back together. And we went back to racing the next day."

In one of the best and strongest entries of the year, John Cannon won the F Production race—the Dix Cup—at Watkins Glen in his Elva Courier, less than a second ahead of Diffenderfer's Siata. Jay was third and Paul Richards fourth in a Fiat-Abarth entered by Team Roosevelt. Mark had to settle for fifth in the field of 39 starters.

Canadian-domiciled John Cannon was extremely fast and Mark had a lot of trouble beating him. He represented the first big challenge that required Mark to ratchet his skills up to the next level. Dave Lawton was there: "Mark spent a lot of time figuring out what it was in Cannon's technique that made him so quick. His first reaction was that he's got a different rear end ratio or a better engine. Mark soon realized that no, Cannon's car wasn't any better than anyone else's; he was really a naturally gifted driver."

London, England–born Cannon was just three months younger than Mark. He was working as a car salesman in Montreal, where he met and married Pat Billings in 1959. They went to a race at Ontario's Harewood Acres on their honeymoon. He bought a Morgan that year and did a few races before replacing it with the Courier, intending to concentrate on SCCA races in the States. Pat remembers Mark and Jay Signore as the fastest competitors in the class. In Pat's memory, "Mark was a darling guy. He was intense, but I never thought he was as tough minded about his racing as was John. John took no prisoners."

Doug Diffenderfer's 62 points scored in winning the 1960 F Production SCCA National Championship nearly doubled the 34 scored by runner-up Paul Richards. Mark was equal third with Ernie Harris from Fort Wayne, New Jersey. It was an impressive result for the rookie from the 53 drivers who scored points in FP. Mark's National season hadn't started until July, and in the four Nationals he ran he had two wins, a second, and a fifth. It gave him confidence going into the new year, and he made a personal commitment to go after the championship in 1961.

Mark had built a wooden deck on top of the green Scaglietti—the perfect place for a party after the race. Mark liked to "curb-walk" the Scag. Barb describes the technique: "On garbage day people would put their garbage can out on the edge of the curb. Mark—putting his engineering to use, figuring just the right angle for impact—could skew it all across a guy's lawn."

Barb describes a memorable encounter with the authorities caused by an excess of exuberance in using the smoker. "Up on Broad Street in the center of Elizabeth, a cop on a motorcycle pulled up alongside us. He takes a handkerchief from his back pocket and rubs his eyes, and says, 'I would have caught you five puffs ago, but I couldn't see.' But Mark had that innocent look—the cop says 'I don't know whether to give you a ticket for a smoking vehicle or what.' Mark says, 'Officer, we just stopped in a gas station—the car was running horrible—and the guy put some stuff in the gas tank and said it would fix it—and ever since it has been smoking.' Cop says to us, 'What are you doing in town?' 'Well we're visiting friends over on Linden Avenue.' Cop says, 'Look—drop them off and get out of here. I'm giving you ten minutes to leave town.' "

Barb recalls that Mark always retained that sense of fun with his very close friends. "We always had a good time. Even if Mark got down a little we wouldn't let him." Mark's sense of humor could often be outrageous, and they were constantly playing little games on each other. One day Barb and Jay tripped the Scag's smoke effect without Mark's knowledge. When Mark pulled out of the paddock, people began to run and a fire truck was called over. Mark and Jay would convoy to the races and race back home. A typical move was to cut through a gas station to come out the other side ahead of the other rig.

Mark's antics were not always without retribution. An unknown party, likely seeking revenge for the Scag's smoke-screen treatment, craftily placed an egg salad sandwich under the driver's seat in a place it couldn't easily be detected. The prank worked, as the resultant extremely unpleasant odor lingered for most of the summer.

Jay believes that Mark figured out how to make the Elva fast pretty much on his own. He saw Mark as a natural driver who was "pretty fair" mechanically. "He wasn't afraid to dive in and do something even though he wasn't trained in it as I was," Jay says. "He was really good with the engineering side. He could visualize what he needed, sketch and draw something up, and come up with a solution to a problem."

CHAPTER 13:
You Can't Tow in the Snow

Mark and Jay were ready to open a new season on the first full weekend of January 1961. The always-innovative Washington, D.C., Region of the SCCA had inaugurated the Refrigerator Bowl races at Marlboro just the year before. The idea of racing in the Washington, D.C., area in the brisk early-January weather met with great enthusiasm, and became a tradition.

The 1.7-mile track in Upper Marlboro, Maryland, was important in Mark's life as the site of his drivers' school and his first important Regional win. The SCCA's Washington Region was a hotbed of racing and had spawned the Lavender Hill Mob, a dedicated group of racers and supporters that included Dick Thompson, Richard "Tex" Hopkins, and Bob McKinsey. In 1955 the Mob had persuaded local contractor Dick Cheney, owner of a third-of-a-mile dirt track in Upper Marlboro, to pave his track and add an extension that created a 0.7-mile road circuit. By 1957, with enthusiastic financial support from the Mob, an additional mile had been added, and the D.C. Region hosted its first National. It was a hugely popular circuit, and the original oval created a distinctive bowl-like turn.

The big news for the 1961 season was the SCCA's realignment of the Production classes to create better balance and more competitive racing—a decision that had only been announced the month before. The Elva Couriers' 1960 success in F Production found them reassigned for the new year to E Production. Everyone was anxious to see how the new alignments would play out on the track.

Although this was only a Regional race, Mark and Jay Signore gave notice that the Courier would be just as tough to beat as it had been in 1960, despite moving up a class. Mark won the preliminary race ahead of the theoretically quicker D Production cars, including Reed Rollo's Alfa Romeo Veloce. The 12-lap feature race looked to be another Mark runaway as he opened a solid lead at the start. But Jay got his Courier flying and the two began to swap the lead on every lap. Jay won the race, with Mark second and Reed Rollo again the first DP car.

The first National of the season was another great adventure, unfolding in Daytona Beach, Florida, on the already-famous Speedway. Bill France had opened the Speedway in 1959, and it was the most exciting new track in racing. France had always envisioned international road racing as an important part of his long-range strategy, and a road course was an integral part of the Speedway's design. SCCA races had been part of the schedule since the year the track opened. Slower classes used a 1.6-mile course, while the faster cars—including the now E Prod Couriers—were on the 3.1-mile circuit that incorporated the infield road circuit and the east banking of the tri-oval.

Dave had arrived at the Donohue home on Valley View Avenue just before Mark got home from his engineering job at the Pulverizing Machinery Company in Summit. Zilly fed them a great dinner before they got on the road, Scaglietti and trailer loaded with race car and supplies. Although Mark had been up late all week preparing for the trip, he told Dave, "Let me drive till I can't stay awake any longer." Shortly after they drove into Delaware he turned the wheel over to Dave, with a warning not to exceed 55 mph as the rig could become uncontrollable. Mark climbed into the back of the wagon where they had a mattress set up for sleeping. It wasn't long before the "Scag" inched up to 58 mph on a downhill grade and instantly the trailer began to swing violently from side to side. Mark reached over the back of the seat and with four hands on the wheel, the friends brought the rig back under control.

After driving straight through the night they arrived at Daytona the following afternoon. With no formalities they were waved through the gate, where they learned the track was available for practice. Mark quickly suited up and was out on the circuit. Only the oval was open and Dave recalls Mark coming off the track with a huge grin, saying, "You've got to try it. It's fantastic." Dave pulled on Mark's driver suit, donned his helmet, and was soon circulating the Daytona International Speedway. Dave and Mark discovered that with the Elva Courier maxed out at 120 mph, the third lane of the banking effortlessly carried the little car through.

Barb and Jay had also made the long tow from New Jersey. For Barb, leaving the frigid cold of New Jersey to go racing in Florida in the middle of the winter was "like going into a new world." The E Prod cars were at the bottom of the totem pole in their race, which included the very quick G Modified Lolas, Lotuses, and Elvas, as well as C and D Production cars. Herb Byrne won the class and finished ninth overall in a twin-cam MGA, with Jay Signore second and Ernie Harris from Fort Wayne, Indiana, third in his Courier. Mark had to settle for fourth in class and 14th overall in the 30-car field. This first

National of the season was one of the few times Mark was beaten in the championship season to come.

The fun in the Florida trip came after the race. The Northeast was experiencing brutal cold and deep snow, and Dave Lawton recalls that the Florida newspapers were playing heavily on the bad weather up north. "Every morning after the race we would meet for breakfast, and with encouragement from the news, we would convince one another that it was too risky to head home through the deep snow and that we needed to stay in Florida another day. We quickly coined the phrase, 'You can't tow in the snow.' "

"So we blissfully stayed in Florida for several extra days," recalls Barb. "Jay worked for his dad, Joe Signore, who was a tough guy. When we returned to New Jersey—we weren't married at the time—Joe had not only fired Jay but had put all his possessions out in the snow in front of their house."

CHAPTER 14:
Winning Streak

Mark came to the Northeast's first National on April 16 at Marlboro on the heels of a pair of Regional wins the previous weekend at Vineland, where he had dominated on both Saturday and Sunday. At Marlboro it was a full and competitive field of E Production cars, and Mark won the five-lap qualifying race on Saturday. On Sunday the 25-car field battled hard in very wet conditions. Mark and Jay emerged in the lead at the end of the first lap and stayed there for a 1-2 finish. Behind them it was tough going, with cars off the track and through the hay bales. John Cannon came through for third place in his Courier ahead of Ed Diehl's Triumph TR3, and Peter Revson finished fifth—minus the hood on his Morgan.

On April 30 at Virginia International Raceway (VIR) for the President's Cup Nationals, Mark was dominant, winning overall in the E and F Prod combined race with a clear lead over the E Prod MGA of Sherm Decker. It was a bad day for Jay Signore, who struggled with a poorly running car. A prominent DNF was Peter Revson in his Morgan. The feature race for the President's Cup—the SCCA's most distinguished race award—featured a classic tactical battle between two important figures in Mark's life.

Although Roger Penske was Mark's contemporary in age and background, he had already established himself at the top rung of American road racing as a premier driver, having won the 1960 National Championship in F Modified in his Porsche RSK. By the end of 1961 he would make his debut in a Formula One car at the United States Grand Prix. At VIR Roger was driving his new Tipo 61 Birdcage Maserati and had fitted extra fuel tanks in order to run the three-hour feature race without a stop for fuel. Penske's primary competition was Walt Hansgen in the Briggs Cunningham–entered Birdcage. When Hansgen pitted for tires, fuel, and two and a half gallons of oil at mid-race, his two-minute lead was sufficient to get him out of the pits still in the lead. Hansgen drove on to win his third President's Cup.

The next day Hansgen, Cunningham, and Alfred Momo were at the Pentagon in Arlington, Virginia, to receive the Cup from General Curtis LeMay, U.S. Air Force vice chief of staff and a great supporter of American road racing. Although newly elected U.S. president John F. Kennedy was unavailable to make the presentation, the President's Cup was exactly that. The original award had been presented to Bill Spear after his 1954 victory in the National at Andrews Air Force Base, direct from the hands of President Dwight D. Eisenhower. The magnificent cup was awarded each year to the winner of the premier National organized by the Washington, D.C., Region of the SCCA. This was Walt Hansgen's third time as winner.

At age 41 Walt Hansgen was the elder statesman of American road racing, although his best racing days still lay ahead of him. Hansgen had been racing since 1951, and since 1956 had been the lead driver for the powerful Briggs Cunningham team. As a four-time National Champion in C Modified—then the premier category—and a driver of international reputation, Hansgen was a mentor to many young drivers. He was an early member of the Road Racing Drivers Club (RRDC), and served for several years as president of the group. Through the RRDC Hansgen helped establish safety standards and pioneered modern racing drivers' schools that were adopted by the SCCA. As a fellow member of the SCCA's Northern New Jersey region, Walt Hansgen befriended Mark Donohue and, recognizing his unique talent, recommended him for membership in the prestigious RRDC.

At Vineland the next weekend Mark won another Regional, and he and Lou met novice driver Michael O'Hara. O'Hara had done his own race preparation on his Elva Courier, but it was not performing up to expectations. At Vineland Lou

Schulz suggested he bring the car to his shop in New Jersey. Lou, discovering that Michael had increased the compression ratio to the point where it actually lowered the performance, made the appropriate adjustments.

O'Hara picked the car up and towed it directly to the next race at Cumberland, Maryland, on May 14. In keeping with most SCCA Nationals, novice races were run on Fridays. The difference in his Courier's performance was astounding, and after he won Friday's novice race, the SCCA stewards were threatening to tear the car down to check its legality. On Saturday he was standing beside Lou Schulz when Mark pulled the triple-zero Courier—Mark loved to have double zero or triple zero as his race number whenever it was available—into the pits after just one or two laps of practice. "Mark could hear something tapping inside the engine," Michael recalls. "It was incomprehensible to me that anyone could have the sensitivity to hear that over the very loud unmuffled engine noise and other distractions."

Lou Schulz put a stethoscope on the engine and discovered a crack in the crankshaft. A replacement engine was sent for, but in the meantime Mark had not completed the five required practice laps. O'Hara suggested that Mark take his car out and the invitation was gratefully accepted. Almost immediately Mark lapped the course five seconds faster than Michael had achieved. O'Hara remembers it clearly: "It was uncanny how fast he was. I hadn't exactly been slow—I was quick enough that they wanted to tear me down. But Mark's talent had to be seen to be believed. He was that fast."

With the new engine fitted to his own car Mark made it three National wins in a row when he decisively won at Cumberland. Jay made it another 1-2 for the New Jersey pals but did it the hard way, coming from the back of the field after a poor start. At the end of a long day of watching racing, Roger DeVore was inching his Austin-Healey 100/4 up the long hill out of the track in painfully slow traffic. Roger and two friends, who were squeezed into the passenger side seat, were heading east for Chestertown, Maryland, where they were students at Washington College. Hearing a sudden roar from behind they looked up in time to see Mark in the Elva driving by on the shoulder of the road at a brisk rate, continuing up the long hill and out of sight. Had he been asked, Mark no doubt would have explained with perfect logic that the race car simply wasn't set up to cool in traffic and there wasn't anything for it but to steam along the best way he could.

Mark was actually practicing the time-honored privilege assumed by race drivers all over the world. Fast driving on the road was, if not a birthright, certainly one that came with being among the racing elite. With few exceptions race drivers drove flat out—in every situation. You didn't have to be in a particular hurry to get anywhere; that was just the way you drove. It was part of the conceit of being an "ace."

Two weeks later on Memorial Day weekend at Bridgehampton, Mark again dominated in winning the E Prod class, and finished fourth overall behind three D Prod cars. Jay Signore and Peter Revson failed to finish, and Tim Mayer, driving a Lotus Elite, finished second in E Prod to Mark. The feature race went to Mark's friend Walt Hansgen, who drove the Cunningham Tipo 61 Birdcage Maserati to victory over the Birdcages of Alan Connell and Fred Gamble.

The next weekend Mark gave the triple-zero Courier—the white car with the three red zeros had achieved popular acclaim and recognition in its own right—a welcome rest. Instead he accepted Michael O'Hara's invitation to co-drive his Courier in the feature 6-Hour Regional race at Marlboro. O'Hara continued to be impressed with Mark's lap times, and after watching carefully from the corners asked him how he managed to carry so much speed through the first-gear hairpin. Mark's answer spoke volumes: He used second gear.

Mark started the race, and by the two-hour point had the little production Elva up to a remarkable second place overall against stern competition that included modified Porsches—the winning car was an ex–Bob Holbert RS60 driven by Pete DeCosta and Holbert's mechanic Bill (Murf) Mayberry. Mark was doing it through fast, consistent driving and was displaying a gift for lapping traffic without losing momentum. The great drive was delayed by a broken throttle cable. After Mark returned to the track, a halfshaft broke, and he parked the car out on the circuit. Michael had a spare that he took out to the car; in the darkness, he replaced it under the watchful eye of an SCCA observer. Mark was able to finish the race.

Weak halfshafts were just one of the chronic maintenance issues that Mark and others racing Elva Couriers dealt with. It was essential after every race to take the pan down, replace the rod bearings, and re-torque the main bearings. The engine would lose 50 pounds of torque off the main bearing cap bolts during each race.

On June 11 a relatively minor eight-lap preliminary race at Vineland produced a result of greater interest retrospectively

than it likely had for the participants or observers at the time. Three of the first four finishers were future Formula One drivers, with Mark winning ahead of Jay Signore. Tim Mayer came in third in a Lotus Elite, and Peter Revson fourth in his Morgan. Later in the day in the feature 12-lap Divisional championship race, things did not go as well. Mark and Jay both failed to finish the race, and Revson won in the Morgan Plus 4 ahead of Norman Cook's MGA, with Mayer third in his Elite.

Bob Sharp, who became a six-time SCCA National champion and a racing legend in his own right, was a keen observer of driver technique. He rated Mark and Tim Mayer very highly at this point in their careers, and believes they employed similar driving techniques. "Mark and Timmy were fast and were already precise, consistent, and thoughtful on the track. Peter [Revson] was fast too, although at this point he lacked the consistency of Mark and Timmy."

The DNF at Vineland ended a remarkable spring of 1961 for Mark, who had raced at virtually every opportunity on the Atlantic coast. Since the Vineland races in April, in a combination of prelims, Regionals, and Nationals, he had run off 11 consecutive wins in his own Elva Courier in a highly competitive and diverse class.

CHAPTER 15:
"The Drift—Its Execution and Its Advantages"

Barb and Jay were now married, and their apartment often served as "party central" away from the track. Mark was a constant presence at these events and often an overnight guest of the Signores. Peter Revson was part of the group, and away from the track he and Mark enjoyed a friendship reasonably free from competitiveness. At the track it was a different story, as Jay Signore remembers: "Mark and Peter were always cranking on each other at the track—at Cumberland one day Mark walked up to the Morgan and pulled on the leather strap saying, 'Pete, this thing is kind of loose, isn't it?' Peter grabbed the strap and unintentionally ripped it out. He was mad at Mark for a while after that." Jay recalls that Peter was "a very competitive guy, and considering that car-to-car, the Morgan was down on the Couriers, he did a heck of a job, drove it very well."

Mark and Peter fought a close battle at Watkins Glen on

June 24, although neither man emerged with a finish. Mark had qualified third and Peter second for the Glen Classic, a Divisional race, and Mark took an early lead from the double overhead cam MGA of Robert Poupard. Poupard took the lead on the second lap and was able to open a gap while Mark and Peter diced hard for second. Peter was out of the race on lap 11 and Mark was out on lap 17 of 22 as Poupard won.

A week later, Mark won the traditional Fourth of July Nationals at Lime Rock, with Peter second. Mark's driving was impressive; according to *Sports Car* magazine's Henry Bostder, "[the race] might well be entitled 'The Drift—Its Execution and Its Advantages,' as Mark Donohue put on a superb demonstration of the Elva's handling and his own driving ability."

Afterward Mark and Rob McCullough, Jay and Barb Signore, and Peter Revson were among a number of friendly competitors from the E Prod race who wandered up on the hill to watch the rest of the races together in a convivial spirit. Suddenly an announcement was made for Mark to report to the chief steward. Mark's engine was being protested by Peter Revson. It was as big a shock to Peter as to anyone present. The protest had been lodged by his mechanic, without consulting Peter. The result of the teardown was that the Courier was once again found to be in complete compliance. Peter was embarrassed and spent the rest of the day explaining to one and all that he had not been party to the protest.

Mark, Jay, and Peter were each determined to win the National Championship, and on July 23 there were important points to be won at faraway Meadowdale Raceway, located in the Chicago suburb of Carpentersville, Illinois. Jay remembers that the three men made an agreement: "We were kind of broke in a way, and we were all really tight in points for the championship, and we all agreed—made a pact—that we weren't going to go to some western race. We would just keep the points the same. Barb and I didn't go—we couldn't afford it. But Mark, unbeknownst to me, and Peter, unbeknownst to Mark or me, made the long haul."

A lack of funds was keeping Mark at home—not to mention his fear that the 1,700-plus-mile round-trip was likely more than the Scag could handle. But during the week Mark Sr. offered his Oldsmobile wagon for the journey, and in his excitement Mark forgot the agreement. He was not alone in his enthusiasm to be in the race. Mark left late Friday night, and early Saturday morning near Chicago spotted a familiar tow vehicle in a diner parking lot. Walking into the

diner, Mark discovered Peter enjoying his breakfast. The surprise was mutual.

The 3.27-mile Meadowdale circuit was an American classic. The nature of the available space meant that runoff areas were minimal or nonexistent, making the circuit challenging and unforgiving. It is well remembered for the Monza Wall, a 180-degree, steeply banked turn that led to a nearly 4,000-foot straight. The track was built in 1958, and track management had soon fallen afoul of the SCCA, which ran no races there in 1959 or 1960, so the July National in 1961 was a return to good graces with the Westport, Connecticut–based club.

Ernie Harris from Fort Wayne, Indiana, was the leading Courier driver in the Midwest, and local experts viewed him as the favorite in E Production. Midwesterners were unimpressed with tales coming from the East Coast of a guy named Donohue running up a string of victories. But Mark proved a sensation, and perhaps a revelation, at Meadowdale on a difficult track he had never seen before. The race was for A, B, C, D, and E Production. Mark easily won his class and was impressive in doing it, as reported by Dic Van der Feen in his *Competition Press* column: "Harris himself was pulverized in the next big event when Mark Donohue (Courier) showed how he's won those 30-odd races on the East Coast. Donohue boggled the imagination, finishing 11th overall in the ABCDE production 12-lapper. He headed all the C & D class cars and only the Ferraris and Corvettes were ahead of him at the finish."

Mark was actually 10th and Peter Revson 11th as they ran 1-2 in E Prod—an impressive showing for both men in the 42-car field. Harris was 3rd in class and 14th overall. The overall race winner was Ferrari driver Denise McCluggage after apparent victor Don Yenko was disqualified for an illegal flywheel in his Corvette (the protest coming from a fellow Corvette driver). The race was characterized by frequent accidents and was eventually red-flagged and ended early.

The feature race at Meadowdale was for B through F Modified cars. Roger Penske won in his Tipo 61 Maserati Birdcage ahead of Peter Ryan in the Comstock-sponsored Sadler Special from Canada and Augie Pabst in his own 2.5-liter Ferrari. The rare and aesthetically pleasing Birdcages were as good as it got in SCCA sports-car racing in 1961. The 2.0-liter Birdcage—the Tipo 60—was an E Modified car, while the Tipo 61, at 2890cc, fit in D Modified for under-3.0-liter cars. Penske finished the season as SCCA National Champion in D Modified. Winner of the F Modified class at Meadowdale was

Tom Payne from Ann Arbor, Michigan. Payne's Porsche RS61 was looked after by Porsche-trained master mechanic Karl Kainhofer from Graz, Austria. Both Penske and Kainhofer were to become close friends of Mark Donohue's, and would play a central role in his future success.

CHAPTER 16:
National Champion

Back on the East Coast the Mark-and-Jay show in E Production became the Mark-and-Peter show as the two again ran 1-2 while Jay fell out in the August 6 National at Bridgehampton, Long Island. The race on this date had traditionally been held at the Montgomery Airport circuit in the Hudson Valley, but when that venue became unavailable, the New York Region of the SCCA switched it to Bridgehampton. Although Mark at first trailed the D Production Alfa Romeos and Porsches, within a few laps he had passed the theoretically faster cars to win the race overall. Peter Revson, while second in E Prod, was seventh overall.

The feature race was a much-anticipated battle between the Tipo 61 Birdcage Maserati of Roger Penske and the rear-engined Tipo 63 Maserati driven by Walt Hansgen—the latter making its first appearance on U.S. soil. While Hansgen and Cunningham had been away in Europe, Penske had won the Nationals at Elkhart Lake, Lime Rock, and Meadowdale. The Cunningham Tipo 61 was driven on this day by Dick Thompson, and other top entries included Peter Ryan in a Lotus 19, George Constantine in a Ferrari Testa Rossa, and Harry Heuer in the Meister Bräuser Scarab. Penske and Ryan brought the battle to Hansgen—rightly remembered as the Master of the Bridge—and when Ryan fell out with gearbox trouble, it was all Hansgen and Penske, with the two men exchanging the lead throughout. Such was Hansgen's reputation at Bridgehampton that Penske's close run to second place gained him nearly as much respect as his previous wins.

Sports Car named Mark the heavy favorite to win the traditional Labor Day National at Thompson, Connecticut, on September 3–4—but this would be a weekend remembered for transmission trouble. Mark was staying in his room in the Lawton household in nearby Pawtucket, Rhode Island, and Dave Lawton helped Mark replace his transmission. Mark had been leading Saturday's qualifying prelim before the transmission packed up. On Sunday, Mark was placed 16th

on the grid. By the fifth lap he was challenging Jay Signore for the lead, but ultimately dropped out of the race with engine trouble. Nevertheless, Mark's overwhelming lead in points—Jay was second—had caused Peter Revson to abandon hopes of winning the E Production championship. He replaced his Morgan with an Elva Formula Junior.

September was a busy month with Mark racing every weekend. At Vineland on September 10, he first won a 10-lap qualifying race before winning again in the 15-lap feature. A week later he entered a Divisional race at Lime Rock where he emerged victorious.

His last National of the year was September 22 at Watkins Glen. The E Production cars raced in the Collier Brothers Memorial—the race honoring the memories of Sam and Miles Collier, who had done so much to pioneer road racing in America both before and after World War II. It was not Mark's day, as two uncharacteristic spins knocked him out of contention for the win. Victory went to Jay Signore, with Mark settling for fifth. Mark also accepted a last-minute invitation from Herrymond Maurer to race his F Production MGA in the Dix Cup. He finished 12th in the 30-car field.

Even before Watkins Glen, Mark had clinched the National Championship in the tough E Production class. Final National points counts showed Mark with 70, Jay Signore with 56, Ernie Harris with 44, and Peter Revson with 26.

CHAPTER 17:
Large Mark Steps Up to the Plate

Lou Schulz had been talking about getting an Elva Formula Junior for Mark to drive, and the car arrived in late October. The radically low Elva 300 was the latest and greatest model for the small British company. Elva had been taken over earlier in the year by Trojan Engineering, which hoped the new car would achieve success in the lucrative Formula Junior market. The car delivered to S&R Motors was chassis # 300/000/01.

With the SCCA season in the Northeast virtually over, Mark and Lou made plans to enter the car at the Bahamas Speed Weeks in Nassau. Hank Thorpe had a parts replacement business in Highland Park, New Jersey, with a small race shop. Mark and Lou knew the new Elva needed specialized work, and asked Thorpe to go through the car. It resided in Thorpe's shop for some time, with Mark an ever-present figure. As the time for departure to Nassau neared, The Coach came to Mark with news that the deal had changed. Lou was a car salesman and had financed the Elva through his floor-plan arrangement with the bank. The terms of the financing did not permit the car to leave the country. There would be no sponsored drive at Nassau after all.

All of Mark's friends knew his parents well as frequent visitors to the Donohue home, where all were welcome. Zilly was gregarious and fun and could charm anyone. Mark Sr., while well liked, was always Mr. Donohue, or Sir, though when not present he was also referred to as "Large Mark"—only in part because of his imposing height. It was Large Mark who now stepped up and quietly purchased the Junior. Even the closest observers were never clear on whether the car was Mark's or Lou's, or when it ceased to be Lou's.

Mark Sr. and Zilly were supportive parents who believed in their children. Although Zilly was the vocal and visible presence at Mark's races, Mark Sr. always encouraged his son to pursue his dreams. Mark maintained a meticulous record of the money advanced to him by his father, and later said that the total was $37,000. He eventually paid the money back, although his father maintained the funds in a separate account in case Mark ever needed the money again.

Under the direction of organizer "Red" Crise, the Bahamas Speed Weeks featured racing for a variety of cars and classes on the Oakes Field circuit, along with various social activities. Entry was by invitation only, and the Nassau Tourist Board picked up the tab for transportation and prize money. A different local resort hotel hosted a party each evening.

Nassau, with its weeklong unhurried schedule of races, was an end-of-the-season phenomenon and a nonstop party for most participants. Red Crise was a colorful promoter, and with the backing of the Nassau Tourist Board had managed since the early 1950s to attract the elite drivers and cars of international racing. Mark towed the Formula Junior to Miami, where he was met by Rob McCullough. The two friends took the boat to Nassau for what was expected to be a great adventure.

The broad enthusiasm for participating in the race can be understood by the fact that race organizer Crise was able to turn away 161 would-be entries for this, the eighth annual Speed Week. Neither Mark nor Rob was impressed with the fabled event, although it is fair to say that their experience was clouded by the amount of work required by the Elva.

The car was fragile, and the extremely bumpy Oakes Field circuit found every weak spot on the frame and broke it. Rob remembers having to repeatedly weld the damage.

These disappointments notwithstanding, Mark made an impressive showing in his single-seater debut. After plenty of time all week to practice (and break the brittle chassis) on the rough 4.5-mile circuit, a five-lap heat race was run on Friday. Mark was a solid fourth behind two Lotus 20s from the West Coast in the hands of Pat Pigott and Jack McAfee, with Roger Penske third in his Cooper T56 BMC. Behind Mark in order were: Charlie Kolb, Gemini 3A; Pete Lovely, Lotus 20; Harry Carter, Lotus 20; and Jim Hall, Cooper T56. Mark did not start the Saturday heat, as he and Rob were busy welding the Elva chassis. Pete Lovely won this heat, with Roger Penske second and Pat Pigott third. Missing Saturday's heat race left Mark well down on the grid for Sunday's 12-lap finale on December 10. Mark worked the Elva through the pack until he reached fourth position among the 25 runners. The three leaders had broken away by this point, and the final result was Lovely, Pigott, Penske, and Donohue.

Although not everything Mark had hoped for, Nassau still represented a good result. It concluded a great year for Mark, who had earned a National Championship in only his second year of racing.

CHAPTER 18:

Respectful Tap

The new road race in America for 1962 was the Daytona Continental. Race organizer Bill France had obtained an international listing and a place on the Fédération Internationale de l'Automobile's (FIA) World Championship for Manufacturers series. Alec Ulmann, whose 12 Hour race at Sebring, Florida, had been a fixture in the international championship since 1953, vigorously resisted the inclusion of a second American race, particularly one to be held in the same state just a month before his own. Although the rivalry continued for many years, ultimately both races found their own version of success. Sebring always attracted the larger crowd because of its established tradition, with the added attraction of a March date that coincided with spring break for American colleges.

The first 3-Hour Continental attracted a great entry and was famously won by Dan Gurney in a red Lotus 19. On

Saturday there was a Formula Junior race, so Mark made the long tow from New Jersey to be part of it. Formula Junior was beginning its third year as an SCCA class and was at the height of its popularity. As a new driver in the class Mark was biting off a great deal. The top teams and drivers had logged many race miles in the finely engineered single-seat cars and knew how to prepare and set them up.

There was a big field for Daytona's Junior race, requiring three 10-lap qualifying heats to determine the starting order for the final. Mark scored a splendid victory with the Elva in his heat, ahead of top drivers with extensive Formula Junior experience. These included Tim Mayer and Roger Penske. Mark had only the slightest relationship at the time with Penske, and was startled when Roger tapped him from behind on the cool-down lap. Mark was initially a little put out until he realized it had been a congratulatory acknowledgment of his win.

The feature race for Formula Junior was for 35 laps on the 1.63-mile short course. Mark took the early lead and held it for the first four laps before being passed by Pete Lovely in a Lotus 22. On the next lap Mark spun and dropped to fourth place, but he stayed with it, and toward the end of the race had regained second behind Lovely. On the next to the last lap he went off the road again and was unable to restart as the carburetor caught on fire. Lovely won, with Floyd Aaskov second in a Lotus 20, and Charlie Kolb third in a Gemini. Years later, recounting the race for his book, Mark would describe the weekend as something of a disaster and downplay his accomplishment. The fact is that he had completely distinguished himself and shown great speed. A heat win and a competitive run in the final were both to be savored.

Mark and Jay Signore had been recommended for a drive with the British TVR team for the 1962 Sebring 12 Hour race on March 24. It was the first time at the famous Florida circuit for either man. The small British manufacturer had ambitiously entered a three-car team. Its latest model, the Mark 3, would be introduced to the public at the New York Auto Show in April. The Mark 3 had a 1588cc MG engine, and at Sebring TVR hoped to compete with the works-supported MGAs and Elva Couriers. The race cars at Sebring were actually lightened Mk 2As with some of the Mk 3 styling.

Lou Schulz had been the key to Mark and Jay obtaining the drive in the TVR. Lou was a TVR distributor and easily convinced the firm's U.S. importer, New Yorker Dick Monnich, to include the New Jersey pair. At the race Lou served as a mechanical adviser to the team. The cars were late in arriving at the Port of New York due to problems at sea. Monnich was unable to arrange air transport from New York to Florida, and the three race cars were driven the 1,300 miles to Sebring by Monnich, sales manager Tony Clark, and Walt Mann, one of the drivers.

On Friday, the day before the 12 Hour race, Mark entered the Elva in the Formula Junior race. Madeline and Rob Mc-Cullough towed the race car from New Jersey and assisted. It was a discouraging day. Mark had to buy a set of both wet and dry tires, and he later said, "That was all the money I had in the world." And the 5.2-mile Sebring circuit proved even rougher than Oakes Field in Nassau. When the frame broke in a practice session and the right front wheel fell off, Rob and Mark were unable to prepare the car to start the race. Mark's friend Walt Hansgen was knocked out of contention for the lead in the Formula Junior event when he pitted with low oil pressure in the Cunningham-entered Cooper-Fiat. Hansgen managed to finish third behind Pat Pigott's Team Rosebud Lotus 20 and Tim Mayer in a Cooper.

Jay and Mark were delighted to be part of the works TVR team for the 12 Hour race, but during practice, they failed to achieve lap times fast enough to please competition director Ken Richardson. Richardson had been associated with BRM in its early days as both a driver and race engineer, and later headed the factory Triumph entries in international endurance racing.

"Mark and I were very mindful that this was a long race on a rough track, and we were deliberately not running the car too hard during practice. It became apparent that the TVR people were not impressed with our lap times, and our position on the team was in jeopardy," remembers Signore. "Mark was down about this until I walked him out to one of the corners. We watched our teammates wail through lap after lap, using every bit of the road and every bit of the car. I told Mark that these guys were going to break their cars for certain. We decided to each do one hot practice lap to show the TVR brass we could and then save the cars for the race."

The TVR was not without its inherent problems. On the long Sebring straights the little cars would reach peak speed and stay there for an extended time. Jay reports that the bodies would lift and the windshield would fall in on the driver. Safety wire was employed to solve the problem.

The race played out about as Jay had predicted. The two team cars were out after 20 and 56 laps respectively. The

Peter Bolton / Mike Rothschild No. 54 entry failed with a broken differential in the second hour, while the No. 56 of Ray Cuomo / Jake Jacobs dropped out with bearing failure after four hours. Jay and Mark were in the only TVR to finish. They were up to 14th position overall after nine hours when, with Mark at the wheel, the No. 55 TVR developed steering trouble. Mark brought the car to the pits and forty minutes were lost repairing a steering arm. They finished 25th overall and 8th in class. Nonetheless, they were still running at the finish, vindicating their original instincts. The overall 1962 Sebring winner was a Ferrari driven by Joakim Bonnier and Lucien Bianchi.

After Sebring the TVR race cars stayed in the country and were campaigned by R.M. Imports. Dick Monnich, who became a close friend of Mark's, based his importing operation in the Hicksville, New York, Ford dealership of Jack Griffith. The Sebring race was the beginning of a relationship between Mark, Dick, and Jack that would take on greater significance in the years ahead.

After the race Rob and Madeline towed the Elva back to New Jersey and Mark, anxious to get back to work, got on an airplane. Before beginning his drive Rob said he would be home first. Mark caught a series of short flights on his way home. When he picked up his car he later described driving as fast as he could to get home. "As I pulled in the driveway of my parents' home where I kept the car, there were Rob and Madeline having just arrived with the Elva in tow."

The Governor's Cup races on April 14–15 brought Marlboro, Maryland, the largest crowd in the history of the track up to that time. Mark again doubled with his Elva and the TVR, and distinguished himself in the Formula Junior race. He was second in Saturday's 5-lap preliminary, and on Sunday was again the runner-up to Tim Mayer's Cooper in a top field of 21 cars in the 10-lap race for national points. Mayer was on his way to winning the SCCA Formula Junior National Championship. It was a cold and windy day but largely a good one for Mark and friends. Jay Signore won the E Production race in his Elva Courier.

The big modified race was for the Governor's Cup. The TVR, entered by Dick Monnich, was completely outclassed. The SCCA refused to allow it to run as a production car as had been hoped, and in D Modified, with an essentially stock 1800cc MG engine, it was running against all the fastest sports-racing cars of the period. Mark brought it home

in 13th place. The Governor's Cup went to Roger Penske in his Telar Cooper-Monaco. The Telar name on the side of the Cooper was causing waves within the SCCA, and at some tracks Penske was forced to cover the lettering with tape. The SCCA was still a year away from embracing open commercial sponsorship.

The TVR found a more agreeable classification at Bridgehampton on June 2. The New York Region of the SCCA held a GT race to international rules as a curtain-raiser to the National that weekend. The race was dominated by Ferrari 250 GTs, with Bob Grossman winning overall. The TVR was quick in Class 2, and Mark led the category until suffering ignition trouble and dropping out. His teammate Rich Schmanske won the class.

Cunningham team drivers Augie Pabst and Walt Hansgen were standing outside the Bridgehampton circuit gate talking as Mark happened to drive by. Augie has never forgotten how Walt interrupted their conversation: "Hey mate! See that guy? He is going to be one of the greatest drivers this country will ever see."

CHAPTER 19:

Wrong Car—Right Girl

The Formula Junior venture had become too much for Mark. The Elva was a car with great potential, and Mark had been fast in it every time out against the best and most experienced drivers in America. But it was an expensive car to maintain and develop, and Mark had neither the time nor the financial resources to keep it up. The Elva chassis was particularly brittle and Mark had become discouraged at the continual repairs. He now set the car aside and tried to find a more rational means of staying in racing. Although drives in the TVR were keeping his season from being a complete bust, the fact that the car did not fit in an SCCA class made it an only occasional, and generally uncompetitive, proposition.

Mark purchased a used Daimler SP250 from racer/car dealer Bob Grossman. The Daimler was not race prepared, so Mark went about making the car track-ready. He received some help from Lou Schulz, but The Coach wasn't enthusiastic about the Daimler, and was disappointed that Mark was not continuing to develop the Elva Formula Junior. John Heyer helped Mark with the car and sums up the experience:

"We all make occasional bad choices in life. The Daimler was Mark's bad choice." Mark debuted the Daimler at Vineland on July 7–8 in a Regional and won C Production. Although it wasn't against top national competition, it was an encouraging beginning for the car.

Mark's life was about to change. The seminal moment occurred at Vineland later that same month. Mark was not racing and had agreed to serve as a corner observer. Renee Rost bumped into him in the paddock and impulsively acted on an idea that had been in her mind for some time. She found a phone and called her sister. Renee and Sue Warren had grown up in Rumson, New Jersey, and Sue was a graduate of Centenary College in Hackettstown, New Jersey. She was now working for an insurance company in Red Bank. She was at home on that quiet Saturday morning in the summer of 1962 when she took the phone call from Renee that would change her life, as well.

"Renee said, 'We're here at a race in Vineland and I want you to come,'" recalls Sue. "I said, no, I don't feel like coming." Renee frequently told Sue she needed to see what was going on in this whole different world of racing, often regaling her sister with the fun they all had at the races and the attractive young men who drove the cars. On this day she was insistent. Sue should find her way to the Vineland without delay; Renee had people she wanted her sister to meet. "You get down here and you get down here now," Renee told Sue. "I remember driving down the Parkway with curlers in my hair," says Sue.

When Sue arrived at Vineland she discovered her sister was right. It was fun, and she had a wonderful day. Mark Donohue, Peter Ryan, and Peter Revson were the young men Renee particularly had her eye on for her sister. It was Mark who appealed to Sue. "When I met Mark, that was it."

Stone Harbor was very near the Vineland circuit, and the Rosts had a house there. It was the center of the fun on race weekends. The Rosts managed to put a lot of racing friends up for the weekends, even if some ended up sleeping on the floors. "Nobody had any money," Sue remembers. "It was just as many bodies as you could possibly fit in a room—male or female, it didn't matter. It was a great time and everyone got along.

"From that day on Mark and I spent every minute of every day and evening together until the day we were married," says Sue. "We always had fun together and did all kinds of crazy things. Mark was a wonderful guy to be with."

Additional perspective on that first meeting is provided by Sue's interview with Bill Levinson for an early-1970s feature article in the *Newark Sunday News*:

Renee decided she wanted Mark for a brother-in-law and arranged for me to come to the track to meet him. It was the first time I had ever been to the track, and Mark wasn't driving, he was an observer stationed at one of the turns to grade other drivers on the way they handled their cars. Mark was one of the top amateur sports-car drivers in the country and had an engineering degree from Brown, but he explained everything in language I could understand. I was very impressed.

The attraction was mutual and immediate as recalled by Renee. "They were drawn to each other and were just having a great deal of fun—Sue came to all his races and I would see her fooling around, wearing Mark's helmet and sitting in the race car. They both seemed transformed in a sense."

CHAPTER 20:
"Mark was such a devil"

C production was a competitive class, and the Daimler's best days as a top car in the category had been two years earlier. The Lotus Super 7 was among an eclectic group of cars in the category that included the Porsche Super 90, the still-powerful-though-dated Jaguar XK120, the Morgan Plus 4, and the Ace Bristol. Mark later described the Daimler as "... a big truck, it was terrible, it understeered and I never really had time to do much with it as I was spending all my time working on the engine."

Rob McCullough was with Mark at Thompson for the Labor Day weekend National. The transmission broke beyond repair in practice. Ray Pickles, a friend of Mark and Rob's, offered the transmission from his street Daimler. The three friends worked late into the night swapping the transmissions from one car to the other. The next day Mark had his best National result in the Daimler, finishing 2nd in C Production and 14th overall out of 26 starters in the race for A, B, and C Prod combined. Dave Clark won CP in a Lotus Super 7 and was 10th overall.

Mark had another opportunity to race the TVR for Dick Monnich on September 15 when Bridgehampton organized its most important race to date, having obtained an international listing for a round in the World Manufacturers Championship. The 1962 championship was contested for GT cars and within four separate divisions based upon displacement. Division I was for cars up to 1000cc, and Division II, where the TVR fit, was for those up to 2000cc. The smaller cars ran a 400-kilometer race on Saturday and the big cars in Division III and IV had their own 400-kilometer race on Sunday. Unfortunately for the race organizers, the top European teams did not send cars since the championships had been sewn up in the respective categories earlier in the year. The entry was made up of domestic teams, in many cases supported by the U.S. importer of a particular model. The three-car TVR team was out of its league against the much faster Porsches and Fiat-Abarths. Mark lasted only a few laps before the car gave him trouble. Bob Holbert won in a Porsche-Abarth. The big car race on Sunday was won by a Ferrari TR LM entered by Luigi Chinetti's North American Racing Team (NART) for Pedro Rodríguez.

The following week on September 22, Mark brought the Daimler to the 15th Annual Watkins Glen Grand Prix, where C Production cars had their own race. Typically SCCA races were named as race one, race two, etc. At Watkins Glen each race was distinguished with a name. The 17 starters in C Production were contesting the Dix Cup—Dix being the township in Schuyler County in which the Watkins Glen race circuit is located. Mark finished fifth and wasn't even the fastest Daimler. Dave Clark, in the Lotus Super 7 in which he had been dominating the class, won ahead of the Daimler of Gary Morgan. Clark ended the season as National Champion in the class. Mark also trailed the XK120 of John Howe and the Lotus Super 7 of Horace Pettit Jr.

The 15th Annual Watkins Glen Grand Prix was won by Walt Hansgen in Briggs Cunningham's Cooper-Buick. It was Hansgen's fourth victory in the classic event. The race marked the first driver fatality at Watkins Glen since Sam Collier's death in the 1950 race. Arthur "Bud" Faust crashed his Lotus Buick in the very fast Big Bend and died instantly from his injuries. Faust was 48 years old and an experienced driver from Kingston, Pennsylvania, having gained particular distinction as a hillclimb champion. The 1962 race was the last of the series to be held on the traditional late-September date. The United States Grand Prix for Formula One was in its second year at the Glen circuit and its date was the first weekend in October. In 1963 the annual amateur race was moved to August to create a longer break between events.

At Vineland in October for the SCCA's South Jersey Region Autumn Sprints, Mark had the opportunity to race a Lotus 22 Formula Junior for local enthusiast John Kalhoven. Jay Signore was also in the race in a Lotus 22 from Lotus dealer Sy Kaback. The two friends finished 1-2, and on this occasion it was Jay ahead of Mark.

Sue and Mark visited her sister Renee and husband Bob Rost in Pittsburgh in November. On the drive back east across Pennsylvania Mark had a suggestion. "Mark said we ought to think about getting married," Sue recalls. "That was the proposal, and four months later we did marry."

Sue remembers that everyone in her family loved Mark. "He was a joy to be with and everyone felt that way. Really, it wasn't just my family. He was just a fellow you couldn't help being attracted to."

Alice Warren, Sue and Renee's mother, was particularly fond of Mark, who returned the feeling. "Mark was such a devil," remembers Renee. "He would get both my mother and himself tipsy and they would get silly beyond belief. She loved it."

The year ended with a trip to Nassau the first week of December where Mark raced the TVR. The Speed Weeks the year before had been a mixed pleasure because of the amount of work required on the Elva Formula Junior. This year was a delight. Although the TVR didn't go even as well as the Elva had, Mark and Sue were having the time of their lives. Impulsively Mark put a phone call through to Pittsburgh. He wanted Renee to know that Sue had agreed to marry him.

Charlie Hayes remembers Mark's joy. "He was almost like an adolescent talking about this wonderful woman he had met named Sue. He was obviously head over heels in love."

The TVR never ran well at Nassau in 1962. Mark completed only three laps of the first heat for the Nassau Tourist Trophy heat race on December 2. The car could not be made ready for the start of the Tourist Trophy later in the day. Roger Penske won the race impressively in a Ferrari GTO ahead of Lorenzo Bandini and Innes Ireland in GTOs. By the end of the week Mark was able to bring the TVR to the start line for the heat race for the Governor's Trophy race. But he never completed a lap, and the two heat races represented the sum total of his racing at Nassau in 1962. Texan Hap Sharp won the Governor's Trophy in his Cooper-Monaco ahead of the Porsche RSK of Bob Holbert. The feature Nassau Trophy on December 9 was won by Scotland's Innes Ireland in a Lotus 19 for Texan Tom O'Connor's Rosebud Racing Team.

The ever-competitive Mark was reasonably sanguine about the disappointing performance of the TVR. Nassau was an anomaly that existed outside the regular racing season, and it had an atmosphere unlike any other event. Although the competition on the track was as intense as anywhere else, the overall end-of-season feel and the constant party atmosphere mitigated racing upsets. Mark and Sue were together and just couldn't help having a wonderful time.

CHAPTER 21:

"Wherever Mark was . . ."

Mark was ready to part with the Elva Formula Junior, having reached the end of his patience and his financial resources with the high-maintenance race car. He took the Elva to Marlboro, Maryland, for the Refrigerator Bowl, organized annually by the SCCA's Washington, D.C., Region. Races were run on both the 1.7-mile road course and the track's original half-mile oval. Mark easily won the preliminary race for Formula Junior on Saturday, January 5, 1963. After the race he had a drink with Charlie Hayes. "I did not have a car for that weekend," Charlie remembers. "Over a drink or two that Saturday night before the race, he told me how much he wanted to sell the Elva. I had recently sold my Ferrari Berlinetta and asked him what he wanted for the car. The number he quoted may have been $3,500. Whatever it was I, mostly joking, offered him $1,500. Mark said, 'Hell, no.' It was about midnight, after a few more drinks, when I took my checkbook out and said, 'I'll write you check right now for $2,500. Mark said, 'Oh, what the hell. I'll take it.' " Charlie raced the Elva the next day.

Before he turned the Elva over to Hayes, Mark raced the car one last time. A 10-lap "Midget Match Race" was staged on Marlboro's half-mile oval track. The total field comprised three Formula Juniors pitted against Bud Brosenne's dirt-track midget V8-60. Donna Mae Mimms captured the atmosphere in her report for *Competition Press*: "It was a very incongruous sight to see Brosenne, replete with face mask, dirt track tires and hand brake, roar around the oval lifting his left front wheel in classic midget fashion (many fans thought this was very courageous), and lead three snarling F-Jrs to the checkered flag. The only serious challenge was by Mark Donahue [sic] who could not find quite enough darting room."

Dick Monnich again invited Mark to race the TVR at Sebring on March 23. It was Sue's first Sebring and she remembers the fun and adventure. "In those days everything

was just a great laugh. Mark was serious when he was on the track, but most of the time we were laughing and having fun." It was just a month before their wedding and a perfect time to be away from cold and damp New Jersey. The Florida sun was great, but for Sue it was all about being together. "Wherever Mark was is where I wanted to be."

The pleasure they found in one another's company seemingly overcame a dismal race performance. The 1963 three-car TVR team was even less successful than the relatively poor showing of the previous year. TVR was not a well-funded team. Mark and Sue did their part by towing the No. 51 team car behind the faithful Scaglietti the 1,200-plus miles from New Jersey. Only two of the three cars entered made the race. Jerry Segerman was listed as co-driver in the No. 51 car with Mark, but never got to drive in the race. Mark was in and out of the pits before retiring after 45 minutes with a blown engine. The No. 53 team car for George McClure / Dick Semko suffered a cracked head and lasted only 30 minutes. Both cars completed seven laps and were the first to retire of the 65 starters.

Mark's friend Bill Claren was racing a Morgan and was paddocked next to the TVR team. In the mid-1950s Claren had founded SCODA (Sports Car Owners Driving Association), the professional sanctioning body for sports cars, and was well connected in the sport. He and Mark had become friends working out of Lou Schulz's S&R Motors. Schulz had been active as a car owner in SCODA, and the two men later worked together when Claren formed AFFDA (American Formula Ford Drivers Association). Claren recalls that at Sebring a self-styled Weber carburetor tuning expert was active in their section of the paddock and had caused his team a setback that was only sorted out just before the start. He speculates that the poor performance by the TVRs may have come from the same source.

CHAPTER 22:

Red Socks for a Wedding

Mark was 26 years old and Sue 23 on the day they were married. For the wedding Mark wore red socks with his formal tuxedo. "It was a time when people were very conscious of dressing appropriately and Mark liked to reserve the red socks for special occasions," remembers Dave Lawton. "It was just another way to bust everyone up."

Renee was Sue's matron of honor at the wedding at the Church of Nativity in Fair Haven, New Jersey, on April 20, 1963. Although it was a Catholic ceremony at the altar, it was not a wedding Mass, as Sue was not a Catholic, although she later converted. Nancy was away in South Africa and missed her brother's wedding, but Mary Ellen was a bridesmaid for Sue. Burge Hulett was Mark's best man and Phil Burrows was an usher. It was a big wedding—Sue and Mark invited everyone they knew, and there were many friends from the racing crowd. The reception was at the Bamm Hollow Country Club in Red Bank where Sue's parents, Alice and Edward Warren, were members. Bamm Hollow was not the bride and groom's first choice for their reception, but they had not made their plans sufficiently in advance and more-desirable locations just weren't available. The club wasn't equipped to host a large reception, but as the mistakes and problems multiplied the young couple decided to laugh it off and enjoy the company of their friends and family.

After the wedding they moved to an apartment in Madison, New Jersey. Mark's affectionate name for Sue was "Suzuki," and mutual friends still refer to her as such.

Mark never missed Mass if he could possibly avoid it. Sue remembers that he would always seek out the local Catholic church wherever they were racing. Jim Haas confirms this and recalls Burge's typical grumbling response: "Oh, no, he's off to Mass again." Dave Lawton brings a thoughtful perspective to Mark's faith. "He wasn't overly religious or at all a zealot. I believe the tradition of Mass helped him keep a personal balance and, in a subtle manner, maintained a connection for him with his life at home as a young person."

CHAPTER 23:

Winning with the Pusher Midget

Mark hadn't raced since becoming a married man, and when he got wind of the opportunity to drive Ken Brenn's Offenhauser-powered Cooper at Lime Rock, he was interested. Brenn had become excited about the potential for a rear-engine car in midget racing when Jack Brabham tested the first rear-engine Cooper at Indianapolis in October 1960. Soon after, Brenn was at a party hosted by Alfred Momo in his Queens, New York, showroom to celebrate becoming a Maserati distributor. While Brenn thought the Maseratis were beautiful, his eye was drawn to a Formula Junior Cooper sitting nearby. Brenn was known as an innovator—a car owner who was willing to explore new worlds. In 1959 he had been the entrant for Rodger Ward when Ward scored an upset victory in a Formula Libre race at Lime Rock in Brenn's Kurtis-Kraft midget against a strong field of road-racing cars and drivers.

Now Brenn bought the Cooper from Momo. At his race shop in Madison, New Jersey, he and shop foreman Dick Briggs shortened the Cooper chassis by 18 inches, fitted a 110ci Offenhauser motor, and went racing. A midget with the engine in the rear was a novelty—a "pusher" in oval-track parlance. Although it was an interesting experiment, none of the drivers Brenn put in the car were able to come to terms with it. Eventually he stopped running it and the pusher found a place in the back of his race shop.

Bill Claren knew Brenn, and when he heard the midgets would run at Lime Rock he thought of Mark right away. It was Claren, as a former publicist for the American Racing Drivers Club (ARDC)—a major sanctioning body for midget racing—and as a former midget driver himself, who convinced Brenn that Mark was the man for the job. Encouraged by Claren, Mark called Brenn, who invited him to come see him at his race shop. When Mark arrived to meet Brenn—the race shop was attached to his construction business—he didn't make much of an impression, with Brenn commenting that Mark didn't look much like a race driver. It was an accurate appraisal. Midget racers—and oval-track race drivers in general—tended to be working-class men, and their rough-and-ready style was considered the norm for race drivers. Mark, in contrast, looked just like what he was: an educated, upper-middle-class preppie dressed in colorful slacks and a sports shirt.

But Brenn had an instinct that Mark was the real thing, and they agreed to do the race, which was just a little more than a week away. Brenn wanted to go testing on the Tuesday before the race weekend. It was a hot July day and Mark showed up at the race shop wearing Bermuda shorts, much to the amusement of the crew. This was clearly not the way a "real" race-car driver dressed.

There is nothing in the world of racing that changes perceptions and attitudes more quickly than being fast—and Mark was immediately and unmistakably blindingly fast in the unusual-looking Cooper. Brenn's regular driver Len Duncan was also on hand and was unable to approach Mark's times. Duncan recognized that road racing was not his forte, but showed his class by being very helpful to Mark. He also displayed his sense of humor when he appeared at the race wearing decidedly out-of-character Bermuda shorts to acknowledge Mark's talent and commitment. Duncan was a champion in his own right, and he was letting it be known that Mark was okay. Realizing how much faster Mark was than anyone else, Brenn instructed his driver not to show his hand in practice.

Midget racing was a serious business and races were fiercely contested. The normal venues for midgets were quarter-mile and third-of-a-mile ovals where they were in their element. The July 27, 1963, race at Lime Rock was a Jim Haynes promotion and featured a unique format. There were three races: a 20-lap ARDC points race for midgets; a 20-lapper for SCCA single-seat Formula Libre cars—with a variety of types entered; and a 47-lap finale combining the ARDC midgets and the SCCA formula classes. The purse was excellent for the time, with $2,000 being paid for the midget main and $2,000 more for the combined feature, with $1,000 going to the winner in each.

After three short heat races, the 20-lap midget race started with 22 top ARDC cars. Everyone was talking about the new fast guy, Mario Andretti, who was driving a Kurtis-Offy for the Mataka brothers. Bill and Ed Mataka were from Maplewood, New Jersey, and their orange midget enjoyed sponsorship from Frank Boeninghaus, a friend and sponsor of Mario's. Although not yet famous nationally, Mario at 22 was already highly regarded in eastern midget racing circles. Ken Brenn left the pits to see the start from turn one. As the cars charged into the fast right-hand bend, the throttle on Bill Randall's midget jammed open and he went up over the wheel of the car in front of him, his midget landing upside down. Ken was the first person on the scene and helped remove Bill from the car. Randall suffered cervical spine fractures and died three days later. He had driven for Brenn in the past and the two men were friends.

In his book with Gordon Kirby, *Mario Andretti: A Driving Passion*, Andretti describes battling in the race with Mark, noting that ". . . the only one that challenged him in that race was me." Media reports say that Mark suffered a puncture on the first lap and was never a factor in the race. The author relies on Mario's story: "The whole race I'm right on him, pushing him. Toward the end, about two laps to go, he drove off the road and got a puncture. It was the right rear, which is not the dominant tire at Lime Rock, but it slowed him down just enough that coming off the last corner I got underneath

him, and won the race."

Race reports differ from Mario's account just as they do with Mark's version, recounted in *The Unfair Advantage*. Mario never mentions the 47-lap feature that Mark won. Mark in turn mixes incidents from the 20-lap "midget-only" race with the feature. No matter. They both won races that day, and the 20-lap event was likely more important in Mario's memory because it counted for ARDC points. Both men were recalling events that were already well in the past, with many races having been run in the interim.

Before the 47-lap combined feature, 19 Formula Libre cars lined up for their 20-lap race. The field was dominated by Formula Juniors, although there were some hybrids in the mix. Notable among those was the ex–Jean Behra Formula 2 Porsche driven by Vic Meinhardt, and George Alderman's ex–Cooper Junior, now fitted with a 1500cc Alfa Romeo engine. Alderman won the race in decisive fashion.

For the feature Andretti was on the pole. Mark was well back because of his poor result in the earlier race. At the end of the first lap Mario led, with the midget of Bert Brooks second, George Alderman third in the Cooper-Alfa, and Mark coming up through the field. On the second lap Andretti and Alderman were missing and Brooks led with Mark now second. Alderman had been off the track and returned at the back of the field before beginning an exciting chase. Mark passed Brooks for the lead on lap four and began to pull away. Andretti never reemerged in the race.

The excitement came from George Alderman's dramatic surge through the field. By lap 13 he was back in second place and now pulled out all the stops in his pursuit of Mark. He set a new Lime Rock lap record at 1:02.5 as he closed to within three car lengths of Mark. But the Alfa engine broke on lap 25 and he was out. Mark continued to run consistent 1:03 laps, and finished the 47 laps a full lap ahead of second-place Ernie de Vos in a Brabham Junior. Third was Reed Rollo in a Cooper Junior; fourth, Vic Meinhardt in the Porsche; fifth, Pierre Mion in a Cooper Junior; and sixth, Jack Walsh in a Formula 2 Cooper.

Although the press played up the story of a midget once again beating the "sporty-car" types, the reality was somewhat different. It was a clean sweep for the SCCA drivers. No conventional midget—and certainly no ARDC regular—made the top six. This is no reflection on the ARDC cars and drivers. They were out of their element on a predominantly right-hand-turn course. Had the race been held on a left-hand-turn oval, they likely would have swept the board.

After the race, well-known ARDC figure Mike Caruso approached Brenn and asked him quietly, "Where did this guy come from?" Ken explained to Caruso where he had found Mark and added, "And the best part of the deal is that he's an amateur and can't accept any money." Mark, overhearing Ken, immediately said with a smile, "I just turned pro." Mark did receive the standard 40 percent of the winnings that went to the driver. He was thrilled.

Mark ran one more race in the car at the one-mile paved oval track at Trenton, New Jersey. The "pusher" understeered terribly, and with only three laps of practice before the start, Mark struggled home in eighth place. Ken Brenn and Mark later went testing at Flemington, but Mark never felt he had learned to set the car up properly for oval racing.

The victory at Lime Rock was important in Mark's career. It was his first professional win and exposed him to a whole new world within the sport of auto racing. He gained great respect for the hard-nosed world of oval-track racing, and that respect was returned.

Mark had developed a reputation as a naturally fast driver. Later in his professional career, many would attribute his accomplishments to his engineering skills and understate his pure talent. But engineering had little to do with the speed he was demonstrating at this early point in his career. "Mark was fast right out of the box," says Charlie Hayes. "It wasn't his education; it wasn't his engineering degree that made him fast. Admittedly he could relate to the engineers on the car better than most guys—but that wasn't what made him fast. There's something transcendental about that ability to drop everything else about yourself and just be in the race car. Mark was just intrinsically fast."

CHAPTER 24:
Marlboro 12 Hours

On August 8 Marlboro hosted its annual endurance race for sedans, and Mark was delighted to accept an invitation to participate as a member of the factory-supported Renault team.

John Norwood, an advertising associate at *Sports Illustrated* magazine, was a first-rate entrepreneur and sometime race driver who knew how to put together a deal. John had been instrumental in Team Roosevelt, backed by Franklin D.

Roosevelt Jr., and best known for successfully campaigning Fiat-Abarths. John persuaded the U.S. Renault importer to enter a three-car team of 1093cc Dauphines to compete in the Marlboro 12 Hour race on August 18. The 1093cc Renault was a limited-production run of the familiar Dauphine with added performance features that included a twin barrel carburetor, rear track rods, a tachometer, and a four-speed manual gearbox. It was available only in white with two blue stripes down each side. Mark was chosen as one of the team's six drivers and was paired with Ron Grable.

The Washington, D.C., Region of the SCCA had been a pioneer in sedan racing in America since the late 1950s. In 1963 the Marlboro 12 Hour was an FIA national Open, and attracted international participation. Volvo had been dominating the race for years and enjoying the publicity. Ford made a big effort at this race, bringing three Cortinas from England and two Holman-Moody Ford Falcons. A change in rules for 1963 accommodated the American compact cars. They were limited in displacement to 260ci (4260cc), and although wheelbase was not specified, eligible cars could not exceed 200 inches in length. Aided by the presence on their driving roster of Walt Hansgen and Curtis Turner, the Falcons were by far the fastest cars in the race, but it was the Cortinas, in the hands of Englishman Jack Sears and Bob Olthoff of South Africa, which brought Ford the victory. Mark and Ron Grable finished 8th in class, 16th overall, in the Dauphine.

George Alderman was standing in the Renault pit when another one of the team's drivers, Charlie Kolb, turned his car over to his partner, Art Tweedale. "Charlie told Art that the car was great and to just get in it and drive," recalls Alderman. "As the car pulled out of the pit Charlie turned to me and said, 'He's in for a surprise when he gets to the end of the straight. That car hasn't had any brakes for the last hour.' "

CHAPTER 25:
"With great sound and fury"

Mark received a break when he was offered the chance to race Jack Griffith's A Production 289 Cobra in some late-season Regional races. It would have never happened if Jack and Bobby Brown hadn't had a falling out. Brown had run off an enviable string of National victories in the Griffith Cobra on his way to the A Production National Championship. On June 15, 1963, Mark was watching from the hillside at Lime Rock when Brown won a National in the car. Mark hadn't been able to obtain a paddock pass for the race and paid general admission to attend. In this lean season for Mark, a drive in a Cobra didn't even enter his imagination.

Jack Griffith was a Ford dealer in Hicksville, New York, on Long Island. As an active member of the Kiwanis Club, he was well acquainted with other local businessmen. Racing legend Phil Walters was a Volkswagen dealer in Hicksville, and Bob Brown Sr. was the local Chevrolet dealer. As a Ford dealer, Jack had read about the Cobra and wanted to get involved. Ed Hugus in Pittsburgh was the East Coast Cobra man and a prime mover with Carroll Shelby in the early development of the car. Ed arranged for a car to be picked up in February. Jack drove the Cobra back across Pennsylvania in a snowstorm—an experience he remembers as an adventure in itself.

At a Kiwanis meeting that spring Jack mentioned his desire to try the Cobra out on a track to Brown Sr., who then mentioned that his son Bobby—a well-established race driver—had rented Bridgehampton for a test day in his Corvette, and invited Jack to come along. Jack and a friend drove the Cobra, and at the end of the day asked Bobby if he would like to drive it. To be polite, and because Jack was a friend of his dad's, Bobby said he would do two laps. Fifteen laps later he came in with, as described by Jack, "a smile from one side of his face to the other." Bobby immediately suggested that they campaign a race-prepared Cobra.

Jack by now was the New York–area Cobra dealer and had sold several stock versions of the car. He now obtained the full race version and went racing with Brown as the driver and ace mechanic George Clark doing the wrench work. Clark had learned the racing side of mechanics working for Frank Dominianni in his Long Island Speed Shop.

It was a tremendously successful partnership, with Brown winning the SCCA National Championship in the Cobra, but by the end of the season the two men had had a disagreement. Although the National season was now over, Dick Monnich persuaded Jack that there was publicity to be gained by running the car in the remaining Regional races in the Northeast. Monnich was closely associated with Griffith through their TVR connection, and it was he who recommended Mark as the driver. "It was not a problem between Mark and me," recalls Bobby. "The problem was between Jack and me. Mark and I talked about it and I encouraged him to race the car."

Mark had never sat in a Cobra until he arrived at Lime Rock on September 28 for an SCCA Divisional championship race. It was the most powerful car he had driven to this point in his career and required its own special handling. Mark impressed all—even the initially skeptical George Clark—by immediately taking to the car. *Competition Press* reported, "A new combination of Mark Donahue [sic] and a Cobra won with ease. Mark, in Jack Griffith's Cobra . . . steamed around the course with great sound and fury, adding much to the spectators' pleasure."

Although Mark had hoped for more races in the Cobra, there was only one other opportunity to drive the car in 1963. It came at a South Jersey Region race at Vineland on November 3. Mark was able to persuade Monnich and Griffith to do the race in part because he had negotiated $100 in appearance money from the race promoter; people were excited about the Cobra and would come to see one run. Mark was again impressive, completely dominating the eight-lap preliminary race. The finale was a letdown when a front spring bolt failed and Mark dropped out of the lead on lap five.

CHAPTER 26:
Cobra Heroics

Chris Economaki's *National Speed Sport News* proclaimed Mark "one of 1963's new Stars." In a page-one article in their January 8, 1964, issue, Mark was pictured in the Ken Brenn midget after winning the ARDC 100-miler at Lime Rock the previous summer. Mark was joined in the photo by Sue and race queen "Miss Greater New York."

On January 5 Mark and Sue were in Upper Marlboro, Maryland, to enjoy the brisk weather at the Washington Region's fifth annual Refrigerator Bowl races. Mark qualified poorly because of problems with the Cobra and started well down in the field for the five-lap preliminary race for the big production car classes. He just pulled off a win, passing Bob Mouat's Corvette on the last lap. The 10-lap final was a close race all the way, with the Cobra and Corvette starting from the front row. Mark seemed to have the race in hand when he spun with just two laps to go. Mouat roared ahead, but Mark was quickly back on track and again passed Mouat on the last lap to win by less than a second.

A five-car match race on the half-mile oval featured Mark

on the middle of the front row, with Ed Lowther in his Lister Corvette on one side and a Buick-powered midget driven by Bud Brosenne on the other. Pierre Mion in a Cooper Formula Junior and Art Tweedale in a Lola were in the row behind. The five cars made up the entire field for the five-lap race. Lowther led until breaking a king pin on the second lap, causing the midget and the Lola to spin off together on the first lap. With Mark now in hot pursuit of Mion's Cooper, the field was reduced to two cars, and the race was flagged off after just three laps.

Mark's win rated yet another front-page photo in the next issue of *National Speed Sport News*. The full-width, top-of-the-page spread depicted a sideways Mark in the Cobra as he took the lead from Mouat, who was only partially visible through the intense tire smoke.

The most important race Mark drove in Jack Griffith's Cobra was his last time in the car. It was a National at Virginia International Raceway on April 18–19. Mark, Graham Shaw, and Hal Keck were all in Cobras, while the fastest Corvette was Dick Lang's. Mark passed Keck on the first lap and Keck, in attempting to re-pass under braking at the end of the long straightaway, hit Mark hard enough to stave in the Cobra's trunk. Mark continued, as did Keck, with an extensively crumpled right front fender. Mark was up to second place behind Lang, who had led from the first lap. Mark passed Lang for the lead on the fifth lap and drove on to a 16-second winning margin from Shaw, with Lang third. Lang lost his third place after a post-race impound revealed altered rear fender walls needed to accommodate larger tires. It was the race of the day, and Mark's winning average speed of 80.64 mph was faster than that of Ed Lowther in the Genie-Ford that won the feature race for sports-racers.

CHAPTER 27:
Staying Connected and the RRDC

As lean a season as Mark had experienced the previous year, 1964 was to prove worse. The Cobra drives had been a big boost and had added to his reputation for being fast and a winner in anything he drove. But Jack Griffith had no interest in campaigning the car for the season. The Cobra was sold to provide capital for Jack's then-burgeoning business importing roller TVRs and completing them as

Griffiths. This conversion primarily involved fitting a high-performance Ford V8 and 4-speed transmission to the light chassis and body of the English sports car.

While Mark's racing stagnated without opportunities in domestic road racing, contemporaries were looking to international racing to further their careers. Peter Revson had abandoned the U.S. scene in 1962 to race in Europe in Formula 3. He had caught on with Reg Parnell Racing, a private team well connected to the British racing industry, and had made his Formula One debut in late 1963 in the Oulton Park Gold Cup. Reg Parnell, one of the great British drivers of the early postwar era, died early in 1964, and the team continued under his son, Tim. Tim announced in March that Revson would join Chris Amon and Mike Hailwood for the 1964 Grand Prix season in the Reg Parnell Racing–entered, BRM-powered Lotus 24.

Also planning to pursue Formula One in Europe was Tim Mayer. Mayer, too, had gone to Europe in 1963 after showing his talent in SCCA Formula Juniors and sports-racers. He had become a protégé of Cooper Grand Prix star Bruce McLaren, and seemed assured of a spot in Formula One for the 1964 season as second driver to McLaren on the Cooper Car Company team. McLaren was in charge of the Cooper entry in the off-season Tasman series of races in Australia and New Zealand. Mayer had continued to impress in the early rounds of the series, but was tragically killed on February 29 during a practice session at Longford, Tasmania, Australia. Mayer, a nephew of Pennsylvania governor William Scranton, was 26 years old and married. His brother Ted was a great supporter of his racing. After Tim's death, Ted maintained his close relationship with McLaren, eventually helping Bruce start his own racing business and becoming a principal in that company.

Mark was still working for the Pulverizing Machinery Company in Summit. Expecting their first child and about to outgrow their apartment in Madison, Sue and Mark were house hunting. Sue was at her mother's house in Rumson for a baby shower when Mark phoned and said he had found a house. He asked her if she would agree to buy it, as he wanted to put in a bid right away. Sue had good reason to feel some trepidation about agreeing without first seeing the property. They had recently looked at a house that had numerous problems, both structurally and with its location. (The only thing Mark had focused on was the great garage.) But over the phone Sue now said "Okay," and Mark put in a bid for the house they eventually bought, at 625 Mountain Avenue in Murray Hill. "It was a great house," Sue remembers.

Although Mark wasn't racing, he was staying close to the sport. At Lime Rock in June he was helping out his club—the Northern New Jersey Region of the SCCA—by serving as course marshal at a race. During a break in the action he was told that there was a young enthusiast who would love to have Mark drive him around the track in his brand-new Lotus Elan. It was his first meeting with Malcolm Starr, who would play an important role in Mark's career in the near future. Malcolm was ". . . underwhelmed." The crew-cut, polite Mark Donohue just didn't fit the image of a flamboyant race driver envisioned by an impressionable Malcolm. "Sue was there and very pregnant. They seemed like a nice normal couple—not exactly what I expected at the time. I soon came to realize that Mark was, in fact, the real deal."

When Michael Warren Donohue was born on July 20, 1964, it was a day of great joy for Mark, Sue, and their families. For Mark it was the brilliant light in an otherwise frustrating year. There were just no drives on the horizon, and with a fresh mortgage on a new house, money was too tight to contemplate buying a race car.

Mark was also maintaining his contact with the sport as a member of the Road Racing Drivers Club, where he was making many friends through his sponsor, Walt Hansgen. Walt, an early member of the prestigious group and a three-time past president, wasn't alone among the veteran drivers in the RRDC in seeing Mark as a potentially major star. Mark was secretary of the club, and his energy and enthusiasm had placed him in the spotlight as head of the annual RRDC advanced drivers' clinic. Other officers in 1964 were Lake Underwood, president; George Constantine, vice president; and Gordon "Tippy" Lipe, treasurer. The RRDC had 80 members who were admitted strictly by invitation. Criteria for membership in the exclusive group was described in a Mark Donohue–bylined article in the April 1964 issue of *Sports Car*: "One must be a competent and accomplished driver, a sincere gentleman, and well liked by the existing members. The judge of these qualities, of course, lies within the club."

The RRDC policy was to push for safer road racing by working with tracks and sanctioning bodies. The club also believed in improving driving and racing skills. The advanced drivers' clinic, first held in 1961, was open only to experienced National-licensed drivers and was always fully subscribed. Mark explained the purpose of the clinic: ". . . to help driv-

ers, already acquainted with driving a race car, drive better, thereby faster, and hopefully fast enough to win." The 1964 event was conducted by Mark at Bridgehampton on July 26. One of the already-experienced drivers enrolling to increase her skills was future star Janet Guthrie. RRDC members assisting Mark with instructional duties included: Walt Hansgen, Bob Grossman, Jim Hall, Howard Hanna, Roger Penske, Chandler Lawrence, Augie Pabst, Lake Underwood, Hap Sharp, Dick Thompson, Carroll Shelby, and Bob Holbert. The New York Region of the SCCA supported the event with flag and communication personnel.

The annual clinic was a great social occasion for RRDC members. Prior to the weekend at Bridgehampton, Sardi's and Le Chanteclair—the two favored New York restaurants and drinking establishments for East Coast sports-car insiders—were busy with the arrival of many RRDC drivers, both active and retired. The RRDC had organized a tribute to Alfred Momo, who had recently announced his retirement. Vince Sardi and René Dreyfus—proprietor with his brother Maurice of Le Chanteclair—were close friends, and they co-hosted the dinner at Sardi's West. Mark was there, and attendees included many of the great drivers who had raced for Briggs Cunningham and Momo—John Fitch, Phil Walters, Sherwood Johnston, Augie Pabst, Walt Hansgen, Ed Hugus, George Rand, Russ Boss, Bob Grossman, Bill Spear, and Bill Kimberly.

CHAPTER 28:
Walt's MG

Walt Hansgen had taken a personal interest in Mark's career. Hansgen had been the lead driver for Briggs Cunningham's team since 1956. With Cunningham closing the team at the end of 1963, he was now entering a new chapter in his racing career. He had made his debut in the Indianapolis 500 in May of 1964, where he had impressed as the fastest rookie in the field. Mark often visited Walt at his Jaguar dealership in Bedminster, New Jersey. Walt had acquired an MGB through his contacts at BMC and attempted to develop the car. With his son Rusty, Walt took the MG to an SCCA drivers' school where he could get some track time. He quickly became disillusioned with its potential as a race car and essentially abandoned the project. Now he offered it to Mark as a car to race during this fallow period.

Mark eagerly accepted and the car went to his home in Murray Hill.

Mark entered the MGB for a Regional at Lime Rock on August 29, with the car classified in D Production. Other cars in the class included the Alfa Romeo Giulia Spider Veloce, Triumph TR4, Ace Bristol, Austin-Healey 3000, and Lotus Elite. He finished an uncompetitive fifth and brought the car home for additional development. Mark had noticed that the other racing MGBs were much lower than his car, and he attempted to bring his ride height down by cutting the springs and bending the A-arms.

Bridgehampton hosted a full FIA International race for the World Manufacturers Championship on September 19 and 20. The event was billed as the Double 500, with one 500-kilometer race for the smaller-displacement cars on Saturday and a second one for the big cars on Sunday. Neither race was blessed with the serious entries from Europe that the organizers had hoped for. The championships in each category had once again been decided during the European season, and there was little incentive for the top teams to send factory-supported cars. Although Sunday's race had competitive entries from Luigi Chinetti's NART and Carroll Shelby's West Coast Cobra team, along with some top American sports-racers running in the prototype class, the race on Saturday featured primarily domestic amateur teams in the 26-car field.

The 1800cc MGB was clearly outclassed in the heavily populated GTII (up to 2000cc) category, with competition that included three Porsche 904s and an Alfa Romeo GTZ. Still, Mark's great talent managed to achieve a qualifying time in the top 10, and he raced hard throughout. Joe Buzzetta and Bill Wuesthoff drove the winning Porsche 904, and Skip Scott, driving solo, brought a similar car home second. Mark was one of a very few drivers to do the distance alone and finished eighth overall, 10 laps down on the winners, and sixth in class. The Hansgen family cheered from the pits and the race was considered a success for the modest entry.

On Sunday it was Mark's turn to root for Walt as he won one of his most famous races in the Mk 4 rear-engine Scarab powered by a 364ci Chevrolet and entered by the John Mecom team from Houston, Texas. Just the week before, Walt and Augie Pabst had co-driven Mecom's 250 LM Ferrari to victory in the Road America 500 at Elkhart Lake, Wisconsin. At Bridgehampton, Augie was in the Ferrari, driving alone. Walt won a dramatic race from competition that included

Lodovico Scarfiotti and Pedro Rodríguez. The big engine in the Scarab was having oiling problems that required lengthy pit stops and great care in the turns, but Hansgen once again demonstrated he was Master of the Bridge, America's most challenging circuit. The 2.85-mile track overlooking Peconic Bay near the tip of Long Island had opened in 1957. Hansgen had won the first feature race that year and was undefeated in top-level sports-car races held there through 1964.

Bridgehampton was a circuit that brought out the best in Mark Donohue, too. But his racing season was over, and his future in the sport up in the air. As a husband and a father he no longer had the disposable income to buy and support his own race car. There was, however, a great deal of recognition for his talent, and he clearly had the desire to continue in his sport. And for the first time there was hope that American road racing might present the opportunity to make a little money—if not a living.

Beginning in 1961, under the leadership of John Bishop as executive director, the SCCA had undergone an enormous change in identity. The club had learned to accommodate a professional racing series alongside its traditional amateur club racing base. Even on the amateur side the club was beginning to define itself more broadly, now accepting types of cars that had previously not been considered proper sports cars—sedans being the prime example. The United States Road Racing Championship (USRRC) had debuted in 1963 and gained strength in 1964. The professional series was for high-end, exotic sports-racing cars, but Mark was confident in his ability to handle powerful cars. He had no prospects, but there was now something to dream about.

Becoming a Professional

Fame usually comes to those who are thinking about something else.

—OLIVER WENDELL HOLMES SR.

CHAPTER 29:

"No, John. I feel perfect"

Mark's friend Walt Hansgen was now well established with John Mecom's racing team as vice president and general manager, and was constantly traveling back and forth from his home in Westfield, New Jersey, to Houston, Texas. After Briggs Cunningham closed his team at the end of the 1963 season, Walt had driven for seven different teams in 1964; his impressive season included qualifying at Indianapolis for the 500 as the fastest rookie and scoring World Championship points in Formula One for Team Lotus at the United States Grand Prix at Watkins Glen. By the beginning of 1965 he was Mecom's number-one driver.

Walt believed in Mark's talent and thought his younger friend just needed the right break. Mark was spending a great deal of time visiting Walt's Jaguar dealership in Bedminster, New Jersey, and developed a taste for martinis—Walt's drink of choice—on visits to the Hansgen home. One day Walt told Mark that he was going to arrange for him to co-drive with him at Sebring that year. Mark refused to take him seriously as it seemed too good to be true. It wasn't until Walt returned from tire testing with a photograph of the handsome metallic blue Ferrari 250 LM that Mark realized the exciting truth. Lettered neatly on the side of the car were the names of the drivers: Walt Hansgen and Mark Donohue.

The annual 12 Hour race at Sebring was on March 27, 1965. John Mecom had entered three cars: the first of the Lola T70s (Mecom had become the U.S. importer for Lola) driven by John Cannon and Jack Saunders from Houston; a Ferrari 330 P for Pedro Rodríguez and Graham Hill; and the only one that would finish—the Ferrari 250 LM for Walt and Mark.

The Mecom team was operated on a first-class basis. John Kalb was the very capable team manager, and John Mecom credits Hansgen for giving the team organization and direction. Sue remembers that the Mecoms were wonderful people to spend time with. "John and Katsie Mecom were so much fun. They always made you feel comfortable."

The Ferrari was the most sophisticated race car Mark had ever driven, and although he struggled in practice, he was helped by Walt's patient coaching and encouragement. Mark was 10 seconds down on Walt's lap times and was finding the non-synchronized gearbox and finely tuned race engine

a challenge to come to terms with. Mark called Walt "the eternal optimist," and recalled in *The Unfair Advantage* that Walt responded to his anxieties with a simple, "Everything will be all right."

The team's Lola T70 had arrived from England a week earlier and Sebring would be a shakedown for the car that Walt would race in the USRRC and the fall series of professional road races. The T70 was not designed to be an endurance car, but represented the state of the art in sports-racers. Sebring was a round in the International Championship for Manufacturers and organizer Alec Ulmann, frustrated with the FIA for their emphasis on GT cars, had chosen to add sizzle to his event by inviting sports-racers to enter alongside the GT and prototype classes. This did not please Enzo Ferrari, who considered the sports-racers with the big American V8 engines little more than backyard hot rods. He refused to bring his factory team, although many top private teams did enter Ferraris. Ulmann's strategy was rewarded by the largest crowd the classic race had ever experienced.

The Ferrari that Mark co-drove with Walt was emblematic of the autocratic Enzo Ferrari and his constant battle with the FIA. The 250 LM had debuted the previous year, allegedly as Ferrari's latest development of the GTO. The Ferrari GTO had dominated world GT racing for the past three years and remains one of the most desirable racing cars ever built. The trouble was that it had never met the FIA's rule requiring that 50 cars had to be produced in order for a model to be eligible for the GT category. Although there were never more than 39 GTOs in existence, Ferrari had bullied the system and created a charade to have the car classified in GT. When the 250 LM was introduced in 1964, Ferrari attempted to classify it as a GT, maintaining that the LM was a continuation of the GTO line. With this the FIA had finally had enough. The GTO was a front-engine car while the engine in the 250 LM was in the back; it would have to race as a prototype. Ferrari's position was too outrageous for even the Italian FIA delegates to support.

Enzo Ferrari, used to getting his way, was infuriated. It was the flash point for his decision to withdraw his team at the end of 1964 and declare that Ferrari would never race again in the Italian national color of red. The Formula One Ferraris that arrived at Watkins Glen and Mexico for the season-ending grands prix created a sensation by appearing in the American colors of white with a blue stripe. They were officially entered by the North American Racing Team, but were attended by the regular works mechanics and team drivers. Lost in the furor was the fact that the 250 LM was a terrific car. John Mecom had taken delivery of his days before the 1964 Road America 500, and Walt Hansgen and Augie Pabst had driven it to victory.

The race at Sebring started under a brutally hot sun, and as it wore on the drivers suffered, with many needing early relief. After two hours, when Walt turned the car over to Mark, they were well placed in fifth, right behind their teammates Hill and Rodríguez in the 330 P2. Dan Gurney and Jerry Grant led the race in their much-modified Lotus-Ford, ahead of the Chaparral 2C of Jim Hall and Hap Sharp.

While the car was being serviced in the pits, Walt gave Mark a quick briefing. The news wasn't good. The clutch linkage had failed and the car would have to be shifted without benefit of the clutch for the remainder of the race. Walt provided a brief primer on the technique involved and Mark proved a fast and adept learner. But the stress of shifting without the clutch and the extreme midday heat—his first stint was between noon and 2:00 p.m.—wore hard on Mark. When he got out of the car they were down to ninth position, but more important, Mark could barely stand up and feared he might collapse, as other drivers already had that day. He sat on the pit wall until he collected himself and then retreated to the Mecom trailer.

The team's Lola T70 with John Cannon driving had led the first lap of the race and ran in the top 10 for the first hour, but by now was out after contact with an off-track runway marker. Cannon approached Mark, and, seeing how much pain he was in, said he would take over the car for the next stint before Mark got hurt. That was all Mark needed to hear to muster his inner reserve of strength. Cannon was a friend, but he was also a driving rival of many years standing. Mark replied: "No, John. I feel perfect." When he took the wheel for his second stint at around 4:00 p.m., he had recovered his strength and the extreme conditions had abated somewhat. He had survived a personal crisis.

The Gurney/Grant Lotus-Ford retired in the third hour and the Hill/Rodríguez Mecom Ferrari 330 P2 moved up to second overall behind the now-dominant Jim Hall / Hap Sharp Chaparral, which had begun to build an enormous lead.

The Ferrari had dropped out of the top 10 by Mark's second shift, which was also when the race took a dramatic turn. The 94-degree heat changed abruptly to a cold torrential rain that hit hard and fast. The flat airport circuit offered little

or no drainage, and water stood four to six inches deep on the circuit and in the pits. Walt Hansgen's son Rusty was watching from above the Mecom pit when the deluge hit. He saw tires floating away from their pit boxes and "the amazing sight of the prototypes going down the pit straight with the water so deep that the front radiator openings were lower than the water level. There were drivers holding their door open to let the water run out of the cockpit as they drove down the straight."

Cars were circulating very slowly, and in many cases the drivers were unable to even see the course. Many of the smaller-displacement cars made up enormous amounts of time on the fussier big-bore sports-racers and prototypes. In the middle of all this, the Mecom 330 P Ferrari was out of the race after eight hours. But the wet track initially suited the 250 LM, and complemented the wet-weather driving skills of Walt and Mark. Mark did an excellent job of keeping the car going while others were spinning or parking in the pits, and regained enough places to bring the car back into contention. With Walt back in the car they were up to third place with only an hour and a half to go. And then the Ferrari began to misfire. *Car and Driver* captured the moment:

> **John Mecom, Jr. strolled down the pit lane, soaked to the skin, his hair still carefully combed, his tie neatly knotted, his expensive loafers in eight inches of water. He chatted politely with a reporter, but his ear was tuned to his remaining entry, the Walt Hansgen / Mark Donohue Ferrari 275 [sic] LM. It had been clutchless from the start and was now faltering with water in the ignition system. It's lovely, ripping-canvas scream was choked and strangling.**

In the pits the decision was made to change the plugs to attempt to cure the misfire. The crew struggled valiantly in the cramped V12 engine bay. The exhaust headers were very close to the plugs and laps were lost in the process. They gave up and sent the car back on the track with only 10 of the 12 plugs changed. Walt and Mark had to settle for an 11th-place finish while the Chaparral 2C scored a great victory, four laps ahead of the Ford GT40 of Bruce McLaren and Ken Miles.

The finish was a great disappointment to the team: Second in class held little consolation after being so well placed so close to the finish. But the race had a larger meaning for Mark. He had proven himself under extreme conditions and had held up his end in impressive fashion. The drive had exposed him to the national and international press as a driver to be watched.

CHAPTER 30:

Mark was a Beautiful Person

The intervention of Walt Hansgen had provided a shining moment in what seemed destined to be Mark's bleakest season. There didn't seem to be anything on the horizon beyond Sebring, other than Walt's assurance of something in the future with John Mecom's team. Then good news came through the intervention of sports-car mechanic Jimmy Carter and a young man Jimmy had convinced to go racing. Just before leaving for Sebring, Mark received a visit at home from Malcolm Starr.

Malcolm Starr was enrolled at Columbia University in Manhattan when he celebrated his 21st birthday. Malcolm had spent his first two college years at Claremont College in the middle of the California car culture without a vehicle of his own. At Columbia he joined a fraternity that just so happened to include young men with some very nice cars. "I came into a little money on that birthday and just had to have a great car," Malcolm recalls.

Malcolm test-drove a Lotus Elan at Cox and Pulver, a small glass-front boutique dealership on Madison Avenue. He wasted little time buying it for $4,200. At Cox and Pulver's garage on East 73rd Street, Malcolm met Englishman Jimmy Carter, late of Lou Schulz's shop in New Jersey, who had been hired to run the service end of the business. Jimmy was gregarious and very social, and showed Malcolm the best of New York nightlife. They became great friends, and Jimmy rode with Malcolm enough in the Elan to become convinced that he was "crazy enough to be a good race driver." With little more encouragement than that, allied with his realization that his aggressive driving was making him dangerous on the road, Malcolm decided to go racing.

Possessing no mechanical skills and little knowledge of the sport, Malcolm realized he couldn't run a car on his own. Jimmy knew that Mark was without a drive. He suggested that if Malcolm bought a proper race car and if Mark could be persuaded to race it in Nationals, it would help maintain the value of the car and that Malcolm could learn a lot from Mark.

They studied the used-car ads in *Competition Press* and found a Lotus 20C being sold by Brooks Frybarger, who had raced the car for Bill Kay and won the national championship in 1964. The Lotus single-seater had a terrific pedigree: Jim Haynes had won the 1963 Formula Junior national championship in it. "It was a thoroughbred car," reports Malcolm. "We were told the motor was an ex–Jim Clark Formula Junior Cosworth Ford 109E block with a steel billet crank. It had two Weber 45 DCOE side draft carburetors—none of the jets were the same—we were told whatever you do, don't change the jets."

The car was located in Millerton, New York, and was being offered at $4,000. Malcolm negotiated the price down to $3,500 over the phone before going to see it. The next step was a visit with Mark. "I went to the Donohue home in Murray Hill in March 1965 and had a pleasant evening with Mark and Sue. It was the first of many very happy evenings with the Donohues. Sue was a gracious and lovely woman."

Mark wanted to do the deal but he spoke very candidly to Malcolm about the dangers and possible downsides. Malcolm remembers with clarity Mark saying that evening, "You have a lot of money tied up in this car, but you have to understand that this is a dangerous sport and you can't take anything for granted. At any moment either one of us can have an accident and the entire investment can be wiped out. You just have to hope you can get out of it in good health."

While Jimmy was a good mechanic and had been instrumental in putting the deal together, he may have been a little surprised that he didn't call the shots. "It was Mark's show and Mark's team," says Malcolm. "It's a good thing it worked that way. Mark kept us organized and made us successful. I think I would have been out of the sport within six races if it had just been Jimmy and me."

The car came with Dunlop tires on the original Lotus wheels. The first thing Mark did was call on Walt Hansgen at his Firestone race tire distributorship to find the largest tire that would fit on the Lotus's wheels, which were seven inches wide in the rear and five inches in the front. Conventional wisdom dictated that the small engine would never pull big tires, but Mark had an instinct based on "what looks right is right." The big tires looked right and worked so well on the small Lotus wheels that Mark decided to go bigger still, ordering a set of magnesium 8-inch fronts and 10-inch rears from American Racing Equipment.

Malcolm had plans of his own—he knew just how he wanted the Lotus painted. It had been red, but Malcolm specified dark green with gold stripes. The result was striking, although the stripes turned out white. Number 29 went on the car as Malcolm recalls, "because I went to Cox and Pulver to buy numbers and two and nine were the only ones they had in stock in sufficient size and quantity." The number had other favorable connotations. The great New York Giants running back Alex Webster wore No. 29 on his jersey, and No. 29 had been on the Mecom Ferrari Mark raced at Sebring. Mark had two garage bays under his house, and the Lotus resided in one of them. Mark towed the Lotus to the tracks behind his red Oldsmobile wagon with 140,000 miles on it. By this point the long-serving Scaglietti had been retired.

The first time out for the Lotus was in late March for Malcolm's first drivers' school at Bridgehampton. Mark was present for all three of Malcolm's drivers' schools and most of his races. Between them they put a great many races on the car over the season but never had to touch the engine. They had been warned never to experiment with the carburetor jets. "Of course, we tried once with miserable results," says Malcolm. "They went back in as they had been. We realized that this was, after all, a well-developed car and a well-tuned engine."

Despite Mark's dominance of the Formula C class, Malcolm remembers their campaign as a very amateur effort. They had virtually no spare parts for the car. Gear ratios were never changed from circuit to circuit. They had been told the engine could rev safely to 11,000, but Mark decreed that they would not push it past 9,000–9,500. The power band began at 6,000 rpm. The SCCA used standing starts for most races and Mark taught Malcolm how to handle them. He counseled against "blipping" the throttle on the grid. His advice was to bring the engine to 9,000 rpm moments before the start and hold it there until the flag fell.

At an early-season Regional at Lime Rock the engine needed the timing chain replaced. It began to rain and Mark was concerned that conditions just weren't right to accomplish the work properly at the track. "Mark said, 'Let's put it on the trailer and take it home,'" Malcolm remembers. "He was protecting my investment. As much as he wanted to race, he was always very considerate of my stake in the enterprise."

On that day Mark was taking the long view of the season while displaying his essential consideration. Malcolm remembers Mark as modest and always calm. "Mark was a beautiful person. I believe his Catholicism gave him a degree of serenity that was an essential part of his personality."

Sue and Malcolm are among those who remember that wherever he was, in America or Europe, Mark would locate the nearest Catholic church so he could attend Mass. If the Sunday race schedule made it impossible, he would make it to Saturday-afternoon services. "He was serious about meeting his obligations as a Catholic," says Starr.

Mark and the Lotus made a big impression in their first National at Marlboro, Maryland, on April 24. The Lotus was immaculately turned out and Mark was the class of the Formula car field in the 30-minute timed race. The only Formula B car to lead Mark's Formula C Lotus was the Cooper-Alfa of George Alderman, which only lasted until Alderman pitted for undisclosed trouble. Alderman returned, but Mark not only won the FC class but won the race overall.

Formula car racing was something of a subspecialty in SCCA events in the mid-1960s. Formula Junior had been enormously popular from 1960 to 1962, but the fields had waned by the end of 1963. Cars had been reclassified in 1964, with Formula B for cars up to 1600cc and Formula C for cars up to 1100cc. Formula Vee was also popular, but the cars were substantially slower. At Marlboro and most other races, a split start was used when the classes raced together to separate the Vees from the faster FB and FC cars.

A week later at Vineland, Mark and the Lotus were second. Such was Mark's dominance in the class that Vineland was the only National he entered in the Lotus that he didn't win.

CHAPTER 31:

Mark's Team

Mark's experiences in Jack Griffith's Cobra left him eager to race a Shelby Mustang in SCCA B Production. He was influenced by Dave Lawton, who saw the fast-evolving interest in SCCA sedan racing as the coming thing. Dave advised Mark that being in on the ground floor of the Mustang racing program could be an important step in establishing his reputation and moving him toward becoming a professional. As happened so often in Mark's life, Dave's advice proved prescient.

The Mustang to have for racing was the extremely rare Shelby GT350R, which was developed and built in Carroll Shelby's shops in California. Shelby was the key American road-racing connection with the Ford Motor Company in directing the enormous commitment they had made to racing. The street version of the car, based on the handsome Mustang 2+2 Fastback, was the Shelby GT350. Even in this relatively tamer version it was impressive.

Chuck Cantwell was the engineer Carroll Shelby employed to develop both cars. Cantwell grew up in Speedway, Indiana, just half a mile from the Indianapolis Motor Speedway. He was an engineer by training and a successful SCCA production car driver when Shelby recruited him away from his job with General Motors Styling. Cantwell recalled that the development of the race version R model from the street GT350 was guided by an agreement Shelby had reached with the SCCA's John Bishop. "According to Carroll, Bishop said we could modify either the engine or the chassis, but not both." Cantwell focused on the engine. With lead mechanic Jerry Schwartz, he added headers with side exhaust, an aluminum manifold, and a Holley carburetor that raised the horsepower from 306 to 325. The car already had an excellent suspension and a close-ratio 4-speed gearbox. Full cockpit instrumentation was added along with Plexiglas windows to replace the glass, a fiberglass fascia beneath the nose that accommodated an oil cooler, and special panels created for improved brake cooling.

Mark first realized the GT350's potential as a race car when he drove the one owned by Ben Poster, a Baltimore, Maryland, dentist and friend from the Courier days. Dr. Poster introduced Mark to Allen Abramson, who owned Archway Ford in Baltimore. They were already sponsoring Hal Keck's successful A Production 427 Cobra. Mark began a campaign, ultimately successful, to persuade Abramson to extend sponsorship to the Mustang.

Mark asked Malcolm Starr if he would be interested in expanding the team by taking the ownership position in the car. Malcolm thought it was a good idea. While Malcolm's ownership was crucial, Mark carefully put together a support program to make it possible to run the car with some hope for success. On April 21 he wrote to his friend Rob "Flint" McCullough in Pawtucket, Rhode Island, outlining the proposal he was putting together. Rob was connected with Providence's Tasca Ford, which was active in all forms of racing. Mark was hedging his bets since he wasn't certain of support from Archway.

Hey Flint,
The enclosed is a brief outline of the situation.
Please keep Malcolm's name confidential until the project becomes a reality (if it does).

We are presently talking this project over with Archway Ford in Baltimore, but no decision has been reached. I have my doubts as the owner is not the enthusiast that is required.
Thanks a lot,
Mark

Mark outlined the plan in longhand:

Mustang Program
Project Outline
The purpose of the project is to campaign a Shelby Mustang in SCCA National races plus misc. local and professional events. The project is set up so that no one individual or firm has to absorb the total cost.
Project Reasoning
It can be readily seen that racing the Mustang in SCCA is going to be a much looked at, publicized, important thing because:
1—This is the FIRST time an automobile which is basically a stock car has been classified as a sports car and allowed to race.
2—This is the FIRST time a car racing in SCCA can be directly equated to a very popular common road vehicle which many spectators will or want to own.
3—Because of points 1 and 2 the Mustang will receive the lion's share of publicity and interest this year from spectators and the press.
4—The car is in a top class and will have good competition and will have to be driven extremely hard to win but is capable of winning.
5—The Mustang will ride the Cobra tidal wave of prestige etc.
Project Details
The mechanics of the project are arranged for maximum benefit and minimum risk for all.
1—The Ford Dealer
Give—He will supply all the parts required to maintain the car. This will have to include non-Ford competition parts where required and tires, brakes, wheels, etc. whenever a side deal cannot be made with a supplier (example—Firestone donating tires).
Take—In return for the above he will be known as the so-called sponsor even though he does not own or is not responsible for the car.

- His name and advertising will go on the car and as much as is allowed.
- Additional advertising schemes can be worked out.
- Much business prestige and fame will be directed his way.
- His name can go on a tow car and/or trailer in larger sizes.
- A separate arrangement can be negotiated concerning a tow car with the name in large sizes, etc.
- The car can be present in his showroom when not being prepared for a race.
- The dealer can make any deals of his own with Ford, etc. However, since only the Dealer can do business with these people, his support of the project is the prime consideration.

2—The Driver

Mark Donohue—qualifications available by request. Experience in:

Elva
Daimler
Cooper
Lotus
Ferrari
Midget
Cobra
Etc.

He will drive the car in the National races.
He will manage the project and serve as PR man.

3—The Owner

Malcolm Starr

- He will retain ownership of the car throughout its campaign.
- He will occasionally compete in Regional events.
- He will sell the car at close of this arrangement.
- He will work with the driver in managing and planning the project.
- He will act as spokesman when required.

4—The Mechanic

George Clark

- He has much experience managing the Griffith Cobra of 1963.
- He will do all the necessary maintenance on the car at his own establishment.
- He will provide the trailer necessary for transporting the car.
- He will receive what appearance money is available for compensation of his efforts.
- He will go with the car to races to perform tuning etc.
- He will benefit by obtaining a reputation of competent race mechanic and thus promote his new business of building race engines
- Part of their establishment includes a fairly complete machine shop so that outside work would be at a minimum.

The concept for the program that Mark laid out to Tasca in April was essentially the one later adopted by Archway. The reason he wanted to keep Malcolm's name confidential as the details were worked out was to protect the young owner from his parents. They didn't know—and never found out—that in addition to the Lotus, he was also the owner of the Shelby Mustang. When the time came to purchase the Shelby, Malcolm didn't have the cash available. The GT350R cost $6,000—the street-version GT350 listed for $4,547—and it was another $500 to have it air-freighted from Southern California. Malcolm borrowed the bulk of the money from his friend Yale Kneeland and the rest from Virginia Morley. Originally from Oregon, Virginia and Malcolm had met when she was a student at Barnard College in Manhattan.

The other principal in the arrangement was George Clark, who Mark had come to know well through their relationship running Jack Griffith's Cobra. Between races George kept the car at Jack Griffith's Hicksville Ford dealership where he was employed. George bought a new station wagon to tow the race car to the tracks. Meanwhile, the Lotus resided between races in Mark's garage in Murray Hill. The cars would converge in the race paddocks to constitute Mark's team. Mark, George, and Malcolm bought yellow Brooks Brothers shirts for $7.50 each and had their first names monogrammed over the number 29, which graced both the Mustang and the Lotus. Malcolm designed and carefully cut out the numbers for the Mustang. Archway Ford's name went on the side of the Mustang, and the dealership's connections at Shelby through their existing sponsorship of Hal Keck's 427 Cobra proved valuable. It was a good situation for Archway: Their name became nationally known as they were seen to field the top A Production and top B Production cars in the Northeast. Although Archway's support for the Keck Cobra was somewhat more extensive than for the Shelby Mustang, their backing was crucial to Mark and Malcolm's program.

Karen Bocsusis, George Clark's wife, was an important member of the team. She owned an Austin-Healey 3000 and had met George through her enthusiasm for sports-car racing. Ford's Mustang was a sensation in the American market when it became available in April of 1964, and Karen was one of the first to own one. George and Mark would often try out adjustments on her Mustang before applying them to the race car.

The entire team would meet up for dinner on Friday evening before a race. Karen recalls Mark's sense of humor and good nature. "Mark would often arrive wearing a moccasin on one foot and a sneaker on the other—typically without socks or, if he wore socks, they would be an outrageous color. Mark was usually seen in white pants with a madras sport jacket. He also favored madras button-down shirts. He was always in a good mood and would have everyone laughing over something."

Sue recalls that Mark's standard response to a request for directions was, "You can't get there from here—the road turns to dirt now and again." And after providing extraordinarily detailed directions he still loved to conclude by saying, "Of course, that's if you drive out the driveway—if you back out it's all the opposite."

Malcolm Starr adds insight to the picture of Mark at this time in his life. "As funny as he was, Mark was, in the parlance of the time, very square. He never talked politics—he was just so absorbed in racing. He enjoyed popular music but had no particular strong musical tastes. He was a very busy guy—he was always working hard. He had just bought a house."

In fact, Mark did have a lifetime musical preference for jazz, cultivated during his college years.

Time was always short as Mark rushed back from his sales calls to make it to the races. As the other members of the crew arrived to load up the Lotus they would find notes from Mark indicating the jobs that needed to be completed before they could all depart for the race track. Mark took a pragmatic approach to the universe of things that needed to be done, and not all the jobs were necessarily related to

loading the trailer or car preparation. Malcolm arrived one Friday evening to find a note that he should mow the lawn. "It was acknowledged that I had limited or no technical skills so Mark assigned to me a duty he thought I could handle. As it happened I had no experience in this area either. I drove the power mower over the lawn outlet for filling the house oil reservoir and broke off the cap."

CHAPTER 32:

Racing the Lotus and the Mustang

Before the arrival of the Shelby there was a National at Vineland on June 13. Mark completely dominated the 1100cc FC field and once again was as fast as the top cars in the 1600cc FB class. The top FB cars were George Alderman's Cooper-Alfa, Gaston Andrey's Lotus 22-Alfa, and Alan Gottlieb's Lotus 22 fitted with a Ford-Cosworth twin-cam engine. Alderman led the race until a water hose burst, giving Andrey the overall win, with Mark second and the decisive winner in FC.

The Shelby GT350R arrived at Kennedy Airport on the Tuesday before the July 4 National at Lime Rock. This traditional race was important to teams and drivers in the Northeast. Mark's desire to be part of the event prompted the extra expenditure for air freight. The GT350R arrived in the classic Shelby white (actually Ford Wimbledon White), with broad blue parallel stripes from nose to tail. The car was taken directly to Frank Dominianni's race shop on Merrick Road in Valley Stream, New York, on Long Island. Frank, a top Corvette driver, was a friend of Mark's through the RRDC and their mutual friendship with Walt Hansgen. Mark had a great deal of respect for Frank, who had been racing since 1950 and had vast experience in engineering race cars. The immediate connection was George Clark, who had gained his early race experience as a mechanic in Frank's speed shop.

Good as the GT350R was, it was still not ready to go on the track. Dominianni proved an invaluable ally to Mark and George in the early days of preparation. "Frankie was about the only person around who had a chassis dyno," recalls Long Island race driver Bobby Brown. By Thursday the car was at Bridgehampton where Mark was able to test it for the first time. Malcolm recalls the Mustang coming down the straight for the first time, "like a motorboat, planing with its nose up." The springs were found to be still too soft and it was back to Dominianni's race shop for further modification.

On Saturday, July 3, the team was at Lime Rock for the big holiday weekend race sanctioned by Mark's Northern New Jersey region of the SCCA. The car had been trailered from Long Island on Friday. Practice and qualifying confirmed that the modifications had improved the Mustang, but there was more Mark wanted done. The 4th fell on Sunday. Since 1960, local blue laws prohibited racing on the Sabbath at Lime Rock because a church was located across the street from the circuit. Track promoter Jim Haynes successfully lobbied the SCCA to change the original Friday-Saturday dates to a Saturday-Monday schedule. The car went back to Long Island Saturday evening after practice and returned late Sunday night. Race day was Monday, July 5. The schedule was less than ideal. Race 7 was for Formula B and C, and race 8 was for A Production and B Production.

Mark was up to the challenge. He won FC convincingly in the Lotus and beat all the FB cars, except overall winner Candido DaMota. After his lap of honor with the checkered flag, he left the Lotus in the paddock and rushed to the false grid where George had the Mustang ready to go. In a great race, he finished second to Ohioan Bob Johnson. At the finish line the nose of Mark's Shelby Mustang had pulled alongside the door handles of Johnson's gray and red GT350R. Martin Krinner was third in another Shelby GT350R, while Skip Scott beat Hal Keck's similar 427 Cobra to win AP. Johnson was a top driver who had been running Cobras and Mustangs for more than a year with support from Shelby.

Mark's team's next race was August 8 at Bryar Motorsports Park near Loudon, New Hampshire. There the big threat was Dean Gregson, who, like Mark, had one of the rare GT350Rs. Gregson ran his with support from Harr Ford of Worcester, Massachusetts. He had won a Regional on the same track two weeks before, and the media now touted a showdown between the Archway Mustang and the Harr Mustang.

The chance to directly compare the cars was keenly anticipated. Malcolm Starr recalls the team preparing for the race with great intensity. "We had not run up against Gregson previously; he was an unknown quantity and we were always going into races worrying about whatever we could worry about." Mark rose to the occasion and won the race because he had prepared himself mentally for the competition. Erika Rhone in *Competition Press* could not resist writing that the

Mustang had "galloped" to a win in B Production.

Once again only the first Formula B car was ahead of Mark's FC Lotus at the finish of the Formula car race. On the tight and twisty Bryar circuit, Mark almost pulled a major upset as he harried the Lotus-Alfa of Gaston Andrey from start to finish despite giving away 500ccs of engine capacity.

These were busy days, with Mark providing leadership for the race team while working full-time in his sales engineering job. He was also the father of a one-year-old. Mark was a loving father but not hands-on, as Sue recalls. "On one famous occasion I managed to schedule Mark to look after Michael for a six-hour block of time while I had dental surgery," she says. "When I returned home, Mark advised me that there were diapers to be changed. It would never have occurred to him to do it himself!"

At Bridgehampton on August 14, the New York Region of the SCCA employed a different format for their National. B through F Production cars were combined with the faster modified classes for a one-hour race at the end of the day. Earlier in the combined Formula race, Mark won Formula C in the Lotus, again beating all the Formula B cars, with the exception of race winner Gaston Andrey in his Lotus-Alfa. Bridgehampton was a very fast track that demanded the utmost skill and commitment. Jimmy Carter had fitted the Lotus with a new set of rings that needed to be seated. This was accomplished by running the engine with the car on the trailer. To cool the motor, Jimmy, Virginia, and Malcolm took turns spraying a hose into the radiator for an hour or so while playing cribbage to stay entertained.

In the combined feature, it was hardly smooth sailing for the Shelby Mustang. Sherm Decker had pole position in his brand-new Lola T70, and was clearly the class of the field. However, it was the first time out for the car and Decker was still working out the bugs. An oil line came loose and liberally coated the track. Mark was close behind and had a lurid slide. Decker pitted to fix the problem and later rejoined the race many laps down. When the extremely potent Lola came up behind the GT350R, Mark made it very difficult for Decker to pass. Mark finished fourth overall and won B Production. The SCCA assessed a 30-second penalty for rough driving as Mark was judged to have blocked Decker. The effect of the penalty was to drop Mark to sixth overall, but it did not cost him his BP win. Bobby Brown won the race overall in a Malibu-Chevy Special ahead of Bob Grossman's Ferrari 250 LM entered by Scuderia Bear. Hal Keck was third and winner of A Production in the Archway Ford 427 Cobra. Behind Mark on the track but moving up to fourth and fifth overall as a result of the penalty were Lew Kerr's Brabham BT8, and Bruce Jennings in an Elva-Porsche. On this most demanding of circuits, Mark's fourth overall among well-prepared and well-driven sports-racers was an indication of his remarkable talent.

CHAPTER 33:

Mark and Walt at the Glen

The National at Watkins Glen on August 21 and 22 offered a real challenge for competitors in classes A through D Production. The Glen 500 featured those classes, and if you wanted to earn National championship points you had to be part of it. While some teams bemoaned running a 500-mile race as part of the National schedule—individual tracks at the time could run any race and class at the distance they chose—many welcomed the challenge of a true endurance test, as witnessed by the full entry the race attracted each year it was run.

A 500-mile race on a road circuit meant you needed a co-driver, and Mark was able to persuade his friend Walt Hansgen to join the team. Mark thought he was in some small part repaying Walt's favor in bringing him onto the Mecom team at Sebring. From Walt's perspective as a professional he was the one doing Mark a favor, since he usually was paid to drive a race car. But Walt cheerfully joined the operation and was an impressive presence.

"Walt was totally charming and very nice to be around," remembers Malcolm Starr. "He certainly helped bring a professional air to the operation. He concentrated on driving and let us run the operation."

Dave Lawton was team manager for the race and worked hard to bring organization to the effort. An endurance race can be a big hurdle for an amateur race team. "We tried to be professional. I had made some quick-fill gas cans for the pit stops. We could dump those 10-gallon cans—it was a 32-gallon tank—we could fill that thing in about 12 seconds. I trained the crew. We did test pit stops with the entire crew involved. I could see that Walt was pleased and happy that this wasn't going to be an amateur operation. It made him feel positive as we got to the race."

As the East Coast Firestone racing tire distributor, Walt helped Mark find oversized Firestone tires for the Shelby Mustang, and the team experimented with subtly expanding the wheel wells to make them fit. It was not a great idea, as the big tires caused problems in the 500 and even bigger trouble later at Daytona in the National Championship Runoffs. This was the first race the GT350R ran on Firestones; the earlier races had been on the Goodyears that came with the car. "Walter was contracted to Firestone and wouldn't hear of driving on Goodyears as it would endanger his tire deal with Firestone," recalls Lawton.

On Saturday Mark won the FC class in the 22-lap, 50-mile Seneca Cup and finished fourth overall behind the top three FB cars. On this high-speed circuit Mark's fastest lap of 1:32.2 was four and a half seconds slower than the fastest lap of the FB-winning Lotus of Candido DaMota. This was Mark's last race in the Lotus until the Runoffs. By winning his sixth National he had scored 54 points, the maximum number possible, since only the best six finishes could be counted. In a dominant season Mark had been second in the only other race he had run in the car.

The 500 started at 1:05 p.m. on Sunday. Mark immediately leapt from his second-row grid spot to lead the A Production 427 Cobra of Bob Nagel and the B Production Corvette of Don Yenko up the hill on the first lap. The six-car entry for B Production was relatively small but featured some strong cars and driver combinations. In addition to Nagel, paired with Bob Mouat in the Corvette, Skip Scott and Edward (Ned) Owen Jr. were co-driving Owen's GT350R, and Martin Krinner and Charles Sofield were in another GT350R sponsored by Dockery Ford. Another strong Corvette entry was from Frank Dominianni, with Janet Guthrie as co-driver.

Mark was in the pits at the end of the first lap. The big tires were rubbing and it cost six minutes—approximately four laps—to determine that the smaller-diameter tire would be needed. The remainder of the race was a flat-out chase to overcome the deficit. Mark stayed in the car for the first hour and 40 minutes and was lapping at a pace that won him back two of the lost laps on the 2.3-mile course. Walt drove for roughly the same amount of time. When he stopped to refuel and change drivers and tires at 4:15 p.m., the No. 29 Mustang was leading BP by two laps and was placed fourth overall, just three laps down to race-leading Archway Ford teammates Hal Keck and Oscar Kovaleski in the 427 Cobra. This stop was delayed slightly when a broken stud was discovered on the left rear wheel, although it was not replaced.

Walt Hansgen brought comic relief to the pits a few laps later when Skip Scott brought the second-place BP Shelby Mustang into the adjacent pit box. As Malcolm Starr remembers, "Skip came in, in a rush, and started screaming at the mechanics—do this, do that, and the crew is running all over the place—Walt is standing there with shades on and says in his simultaneously calm and authoritative voice, 'Take it easy guys, take it easy.' Everyone slows down. Scott is still in the car and he looks around and sees Walt—does a double take—and yells at his crew 'Get back to work!' "

Not satisfied with leading his class, Mark was on a mission to get the Mustang into the overall lead. He almost made it, bringing the Shelby up to second place with less than 30 laps to go. The left front tire was taking a beating and Mark stopped for a replacement with just a few laps to go. Mark, who had driven 131 of the 214 laps, had Walt get back in the car for the honor of finishing the race. The AP Corvette of Paul Sonda and Tom Swindell reclaimed second place overall as Walt brought the GT350R home on the same lap, a clear winner in B Production.

Tragically, the race claimed the life of 34-year-old Harold Woods from Riverton, New Jersey. Woods was driving a Daimler SP250 in D Production. He crashed on the inside of Big Bend—the corner so named in homage to the like-named bend on the original 6.6-mile Watkins Glen road course—on the 70th lap and died instantly when the Daimler flipped and went into a series of rollovers. One side of the floor mounting of his shoulder harness had failed. Woods's wife and two children were not present at the race.

The next weekend Mark and George towed the Mustang across the state of Pennsylvania to the airport circuit at Connellsville for a National organized by the Steel Cities Region. Mark dominated the race and appeared set to win when a piston broke on the last lap and destroyed the engine. The incident caused some friction between Mark and George. Mark had been agitating to overhaul the motor while George had the usual mechanic's attitude: If it was running well you should leave it alone. Shelby Racing did provide a replacement engine, but the relationship with the West Coast racing operation was always tentative in the minds of Mark and his teammates.

Malcolm Starr remembers that Mark often wondered if they were getting everything the Shelby team could provide. "They were the last word on that kind of car. Anyone who challenged them wasn't a buddy. Mark was a challenge—a reflection on them. They wouldn't offer everything they knew. They always held back key information. Things such as 'What suspension setting are you using? What shock settings? What spring rates are you using?' Things like that. You couldn't be sure of the information you were getting."

The reality may have been somewhat different. Chuck Cantwell, the chief engineer on the racing program at the time, remembers Mark and his race operation as an ally, the great exponent for the Shelby Mustang racing program on the East Coast. Many parts flowed west to east to help Mark continue to succeed. At Shelby the relationship was considered strong. The truth likely lies in the very nature of competitive racing, with development occurring on virtually a day-to-day basis. It is integral to the racer's inherent paranoia to believe that the other guy has the latest trick part that you feel should be on your car.

In a busy year, Mark remained close to his friends and their activities. Burge Hulett had purchased a crashed Lotus 23. Dave Lawton straightened the frame for him. At least two years of work had gone into the car, with various engineering updates to accommodate a different engine and other modifications. Because Mark was running the bigger tires on the Formula C, Burge wanted to run them on the 23 as well. The final touch was a handsome new body, built by Dave to encompass the larger wheels. They took it to Lime Rock for a shakedown and Burge turned a best lap of 1:11—a good Lotus 23 time then was 1:08. When Burge and Dave asked Mark to try it out he immediately did a 1:04.

Despite his tight budget Mark could not resist a good deal on a Mercedes-Benz 300SL for a daily driver. Purchased from the original owner, the car was a little rough. Mark picked it up for $3,500 and had it repainted and reupholstered. Mark's brother-in-law Bob Rost remembers the black gullwing was Mark's pride and joy. When Mark first bought the car he told Bob to drive it, sure that he would love it. They were in Rumson, New Jersey, where Sue and Renee had grown up. Bob told him that it would be a nice car if there was a place to drive it fast enough. Mark and Bob agreed that at slow speeds, there was nothing very special about the car, but at higher speeds it lightened up and became a real pleasure. Mark decided he needed a high-ratio rear but knew they were very rare. Bob, a lawyer by training who spent most of his career in business management, had an automotive dealership. He knew that Sam Coe, a foreign-car specialist in the north hills of Pittsburgh, had the ratio they needed. Bob obtained it for Mark, who was thrilled by its effect on the car's performance.

On a visit to Sue and Mark's home in Murray Hill, Dave Lawton drove the 300SL and agreed that it was a terrific car. Mark needed to sell it to buy a new house and told Dave he could have it for what he had put into it: $6,500. Although Dave was sorely tempted, he declined. Fortunately, Mark soon found another buyer.

The new house the Donohues were looking at was in Stony Brook, New York, on Long Island. Mark was spending an increasing amount of time doing part-time engineering work for Jack Griffith on his TVR/Griffith production business. He now left his position at the Pulverizing Machinery Company to accept Griffith's offer of a full-time position. The Donohues' move to the new house in Stony Brook was completed in January of the following year.

CHAPTER 34:
Road America 500 in the Big Lola

Walt Hansgen continued to try to bring Mark into the Mecom Racing team. The Road America 500 on Labor Day weekend provided the perfect opportunity. The race was the final round in the SCCA's professional United States Road Racing Championship (USRRC). Walt, a three-time past winner of the race, had won the 500 the previous year driving the Mecom 250 LM Ferrari with Augie Pabst—the same car he and Mark had shared at Sebring. This time Walt and Mark would be in the even more potent Lola T70 sports-racer. Mecom was the U.S. importer for Lola and they were developing the car for the fall series of sports-racer events.

Going into this final race, the 1965 USRRC was still open between Jim Hall in the Chaparral 2C and George Follmer in his Trans Ocean Motors Elva-Porsche. The somewhat controversial point system gave equal points in each race to the over-2.0-liter category and to the under-2.0-liter cars, and each man had dominated his class. Hall needed to win and have Follmer finish no better than third in the under-2.0-liter class in order to repeat his 1964 championship. Two Chaparrals were entered, and Hall was prepared to drive both of them if necessary. Follmer was taking the same approach.

He started the race in his Lotus 23-Porsche but also co-drove an Elva-Porsche with Joe Buzzetta.

Walt had qualified the Lola on the pole with a time of 2:27.8, and Jim Hall joined him on the front row of the 56-car starting field. The Chaparral beat the Lola into turn one of the four-mile-long circuit—but when the cars reappeared at the end of the second long straight, braking hard on the downhill run into turn five, Walt had regained the lead. As the two cars completed lap one of the 125-lap grind, Walt had a slight lead—so slight that some thought Hall was ahead. This proved a matter of academic interest because the Chaparral never trailed again during the entire 500-mile race. Walt stayed with Jim through the 16th lap, when a large crash back in the field blocked the track and brought out the first red flag in Road America history. Clint Lindburg had flipped his Elva Mk 5 between the carousel and the kink and had come down on top of the Apache Special of Jack Ensley. The track was blocked, and Cheetah driver Budd Clusserath stopped and bravely pulled Lindburg out of his burning car. Lindburg's burns were minor and Ensley got away with a broken arm. Road America historian Tom Schultz was there, and reports that the restart was delayed by Clusserath. After his heroic actions, the Hammond, Indiana, driver "sat down at the side of the hill, causing consternation for the rescue crew, who could not find a driver in the Cheetah, and got all worried that Clusserath was injured and lying somewhere! It took them a while to find Budd whiling away the time!"

After the restart, the order remained the same until Walt pitted to turn the Lola over to Mark on lap 27. Mark reentered in fifth place and brought the Lola up to third before ending his race in the pits on lap 44 with a broken suspension.

Hall's win was typical of the Chaparral domination all year—they won 16 of 22 races entered. But Follmer won his class, too, and became the SCCA's United States Road Racing Champion for 1965. Follmer's championship was well deserved, as he had been the dominant driver in a very competitive division and had won one round outright. But the rules were unpopular and were subsequently changed to ensure that future championships would go to the driver with the most points in overall competition.

The race gave Mark his first taste of big-bore sports-racing. The recent trend to mate ever bigger American V8s with a sophisticated British chassis was fast making sports-racing cars the hottest thing in road racing. Despite the Lola's failure to finish the race, Mark had gained valuable experience and exposure.

"Walt was a big influence on Mark," recalls John Mecom. "He treated him like a son and couldn't do enough for him. He believed in his talent and wanted him to succeed. In return, I would say Mark idolized Walt. He even began talking like him—it was from Walt that Mark picked up the habit of calling everyone 'mate' or 'matey.'"

CHAPTER 35:
Clinching Championships and Painting the Mustang

Mark had clinched the Formula C championship in the SCCA's Northeast Division with the maximum possible score of 54 points with six victories in the Lotus. Mark also had sufficient points in the GT350R to assure an invitation to the Runoffs, but he had promised Archway Ford and his other supporters the Northeast championship. Mark won another National at Marlboro on September 26. It was a good day for Archway: Hal Keck's A Production Cobra and Mark's Mustang ran closely together for a 1-2 overall finish. To clinch the championship, though, Mark needed one more win. He made the decision to go out of division for a late-season National the following week in Bainbridge, Georgia. It had come down to this final race to decide the Northeast Division championship between Mark and Don Yenko.

Bainbridge is just 40 miles north of Tallahassee, Florida, and the distance involved made it impossible for either Mark or George to take the time off from their jobs to tow the car. Mark solved the problem by hiring two of George's friends to transport the car and trailer behind George's Oldsmobile. Mark and Sue flew to the race, as did George and Karen. Although located at the former Bainbridge Air Base, where the Air Force had trained pilots until its closing in 1960, this was not a typical airport track. The 2.6-mile road course used access roads and streets through what had been a military housing neighborhood. Unfortunately, it was a weekend of organizational and logistical chaos for the sponsoring Dixie Region of the SCCA, with an almost complete breakdown of communications. Mark won the race with Don Yenko, who

had made the long tow from Pittsburgh, suffering mechanical problems with the Corvette.

Back home, Mark did not have the opportunity to bask in his championship for long. Word soon came that on the tow home the trailer and George's Olds had been comprehensively wrecked. Mark said the Oldsmobile looked like "there had been an explosion in it with the top and sides bowed out and the windshield gone." Fortunately George's friends were not injured. The driver had lost control crossing a bridge and the entire rig ended up in a swamp. The race car suffered only superficial damage, but the necessary bodywork provided the opportunity to paint the car for the upcoming Runoffs. The No. 29 Mustang which ran all season in the traditional Shelby paint scheme was transformed to a beautiful blue, with the stripes now white.

Malcolm only raced the Shelby Mustang once. It was an October Regional at Lime Rock, and Malcolm found the car a real handful in practice. He had a particularly difficult moment in full view of the pits with the car completely sideways and off the road in the fast downhill bend leading to the pit straightaway. "People were saying I was in way over my head and that I shouldn't be in the car. I had qualified well back. Once again Mark was terrific. He spoke to me very calmly and assured me that I could do this and it was just a car that I needed to adjust to."

Mark's calming presence was just the right touch. It was Malcolm's day as he broke the track record for B Production while winning the class. It was the only time his parents ever saw him race. Malcolm put his mother in the car for the victory lap. There was no real seat, so you essentially sat on the floor and held on to whatever you could. "She never tired of telling the story—although seldom in my presence," Malcolm recalls. "The awkward thing was that neither of my parents knew I was the owner, so we all had to watch what we said in their presence."

Malcolm had provided a critical bridge in Mark's career, but Mark was equally important to Malcolm's life. "Mark was like an older brother to me. He had so many people in his life who adored him and wanted to help him. I was sort of a bystander inserted into his life at the right time and, by accident, I was his lifeline. There was great admiration for him and people wanted to help Mark because they liked him and respected him so much. Mark was a man of such integrity."

CHAPTER 36:
Runoffs at Daytona

The American Road Race of Champions (ARRC) was one of the best ideas to come out of SCCA amateur racing. Debuting in 1964, the event that became known as the "Runoffs" eventually replaced the system of crowning National champions in each class strictly through points accumulated throughout the year. The old system was unfair geographically, favoring teams and drivers with sufficient resources to chase points all over the country.

It was not until 1966 that the Runoffs winner would be considered the National Champion. Under the interim system in effect in 1965, the SCCA divided the country into six geographic divisions. Each division held its own series of Nationals and, in a cumbersome arrangement, a "national champion" was declared in every class in each division, thus devaluing the title. Technically, therefore, Mark could be seen as a national champion in 1965 in both B Production and Formula C (if only one-sixth champion in a true sense). Effectively the winner of the Runoffs was considered the de facto National Champion.

The top three finishers in points in each division were invited to the year-end Runoff, where a true National Champion would be determined in a single-race "shoot-out." The format was so successful that it continues to exist well into the 21st century, with only minor tweaks and adjustments. Mark's first entry in the Runoffs was in its second year. It had debuted on the West Coast at Riverside and now came to the East Coast. The original plan was to alternate coasts each year. Later the event found a home through 1993 as an annual fixture at Road Atlanta in Georgia. It moved to the Mid-Ohio circuit for a twelve-year run before moving again, in 2006, to Heartland Park Topeka in Topeka, Kansas. For 2009 it was announced for Road America in Elkhart Lake, Wisconsin.

The idea was conceptualized and developed by Tommy Edward Van Hoozier of the Eastern Tennessee Region of the SCCA. The inaugural 1964 event was conducted by the California Sports Car Club Region of SCCA and sponsored by *Sports Car Graphic* magazine. Each entrant received a free double room for four nights in Riverside as guest of the sponsor. No entry fees were charged, and garage space was provided for free. The SCCA established a travel fund to be used for reimbursement of a portion of travel expenses.

At Daytona on the last weekend of November 1965, the second edition of the Runoffs attracted 81 Divisional champions among the 221 cars and drivers entered. Practice began on Thanksgiving Day—Thursday, November 25—and continued on Friday with official qualifying. Five of the races were run on Saturday and six on Sunday. A 1.63-mile configuration of the Daytona circuit that avoided most of the high-speed banking was used for the smaller-displacement classes. The full 3.1-mile combined road circuit and banked speedway was used for the bigger cars.

In June Malcolm had received notice from the Selective Service Administration that he had been drafted into the U.S. Army. He opted instead to enlist in the Marine Corps Reserve, and was scheduled to report for duty on December 16. After his race in the Shelby GT350R at Lime Rock, Malcolm had spent six weeks on the West Coast with Virginia before going directly to Daytona. When he arrived, the team was in a state of readiness, with Dave Lawton as crew chief providing a steadying hand. Mark was the only driver at the race who was a divisional champion in two classes, and was considered a favorite in both.

Unlike today's Runoff format where every one of the SCCA's 20-plus classes gets its own race, in 1965 the classes were grouped together the same way they were at a regular-season National. Mark qualified fastest in class for both races. This placed him eighth on the grid for the formula-car race behind the seven fastest Formula B cars. For the combined A and B Production race, however, Mark had the Mustang on the front row. He had qualified faster than any of the A Production cars except the Cobra of Hal Keck.

The Formula cars were the third race on Sunday and ran on the 1.63-mile short track. Mark in the Lotus battled closely with Larry Skeels, Central Division champion, in a Cooper, and Karl Knapp, the Pacific Division champion, in a Le Grand. Mark worked his way into the lead but it was short-lived. Suddenly the gearbox was acting up—third gear was lost—and Mark dropped to third, well off the lead pace. Knapp retired from the lead with input shaft failure and Skeels won the race, with Mark second. The great run of reliability for the game Lotus 20, which had been so strong all season for Mark and Malcolm, had ended at the worst possible time.

After the disappointing finish Mark had an hour to prepare himself for his next race. The two Archway cars from the Northeast were impressive on the front row, and equally impressive as they dominated the first half of the 25 laps.

Dogging Keck closely, Mark was holding a comfortable lead from the other B Production runners. Suddenly Mark began to drop off the pace as the GT350R experienced a severe tire rub on the high-speed banking. While a Cobra driven by George Montgomery passed him, Mark still led B Production—but Jerry Titus in the GT350R from Hi Performance Motors in California was now right on his rear bumper. It was an exciting battle, with Mark doing all he could to keep Titus behind him. It ended when the right rear tire burst on the 18th lap and Mark was out. Titus won, with Bob Johnson's GT350R second and Don Yenko third in the Corvette.

Although the press reported Mark's account that the tire had picked up broken glass left over from someone else's crash on the first lap, Malcolm Starr knew the real story: "Mark was one of the two or three smartest people I have ever known, but his analytical approach sometimes caused him to overanalyze or over-engineer a problem to the unintended detriment to the cause of winning," he observes. "The trouble came when we didn't have the opportunity to test a theory. Most painfully for us was at Daytona where Mark fitted a bigger tire than could survive the race. It cost us the National Championship. We could see from the pits Mark leading Jerry Titus into the turn past the pits—they were both flying—Titus was braking very, very deeply into the turn but Mark knew that if he stayed ahead he would be faster out of the turn. We had spent the entire weekend trying to beat out the interior wheel wells. We were actually grinding away the side of the leaf springs to give us more room for those big tires. The tire was flexing enough on the banking that it was rubbing, and eventually it burst."

Jerry Titus was the technical editor of *Sports Car Graphic* and a very quick driver. He was 37 years old when he won his National Championship, and, like Mark, on the cusp of becoming a full-time professional.

It had been a great year for "Mark's Team," despite the disappointments. The team regarded the loss of the B Production title with particular poignancy, since the Mustang had been faster at the Runoffs than even all the A production cars, with the exception of Hal Keck's Cobra. But two divisional championships and season-long dominance in the Northeast had increased Mark's standing substantially. As the year ended, Mark and members of the team were joined by Walt Hansgen, Allen Gottlieb, and other competitors and friends at a farewell party for Malcolm Starr as he left to begin his Marine Corps duty.

CHAPTER 37:

Man of the Year

In January 1966, Mark, Sue, and 18-month-old Michael became New Yorkers when they moved to their new home on Long Island's north shore in the picturesque unincorporated hamlet of Stony Brook. Mark traded his position as a sales engineer for the Pulverizing Machinery Company in New Jersey for a new job as an automotive engineer for Andrew J. (Jack) Griffith's fledgling automobile business. Jack Griffith imported the British TVR chassis and had originally fitted Ford V8 engines to create the Griffith sports car. During Mark's period with the firm Griffith had moved on to Chrysler powerplants and drivetrains. Mark was busy setting up an assembly line, dealing with the multiple problems and issues attendant to the project. When Mark first arrived at Griffith on a full-time basis, the factory was at 1478 Old Country Road in Plainview, just off the Long Island Expressway, a pleasant 25-mile drive from his new home in Stony Brook.

Developing the Griffith was a challenge. Leonard Bailey, a test driver and engine builder for the Griffith project before Mark joined the firm, described the car: "The Griffith proved to be quite a handful to control, [it] went like a rocket ship on the straight, but wouldn't stop or turn." An experienced race-car driver, Bailey concluded, "I can truly say that the Griffith was the worst-handling car I ever drove."

The relationship between Mark and Jack dated from their earliest connections with the TVR in 1962. In fact, it was through Griffith that Mark knew George Clark, who had been the mechanic on the Griffith-owned Cobra that Mark raced in 1963 and early 1964. Clark had been part of the Griffith car operation but had fallen out with one of Jack's partners and returned to work at Griffith's Hicksville Ford dealership as a line mechanic. Mark's friend Lou Schulz, who had recently sold his foreign-car business, joined him at the Plainview plant as sales manager.

As the year began, Mark's best prospects remained in amateur racing, and he brought the Ford Mustang to Marlboro for the annual Refrigerator Bowl on January 9. This regional event was local SCCA racing in its most lighthearted manifestation, and a race that Mark had long supported. It was the last time Mark would go racing in such an entirely informal spirit.

Mark dominated the A–D Production races in the Mustang. In freezing weather—the temperature had dropped 20 degrees overnight—he won both the prelim and feature events and established a new course record for B Production at 1:35.2. Bob Tullius finished second and won D Production in both races in his Triumph TR4. Mark's class record compared to the new outright record for the 1.7-mile course set that day by Charlie Hayes at 1:26.1 (71.1 mph) in his Oldsmobile-powered McLaren-Elva.

Later in the month at the 22nd annual convention of the SCCA in Detroit, Mark was presented the Kimberly Cup as the most improved driver. It reflected the growing impression he was making within the sport, underscored by winning divisional championships in both Formula C and B Production. Mark's friend Walt Hansgen was also honored that day: In Formula One driver Bruce McLaren's keynote remarks he named Walt one of the world's greatest drivers outside of Grand Prix racing.

More recognition for Mark's 1965 exploits came in February when Frank Blunk, motorsports editor at the *New York Times*, announced that Mark was the recipient of two of the prestigious newspaper's annual awards. Mark was named Man of the Year in amateur racing and winner of the Sportsmanship Trophy.

At the meeting in Detroit, the SCCA announced the creation of a new series of professional road races for sedan cars. The Trans-American Sedan Series was set to debut in March 1966 as a preliminary race to the 12 Hours of Sebring. The series very quickly became a popular success with entrants and race fans. A minimum purse of $5,000 per race was guaranteed, with just two classes specified—the under- and over-2.0-liter classes. Maximum engine size was limited to 305 cubic inches, or 5.0 liters. This was a clear nod to the emerging "pony" cars that Detroit was quickly embracing as the next big marketing front. History would prove the series to be a long-running success in SCCA professional racing history.

The club also announced a 10-race schedule for the 1966 United States Road Racing Championship. Although not on Mark's personal horizon in January, the fast-evolving big-bore sports-racers of the USRRC would soon become a consuming occupation.

Other important influences converged even sooner. Ford Motor Company was deeply committed to winning the International Sports Prototype Trophy, and, more particularly, the crown jewel of that series—the Le Mans 24 Hour race.

CHAPTER 38:

"I owe it all to one man"

Ford had won the 1965 World Manufacturers Championship for Grand Touring cars but for the second year running had not won at Le Mans. The failure to win this preeminent event overshadowed what should have been seen as a brilliant year. Ford had broken the dominance of the Offenhauser engine with their first win at the Indy 500—by Jim Clark in the Lotus-Ford—and had continued their supremacy in NASCAR. Their Manufacturers Championship had been won by the Cobras at the expense of archrival Ferrari. But at the top of the corporate hierarchy, only a win at Le Mans could be seen as justification for the enormous expense and resources the racing program consumed. Leo Beebe was the Ford executive with responsibility for the program's eventual success. Despite the fact that he lacked any real background in racing, Beebe ultimately made it happen.

The Ford GT40 was the car originally designed and developed to win at Le Mans. While inspired by the Eric Broadley Lola GT, the GT40 was designed and produced by Ford engineers under the leadership of John Wyer at Ford Advanced Vehicles in Slough, England. The new GT40s had made only limited appearances in 1964, debuting in May at the Nürburgring 1000 Kilometer race in Germany, where they showed their potential but failed to finish. At Le Mans in June, the high-profile cars, even with their top-level drivers, again failed to achieve a finish. An ill-advised decision to run the cars just two weeks later at the Reims 12 Hour race in the Champagne region of France—with no time to address the developmental problems that were resulting in non-finishes—was a sure recipe for a similar failure.

The pressure at Ford to perform in the high-stakes game of international endurance racing was intense. The prototype GT40 had made a better than reasonable showing for an untried car, but Ford's high expectations and insistence on results made this not good enough.

In its earliest incarnation the Ford GT40 Mk I was powered by a 256ci pushrod Indy engine, although later Mk I models were fitted with Ford's more familiar production-based high-performance 289ci (4.7-liter) engine. After the disappointments of 1964, Ford made the decision to immediately develop a car—eventually to become the Mk II—that would be powered by the 427ci (7.0-liter) engine that had performed with great success in NASCAR. These cars were under development all season, so for 1965 the program continued primarily with the original 289-powered Mk I. Carroll Shelby was given operational control of the Ford racing program from his California base, while Wyer's British operation was assigned the task of building a minimum of 100 Mk Is for homologation as customer cars eligible to compete in the Sports category. The season opened with a great victory for the GT40s at Daytona, then a 2,000-kilometer event, but that excellent result was not repeated. The Manufacturers Championship was contested in the GT category, and it was the Cobra that brought Ford that prize. Another failure to win Le Mans—despite a great show of speed in the debut of two 427-powered cars—placed tremendous pressure on everyone involved going into 1966.

For the new year, Ford's entire focus was on the 427ci–powered Mk II, although the original Mk I with the 289 remained a popular car among private teams. Both the 289 and 427 engines had their origins in production-line engines. While highly modified, these were "stock-block" engines, a contrast to the purpose-built race engines used by most of their competitors. The 427 was already well tried in NASCAR, and was further developed for road racing by Ford's Engine and Foundry division under the direction of Gus Scussel. The 427 that went into the Mk II came in at 550 pounds, lighter than the 602-pound NASCAR version. By comparison, the 289 engine in the Mk I GT40 weighed 432 pounds (all weights reported are dry, less exhaust manifold, air cleaner, and clutch).

Engineering and building of the Mk II was done at Kar Kraft, Ford's in-house specialty builder in Dearborn, Michigan. The cars went on to the Shelby shop in Los Angeles, California, for the finish work and testing that would make them real race cars. Phil Remington was the master fabricator and practical engineer for Shelby, and Carroll Smith was the crew chief. Ken Miles was the primary test driver, with most of the development conducted at nearby Riverside International Raceway.

Ford's recent experience indicated that no single team could effectively field more than two cars for a given race, although this principle was frequently ignored as the season developed. Three teams were chosen to carry the works banner at the races: Shelby, British-based Alan Mann Racing, and Holman-Moody of Charlotte, North Carolina. Ford also believed that running the cars through three separate organizations would add to the competitive mix while still benefiting

common development and race-to-race improvements. But the arrangement didn't produce a complete on-track free-for-all. There was a discreet but clearly stated agreement that the Holman-Moody cars were to be subordinate to the Shelby team cars, and only to finish ahead of them in the event that a Shelby car faltered. Above all, nothing short of a Ford winning Le Mans would be acceptable.

Ford had selected Walt Hansgen as a driver on the Holman-Moody team. Secure in his position with Mecom Racing, Walt was determined to have the driver of his choice paired with him in the Ford for the season opener at Daytona on February 5–6. This was arguably the crucial break that set up Mark Donohue for everything that followed in his career. Mark would later say in the *The Unfair Advantage*: "One of the greatest lucky breaks that ever came to me in my racing career was getting to drive the factory Ford GTs, and I owe it all to one man—Walter Hansgen."

Holman-Moody—formed by John Holman and Ralph Moody in 1957 and considered the virtual Ford works racing operation for many years—was a powerhouse in NASCAR but had comparatively little road-racing experience. Hansgen was well known to the team because of previous drives for them and enjoyed a close personal rapport with John Holman. Walt Hansgen needed every bit of that rapport and all of his famous determination to get Mark into the car. The first hurdle was Jacques Passino, the Ford executive with direct operational responsibility for the racing teams. Mark recounted that Passino was "downright negative" at the prospect of having him on the team, preferring to pair Hansgen with Ronnie Bucknum, the experienced and highly regarded veteran who had led Honda into Formula One racing in 1964. Hansgen resolved the impasse by informing Passino and others at Ford that if he couldn't have Mark in the car with him, he wasn't interested in doing the race.

When Mark received the call from Ford—a call he described as less than enthusiastic—he was delighted to learn that the offer included a $1,000 fee plus expenses. Mark would have done it for nothing. He was beside himself with excitement at the prospect of the drive, saying, "I was so thrilled I just couldn't cope with it. I was afraid to even dream about it. I didn't even want to tell anyone because I was so afraid it wouldn't happen."

Mark still had to pass muster with John Holman, who was not a man to be taken lightly. Holman asked Mark if he had ever driven 200 miles per hour, and the answer was no.

Unimpressed, Holman wanted to know if Mark had ever driven on a high-banked track. Although Mark had raced his Mustang on the high banks of Daytona, he assumed that wouldn't impress the tough team owner and again replied no. John Holman went to his friend Walt Hansgen and told him to get someone else because Donohue wasn't going to cut it. Mark was hugely impressed with the manner in which Walt handled it: "Walter didn't argue or even make much of a comment. He just said, 'He'll be all right.' "

And so it was settled. *Car and Driver*'s Brock Yates would later write that Walt ". . . convinced the Ford Motor Company that a squeaky-voiced, crew-cut kid in Bass Weejuns named Mark Donohue was good enough to drive their cars at places like Daytona, Sebring, and Le Mans."

Holman-Moody's driver pairings for the 24 Hours of Daytona—this was the first year that the race was 24 hours in length—were Californians Richie Ginther and Ronnie Bucknum in a car with an experimental automatic transmission, and the New Jersey duo of Walt Hansgen and Mark Donohue. Shelby fielded three cars for Ken Miles / Lloyd Ruby; Dan Gurney / Jerry Grant; and Bruce McLaren / Chris Amon. No works Ferraris were present, but Luigi Chinetti's North American Racing Team fielded a 365 P2 upgraded to P3 specs for Pedro Rodríguez / Mario Andretti and a 250 LM for Jochen Rindt / Bob Bondurant. A second 365 P2 was entered by Jacques Swaters's Ecurie Francorchamps, the Belgian Ferrari concessionaire, for Lucien Bianchi / Gerard Langlois / Jean Blaton (racing under the pseudonym "Beurlys"). A single entry was the very fast Chaparral 2D from Midland, Texas, for Joakim Bonnier / Phil Hill. Although much lighter than the Fords, the Chaparral's aluminum 327ci Chevy was giving away 100 cubic inches to the Mk IIs.

The remainder of the strong 58-car field was made up primarily of the Sports and Grand Touring classes. One of the most interesting GT entries was a Chevrolet Corvette fitted with a 427ci engine entered by Roger Penske for Dick Guldstrand / Ben Moore / George Wintersteen. This was Roger Penske's first effort as an entrant, and he had secured a modest amount of sponsorship from the Sun Oil Company.

CHAPTER 39:

"Goldy, what do you need to win?"

Before Dick Guldstrand became the first professional driver for Roger Penske, he was already a legend in Corvette racing on the West Coast. He had won the Pacific Coast Championship in 1963, 1964, and 1965, and in 1964 had been named the California Sports Car Club SCCA Region Driver of the Year. His considerable talent as a driver was supported by a strong background in engineering, including work in the aerospace industry. He was a product of the California hot-rod culture, well connected with the West Coast speed shops, such as Iskenderian, Kurtis, and Edelbrock, and he had raced jalopies and sprint cars before he found his way into road racing. By the mid-1960s few people knew how to make a Corvette into a race car any better than "Goldy" Guldstrand.

Chevrolet engineer Zora Arkus-Duntov, renowned as the "Father of the Corvette," contacted Guldstrand and persuaded him to go to Philadelphia to meet Roger Penske. Arkus-Duntov had been a champion of Guldstrand's career on the West Coast, helping him connect with longtime sponsor Baher Chevrolet in Manhattan Beach, California. He believed Goldy was just the man to execute Roger Penske's ambitious plan to run the prototype 427ci engine in a Corvette for the major endurance races. The 427 engine was a prototype of the L88 that had been in development at General Motors for several years. It didn't become an option in production cars until April 1966, and the engine provided for Penske's use was one of a very few of the special prototypes in circulation. It was a measure of the confidence that GM racing—and especially Arkus-Duntov—had in Roger Penske. The engine had to run with cast-iron heads, as the aluminum heads designed for the engine were not yet homologated.

Guldstrand couldn't believe how cold it was in Philadelphia when he got off the plane from Los Angeles. Roger was there to meet him, and the first thing he said when they sat down for breakfast was, "Goldy, what do you need to win?" This set the tone, and no resources were denied in developing the car.

At the General Motors Corvette plant in St. Louis, Missouri, Goldy watched the final assembly of the very special Corvette as it came off the line. The production order included J-56 brakes, a 36-gallon fuel tank, F-41 suspension, prototype

2.73:1 positraction rear axle, TI ignition, M22 transmission, off-road exhaust, a teakwood steering wheel, and a special prototype cowl induction hood. There was no radio or heater, and the car was finished in rally red.

"Just about the whole plant was out in the parking lot to see me off—they were really behind the whole thing," Guldstrand recalls. "It was December and plenty cold—they wrapped me in furniture blankets and off I went. I drove the car to Roger's shop in Newtown Square, Pennsylvania."

At the Newtown Square shop on Route 252 the real job of building the Corvette into a race car began immediately. Bill Scott and Bill "Murph" Mayberry worked with Guldstrand and GM engineer Gib Hufstader—described by Guldstrand as Arkus-Duntov's right-hand man—and played a key role in making the engine and chassis work together. Scott, a Sun Oil Company employee, was a longtime friend of Roger Penske's, and Mayberry was a mechanic who worked for George Wintersteen.

Elmer Bradley was vice president of marketing for Sun Oil and had purchased a Corvette from Roger's Chevrolet dealership. When he was in for service, Roger showed him the race car and explained their plans for Daytona. Roger suggested that if Sun would provide fuels and lubricants for the car, along with personnel to help, he would put a Sunoco decal on the front fenders. The deal was struck.

Guldstrand, Wintersteen, and Moore won the GT class and finished 12th overall, but it didn't come easily: The Penske Corvette suffered massive front-end damage in the middle of the night. "Wintersteen ran into the back of a Morgan around midnight," Guldstrand recalls. "Roger sprang into action; he woke me up and told me to get into the car. Well, I couldn't see a thing as the headlamps had been wiped out, and pretty soon they black-flagged me. Roger always had great ideas and what he did was tape flashlights to the fenders." This satisfied the officials but didn't provide any real illumination. "I just followed the red taillights of some pretty quick cars until it started to get light. But the radiator had been damaged too, and pretty soon it was leaking pretty badly." Once again Roger was at his best, locating a Corvette in the paddock and persuading the owner to sell the radiator off his car. The big red Corvette roared on and made Roger Penske a class winner in his first race as an entrant.

Although George Wintersteen and Ben Moore were not professionals, they were competent amateur sports-car drivers and friends of Roger's. Wintersteen played an important role in the early days of Penske Racing, as his enthusiasm and energy were a catalyst for making things happens for the tiny team. The lease for the original garage at Newtown Square was at the time in Wintersteen's name, although he had inherited the space from Roger. Eventually, as Penske Racing expanded, the lease reverted to Roger.

CHAPTER 40:

1-2-3 for Ford

While Penske Racing was having its maiden race, the 1966 Daytona 24 Hours was also a debut for Mark as he joined the high-profile Ford racing operation for the first time. His introduction into the team was eased by the warm welcome he received from veteran Holman-Moody mechanic John Sulley. "I first met Sulley on the boat to Nassau in 1961," Mark remembered. "He was a top guy, having been on Freddy Lorenzen's NASCAR car, and when he recognized me it meant a lot toward fitting in on the team." Vern Houle was also working on the car, and Mark was impressed with his professionalism and enthusiasm. "I realized we had the makings of a good team because Vern, Sulley, Walt, and myself all got along. Walter taught me at that time that it was good to be around the car as much as possible. You show the mechanics that you are interested in what they are doing."

Walt Hansgen, who had never driven the Ford GT before, impressed the Ford personnel by immediately lapping as fast as the team's chief tester, Ken Miles. Eventually Miles qualified on pole at 1:57.8, with Walt third fastest at 1:58.2. They were split by Jo Bonnier's 1:58.0 in the Chaparral 2D.

Mark was extremely nervous before the start, conscious that this was his big break, and that if he couldn't come up to speed the chance was unlikely to come again. His biggest worry was the brakes. The Mk IIs were very heavy at nearly 3,000 pounds, and slowing from 180-plus mph required a great deal of braking power.

Walt was a steadying influence. Just as he had at Sebring the previous year in the Mecom Ferrari, he counseled Mark not only on driving techniques but also on the mental approach needed for an endurance race. Although Mark wasn't yet able to achieve the ultimate lap times of Hansgen, Gurney, Grant, Miles, McLaren, and other experienced hands, he realized in the pre-race team meeting that he could achieve the assigned target lap time for the race pace. He also realized that he would have to drive flat out on every lap to do it. The lead drivers on each car were asked to pick a lap time that they thought would allow them to complete the race and win. Walt Hansgen picked 2:06 (as this was the fastest time Mark had been able to turn), Dan Gurney chose 2:08, and Richie Ginther went with 2:10. Ken Miles selected a 2:04 pace and later said, "This whole business of driving long-distance races is really like playing roulette, and I just happened to pick the right number."

In the race, Bonnier led briefly, but the Chaparral soon fell off the pace with a series of minor problems; he became a non-factor as the Miles/Ruby Ford GT assumed the lead. Walt turned the big Ford over to Mark in second place, a position they held for much of the race, though they also led for eight laps during pit-stop turnovers. Eventually team orders came into play—per the agreement that the Holman-Moody cars were to be subordinate to the Shelby team cars—and the Gurney/Grant car was allowed to assume second place at the finish behind the winning car of Miles/Ruby. Gurney and Grant were running on equal terms with Mark and Walt and therefore were given the honor of finishing second. Hansgen was furious, but Mark admitted to being "elated" to just finish third in such a prestigious race.

The two Ford teams were great rivals. The executives in Dearborn, Michigan, were not above playing one against the other to sharpen the competitive edge. One of the important differences in their setups was that Holman-Moody was a Firestone tire team—and Walt Hansgen was a Firestone race-tire dealer. Shelby was committed to Goodyear. Goodyear was just beginning to be a force to be reckoned with in racing, while Firestone had long been the American racing tire. The battle between the tire companies was as intense as any competition in racing at the time.

The 1-2-3 result was a huge shot in the arm to the Ford program, as the lead car beat the fourth-place Ferrari of Rodríguez/Andretti by 14 laps. The upcoming Sebring 12 Hours would be key in evaluating where Ford's Le Mans program stood. Mark's position on the team was secured and his confidence was soaring.

Birth of the Can-Am

Just a week after Daytona the SCCA made the second of their blockbuster race series announcements. Though Mark Donohue likely gave little thought to any possible personal involvement, the new series would make his name known around the world.

Along with the Canadian Automobile Sport Clubs (CASC), the SCCA announced the Canadian-American Challenge Cup (or Can-Am), a five-race series (a sixth race was added a few weeks later) for two-seat unrestricted sports-racers sanctioned by the FIA. These would be formally known as Group 7 cars, or "big-bangers" in popular parlance. Unlike the detailed regulations governing Group 6 Prototypes (such as the Ford GT Mk II and Ferrari 330 P3), the original FIA regulations provided only minimal restrictions for Group 7. Those included requiring full fenders, a windshield of unspecified size, two usable seats, doors, head- and taillights, rollbar, self-starter, dual braking system, and the use of commercial fuel. These rules closely matched the SCCA regulations for modified cars. As the Can-Am caught the imagination of race fans, it wasn't long before all race cars of this type became known as "Can-Am cars."

Top-level American road racing had evolved in the early 1960s from the high-performance sports cars of the 1950s to a new breed of purpose-built sports-racers. Rear-engine sports cars were introduced into American road racing by the Cooper Monaco, followed soon by the even more sophisticated Lotus 19 (Monte Carlo). These British constructors truly changed the face of racing by designing and producing two-seat sports cars that borrowed heavily from the technology and even the parts bins of the respective companies' Formula One Grand Prix teams.

While the successful USRRC series for the same category of cars had left the SCCA poised to implement the Can-Am, the true genesis of the famous series was the fall series of professional road races for modified sports cars that had evolved informally. Riverside, California, had shown the way, and was soon followed by Laguna Seca in Northern California, and on the East Coast by races at Bridgehampton, Long Island, and Mosport Park in Canada.

As early as 1962, American teams began replacing the already potent 2.5-liter Climax engines with small-block

American V8s. In Europe, Ferrari, Maserati, and Porsche were also building sports-racers designed to win the classic long-distance events that comprised the FIA's World Championship of Manufacturers. A great deal of the interest in top-level American racing in the early 1960s came from the mixture of the thoroughbred European cars with the American specialty-built cars, which featured ever larger American engines, typically in the back of small British chassis, including Cooper, Lotus, and Brabham. And American chassis builders were also emerging to feed the enthusiasm for the evolving sports-racer class. Among the most notable were Genie, the Kjell Qvale / Joe Huffaker alliance from northern California; Bob McKee in Illinois; and Chaparral, the already-famous team from Midland, Texas.

The years 1961 and 1962 had been a time of great transition in American racing, and the changes went beyond the rapid development of race-car technology. The SCCA, under the firm guidance of executive director John Bishop, embraced professional racing as an important element of the organization's future. At the end of 1962 the SCCA announced a dedicated professional road-racing series for sports-racing cars, beginning in 1963. This was the catalyst for the real growth of the sports-racer industry. The United States Road Racing Championship (USRRC) was a very competitive proposition and created great excitement among enthusiasts, drivers, and entrants. The series was a catalyst for rapid advancement in the development of the sports-racers.

The success of the USRRC—which began its fourth season in 1966—certainly helped foster the Can-Am. The big difference was the Can-Am's full FIA sanction, which opened it to any international team or driver. The USRRC was a National series, and the teams competing in it contributed the depth that made possible a full field of cars for the Can-Am. The best of those teams could compete on even terms with the Europeans.

The great ideas and programs coming out of SCCA headquarters in Westport, Connecticut, were reflective of a particularly golden period in the club's history. At no time before or after did the professional staff have the autonomy they enjoyed during the 1960s. The board of governors was concerned with club racing, and had full confidence in the staff to run professional racing. As a result, John Bishop and SCCA competition director Jim Kaser were able to cultivate relationships with track owners and promoters while responding to the industry and the needs of the racing teams—all with minimal interference from the board.

CHAPTER 42:

Greatest Loss

Between Daytona and Sebring, Walt Hansgen had Can-Am very much on his mind. On March 15 he was at Riverside, California, testing tires for Firestone and shaking down the Mecom team's new Lola T70—the Mk II version of that successful chassis. The Lola was fitted with a 289ci Ford, prepared by Ryan Falconer. During the test day he was decisively faster than the lap record set the previous fall by Bruce McLaren in his McLaren-Olds. McLaren's official record (an official lap record can only be set during a race) stood at 108.083 mph, while Walt had turned a lap at 109.027. During the test he also ran off nine consecutive laps at an average speed of 108.333, also faster than the lap record. John Mecom and team manager John Kalb were expecting to make a big splash in the Can-Am. Walt had won the Laguna Seca round of the Fall series and as team leader he, too, expected great things for Mecom in 1966.

The recently announced SCCA Trans-Am Sedan series was inaugurated at Sebring on Friday, March 26, with a four-hour race held as a prelim to Saturday's 12-hour main event. It was an appropriate venue for the first race in a series that would run well into the next century—and it helped establish Mark Donohue's personal legend. As early as 1959, Sebring promoter Alec Ulmann had pioneered small sedan racing as a preliminary event. Bill France had done the same at Daytona, and Lime Rock and Marlboro were other tracks where sedans had been featured. The smaller-displacement cars—particularly the Lotus Cortinas—had been dominant at the events, and it was a 2.0-liter Alfa Romeo driven by future World Champion Jochen Rindt that won the first Trans-Am race over a starting field of 44 cars. The Alfa had been rolled over in practice the day before by Rindt's teammate, Roberto Bussinello, and the Autodelta team considered withdrawing the car. But with some overnight panel beating and fresh glass all the way around, the car was sent out for Jochen to make a solo drive. Rindt's drive through the field was spectacular, featuring his extremely sideways style. Although the Mustangs and Barracudas had featured early, it was a Dodge Dart driven by Bob Tullius that maintained some honor for the big-displacement cars by finishing second.

At Sebring, Ford anticipated a much greater challenge in the 12-hour race than they had seen at Daytona, where NART had carried the flag for Ferrari with year-old cars. There was also a feeling that the high-speed, relatively smooth Daytona circuit had favored the heavier and lower-revving Fords, and that the factory-entered Ferraris would come into their own at Sebring. David Piper, a prominent British private entrant of Ferraris, told *Road & Track*'s Dennis Cipnic, "What Ford has done is succeed in building a car which is perfectly able to run short, quick laps, and a suspension set up to take the 1.8 gs sustained on these smooth bankings. They will not be able to put these factors to use elsewhere." Mark had a different point of view, which he shared with Vince Slavin of the *Newark News*: "We'll have a better chance in France than in Florida because of the layout. There are longer straights at Le Mans where we can walk away from the Ferraris."

Shelby American entered two Mk IIs for Sebring. Ken Miles and Lloyd Ruby were paired again but this time in a special one-off roadster version of the Mk II known as the X-1. At 2,300 pounds the roadster was considerably lighter than the coupes, although its aerodynamics were inferior. Dan Gurney and Jerry Grant were in a more-conventional Mk II. Walt and Mark were in chassis No. 1032 (they had driven 1031 at Daytona), while A. J. Foyt and Ronnie Bucknum drove the second Holman-Moody car, fitted with an automatic transmission. There were an additional nine privately entered Mk I GT40s running in the Sports category. Sefac-Ferrari, the Ferrari factory team, entered the latest 330 P3 for Mike Parkes and Bob Bondurant, and a Dino 206 S for Lorenzo Bandini and Lodovico Scarfiotti. NART again had Mario Andretti and Pedro Rodríguez in the 330 P2 they had brought home fourth at Daytona. Factory-entered Porsche 906s were for Hans Herrmann / Joe Buzzetta and for Gerhard Mitter / Günther Klass. Chaparral arrived with 2D Coupes for Bonnier/Hill and for team principals Hap Sharp / Jim Hall. Chaparral had won the race the year before in the 2C—a sports-racer—and expectations were high for their success.

Mark happened to be in the Penske hangar on the Webster Straight during qualifying and Roger asked him to drive the Sting Ray coupe. "I had a black helmet and Mark wore it when he took the car on the track," remembers George Wintersteen. "You could enter the track from wherever you were paddocked, and this obviated any close examination by the officials of who was in the car." Mark qualified the big Corvette at a 3:21.2—3.8 seconds faster than the next car in the over-5000cc GT category. Jack Deren, a longtime Penske mechanic who had helped build Roger's Formula One–based Zerex-Special, was working on the Corvette and recalls, "When Mark got in the car we weren't even certain from where we were paddocked whether it was qualifying or an untimed practice session. It was as casual as that."

Back in the Ford compound Mark was preoccupied with the poor braking of the big Ford GT, telling Slavin, "Sebring is really tough on brakes. We'll be changing the front pads about three times and the discs once." Mark was determined to bring his engineering skills to bear on the problem, while Walt was content to allow the mechanics to do their best with the brake balance setup and to "let it fall where it will." Walt qualified the car fourth for the Le Mans–type start and was now focused on the race. The success at Daytona had increased Mark's confidence, and he had some ideas he wanted to try. After having the brakes set to his specifications, just before the start of the race he had the mechanics add even more proportion to the front brakes—with no chance to try them out. When the race started Walt was clearly struggling mightily with the car.

The early portion of the race was a disaster, as Walt fell back and then went off the track, hitting some hay bales and knocking the door loose. He pitted to have the door fixed and then came back in again and got out of the car, demanding that the brakes be fixed. Eventually the brakes were brought back to a manageable level, but Walt was furious and clearly felt Mark had put him in a bad position. They were many laps down and, although they persevered and ran fast from that point on, they could never catch the leaders.

Dan Gurney was the story of the race. Starting dead last after his Ford GT failed to start from pole position, he drove through the field in dramatic fashion and lowered the lap record to 2:54.8 in the midst of maximum race traffic. He passed 26 cars on the first lap, 10 more on the second lap, and an hour and a half into the race had taken a commanding lead that he and his co-driver Jerry Grant maintained throughout the race.

The race was not without its share of tragedy, claiming the lives of five people in two separate accidents. At about the three-hour mark, Canadian Bob McLean, in a GT40 entered by the Comstock team, had just exited the pits when he crashed exiting the right-hand bend after the esses. The car struck a utility pole and came to rest upside down where it burned fiercely for 20 minutes. McLean died in the car. In the last hour of the race, Mario Andretti in the NART P2 Ferrari was contesting fourth place closely with Don Wester's Porsche

906 when the gearbox broke in the Ferrari, causing Andretti to spin into Wester's path. The cars made contact and Wester's Porsche went off the road, hitting several spectators who were viewing the race from an unauthorized area. Four died and Wester suffered cuts and bruises and a broken ankle.

Through attrition, Mark and Walt looked set for a third-place finish behind the two Shelby Fords when Dan Gurney had the worst possible luck. On the final lap, the Ford engine broke and Dan was out just before the start/finish. Had he left the car sitting he would have been classified second; instead, he chose to push the heavy Ford the remaining quarter of a mile to the finish line. This was against regulations and the car was disqualified. Mark and Walt inherited second place but there was no cause for elation. In addition to Gurney's bad luck, the Parkes/Bondurant P3 Ferrari that had run a strong second place was out when the transmission gave up after eight hours, and the Andretti/Wester accident had eliminated two other front-running cars. They were 12 laps down to the Miles/Ruby winning open roadster. Walt was still angry enough that he couldn't talk to Mark.

Mark described himself as heartbroken, and the two parted with the issue unresolved. Had not fate intervened they likely would have sat down and cleared the air at their next meeting. Walt, famously loyal to his friends, cared very much for Mark and was determined that he succeed. The Sebring incident would have been long forgotten. As it developed, Mark was to carry the unease of their parting with him the rest of his life.

Walt left early on Sunday morning after the race to catch a plane for Indianapolis where he gave the new Mecom Indy Lola its first test at the Speedway in preparation for the 500. After the test Walt returned to his home and family in Westfield, New Jersey, for just two days before leaving for France for the April test days at Le Mans.

Mark's services weren't required at the test day, although he was confirmed to be Walt's co-driver for the 24-hour race in June. Ford was using the test day to evaluate the new J-car, the first Ford sports prototype to be developed entirely in the United States, and the car they expected to be the successor to the Mk IIs. Walt went out in one of the Mk IIs to establish some base time laps to compare to the J-car. It had been raining hard all day and the track was still wet when the car got out of shape approaching the high-speed right-hand bend after the pits. Walt Hansgen, a masterful rain driver, was able to maintain control and drove down the escape road rather than attempt the 150-mile-per-hour bend. What he did not

know was that the apparent "escape road" was nothing of the sort. Two large piles of sand had been placed on the road for construction purposes. The impact was enormous.

The Ford GTs did not have a rollbar or any sort of integral protective cage as the structural strength of the monocoque chassis was thought to be adequate. It was more than 20 minutes before Walt was extricated from the car. He was initially taken to a local Le Mans hospital and then by helicopter to the U.S. Army 34th General Hospital in Orleans, France. There he received the best possible care, but never regained consciousness. The accident was on Saturday, April 2. Walt died five days later on Thursday, April 7.

Mark learned about the crash at the breakfast table of Rob and Madeline McCullough in Pawtucket, Rhode Island. He and Sue were staying with the McCulloughs for the wedding of Dave Lawton and Judy Hartley on April 2 in nearby Providence. Although he still didn't know the extent of Walt's injuries, Mark was visibly distressed. He could not, however, send Judy and Dave off on their honeymoon without a signature Mark Donohue touch. Mark filled the air ducts of Judy's new 1963 Pontiac Tempest convertible with confetti. "The car dispensed confetti all the way to Florida and back" remembers Judy. "The faster you went the more confetti. In fact, we had traces of it as long as I owned the car."

The evening after the Lawton wedding, Mark, Sue, and 21-month-old Michael drove more than 400 miles to Upper Marlboro, Maryland. George Clark towed the Mustang from New Jersey, and Mark made arrangements with the race stewards to miss practice and qualifying and start at the back of the field for the Governor's Trophy on Sunday, the third of April. He finished fifth overall and fourth in B Production. Don Yenko won the class in his Sting Ray behind overall winner Hal Keck in the Archway 427 Cobra. Second and third ahead of Mark were Peter Haydon in a Lotus Elan and Frank Dominianni's Sting Ray.

Meanwhile, Walt Hansgen's wife Bea and children Beverly and Rusty had rushed to France. After Bea returned to the family home in Bedminster, New Jersey, Mark called on her with a particularly awkward duty on behalf of John Holman. Holman, through Mark, offered to pay for the funeral expenses. Bea firmly and immediately turned down the offer. Ford had behaved badly in the wake of Walt's death. They immediately circulated a story that falsely portrayed the driver as being the cause of the accident. When the family arrived in France the official stance from

Ford was cold and non-supportive. The offer to pay for the burial was seen as a final insult, but Bea would not have accepted Holman's gesture even if the circumstances had been less charged.

Mark never forgot Walt, and remained close to his family. Rusty Hansgen, just 19 years old at his father's death, was always welcome anywhere with Mark. Mark also established the Walter E. Hansgen Memorial Foundation scholarship, awarded annually to engineering students.

While devastated by his friend's death, Mark never considered quitting himself. He believed that race accidents did not bear contemplating too deeply. "Walt could have had the same accident and gotten away with it," he observed. "You never know, and it isn't something you think about."

CHAPTER 43:

Roger, Mark, and Karl

Walt Hansgen's death affected the American racing community profoundly. At age 46, Hansgen had long been a senior statesman among race drivers, and was almost a father figure to many. As an active driver since 1951, he had touched the lives of a great many people within the sport. He was enormously popular with the media, race organizers and officials, mechanics, race workers, and particularly among his fellow drivers—none more so than Mark Donohue.

The world of racing turned out in an impressive tribute for Walt's funeral on Tuesday, April 12, 1966. The service was conducted at the Somerset Hills Lutheran Church in Basking Ridge, New Jersey, with interment at the New Germantown Cemetery in Oldwick. Mark later recalled being approached during the day by a visibly grieving Roger Penske, who greeted Mark warmly. Penske remembers Hansgen as "one of my idols and a great person."

Roger Penske had retired at the end of the 1964 race season after an enormously successful career as a race driver. Penske was no ordinary driver. When he announced he was finished, he was rated among the elite of American road racers. He was one of those very rare athletes to quit at the very zenith of his career. In fact, the argument may well be made that as a racer Penske was only beginning to come into his own when he stopped, his greatest achievements as a driver ahead of him. He became team manager for Chaparral, which only

added to his knowledge and experience.

While Roger Penske had a passion for driving race cars, he had a clear vision of his greater goals. At 27, he was already a success in business: He had thrived in a sales position with Alcoa before becoming general manager of McKean Chevrolet in Philadelphia, Pennsylvania. When the opportunity to purchase the dealership presented itself, he never hesitated, even though the financing package required him to give up racing. Though he was moving forward to build an ever-expanding business empire, he had no intention of leaving racing entirely behind him.

Roger had followed his successful debut as an owner/entrant at the 24-hour race at Daytona with another GT class win at Sebring and a ninth overall finish. The 427 Sting Ray coupe now was painted in Sunoco colors and driven by Ben Moore and George Wintersteen. The team ran a second car for Dick Guldstrand and Dick Thompson after Roger Penske persuaded General Motors to part with one of their two remaining Corvette Grand Sports (GS#001). The cars were now in conflict with GM's official no-racing position and needed to be in private hands if they were ever to see the race track again. Two Grand Sports had been converted from the original coupe design to roadsters. It was in this form that Penske fitted the car with a 427. The car was very fast in the race, but an off-course excursion by Thompson resulted in a DNF.

At Sebring Roger encountered Karl Kainhofer, who was working with Ford's Kar Kraft on construction of the J-car. Karl had grown up in Graz, Austria, and was a Porsche-trained mechanic. He had worked initially on Roger's RSK Porsche and eventually prepared other of Roger's race cars in the late 1950s and early '60s. Now the two men discussed a reunion and Roger's plans to become a serious entrant. A deal was struck, and upon his return to Michigan Karl immediately left Kar Kraft. He packed and moved to Pennsylvania, his family following two months later. Karl was the first employee of Roger Penske Racing Enterprises. "We shook hands on a deal and worked continuously on the basis of that handshake for 32 years," says Karl.

Accompanied by Karl and Bill Scott, Roger visited John Mecom's race shop in Houston, Texas, where Roger placed an order for a new Lola T70. Penske had established close ties with the Lola importer as lead driver for Mecom's racing team in 1963.

On that sad day in New Jersey at Walt Hansgen's funeral,

Roger had told Mark that he was looking for a driver for the race team he was putting together. He asked Mark if he was interested in trying the arrangement on a race-to-race basis. The deal was modest—fifty dollars a day plus expenses. Soon after, Mark called on Roger at his race shop in Newtown Square, Pennsylvania, to accept.

This was the beginning of a relationship that was to become one of the most famous alliances in the history of American motorsports. In the 1960s and '70s one could seldom utter either man's name without immediately associating it with the name of the other. Penske-Donohue came to mean blue race cars with the number 6, Sunoco colors, an advanced state of preparation—"the unfair advantage"—and a winning tradition. This is how the Penske racing team legend began.

Mark was greatly affected by the loss of his friend and mentor, and until talking to Roger was seriously contemplating retiring. Years later he told Hal McCoy for the Dayton (Ohio) *Daily News*: "Walt Hansgen taught me all I know. Walt could put it into words—tell you how to drive—and you could get into the car and put to use in racing what he had put in words. Not many people can do that. I wish Walt were here now. I thought I would quit after Walt was killed, but Roger picked me up."

Mark later told *Road & Track*'s Mike Knepper: "Right from the start I realized there was a great opportunity to learn from an association with Roger. It wasn't a hard decision to make."

Roger Penske was negotiating with the Sun Oil Company for additional support, and that sponsorship was formally announced on May 10, 1966. One of the most valuable parts of the agreement was that Sun Oil would fund two full-time personnel to augment the team. Roger asked especially for Bill Scott, a machinist and fabricator of great talent at Sun Oil and a personal friend who had been involved in Roger's own racing days. The other new member was Bill Preston, who acted as official Sun liaison to the team, responsible for protecting the company's interests. Sun wanted no product failures. Preston was responsible for ensuring that Sun Oil products were the only ones used in and displayed on the car, and he made sure the fuel arrived at each track on time.

From Sun Oil's perspective, the Lola was a more interesting car than the Corvette because it would be competing for overall race wins—and the accompanying publicity—rather than for class wins. Sun Oil effectively funded Penske's purchase of the Lola.

When Mark visited the Newtown Square shop in late April, the new Lola T70 Mk II chassis had arrived, and Karl Kainhofer was busy preparing it as a race car. Karl had arrived at the small two-car garage with two hand-carried boxes of tools. Otherwise the shop had little more than two workbenches, a drill press, a vise, and some gas welding equipment. There was a pay phone in the corner, two bay doors containing the only windows, and a side door. "Bill Scott was essential to getting the operation going," recalls Karl. "Without Scotty I don't know if we could have made a go of it in those early days." The magnificently equipped Sun Oil machine shop where Scotty worked as a fabricator and machinist was just half a mile away.

The Lola T70 represented the state of the art in 1966 for sports-racers. It was the perfect embodiment of a sophisticated British-designed and -built chassis intended for mating with a big American V8 powerplant. There were a number of teams running the Lola T70s in 1966, but Penske's idea for separating his team from the field was to fit an engine that no one else had made work. The small-block 283ci Chevrolet engine—typically enlarged to 333ci—was the standard with most teams, although Mecom Racing was among those preferring the 289ci Ford. Penske's experience with the 7.0-liter, 427ci Chevy at Daytona and Sebring convinced him that it would be sensational in the Lola.

By the time the car was ready the 1966 USRRC was well under way, with the first rounds of the series already run. The Penske plan was to enter the remaining USRRC rounds and other Group 7 races with the longer-term goal of tackling the inaugural Can-Am in the fall. Mark's ability to make a major contribution to the team outside of the race events themselves was severely limited because of his other obligations. He was living on Long Island and had recently accepted additional responsibilities at Griffith Motors, where he was helping the fledgling manufacturer with their transition from the facility in Plainview, New York, to expanded space in Bridgehampton.

Mark still had his foot in amateur racing as he pursued a sufficient number of SCCA Nationals in the B Production Mustang to ensure an invitation to the end-of-year Runoffs. Mark very much wanted to win the National Championship in the Mustang. He was also fully committed to the Ford prototype program.

CHAPTER 44:

"A driver doesn't want to appear concerned with his own safety"

Mark felt somewhat adrift after Walt's death. "I was lost for a while," he later recalled. "He was really able to talk to me. We talked the same language." John Holman had overcome his initial skepticism about Mark and understood the painful loss the younger man was experiencing. Mark came under Holman's influence, flattered that the legendary figure seemed to take him under his wing. He later was to say that John Holman and Walt Hansgen were remarkably alike. Mark thought they looked alike, held many similar views, and even talked the same way. When Holman asked for his engineering opinion of the Mk II Ford, Mark was eager to respond. On April 15, just three days after Walt's funeral, he wrote to him on Griffith Motors letterhead:

Mr. John Holman

Holman & Moody

Charlotte, North Carolina

Dear John,

You asked me for my ideas about the car. It seems far easier to write them down in outline form rather than discuss them on the phone at the outset.

Mark II Ford—Comments After Sebring

Lighting and Instruments

Possibly the bottom pair of running lights could be regular type headlights as on the top in order to increase the night vision. The alternator capacity should be checked first to see if this is possible.

A more secure way of fastening the number identification lights would be desirable.

The white transmission oil pressure light should be changed so that:

In the daytime it is clearly visible to the driver if it should come on. Thus no shield should be over it to direct light downward.

It comes on only in event of failure (O pressure) or a much lower pressure than is presently used.

All tach should be equipt [sic] with a tell tail [sic]. Although this is a relatively minor item it does help the driver in many ways.

As at Sebring, all switches should come on by pulling down.

Some checking should be made of the headlight mounting arrangement as our right side unit seemed quite loose.

A double angle mirror for night lights is an absolute must.

Chassis and Suspension

Some consideration should be given to the use of the new Firestone 16 inch Indy tire. This may not be possible with the standardization of the 15 inch combination. That tire will be available by then and may prove advantageous from a brake cooling point of view.

Also consideration should be given to the Firestone 1200x15 tire, as it is faster. Perhaps this route is impossible politically due to its small diameter.

Due to the lack of time in France for much practice, it seems like a good idea to try and test the particular car to be run in the States before the trip over. During the testing, one could attempt to achieve the following:

Bed in more than enough brake pucks for practice and the race.

Jack the suspension to eliminate cross jacking and achieve the proper legal height at the proper alignment settings.

Experiment with a few sway bars, shock settings, and front height settings.

Shake down the car again for leaks, etc.

It would not be overly strenuous on the car as any desire to change the car to break it seems unnecessary after the Sebring race. The above type of test would preclude that the brake situation is considered adequate from the dyno tests.

Once accomplished, the practice in France would be to bed in the engine, adjust to the course and obtain an adequate tire and gas mileage figure only. This would sure simplify matters when the heat comes on! The best courses nearby are Danville or Bridgehampton. I favor the latter.

After my error on adjusting the balance bar at Sebring, it seems necessary to install pressure gauges on the front and rear calipers to pre-set the balance. The desired pressure readings would of course be dependent upon the piston and lining area front and rear, as equal pressure might not be equal to brake force. Of course Ford has already worked all this out and the information should be readily available.

A driver doesn't want to appear concerned with his own safety so I make these comments as a bystander.

Seat belts—Some additional belting running forward along the sides of the driver might be helpful in preventing the hook up button from riding up if one moves around a bit.

Doors—A side opening door without the extension in the roof ought to be considered for better exits in the upside down position. Normal entry and exit would be hampered but that is not important.

Roll Bar—Perhaps a form of roll cage should be considered.

Because of the tremendous effort you people put into the cars, by race time everyone is kind of destroyed physically. Perhaps if there was one guy who was kind of fresh, he could instruct the crew in step by step motions and insist on keeping unnecessary people out of the pits (like you and the cameramen).

Also the crew should practice disc changing if they haven't already done so.

The above kind of sums up my thoughts on the matter. I want you to know that I'd still like to drive for you—if you want me. I'd also like to do the testing, if you decided to go thru with it. I'll call you after you've had time to read this letter.

Sincerely

Mark Donohue

Chief Engineer

Mark's letter to John Holman is fascinating and certainly tempts interpretation and technical speculation. On a purely human level, it reflects a young man anxious to impress—but not wishing to offend or overstep. John Holman was a tough customer, and while he had obviously opened the door to some confidences and rapport, Mark was treading carefully. Perhaps most poignant is the reference to safety issues: "A driver doesn't want to appear concerned with his own safety . . ." This revealing line reflects the aesthetic of the era: A driver never complained or appeared to give a thought to anything that could be interpreted as outside the "code."

The code, of course, never existed in writing but was a prevailing attitude not unlike the phenomenon described by Tom Wolfe in his 1979 book, *The Right Stuff*. Wolfe portrays the experience of the original seven Mercury astronauts who pioneered the American space program. All veteran test pilots, the astronauts were strong individuals bonded by a common attitude regarding the danger of their chosen profession. The overlap between pilots and race-car drivers is apparent throughout history. Aviation and racing appeal to a similar personality type, and each discipline requires remarkably parallel mental and physical attributes. Inevitably, race-car drivers wanted to fly and pilots wanted to race. This extended to the astronauts—Alan Shepard crewed for friends at Nassau, and Gus Grissom and Deke Slayton were among those who owned performance sports cars and were greatly frustrated by NASA's refusal to allow them to compete. Grissom and Gordon Cooper were co-owners with Jim Rathmann of a USAC Indy car. It is a delightful turn of history that Grissom's son, Scott, became a race-car driver of great talent and achievement.

A hint at the attitude implicit in the racing driver's code is also touched on in Ken Purdy's 1965 book, *The New Matadors*:

> Most drivers don't want to talk about why they drive, and will not. When politeness requires, they will make an answer, but it may have little connection with reality. They don't want to talk about it, and they do not approve of others who do, within or without the club, but particularly within it. They should not be criticized. Anyone practicing a peacetime profession which has taken the lives of, say 200 men in our time, is entitled to keep his thoughts on the matter to himself.

The John Holman letter never refers directly to Walt Hansgen. His death was likely all too recent and painful for both men. But Walt's influence can be seen throughout in Mark's meticulous attention to detail. Walt's violent crash demonstrated that the integral strength of the Ford's monocoque structure was not sufficient to protect the driver as had been believed. Soon all the Mk II cars were fitted with roll cages.

Mark was invited to the test sessions conducted by Holman-Moody at the Ford test track at Kingman, Arizona, and at Riverside, California. He was joined by NASCAR drivers Dick Hutcherson and Marvin Panch under the crew chief leadership of John Wanderer. They focused on brakes at Riverside and at Kingman did a 24-hour reliability test, spreading it over three eight-hour days. Mark was intense by nature. At this early chapter in his professional career he was surprised at the casual attitude taken by Panch and Hutcherson when they weren't in the race car, although they were competitive with one another during the actual testing. All three men got along well, and it was the beginning of a relationship that would continue through Le Mans that year. Hutcherson had just completed his rookie year in NASCAR and was under contract with Holman-Moody. Mark later told Bill Preston that when Hutcherson asked him about the Ford deal at Le Mans, Mark had explained that it was $1,000 to drive with Ford paying all the expenses, plus another $1,000 if they won. Hutcherson replied in a slow southern drawl, elongating "hell" to sound like *heeell*: "Hell, I can make more money than that at the track in Myrtle Beach on a Saturday night. I ain't going." He did though.

Panch was also slated to drive at Le Mans until he received a call from Bill France urging him to race instead at Charlotte in the World 600. Ford was telling Panch to turn the NASCAR drive down, and advised him to inform France he wouldn't do it unless it was in a top car. France arranged a drive for Panch in a Petty Plymouth. Panch accepted it and won the race. He retired at the end of the year after a great career that included a win in the 1961 Daytona 500. He was one of the very best road racers among the NASCAR regulars, having won Watkins Glen in 1965.

Mark's letter to John Holman was signed "Chief Engineer," his new title at Griffith. On April 12, Jack Griffith announced in a press release that Mark had been appointed to the new position with increased responsibilities, saying, "We have been very impressed with Mark's ability to translate a race driver's awareness of handling and performance qualities into engineering terms that are applicable to production automobiles." This same month, the Griffith production line and offices moved further out on Long Island from Plainview to a new space in Bridgehampton. Mark was setting up a production line for the new Griffith 600 series while continuing to engineer the car itself. Like previous Griffiths the new car started with a TVR chassis, but this time Jack Griffith's new European partner was Intermeccanica. The Italian firm shipped cars to Griffith, complete with chassis and the handsome John Cumberford–designed body. On Mark's assembly line, the car was fitted with a 273ci Plymouth V8 and drivetrain. Mark did the final engineering and test driving. Jack Griffith recalls that he enjoyed a friendly relationship with Roger Penske and was happy to make Mark's time available to pursue his racing career.

CHAPTER 45:
Debut Race for Penske-Donohue

The USRRC and the much-anticipated Can-Am were not the only venues in North America showcasing the big Group 7 sports-racers. On consecutive weekends in late May and early June, Le Circuit Mont Tremblant–St. Jovite in Quebec, Canada, and Mosport Park in Ontario, Canada, were hosting 200-mile races with FIA international listings. Roger Penske decided to make those races the debut for the Lola and the 427 engine.

When Mark returned from testing with Ford he found that work was well along on the Lola, and Penske team hopes were high for the 427. Karl Kainhofer had brought a steadying and professional influence to the operation. Mark learned very quickly to appreciate Karl's patience, as he was still struggling to bring his own technical knowledge to a practical level. He later divined that Karl had likely been several steps ahead of him while never indicating so. Karl and Mark rapidly developed a friendship that would endure until the very last moments of Mark's life.

Bill Preston knew that Mark was still finding his way with the Penske operation. "Mark was still contracted to Ford through Holman-Moody to drive the GT40s for '66 and '67. Roger was a Chevrolet dealer, so naturally needed to use Chevrolet engines and cars. This meant that he wasn't trusted by either camp, which I am sure made things difficult for him."

The Labatt 50 race at Mont Tremblant demonstrated what a steep learning curve the team faced. Group 7 racing was at its apogee in the middle of 1966, and most of the rival teams had their programs well advanced, with their cars long since developed. Despite his experience with the big Fords, Mark too was treading on almost new ground. He had shared the Mecom Lola T70 with Walt Hansgen the previous year in the Road America 500, but this was precious little experience in these high-horsepower, relatively light, and low-grip cars that required their very own technique to go fast. At St. Jovite and Mosport, he was facing veteran European teams that he would see again in the Can-Am, plus the best of the American teams who had already completed four rounds of the USRRC. Admittedly, everyone was constantly adjusting to the sport's fast-paced changes, but with a brand-new team and an untried chassis/engine combination, the Penske operation was biting off a great deal. The primary problem, inherent to the wet sump oil system, was getting the big engine properly lubricated and maintaining oil pressure. Great efforts were expended in creating new baffles, rerouting oil lines, and every other idea the hardworking crew could dream up.

There were various other teething problems, inevitable with a new car and a new team. Mark found himself at the St. Jovite start line with no tachometer, dry tires on a wet track, and brakes that had not been bedded in. "Roger always wants new parts on the car," said Mark. "So Karl was told to install new, unburnished brake pads." It did not go well. The green brakes forced Mark off-line to avoid running up the back of John Cannon's Genie. Off the line, where it was very wet, Mark's dry compound tires did him no good, and off-line became off-the-road. He recovered well, but the excursion resulted in a holed radiator. In those very wet conditions it was difficult for Mark to discern that water was coming from the radiator, and by the time he brought the car into the pits the engine was fairly cooked. Mark thought this might have been the end of his racing career with Penske, but Roger was very encouraging and asked him to help get the car ready for Mosport the next weekend.

Bruce McLaren won at Mont Tremblant–St. Jovite in dominant fashion, lowering the previous lap record by more than a second, and his teammate Chris Amon had been a strong second until the engine failed late in the race. There was a great deal of carnage from a start-line accident combined with a generally high rate of attrition. Chuck Parsons finished second in his Genie, and Skip Barber drove a remarkable race in the difficult conditions to finish third and win the under-2.0-liter category in his Brabham BT8.

Both McLaren team cars were powered by Oldsmobile engines, and the McLaren chassis was state-of-the-art for Group 7. They were also the most professional and best-prepared team at the event. McLaren was a veteran Formula One driver who in 1959 had been the youngest man to win a World Championship Grand Prix. He had continued through 1965 as a top-line Formula One driver with Cooper, and now, in partnership with American Teddy Mayer, was on his own as both a Formula One constructor and a sports-racer constructor. The sports-racer side of his business had been

up and running since 1963, and by the time the McLaren Mk 1A began making news in 1964, there was a strong customer demand. Bruce's small race shop could not keep up, so he wisely made an arrangement with the Trojan Group to produce customer cars under license. The cars were marketed as McLaren-Elvas since Trojan had taken over the assets of the well-known Elva Company. Trojan built 24 of the original Mk 1As, and eventually 28 more of the Mk 1B (the cars, latterly identified as the Mk 1B, were at the time generally referred to within the racing industry as the Mk 2). Bruce McLaren's technical and practical engineering skill provided him more knowledge of how to make a big-engined sports-racer work than just about anyone in the world.

The possible exception, the American Chaparral team, was preoccupied in early 1966 with developing their Group 6 endurance car. It would not be until the advent of the Can-Am in the fall that they would show their hand with their latest Group 7 challenger.

The Penske team worked all week before Mosport to be race-ready, and was still at it late Friday evening. Mark and Karl together drove the transporter through the night. They loaded up at the shop in Newtown Square and started the 500-mile drive at 1:30 a.m., arriving at Mosport Park near Toronto on Saturday morning. The entry was stronger at Mosport than the previous week, with the addition of John Mecom's Lola T70 Ford for Jackie Stewart and the similar car from All American Racers (AAR) for Jerry Grant. Stewart and Grant had missed St. Jovite in favor of the Indianapolis 500, where Stewart came within six laps of winning as a rookie for team owner Mecom. Teammate Graham Hill—in the car originally intended for team leader Walt Hansgen—did win, making him a rookie winner for rookie team owner John Mecom.

The race at Mosport was run in two heats, and Bruce McLaren dominated both, underscoring the clear superiority of the McLaren chassis and overall setup. Lothar Motschenbacher saved some pride for the American contingent by finishing second, ahead of McLaren driver Chris Amon. The Penske team continued to struggle with the 427's oil issues, although Mark was able to make a better impression than the week before. On only the sixth lap of the first heat, Mark was following Jerry Grant when Grant's Lola got on to an oil spill at the very difficult turn 2A and went off the track, sliding down the hill. The crash demolished the Lola and injured Grant—but also, tragically, struck 37-year-old Gordon Harrison at his flag marshal post. He died almost immediately. Harrison was an avid bicyclist who had become fascinated by racing and was a pioneer member of the Canadian Race Communications Association (CRCA). He was also the current competition chairman of the Ontario region of the Canadian Automobile Sport Clubs (CASC).

Mark was shocked by the violence of the accident and well aware that oil on the track had caught Grant out. He was also aware of an inch of oil gathering in the passenger seat of his Lola and feared that he may have been the culprit. "I didn't think I was spilling any, or I would have spun in it myself," Mark later recalled. "But still, I thought, 'Grant has just killed some guy, and here I am carrying around a gallon of loose oil. Maybe I contributed to the accident.'" The engine was now smoking and Mark pitted to tell Roger what was on his mind. They agreed it was time to retire the car.

A week later, Mark left for France with Ford. When he next saw the Lola, the 427 had been replaced.

CHAPTER 46:
"The greatest triumph in the 65-year history of the Ford Motor Company"

For Le Mans, Ford had to scramble for drivers to make up an armada of eight Ford GT Mk IIs, backed by five privately entered GT40s running in the Sports category. The driver lineup had been diminished by a series of accidents—the most tragic being Walt Hansgen's death in the April test days. Less than two weeks before the race there was a serious crash at Spa in the Belgian Grand Prix that left Jackie Stewart hospitalized. Lloyd Ruby crashed his airplane on takeoff at Indianapolis, putting him in the hospital for several months. Finally, at the Milwaukee USAC Indy car race, A. J. Foyt bailed out of a burning car, suffering burns too severe to allow him to compete.

Australian Paul "Hawkeye" Hawkins was one of the new recruits brought on board to fill the seats. When Mark learned that the new man—whom he had never heard of—would be his co-driver and have the honor of starting the race, he complained to John Holman. Mark not unreasonably saw himself as a veteran of two successful endurance races—plus extensive testing—for Ford. Holman's explanation that

Hawkins had previous race experience at Le Mans didn't impress Mark, as, in his words, it had been "in an MG."

Actually, Hawkeye had twice driven the 24 Hours and in 1965 had won his class and finished 12th overall with John Rhodes in the very quick Austin-Healey Sebring Sprite. Hawkins had at least as much race experience as Mark, and a great deal more on the international scene. It is a credit to both men that they ultimately found common ground as friends. Sue was with Mark at Le Mans—her first trip to Europe—and remembers that Paul and Mark hit it off almost immediately, initial differences being quickly put aside. They had a lot of fun together at Le Mans and later.

Hawkeye was one of the great personalities of racing in the 1960s, and his exploits off the track were legendary. When he was on the continent, Hawkins often stayed with American racing journalist Randy Barnett and his family at their home near Darmstadt, Germany. He was a fine person and a great deal of fun, Barnett recalled. "On the way to a race, he would always stop in at my office in *Stars & Stripes* to use our Telex machine and read the papers, and to visit the Press Club to get a beer or two." His biographer, Ivan McLeod, said of Hawkins, "He could drink like a fish, swear like a trooper, and next morning go out to win the race."

The hugely talented Hawkins often made news for the wrong reason. He had, the previous year, made his World Championship Formula One debut at the Monaco Grand Prix in an ex–Jim Clark Lotus 33 (chassis R8) entered by a private team. By lap 79 he was running in ninth place when he had the misfortune to land the Lotus in the bottom of the harbor of Monte Carlo, a feat achieved only once before, a decade earlier, by Alberto Ascari. After swimming to the top, Hawkeye watched the remainder of the race from a yacht in the harbor, gin and tonic in hand. Hawkins was also known for his liberal use of M80 firecrackers to speed along a slow-moving waitress or just to liven up a bathroom visit by one of his mates. Perhaps it isn't such a surprise that he and Mark ended up great friends.

The other two Holman-Moody entries were for Ronnie Bucknum / Dick Hutcherson and Mario Andretti / Lucien Bianchi. Bianchi was a highly regarded Belgian driver who had previously won at Sebring and the Tour de France. Andretti's place on the team was recognition of his place as the fastest-rising star in American racing. From Mario's perspective it was an opportunity to refine his road-racing skills and to increase his exposure on the world stage.

The three Shelby-entered Mk IIs were for the familiar pairings of Gurney/Grant and McLaren/Amon, plus Ken Miles now joined by Denny Hulme, who was subbing for the injured Lloyd Ruby. Alan Mann Racing had two Mk IIs for Sir John Whitmore / Frank Gardner and for Graham Hill, who was supposed to drive with Dick Thompson—but didn't. Thompson was unfairly excluded from the race by the organizers because of a practice incident. Australian Brian Muir was brought in on very short notice to fill the final seat.

Impressive as the Ford presence was, they were up against formidable opposition from Ferrari, Porsche, and Chaparral. Ferrari's total turnout of cars was even more numerous than Ford's, but their front line was represented by just three of the twin-cam 4.0-liter P3s. The works team was looking after two coupes for John Surtees / Mike Parkes and Lorenzo Bandini / Jean Guichet. The third P3 was a roadster on loan to NART for the race and to be driven by Pedro Rodríguez / Richie Ginther. Lodovico Scarfiotti was named as a reserve driver for the P3s, team manager Eugenio Dragoni implying that John Surtees may not yet be sufficiently recovered from the serious injuries he had suffered the previous year in Canada in the Group 7 Lola. Surtees, however, had just demonstrated his fitness by running off four consecutive wins for the team, including a dramatic Belgian Grand Prix victory just the week before. Surtees was not pleased and took the matter up directly with Dragoni. Tempers flew, and upon failing to gain the support of Enzo Ferrari, Surtees withdrew on principle—never to return to the team. Carroll Shelby had gotten wind of the upset and attempted to induce him to drive one of the Fords. At that point, though, Surtees still hoped to work things out with Enzo Ferrari and declined. As a result of the dispute, Ferrari was weakened for the Le Mans race, and likely also lost the 1966 World Championship because of it.

Porsche had five Carrera 6s (Type 906) cars entered, and, by virtue of their reputation for reliability, were considered a potential overall winner. The truth in this was demonstrated by their eventual finish in fourth through seventh places and a clean sweep of the 2.0-liter category.

Although there was just one Chaparral up against all of these major players, their chances for a win were taken very seriously, thanks to the win at the Nürburgring 1000 Kilometers just two weeks previous. After the disappointing results at Daytona and Sebring earlier in the year, the team had gone back to Midland, Texas, where a comprehensive development program was undertaken that made the 2D a winner. Victory by Phil Hill and Jo Bonnier at the 'Ring was a classic moment in American racing history.

The race for Mark and Paul in the bronze Ford with the green nose—each Mk II was painted in a different stock Ford color—effectively was over on lap one. At the 4:00 p.m. start, Paul ran across the road with the 55 other starters, leapt into the car, and accelerated away smartly. Too smartly, as it developed, as his aggressive move off the line broke an axle shaft. He was the first car to pit and stayed there a long time while it was being fixed. He did a couple of laps and came in with more problems. Mark eventually got in the car and one problem after another culminated in a very big one: The entire rear body section came off at more than 200 mph, sending the big Ford airborne. Mark drove carefully to the pits and, after overcoming an attempt by the officials to disqualify the car, went back on the circuit armed with wire, pliers, and "racer's tape" to find the body in the woods. He secured it well enough to limp back to the pits, but it was all for nothing. The broken axle had put strain on the differential, which ultimately caused the car to be retired. Remarkably, the same thing had happened to Hawkins in practice when the body came off at 200 mph on the Mulsanne straight. Hawkeye had managed to keep the car from hitting anything solid, although it pirouetted down the straight in spectacular fashion. It was all captured on television, making Paul the celebrity of the moment and contributing to his growing legend. It was one of the shared adventures of the weekend that created a bond between the two men.

Eight of the Mk IIs failed to finish at Le Mans in 1966, but the three that did were first, second, and third. The Miles/Hulme car and Gurney/Grant had led much of the race with strong opposition from the Ginther/Rodríguez P3 Ferrari, until it failed in the middle of the night. As dawn broke, the Fords occupied the first six positions, with Gurney/Grant in the lead. At 9:00 a.m., with Jerry Grant at the wheel, the car that had been fastest in practice and had set the fastest race lap expired with a blown head gasket. With just two hours to go it was clear that Ford would win—but which car should it be? The light blue car of Miles/Hulme had led much of the race, but the black McLaren/Amon car was on the same lap. Miles had won at Daytona and Sebring and had been central to Shelby's test program, and many felt he deserved the win. Others were put out by Miles for defying team orders and dicing hard with Gurney at both Sebring and in this race.

With the apparent agreement of the race officials, Ford decided to stage a dead heat. This would be a historical first at the classic race and present a great photo opportunity—graphic proof of Ford dominance. At their last pit stop the drivers were told to form up on the last lap and finish side by side. It did not play out as planned. The organizers rescinded their agreement for a dead heat, decreeing that in such an event the car that had started further back on the grid would be declared the winner since it had traveled the greatest distance. That was the McLaren/Amon car, which had started fourth, some 20 feet behind Miles/Hulme. The canny Ken Miles anticipated this outcome, and as the cars approached the finish line side by side, Miles suddenly braked hard, allowing McLaren to cross the line first and claim the win without dispute. This was Miles's way of protesting what he believed to be an unfair and inappropriately contrived result.

Despite the internal squabbles, disappointment, and criticism over the finish, nothing could diminish this great victory. Ford had finally won Europe's greatest race. In his history of Ford racing, *The Dust and the Glory*, author Leo Levine called it "the greatest triumph in the 65-year history of the Ford Motor Company."

The 1-2-3 finish at Le Mans also clinched for Ford the FIA's International Challenge for Sports/Prototype cars. The final tally was 38 points to 33 for Ferrari. Additionally, the good work of the Mk I GT40s, run primarily by private teams, produced a win in the International Championship for Sports Cars. Victory at Le Mans was the big prize for Ford, however: Without it, the rest wouldn't have mattered.

CHAPTER 47:

A Particularly Hot Day at Watkins Glen

When Mark returned from Europe, he found substantial changes to the Lola. Karl had fitted a new Traco-built 333ci engine based on the small-block 283 Chevrolet. The first race with the new engine was at Watkins Glen for the SCCA's USRRC on June 26. This was the fifth round in the series, although only the first appearance for the Penske team. The early-season races had been won by: Canadian John Cannon in a Nickey Chevrolet–entered Genie-Olds (known as the Vinegaroon II) at the Stardust circuit in Las Vegas, Nevada; John "Buck" Fulp from South Carolina in his Lola T70-Olds at Riverside in California; Maryland's Charlie Hayes in a McLaren-Chevy at Laguna Seca; and Oregon's Jerry Grant in the Santa Ana, California–based AAR Lola T70-Ford at Bridgehampton, New York. The series was gaining strength from race to race, and at Watkins Glen featured its best entry of the season.

Jerry Grant had been the fastest man all season, despite winning only the most recent race at Bridgehampton. When he put the AAR Lola on the pole at Watkins Glen with a course-record 1:15.0 (110.4 mph), he was heavily favored to take his second consecutive win. The car was brand-new, as Jerry's accident at Mosport earlier in the month had destroyed the original AAR Lola. Jerry reported that the Gurney-Weslake heads on the 305ci Ford motor produced as much as 70 horsepower more than the predecessor Ford engine—perhaps as much as 550 horsepower. Sharing the front row of the starting grid with Grant was Buck Fulp at 1:16.2. Mark was third with a 1:16.4, alongside Mike Goth's McLaren-Chevy with the same time.

Grant's time was more than a second faster than the lap record for the sports-car version of the Watkins Glen circuit, set the previous year by Jim Hall in the Chaparral. The US-RRC race used a chicane at the end of the long straightaway, while the Formula One circuit ignored the chicane and went immediately into the high-speed loop that followed.

Ron Fournier was at Watkins Glen as a crewman on Canadian Ludwig Heimrath's 427ci Ford–powered McLaren and observed the small Penske race team. "It was the first time I had seen Mark, Roger, and Karl together," he says. "I knew Karl because we had worked together at Kar Kraft. I remember seeing that small group meeting at the end of the day—they were gathered around like Indians at a campfire, discussing what the car was doing and what they could do to improve it. I was really impressed with that, thinking, 'Wow, these guys are really serious.' While most other teams were off drinking beer they were going over every aspect of the car. It was amazing to see how completely professional they were in the presentation of the car and everything they did."

Working out of Glen Chevrolet—owner Nick Fraboni was on the Grand Prix Corporation's board of directors, and his dealership on Franklin Street was Penske team headquarters at Watkins Glen for many years—the decision was made the night before the race to make a major change to the Sunoco Lola brake system. The team had tried Airheart sprint car brakes unsuccessfully and had to switch back to the normal

Girlings. "We needed to test and bed the brakes but the Lola had no headlights," Bill Preston remembers. After a brief discussion about asking the local police for permission, we decided to use a Chevy sedan to run behind the Lola to provide illumination and we ran up and down a road near the shop."

Grant led at the start but Mark came by him on the second lap. Grant was troubled by a sticking throttle and pitted for adjustments on lap seven of the 87-lap, 200-mile race. Two laps later, Mark was lapping slower cars in the chicane when the left side of the Lola made contact with a Porsche and he spun to a stop. The incident was minor, but Mark noticed the left-side filler cap had popped open and that fuel was spilling into the cockpit. To secure the fuel cap he had to undo his harness in order to reach across from the right-side driver's seat. The stop was brief and he returned to the track, charging hard to regain lost position.

On the 19th lap, already back up to fourth, Mark was fully committed as he entered the blind left-hander at the top of the hill in the middle of the esses. Moments before, in the same high-speed left-hand bend, John Cannon—running third in the Nickey Chevrolet Vinegaroon—was trying to lap the leading under-2.0-liter Porsche 906 of Joe Buzzetta. Buzzetta, not expecting Cannon to attempt the pass in that spot, held the line through the turn. Cannon made his move from a length and a half behind, and as he tried to force his way through on the inside left, made heavy contact. Both cars were damaged, the Porsche coming to rest off the track on the right side. Cannon's Genie slid further through the esses and came to a stop broadside on the race track.

Mark arrived on the scene within a heartbeat and attempted to lessen the inevitable impact by braking and turning left. Although he hit Cannon's car very hard, his reaction had reduced the impact, and the contact made was side to side instead of straight in. Cannon told his wife Pat that Mark's instinctive move had saved his life. The crash ruptured the Sunoco Lola's fuel tank, and, already on fire, the car continued to slide, coming to a stop in the middle of the road at the point where the track begins to turn right.

Mark was barely clear of the Lola when it exploded. Fuel from the open cap had collected on the floor pan and ignited. Although he jumped out as quickly as he could, he suffered painful burns. The fire was so intense that the car virtually melted into the pavement. The race was stopped for more than an hour. Mark, protesting that he was fine, was taken by

ambulance to Schuyler Hospital in nearby Montour Falls. He wasn't there long. When Roger came by Mark said he wanted out. Roger had him on a private plane within the hour, and back on Long Island before dark. Sue met the plane at the local airport.

"My head was spinning and my stomach was jumping, but I kept control," Sue remembers. "Mark was all bandaged up and he was drugged, but he recognized me and was able to talk to me, and we took him home instead of to the hospital." Dr. Dan Damianos, Mark's personal physician, called at the Donohue home in Stony Brook, and after examining the patient had Mark admitted to St. Charles Hospital in nearby Port Jefferson. Despite second- and third-degree burns to his legs and one hand, and first-degree burns to his face, Mark never complained. "He just ignored personal pain and discomfort," Sue recalls. "It was always that way."

It had been that way since childhood. At age five Mark had explained to his sister Nancy, awestruck that Mark hadn't cried after a painful medical procedure, "You just say to yourself you won't, and you don't. You clamp your teeth." It had been a particularly hot day at Watkins Glen and Mark had elected to not wear a face mask, or gloves, or Nomex underwear under his Hinchman flameproof cotton one-piece suit. The experience made him a believer in wearing all available protective gear.

Back at the track, Karl and Al Holbert loaded the burnt-out Lola on the flatbed truck and arrived back in Newtown Square that evening. Behind closed doors they dismantled the remains of the car. According to Karl there wasn't much to salvage. "We may have saved the block—the rest of the engine was either gone or junk. I did unscrew the gearshift knob and still have it. It was burnt too." Everything else went to the dump at Sun Oil. The dismantling job was such filthy work that Karl and Al had to throw their work clothes away.

With the Lola destroyed, it was a time of crisis for the young Penske team. Without funds to replace the race car, Roger Penske was contemplating ending the season. He phoned his contacts at Sun Oil Company from Watkins Glen and reported what had happened. "After the accident at Watkins Glen and the fire and the car burned, I went back to Sun Oil and I said, 'Look, we've got a great driver here—give me enough money so I can get another car,'" remembers Roger. "It was a crisis—like just about anyone getting started with a racing team, I had borrowed just about everything I could to get that team going—you have it in your blood that you want to go racing. Donohue was driving for practically nothing—he certainly wasn't the cost. Without Sun Oil and their ability to say, 'We won't let you down when you're down, we want to build you up,' it just would not have been possible."

It didn't take Sun Oil long to decide they liked what they had seen so far and were committed to the program. They advanced sufficient money for Roger to purchase a new Lola.

A week later Mark was out of the hospital and insisting on racing at Lime Rock. Sue recalled the episode for Bill Levinson in the Newark *Sunday News*:

> This was one of the few times I interfered with Mark. Most of the time I take the attitude that I married a racing driver, and as long as he's happy in his career, it's up to me to be happy with it, too. But this time I told the pit crew to stop working on the car. Then I reminded the race doctor that Mark had been under drugs for close to a week, so the doctor gave Mark a hard time, too. But I don't think either one of us could have stopped him. Mark finally stopped himself when he realized that his hands were so burned he couldn't hold the wheel. But, to show the accident hadn't cost him his nerve, he started planning that "Crash and Burn" party.

When a film of the crash became available, it was the centerpiece for the well-remembered "Crash and Burn Party" that Mark and Sue threw for friends and family at the house in Stony Brook.

CHAPTER 48:
Growth for Penske Racing

During the summer of 1966, Roger Penske was becoming increasingly involved in racing. On July 18 he was appointed Firestone racing tire distributor for the northeastern United States. After Walt Hansgen's death in April, his wife Bea had decided to liquidate his businesses, including the Jaguar dealership in Bedminster, New Jersey, and the Firestone racing tire distributorship. When Firestone appointed Penske Enterprises as their new distributor, Roger asked Norman Ahn to head up the operation. When Ahn, a friend of Bill Mayberry's, had helped out on a volunteer basis with the Penske Corvette at Sebring earlier in the year,

he told Roger that if a professional position ever became available, he would be interested. They now agreed that he would come to work on September 1, but Roger also asked Norman to help Karl with the Can-Am program until the end of the year, and to take over the Firestone business out of the Chevrolet dealership on Walnut Street in Philadelphia on January 1.

In the interim, Roger's brother David managed the tire business. Ahn became a central figure in Penske Enterprises and eventually owned the tire dealership. Penske Corporation executive vice president Walt Czarnecki later described him as "the most detail oriented person I have ever known." According to Mark, "Norman was just a very talented guy and Roger was able to see this immediately. Roger's talent was that he was able to spot talent. Norman had a similar aesthetic to Roger and could not only get things done but accomplish them in the same vision Roger had."

Penske was also observing the SCCA's Trans-Am. In its first year, the series had already captured the imagination of the media and quickly became a great fan favorite. Race circuits were lining up for a date in the series. As a result, Ford's Mustang and Chrysler's Barracuda were already gaining valuable exposure among performance-oriented buyers. As a Chevrolet dealer and as a racer, Roger was intrigued by the potential for the Camaro, Chevrolet's recently introduced answer to the Mustang. Mark, immersed in his own Mustang program, likely knew as much as any private entrant about how to develop this type of car into a competitive race car.

Meanwhile, news out of London during the summer of 1966 would have a profound impact on American racing in the coming years. The Royal Automobile Club (RAC) announced that henceforth they would no longer organize or sanction races for Group 7 cars, even as that category was enjoying its greatest popularity. The announcement came as a shock, since Group 7 was just as enthusiastically followed by British motorsports fans as by their American counterparts. The RAC cited the oil companies' unwillingness to support the plethora of top-level racing formats in the United Kingdom. With Formulas One, Two, and Three all demanding budgetary support, the influential industry sponsors felt something had to give. While the effect on Group 7 racing generally, and the soon-to-launch Can-Am in particular, was largely missed at the time, the long-range impact was profound. With a market now limited to North America, the incentive for most British race-car constructors to develop the big sports-racing cars was largely gone. It also meant that private British teams were not fielding Group 7 cars for domestic racing. Within just a few years the impact could be seen in a declining Can-Am series.

CHAPTER 49:
Dockery Ford

Despite his increasing involvement in professional racing, Mark was keeping one foot in the amateur ranks. The near miss for an SCCA National Championship at the 1965 Daytona Runoffs the previous December still rankled. He planned to keep racing the Shelby Mustang, though he'd have to do it with a different support team. When Malcolm Starr prepared to report to the Marine Corps the previous December he came to terms with his finances. Although Malcolm, as the outright owner of both the Lotus 20 and the Mustang, had been the major support to "Mark's Team," he had in fact borrowed from his friend Yale Kneeland and girlfriend Virginia Morley in order to purchase the GT350R. He had the cash to return the $1,000 he owed Virginia, and resolved the debt to Yale by signing the car over to him. Yale followed Malcolm's path of racing in drivers' schools and Regionals while making the Mustang available for Mark to race in Nationals. Although sponsorship from Baltimore's Archway Ford was gone, Mark had attracted a more-desirable arrangement with Dockery Ford of Morristown, New Jersey.

Bob Dockery had grown up in the dealership world and was a tremendous racing enthusiast. He had a Shelby franchise as part of his Ford dealership. Having sponsored Marty Krinner in his GT350R throughout 1965, it appealed to him to have a two-car team in 1966. The Dockery facility provided a place for the Mustang to be worked on, and Bob brought George Clark on the payroll to help stabilize the relationship. Dockery also provided a handsome new Ford F-250 truck and a trailer, painted in a matching dark blue, to support the team. The truck was fitted with a "plumber's body" (or utility body) that provided space to fit a spare engine and transmission, along with other parts.

Bob and Mark were very close in age, and the two found an immediate rapport. "I soon discovered how very smart he was," Bob says. "Mark really understood race engineering and was way ahead of everyone at the time. He could sort

out a car very quickly and would set his car and Marty's up at every race." While Mark was the setup expert, Marty Krinner, a brilliant engineer, built his own engines as well as Mark's, according to Dick DiBiasse, a legendary engine man who was associated with Mark in a number of racing projects. "Marty Krinner was one of the nicest guys in the world and a great engine builder," says DiBiasse. "Mark learned a lot from him."

Once again, Mark set the tone for the team. When the cars would come off the trailer on Saturday morning at the track, it was all business. There was a specific warm-up schedule, and after practice and qualifying the team never stayed in the paddock. "Mark had made an arrangement with a local garage at every track—often a Ford dealership. We would load up after the last track session and head to the garage where the cars were worked on. We never did our business at the track," recalls Dockery.

The team went out of division for the Central Division National at Mid-Ohio on July 17. Mark couldn't match Don Yenko's very fast Corvette and brought the Mustang home a secure second. Mark needed points to qualify for the Runoffs, and so with George Clark, he towed the Mustang to Connellsville, Pennsylvania, for the Northeast Division National on Connellsville's airport circuit on July 24. It was a wet weekend and rained particularly hard on race day. In the combined A and B Production race Mark finished behind three AP Cobras (Ed Lowther, Hal Keck, and Bob Grossman), but won B Production decisively to gain maximum points.

After the race Mark approached Walt Hane, who he had raced against but never met. Hane, with his 14-year-old son Chip as his only pit crew, had made the long tow north from his home in Maitland, Florida, to race his GT350R at Mid-Ohio and Connellsville. Although Hane's results had been discouraging, Mark managed to lift his spirits. "He told me not to worry," Hane remembers. "He had seen me drive. He said we would get it together and be very competitive. That remark greatly offset my depression from the trip. We went back to Florida determined to get the car and driver working much better."

CHAPTER 50:

First Win for Mark and Roger

T owing a race car from Philadelphia to Pacific Raceways in Kent, Washington, is a significant task today. But in 1966 it was a formidable undertaking because there were many long stretches where the interstate remained to be built. Karl Kainhofer and 19-year-old Al Holbert made the 2,854-mile drive to the sixth round in the USRRC series on July 31, 1966. In the 1980s Alvah Robert Holbert would become one of America's great race drivers. His father, Bob, had been a dominant Porsche racer in the 1950s and '60s and won the 1963 USRRC. Bob Holbert was one of the first authorized Porsche dealers in America, and the dealership he operated in Warrington, Pennsylvania, exists today under the guidance of his son Larry. In 1959, Holbert had sold Roger Penske the Porsche RS he had successfully campaigned in 1958. It was Penske's first serious race car. The men remained close, and Al's summer job with Roger's racing team was a natural. Al was attending Roger's alma mater, Lehigh University. En route to Kent, Karl did all the driving but reported that Al was good company.

Pacific Raceways, just 20 miles from Seattle in the foothills of the Cascade Mountains, was opened in 1960 by the Fiorito family. Dan Fiorito Sr. owned a road construction company and was inspired to build the circuit by his desire to give teenagers an alternative to high-speed driving on public roads. His sons, Dan Jr. and Joe, worked alongside the construction crew to build the track during their 1959 summer break. They created a 2.25-mile, nine-turn circuit, with an elevation change of more than 125 feet in the midst of the beautiful Pacific Northwest forests. Just before the 1966 USRRC, the track's infrastructure was significantly upgraded thanks to fresh financial resources from the Seattle-based Bardahl Oil Company.

This was Mark's first visit to the track and the first run for the new Lola T70 (chassis No. SL71/32) that replaced the car ruined at Watkins Glen. Seattle's own Jerry Grant was heavily favored and qualified fastest—as he had in four of the previous USRRC rounds—setting a new lap record at 1:19.5 (101.9 mph). Mark qualified fifth at 1:21.4 and was on the second row of the 3-2-3 grid with Mike Goth's McLaren. Grant in the AAR Lola shared the front row with the McLarens of

Charlie Hayes and Lothar Motschenbacher.

Gerald Wayne Grant, from Seattle, Washington, was pure talent and naturally fast. He first raced in the mid-1950s and made a major impression in SCCA racing in the Northwest and in Canada in the early '60s, putting together an impressive record of wins in just about any car he ever sat in. By this period in Jerry's life he was fully committed to racing as a profession and employed by Dan Gurney at All American Racers in Santa Ana, California. While Gurney was his biggest booster, Jerry's talent was apparent to all. Ken Miles, a savvy and often-blunt observer, considered Jerry one of the three best drivers in America.

Hayes, Motschenbacher, and Goth each experienced early delays, bringing Mark up to second place by a third of the way through the 68-lap race. Grant was dominating with a comfortable 11-second lead on Mark, when on the 42nd lap, a brake pad disintegrated on the entrance to a 170-mph left-hand bend. Though Grant managed to save the car after an alarming slide, Mark was now only four seconds behind. Two laps later Mark took the lead and Grant fell back as the car deteriorated. He was soon out with a broken ring and pinion. Mark won the race with a lead of more than a minute from John Cannon in the Nickey Chevrolet-McLaren.

This historic first-time win for the Penske-Donohue-Kainhofer combination was well worth celebrating, particularly on the heels of the near disaster at Watkins Glen. It was a brand-new car and Mark's first victory at this level. "That was really the start," says Roger Penske. "And I think Mark was really surprised himself at how good he was at that point."

In typical fashion, Mark downplayed the win, feeling he owed it to Grant's bad luck. The truth was that he had driven a well-judged race, and his pace had been just right—as quick, or quicker, than anyone but Grant.

After Kent, Mark took an indirect route home. He accompanied Karl and Al in the flatbed truck as they plotted a southeastern route to Midland, Texas. It's a long drive south from the state of Washington to west Texas, and the bench seat in the truck just barely accommodated the three men. Karl remembers that for long stretches Mark would sit in the open cockpit of the race car and doze or read his magazines. Mark later told Dave Lawton, "I just lay back in the seat of the Lola and watched those beautiful Rocky Mountains roll by. The air was great and it was the first relaxation I had had all year."

Roger Penske and Chaparral Cars' Jim Hall had a long and close relationship. Roger had driven with great success for Jim in the Chaparral, ending his career by sweeping the 1964 Nassau races for the Texas team. After his retirement as a driver, Roger cut his teeth as a team manager with the Midland team. The two men were among a select group of people with access to General Motors factory race engineering and equipment. It was a natural for them to agree that Mark should bring the Lola to Chaparral's private Rattlesnake Raceway test track for evaluation. For Chaparral—who had given the USRRC a miss in 1966 in favor of campaigning the Sports Prototype coupe in the World Championship rounds—it was an opportunity to take a close-up look at what they were up against in the upcoming Can-Am. Most of the top teams would be running the same model T70 Lola that Mark and his small team brought to the Chaparral facility. For Roger it was a chance to expose Mark to the professional setup and engineering skills of the well-established and experienced Texas team.

Although Mark had just won a round in the USRRC, he still wasn't a well-known driver and had never met Jim Hall. His experience with the Ford program and the small number of Group 7 races had barely established him as a professional. While Hall and others at Midland treated him well, he was never shown the new Chaparral race car. Both Mark and Jim drove the Lola at Rattlesnake and Mark was able to observe how a major team went about engineering a car. Karl was impressed by the professional approach at Chaparral and their ability to rapidly adapt what they learned in testing through their extensive fabricating and engineering facilities. At the time, the Penske shop in Pennsylvania was little more than a two-car garage.

Mark saw a skid pad used for the first time. It made a big impression on him as a practical way to set up a car. "Skid pads were commonplace to GM and Chaparral at the time, but this was the first time I had ever seen one," Mark later said. Mark would become a major advocate of skid-pad testing as he learned to utilize them in developing a race car. Mark used his time in Midland to observe and learn. He wisely kept his counsel and appreciated the opportunity for what it was. In addition to Mark's fast "leg-up" on the learning curve of race engineering, the Lola benefited directly from additional development at Midland. Chaparral was on the cutting edge of race-car aerodynamics, and when the Lola returned to the shop in Newtown Square, it sported a tail spoiler and a nose dam.

From Texas Mark flew directly to New Hampshire where he was racing the Mustang that weekend at Bryar Motor-

sports Park, leaving Karl and Al to complete the haul back to Pennsylvania. Once there, the engine was shipped to Detroit where Roger had arranged for Chevrolet engineers to examine it carefully. They were impressed with the power that the little Traco shop had developed from the small-block Chevy. The travel schedule was tight, but Mark was back in time for the event on August 7. The 50-lap race for the big Production cars on the 1.6-mile course was being run as a benefit for the cancer ward of Children's Hospital in Boston. Don Yenko again won BP in his Corvette, but in the early laps was pursued closely by Mark and Bob Colombosian in a Lotus Elan. Mark and Colombosian tangled in the Clubhouse turn and Mark was off the road. By the time he brought the car back on the track he was never a threat, and was fortunate to finish fifth.

Bob Dockery recalls Mark's droll sense of humor and distinctive approach. "Mark was very serious about his racing but he was a great deal of fun. He had a type of humor that kept you guessing as to when he was kidding or not. He would show up with a black shoe and a blue shoe and never give it notice. You never really knew if it was a gag or not. He could also take a good kidding. He was notoriously tight with his nickels and dimes and somehow never managed to fit into the rotation we had of picking up the dinner bills for the eight or ten people we always had with us. One evening in Loudon, New Hampshire, Mark went to the men's room after dinner and we all jumped up and got outside and in the cars. When Mark came out of the men's, he was the only one left and was presented the bill. He took it all in good spirit."

A little more than a week later, on Wednesday, August 17, Mark's Ford teammate Ken Miles was concluding a long day of testing at Riverside with the prototype J-car. The J-car was designed, built, and developed entirely in America by Carroll Shelby's team to comply with Appendix J of the FIA's new regulations, and was seen as the replacement for the Mk II Ford GT. At the end of the mile-long straight, Miles braked from 180 to approximately 100 mph on his normal line when, inexplicably, the Ford began flipping violently. Miles was thrown clear of the wreckage but was dead before anyone could reach him. His death was heartbreaking to the entire American racing community, and the loss was perhaps most poignantly felt on the West Coast, where the English-born driver had lived and created his legend. With Walt Hansgen's death at the Le Mans test days in April, testing accidents for the Ford Le Mans program had taken the lives of two of America's most senior and respected drivers. Hansgen was 46 and Miles was 47. Both Hansgen on the East Coast and Miles on the West had been intimately involved in the growth of road racing in America. Each had been influential both on and off the race track.

That weekend Mark had Ken Miles and Walt Hansgen very much on his mind as he headed off to Watkins Glen for the Glen 500 National on August 21. The previous year he and Walt had teamed to win their class in the Mustang in this same race. So much had changed in Mark's life and racing career in that brief year. He had been the slightly awed amateur, thrilled to have the consummate professional sharing the wheel with him. Now he was the pro, the driver in the race with the reputation as the "up and coming man," and likely aware that his days on the National circuit were nearing an end. This year Martin Krinner joined him in the car. The Dockery Ford–backed teammates were both chasing points to make it to the Runoffs.

For 1966 the race had been shortened by adjusting its length to 500 kilometers instead of miles. This was still a challenging distance, as most Nationals were roughly half an hour in duration. The SCCA had not yet mandated maximum lengths for National races, and distances were at the discretion of the promoter. The long races, while attractive for the promoter, had become unpopular with the competitors waging a season-long campaign. An endurance race demanded a different approach and different equipment than were called for in the typical sprint-race format of most SCCA Nationals. It was not a good day for the Dockery Mustang, and Mark and Marty were out after just 31 of the 135 laps. Sam Posey and Ray Caldwell won the 500 in a Porsche Carrera GTS (Type 904).

CHAPTER 51:

Prelude to the Can-Am

Despite Mark's win at Kent, he had entered the USRRC season too late to have any hope for a meaningful placing in the point standings. Instead, the Penske team's focus was very much on the Can-Am, with the two remaining USRRC races regarded mainly as a tune-up for the big series. The final USRRC round was the grueling 500-miler at Road America just a week before the Can-Am opener at St. Jovite on September 11. The only top teams going to Wisconsin were those in contention for the series championship. The Penske team chose instead the race at Mid-Ohio on August 28.

The USRRC was never more closely contested than in 1966, and the entry for Mid-Ohio, the penultimate round, was the strongest of the year. As a late arrival to the series, Mark was the potential spoiler in the final point battle. That certainly seemed the case in qualifying when Mark won pole position with a lap at 1:37.8 (88.34 mph), while recording 161.1 mph through the speed trap. John Cannon equaled Mark's time in his McLaren, but the honor of pole position went to Mark because he had set the time first. Fast man Jerry Grant arrived late after transport trouble on the way from California, and in an abbreviated session with a smoking engine ran only a 1:43.2 for a spot on the sixth row of the grid. Unable to sort out the engine, Grant withdrew before the race.

The soon-to-be-famous Penske/Donohue partnership was still finding its way as the two men came to know each other as race partners. As a recent driver of championship caliber, Roger could identify with Mark's perspective on problems faced in the cockpit. "One day Roger criticized Mark for missing a shift and 'zinging' the engine," recalls Bill Preston. "They hammered out an agreement that Mark could miss one shift a weekend without Roger saying anything." Another Preston anecdote reveals the easy informality and rapport that was growing between the pair. "One day, after qualifying, Mark complained to Roger that the Lola wasn't fast enough. Roger told him, 'Go back to the motel, fill the tub with hot water and soak your right foot in it to get it good and heavy.'"

The McLarens of Cannon, Lothar Motschenbacher, and Ludwig Heimrath all outdragged Mark's Lola off the line, but Mark was a close second to Cannon by the end of the first lap. Mark took the lead on the fifth lap and set a fast pace, although Cannon and Motschenbacher maintained close contact. The Sunoco Lola was emitting strong fumes and the closely pursuing drivers began to suffer. When Cannon stopped at mid-race with terminal engine trouble he reported that he could not have held out long from the fumes. And on the 60th of the 85 laps, Motschenbacher, too, was exhausted and suddenly fell half a minute off Mark's pace. From there Mark seemed destined for a smooth run home for a second consecutive win. It was not to be. On the 77th lap he pitted with a near-flat left rear tire, and two laps later was out of the race with engine trouble. Motschenbacher's perseverance was rewarded with the win, followed by steady Chuck Parsons in second and Buck Fulp third. Motschenbacher's Oldsmobile-powered McLaren was sponsored by Nickey Chevrolet and owned by Dan Blocker, the popular actor who played the character "Hoss" on the hit television show, *Bonanza*.

Parsons went on to win the Road America 500—the USRRC season finale—with a great solo drive, and with it captured the 1966 United States Road Racing Championship. Mark's only points in the eight-race series came from his win at Kent. Those nine points placed him in a tie for seventh place in the final series standings. Parsons was a more than worthy champion. He was one of the great American road-racing drivers of the 1960s, and, in the memory of many, the most popular among his fellow competitors. Parsons was naturally talented and fast in anything he drove. He was also a smart driver, and his USRRC crown came through perseverance against teams with substantially more resources. Randy Hilton from Carmel, California, was the car owner and Bob Smith the chief mechanic, supported by Gil Munz. Hilton's son John was team manager. While the team was anything but ostentatious, it was effective. They had started the season with a Genie Mk 10, and after Watkins Glen had switched to a new McLaren Mk 1B. Chuck and his wife Sherry towed the race car around the country behind their Ford station wagon.

It had been the best year yet in the American professional sports-car series. With the European teams—and Chaparral—set to make their appearance, the inaugural Can-Am was shaping up to be something very special indeed.

CHAPTER 52:
The Way They Got Paid

The Canadian-American Challenge Cup (Can-Am) was sponsored by the Johnson Wax Company, and their energetic promotion of the series was a key part of the success story. They hired Stirling Moss to serve as commissioner of the series, and his visibility and ability to generate publicity made him a great choice. Earlier in the year Al Bochroch had left Gray & Rogers, a Philadelphia advertising agency, after 14 years as a senior vice president. He now joined the Can-Am as communications director. Johnson Wax also provided $25,000 to the season-end point fund. Along with the $5,000 committed to the fund by each race organizer, this created a season-end "pot" of $55,000

designed to maintain the participation of entrants throughout the entire series.

Starting money, however, was a hotly debated issue. The SCCA and the CASC—sanctioning bodies for the Can-Am—were embroiled all summer in discussions with Teddy Mayer and Bruce McLaren on the issue. The Can-Am's position was that the prize money at individual races, along with the end-of-season financial rewards, should be incentive enough for the teams to participate. Mayer, negotiating for his own McLaren team, as well as John Surtees and Eric Broadley's Lola operation, argued for the European tradition of "starting money." The dispute carried on through most of the spring and summer, much of it fought out in the media.

Starting money—called "appearance money" in America—was deeply ingrained in the European racing system where race purses were modest. Starting money represented the principal financial outlay for race organizers. The system ensured them a full field of cars—and the star drivers. The teams and drivers benefited from the assurance that whatever bad fortune might befall them in the race, they were guaranteed sufficient money to cover their costs and perhaps turn a small profit on the race. This approach worked in Europe, where motor racing was established as a major sport with a loyal following of fans who could be counted on to turn up at the traditional events.

Can-Am race purses ranged from a minimum of $20,000 to a maximum of $40,000, and, in principle, neither transportation nor starting money was paid. While this was the ideal, individual Can-Am promoters would often find sufficient funds in the form of appearance or expense money to quietly induce particular drivers or teams to participate in their race. Drivers were paid in a variety of ways according to their deal with the owner or entrant of the car. Penske's arrangement in 1966 for distribution of prize money is said to have been 50 percent to Roger, 40 percent to Mark, and 10 percent to Karl.

What helped make the Can-Am work financially, particularly for European teams, was the tight schedule that squeezed the six races into a nine-week period. The season-end point fund of $55,000 was an added incentive. The Johnson Wax Can-Am trophy went to the driver who scored the most points in the series. Points in each race were earned by the first six finishers, using the same points system that Formula One did at the time—9-6-4-3-2-1. Only the top 10 point scorers shared in the season-end point fund. The total potential winnings made it a losing proposition for all but the elite and dominant teams. In 1966 it didn't matter. The enormous enthusiasm and momentum for the series brought the teams out in greater variety and depth than anything previously seen or would ever be repeated in Can-Am history.

CHAPTER 53:
Wake-Up Call in Pawtucket

Before tackling the Can-Am, Mark still needed points in the Mustang to assure an invitation to the November Runoffs in the B Production class. Mark wanted an SCCA National Championship to climax his amateur career. The traditional Labor Day National at Thompson was his last appearance in an amateur event except for the season-ending Runoffs. Saturday was hot and beautiful with Mark in top form during practice at this familiar venue.

It was little more than 30 miles from Thompson, in the northeast corner of Connecticut, to the Lawton home in Pawtucket, Rhode Island. Mark, as usual, was staying the weekend at the Lawton home, and this time he brought along most of the Dockery Ford team. As always there was work to be finished on the race car, and George was up until 3:00 a.m. in the family garage, putting new head gaskets on the GT350R. George, exhausted from working all day in the hot sun, was concerned that if he waited until morning to finish the job, he wouldn't wake up in time to complete it before leaving for the track. When the work was done he warmed the Mustang up before re-torquing the heads. The upscale residential neighborhood went from pin-drop quiet to ear-shattering, straight-pipe-staccato loud as the noise reverberated between the two adjoining houses. The police arrived in short order, just as the engine reached operating temperature. After receiving firm promises that the motor would not be run again that night, the police left, and George finished re-torquing the heads.

On Sunday Mark got the win he wanted in his final SCCA National. And he needed the points. His limited National schedule had only yielded 29 points—just enough to qualify him for the Runoffs at Riverside, California, in November.

Getting to the track was always an adventure, as Mark believed in flat-out motoring. You could not race in SCCA without a valid state driver's license, and Mark was always in

jeopardy of losing his. Sue and Karen Bocsusis both remember the day the Donohues pulled off a seemingly practiced acrobatic feat. Karen tells the story: "We were towing the race car with the station wagon and Mark, as always, was driving way over the speed limit. Sue was in the front seat beside Mark with George and me in the back. Suddenly the sirens and red lights came on behind us and as Mark slowed down he and Sue—who was very pregnant—performed a pirouette in the front seat that had Sue behind the wheel by the time the car came to a stop. Sue got the ticket, as Mark was at a point where he would have lost his license with one more conviction."

CHAPTER 54:
Advancing the Science

The Can-Am was launched at St. Jovite on September 11 at the very peak of Group 7 racing. The fields were large at every race venue. Enthusiasm among entrants, race organizers, the media, and the paying public converged to make the inaugural 1966 season a success.

The Circuit Mont Tremblant at St. Jovite, Quebec, just 90 miles northwest of Montreal, was opened in 1964 in a 1.5-mile format, and the following year was expanded to its fully envisioned 2.65 miles. Group 7 racing was the feature attraction from the outset, and the 1965 race was won by John Surtees in the factory Lola T70. The track captured the imagination of drivers and was a favorite for spectators because of its excellent viewing areas and its location in the breathtakingly beautiful Laurentian mountain range, bordered by Lake Moore and Devil River (La Diable).

Mark's debut race for Roger Penske at the circuit in May had been fraught. The team that returned just three months later for the first Can-Am series race had matured almost beyond recognition. The Traco 333ci Chevy was a proven performer, and Mark and the Lola had displayed their worth in the few USRRC races they contested. The Can-Am would be a big step up in competitiveness, and the small Penske team promised to be a major factor.

Mark was one of eight drivers to break the lap record in qualifying, and he lined up the Lola in the middle of the third row between the McLarens of John Cannon and Bud Morley. John Surtees captured pole position in the factory-team Lola, just a tenth of a second ahead of Bruce McLaren in his

McLaren Mk 1B. McLaren's teammate Chris Amon, in an identical bright red car, filled out the extremely competitive front row. On the inside of the second row, and fastest qualifier of the USRRC regulars, was Lothar Motschenbacher in the Nickey Chevrolet McLaren Mk 1B. Alongside him as fifth fastest was Parnelli Jones driving a Paxton supercharged 289ci Ford-powered Lola T70 for U.S. Lola importer John Mecom. Jones's teammate George Follmer was 10th on the grid with a normally aspirated 332ci Ford in his Lola. He sat next to another Ford runner, Dan Gurney, in the All American Racers (AAR) Lola with a 305ci version fitted with the special Gurney-Weslake heads. Gurney did not make the start as his engine spun a bearing in the warm-up session. AAR teammate Jerry Grant, who qualified 13th, had made a remarkable engine change in his Bardahl Lola during practice. Frustrated by the lack of power in his near-stock 289ci Ford, he borrowed a 364ci Traco Chevy from Chuck Parsons, who was 11th on the grid. It was not an ideal setup for Grant's Lola, as the extra weight of the engine disrupted the suspension settings. Sixteen McLarens and 11 Lolas dominated the 34-car starting grid. Ford and Chevrolet each had engines in 15 of the cars.

The sensation of practice was a spectacular accident by Paul Hawkins. The colorful Australian and his car's owner, Jackie Epstein, had become great friends of Mark and Sue's, and were frequent houseguests whenever they were on the East Coast. On the second day of practice, with a fierce wind blowing, Hawkins crested a hill at some 170 mph. The combination of speed and lightened balance caused the undertray of the Lola to behave like a sail. The car flipped into the air, reaching an impressive height, and flew 150 yards before landing upside down. The rollbar was torn off, and Hawkeye later recalled the sensation of his helmet grinding away as the car slid a considerable distance. Sam Posey, making his Group 7 race debut in a recently purchased McLaren Mk 1B, witnessed the flip and stopped to render assistance. Posey helped the workers carefully extricate Hawkeye from the upside-down Lola. In his book, *The Mudge Pond Express*, Posey recalled the silence as Hawkins examined his bloody scalp. Finally the normally loquacious Hawkeye was heard to whisper, "Bloody 'ell. Never thought I'd see the day when a bloke could get upside down on the bloody straightaway."

On the last day of practice another Lola took flight. Coming over the same rise, British Overseas Airways Corporation (BOAC) pilot Hugh P. K. Dibley left the ground and flew at

least as far as had Hawkins. The difference was that Dibley's Lola never flipped over but landed and bounced again through the air, landing on top of a tree stump in a spectator area. No one was hurt, although the chassis was torn in half.

The accidents caught everyone's attention. Aerodynamics were just coming into vogue in racing and were clearly still a black art with unpredictable side effects, although the science would advance rapidly. Despite being such a close observer to the Hawkins incident, Posey was apparently undeterred. In his maiden race in this very demanding type of car, he impressively qualified in the top half of the field.

The pivotal race moment came with an upset at the start, with Mark one of the drivers victimized. Parnelli Jones couldn't find the right gear, and his slow start off the second row created major havoc behind him. Masten Gregory, Ronnie Bucknum, and Skip Scott were all eliminated immediately by crash damage that included wrecked radiators and broken gearboxes, and Mark's Penske Lola was knocked out with a broken steering arm.

It was a good race for the series opener, although John Surtees controlled the pace from the lead almost the entire way. Bruce McLaren kept it close in second while the greatest excitement came from Chris Amon, who, after a pit stop, roared back to run with the leaders. Amon was impressive—setting a new lap record, a full second quicker than Surtees' qualifying time—but Surtees always seemed to have it in hand. The remaining points-earning places, fourth through sixth, were taken by USRRC regulars John Cannon, George Follmer, and Chuck Parsons.

Norman Ahn, hired to head the new Penske Firestone race tire business in 1967, was Karl Kainhofer's primary—and usually sole—helper on the Sunoco Lola during the Can-Am season. Al Holbert was back at Lehigh University for the fall semester. Back at the shop, master fabricator Bill Scott was on loan from the Sun Oil Company and occasionally appeared at the races. Ahn fit easily into the Penske team aesthetic, projecting a neat and well-put-together persona, just as Roger, Mark, and Karl did. Karl credits Norman for keeping the car in spotless cosmetic condition and for helping to create the Penske team image for beautifully turned-out cars. Karl, Mark, and Roger shared a predisposition toward immaculate presentation. Among race mechanics Karl was often affectionately addressed as "Slick and Smooth," in reference to his oft-repeated refrain that a car must be "slick and smooth and square with the bottom."

After St. Jovite, Karl and Norman headed directly to the next race, tracing a route through New England and catching a ferry to Long Island. Mark had suggested to Roger that rather than going back to Newtown Square, they should bring the car to Jack Griffith's Hicksville, New York, Ford dealership. It was there that the car was repaired and made ready for round two at Bridgehampton, just a week after St. Jovite.

At Bridgehampton the race entry was bigger still—and the most exciting additions to the field were two Chaparrals. It was rumored that the non-appearance of the Midland team at St. Jovite was related to the testing done on the Penske Lola the previous month. The performance of the Penske Lola in their testing at Rattlesnake Raceway had convinced Jim Hall and Chevrolet that the new Lola would be so formidable in the hands of John Surtees that they needed extra time to develop an answer. The "something extra" was immediately apparent at Bridgehampton.

The Chaparral 2E that appeared at Bridgehampton—the car that had been kept out of Mark's sight in Midland—was a sensation. Hall's new cars featured a tall, suspension-mounted, hydraulically actuated wing that immediately advanced the science of aerodynamics in race-car application to a new level. The 2Es, continuing their development of automatic transmissions, were fitted with 427ci aluminum-block engines of advanced design. It was clear that the entire game would now be played at a higher level. The cars did not disappoint in qualifying, and Jim Hall broke the lap record to gain pole position.

The Firestone and Goodyear battle was being fought as hard in the Can-Am as anywhere in racing. As a distributor, Roger Penske was obviously on Firestones, as were Chaparral, McLaren, Surtees, and Mecom. Dan Gurney's AAR team was the top runner on Goodyears. Most Goodyear- and Firestone-fitted cars were running 15-inch rims. A combination of 9:50x15 fronts and 11:90x15 rears was typical on Goodyear-shod cars, while those running Firestones used 9:20x15 fronts and 12:00x15 rears. The Penske Sunoco Lola, along with Chaparrals, were exceptions. They were running 16-inch rims with 10:10x16 fronts and 12:10x16 rears. These special tires had a very low profile, making them no taller than the standard 15 inches, and were first fitted to the Sunoco Lola at Bridgehampton.

The Penske crew was faced with an immediate challenge: The center holes in the new wheels were too small to fit the Lola hubs. They needed a precision metal lathe, so the crew asked a local Bridgehampton police officer where they might find one on eastern Long Island. They were directed to the home and workshop of Norman C. Pickering in Southampton. Bill Preston, Bill Scott, and helpers headed there with the eight wheels.

It was a remarkable encounter. Pickering is a legend in the music business as an inventor and acoustical engineer, having helped give birth to the high-fidelity sound industry through his inventions and designs. Pickering had a handsome workshop that included an Austrian lathe of very high quality. "Scotty was delighted with it and went right to work on the wheels," remembers Bill Preston. "The rest of us were just standing around and enjoying the gracious hospitality of the Pickerings when we noticed that Mr. Pickering had just received delivery of a crate containing an elaborate garden shed in kit form. A concrete slab had been poured, and with nothing else to do, we offered to assemble it on the slab. Mr. Pickering promptly sent Mrs. Pickering for a cold case of beer, provided hammers and nails, and we did the job."

The first indication that the debut of the Chaparral 2E would not go smoothly came in practice when a wing bracing strut failed and Phil Hill's car crashed. Hill went out in Hall's car and the same thing happened, this time with minimal damage. Hall surrendered his seat, and the pole position he had earned, to Hill, who lined up fifth in the second row with an identical time to Chris Amon's. The front row featured Dan Gurney, now on pole, with Surtees in the middle and McLaren on the outside. Mark was sixth fastest and occupied the inside of the third row. Most of the field was the same as at St. Jovite, although Al Unser had moved into the Mecom Lola previously driven by Parnelli Jones. The first 20 spots on the grid were established by time. The remainder of the 30-car field had to run in a 15-lap qualifying race—won by Bud Morley—to get into the race. By filling the last spots in this manner the organizers were able to offer what was essentially a consolation race for those who would be excluded from the main event. It also provided added entertainment for the spectators. The need for a consolation race was a testament to the depth of the field at this early date in Can-Am history.

Sunday was Dan Gurney's day. Along with his mechanics, Larry Stellings and Wayne Leary, Dan had the car ideally geared and set up for the difficult and very fast circuit. Gurney was a prodigious talent at the peak of his career, and Bridgehampton was a perfect stage to display his craft.

John Bishop recalled that "only Dan Gurney was ever as impressive at Bridgehampton as Walt Hansgen." It was high praise indeed.

But it wasn't easy for Dan. At the drop of the flag on the rolling start, Phil Hill charged from the second row to battle aggressively with Dan's Lola. After 150 miles, another wing failure forced the Chaparral driver to ease the pace and drop to an eventual fourth-place finish. Chris Amon now applied the pressure, but the determined Gurney held him off to win by two-tenths of a second. McLaren was third.

A lap down, Mark was the best of the rest. A solid if un-spectacular drive had netted fifth place and his first two series points. Before the race Mark had told Al Holbert, "We feel our car is about the best prepared, and we're going to run to finish and hope we're right up there at the end." Still another lap down was the steady Chuck Parsons in sixth. Dan's AAR teammate Jerry Grant just missed the points in seventh, while Sam Posey was an impressive eighth in only his second race in the big cars. John Surtees had only been a factor briefly, retiring with an oil line failure inside of 10 laps.

For the Bridgehampton organizers the race was an enor-mous success, with a gate more than double anything the circuit had seen in its 10-year history.

Up to now Mark had only succeeded in identifying himself and the team as among the best of the second tier. His status was about to be elevated.

CHAPTER 55:
"To finish first, you must first finish"

To finish first, you must first finish," was an old racing maxim that came to be identified with Mark Donohue and Roger Penske. It may well have first applied at the 1966 Canadian Grand Prix on September 24, 1966—the third round in the Can-Am, and the third race in as many weekends. It certainly was never more apt.

The tightly packed schedule made it an exhausting week for Kainhofer and Ahn. The first practice at Mosport was on Thursday, and it was especially important, as the fastest quali-fiers that day were guaranteed the first 10 spots on the grid. The drive to Mosport from Newtown Square is remembered by Norman and Karl as an endurance test.

It rained hard all day Thursday, and Hall and Hill decided

not to take out their Chaparrals. Surtees blew an engine before he could post a representative time. Therefore, these three aggressive drivers had to qualify on Friday, and could only earn a starting spot of 11th or worse. Mark, who took part on Thursday, again qualified a more-than-respectable sixth, on the inside of the third row. The two cars on the row ahead of him were a surprise. Sam Posey took advantage of the wet conditions to display his talent, and qualified fifth alongside series newcomer Denis Hulme of New Zealand. Hulme, who in time became the winningest driver in the history of the series, was driving a Lola for Irish entrant Sid Taylor. Dan Gurney was on the pole, and the McLaren duo completed the front row. Although fastest in the dry on Friday, Hall, Surtees, and Hill lined up for the race in the middle of the grid. Mosport limited the starters to 30 cars from an entry of more than 45. With the first 25 spots set, a consolation race was run on race-day morning, with the first five finishers moving forward to take up the last five spots on the grid for the big race. Earl Jones won the consolation in Charlie Hayes's spare McLaren.

In the scramble into the first corner, John Surtees, knif-ing through the pack, was turned sideways, setting off a multiple-car accident and forcing a restart. Surtees at first blamed Sam Posey for the accident, but he later showed Sam a series of exculpatory photos of John Cannon hitting Surtees' car from behind. The bottom line was that several contenders were immediately eliminated, including Surtees, Lothar Motschenbacher, Brett Lunger, and Skip Scott, while many more cars bore the scars of the incident.

Gurney led initially after the single-file restart, and then Amon took the front spot. His lead was hotly contested deep into the race by McLaren, Hulme, and Gurney. Mark was just outside this pitched battle and never ran lower than sixth place throughout. His steady pace was rewarded: McLaren and Amon were each eliminated in separate incidents by cars they were lapping, while Hulme broke a halfshaft. Dan Gurney appeared set for a second consecutive win when the crankshaft in his Ford broke, although at the time it was reported that the problem was a flat battery. Mark assumed the lead, and just as smoothly as he had the entire race, drove the Sunoco Lola to the checkered flag a full two laps ahead of the struggling Chaparral of Phil Hill (teammate Hall had dropped out with engine trouble). Chuck Parsons was third, Earl Jones in the borrowed McLaren fourth, Paul Hawkins fifth, and Canadian Eppie Wietzes sixth—seven laps down in a Ford GT40. Only 11 cars made it to the finish.

With Sue not in attendance, it was Roger's wife Lisa who got the ride with Mark and Karl on the victory lap. It was a great victory for Mark, for Roger, for Sunoco, and for the series. It was typical of Mark's chronic self-effacement that he gave little moment to the importance of the achievement, seemingly embarrassed at having inherited the win through the misfortune of others. But attrition is an integral part of racing, and Mark deserved every accolade: He had kept his head throughout and had been one of the fastest cars all weekend. For a guy who had started the season at the Refrigerator Bowl in Marlboro, Maryland, a win in the Can-Am was a very big deal indeed.

Better still, the first half of the Can-Am was over and there was a new points leader: Mark Donohue, with 11 points. Although McLaren and Amon were each just one point behind, and Gurney, Surtees, and Hill just two back, Mark had three full weeks to savor the status. The second half of the series was on the West Coast, and the teams had almost three weeks to repair the damages and make the long trip to northern California for round four at Laguna Seca.

CHAPTER 56:
"A driver of major importance"

Karl had celebrated the big win at Mosport by flying back to Philadelphia on Roger's plane—Norman pulled solo duty driving the rig. The Kainhofer/Ahn tandem was back at the wheel of the Sunoco blue Chevrolet truck, with the Lola in back, for the long drive across America for the West Coast leg of the Can-Am season, beginning at Laguna Seca on October 16. The team's West Coast base was in the Halibrand Engineering shop in Torrance, California, where they occupied a guest bay.

Mark, having never seen the Laguna Seca circuit, was happy to be eighth on the grid after qualifying. He was just a tick over two seconds slower than Jim Hall's top qualifying 1:05.4. Hall shared the front row with teammate Phil Hill—the best performance for Chaparral to date. During the three-week break, further development had been carried out on the Chaparral 2E, which now sported an even larger wing, with side plates for added stability. The grid demonstrated how competitive the series was: Bruce McLaren and Dan

Gurney were on row two, and McLaren's time was less than two-tenths of a second off pole. Chris Amon and Denny Hulme made up the third row, with John Surtees—beside Mark on the fourth row—just a second and a half off pole. After qualifying with a 1:08.1, Chuck Parsons told Charles Fox for *Car and Driver*, "That's quicker than I ever went here before. Running like that I would have made the front row of any USRRC grid this season. But with this bunch you do your damnedest and there's still nine guys ahead of you."

The first 20 cars made the race on qualifying times, and the remaining 12 positions were decided in a qualifying race that Parnelli Jones won in John Mecom's Lola. Mecom also had Jackie Stewart on the team, but the supercharged Ford in his Lola failed and Stewart didn't race. Mecom was disgusted by the performance of his Ford engines and had a Chevrolet, borrowed from Roger Penske, fitted to Jones's car. Parnelli had started at the back of the qualifying race and was in the lead by the second lap.

As was the custom at Laguna Seca, the feature race—the Monterey Grand Prix—was run in two heats of 100 miles each. Mark picked up spots in the early laps and ran as high as fourth place for a period. He finished sixth in the heat, a lap down behind Hill and Hall's dominant Chaparrals and McLaren, Surtees, and Hulme. The second heat followed 45 minutes later and featured an amazing charge from the back of the field by Parnelli Jones, who had not finished in the first heat. By the 16th lap he had passed Mark to take away fourth place and set after Surtees, who was trailing the two Chaparrals. They battled hard for many laps, ultimately colliding when Jones forced his way through on the inside of a fast left-hand bend. Surtees was knocked out of the race, and Jones eventually caught and passed Hall and Hill to win the heat. Mark finished the heat and the overall race fourth. Phil Hill was the overall winner, with teammate Hall second and McLaren third. Parnelli's failure to finish in the first heat dropped him to 21st overall on aggregate.

After the race Bill Preston and Bill Scott were leaving the track in a U-Haul Ford Econoline van, with Mark and the rest of the crew following in a Hertz Chevy sedan. Mark began playfully bumping and pushing the van, and Scotty, concerned about the partially full gasoline drums on board, leaned out the window to tell him to knock it off. When Mark kept pushing, Scotty turned to Bill and said, "Hit the brakes." No damage was done to the van, but all four headlights on the Chevy were wiped out. "Mark returned the car to Hertz and attempted to park it against a wall where the damage couldn't be seen," remembers Bill. "But Hertz was too smart for that and Mark had to pay."

The results after the Laguna Seca round showed Phil Hill as the fourth different winner in four races and now vaulted him into the points lead with 18. Mark was tied for second with Bruce McLaren at 14 points. During the two-week break before Riverside, Mark returned home, but Karl and Norman remained with the car at the Halibrand shop in Torrance. One of their tasks was to replace the 333ci engine in the Sunoco Lola with a 377ci, Traco's latest incarnation of the small-block Chevy. For this race Riverside reverted to the full 3.275-mile configuration that had last been used for a major race in 1961. This meant the return of the famous one-mile straightaway. In practice, Mark in the Sunoco Lola and Charlie Hayes in the Nickey McLaren-Chevy recorded the highest speeds at more than 195 mph. But Mark's top speed for the race would drop to the mid-180 mph range after the more-reliable 333ci engine went back in the Sunoco Lola and a lower top gear was fitted.

The traditional October race at Riverside was the progenitor of the Can-Am. The enormous success of the 1958 *Los Angeles Times*–sponsored U. S. Grand Prix for sports-racing cars represented the beginnings of what became the informal fall series and had now emerged as the biggest series in American road racing. Riverside was the series gem for its history and its location, so close to the huge media market of Los Angeles and the California car culture. The largest purse in the series didn't hurt either. One of the reasons the *Los Angeles Times* made this race such a promotional success was its willingness to pay starting money—supposedly contrary to the Can-Am ideal—to ensure the presence of name drivers. According to *Competition Press & AutoWeek*, Surtees got $8,000, which made it possible for him to field a two-car team. His second driver was Graham Hill, who had won the Indianapolis 500 earlier in the year for John Mecom. Teddy Mayer wasn't left behind, and the McLaren team received $6,000 according to the same source. A. J. Foyt was said to have received $1,500 just to appear.

Foyt and Mario Andretti were making their first Can-Am starts, and they were running Ford-backed Lolas with experimental 427ci engines—Mario's fitted with an automatic transmission. Mario's Lola, fielded by the Mecom team, qualified just one position behind Mark, who was 12th on the 38-car starting grid. A. J.'s car had mechanical troubles, and he had

to make the grid from the consolation race on Saturday. But Foyt failed to finish that race too—won by Masten Gregory—as did Parnelli Jones in the Mecom Lola. This wouldn't do for race chairman Glenn Davis—Heisman Trophy winner and Mr. Outside to Doc Blanchard's Mr. Inside in the famed Army football backfield of the 1940s. The huge investment in promotion had promised that both drivers would be in the field, and some sleight of hand was employed to ensure this would be the case. The five slowest cars to finish the consolation race were suddenly declared "too slow." Allowed to start in their place, along with Foyt and Jones, were Jerry Titus, Ludwig Heimrath, and Billy Foster.

John Mecom had said he would never use a Ford engine again after the team's struggles with blown engines and the Paxton supercharger, declaring he was ready to use the engine as a boat anchor. Ford rose to the occasion at Riverside and was conspicuous with full factory support, including the presence of racing chief Roy Lunn. Mecom also used Ford engines in his Lolas for Parnelli Jones and Jackie Stewart.

Bruce McLaren had appeared at Laguna Seca with Hilborn fuel injection on both of his team cars—everyone else was using Weber carburetors—and the system worked well in qualifying at Riverside, as Bruce captured pole position with John Surtees alongside. Mark, with the 12th-fastest time—his poorest qualifying result of the series—was back on the sixth row alongside Denny Hulme. The 377ci Chevy fitted for qualifying had not performed to Mark's satisfaction.

It turned out to be one of the most memorable Can-Am races ever run. Phil Hill's Chaparral was eliminated early with fuel vaporization. Hall experienced similar trouble but adjusted his driving style to bring a great battle to John Surtees. As other favored cars fell by the wayside, the two traded the lead almost on a lap-to-lap basis. Surtees won, with Hall second and Graham Hill third. Mark drove one of his finest races to finish fourth, on the lead lap. He had again driven smart and persevered on a very hot day that had wilted other drivers. Before the start he had told Chris Economaki, "This is a 200-mile sprint race. I'll drive as fast as I can but we need to finish." George Follmer was fifth and Peter Revson, in his Can-Am debut, sixth, driving the Drummond Racing McLaren-Ford.

Surtees became the first to win two races in the series, and now had 18 points to tie Phil Hill for the Can-Am lead. Mark was just one point back with 17, and Bruce McLaren had 14. It was wide open heading for Las Vegas for the season finale.

Many were pulling for Phil Hill to be the Can-Am champion, and for good reasons. Hill represented something very special to American road racing. He had been an early participant in the rebirth of road racing in America, particularly in his native California, where by the early 1950s he was clearly the man to beat on circuits at Pebble Beach, Torrey Pines, Carrell Speedway, and Palm Springs. Epic drives in the Carrera Panamericana—Mexico's answer to Italy's Mille Miglia—proved his mastery of rugged road racing under the most trying circumstances, and honed his intuitive skills and ability to concentrate for long periods of time. He joined the works Ferrari team in Europe for the 1956 season, and his victory at Monza in the1960 Italian Grand Prix was the first European Grand Prix win for an American in 39 years. The quiet but intense man from Santa Monica simply did it all, and he did it with grace and style. Phil Hill was the first American World Champion when he won the Formula One championship for Ferrari in 1961, the first to win the classic Le Mans 24 Hour race, and the first since Jimmy Murphy in 1921 to win a major European Grand Prix. It would be difficult to think of another man who so exemplified what was fine and admirable about Grand Prix drivers in the postwar era. Great drivers they were, certainly, but the best of them were so much more; they had grace and wit, and myriad interests and enthusiasms—all of which Phil Hill had in abundance. America never had a finer champion in any sport.

The Stardust Grand Prix on November 13 brought all of the season regulars to the final shoot-out to decide the Can-Am championship. Stardust International Raceway had opened just the previous year, built by the owners of the Stardust Hotel to attract people to the great church of gambling in the Las Vegas desert. The track was situated on 480 acres, approximately five miles out in the desert from Las Vegas, although the site has long since been overcome by urban sprawl. The road course was three miles around and featured several challenging high-speed bends. Jerry Entin is a driver with fond memories of Stardust: "It was laid out very nicely, all open desert, and if you happened to go off you would have a car full of small rocks and sand, but it was a very safe course as the desert sand stopped you very quickly."

Mark had a different view of the circuit, which he considered featureless to the point of treachery. As he explained to Charles Fox, "You go into a turn here with virtually no indication of where to brake, and come out of it looking to

see where the road goes next. It's just that easy to get lost for a fraction of a second."

The Chaparrals were again fast on the first row of the grid, with Hall on pole. Mark in 14th was farther back on the grid than at any race in the series. John Surtees was fourth behind the Chaparrals and Chris Amon, but at the start he took the lead in the first corner. He would hold onto it for the rest of the race. The Chaparrals had major problems with their wings and dropped from contention. Bruce McLaren, who had reverted to Webers on his Chevrolet engine, finished second. And Mark finished third—for the fifth consecutive race he had finished in the points by dint of smooth and fast driving.

The championship belonged to John Surtees with 27 points. Others had been faster at times, but "Fearless John" was the fastest when it mattered most. He won half the races—all three that he finished—and only bad luck kept him from running away with the series. Runner-up was Mark Donohue. Despite all the experienced drivers, emerging technology, and highly publicized teams, it was Mark who was there all the way through. The only race he didn't finish in the points was the very first round at St. Jovite, where he was eliminated in the first corner by someone else's accident.

"Donohue had emerged as a driver of major importance," Sam Posey was to say later. And it was true. Suddenly Mark was news. He had demonstrated the maturity and sense of pace of a winner. The second-place slice of the points fund pie was $10,450—a fraction of the team's total winnings in the series. By earning prize money in five of the six races, the Penske team brought home more money than any other single-car team—perhaps more than the two-car teams of McLaren and Chaparral.

For John Surtees, the Can-Am was a highlight of a remarkable year and the completion of a brave comeback. Surtees had clearly returned to the form and stature that he had enjoyed before the Mosport accident.

At the time of his Can-Am championship, John Surtees was at the height of his considerable talent. Mark called Surtees "Racing's Superman." Only Jim Clark and Dan Gurney were considered in the same breath with John when people discussed the greatest driver in the world. No one in the sport possessed more intensity and focus than did Surtees, and he displayed a more complete commitment to his racing than most drivers of his era.

The man who finished runner-up to Surtees in that first

Can-Am was already displaying many of these same traits. Although it was still early in his professional career, Mark Donohue would soon be respected and admired in much the same way as was Surtees, and for many of the same reasons. "Mark soon proved himself not only to be quick but also to have a good head on his shoulders," recalls John Surtees. "He was good to race with because you could be pretty sure that he wouldn't endanger you on the track by doing a stupid move."

The evening after the race there was a big party at the Stardust Hotel in downtown Las Vegas. More than 400 people attended, including drivers, team owners, mechanics, race officials, and other industry figures. Sam Johnson, president of the Johnson Wax Company, made the presentation of checks and other awards, assisted by Can-Am commissioner Stirling Moss. The big prize to John Surtees was the Johnson Wax trophy—an unusual and original sculpture in the style of a fixed mobile that actually floated in the air—by Venezuelan artist Alberto Collie. It was a night of great festivity, but one celebration was unexpected. Paul Hawkins had noticed the dramatic fountain outside the hotel spouting water all the way to the second floor where the party was being held behind enormous panoramic windows. Aided and abetted by team owner Jackie Epstein, Hawkeye stopped on his way to the party and bought a giant box of laundry detergent. On his way into the party he quietly deposited the entire contents into the fountain. In his book *Hawkeye*, Ivan McLeod quotes Epstein: ". . . the organizers had their backs to the window. We all stood there, all very solemn and clapping politely, and this fountain was erupting. It was getting higher and higher past these windows, and of course eventually the whole place burst out in fits of laughter, and of course the organizers couldn't see it."

The next day, Karl and Norman had a companion for the long tow back to Pennsylvania. Roger hired Peter Reinhart to join the team immediately after Las Vegas. Reinhart, a German who had been working with Lothar Motschenbacher and the Nickey / Dan Blocker team, was destined to play an important role in the Penske team's early growth.

The first Can-Am had been an enormous success. It worked for the sanctioning bodies, the tracks, and the teams and drivers, elevating all of them. Series public relations director Al Bochroch told Sam Posey at the victory dinner that he hoped future Can-Ams would be even more successful, and that he expected that it would eventually be the biggest thing in rac-

ing. "But you know," Bochroch told Posey, "it will never be the same again, because this was the first." Bochroch's hopes for the ultimate success of the Can-Am never fully materialized, but he was completely correct about how special the first year had been. The 1966 Can-Am was the most competitive it would ever be, with the biggest fields and the closest racing. The series had peaked in its debut year.

CHAPTER 57:

Unfinished Business

For Mark there was still more to do. He had worked hard to qualify for the SCCA Runoffs, and wanted very badly to cap his amateur racing career with a national championship.

This was the third year of the Runoffs and the first year that the race officially decided the national champion. The single-race shoot-out format brought together the top cars and drivers from each geographical area of the country. The 1966 showdown was on the West Coast at Riverside International Raceway.

At technical inspection Mark faced a crisis. The SCCA would not allow the Mustang's enlarged wheel wells that had been created to accommodate the large Firestones. Mark quickly found a pay phone and called Chuck Cantwell at Shelby for advice. Chuck instructed him to measure the exact dimensions that were needed. Chuck then created "factory" drawings and blueprints. They were complete with stamps providing tolerances that would meet Mark's needs. The documents were "aged" and then copied. A courier delivered them to Mark late the same day. The SCCA accepted the "proof" the wheel wells were within original specifications and passed the car.

Official practice began on Wednesday afternoon, November 23. Mark had major engine problems and by race time was on his third engine of the week. Fastest qualifier for the BP class was Walt Hane in a GT350R, while Mark was fifth of the 20 entrants in BP. The race combined AP and BP and utilized a split start, with the BP cars taking the flag 30 seconds after those in AP. Don Yenko in his Corvette took the lead off the start, but by the end of the first lap had been demoted to fourth by Mark, Hane, and Ron Dykes in a Sunbeam Tiger. The opening laps were fiercely contested, with Mark in the middle of it until the engine lost top end power, dropping him slightly off the pace of the top three. On the fourth lap Dan Gerber in a Shelby GT350R tangled with another car on the start/finish straight, resulting in an enormous crash that blocked the track and forced a red flag. When the race resumed, Yenko was the apparent winner on the track—but he had ignored a black flag for numerous laps, and that, along with a few rude gestures to the flagman, caused his disqualification. Walt Hane—the Maitland, Florida, man who Mark had encouraged earlier in the year—was the winner after a race-long battle with Ron Dykes.

More than 20 minutes had passed before the race could be restarted after the red flag, and three drivers were discovered working on their cars during this period. One was Mark, and along with the others he was disqualified. Suddenly it was over. The long trip, the obstacles in tech and in practice, and the pitched battle on the track—were all done, and for nothing. Mark's amateur career ended with an emphatic anticlimax.

CHAPTER 58:

Success in the Bahamas

Roger and Mark decided to run one last race before the year was out. Both remembered the unique combination of fun and competition at the Nassau races. Roger had won the Nassau Trophy in 1964 for Chaparral, his last race before retiring as a driver. The Nassau they found in 1966 was a faded version, and the races ended the 13-year run for promoter Red Crise's Bahamas Speed Week. The party scene was still great, though, and the entry was more than decent despite being diminished in quantity.

Norman Ahn and Peter Reinhart left Newtown Square on Thanksgiving Day to drive to Miami, where they put the Lola on the boat to Nassau. The Sunoco Special Lola was fitted with a 359ci engine for this race. Karl and his family arrived by air, as did Roger. Mark came without Sue, as she was due to deliver their second child within a month.

Chaparral won the two previous Nassau Trophy races with Penske in 1964 and Jim Hall in 1965. The team brought only one 2E in 1966 for Hap Sharp, whose most recent race had been at Sebring in March. In Richard Falconer and Doug Nye's book, *Chaparral*, Hall expressed the lack of enthusiasm that many people had developed for the event:

. . . it was an old airport, rough as hell . . . I never particularly enjoyed it . . . In those days it wasn't a very nice place . . . The locals were rude; it was no fun to be there. And the service in the hotels was terrible. . . . It was hard to be a serious racer there. . . . The schedule was never adhered to, the track wouldn't be ready, the fences wouldn't be up. It was so poorly run. . . .

Despite the problems, the entry was strong, in part because certain Can-Am teams and suppliers still had something to prove. Although Surtees and the McLaren team were absent, along with Dan Gurney and Chuck Parsons, Ford largely underwrote the participation of a number of cars. The two Drummond Team McLarens were fitted with developmental Ford 351ci engines for Peter Revson and Skip Scott; A. J. Foyt was in a Holman-Moody–supported Lola fitted with a 427ci engine, as were Mario Andretti and Billy Foster. Andretti owned the Lola his friend Foster was driving, while his own car had come from John Mecom, who had announced his withdrawal from road racing after the last round of the Can-Am. Additional strong cars included Pedro Rodríguez in a Ferrari Dino 206; Brett Lunger in a McLaren-Chevy; Charlie Kolb, Lola-Chevy; Buck Fulp, Lola-Chevy; Dick Brown, McLaren-Ford; and Sam Posey's McLaren-Ford.

The format at Nassau was always unusual and subject to last-minute changes. This year the schedule was really thrown up in the air when the ocean freighter that had been engaged to bring the cars from Miami to Nassau was impounded for nonpayment of taxes. By the time the cars were loaded on a substitute boat, the traditional weeklong schedule had to be abandoned. The big cars were now scheduled for three races: The Governor's Trophy on Friday; The Nassau Classic on Saturday; and the feature Nassau Trophy race on Sunday—the only race where prize money was at stake. Hap Sharp was fastest in practice, with Mark second. Peter Revson filled out the front row for the Governor's Trophy. The 25-lap, 112.5-mile race was combined with the Nassau Tourist Trophy for GT cars. The pairing created an unlikely and dangerous mix of cars, with the overpowering Can-Am cars lapping Mini Coopers, MG Midgets, Volvos, and the like.

Mark took an immediate lead from Sharp. Almost inevitably several big cars came to grief attempting to get by the often poorly driven smaller cars. It cost Mark the Friday race. As he attempted to lap Fernando Irego's Volvo 122S, the Puerto Rican driver chopped him off and the Sunoco Lola was sent hurtling off course. Mark drove back to the pits where the minor damage to the car was repaired. He returned to do five more laps just to see that everything was all right. Many other top cars took the race even less seriously, turning it into a virtual practice session. Red Crise argued with the teams to get them on the track but they largely ignored him. The cars needed to be conserved for the big race on Sunday when money would be at stake.

The Nassau Classic on Saturday was just four laps long. Again, the race held little meaning save as a warm-up for the next day, and only seventeen cars started. A. J. Foyt led all the way, with Mark second.

Sunday brought the feature race, the 56-lap, 252-mile Nassau Trophy. A Le Mans–type start was used, and each car was required to make a pit stop. Forty-eight cars started, and tragedy struck almost immediately. A Ferrari 365 P2 driven by Venezuelan Rodrigo Borges Zingg crashed violently in turn one of the second lap. The car burst into flames. It took almost 10 minutes for an ambulance and fire truck to be dispatched as the race continued with the burning car on the edge of the circuit. Then the fire truck proved too large to pass through the tiny exit arch under the footbridge. When the fire team finally arrived at the scene of the crash they found that their water hose had holes in it. The 21-year-old Zingg had managed to exit the Ferrari but he was grievously burned and succumbed to his injuries six weeks later.

Mark and Roger decided on a secret strategy to allow them to make the briefest of pit stops. Bill Scott fabricated an aluminum fuel tank, boosting capacity to 65 gallons and obviating any need to take on more gas at the mandatory pit stop. The extra tank was mounted on top of the side pod and flowed into the fuel cell through gravity. This created a weight penalty in the early laps and, worse yet, the untested vent hose wasn't located high enough. Mark was being sprayed by the fuel and vapor sloshing out, and later reported that he very nearly had to pit from the noxious fumes. In typical Donohue fashion he soldiered on, and the problem lessened as the fuel drained down. Despite all this Mark held a close and steady third behind race leader Peter Revson and his teammate Skip Scott. Mark lost crucial time when he had to run wide to avoid yet another Volvo spinning in the tricky and colorfully named Blackbeard's Bend. "I got off the track and spun in sand," Mark told *National Speed Sport News*. "[I] picked up a section of tree and left some of my car there." Indeed, a large section of fiberglass on the front fender and

spoiler was ripped away from the Sunoco Lola.

Mark picked up his pace dramatically, but it was almost not enough. Near the 40th lap the Drummond team cars pitted for fuel on consecutive laps, turning the lead over to Mark. When Mark finally made his mandatory stop with just three laps to go, his lead was not sufficient to keep Scott, who had made the better of the Drummond Team stops, behind him. The pit-stop rule only required that the driver exit the car. Mark loosened his safety harness as he entered the pits, two large crew members lifted him from the car, put his feet on the ground, and then put him back in. He was away in just 7.5 seconds, but Scott had come by and now led by 15 seconds. Mark seemed destined to finish second when on the 54th lap, Scott was forced off the track and spun when attempting to lap the Cheval-Chevy of Paul Layman. Mark flashed by and came home to win by 4.5 seconds from Scott, with Revson third.

Hap Sharp had made a terrible start and spent the entire race catching up before crashing badly on the next-to-last lap when a bolt sheared off the wing. Sharp suffered only a cut hand, but the 2E was severely damaged. This gave fourth to Buck Fulp, while Sam Posey finished fifth. The rough circuit and the hazard of cars traveling as much as 80 mph slower made Nassau feel like a battle. "It was quite difficult with the slower cars," said Mark in victory circle. "We owe our good fortune to Roger's fuel strategy, plus we were fortunate when Skip Scott spun."

It was a great way to finish the season for the Penske Team. A win at Nassau was always a big publicity score, despite being a stand-alone race. Although Skip Scott's bad luck with lapped traffic had made the win possible, Mark had suffered an even worse setback earlier in the race for the same reason. Later Mark and others would evaluate this first year for the Penske-Donohue combination as "less than spectacular." This conclusion can only be supported in comparison to the great success the team enjoyed in later years. In fact, 1966 had been a year of great accomplishment for the small team: A race win in the USRRC, a race win in the Can-Am, and second place in the series standings, along with the season-end victory at Nassau would be the stuff of dreams for most.

The Sun Oil Company agreed. They ran a full-page ad that appeared in *Road & Track* and other publications. In small block letters it began, "We don't mean to brag, but," and then in giant letters that dominated half the page, "WE WON". The rest of the page featured photos of Mark in the Lola and a list of accomplishments by the Sunoco Special.

The Nassau experience ended in bittersweet fashion. Swamped by well-wishers and autograph seekers after the victory ceremony, Mark was so busy giving attention to each person that by the end of the day, he found himself the last person left at the circuit with no way to get back to the hotel. He begged a ride back in the rear of a garbage truck. "By then I was really feeling sorry for myself," Mark later recalled. While Mark was able to see the humor in the anticlimactic end to the day, the poignancy of the situation contributed to his subsequent careful evaluation of where he was going.

Over the Christmas holidays Mark looked carefully at his racing within the total context of his life. He wasn't making much money at it, and he had less faith in his ability as a driver than did most observers. About to become a father for the second time, Mark considered other means of making a living that did not include being a race driver.

Mark's primary source of income was his job as chief engineer at Griffith. The small company was strained to the limit for capital, but Mark didn't know it. His energy was focused on developing the cars and solving the assembly problems. "It was great to hear Mark talk about the challenges he was facing in setting up an assembly line and all the other issues he was dealing with," says Dave Lawton. "He was immersed in making that operation work."

CHAPTER 59:
Evaluating the Future

The new year of 1967 began for Sue and Mark in splendid fashion. David Neary Donohue was born January 5, 1967, and brought home to 8 Barnwell Lane in Stony Brook, where he was greeted by his two-year-old brother Michael. The subsequent baptism at St. Peter and Paul Church in nearby St. James, New York, was a joyous family occasion. Mark Sr. was David's godfather and Mark's sister Nancy was godmother.

Mark's position as chief engineer at Griffith Motors had reached a crisis. The company was bankrupt and Mark felt he was left holding the bag. Unbeknownst to him, Jack Griffith and a partner had named Mark as a principal in the business. When the creditors came around, the two had disappeared. The sudden turn of events at Griffith caught Mark by surprise. Immersed in his engineering duties and responding daily to

new challenges presented by the ambitious venture, Mark was removed from the financial realities closing in on the fledgling company. Mark was warned by Jack, just in time, that his own personal property was in jeopardy of being attached. It was an unhappy ending to a project that Mark had thrown himself into with great energy. Mark held no long-term bad feelings toward Griffith. He knew Jack to be a good man who had simply gotten into a complex international business arrangement without sufficient resources to weather the vagaries of a complex start-up operation.

It was a difficult period. Mark was coming off a year when he had gone from the purely amateur ranks to very professional drives for Ford and Roger Penske. Mark made more money in his few drives for Ford than he did in an entire year on his regular job. Though the Ford drive offered a per-race fee of $3,000 for 1967—up from $1,000 the year before—there wasn't a future there since there were only so many races, and Mark wasn't needed for all of them. From a racer's perspective, the Penske deal was more attractive: It entailed more events, with Mark clearly the lead driver. But Roger was only paying him $50 a day for racing and testing, clearly insufficient for a mature man with a wife and children. So Mark was considering a range of options that included quitting driving. He was always his own greatest critic as a driver. The race at Nassau had left him feeling there were other drivers with more talent and a willingness to make a bigger commitment on the track. He later recalled thinking he should give up racing. "I remember thinking about it on the cool-off lap," Mark said. "Scott and Revson were much faster—much more capable drivers—and the only reason we won was because Roger psyched everyone out."

While it is not uncommon for race drivers to experience moments of self-doubt even in the heat of battle, most overcome these feelings once the passion of the race cools—particularly when the result is as positive as it was at Nassau. There is no evidence to suggest that others shared Mark's doubts regarding his ability. Roger Penske, a shrewd evaluator of talent, believed firmly in Mark as a driver, as did rival teams and experienced members of the media.

One of the options Mark was considering was a quality-control job at Kar Kraft, Ford's in-house race shop in Detroit. He drove to Philadelphia to tell Roger Penske what he was thinking. Roger was unimpressed with the Kar Kraft offer, advising Mark that he would be no more than a small cog in the Ford race operation. On the spot he offered Mark a salaried position plus a percentage of his race winnings, saying he would pay what Mark was currently making, plus 25 percent. Mark took time to discuss it with Sue and with his parents, since he feared becoming a professional race driver would be irresponsible to his wife and children. To his surprise, they were not opposed to his making a full commitment to racing. Mark knew few drivers were salaried; most were dependent on what they could make in prize money. For his family the offer of a salary took some of the uncertainty out of his becoming a professional driver.

At least two other factors were important to Mark's decision. First, he had great faith in Roger's ability to put him in the right equipment. He told his friend Dave Lawton, "Look, I'm driving the best equipment that's out there. I don't have to have the best driving deal—I'm catching it the other way with the best equipment."

Mark also knew that the chemistry between he and Penske was right. Roger was an excellent manager, but one who would still allow Mark to follow his own instincts with little interference. Mark knew he would be able to engineer the car and the setup the way he wanted, and that if he needed something more, he would have a good shot of being able to talk Roger into it. Mark believed that he and Roger shared "a mutual sensibility" and a willingness to not get overly involved in each other's responsibilities. Mark had observed Roger's talent for delegating authority and saw how it would help him. With his acceptance of the offer, the relationship between Mark Donohue and Roger Penske took a critical turn.

Additional measure of Mark's increasing stature within the sport was the FIA's announcement of their "graded" list of drivers for the 1967 season. Mark was one of 9 Americans among the 30 international drivers listed—the others were Bob Bondurant, Ronnie Bucknum, Richie Ginther, Dan Gurney, Phil Hill, Lloyd Ruby, Peter Revson, and Skip Scott—illustrating the prominence American drivers enjoyed internationally in this period. Being graded could be a mixed blessing, as it curtailed a driver's ability to participate in non-internationally sanctioned events outside his own country. The FIA represented the list as a means to protect local national events from being "cherry-picked" by the top stars. At the same time, it gave the FIA control and lent added weight to their international sanctions.

Mark focused his attention on the Penske race shop in Newtown Square, although it would be summer before he and Sue sold the house on Long Island and moved to suburban Philadelphia. With the first USRRC race for the Group 7 Lola not until late April, Roger Penske now took a serious look at the Trans-Am series.

Ford had won the inaugural Trans-Am series in 1966 with the Mustang on the strength of a fully supported factory effort run by Carroll Shelby's team. Primary opposition had come from Chrysler, with points scored separately by their Plymouth and Dodge divisions. In the marketplace, the Mustang was setting the tone for the pony cars that were now the rage in the U.S. auto industry. Chevrolet dealers around the country had been eagerly awaiting General Motors' response. Now they had it.

The Camaro, introduced in the fall of 1966 as a 1967 model, was initially available with a 250ci six-cylinder engine, or in V8 form with a 327ci or 350ci. None of these would do for the Trans-Am series, which specified a maximum engine size of 5.0 liters (305ci). Roger Penske—a Chevrolet dealer who understood the marketing value of racing—had a close relationship with Vince Piggins, the head of Chevrolet engineering, and was able to influence him to develop a high-performance production version of the Camaro. The resulting package was RPO (Regular Production Option) Z28. The required engine size was achieved by mating the shorter-stroke 283 engine crankshaft with the 327 bore, producing a displacement of 302ci. A production run of 1,000 cars allowed the Z28 to be homologated. The street version of the car had front disc brakes with—theoretically, at least—optional four-wheel discs. Another option that was hard to come by in real life was a larger fuel tank. Other options that were generally available included close-ratio 4-speed gearboxes, a larger radiator, and bucket seats. The Z28 was an immediate hit with performance buyers, instantly recognizable by the two broad parallel stripes that ran the length of the car. The visual appeal of the car was enhanced by a small rear spoiler and front-mounted valance. Considered a pure styling statement by some, the spoiler and front valance had, in fact, been designed by Paul Van Valkenburgh in GM's research and development department.

The Trans-Am had started with relatively little fanfare the previous March at Sebring. By the end of the year, however, it was big news, and Ford was determined to maintain its winning edge in 1967. The Mustang had enjoyed three years of development as a race car and Shelby had a well-honed operation. The Penske team faced a huge challenge in bringing the Camaro to the track, let alone winning races with it.

Roger figured that Mark's experience with the Mustang would give the team a big leg-up in developing the Z28. Mark had a more realistic sense of the challenge ahead.

CHAPTER 60:

Juggling Fords and Chevys

The first race on the calendar was at Daytona on February 3, leaving very little time to prepare a car. Roger's longtime friend George Wintersteen picked up an assembly-line stock Z28 in Detroit on January 10 and drove it back to the shop in Newtown Square. The team immediately began to strip the interior and install a roll cage. Traco provided a race-prepared version of the 302 engine and Mark specified the spring rates—ultimately relying as much on instinct as science. Roger and the engineers at Chevrolet were pressing Mark for a decision on springs, and Mark just wasn't certain. Concerned that Roger may be losing confidence in him, Mark went with his best judgment and had a Philadelphia spring shop make a stiff set, specifying only that they be ". . . say, four leaves, and yea thick." Mark's instinct proved to be correct, and the experience bolstered his confidence in his ability to set up a car for racing. At the last minute Mark and Wintersteen took the car to Bridgehampton to test. Mark didn't think the car was right, although the late-January weather conditions (ice on the track in places) and the early setting sun made it difficult to gain a real sense of what they had.

In fact, the car was surprisingly good, but last-minute complications nearly thwarted Mark's debut in it. Ford balked when they got wind of Mark's entry in the Camaro for Friday's Trans-Am curtain-raiser, the Daytona 300. Mark was a member of the powerful Ford team defending its World Manufacturers Championship, and he was entered to co-drive a Holman-Moody Mark II in the 24-hour race with Peter Revson. Mark, along with Ronnie Bucknum, had been doing testing at Daytona for Ford in January in the latest development of the Mk II at $200 a day. His fee for the race was $3,000—an important amount to Mark. Ford told Mark they couldn't take the chance of his being hurt in the Trans-Am and thus unavailable for the big race. The unspoken truth was that Ford feared the adverse publicity should Mark win the Trans-Am in a Chevrolet. Mark went to Roger with the dilemma, and Roger had the answer. He told Mark he would

pay him $3,000 to drive the Camaro, and to hell with the Ford deal. Ford backed down. Top-line drivers were hard to find, and Mark was now too ingrained in Ford's development and engineering system to be left off the team. Mark must have mused at the contrast with the previous year's race, when he had barely passed muster with Ford. Only Walt Hansgen's persistent promise—"He'll be fine"—had kept Mark on the team. Now he was considered indispensable.

The greatest rivalry in Trans-Am at the time was not Ford versus Chevrolet, but Ford versus Mercury. The big-budget Trans-Am teams represented two competing divisions of the Ford Motor Company. Mercury was running a two-car team of Cougars under the leadership of veteran NASCAR car builder Bud Moore of Spartanburg, South Carolina. Parnelli Jones and Dan Gurney had put the Cougars on the front row for Daytona, while Jerry Titus and Dick Thompson headed the Shelby Mustang lineup.

In qualifying Mark was delighted to find that the Camaro was at least competitive, exclaiming, "Doggone, if the car wasn't fast!" The handling was reasonable for the high banks of Daytona, where Mark had learned that ". . . if the car is sprung stiffly for the banks and fast on the straight, you can just drive it around with no problems." Again Mark revealed his disinclination to give himself credit for his driving. "Drive it around with no problems," indeed. For Mark it was always important to minimize his great talent by implying some advantage of setup, power, or luck.

He qualified the Camaro third at Daytona, less than a second off Gurney's pole-position time. When the race started Mark caused a sensation when he stole the lead into the first corner. He led briefly, but after 14 laps was out with a persistent misfire, initially diagnosed as an electrical issue that later proved to be a fuel problem. The two fuel tanks that the team had welded together to create a 37-gallon capacity apparently hadn't been cleaned sufficiently. Brakes would eventually become the big challenge for the Camaro, but at Daytona Mark didn't last long enough to discover this. The Cougars and Mustangs took turns leading but dropped out or were delayed with lengthy pit stops. Bob Tullius won in a Dodge Dart that he was running on a very limited budget after Chrysler Corporation had withdrawn from the Trans-Am after just missing winning the 1966 championship. Remarkably, a Camaro from Canadian independent Craig Fisher was second. Parnelli Jones was third and Jerry Titus fourth.

While the relationship with Sun Oil remained strong and

growing for the Group 7 car, Penske received no sponsorship from the oil company in 1967 for the Sunoco Camaro. The car was painted in the blue and yellow colors and had a large Sunoco logo on the side, but the arrangement was unspoken and purely prospective on Roger's part. There were no Sun Oil personnel augmenting the race team at Trans-Am events as there were for the USRRC and Can-Am with the Lola. Roger Penske was never afraid to make bold moves or to take the long view, and indeed his decision paid off, as Sunoco later formally joined the effort as a sponsor.

The Trans-Am cars were eligible to run the next day in the 24-hour race. With Mark driving the prototype Ford, Roger put George Wintersteen, Joe Welch, and Bobby Brown in the Camaro. They qualified a respectable 22nd in the 58-car field and finished 26th, although they were not running at the finish due to last-minute problems.

When asked about the Chevrolet–Ford rivalry and if he harbored animosity one way or the other, or if it was awkward to move from one team to the other, Mark was clear in expressing a very different point of view: "No, I absolutely don't have a problem with it because it really comes down to the point that Ford and GM are made up of people, and it's the people you work with that you form the loyalties to."

The Mercury division of Ford Motor Company was jealous of the attention going to Ford in prototype racing and wanted in on the promotion. Of the six Ford GT IIs entered—three by Holman-Moody and three by Shelby—two carried the Mercury name plate. The Holman-Moody "Mercury"—chassis No. 1016, finished in gold with two thin black stripes—was driven by Mark and Peter Revson. Holman-Moody also fielded Mk IIs for Denis Hulme / Lloyd Ruby and for Mario Andretti / Richie Ginther. The three Shelby-entered Mk IIs were for Dan Gurney / A. J. Foyt in a Mercury-branded car, and for Bruce McLaren / Lucien Bianchi and Ronnie Bucknum / Frank Gardner in Fords. Mark's friend Paul Hawkins was also part of the driver strength for possible reserve duty, although he did not drive in the race.

Ford catered well to their personnel for Daytona, providing facilities behind the pits with folding cots and attendants to make up the beds. A hospitality area served food throughout the 24 hours, with the menu changing on an hourly basis. This level of attention to driver and mechanic comfort was startling, and seen by many as an example of Ford excess. More-perceptive eyes saw it as an example of excellent preparation and commitment—and perhaps a harbinger of the future.

Mark and Peter had a difficult time in the Holman-Moody GT II. A shock absorber mount tore loose from the chassis on the banking at near top speed. It was a bad experience, and Mark did well to avoid crashing and to bring the car to the pits. The car was repaired, but the transmission output shaft between second and third gear failed and was replaced twice before it put Mark and Peter out for good in the middle of the night. Although Mark had been warned that it was just a matter of time, he was still disappointed when he was woken only to be told it was over. "Someone woke me up to tell me the car had failed," Mark later recalled. "When I went around to the garage, there it was, parked and forgotten."

Remarkably, the same shaft troubled every Mk II. It was a bad day for Ford, with the highest-placed Mk II in seventh place with Bruce McLaren and Lucien Bianchi. A Mk I GT40 was fifth with Dick Thompson and Jacky Ickx. Archrival Ferrari had swept the first three spots with Lorenzo Bandini and Chris Amon in the winning 330 P4. The latest Chaparral, the 2F—which boasted a 7.0-liter Chevrolet engine and a huge suspension-mounted wing—was impressive, leading the early stages of the race with Phil Hill and Mike Spence. Its great performance ended when Hill encountered broken pavement that pitched the rear of the car into the wall, breaking the suspension. The disastrous race for Ford was made all the worse when Ferrari driver Chris Amon—who had shared the winning Ford with Bruce McLaren at Le Mans the previous year—said of the 330 P4, "It's beautiful. By comparison the Ford Mk II is a truck."

Once again the careers of Mark Donohue and Peter Revson intersected. They had been keen but friendly rivals as early as 1961 when they were both chasing the SCCA National Championship in E Production—Mark in his Elva Courier and Peter in his Morgan. While Mark suffered the frustration of the slow climb to recognition through the SCCA ranks, Peter had gone to Europe on a minimal budget to make his reputation—barnstorming in Formula 3, towing his race car behind a Volkswagen microbus, and sleeping in tents. Although they respected each other, there was always an edge between the two men, and they would never be close. Sam Posey, who was close to both men, observes, "They were more rivals than friends although they had similar backgrounds." Peter Revson's family had a sizable fortune, but, contrary to popular perception, Peter and his brother Doug had little access to the money that could have paved their way more quickly in the sport. Posey adds further perspective: "They both had that funny relationship with money. Mark always came across as someone who had no money, but that wasn't entirely true. Mark's dad—if he wasn't wealthy, he was certainly well-to-do. Revson had the money but couldn't get his hands on it."

Racing in Europe had honed Peter's talent and hardened his approach. Finding themselves paired in the big Ford at Daytona, Mark and Peter had, through different routes, reached a similar level in their careers. While Mark had established more of a name in America, Peter was better known in Europe. A career in Formula One remained Peter's avowed goal.

Revson's role on the Ford team took an unexpected turn when, shortly after the 24-hour race, he arrived at Daytona for a test day in the Mk II. Mark was not present. A tire deflated on the banking at 185 mph, and Peter had a spectacular and chilling accident. He was fortunate to step out of the car uninjured. Walt Hansgen's fatal accident the previous year at Le Mans testing had prompted Ford to fit the Ford GTs with integral roll cages. Although unhurt and not at fault, such were the politics in Ford racing that the accident cost Revson a prominent place on the team.

With Sebring on March 31 still more than a month away, work on the Camaro continued in Newtown Square. Mark was still living on Long Island and commuting home on the weekends, with the family move from Stony Brook to the Philadelphia area set for late June. Mark was not called on for Ford testing during this period and was able to concentrate on the Camaro and the Lola.

The Sebring race organization suffered severe criticism after the fatalities of the previous year. Race director Alec Ulmann and race secretary and vice president Reggie Smith worked hard to resolve safety issues, placing modern safety barriers and making the most significant alterations in the circuit's history.

Ford brought only two prototype race cars to Sebring for the 12-hour race but paid Mark to be on hand as a reserve driver. While happy to be paid for his reserve role, Mark was disappointed that Mario Andretti was selected ahead of him to co-drive with Bruce McLaren. Although Mario was better known, Mark thought he was a more experienced road-race driver and believed that he would have been the right choice for an endurance race. With only sideline duties for Ford, Mark was free to concentrate on the Camaro and

the Trans-Am race the day before the 12 Hours. The Penske team was rewarded with a promising second place to Jerry Titus in the Shelby Team Mustang. The four-hour Trans-Am was a grueling event on the rough 5.2-mile circuit, with Mark sharing the car with George Wintersteen. It was a tribute to the young Penske team that in a starting field of 61 cars, they were able to bring the Camaro home in second place, and on the lead lap, in only the second race for the car. Mark, in typical fashion, downplayed the achievement and privately decried the poor handling—the stiff setup that had worked so well on the Daytona banking was not good at all on the rough airport concrete of Sebring—but it was a fine result nonetheless.

The sensation of the 12-hour race was the debut of the Ford Mk IV GT, which did indeed win, driven by McLaren and Andretti. For Andretti the win came just a month after the USAC sensation had stunned the NASCAR regulars with a win in their biggest race, the Daytona 500. Now Andretti had won for Ford again, but this time in a major international sports-car endurance race. It was a pivotal period in Mario Andretti's increasing recognition as a major star on the international stage.

The winning Mk IV was very much a derivative of the J-car that had been under development throughout the previous year by Carroll Shelby. After the Fords were outpaced by Ferrari at Daytona, it was full speed ahead on getting the J-car into racing shape. The work was done at Kar Kraft in Detroit by Phil Remington, who arrived from Shelby with a team of fabricators. The combined team produced a new and very aerodynamic shape around the honeycomb J-car chassis, and in record time the Mk IV was born.

A. J. Foyt and Lloyd Ruby were second at Sebring in a Mk II, despite spending the last 27 minutes of the race sitting in the pits with a seized camshaft drive. The clean sweep and debut win for the Mk IV were good for Ford morale, but the achievement was dampened by the lack of factory-entered and -supported Ferraris. Sebring organizer Alec Ulmann was unwilling to meet Enzo Ferrari's demands for starting money. "The Americans need me more than I need them," Ferrari was quoted as saying. Even the NART team, which frequently held up the Ferrari banner in these situations, failed to appear. Ferrari's absence was not strictly an appearance-money issue. They feared their cars and equipment would be attached to legal actions from the fatalities of the previous year. The highest-placed Ferrari at the finish was the very stock-appearing 275 GTB Spyder of Denise McCluggage and Marianne "Pinky" Rollo in 17th place.

With Ferrari out it was up to Chaparral to bring the battle to Ford, and the 2F did exactly that. Jim Hall subbed for Phil Hill, who had to have an emergency appendectomy after practice. Hall was managing the team and preferred having Hap Sharp take over for Hill, but Sharp's FIA license wasn't up-to-date. Hall and Mike Spence battled the Mk IV until the gearbox broke. Spence in the Chaparral did have the consolation of setting fastest lap.

The Penske Camaro was not in the 12-hour race, but Roger entered George Wintersteen and Joe Welch in the team's 427 Sting Ray. They led their class at one point, but finished second in class and 26th overall after Welch spun and damaged the starter motor. He had to return to the pits on foot for a new starter and then replace it on course.

Mark left early the following week for Le Mans, where he was delighted to join the Ford team at the April test days. "I considered it quite an honor to get sent to France for a weekend of testing," he recalled. He drove the same Mk II he had shared at Daytona with Peter Revson. Bruce McLaren tested a new Mk IV, logging a relatively slow best lap of 3:36.1 as he concentrated on chassis setup and data acquisition. Mark was quicker in the Mk II with a 3:32.6 best lap, although his 202-mph top speed through the speed trap at the end of the Mulsanne straight was three miles an hour slower than Bruce in the Mk IV. Testing was greatly curtailed by prevailing rain that provided only brief opportunities for dry laps over the weekend. Lorenzo Bandini and Michael Parkes in Ferrari 330 P4s each had faster times than either Ford, as did John Surtees in the works Lola T70-Aston Martin coupe. Mark and Bruce's lap times were deceptive, however: Ford engineers were deliberately not showing their hand. The cars were heavily instrumented to evaluate maximum performance on each section of the track. None of the fast sections were put together in a single lap, so only the Ford team knew that the Mark IV was going to be very, very fast in the race.

It had been just a year since Walt Hansgen had fatally crashed at these same test days, and tragedy struck again in 1967. Roby Weber died after his works Type 630 Matra-BRM crashed on the Mulsanne straight and burst into flames. Shockingly, the fire truck that arrived on the scene almost immediately had neither hoses nor extinguishers operating. It was a nightmare on par with the debacle at Nassau. Jacques Robert Weber, 27 years old and planning to be married three

days later, was one of the most promising of the new generation of French race drivers.

Once back in America, Mark and Bill Mayberry worked to improve the brakes on the Camaro. The SCCA-approved system employed the standard front discs and rear drums. The brakes would work adequately until they overheated; then they would have to be stroked gently until they came back, partially or entirely. It was not the aggressive setup needed to win races. After Sebring, Bridgehampton was the venue for more testing.

Meanwhile the Trans-Am series continued. The next race, the Green Valley 300, was held on April 16 in Smithfield, Texas. The Green Valley circuit, a tight 1.6-mile track, was on land owned by local dairy farmer William McLure. Dan Gurney won for Bud Moore in the Mercury Cougar over teammate Parnelli Jones by a margin of three feet. The nearly four-hour-long event is remembered as one of the most brutally hot and humid races anywhere. Gurney later said it was the most physically difficult race of his career. Mark drove a strong and steady race to bring the Camaro home fourth, albeit six laps down. The Camaro was running Sebring gear ratios that didn't suit the very short straights at Green Valley. The Mustangs were fast, with Dick Thompson finishing third and setting fastest lap. His teammate Jerry Titus had an extraordinary race, coming from 28th on the grid after a practice-day rollover to lead the race after only three laps. Titus was eventually overcome by the heat and delayed sufficiently to finish fifth on the same lap as Mark. In only its third Trans-Am appearance the Camaro clearly wasn't up to speed with the Cougars and Mustangs, but Mark's steady drives had Chevrolet tied with Mercury at 15 points for second place in the Manufacturers Championship. Ford led by just one point with 16.

The lack of the right gear ratios in the Camaro illustrates the still-nascent status of the Trans-Am program for Team Penske, particularly in comparison to the well-financed and -equipped Mercury and Ford operations. Ford and Mercury were factory teams with enormous resources and experience. Penske Racing was a truly private effort with, at this juncture, only modest assistance from GM engineering. It's likely that the Ford teams didn't know the correct ratios either until they arrived at Green Valley, but they had the resources to stock all types of ratios in the transporter, ready and waiting if changes were needed. The other complications included Mark's other commitments: He was still living on Long Island, far from the day-to-day operations, and he was still involved with the Ford Le Mans program.

CHAPTER 61:
Mark and Twiggy in Victory Lane

By April nearly five months had elapsed since the Group 7 Sunoco Lola had last seen action, but now the team had three races on consecutive weekends. For the first event in the eight-race 1967 USRRC, Karl Kainhofer and Peter Reinhart towed the team's new Lola Mk III as a rolling chassis to Stardust Raceway in Las Vegas, while Traco freighted the 359ci Chevy race engine from their shop in Culver City, California. Although the team stayed at the Stardust Hotel, the race car was headquartered at the Desert Inn golf shop. Frank Catania, a friend of the Penske team through his relationship with George Bignotti, owned the golf shop, which featured a spotless and well-equipped maintenance shed behind it next to the hotel. Howard Hughes had lived on the ninth floor of the hotel for many years, and in 1966 had purchased the famous resort for seven million dollars. Hughes had some interest in racing, and made his last appearance in public at Watkins Glen in 1961 for the United States Grand Prix.

Sun Oil engineer Jerry Kroninger was attending his first race, and Mark picked him up at the airport in a rental station wagon. It was Jerry's first experience riding with Mark on public roads, and it taught him to avoid those situations whenever possible in the future. "I think Mark had more confidence in other drivers on the road than was warranted. He was always great to be with and I would jump at any opportunity to ride with him in the race car. But I was uncomfortable with him on the highway." This was not a universally held view. Master fabricator Ron Fournier, who was soon to join the team, rode many miles with Mark in varied circumstances and was completely at ease, finding him remarkably alert and in control. "You never worried with Mark driving; I always felt totally secure. He was awesome."

The previous fall's inaugural Can-Am series had shown teams and drivers what it would take to succeed in Group 7 racing. The entries had been enormous, often requiring a consolation race to determine who would start in the main race, but those days were already over. The boundless enthusiasm and optimism for the category was tempered with the realization that rapidly developing technology and the expense that went along with it was polarizing the field between the haves and have-nots. Though entries were down in 1967, there were still plenty of quality teams to provide a full grid.

The three West Coast USRRC races quickly established that the best of those teams was Penske Racing, and that the Sunoco Special Lola T70 with Mark Donohue at the wheel was ready to pursue the 1967 United States Road Racing Championship. Fewer cars were powered by Ford in the 1967 season because teams and drivers without factory support realized that the Chevy engine in its various derivatives and displacements was less expensive to develop for racing. More independent speed shops were working with the small-block Chevy engine than were working with the Ford.

At Stardust Sam Posey qualified his McLaren on pole position, with George Follmer's Lola and Skip Scott's McLaren next. Mark was fourth on the grid, followed by Peter Revson and Chuck Parsons. Revson, a Goodyear-contracted driver, was with the Dana Chevrolet team out of South Gate, California. The two-car team was heavily supported by the tire company and managed by Peyton Cramer. Before becoming a principal in Dana Chevrolet, Cramer had been general manager of Shelby American. Revson's teammate Bob Bondurant did not start the race after his car was damaged when he became caught up on a high-speed bend in oil dumped by Australian Frank Matich's Matich-Olds. Defending USRRC champion Chuck Parsons was racing independently, having purchased the McLaren from Randy and John Hilton, who now were sponsoring a Mustang in the Trans-Am for Scooter Patrick.

At Stardust Mark and George Follmer broke away best at the start. When George went off course in the last corner and caught a stone in his oil cooler, Mark was in the lead at the end of lap one. Race officials were blamed for not warning the drivers that a preliminary race had left the turn well oiled and still slippery. "They just didn't tell us about it," Mark told Leon Mandel for *AutoWeek*. "Had I been first into the turn I probably would have done the same thing as George."

With Follmer gone, Mark and the Sunoco Special simply motored away and were never threatened. Sam Posey recovered from a terrible start to finish second, with Bill Eve in a Lola third. Lothar Motschenbacher had looked set for second place in his McLaren but had engine trouble and struggled home fourth. Mark's win appeared easy, but the engine block split at the very end of the race. The entire weekend, in fact, had been more difficult than was apparent to most observers. The new engine and new chassis had not been tested, and Mark spun several times during practice as he sought the right handling setup. Development on the Lola at this time was primarily focused on finding the ideal rear anti-rollbar size. "George Follmer was putting great big anti-rollbars on the rear of his Lola, so we copied it, and we went faster too," Mark later revealed.

The Stardust organization had worked to upgrade the two-year-old facility with landscaping, a new tower, and improved toilets. The crowd, however, was disappointingly small, and the organizers could only hope for improvement in the fall with the Can-Am.

At Riverside for round two, the organizers reverted to the shorter 2.6-mile version of the circuit. George Follmer was fast qualifier, with Mark second. Just as at Las Vegas, George and Mark broke away, and it wasn't until the fourth lap that Mark took the lead, as Follmer struggled with a transmission that kept popping out of gear. Mark soon established a comfortable six-second lead, and the two cars held that position until George's Chevy engine lost oil pressure and he was out. After the race Mark told the media that Follmer was a continual threat. "Until George went out, it was quite a strain. All it would have taken was one slip in traffic and he would have been by." Bondurant and Revson were second and third for Dana Chevrolet and Motschenbacher was fourth.

In the victory circle Mark was joined by Twiggy—Leslie Hornby—the waiflike British fashion model and media sensation, who was accompanied by an entourage. She was at the race as a guest of Carroll Shelby. Unkind onlookers could not resist comparing Twiggy to the voluptuous Linda Vaughn, a familiar presence at NASCAR and drag-racing ceremonies.

Creating as much news as Mark's win, and even Twiggy's appearance, was the non-start of Masten Gregory. The veteran Gregory—one of the most naturally talented drivers to ever sit in a race car and a pioneer in the 1950s for American drivers in Europe—was contracted to drive for Chicago-based Carl Haas in the Simoniz Wax-sponsored McLaren. Gregory was living in Paris, and when he arrived in California, he failed to accurately note the time change. On race day he arrived at the track after the race had started. Charlie Hayes was working for Haas and remembers that fifteen minutes before the start and with the car on the grid, Carl realized

Masten was not going to arrive on time. "Carl said, 'Charlie, get your helmet, you're driving,'" Charlie recalls. "I was all for it, but I literally couldn't fit my six-foot-three frame into the cockpit that was set up for Masten, who was at least seven inches shorter. It was a frustrating moment for both Carl and myself—I had the previous year set a qualifying record in the race. I really wanted to drive that car." Haas was understandably furious.

For Laguna Seca on May 7, Karl and Peter fitted the Lola with a new transmission and engine, as well as a modified front spoiler that worked well on the ups and downs of the 1.9-mile circuit. After qualifying, Follmer at 1:06.2 and Motschenbacher at 1:07.0 were on the front row, and Mark's time of 1:07.2 was equaled by Peter Revson to place them on row two. Much was made in the media about Mark seldom qualifying fastest, but Karl Kainhofer offers the best perspective: "Mark was very fast. Some may have been faster. But it was just not the Penske team's way to focus on a fast qualifying time. It was all about being prepared to win the race, and Mark played a big role in emphasizing that approach." Bill Preston recalls that Roger specifically counseled against risking wrecking the car or blowing an engine to achieve pole position, saying, "They don't pay any money for qualifying. What counts is where you finish on Sunday."

It looked like another Mark runaway as he powered the Sunoco Special into an immediate lead from the second row of the grid. Mark was 40 seconds ahead of second-place Motschenbacher, with only 20 of the race's 80 laps to go when he encountered fuel starvation. The right-side tank wasn't drawing properly, so he headed to the pits to refuel. When he returned to the race he was in second place, and the stop ultimately cost him a third consecutive win. Mark had to stop again for fuel with just a few laps remaining, which allowed Mike Goth's Lola into second place. Mark salvaged third place, with John Cannon and Skip Barber fourth and fifth in McLarens. Lothar Motschenbacher won the race in his McLaren.

The healthy crowd at Laguna Seca was a sharp contrast to the disappointing turnouts at Riverside and Las Vegas. It remained to be seen whether two separate Group 7 series could provide race organizers with two healthy race dates. Not all tracks had races in both series, and those without a Can-Am date were happy to have a round of the USRRC. Low attendance wasn't necessarily a reflection of the series' popularity. Promotion for the Las Vegas and Riverside races had been extremely poor.

All of the teams now had two weeks to recover from the three-races-in-three-weeks grind on the West Coast, and to make the long haul east to Bridgehampton. Back in Newtown Square great things were being achieved by a small group of individuals. It was typical for Mark, Karl, Peter, Scotty, Bill, and other team members to sit on the garage floor and toss out suggestions for improving performance. "Anyone could make a suggestion. If experience or logic did not rule the idea out, the team would try to implement it for the next race. This was nearly completely democratic," Bill Preston recalls.

An excellent crowd turned up at Bridgehampton on May 21 despite cool and overcast weather. George Follmer was the fast qualifier for the third time in four races with a time of 1:32.6. His average speed of 110.8 mph illustrated how fast this extremely difficult and bumpy circuit was. Motschenbacher was second with a 1:33.8, and Mark third with a 1:34.2, sharing the second row with Bondurant at 1:34.5. It was a tight grid with Revson next at 1:35.0, followed by Posey at 35.2, Mike Goth at 35.8, and Masten Gregory at 36.4. It was the first time in the series that pole position had been captured with a time faster than that seen at the previous fall's Can-Am, which spoke well for the quality of the entry.

Competitive as the grid was, Mark once again demonstrated the command he had shown in the three previous races. He was second by lap two, and Mark and George provided the greatest excitement of the race as they ran together well clear of the rest of the field. Mark took the lead by slipstreaming past George on the long pit straightaway before the downhill. The close dice continued until George spun in Echo Valley and was unable to restart the Lola. He lost several laps and ultimately finished ninth. Prior to the spin Sam Posey had flipped in his McLaren, and Mark was impressed by Follmer's reaction. "If there were a sportsmanship award it should go to George Follmer," Mark later told the press. "When Posey flipped and the ambulance was on the course I backed off a bit in an area where I didn't have to—there were no flags displayed—and George went by me. A few seconds later he backed off and motioned me back into the lead and we started racing again. I'm not too sure I would have done the same."

"It was only fair," remembers George. "I was close behind Mark and did not see the yellow flag until I was by him. I had passed under the yellow—it wasn't a legitimate pass—so I waved him back by."

The 70-lap, 200-mile race was one of attrition, and Mark sailed on ahead while others fell by the wayside. The Sunoco Special took the checkered flag four full laps ahead of second-place Masten Gregory. That result did not salvage the colorful veteran driver's seat in the Haas McLaren. With the USRRC season now half over and a month before the next race, Haas took the opportunity to find a new driver.

CHAPTER 62:

Chasing the Cougars and Mustangs

The Trans-Am had taken off and was one of the hottest items in racing. The media, spectators, and particularly the automotive industry could not get enough of it. Every track wanted a race, and those without a Trans-Am series date were organizing races for the category anyway. It was nominally an endurance series, but the races were being contested as flat-out sprints. To be competitive the top cars had to be driven very close to their top lap times from start to finish. Unlike pure race cars and prototypes, the Trans-Am sedans could take the punishment because they were inherently "overengineered," having been originally designed as street cars intended to last for many years, and miles. Even when modified for racing, the Trans-Am sedans could be driven close to their limit for hours on end.

On Memorial Day, May 30, Lime Rock Park, under the management of racer Jim Haynes, held its first SCCA-sanctioned professional event: round four of the Trans-Am series. The Indianapolis 500 the same day drew away Parnelli Jones and Dan Gurney from the Mercury Cougar team, opening seats for Peter Revson and Ed Leslie. Leslie put his car on the pole and Revson was on the outside of the front row, with Shelby Mustang team leader Jerry Titus in the middle. While Titus grabbed an early lead off the start, teammates Dick Thompson and Bob Johnson had incidents while trying to squeeze between the Cougars from row two, immediately eliminating Johnson and eventually putting Thompson out.

Mark had said before the race that he was just hoping for a high finish. The handling still wasn't there on the Camaro. Mark was not one of the fastest runners on this day, but he overcame a bad start to finish second in the four-hour race. Revson had trailed Titus for more than half the race, and when the Mustang pitted to change a fan belt, he took the lead and won by two laps from Mark. Titus was third, on the same lap as Mark. There was no Drivers championship in the early years of the Trans-Am, and the Manufacturers Championship was everything. Mark had kept Chevrolet close.

Jim Russell and Greg Pierson had driven to Lime Rock in Jim's new 427 Cougar to see the race. Mark was eager to see the Cougar, and had pulled strings with Ford's Jacques Passino for his friend to obtain an early one. Jim's 427 was the fifth unit of the much-in-demand model to come off the production line. After the race, Mark, in his Cadillac convertible, drove his boyhood friends to the spot in the now mostly deserted parking lot where the special Cougar was parked. When Mark spotted the car he accelerated hard, and then threw the Cadillac into a broadside slide, stopping just feet away alongside the new Cougar. Once again Mark had achieved the desired effect.

Two weeks later came round five of the Trans-Am at Mid-Ohio. Mark had a conflict with his commitment to Ford at Le Mans, so Roger put George Follmer in the Camaro. It was the first of many times that George would be part of the Penske team. NASCAR star David Pearson qualified the Cougar on pole but led only the first lap as Jerry Titus brought Mustang back to victory lane with Pearson second and Follmer third in the Camaro. "It was my first time racing with the Penske operation," remembers George. "We had some trouble toward the end of the race with the shims falling out of the front end, and I had a camber change in every corner." Mercury now led the Championship points table with 30 points ahead of Ford with 29 and Chevrolet with 25. Immediately after the race the Camaro went to Detroit where Mark would join it for testing at the General Motors proving grounds upon his return from Le Mans.

CHAPTER 63:
With Bruce at Le Mans

The Ford presence at Le Mans in 1967 exceeded even the impressive display of the winning effort the previous year. It was an organizational and logistical achievement of major proportions, as Ford brought cars, equipment, and personnel to the Sarthe circuit in unprecedented numbers: 14 drivers along with their wives were supported by 19 men from Shelby American and 27 more from Holman-Moody.

This number did not include 20 additional support people for timing, scoring, and signaling, or the 34 executives from Ford Motor Company. The team had taken over most of the local Peugeot dealership and had equipped it with their own comforts, including coffee and Coca-Cola machines and water brought along from home. In *Hawkeye* Paul Hawkins summed it up this way: "They even had their own toilet paper specially brought over from the States. We were looked after like kings—the best hotels in Le Mans, special caterers at the circuit, and caravans for us to sleep in out there."

The importance of being part of the Ford team was not lost on Mark, who said, "Imagine how prestigious it was for me, what an honor I felt to be driving on a team with all this equipment, all these engines, all these transmissions, engineers, team managers, caterers, butlers—it was just larger than life."

Mark and Sue arrived together on Tuesday after visits to Amsterdam and Paris. Sue recalls this as a happy time: "Racing was fun. Going to the track with Dee Ann Andretti and some of the other driver's wives, we all had a great time together." Practice began on Wednesday, and Mark quickly immersed himself in the activities. Although Mark had always been part of the Holman-Moody team, he was now assigned to the Shelby operation, paired with Bruce McLaren in a Mk IV. "I was shuffled to Shelby's team," Mark later recalled. "It didn't matter as far as Ford was concerned, because the paycheck always came from the same place, but there was a lot of subsurface rivalry between the two teams."

Indeed, the rivalry between the two Ford race teams was strong and sometimes bitter, but it was not uncommon for Ford-contracted drivers to be moved between teams to suit a particular need or to create a favorable driver match. Mark came to realize that the assignment was good for his career in the long term, as he formed a relationship with the engineers and other personnel at Shelby. Shelby was running another Mk IV for Dan Gurney and A. J. Foyt. Mark's friend and 1966 co-driver Paul Hawkins, who had scored a great win the previous month in the Targa Florio for Porsche, was sharing a Mk IIB with Ronnie Bucknum. The Holman-Moody Mk IVs were for Mario Andretti / Lucien Bianchi and Lloyd Ruby / Denis Hulme. The Holman-Moody Mk IIB was driven by Frank Gardner and Roger McCluskey. There was also a single Mk IIB for Ford France's Jo Schlesser and Guy Ligier. The team was completed by reserve drivers Skip Scott and Peter Revson.

Practice brought its challenges, especially for McCluskey,

Foyt, and Ruby, who were seeing the difficult 8.38-mile circuit for the first time. McCluskey, the newest member of the team, was brought in to replace Richie Ginther, who had unexpectedly announced his retirement from driving at Indianapolis just three weeks earlier. McCluskey faced the additional challenge of having never previously driven a Ford GT, even in testing. Ford, in a misplaced belief that oval-track drivers were more professional than road racers, had decided to replace Peter Revson and Skip Scott for Le Mans with McCluskey and the other oval drivers. Like Mario Andretti, these drivers were primarily oval racers, and the adjustment to a long and difficult road course would draw deeply upon that professionalism. It was a mistake for which Ford would pay a high price during the race itself.

Mark did not sense a great deal of warmth from Bruce McLaren, later saying, "I didn't know Bruce at all then. . . . Bruce obviously didn't know anything about me either, because he didn't seem very happy about being teamed with me." As an established Grand Prix star and the winner of the race for Ford the previous year, Bruce called the shots on the car setup and shared few of the details with Mark. He qualified the yellow No. 2 car on the pole and did it in spectacular style during night practice. The car reached 215 mph on the Mulsanne straight, achieving a lap of 3:24.2, and a 147.316 mph average for the 8.14-mile circuit. Bruce also was asked by Dan Gurney to practice the car he was co-driving with A. J. Foyt, and that car was also set up to Bruce's specifications.

Ferrari and Chaparral again provided the main competition. Chaparral brought two of the latest 2F model, and the lead car was driven by Phil Hill and Mike Spence. Unlike Ford, which had only run Daytona and Sebring prior to Le Mans, the small team from Texas had been in Europe all spring, contesting the championship rounds at Monza, Spa, the Targa Florio, and the Nürburgring. Their perseverance was to be rewarded by victory at Brands Hatch the month after Le Mans.

Ferrari matched Ford with seven top-line cars, three of which were P4s. The Ford–Ferrari rivalry remained intense. Enzo Ferrari had vowed to beat the American team this year after Ford broke Ferrari's long dominance at Le Mans in 1966.

Ronnie Bucknum led the first lap and the first hour of the race in the Mk IIB until slowed by a fractured water pipe. The Chaparral led briefly, but by the third hour the red Gurney/Foyt No. 1 Mk IV was in the lead. Mark and

Bruce maintained a steady position in third or fourth, and were a strong third when the clutch failed at 2:00 a.m. The half-hour-long repair in the pits cost them any realistic hope of winning, but they were still running strongly in fifth place when near disaster struck at 8:00 a.m.: A latch came undone and the rear bodywork flew off the car at over 200 mph on the Mulsanne straight, with McLaren at the wheel.

"It seemed as if everything was happening to Bruce," Mark later said. "He had the rear body section fly off on him as it had on me the year before, only this time it got smashed up a lot worse, and by the end of the race it was half tape." Bruce, like Mark the year before, was sent out in the race car with duct tape, bungee cords, and pliers to find the missing body section and bring it back to the pit. While the mechanics were making repairs, A. J. Foyt made a scheduled pit stop in the race-leading Mk IV. According to author and driver Leo Levine, Foyt was stunned at the sight of the yellow car in the adjacent pit: "Man, I saw that yellow rear end laying back there and I thought 'My God, where's the rest of that car!' It really shook me up, I'll tell you."

By then the Ford strength was greatly depleted. Just before the halfway point in the race—between 3:00 and 4:00 a.m.— three team cars were eliminated within a matter of seconds. Andretti had taken over the second-place car from Bianchi and new brake pads had been fitted. At more than 150 mph Mario began to slow for the approach to the Esses when one front brake locked, throwing the car into a wild spin. The car bounced off the wall on both sides of the track and came apart on impact. Pieces of the Ford were scattered over the track, with Mario in the driver compartment in the middle of the road. Two cars managed to slip by as Mario hastened to exit the car. He was just safely clear and had collapsed on the side of the road, badly bruised and in shock, when Roger McCluskey came over the rise. Fearing that the driver might still be in the car, McCluskey chose to put his Ford into the wall rather than risk injuring or killing another driver. Jo Schlesser in the Ford France Mk II was the next car on the scene, and he also crashed while attempting to miss the two wrecked cars. Just as quickly as that, three of the seven Fords were eliminated.

It was left to Dan Gurney and A. J. Foyt to win the race for Ford, and they did it with a steady and disciplined drive at a record average speed of 135 mph. The two notoriously hard-charging drivers had managed to temper their desire to be the fastest in order to be the winners instead. It was a great win for Dan, who had suffered many previous disappointments at the great race, and equally so for A. J., who had won in his first appearance. Just two weeks earlier Foyt had taken the third of what would become four Indianapolis 500 victories. He had now won the two greatest races in the world. Dan was just a week away from achieving a double of equal historic importance: On June 18, on the great Spa-Francorchamps circuit, he won the Belgian Grand Prix in his Eagle, becoming the only American to win a Formula One Grand Prix in a car of his own construction.

Mark and Sue arrived home from Europe to learn that a buyer had been found for their house on Long Island. The terms of sale required that they move out in just a week. With David just six months old and Michael barely three years, the bulk of the arrangements were left to Sue as Mark was off to test the Camaro. Sue had to get the household packed and moved to the new house at 3002 North Providence Road in Media, Pennsylvania. As the pace of Mark's career picked up, Sue was increasingly without the benefit of Mark's presence at home. Mark was aware of this, noting to *Road & Track*'s Al Bochroch: "Sue's really great about my racing. When she married me she knew I wanted to race but neither of us realized I would be doing it full time."

"Sue and Mark's new home in Media was a really neat, stone farmhouse with a beautiful winding road leading to it," recalls Ron Fournier. "My wife Sue and I were new to the area and so were the Donohues, and we became great friends. What little we socialized was with them. We had no children at the time and they had the two little boys."

At the General Motors Proving Ground where the Camaro had been delivered direct from Mid-Ohio, Mark had access to the skid pad and the enthusiastic cooperation of top GM engineers. The car was instrumented for data acquisition, and, in addition to the skid pad, other parts of the facility were utilized. Mark learned a great deal about how GM operated and the potential their resources represented. He also realized that while the engineers could help identify what the car was doing and accurately measure drag, lift, and other parameters, they were not equipped to tell him what to do about it. Mark was later to say that he realized, "All right, now I have to decide for myself what to do." The GM engineers learned a great deal about the unique needs of a race car. This shared knowledge would come into play as the season progressed.

CHAPTER 64:
The Psychological Barrier

Living in Media just down the road from the shop in Newtown Square seemed the ideal arrangement for Mark, with his young family and growing responsibilities at Penske Racing. The short commute replaced the back-and-forth to Long Island some 170 miles away, and promised more time with the family and easier access to the shop. But this seemingly ideal arrangement was to prove a very different reality for Sue and Mark's family life. Being so close to the race shop meant that Mark spent even more time there and less at home with his family. It was only with the move to Media that Mark began to have an impact on the day-to-day operations of Penske Racing. As he took to his new and expanded role with the race team, his hours at the shop expanded dramatically.

After four rounds of the USRRC in the span of a month, there had been a full month between Bridgehampton and the next race at Watkins Glen on June 25. The 20th annual Watkins Glen Grand Prix was a return for Mark to the site of his enormous crash the year before. In practice and qualifying, Sam Posey and Lothar Motschenbacher had vied for pole position, and late in the final session Sam seemed to have it cinched with a 1:13.9 to Lothar's 1:14.2. The track had become extremely oily and slippery, and Lothar was persuaded not to try for a faster time, as all along the pit lane the teams were convinced that a fast time was now impossible on the high-speed circuit. Bob Kovacik, reporting for *Sports Car Graphic*, heard Roger Penske say to Mark, "I know it's slippery out there, Mark, but try to do it." And Mark did. In the last minutes of the session he turned a 1:13.7 to win the pole. Posey and Motschenbacher were second and third, and Chuck Parsons fourth in a new ride. Carl Haas had hired Chuck to drive the Simoniz-sponsored McLaren-Chevy after dropping Masten Gregory. Despite this episode Carl Haas held no grudge against Masten. They remained close friends, and Carl later provided major support during a difficult period in Gregory's life.

As Mark became more well known, it was less common for reporters and statisticians to misspell his name by substituting an *a* for the second *o*. Even so, someone should have briefed the uniform maker. At Watkins Glen Mark's white Nomex driver's suit was clearly embroidered in script as *Mark Donahue*.

Sam Posey pursued Mark aggressively in the early laps, staying just a car length behind until they encountered lapped traffic, when Mark opened a gap that he would extend throughout the race. Sam actually led for one lap when he made a great restart after a mammoth accident by Bob Bondurant.

Mark and the Penske team had, even at this early page in their history, achieved a certain status and reputation within American sports-car racing that seemed to defeat teams even before the race started. Sam Posey described it as ". . . some kind of psychological barrier." The cool approach personified by Mark and Roger, the extreme level of preparation evident in the highly detailed and beautifully turned-out race car and support vehicles, and the implied connection with insiders at General Motors all conspired to create an aura that said "This is the team to beat." The reality of the GM connection was that little or no technical data, and certainly no financial support, flowed between Detroit and Newtown Square. There was some technical feedback for the Trans Am team, but nothing for the Group 7 car. The Penske Team managed a presentation at the circuit that belied the very small operation it actually was. None of this would have meant a thing if they hadn't been winning races.

Mark won the race in front of the biggest crowd for any race in the series. In the victory circle he received a kiss and was presented the laurel wreath by Miss New York State. Mark finished a full minute ahead of Sam Posey, while Skip Barber was impressive in finishing third in his McLaren. Don Morin, who had won the SCCA National Championship the previous year in Formula B, was fourth. Motschenbacher fell back early in the race, hampered by a broken seat, and was fifth. Bob Bondurant suffered a career-ending crash of mammoth proportions when he lost the Dana Chevrolet Lola at 150 mph near the exit of the esses, just past where Mark had crashed the previous year. The Lola flipped end over end and both of Bondurant's legs were broken. He also suffered a concussion, fractured ribs, a broken shoulder, and facial cuts and bruises.

Bob Bondurant's crash and subsequent retirement deprived American road racing of one of its greatest drivers. Bondurant was born in Evanston, Illinois, but became famous as a West Coast road racer with a reputation as a smooth and fast Corvette driver. He joined the Shelby American team in 1963 and became internationally known for his exploits in the Cobra that won the World Championship for Manufacturers

for Ford in 1965. He had a factory drive for Ferrari in Formula One at Watkins Glen in 1965, and ran most of the 1966 Grand Prix season in Europe in a privately entered ex-works BRM. The handsome, well-spoken Bondurant was immensely popular and had great technical and analytical insight. Lying in the small Schuyler County hospital in downtown Montour Falls the week after his accident, he said he would now stop racing and act upon his long-held dream to create a racing school. He succeeded admirably in this ambition and is today better known for the Bob Bondurant School of High Performance Driving than for his distinguished career as a driver. When Bondurant left upstate New York to return to California, he did it in style. Dana Chevrolet arranged for four first-class seats on a TWA plane to be taken out and a bed installed for Bob's comfort.

At Kent, Washington, on July 18, Mark won his fifth race of the six rounds and clinched the 1967 United States Road Racing Championship with two races still remaining. Roger Penske, detained by business elsewhere, missed a victory circle celebration enlivened by the presence of Ann Randall, *Playboy* magazine's May centerfold feature.

The race had been another dominant performance for the Sunoco Lola, but with Firestone on strike there were tire worries. The team had only two sets of tires for the weekend, and when the race set was fitted they were found to be out of round. There was no alternative but to fit the used practice tires. Jerry Grant had returned to the series in a Lola T70 Mk III, and on his home track took pole position. Mark was second, and George Follmer filled out the three-car front row. By the third lap Mark was in the lead and was never headed as he won from the Dana Chevrolet duo of Peter Revson and Lothar Motschenbacher, who had taken over the second Dana team car after Bob Bondurant's retirement. Mark lapped the entire field, and later celebrated with a bottle of champagne as he told the assembled media that the dominant victory was only made possible by Roger's absence. "If Roger had been here he would have slowed me down after I got a good lead," Mark told *AutoWeek*'s Bill Sendelback. "But I wanted to lap the field and I wanted to push the car throughout just to prove it could take it." Mark explained to *Sport Car Graphic*'s Bob Kovacik, "Roger always wants to win at the slowest possible speed." The comments belied the smoothness of Mark's drive. He was fast but deliberate, and made the right choices in traffic situations. Despite punctures for several other cars that picked up debris from an early race collision, the practice tires on the Lola never gave trouble.

Second-place finisher Peter Revson was headed to Hawaii after the race to watch the finish of the Transpacific yacht race. Peter invited Mark to join him, but Mark had to decline. "Penske would never let me do something like that," Mark told the *Seattle Times*'s Walt Parietti. The comment reflects the relationship between Roger and Mark. While they enjoyed a genuine friendship, it was a big brother to little brother relationship—particularly since Roger was Mark's employer. And although he had not mentioned it to Parietti, there was another good reason not to join carefree bachelor Peter on a spur-of-the-moment trip: Mark was a married man, already finding precious little time to be home with Sue and their two sons.

With two rounds of the USRRC to go, the Penske team, as they had the previous year, declined to go to Road America for the 500-mile race. Instead, Karl and Peter towed the Lola down the coast to Riverside to test tires for Firestone and prepare for the upcoming Can-Am. Mark was enjoying the opportunity to log a lot of laps on the circuit until a brake failure put him off the road and through the catch fencing at turn seven. Mark was unhurt and Karl was quickly on the scene. After a quick assessment of the car he told Mark, "I'm glad you didn't make a mistake." The incident gave Mark a fresh appreciation for Karl's character, as he realized that Karl was being completely candid in assuming blame for the accident while being protective of Mark as a friend. It was a revealing moment that Mark would frequently revisit. Mark came to see Karl as virtually infallible professionally as well as a loyal friend. The Lola, although extensively damaged, was rebuilt around the same tub.

CHAPTER 65:
The Captain and Captain Nice

By mid-1967 Mark had attained star status. The Martini & Rossi Trophy was a well-publicized racing fixture whose organizers polled members of the motorsports press on a quarterly basis before presenting the American Driver of the Year award—and a check for $7,500—at season's end. The second-quarter poll found Mark ranked second in the balloting behind only A. J. Foyt. Mario Andretti had won the first quarter (and would at year's end be the award

winner), and others receiving votes included Richard Petty, Dick Hutcherson, and Bobby Unser. Mark's face was featured in full-page ads from Sunoco in virtually every motoring publication in America. He was a media darling, and it was that summer that he was first dubbed Captain Nice.

"Captain Nice" was not a name ever used in addressing Mark. It was a media creation, possibly coined by John Hearst Jr., a prominent motorsports journalist and a member of the Hearst publishing family. The moniker gained popular usage as a supposed insider's way to refer to Mark. The simpler title of "Captain" was reserved exclusively for Roger Penske. Most members of the team, including Mark, informally addressed Roger as Captain, and referred to him as "the captain." That original core group still calls him by that name to this day. Bill Scott is credited with beginning the practice in the very early days of Roger's racing. The working press picked up on this, and the newer reference to Mark as Captain Nice juxtaposed the two personalities. Roger had a reputation for not suffering fools gladly, while Mark suffered many of them—if not gladly, at least politely.

With the crew Roger was the unquestioned leader. There was respect and a great deal more. The Captain could motivate and extract tremendous effort from those around him, while still maintaining a genuine bond. He was demanding but reasonable. Karl Kainhofer explained it at the time to *Road & Track*'s Al Bochroch: "Roger is two steps ahead of you. He's always trying to improve on what you think is perfect. But he will also listen to you and change things in a second if he thinks your idea is better."

Mark, too, appreciated Roger's unique qualities, telling Bochroch, "Roger expects your best, but you could not drive for a more understanding guy. He's hard but he knows what's going on, and he can tell you more from the pits than anyone I've seen."

While Karl started the long haul home from the West Coast with the wrecked Lola, Mark and the Trans-Am team had back-to-back races on the East Coast. With George Follmer having filled in at Mid-Ohio while Mark was at Le Mans, it had been more than two months since Mark's last race in the Camaro. Mark was never a factor on the familiar Bryar Motorsports Park course in New Hampshire on August 6, suffering a long delay in the pits with wet electrics. On the 93rd lap the left rear axle broke as Mark entered a diving corner. The back of the Camaro bounced into the air and the car spun out of the race. The same thing had happened the day before in practice and had pitched the car violently into a guardrail.

Peter Revson's commitment to the sport and dedicated professionalism were never more apparent, as he drove a well-judged race in the pouring rain, winning for Mercury. His younger brother Doug had died just one week earlier in a Formula 3 race in Denmark at the Djürsland Ring circuit. The accident also claimed the life of track owner Jens-Christian Legarth, who was struck by Revson's car. Douglas Martin Revson, 26, with his spirit and sense of fun, was mourned by the racing fraternity. Sam Posey recalls the essential difference between the brothers. "Doug was charismatic—women were more likely to be attracted to him than to Peter. It wasn't that he was a great deal more handsome; it was just that Doug was so relaxed and fun to be with. Peter was, by comparison, pretty tightly wound." Their sister Jennifer Revson agrees with Posey's appraisal: "They were completely different personalities. Peter was reserved and somewhat conservative—Doug was far more of a daredevil."

The Sunoco Lola was king of the sports-racer world, but the Camaro had yet to win a race. The series was now half over, and Mercury led with 39 points to Ford's 35, while Chevrolet lagged behind at 28.

CHAPTER 66:
The Big Garage in the Sky

With the race at Marlboro, Maryland, coming up the following weekend, the next few days produced hectic development on the Camaro. The car's handling had been terrible all season, and now the axle breakages generated significant assistance from General Motors Research. Unlike the Group 7 program, General Motors was prepared to provide technical support for the Trans-Am, albeit with as much cover as possible. Mark and Roy Gane were at Marlboro early in the week, where they were joined by GM engineer Jim Musser. Musser arrived with a technician and a special tool truck from Research and Development that Paul Van Valkenburgh described in his book, *Chevrolet = Racing?* as "... equipped with everything! Air compressor, arc welder, gas welder, 110-volt generator, engine hoist, floor jacks, dozens of electric and pneumatic hand tools, drawers of parts, and individual tool chests. And yet, with all the panels closed up, it looked like an old vegetable truck."

Musser had also brought along a huge quantity of springs of different rates. They tested for two days, and by trial and error found the critical spring rates. It was Mark and Roy doing all the wrenching while Musser and the technician stood by and made suggestions. Given GM's official anti-racing stance, it was not deemed appropriate for anyone from the company to be seen actually working on the car. Mark had even taken the precaution of obtaining a set of Pennsylvania license plates that were fitted to the already anonymous-appearing GM truck.

An important addition to Penske Racing was the arrival of Ron Fournier as fabricator. Fournier had worked at Holman-Moody on the Ford GT program, and later with Ford's Kar Kraft operation. Ron was now immersed in the redevelopment of the Camaro.

During that crucial but short week between Bryar and Marlboro, the team accomplished an incredible amount of development and preparation. Back at the shop the car was completely stripped and rebuilt. General Motors had anticipated the need for stronger rear axles and provided replacements that had already been broken in on a dynamometer. Gib Hufstader had supplied sturdier axle shafts and prepared the positraction limited-slip rear axles with extra clutch plates shimmed to prevent slippage. Bill Preston had not realized the extent of GM's involvement in development until he stopped by the race shop in Newtown Square and saw numerous crates containing axles and transmissions. When he asked where they came from, Mark replied, ". . . from the big garage in the sky."

The team also constructed a completely new integral roll cage that substantially stiffened the chassis. Master welder and fabricator Ron Fournier performed the specialized work. He convinced Mark that the roll cage had to be attached to all the upper structural members of the car, tying it all together to add torsional stiffness without sacrificing lightness. The new springs and rear anti-rollbar also dramatically improved the car's handling. The Camaro had always been fast. Now it also handled, and Mark went to Marlboro with high expectations.

The Washington, D.C., region of the SCCA had long supported the track at Upper Marlboro, Maryland, and had pioneered sedan racing in America. The Marlboro 12 Hours had great tradition and attracted international entries. The race had played a key role in bringing sedan racing on road circuits to the forefront. Now the 12-hour event was abandoned to accommodate the Trans-Am format with a Double 300. Two separate races of 300 miles each, the opener for the under-2.0-liter cars and the final for those over 2.0 liters, provided a close approximation of 12 hours of racing on the 1.7-mile circuit, just 15 miles from the nation's capital. This was home ground for both Mark and Roger—a track where they had learned and practiced their craft.

Back in Newtown Square the team worked on modifications through Friday and missed the first day of practice. Mark was under tremendous stress—partly from sleep deprivation, but also because of the pressure he felt to make the Camaro competitive with the Mustangs and Cougars. Along with Roy Gane and Ron Fournier, Mark worked night and day. "We went without sleep for days," Mark later recalled. "We sent out for sandwiches and showered under a hose in the driveway." When they were ready they loaded up, and Mark helped drive the transporter through the night to Marlboro.

When Mark arrived on Saturday everyone in the paddock soon knew it was going to be a new ball game. He put the Camaro on the pole with a 1:32.9. Ed Leslie got the Cougar he would share with Peter Revson on the front row with a 1:33.0, and Shelby Mustangs occupied the second row for Dick Thompson / Ed Lowther and Jerry Titus / Jim Adams. The length of the race had every entry listed with a co-driver, and Mark and Roger chose Craig Fisher. The Canadian driver had been campaigning his own Camaro in the series and had posted excellent results. Bud Moore paired NASCAR stars Lee Roy Yarbrough and Cale Yarborough in the second Mercury Cougar. Mark was impressed with their rapid adaptation to road racing, saying he doubted he could do as well if he tried the Grand National circuit.

Leslie took the lead and Mark followed him closely for two laps before outbraking the Cougar at the end of the main straight. Mark soon began to open a gap and pulled away from the rest of the field as the race progressed. Fisher relieved Mark for an hour in the middle of the race and they built up a lead at one point of three laps over second place. The Camaro was clearly the fastest car on the straight, although it gave away a little to the Cougars and Mustangs on low-end torque. Pit stops were very efficient—the car stopped twice and the total time to change drivers, tires, and add fuel was only a minute and fifteen seconds for both stops combined. It was here that Roger Penske excelled, even with limited experience and personnel. Only one or two of the pit crew were professionals, and the team relied on "weekend warriors"

to cover the myriad needs of a Trans-Am pit stop. These included everything from tire changes and fueling to such minor but important tasks as handing the driver a cup of water. The magic in a Penske pit stop was in its organization and attention to detail.

After 177 laps and 4 hours and 45 minutes of racing, Mark took the checkered flag to achieve the win Chevrolet and Penske Racing had been striving for all year. The independently run Mustang of Clarence Mathews from Fresno, California, driven by Allan Moffat and Milt Minter was second, two laps down and ahead of the factory-supported Shelby Mustang of Jerry Titus / Jim Adams. None of the Cougars finished, and there was a sudden new look to the points table. With 7 of the 12 races now run, Ford had recaptured the lead with 41 points, ahead of Mercury with 39. Chevrolet was now in real contention with 36 points.

It was a busy time. Beginning with the August 6 Trans-Am at Bryar, Mark raced on 11 consecutive weekends. On August 20 at Mid-Ohio, he was back in the Sunoco Lola for the last race in the USRRC, a championship he had clinched at Kent. The Lola T70 Mk IIIB was a completely new car after the testing accident at Riverside. The new Lola was lighter than its predecessor and featured a slightly longer nose. Both the front and rear suspension were altered. A new car is always suspect, and the opportunity to put race miles on it before the Can-Am—now just two weeks off—was welcome. The chassis wasn't all that was new. Karl had fitted the latest weapons in the team's arsenal: a 427ci Chevy from Traco and the latest 5-speed Hewland LG 600 transmission. Mark reported the engine to be "right out of the crate," with only the addition of Webers to help it produce a modest 530 horsepower.

Mark did not appear until late in the first qualifying session at Mid-Ohio and recorded an unremarkable lap. The Lola's windscreen had been destroyed in transit to the race, and Mark was given permission to qualify without it, although the SCCA was clear in stating he could not start the race without one. A replacement was put on a plane in Philadelphia, and Roger's personal pilot, Manny Lynn, drove to the Cleveland airport to pick it up. Lynn was a popular member of the Penske team, and Mark, who always loved a play on words, called him "just plane Manny."

In final qualifying Mark turned a pole-winning lap of 1:33.4, a second and a half faster than the second and third qualifiers. Charlie Hayes in his McKee Cro-Sal Olds and Chuck Parsons in the Simoniz McLaren had turned identical times of 1:35.0. Sam Posey's debut in the new Caldwell during the first qualifying session was beset with development problems. He took over his regular McLaren which was to have been driven by newcomer and teammate Brett Lunger. Lunger's best had been a 1:44.2, while Posey put the car on row three with a time of 1:36.6.

Sam Posey was pursuing the brave course of developing and racing a Group 7 car of original design. Although Ray Caldwell was a successful designer of Formula Vee race cars through his Autodynamics business in Marblehead, Massachusetts, it was a considerable jump into the increasingly sophisticated world of Group 7 racing. Posey was a remarkable individual who approached the sport from the romantic tradition and brought great passion and enthusiasm to the racing scene. Although fascinated by scientific and engineering challenges, he personally was not technically oriented, and his considerable driving skill was largely intuitive. Sam Posey was an artist by inclination and training and graduated from the Gunnery School near his home in Sharon, Connecticut, and from the Rhode Island School of Design. His articulate and engaging interviews enlivened the sport and made him a great media favorite.

Mark dominated the Mid-Ohio race with speeds through the trap in the 154-mph range. His pursuers followed him closely in the early laps until they approached the backmarkers. When other top cars would catch a backmarker at the end of a straight, they would either pass under braking or, more typically, set them up through the corner and pass under acceleration on the exit. Mark never wasted time in this manner; he passed cars whenever and wherever he found them.

Mark's lead suddenly increased dramatically, demonstrating his great skill and what made him special as a driver. Although he lost second gear during the race it did not slow him appreciably. Neither did the Firestones rubbing on the fenders. The latest wider tires had been rejected after practice because they rubbed. The team had reverted to the next size down, but even these rubbed, and at the finish all four fenders had holes above the tires. Sue joined Mark in the Lola for the checkered-flag lap.

Charlie Hayes drove an excellent race in the McKee, keeping the pressure on in second place until running out of gas on the last lap. After the race Hayes told *Sports Car Graphic*'s Bob Kovacik, "That guy flat outdrove me. He's a great driver." When Kovacik repeated what Hayes had said,

Mark's jaw dropped, his eyes popped open in amazement, and he exclaimed, "He did?" Although Mark had achieved stardom in the eyes of many, the notion hadn't worked its way entirely into his own self-perception.

SCCA Nationals star Jerry Hansen, making a rare appearance in a professional race, finished second. Lothar Motschenbacher had a frightening crash in the Dana McLaren when a halfshaft broke. The car flew through the air and overturned after striking a post very close to the spectator area. The fuel cells ruptured but the gas did not ignite. Two teenagers were very slightly hurt when doused with fuel, one spraining an ankle trying to run. Lothar escaped with torn rib ligaments.

The U.S. Championship for the big sports-racers was now complete, and Mark had totally dominated, winning six of the seven races he contested. He scored 58 points compared to the 21, 17, and 13 registered by the second-through fourth-place drivers, Motschenbacher, Posey, and Barber. Celebrations were minimal as the championship had been clinched a full month earlier at Kent. And Mark's spirits were dimmed when he learned that his friend Martin Krinner had been fatally injured in the Watkins Glen 500 on the same day as Mid-Ohio. Just a year before, Mark and Martin had co-driven the Dockery Ford in that race. Krinner's death was uniquely tragic: He had exited his car on the side of the track and was walking to the fence with his back to the track when a Corvette ran off the road and struck him. When the news reached the pits, Bob Dockery called in the team car—driven by Malcolm Starr—and retired on the spot. Bob never attended another race. Mark, too, was deeply affected by Krinner's death. Marty was an experienced and practical engineer who taught Mark a great deal about race-car dynamics.

There was another Trans-Am race before the much-heralded Can-Am, and the team towed west to Castle Rock, Colorado. The 2.85-mile Continental Divide Raceway was hilly and twisty. Mark qualified the Camaro third behind the Mustangs of Milt Minter and Jerry Titus, but this was not to be his day. He initially ran a strong third but was forced to pit early when a gas-tank strap broke open. Later he had a flat tire, and the two unscheduled stops put him well back. Mark persevered to finish eighth overall, but he was fifth in the over-2.0-liter category, enough to give Chevrolet two points. They needed them, as Jerry Titus won the race in the Mustang and Ed Leslie was second in a Cougar. Titus had just resigned as technical editor of *Sports Car Graphic* to focus solely on his racing. While Titus was a talented driver, he was also a natural publicist with a wry appreciation for the media potential of an obscure joke. The Shelby team cars were entered as the Terlingua Racing Team, carrying forward a long-running gag between Titus, Shelby, and other insiders in Ford racing. Terlingua is a ghost town in southwest Texas, and Titus and Shelby had previously named the town as the site of a fictitious race that garnered extensive publicity before editors cottoned on to the joke.

CHAPTER 67:
Orange McLarens

The second edition of the Can-Am had been launched in February with a gala publicity event in New York at the Tavern on the Green in Central Park. Two Can-Am cars were driven briskly through the park roads by Phil Hill and Bruce McLaren behind a police escort. Hill got his foot caught under the brake and spun into the shrubbery. Six months before the first race, this event was designed to keep the Can-Am and sponsor Johnson Wax in the public eye. John Bishop, the SCCA executive director, announced that Road America in Elkhart Lake, Wisconsin, would replace St. Jovite as the season-opener. The Mont Tremblant circuit had been unable to come to agreement with the Montreal Motor Club sanctioning body regarding financial arrangements.

Mark was excited about the challenge represented by the Can-Am. He told Al Bochroch for *Road & Track*, "The Can-Am is the greatest. The USRRC was fine but it was like playing tennis with your wife. When you run with those international guys and they smoke you off, you really try harder."

The beautiful, rolling 4.0-mile Road America circuit with its long straights and square corners was in many ways the ideal venue for Group 7 cars. Despite not being in on the inaugural year of the Can-Am, promoter Clif Tufte became the series' greatest proponent, and many consider the track the spiritual home of the big-banger cars. The entry for the first round in the 1967 series on September 3 was strong, with virtually every team that had contested the just-completed USRRC accounted for, plus the European entries that made the series truly international. Defending champion John Surtees was back with the latest Lola T70 Mk IIIB, and the McLaren team, which had just fallen short in 1966, appeared

with a new look. The team's M6A McLaren cars immediately made obsolete every McLaren customer car. Their color had changed from red to orange, and it was in this unique shade that the team would become the Can-Am's most enduring legend. Bruce McLaren's fellow New Zealander Denis Hulme, who was on his way to becoming the 1967 World Champion for Brabham in Formula One, joined the team in the second car. Can-Am races had a full international listing with the FIA and were carefully scheduled to never conflict with a Formula One date. Although relatively few active Formula One drivers competed in Can-Am, the organizers always hoped for more, and disingenuously promoted the biggest names in Formula One Grand Prix racing as anticipated Can-Am participants.

While Mark's dominant performance in the USRRC had made the Penske team the hope among the American entries, there were two other important American teams that had not participated in the USRRC. Dan Gurney's All American Racers was running just one car for Dan himself. It was the latest Lola T70 Mk IIIB, in this case fitted with a 377ci Ford. The other big team was Chaparral, and they too were running just one car for team principal Jim Hall. The Chaparral 2G was a development of the 2E, essentially based on the earlier car's aluminum chassis. The 2G was powered by an aluminum-block 427ci engine.

The Penske Lolas were identically turned out in Sunoco colors for Mark and George Follmer. Chris Amon had been scheduled for the seat in the second car, but his contract at Ferrari prohibited him from racing for any other team. Mark had not been at all happy with the prospect of Chris joining the team. It wasn't because he was afraid of having a quick driver alongside him; what troubled Mark was the implication that Roger thought Mark couldn't get the job done against the European drivers and needed to bring one into the team in order to win. Mark had a distinct preference for one-car teams, as he believed having two cars spread resources too thin. But Follmer was a choice he could live with, even though he rated George to be a better driver than himself. He believed that George's pure talent could overcome poor handling and consistently get the best out of a car.

Mark was in the T70 IIIB he had debuted at Mid-Ohio, with the 427ci engine and aluminum heads. George's car was the USRRC chassis damaged at the Riverside test day, now rebuilt and fitted with the reliable 365ci Chevy. All Penske engines were built by Traco. Karl Kainhofer headed an expanded corps of five mechanics dedicated to running the two cars. Roger Bailey was crew chief on Follmer's car, assisted by Al Holbert, while Peter Reinhart worked with Karl on Mark's car. Bill Scott remained an important member of the crew.

Bailey, originally from Peterborough, England, had a background in Formula One with Cooper, and was working in the Ford racing program when Roger Penske offered him the job looking after Chris Amon's car. Bailey and Amon were sharing an apartment, and Chris encouraged him to take the job, saying they would have a great time in America doing the Can-Am. It was after Bailey arrived at Newtown Square that Amon had to decline the drive. "I was already in America and wondering if I should stay," remembers Roger. "But by then I had really gotten to like Karl Kainhofer and Mark."

"I had one of the best periods in my racing life that year," Bailey continues. "We had a great time; it was a very cohesive, tightly knit little team and Mark was a real leader. He led by example and that brought out the best in everyone. When we were working, Mark was working." Bailey also remembers Karl as an exceptional individual. "Karl had a great, very dry, sense of humor," says Bailey. "He was a terrific mechanic and just a fine person."

Another American team with a new look was Dana Chevrolet. The California team run by Peyton Cramer had evolved during the USRRC season. After their McLarens had been destroyed, first in the Bondurant crash and then in the Motschenbacher accident, the strong pairing of Peter Revson and Lothar Motschenbacher now drove the latest Lola T70 Mk IIIB.

The Can-Am's under-2.0-liter category had been an important part of Group 7 racing but entries had begun to wane as separate recognition and prize money was no longer paid for the smaller-engined cars. Peter Revson gave the category a boost by honoring his brother Doug, who had been very active in the smaller cars, through the establishment of the Doug Revson Memorial Trophy for the highest-placed under-2.0-liter driver in the series.

McLaren and Hulme quickly established the superiority of the new McLarens. Tires were part of the story, and Bruce was at the circuit early in the week testing the latest Goodyears. The new tires were 2.5 inches wider with a profile one inch lower than the previous version. Goodyear had stolen such a jump on Firestone—still suffering from time lost during a company-wide strike earlier in the summer—that Surtees

switched brands in the middle of the weekend. Bruce with a 2:12.6 and Denny with a 2:12.7 were the fastest qualifiers, almost two seconds quicker than Gurney at 2:14.4. George and Mark were next on the grid, with George a tenth of a second faster at 2:15.7. Mark had experienced oil surge with the 427ci Chevy during first qualifying and had struggled to get into the mid-2:17 range. Karl and Peter replaced the 427ci engine with a 359ci Chevy for the final qualifying, and Mark picked up two seconds to qualify fifth. Chuck Parsons in Carl Haas's Simoniz Lola—winner of the recent Road America 500—was an impressive sixth at 2:16.6, ahead of defending Can-Am champion John Surtees, next at 2:16.9. On the fourth row with Surtees was Peter Revson at 2:17.2, and the fifth row comprised Jim Hall in the Chaparral and Revson's teammate Lothar Motschenbacher at 17.4 and 18.6 respectively. The fastest 19 qualifiers broke the lap record of 2:22.3 that Peter Revson had set just the month before during the Road America 500.

On race day a tremendous crowd witnessed and added to the intense excitement that the thunder of 30 Group 7 cars charging into Road America's first corner produces. Exiting turn 14 and charging up the hill on the start/finish straight at the end of the first lap, the two McLarens were out front with Hulme in the lead. Gurney was a close third followed by Mark, who had passed George in the other team car. Gurney brought the race to the orange McLarens, but pitted briefly after only five laps. After 20 laps the Lola's Hewland gearbox failed and he was out. Surtees moved up aggressively to take third, which became second when McLaren retired with oil system trouble. While Hulme expanded his lead, Surtees in second had opened a nine-second lead on Mark, which he held until mid-race when Mark began to whittle down the gap. By the 40th lap Mark was right on the tail of "Il Grande" John, but as he explained to Charles Fox for *AutoWeek*, "Catching John was one thing, passing him was another. I don't think I could have gotten around him in the time we had left."

Trouble struck five laps later, as Surtees and Mark descended the hill at the end of the long straight at speeds approaching 180 mph. Under heavy braking for the sharp second-gear left turn five, they spotted the McLaren of John Cordts sitting sideways on the exit of the turn. Cordts's engine had blown and he spun in his own oil moments before the battle for second place appeared. Surtees hit the oil first and spun immediately, but was unable to correct his spin for fear of slamming into Cordts's inert car. Mark later said he thought he was going to sail right over the top of John's car, but he managed to dive to the inside of the corner and avoid spinning or making contact. With just five laps to go Mark was now second. He finished there with Surtees recovering to finish third and Jim Hall fourth in the Chaparral, a lap down. Follmer in the second Sunoco Lola had run strong in fifth place until the radiator was punctured by debris on the track. He pitted, and though the radiator was replaced by Karl and Peter in record time, too much time was lost and George finished 18th.

The first round of the Can-Am was over, and the McLaren team had set a new benchmark for what it would take to be competitive. As Mark told Mike Kupper for *AutoWeek*, "They just walked away from us and we thought we were ready. Our car ran as strong at the end as it did at the beginning. We didn't have any problems but we just weren't fast enough." There were two weeks until the next round, a thousand miles east at Bridgehampton.

CHAPTER 68:

"Damn that Penske and his sneaky strategy . . ."

Before Bridgehampton, Mark spent his weekend on the other side of the country in Modesto, California, for the ninth round of the Trans-Am. The race and all that led up to it are remembered as one of the most difficult and frustrating episodes in the Penske team's season.

Mark and Roger now believed that they needed an all-new race car to compete in the Trans-Am. Despite the breakthrough win at Marlboro they knew the competition was still ahead of them in applying the subtle preparation tricks that were needed to consistently run at the front. "If we were going to uphold the honor of Chevrolet, we had to put together something more special than our converted street sedan," Mark later said. The season to date had taught them a great deal about what it took to be competitive, and one of the things they had learned was how to lighten the car. Acid-dipping body parts to thin and lighten the metal was already in general use, and using the same shop that did the dipping for Shelby, the Penske team, with Ron Fournier in the lead role, built a superlight car that incorporated everything they had learned to date. Because the original Camaro had been so well developed, they decided to run a two-car team

for the rest of the season. Craig Fisher and Tom Greatorex were sent to California with the original car on a trailer. In the meantime it was full speed ahead to have the new one ready for Modesto. Progress was slower than expected, and finally the decision was made to air-freight the unfinished car to California and make it race-ready on-site.

Disaster struck on the long tow west when Craig Fisher dozed off at the wheel and the tow truck and trailer went over a cliff outside Reno, Nevada, on Friday evening of race weekend. No one was injured, but the race car was massively damaged and the truck and trailer were a complete loss. Now it became imperative to finish the new car. It was painted and the wiring completed the night before qualifying, but the troubles were not over. The 3.0-mile circuit was a concrete airstrip at the Naval Air Station just two miles outside Crow's Landing, California, 25 miles down the road from Modesto. Not knowing the circuit, the team had chosen a poor rear-end ratio. They had no spare differential, and Mark and Roy quickly realized they were geared all wrong. Mark was slow, and rather than persevere with the wrong setup, he left the track before qualifying was over to find a replacement. The choices were limited on a Saturday afternoon, but Mark did locate another differential and late that evening drove more than 200 miles to retrieve it. On Sunday morning the team replaced the differential, but even that was a struggle. Because the special rear-axle shafts on the car were the only ones they had, the entire rear end had to be disassembled to make the change. In Sunday morning's final qualifying session Mark discovered that he still didn't have a low-enough ratio; the engine would only reach 6,000 rpm on the straight. Mark qualified seventh, more than three seconds slower than the pole time of Jerry Titus in the Mustang.

Titus and his Shelby Terlingua Mustang ran away with the race, and Peter Revson finished second in the Cougar. After all the heartache involved in making the race and using the wrong gearing, Mark did well to finish third. Roger had been concerned about tire wear on the extremely abrasive concrete track, and when forced to concede top speed to the opposition, he and Mark had chosen to run a tactical race. Running a conservative pace to save fuel and tires, the Camaro required only one pit stop compared to three for the other cars. Titus, writing in *AutoWeek*, said: "Damn that Penske and his sneaky strategy to run the race on one stop, and Mark to hold a pace that would save tires." Titus and others had not recognized that the strategy had been forced on Mark and Roger by the wrong gearing. To the outside observer, despite all the strain and troubles, the Penske Trans-Am program appeared under control.

Blair Camp, Mark's boyhood friend from the Jersey shore, was now selling Piper Cubs on the West Coast and had attended the race at Crow's Island. Mark was keen to evaluate the wreckage from the trailer and car that had gone over the cliff outside Reno, and Blair flew him there the morning after the race. The Camaro was severely damaged, but Mark measured the chassis carefully and declared that the car could and must be rebuilt. This was an unpopular choice from the crew's standpoint, but Mark was adamant. He knew how much work had gone into making that car competitive, and he was unwilling to abandon it. The Camaro was taken to an Oakland Chevrolet dealer where Roy Gane did most of the work, assisted by volunteers. Later the car was finished at another Chevy dealership in Seattle. Mark was intimately involved in the rebuild, tracking down the necessary body panels and other parts. He kept the intensity level high enough for the car to be finished in time for the Las Vegas Trans-Am in early October.

CHAPTER 69:

Broken Tracos

For round two of the Can-Am at Bridgehampton, everyone was quicker than they had been in 1966, and the McLarens were fastest of all on the fast and windswept track. Mark and George both used 365ci engines in the Lolas, but George was faster in qualifying. His 1:31.17 had him on the second row alongside Jim Hall in the Chaparral with a 31.02. Mark was in the middle of the third row with a 31.50, slower than Chuck Parsons in the Simoniz McLaren at 31.46, but ahead of John Surtees in the works Lola at 32.08. Denny Hulme and Bruce McLaren were fastest at 29.85 and 30.17 respectively, and were joined on the front row by Dan Gurney in his AAR Lola at 30.85. Gurney was the only fast Ford runner. Mario Andretti, 23rd on the grid with a 36.16, was the next-fastest Ford in the factory-backed Honker II out of the Holman-Moody shop. Despite great hopes, the car hadn't been properly developed and wasn't very good. Its unusual name derived from team leader John Holman, who had been a truck driver as a young man and earned the "Honker" sobriquet for his delight in using its horn. The race car had sponsor Paul

Newman's name painted prominently on the nose, prompting Andretti to famously suggest, "They should put my name on the nose and let Newman drive it." Newman was still several years away from launching his own racing career, one that would distinguish him as a very serious driver.

Mike Spence was making his Can-Am debut for Canadian Eustache Soucy in a McLaren. Spence had never been to Bridgehampton, and knowing Mark's reputation on the difficult circuit, Mike asked Mark to show him the way around. Bill Preston climbed in the backseat of a Chevy Caprice as Mark showed Mike where to place the car for each turn. "Then he sped up and the first thing the poor car did was shed all four wheel covers as we howled around the course," Bill recalls. "Then Mike took over and repeated the performance. When they finished the Chevy had neither tires nor brakes."

Despite being only seventh on the grid, Mark was up to third place at the end of the first lap. George was following closely in fourth behind the two McLarens. Dan Gurney had injector problems right at the start and became a non-factor. Mark, although never close to the leading Hulme and second-place McLaren, maintained a comfortable third through the first half of the race. Then on lap 38 Mark rolled into the pits, the Lola covered in its own oil. The Traco Chevy had broken a piston, thus ending a remarkable run of reliability for the Sunoco Special Lola. It had been more than a year since the Lola had suffered an engine letdown at the USRRC round at Mid-Ohio in August 1966.

Mark's oil caused his teammate to spin, but George recovered to finish a fine third ahead of John Surtees in fourth. Motschenbacher and Parsons in fifth and sixth captured the remaining available points positions. Mike Spence had proved a fast learner, putting the older McLaren in a solid fifth place when the gearbox broke just a few laps after Mark dropped out. Lodovico Scarfiotti's seventh place in the NART Ferrari P3/P4 was a fine effort in a car designed for endurance racing—not to mention one ceding two liters in engine size to most of the field. Scarfiotti's result illustrates the tremendous attrition that affected Can-Am. Only 13 of the 31 starters were running at the finish of the 200-mile, 1 hour and 50 minute race. Can-Am cars were fragile. The highly stressed big V8 engines and the even more stressed chassis were subject to failure even in the hands of the most experienced and professional of the teams.

The next race at Mosport on September 23 was on Saturday, which meant a very short week for the teams to recover from Bridgehampton, tow northwest to Ontario, and begin practice on Thursday. The 2.46-mile Mosport Park circuit was on a par with Bridgehampton for degree of difficulty, and remains a true test of driver ability. Neither Mark Donohue nor George Follmer had much opportunity to demonstrate their considerable talents on this weekend, the worst of the season for Mark. In qualifying on Friday his left rear stub axle sheared and he hit the bank at Moss Corner. Mark had just begun to get up to speed before the accident, and although the damage was minimal he was stuck with a slow time that left him 17th on the grid.

Minutes later George had a more spectacular crash as his Lola took off over one of the crests on the very fast uphill back straight. It hit a light pole and spun back across the track for more than 200 yards. The car at first glance appeared impossible to fix for the race the next day. Roger, always at his best in a crisis, was still in Philadelphia, and immediately went to work finding the right pieces. He phoned George Bignotti, who confirmed that he had a Lola door, side panel, and seat section. Manny Lynn, with Sunoco's Bill Preston on board, never had to shut off the engine of the Piper when Bignotti met them at the Indianapolis airport. Roger also mobilized a truck from Philadelphia, and within 12 hours a spare tail section was at the track.

"Roger woke me up at night," Ron Fournier recalls. "He told me what had happened and told me to come with the parts. Someone from the dealership met me with a pickup and we drove to Mosport. We drove all night and got there just in time. I was able to fix George's tub by putting in a fabricated patch. Karl was amazing. He anticipated what I was going to have to do and when I arrived he had prepared the car for me in a way that I was able to hit the ground running."

Karl, Peter, Scotty, Roger Bailey, and Ron had worked their magic, with Mark and George working alongside them until 2:00 a.m., and both cars made the race start. Mark never emerged from the depths of the pack, and was soon out of the race with a blown head gasket on the 350ci Traco Chevy. George, with a 365ci engine in his repaired Lola, salvaged something for the Penske team with a strong drive into sixth place at the finish.

"Roger was genuinely grateful for the effort I made driving all through the night," recalls Ron. "As a reward he insisted I ride back in the company plane rather than make that long drive."

"Even people in racing can't believe how much drive [Roger] has and how he can instill this drive in so many people," Mark wrote in *The Boys of Indy.* "His capacity for coping with an unforeseen or unusual challenge is extraordinary."

The McLarens were again the class of the field at Mosport. Denny Hulme won his third straight race despite an accident on the next-to-the-last lap caused by a faulty steering box. Hulme struggled home the winner with only three wheels turning—the fourth was stuffed inert in the body and suspension. Teammate McLaren was again the runner-up despite starting nearly half a lap down after a fuel leak forced the team to replace his tank before the start. Bruce spectacularly carved his way through the entire field to make the finish another Team McLaren 1-2, with Mike Spence third in his comparatively ancient McLaren.

The 1967 Can-Am was now half over. Mark had only 6 points, while Hulme led with 27. There were now three weeks until the West Coast half of the series began at Laguna Seca—time for the Penske team to regroup and attempt to turn the tide.

One of the realities of the first half of the series was that two of its most important supporters had suffered major setbacks. The two biggest rivalries in the series were between Ford and Chevrolet in cars and engines, and Firestone and Goodyear in tires. This competition was at the heart of what was making Can-Am work. It not only was the source for much of the sponsorship money that kept the teams afloat, but also the technology and hardware that kept them competitive.

Firestone's poor performance in the early races had discouraged the company, already beset by labor issues that had slowed development. The week before the 1967 Can-Am opened, Raymond Firestone, chairman of the board, formally announced that his company "[would] not enter into any new contracts to purchase race cars, or pay car owners, drivers or mechanics for using our products." He made it clear that Firestone was not getting out of racing, but he was serious in halting the escalation of team and driver support, calling the decision "a matter of sound business judgment. We have concluded that we will no longer be able to justify the spiraling multimillion-dollar expenditures if they were to continue to grow in accordance with the experience of recent years." A careful observer could recognize that the boom years were over. Without two competing tire companies, the subsidies would disappear, along with the flow of free tires and technical support.

There was further reason to be concerned on the car and engine front. Ford had started the season with great expectations, but one by one, the touted teams and cars had either failed on the track or not even found their way to the starting grid. Only Dan Gurney's team was holding up the Ford honor, and even Dan wasn't winning races. After winning Le Mans two years running and the Indianapolis 500, there were signals that the Dearborn company's unprecedented commitment to racing was on the downturn. The Can-Am looked as if it would become a series dominated by Chevrolet engines.

CHAPTER 70:

Hard Work and Sweet Success

The Bridgehampton Can-Am had conflicted with the next Trans-Am at Riverside, where veteran driver Bob Johnson raced the Penske Camaro. David Pearson and Ed Leslie swept the first two places for Cougar, but Johnson did a fine job bringing the Camaro home third. The Shelby team protested Bud Moore's team when the Ed Leslie Cougar was found to be 19 pounds underweight. The protest was denied because the scales were not certified. The Sunoco Camaro was of legal weight, but SCCA technical inspectors found body panels only one-third of the thickness specified. No penalties were assessed, but the teams were warned that all must be in order before the next race.

The Trans-Am Championship was out of reach for Chevrolet—Ford and Mercury were fighting it out to the final point—but all of the Penske team's hard work had developed the Camaro as a competitive proposition. Roger and Mark were determined to finish the season on a high note. The last two races were just a week apart, with Las Vegas on October 1 and Kent, Washington, the following weekend.

Roger rented Sears Point Raceway in the San Francisco Bay area for private testing. Blair Camp called Jamie Weissenborn and asked him if he wanted to go along for the day. After takeoff from the San Carlos airport, the Piper Cub was soon over the race track where Blair buzzed the pit area to get Mark's attention. Mark cleared the straightaway where his boyhood friends landed to spend the day at the track.

At Stardust Raceway the Cougar and Mustang teams were loaded with everything in their arsenal for the final push

to the championship. Bud Moore's Cougar team, leading Mustang by just one point, fielded three cars for Parnelli Jones, Peter Revson, and Allan Moffat. The Shelby Mustang cars were for Jerry Titus and Ronnie Bucknum. Mark and Parnelli captured the front row with identical qualifying times of 1:50.0—98.182 mph. The 350-mile Stardust race was run at night with the flag falling at 6:00 p.m., just as the sun was setting. Jones charged into the lead followed by Bucknum from the second row. Mark settled into third place and the race was on. As darkness followed twilight, Mark moved into second place and dogged Jones closely. Parnelli's tires were not up to the stress and he pitted early. Mark was in the lead, which he held virtually the rest of the way for the victory. The biggest drama occurred when Mark attempted to indicate that the car should be checked for a sticking throttle. The pit crew misunderstood his signal and added oil to an already-full system, causing the Camaro to blow out the excess oil over a number of laps. Bucknum brought the Mustang home second, and now the points battle had shifted to Ford over Mercury at 63 to 61.

Prior to the final race at Kent on October 8, Roy Gane spent the week at Alan Green's Seattle Chevrolet dealership—Green was sponsoring his own two-car team of Camaros in the Trans-Am—finishing restoration of the original car that had been severely damaged in the towing accident. The car was completed for Bob Johnson and Craig Fisher to race. Putting the final touches on it was only a small part of the hectic week. After Las Vegas it was discovered that all four Penske engines had a chronic valve-train problem that had to be fixed before going to Kent. While Roy Gane towed the race car to Seattle, Mark borrowed a truck from George Follmer and took the engines to Traco in Culver City. Getting other essential parts—special rocker-arm pivot balls—required a confrontation with Chevrolet. Mark obtained the necessary key parts overnight from Vince Piggins, after insisting that if they could not be expedited, the team would not appear at Kent. The incident marked the beginning of Mark's gradual emergence as the forceful figure that he would become in the race operation. Traco did their magic to rebuild and dyno the engines. Mark personally drove the truck to Kent with the rebuilt engines for Roy Gane to fit to the cars.

During the week before the race Mark broke away from the work at Alan Green's Chevy dealership for lunch with *Competition Press*'s editor Bill Finefrock and *Auto Week of the Air* producer Jerry Smith. Looking up from his sandwich Mark spotted a car in the restaurant parking lot with a blazing fire inside. He rushed to the car with a pitcher of water and managed to extinguish the blaze. When the owner arrived all he could do was curse and pound his fists on the hood. It became clear that no thank-you or other acknowledgment would be forthcoming, so Mark said, "Sorry I had to make such a mess of your car," and returned to finish his lunch.

For Shelby's Mustang team and the rival Bud Moore Cougar outfit, the battle for the championship had come down to the final race. No matter what Mark did in the Camaro, the Trans-Am title would go to whichever of these fiercely competitive Ford division teams finished ahead of the other. Shelby's hopes were set back in the early laps of qualifying when team leader Jerry Titus got upside down at high speed in his Terlingua Mustang. The car was a thorough wreck, and Chuck Cantwell and his crew began a thrash to find a replacement. Several Mustang privateers stepped forward to offer their cars in order for Mustang to help Ford clinch the championship. John McComb's was chosen, and after Titus qualified it, the team spent the night before the race going through the car. Mustang's other hopes were on Ronnie Bucknum in the second team car, as well as Clarence Mathews' Milt Minter Mustang, which was considered a quasi team car. Cougar felt reasonably confident with Dan Gurney and Parnelli Jones, plus a third team car for Allan Moffat. Ed Leslie sat in the pits ready for relief duty should he be needed.

During qualifying Mark was dismayed—he called it an "unhappy surprise"—to find that Parnelli's Cougar had a set of special Firestone tires that were not available to the Penske team. Jones's teammate Dan Gurney had the latest Goodyear Blue Streak tires on his Cougar and Mark was two seconds adrift. Despite Roger's status as a Firestone race-tire distributor, Mark felt they were not getting the best deal and decided to fit the Goodyears for final qualifying. The difference was immediate: Mark put the Camaro on pole with a 1:29.2, with Dan and Parnelli at 1:30.3 and 1:30.6 respectively. When Roger arrived on race day he initially ordered the Firestones back on the car. Mark resisted, arguing, "Wait a minute! Why? We don't have a deal with either tire company. Are we going to win this race for Chevrolet or are we going to play favorites with Firestone?" The Goodyears stayed on the car.

The Cougar race plan was for Dan and Parnelli to keep the Mustangs behind them no matter what. At the start Mark

motored away and drove to a convincing win, having lapped every other car in the race. The Cougar team strategy worked well until mid-race, when first Dan and then Parnelli had setbacks. But the Mustangs were having their own troubles, and it was back and forth until the end when Ronnie Bucknum brought his Mustang home second, giving the Trans-Am Championship to Ford for the second year running. Gurney was third, followed by the second Team Penske Camaro, with Craig Fisher and Bob Johnson co-driving. Gurney might have pulled off the championship for Mercury if he hadn't been beset with troubles, including a smashed windshield that he held together with one hand while driving with the other. He was also handicapped by a stop for a tire punctured by a sharp rock and a lost fuel cap that brought about a black-flag stop. Roy Gane, who had worked so hard preparing for the race, rode with Mark on the victory lap.

Race day had also been a success for the Kent organizers. Track manager Larry McCue reported that the crowd count had exceeded the very successful totals recorded at the US-RRC race in July. The Trans-Am had really caught on and race fans were supporting the series at virtually every venue.

The final Trans-Am points table had Ford with 64, Mercury 62, Chevrolet 57, and Dodge 11. In their first year in the series the independently funded and run Penske team had developed their car to become the fastest by season's end. It was a team effort by the small group of people involved, with Mark the tireless catalyst and hands-on man pushing to develop the car. Mark's driving was superb. He had started ten races in the series and won three, including the last two.

The series had been bitterly contested throughout between the two Ford divisions, but the end-of-the-year strength of the Penske Camaro in Mark's hands had added an additional competitive element. All the teams had evolved rule-bending measures that included sandblasting and acid-dipping for body lightness, as well as chassis bracing and engine tricks. SCCA technical inspection was challenged to keep up with the rule benders and often had little choice but to look the other way on underweight cars and other fairly obvious unapproved modifications. They were under pressure from the track promoters and, to a certain extent, their own leadership in the sanctioning body to keep the big names in the race. The teams knew it and were not averse to playing hardball by threatening to withdraw a car along with its star driver rather than make the adjustments to bring it into compliance. The Trans-Am had become big-league seemingly overnight, and the less-well-funded independents were having a tough time keeping up. It was all a mere hint of what was to come.

CHAPTER 71:

Oh, for that Last Drop of Sunoco!

After a three-week break the Can-Am circus reassembled at Laguna Seca to begin the West Coast half of the six-race series. The Penske team made the long tow across the country in two Ford trucks. "They weren't enormous trucks," says Roger Bailey. "Each had a slanted bed where the cars rode at an angle with a tarp over them. There was a bench seat in the front with room for three people. George McKean, who had sold his Philadelphia Chevrolet dealership to Roger Penske, rode in the truck with Al Holbert and me. He was a terrific guy who knew everyone. We rode up through the Redwoods and visited a couple of other National Parks on that trip. George knew all the best places to stay."

The complete domination by the McLaren team of the early races had discouraged many, but the race at Laguna Seca attracted a strong field, and Ford appeared to be having a better look-in. Dan Gurney broke the McLaren hold on pole position in his Ford-powered Lola, and Bruce was second with Denny Hulme third. Parnelli Jones had entered the series and put his Lola, powered by a Ford four-cam Indy engine, on the second row with Hulme. Mark was back in 9th and George on the row behind in 11th starting position.

Firestone was trying hard to overcome Goodyear's edge but seemed to run into one problem after another. Much-needed new 12.5-inch-wide rear tires were finished the week of the race but were shipped to Los Angeles instead of Northern California. By the time the shipping problem was sorted out, the teams who got the first batch—including Penske—received them early Saturday in time for final qualifying. Mark shaved a second off his time. The second batch didn't arrive until that evening.

The traditional Monterey Grand Prix two-heat format was abandoned in favor of a single 201-mile race over 106 laps of the 1.9-mile circuit. Dan jumped out to an early lead, but after eight laps the Ford overheated and Bruce took over the lead, with Denny second. Jim Hall had the Chaparral in a solid third with Mark close behind. On the 76th lap the Chevy engine in the Sunoco Lola blew up for the third consecutive race—a bitter blow still remembered by the team as one of the lowest points in its history. Hulme lost his engine a few laps later, and the race ran out with McLaren overcoming the extreme heat to win from Jim Hall. George Follmer held up the Penske team's honor with a fine third place. The heat was felt by all of the cars and drivers as only 9 of the 31 starters finished.

Two weeks later at Riverside the tide turned for Mark. Although only 10th on the grid, with George again right behind him on the sixth row in 12th, the Penske cars were set up to be fast in the race. Qualifying had appeared to further Ford hopes, with Gurney again capturing pole position and Parnelli Jones sixth. But even more exciting for Ford was that the Holman-Moody Honker II was finally showing speed, as Mario Andretti qualified it fifth on the third row beside Jones with an identical time. Still another Ford entry appeared for the first time as Jerry Titus debuted Shelby American's King Cobra and qualified it a reasonable 13th in the 39-car starting field.

Riverside was the most exciting race of the Can-Am season. This was the 10th annual Times Grand Prix, and the publicity machine of the Times-Mirror group, along with expert promotion by track director Les Richter, produced a crowd of more than 80,000 people who endured dust storms that at times reduced visibility to 100 yards or less.

Gurney jumped into the lead from the rolling start but was out on the third lap with a blown engine. At turn eight the chicane was delineated by white-painted tires embedded halfway in the pavement. A tire at the apex of the turn was struck by one of the lead cars and launched in the air to impact Hulme's McLaren. Hulme pitted and had the damaged body piece removed, but race officials refused to allow him to continue. Parnelli Jones—with the George Bignotti–maintained Double Overhead Cam Indy engine—led briefly for Ford but fell back when his tires overheated. Mark and George finished a satisfying third and sixth—Follmer was two laps down as a result of suffering body damage from the same flying tire that eliminated Hulme—but the real story was a brilliant race at the front between McLaren and Hall. They exchanged the lead throughout, though at the end the result was identical to Laguna Seca, with Bruce first and Jim Hall second. Between Mark and George were Parnelli in fourth and Mike Spence fifth.

With just one round to go, McLaren team leader Bruce McLaren had now won two races in a row and taken over the series lead from teammate Hulme, with 30 points to Hulme's 27. No one else was in the hunt to be Can-Am champion.

On November 12 at Stardust Raceway the series ended with great disappointment for Mark, despite a second-place finish. Second can sometimes feel great, but not when you have led the race for 165 of 210 miles only to run out of fuel in the last half-mile. Mark lost a 21-second lead over John Surtees on the last lap, coasting across the finish line not far ahead of Mike Spence in third. Mark had qualified seventh and driven a decisive race to take the lead as other cars encountered trouble. Mark recalled the feeling of leading Surtees. "I was in the lead! I was beating him!" *AutoWeek*'s Charles Fox credited Mark with "holding off Surtees for the entire race in an incredibly stylish display." Despite the disappointment Mark said the race was a great confidence-builder "because Surtees was the Superman then." John Surtees recalls that it was a satisfying victory. "We had a bad year with many engine problems and the modified car not working," says John. "The Vegas race I did in my 1966 car that luckily had sat in the workshop of Carl Haas, and I recall the satisfaction of bringing it home after some skirmishes with Jim and Mark."

Firestone was relieved to score a 1-2 finish after being dominated by Goodyear in the first five rounds. Both McLarens failed to finish, but Bruce McLaren was crowned 1967 Can-Am champion at the gala awards dinner that evening at the Stardust Hotel. Mark tied John Surtees for third in points with 16.

Despite the near win in the final race at Stardust, Mark and the entire Penske team did not have a good feeling about the 1967 Can-Am. Although two seconds and a third were reasonable results in the face of the overwhelming superiority of the McLaren Mk 6A, three DNFs were not up to the Penske standard. Worse yet, it was clear that the Lola's day as a competitive proposition was over. McLaren had come to the series with cars more advanced than any other team could produce. They had learned from the previous year, and through extensive testing and development—and, ultimately, by outstanding driving from two Grand Prix aces—had dominated. Chaparral had given them something to think about on the West Coast, but everyone else, including Penske, was running outdated or underdeveloped equipment. There were some exciting new cars introduced, but too late to have

an impact. Most teams were using practice and the races for badly needed development. McLaren had done their homework before they ever left England.

Roger Penske had already decided to buy the McLaren M6A that Bruce was racing. He and Bruce had agreed on a deal before Las Vegas, and when the race was over it became his property. Roger also purchased an unfinished M6A chassis that was kept in reserve. The Lola T70 that Mark had driven was purchased by Wallis Engineering, and Follmer's car went to prominent SCCA amateur driver Jerry Hansen. Hansen took the car to Daytona where he won the American Road Race of Champions, known even then as the Runoffs.

McLaren's domination notwithstanding, the 1967 Can-Am was an unqualified success. Although the size of the fields was down somewhat from the previous year, the overall quality had improved, and the entrants had provided great technical variety and innovation.

It was a thrilling time for Group 7 racing, and the SCCA had produced a series that was just right for the time. But the sanctioning body also helped create a false euphoria that contributed to the Can-Am's subsequent decline. In addition to their continued insistence on promoting participation by star drivers who had no real expectation of, or prospect for, being involved in the series, they also misled the public and teams with their inaccurate claims for purse money. At the beginning of the season the SCCA issued a press release stating boldly that the total Can-Am purse had been increased to $456,850 by contingency monies. This was certainly an impressive number, but the reality was very different. Firestone and Goodyear, for example, each paid $15,000 contingent on a car using their product, displaying their decals, and winning. But since no car could use both companies' tires, the real amount that any team could collect was only half of the combined $30,000 counted in the SCCA's total. The same math held true for money from spark-plug and oil suppliers. Only a small part of the contingency money could actually be paid, but the sanctioning body continued to inflate their "total purse" with phony figures. Although they succeeded in creating a sense of "bigness" for the series, they simultaneously created a false aura that led many small- to medium-size teams down the garden path. When the excitement and glory passed and the bills arrived, reality set in and teams disappeared.

In late November Roger Penske announced a switch from Firestone to Goodyear tires. This entailed a great deal more than switching race tires, although the pre-race swap on the Camaro at Kent had foreshadowed the move. Penske had been the Firestone racing tire distributor in the Northeast since early in 1966. Norman Ahn was running the business, which now became a Goodyear distributorship.

McLaren's chief engineer Tyler Alexander came to Newtown Square to go over the car with Mark and Karl. "I knew how good the car was," said Mark. "I naively wondered how they could build something better. Tyler was pretty relaxed about it all." Over the winter the McLaren M6A-1 was fitted with a 427ci engine and taken to Riverside for testing. The primary purpose of the test was to see how the bigger engine worked in the car. (The McLaren team had used the smaller-block Chevy in their successful run in the cars.) "We knew McLaren would come back with something special in the new year," Mark said. "But we figured the 427ci big-block would be our equalizer."

Mark had gone directly from Las Vegas to help master of ceremonies Stirling Moss open the San Francisco Foreign Car Show on November 14. He remained in constant demand for personal appearances.

Although by the end of the 1967 season Mark was beginning to assume greater responsibility for Penske Racing operations, Roger was still calling the shots and making most of the arrangements. It was not yet "Mark's team," as it would become.

CHAPTER 72:

Outstanding Young Man

At the SCCA's convention on January 25–28, 1968, in Atlanta, Georgia, Mark officially accepted his trophy as 1967 United States Road Racing Champion. The host Atlanta Region had come up with a special event for the fun and amusement of attendees—The International Grudge Slalom. Baker Motor Company, the local BMC dealer, in cooperation with British Motor Holdings, loaned four MGB roadsters, and 155 SCCA members competed on a slalom course near the convention hotel. Among the marquee names were Dan Gurney, Gus Hutchinson, Huschke von Hanstein, Jerry Titus, Peter Revson, and Bob Johnson, as well as Mark and Roger. It was all lighthearted and fun on the surface, but racers become serious anytime they sit behind the wheel. Dan Gurney set the fast time early at 28.651; no one bettered it

until Mark got into the MGB, and barely beat Dan's time with a 28.641. Hutchinson was third with a 28.752, while Roger showed he hadn't lost any of his skill by turning a 28.913 to finish fourth ahead of Titus, Johnson, and the rest. Mark graciously attributed his quick time to the advantage of having raced the Hansgen MGB at an early point in his career.

Roger and Mark were busy laying plans for the most ambitious season to date for Penske Racing. The newly acquired McLaren M6A would be used to defend the USRRC championship as well as pursue the Can-Am in the fall. The team's Camaro had emerged as the fastest car in the 1967 Trans-Am series, and the hope was to carry this momentum forward to a championship in 1968. Finally, they had placed an order with Dan Gurney for a new Eagle from his Santa Ana, California, All American Racers shop. Mark and Roger were ready to go racing in USAC.

Living close to the race shop was not the boon to quality family time that Mark and Sue had anticipated. Mark was spending long hours in the Newtown Square shop as his hands-on involvement with every aspect of team logistics increased. Mark was not unaware of the trade-off his commitment to racing represented to his time at home with his young family. In a January 1968 feature in the Delaware County (PA) *Daily Times*, Mark told John Plaisted that his one beef with the life of a professional driver was the time spent away from home: "One race usually equals about a week away from home. I raced 31 times last year, so that made 31 of the 52 weeks somewhere else." He admitted that he had no other plans beyond racing. "I always rely on the advice of my father. Do your best today and tomorrow will take care of itself."

Mark was making an impact on his new community. The Media Area Junior Chamber of Commerce announced that Mark was the recipient of their Outstanding Young Man Award. The presentation was made at the group's annual Distinguished Service Award banquet in Upper Providence on March 21. Thirty-one-year-old Mark was described by Joseph Adcock for the *Philadelphia Inquirer's* Sunday magazine as ". . . a boyish-looking young man with a blond crew cut and apple cheeks."

CHAPTER 73:

Trans-Am on the Enduro Circuit

In 1967 Roger had run the Trans-Am Camaros in full Sunoco colors without any sponsorship help from the oil company. The approach paid dividends. When the team had become strong late in the season, he approached his contacts at Sun Oil and said that he was now able to present a program in which he was confident of winning the 1968 Trans-Am championship. Sun had not been blind to the exposure they had already gained, and a deal was struck for the new year. John Hilton, who had previously sponsored Chuck Parsons in the USRRC and Can-Am, brought a financial interest to the team, and the Camaro carried the Penske-Hilton logo throughout the season.

The big, if not universally popular, news was that the first two rounds in the 1968 Trans-Am championship would be run as a category within the classic endurance races at Daytona and Sebring. There were other important changes. The SCCA declared that the over-2.0-liter-division cars would no longer conform to FIA Group 2 regulations. They would now be subject to specific SCCA rules unique to Trans-Am. This was generally well received as, in theory, it made it more practical to enforce rules and to create a relatively level playing field. One of the changes was that all engines could be bored out to 305ci to equate to the 5.0-liter maximum allowed. Rim widths were standardized at eight inches, as was minimum weight at 2,800 pounds, less fuel and driver. Plastic or aluminum bumpers were now permitted, and allowances were made for enlarged wheel wells to accommodate the bigger rims and tires.

Team lineups were different too. Ford's Lincoln-Mercury division had dropped out and Bud Moore's Cougar team was gone. New to the series was the American Motors Company with a factory-backed team of Javelins. AMC selected veteran driver and Milwaukee advertising executive Jim Jeffords to head the program. Jeffords turned to Chicagoan Ronnie Kaplan to build and run the cars. The two men had been a team in the late 1950s when Jeffords was the ace driver for Nickey Chevrolet race cars prepared by Kaplan. The Javelin team debuted at Sebring.

Early in January the Penske team, ready with modifications that conformed to the new rules, spent several days testing

at Daytona. Smokey Yunick had a race shop in Daytona Beach, and Mark, unaware of a rivalry between Yunick and Roger Penske, phoned to ask if they could use some space at the shop. Yunick agreed, and along with Roy Gane and Peter Reinhart, plus Frank Coon and Jim Travers from Traco, they used a small shed in Yunick's operation as their base for testing. "Later I discovered that there was some sort of rivalry among Smokey, Roger, and [Vince] Piggins, but I didn't know—I didn't even care," Mark later recalled. "All I wanted was space to work on our car, and Smokey seemed to be a straight shooter, in spite of what anyone said."

Mark eventually realized they weren't entirely welcome in the "Best Damn Garage in Town," but was just happy to have a place to work and focus on developing the new car. "I felt they didn't really want us there," he remembered. "Maybe they just wanted a good look at our car."

On Thursday before qualifying for the 24-hour race on February 3–4, Roger drilled the pit crew relentlessly on pit stops, measuring incremental improvements on his stopwatch. Mike Gremaud of *AutoWeek* observed a practice stop with the crew filling an empty tank, checking the oil, and cleaning the windshield in 22 seconds. "You look like you're asleep," said Roger. "Let's do it again." The crew repeated the procedure and got it down to 15 seconds before the drill was switched to include changing tires. Roger had told Mark the day before, "We didn't come down here to wear our good clothes." After seemingly endless practice stops, the crew had finally satisfied Roger's standard. Mark remarked to Gremaud, "See, you don't know the meaning of work until you've been with Roger." Most revealing is that no one, whether an employee or a "weekend warrior" volunteer, complained. Roger had the rare leadership quality that imbued the crew with his spirit and sensibility. They were a team.

In qualifying on Friday, Mark was the fastest Trans-Am runner, and put the Camaro 20th in the starting field of 63 cars. Jerry Titus was 22nd at the start, and he and Ronnie Bucknum made the biggest impression for Trans-Am cars in the race, as they brought the Shelby team Mustang home fourth overall. Mark and co-drivers Bob Johnson and Craig Fisher suffered damaged cylinder heads and lost time having them replaced. They finished 12th, many laps behind the Mustang but second in Trans-Am points.

With Trans-Am cars making up fully a third of the 63-car starting field, Bill France was happy to have struck the agreement with the SCCA to run a qualifying round of the series as part of the race. International prototype racing was recovering from the blow dealt by the announcement the previous year that beginning in 1968, the big-engine Fords and Chaparrals were effectively banned from competition. The new rules placed a 3.0-liter limit on the Group 6 prototypes, and limited the so-called "sports 50" class—Group 4—to 5.0 liters. The Mk II and Mk IV Fords, along with the Chaparral, were now a thing of the past, and from an American perspective much of the glamour was gone from endurance racing. At Daytona John Wyer ran a team of Mk I GT40s that were the only competition for Porsche. In the end, Porsche 907s swept the first three places. Vic Elford and Jochen Neerpasch did most of the driving in the winning car, although Jo Siffert, Hans Herrmann, and Rolf Stommelen all had a turn at the wheel and shared in the win.

The Daytona result was disappointing for the Penske-Hilton team, so they went testing at Sebring two weeks before the 12-hour race. It was an open test day, and Mark in the Sunoco-Camaro was a full two seconds faster than Titus in the fastest Mustang. Mark's 3:03.4 (102.07 mph) was the first lap in a Trans-Am car to exceed 100 mph at Sebring. Al Unser was also present, driving the Smokey Yunick Camaro that had famously failed tech inspection at Daytona three times. Unser's best time was 3:08.4. Mark pronounced himself happy with the car and said the team was ready.

At Sebring for the 12-hour race on March 23, the team ran two Camaros. In addition to the new car raced at Daytona, the team prepared the 1967 car with updates to make it into a '68. The car had been so extensively acid-dipped that it was now very close to the minimum allowed weight, something Mark didn't want the competition to know. Mark solved this by first having the new car, number 15, presented for inspection. When it returned to the team's hangar out on the Webster straight, the number 16 was put on the car, and it returned to tech to be inspected and approved. The lightweight car was never weighed. The same trick was used in qualifying, where the lighter Camaro ran with both numbers. Mark laughingly commented, "That car really got a workout." The purpose of the charade was to keep Ford from realizing how close they had come to the minimum standard. "It was funny to think we could put one over on them like that," said Mark.

Craig Fisher again drove with Mark, who qualified 13th on the 69-car starting grid with a 3:01.2. Lloyd Ruby and Al Unser were co-driving the Yunick Camaro. Ruby had equaled Mark's time, but started 14th because Mark had turned his

lap first. Fisher placed the second team car, also driven by Bob Johnson and Joe Welch, 17th on the grid, at 3:01.7. On Friday evening Mark and Roger were busy with the crew, so John Hilton escorted Sue Donohue and Lisa Penske to dinner at the upscale Kenilworth Hotel. In an amusing feature story for *AutoWeek*, Judy Stropus described the array of period dress seen at events over the weekend. The clothes ranged from "long fashionable evening gowns to grungy dungarees topped with scruffy shirts and surrounded by rings of 'hippy' beads." At the track it was high plastic boots, mesh stockings, and short skirts.

The race result was more than satisfying, with the Penske Camaros heading all the Trans-Am entrants with an overall 3-4 finish, although the Jerry Titus / Ronnie Bucknum Shelby Mustang was fifth on the same lap. Mark drove 9 of the 12 hours in the lead car, and Fisher drove both cars. Roger paid close attention to what was happening on the circuit. Whenever Mark would turn a quick lap he would hang out a pit board that read "6,300"—a not-so-subtle reminder of the rev limit they had agreed upon. Only two prototype Porsche 907s were ahead of the first three Trans-Am cars, with the winning car driven by Jo Siffert and Hans Herrmann. Mark called the crowd response to the third-place finish "unbelievable; it was one of the greatest things that ever happened to me in racing, to experience the enthusiasm for what we had done."

Mark's old friend and mentor Charlie Rainville made a strong showing at Sebring, where he co-drove a Mercury-Cougar with Bruce Jennings. The pair had the ex-factory car up to eighth overall and fourth in the Trans-Am class nine hours into the race when the flywheel exploded through the hood. The popular Rainville rode out the multiple flips as the car was destroyed. Charlie emerging unscathed.

AMC made a creditable debut with the Ronnie Kaplan–run Javelins. They had an impressive driver lineup, with Jerry Grant and George Follmer in the fastest-qualifying Javelin, while Peter Revson and Skip Scott brought the team their best finish in 12th position overall. After two rounds of the 1968 Trans-Am, Chevrolet and Ford each had one race to their credit. Just as Ford was determined to defend their title, Roger and Mark were confident they could bring the championship to Chevrolet and fulfill Roger's promise to Sunoco.

Jerry Titus was an outspoken critic of endurance racing and had lobbied against the Trans-Am including the two long races. He maintained that Roger Penske, by agreeing to run the Camaro in the races, had forced Ford to participate. After

Daytona, in his column in *AutoWeek*, Titus had gloated upon the pleasure of winning the race, emphasizing that "Roger Penske, who forced us into participation because he logically concluded he had some real advantages going there, looks rather good with crow-feathers sticking out of his mouth." After Sebring, Penske Racing replied with a letter to the editor that explained:

> **We at Penske Racing lead a tenuous existence. We work in the shadow of Ford's monstrous vans, struggling painfully against a tide of factory support. Our independence has compensations—living poor, we subsist on a meager diet, and the crow that Jerry Titus had us eat at Daytona tasted almost like roast turkey. We wonder if Mr. Titus, living as he does the rich life on the Ford factory gravy train, found his double dose of large blackbird pie at Sebring equally digestible.**

The letter reflected an important investment by the Sun Oil Company for the 1968 season by engaging Professionals in Motion, a New York public relations firm, to represent the team and its sponsors. Roger had known the firm's principal, Fred Marik, since their teenage days in Cleveland, Ohio. Marik made an immediate impact on the professional presentation of the Penske story, and the firm played an important part in creating the positive public image enjoyed by Penske Racing. It also helped to position Mark as an emerging media star.

CHAPTER 74:
Mexican Trouble and California Dreaming

The motorsports media couldn't resist referring to the USRRC as a "tune-up" to the big show in the fall. With the Can-Am receiving so much hype and attention, it was impossible for the national professional series for Group 7 cars not to appear second-tier. The SCCA did what it could to help race promoters, mandating a purse increase from the previous $10,000 minimum to $15,000, as well as introducing an end-of-season point fund. The series also became international, with a race in Mexico City and one at St. Jovite in Canada.

The season-opener in Mexico City was also the race debut for the Sunoco McLaren with the 427ci engine. Mark and Karl

had taken the car to Colorado's Continental Divide Raceway to test at a high altitude similar to that of the Mexican capital, and it was with great expectations that Karl and Peter crossed the border.

Mark was fast and smooth on the demanding 3.1-mile circuit, and was heavily favored because of his dominance of the previous year's USRRC. The competition was keen. Carl Haas was now the Lola distributor for North America, and with sponsorship from the Simoniz wax company was running two new cars for Chuck Parsons and Skip Scott. McLaren was selling customer versions of the Can-Am-dominating M6A, and Lothar Motschenbacher had his new Mk 6B fitted with a Gurney-Weslake 377ci Ford. Another Gurney-Weslake Ford was in the Shelby American–run Lola for Peter Revson. Sam Posey's Caldwell DL7 had shown occasional promise during the previous fall's Can-Am, although it was suspected that Posey's considerable talent and determination were masking the car's inherent problems. A new McLaren was in the hands of local Mexican star Moises Solana. Solana was a quick driver with Formula One experience and a man to be reckoned with, particularly on home ground. His car had arrived late and he did well to qualify seventh fastest on the inside of the fourth row, alongside his brother Hernán in a Lola Mk 3.

Mark was fastest in the first qualifying session, although he ended his run parked alongside the track with a blown engine. One of the oil pumps in the dry-sump system had failed, and the crank and number-four rod had been ruined. Jim Travers and Frank Coon, the Traco partnership, personally rebuilt the engine with new parts flown in from Los Angeles by Traco employee George Bolthoff. It was no use. During the Sunday morning warm-up, Mark experienced the exact same failure, and the car was unable to start the race. "The week was a total disaster," Mark recalled. "Roger had arranged everything in his own fantastic way, spending all those dollars to get the equipment there and flying all those people in, and getting the engine rebuilt, and because of one tiny mistake we never even started the race."

Moises Solana won a popular victory ahead of Skip Scott, Peter Revson, Sam Posey, Bud Morley, Lothar Motschenbacher, and Jerry Entin. Other than some difficulties with customs at the border, the race was a great success. The organization was flawless, the weather beautiful, and the women of Mexico City even more so.

A week after Mexico City the racing world was stunned

when Jim Clark died in a crash on April 7 at a Formula 2 race at the Hockenheim circuit in Germany. Clark was the dominant driver of the 1960s and enjoyed enormous popularity throughout the world. As lead driver for Team Lotus he had won the World Drivers Championship in 1963 and 1965, as well as the 1965 Indianapolis 500. At a time when fatalities were an all-too-regular staple of racing life, Clark's death managed to shake the racing community to the core. His personal modesty and genuine warmth had made friends of even the fiercest rival.

After the extreme disappointment of Mexico City, Mark and Roger had imbued the entire team with the need to dominate round two of the USRRC at Riverside on April 28. The big technical change was the availability of the all-aluminum 427ci Chevrolet engine which was actually 30 pounds lighter than the well-proven 327-based, small-block engines. The only teams with immediate access to the new engines were Penske, Chaparral, McLaren, and Surtees. Jim Hall was present at Riverside with the Chaparral 2G that featured an updated automatic transmission along with the new 427 engine.

Mark set the pace in Friday's qualifying session with a 1:19.4 lap on the 2.6-mile version of the Riverside circuit, but Jim Hall bettered the time in Saturday's final session with a 1:19.0. On Sunday morning when the Chaparral was restarted after the warm-up session, the transaxle broke. The team from Midland could not make it right in time for the start, and Mark was left to dominate the race, lapping the entire field except for Lothar Motschenbacher. It wasn't all easy. With just two laps to go, the Sunoco McLaren came to a stop on the course with a dead ignition system. Mark reported later that he hit every switch in the cockpit: "One of them was the right one. I don't know which." The engine fired and Mark drove on for the Sunoco McLaren Mk 6A's first victory. Sam Posey was third, Chuck Parsons fourth, Moises Solana fifth, and Dan Gurney protégé Swede Savage sixth in the AAR-entered Lola-Ford. Jerry Entin was seventh, just missing scoring points for the second consecutive race.

Out of the race car Mark Donohue did not project the stereotypical race-driver look. *Road & Track*'s Mike Knepper would later write: "Great racing drivers are supposed to look and act like heroes, not regular people. Here was a boyish grin and a plump, round face topped by a bristle of closely cropped blond hair in a style that hadn't been in style for five years," wrote Knepper. "Yet the crew cut hair went perfectly with Mark's chinos (two inches too short), white socks and penny loafers."

Round three of the USRRC followed just a week later at Laguna Seca on May 5. Mark was in the pits for Friday's practice, but Karl and the rest of the team did not arrive until that evening with the race car. A new engine had been fitted, and Mark pointed out the difficulty of preparing a new race car so far from home base. Jim Hall also missed Friday qualifying, and on Saturday set pole position with the Chaparral at 1:02.89, beating Lothar Motschenbacher's Friday best of 1:03.41. Mark gridded third with a 1:03.87. It was apparent that Motschenbacher in his 377ci Ford-powered McLaren 6B was the only competitor in the 22-car field who could run with Hall and Donohue.

Mark was already creating a reputation for being able to set up a car. Ron Fournier saw it firsthand. "Mark was great to work with because he was mechanically a very clever guy," he says. "Although he wasn't an automotive engineer he was a really talented mechanical engineer. He knew what to do. The only guy I ever saw who was as good as him in being able to set up a car was A. J. Foyt—he was pretty amazing too. Mark could go out and hot lap a car and come in and tell you which tire was down three pounds, or which spring rate to go up or down, which shock was a little too stiff. Once Mark learned something it was planted in his brain and he could use that information time and time again. He only got better at it."

Mark passed Lothar at the start and when he passed the Chaparral on the last corner of the first lap, he was in the lead. Hall pursued Mark closely for the first 25 laps of the 80-lap race on the 1.9-mile circuit before beginning to fall back with handling problems. Lothar now took up the pursuit and chased Mark hard throughout the remainder of the race, with the two separated at times by mere inches. At the end Mark was the winner, and both he and Lothar had lapped the third-place Chaparral. Chuck Parsons was fourth, Bud Morley fifth, and Jerry Entin's consistent driving in his Lola was finally rewarded with a spot in the points in sixth.

Karl Kainhofer began the long tow back east with the McLaren to prepare for the next round of the series at Bridgehampton. Mark now turned his attention to the Camaro, as the third round of the Trans-Am in Oklahoma followed Laguna Seca by just a week.

On May 7, just two days after Mark's win at Laguna Seca, Mike Spence died at Indianapolis from injuries suffered in a crash practicing for the 500. The English driver had become very popular in America for his drives for the Chaparral team, and was mourned by the American racing community. Little more than six months before Mark had taken him around Bridgehampton to show him the line. Spence had been a teammate to Jim Clark in Formula One and had rejoined Team Lotus to race in the 500 after Clark's death almost exactly a month earlier.

CHAPTER 75:

Sunoco on Ice

When Sun Oil became an official sponsor of the Penske Camaros in 1968, part of the arrangement was that the personnel provided by Sun would be present for all of the Trans-Am races. During the previous two years they had only accompanied the team to races for the Lola.

Jerry Kroninger had been splitting duties with Bill Preston for Sun in 1967 but now would be at all the races. In fact, he attended 26 races in 1968 and remained an integral part of the Sunoco/Penske alliance as long as that sponsorship lasted. Mark immediately lobbied Jerry for technical help on improving fuel mileage. Typically the cars stopped three times during a Trans-Am race, but Mark pointed out that if the fuel could be made to go just a bit longer, they could forgo the last stop—a big competitive advantage. Jerry, a Penn State grad in mechanical engineering with a master's degree from the Chrysler Institute of Engineering, had been with Sun Oil since 1960. He assured Mark that if the petroleum industry had an answer for extending gas mileage it would have already been implemented. "Mark was motivational," recounts Kroninger. "He was determined that there was a solution to going further on a tank of gas, and his persistence on the point eventually gave me an idea."

Kroninger found an answer by approaching the problem from another perspective, reasoning that if they could some-how squeeze an extra gallon of gas into the 22-gallon tank, it would effectively produce the same result. Jerry knew this could be achieved by increasing the fuel's density by cooling it dramatically. "I told Mark what my idea was, and he said, 'Great, let's figure how to do it.'" Jerry worked on the application all winter, and on May 12 at War Bonnet Raceway Park in Mannford, Oklahoma, all was ready. This was the first regular-format Trans-Am race of the season where fast pit stops and maximum fuel loads would be essential.

Standard Sunoco fuel drums held 55 gallons or 30 gallons. Kroninger placed a 30-gallon can inside the larger 55-gallon drum. The surrounding space was filled with dry ice mixed with acetone to provide a cooling bath. On race morning Jerry would find a source for dry ice—often a local dairy farm, as dry ice was used extensively in the milk business—and the dry ice was added to the acetone bath. The gasoline would drop from a typical ambient temperature of 70 degrees Fahrenheit to 0 degrees. The resultant increase in density made it possible to put 23 gallons of Sunoco into the Camaro's 22-gallon tank.

The War Bonnet circuit outside of Tulsa was 2.3 miles around. It was narrow and rough and the weekend was plagued by rain, with the resultant mud making access roads and the paddock a quagmire. Mark and the team, running just one car, had the circuit booked for testing on Friday and arrived at the facility before the worst of the rains. Getting in and out of the track over the next couple of days was a challenge. Mark called it "Mud City."

On race-day morning, gone was the Penske team's familiar 200-gallon tank laid horizontally on a three-and-a-half-foot-high stand. In its place was a six-foot rig of an entirely new and obviously sophisticated design that held Kroninger's new storage tank. The design and elevated height increased the pressure head and reduced fueling time to 8.5 seconds from the previous standard of 11 seconds. What really dropped jaws and brought incredulous stares was the frost forming on the outside of the Sunoco container. The dry ice/acetone bath was doing its job of cooling the Sunoco 260 gasoline in the inner tank, but at that moment no one on pit lane understood the reason for the frost or the concept behind it. Mark was pleased beyond words and beamed with delight as he stood on the fueling rig.

The rain had stopped for Sunday, and a special two-hour qualifying session that morning had Parnelli Jones on pole position with a 1:36.0. Mark was next at 1:36.6. George Follmer and Peter Revson had the Javelins—now fitted with dual carburetors—next, with Jerry Titus fifth in the second Shelby Mustang. In the race Jones took the initial lead; he was passed by Mark on lap 6 and then regained the lead on lap 15. The two cars remained close together until the Mustang pitted with electrical trouble, which cost it two laps. Then the Titus Mustang's engine blew and Mark soon had a one-lap lead on the entire field.

On lap 70 of 110 Malcolm Starr had a major accident, his Mustang sliding through the off-track mud and knocking down two chain-link fences before striking a spectator's Mustang. Two people, including a 10-year-old girl from Tulsa, were slightly injured, and the accident brought out an immediate red flag. Parnelli Jones and the chief steward engaged in a dispute that became physical over whether Parnelli had responded appropriately to the red flag. Javelin team director Jim Jeffords protested the lack of action on the Jones incident, which led to further arguments. After a 90-minute delay the race was restarted and Mark won decisively from Follmer, Jones, and Revson. While Ford and Javelin principals continued their protests and arguments, the Penske team celebrated Mark's third race win in as many weeks.

Penske Racing hoped to make it four wins in four weeks at the Bridgehampton USRRC on May 19. Although Lothar Motschenbacher qualified a tenth of a second quicker, Mark again dominated the race and was 14 seconds ahead when Lothar's transmission broke. Mark had a full 75-second lead on Skip Scott when a halfshaft broke on the Sunoco McLaren and Mark was out after a nasty downhill slide. Scott went on to win ahead of Chuck Parsons, giving team owner Carl Haas a 1-2 finish for the Simoniz Lola team.

In *Sports Car Graphic* Karl Ludvigsen compared the approaches of the two major teams contesting the 1968 Trans-Am. He observed that Ford prepared the team Mustangs like long-distance Mk II prototypes, whereas Penske's preparation of the Camaros resembled that of Can-Am sports-racers. He described the Sunoco Camaros as ". . . stark, lean, immaculate, essential, pure racing machines."

"I never remember a day when Mark would come into the shop in a bad mood or any way but upbeat," says Chris Franzese. Chris grew up in Watkins Glen as a member of the family that owned and ran the Glen Motor Inn where Mark and the rest of the team always stayed. He had just graduated from high school and worked that year for Penske Racing in the Newtown Square shop. "Even at the track, if things didn't go according to plan, nothing would bother him. He was always meticulous and focused in what he did and was very much the catalyst for the whole team."

Mark had a very special Z28 Camaro as his personal street car. The Z28 was a fast road car, and in its earliest incarnation in 1967 and 1968 was considered as close to a race-prepared car as could be purchased directly from a dealer. Mark's Z28 was even more special, with its Traco-built engine and other performance enhancements. It was the car's special race tires that got the attention of Jim "Crabby" Travers and Jerry Kroninger on the drive to Lime Rock for the Trans-Am on Memorial Day. Mark and Jerry had met Travers's flight from California at the Philadelphia airport, and the three men drove north on the Jersey Turnpike in pouring rain at 70 to 75 mph. Mark looked over and, as remembered by Crabby, said casually, "Guess what, mates! We are hydroplaning—see!" And with that, to the considerable consternation of Travers and Kroninger, Mark illustrated the point by turning the steering wheel abruptly in a series of full-lock right and left movements while the Camaro continued in a straight line.

The incident reflects Mark's playful side, which was not necessarily the image he projected to the public. David E. Davis, one of the most entertaining writers on motorsports, provided a tongue-in-cheek analysis in *Car and Driver* of who was "in" and who was "out." Davis said stock-car driver Coo Coo Marlin was in, "because anyone named Coo Coo Marlin has to be 'in,' " and declared that Mark was "out"— "until he stops being so goddamn wholesome and ages a little." Davis also proclaimed that Paul Hawkins was "'In' beyond anyone's wildest dreams." Motorsports writers liked their race drivers wild and wooly. Mark's wry sense of humor was likely gratified by the fact that even an insightful observer like Davis was deceived by his serious facade.

On race-day morning Mark loaned Jerry the Z28 to make his pickup run for dry ice. Jerry expected to have great fun at the wheel of this ultrafast car on the winding New England roads. Instead he found himself the cause of traffic bottlenecks as he was unable to even approach the speed limit in the wet conditions. The combination of torque and virtually slick tires made Mark's Z28 a terrible car to drive in wet weather.

Ron Fournier remembers the Z28 too. Mark was fascinated by Ron's fabricating talent and wanted him to teach him to weld. "Ron, if you will teach me to weld I'll teach you how to drive a race car," Ron recalls Mark saying. What Ron didn't have the heart to say was that he had no desire to drive a race car—he only liked to build them—but he gladly gave Mark welding lessons. A week or so later, Sue and Ron Fournier were at Mark and Sue's house for a pizza party. "We played with the kids for a while and then it was time for Mark and me to head back into Newtown Square to pick up the pizza," Ron says. "That Camaro Z28 was brand new and he said, 'Here, Ron, you drive.' We were headed back on that twisty road with the pizza on Mark's lap when we approached a very sharp right-hand turn and I was staying tight to the right side. Suddenly, Mark reached over with his left hand and turned the wheel so that we ran wide into the opposite lane. I thought this was my driving lesson, and when we got to his house I said 'What was that all about? Did I have the wrong line?' Mark laughed and said, 'No. There was a big puddle there and I didn't want to get the car dirty. I just washed it.'"

Mark completely dominated the three-hour Lime Rock race on May 30 with pole position and a two-lap race-winning margin over second-place Jerry Titus in the Shelby Mustang. Arthur Kelley in the *Boston Globe* described it as "an example of perfect driving in a perfectly prepared racing machine." Peter Revson was third for Javelin, an additional lap down.

It was just a week until Mark joined Karl and the Sunoco McLaren at St. Jovite in Quebec for round five of the USRRC. Mark and Lothar were again 1-2 in qualifying, with Mark the faster on this occasion. It began to rain just before the start and continued to come down hard throughout the race. Mark displayed his considerable rain-driving skills, leading throughout and eventually lapping Motschenbacher, who finished third. But it was John Cannon who impressed the most. Cannon had qualified his older Mk II McLaren-Chevy eighth on the grid but showed that he too had a special talent for racing in conditions that Mark described as "like driving on glare ice." Cannon passed Lothar and came within 15 seconds of Mark before Roger put out the "get moving" sign. Mark responded by substantially opening his lead over Cannon, who was the only other driver to finish on the lead lap. The win in the rain meant a great deal to Mark, who felt it helped establish his credentials within his own team.

"Up to that point I don't think either Roger or our guys had a great deal of confidence in me," Mark said. "But everyone knew that if you could win in the rain in those big cars, then you were some kind of Superman." The decisive win over Cannon, who Mark had recognized as a major talent as far back as Elva Courier days, was part of the satisfaction. Mark's quote is characteristic of his reluctance to acknowledge the stature he had attained. Roger Penske and Karl Kainhofer were already on record as recognizing his exceptional talent, and Roger considered Mark indispensable.

In later recalling the Laguna Seca victory, Mark described the technique he used to be so consistently fast in the rain. "You thunder down the straight just as fast as you would if it is dry. And you can brake just as hard. But then you have

to really tiptoe through the corners. Then as soon as you get the car straight you repeat the process—you go just as fast as you can, and then you brake as hard as you can, and then you tiptoe through the corner. A lot of people never understand this. They feel that the way you adjust to the rain is to drive more slowly everywhere, including down the straights. It's a different mode of driving in the rain and you have to adjust to it."

CHAPTER 76:

USAC Debut

Indy car racing had been on Mark and Roger's minds for some time, and with the delivery of the Eagle chassis they were now ready to experience USAC racing. The United States Auto Club and Indy car racing were essentially synonymous in 1968, and had been since the sanctioning body was formed in 1956 when the American Automobile Association (AAA) abandoned their central role in American racing. Oval racing for single-seat cars was the primary focus of USAC, with the Indianapolis 500 the crown jewel in the Championship car series.

USAC had dabbled in road racing in the late 1950s and early 1960s when the SCCA was still opposed to professional racing and was active in stock-car racing, rivaling NASCAR, particularly in their traditional Midwestern stronghold. What was relatively new for USAC was including road courses in their top series for Champ cars. The series had traditionally been run on ovals and dirt tracks, and the fairground tracks at Springfield, Illinois, and Syracuse, New York, had been as much a part of the championship as paved tracks. Road racing was a different culture, and USAC loyalists felt no better about including road circuits in their championship than they did about the influx of road racers at the Indy 500. The Champ cars had debuted at Mosport only a year before, as the Canadian track joined Riverside on the roster of road circuits on the Championship trail.

As road racers it made sense for Mark and Roger to make their first Champ car entry at Mosport, a circuit well known to the team. The Telegraph Trophy on June 8 was run as two 40-lap heats of approximately 100 miles each. Mark wasn't the only road racer in the field. Formula One star Dan Gurney had a long history in USAC racing. His combination of technical insight and international perspective had pioneered many changes in Indy car racing. He was an advocate of "stock-block"–based engines, and the 5.0-liter Gurney-Weslake Ford in his Eagle chassis was a proven winner. Mark and Roger were trying a similar combination, although the stock-block engine in their Eagle was a Traco-prepared Chevy. Dan put his Eagle on pole position with 1:21.55, almost a second quicker than second-fastest Mario Andretti. Mark qualified only 11th from an original entry of 25 cars and an actual starting field of 17. His time was 5.5 seconds slower than Gurney's, but the team expected to be better in the race as the car was completely untested. They missed Friday practice while Karl Kainhofer installed the just-arrived engine. Mark had run only the final qualifying on Saturday morning before the race.

Mark drove a strong first heat to finish sixth, although he was lapped by winner Gurney and runner-up Andretti. The second heat was even better, as Mark finished fourth behind Gurney, Andretti, and Ronnie Bucknum, and ahead of Al Unser. His official position on aggregate finishes was fifth overall. The footwell of the Eagle generated intense heat from poorly located oil and water piping. Mark stoically ignored the pain throughout the race, but he suffered burns to his right foot and left Mosport with it wrapped in bandages.

Saturday evening after the race Roger and Mark flew to Mid-Ohio for round five of the Trans-Am. The Mid-Ohio race had been delayed a week after President Lyndon Johnson appealed to the nation to observe Sunday, June 9, as a day of mourning for Senator Robert Kennedy, who had been assassinated in Los Angeles on June 5. Qualifying at Mid-Ohio had been missed in favor of the Mosport USAC race on Saturday, and Mark started at the back of the 19-car field. It wasn't certain until just before the start that Mark would be able to drive, but once in the race car he ignored the painful burns suffered at Mosport. It was a three-hour race, and Mark was confident that he had plenty of time to work his way to the front. In fact, the Sunoco Camaro was ninth at the end of lap one and in the lead by lap 10. Mark won, a full lap ahead of Jerry Titus in the Mustang and two laps ahead of Peter Revson in the Javelin. Columbus, Ohio's, Bob Johnson drove the second Penske Camaro and finished fourth on his home circuit.

CHAPTER 77:
Leading by Example

The Trans-Am teams headed east to Bridgehampton on June 23 for the second of two back-to-back weekends necessitated by the Kennedy day of mourning. Sam Posey joined the team to drive the second Camaro after arranging with Roger to run four races. Mark won again, and Sam barely missed beating George Follmer in the Javelin for second after a blown tire forced an unscheduled pit stop late in the race. Posey remembers observing a clear message from Mark on the first lap as the cars headed up the straight tightly bunched together. He deliberately turned his rearview mirror up, announcing to all pursuers "that he didn't much care what they had in mind."

Though it still represented the ultimate driver's challenge in North America, the Bridgehampton circuit was criticized for its rough surface and crowded paddock conditions. Even greater complaints came from team principals who found it a challenge to find accommodations for corporate guests and sponsors, not to mention crew members and other personnel. A large and high-profile race in June on the fashionable tip of Long Island wasn't making anyone happy. Like Watkins Glen, the original Bridgehampton race organizers had established an accord with local interests by extending the tourist season—not by competing for limited resources at the beginning of summer in the Hamptons, when available hotel rooms and restaurants were already pressed near the limit.

For Sam Posey, being part of the already-legendary Penske team was momentous. "I had only raced previously with my own set-up, so this was the first time I was part of another team. To see those cars being unloaded from their slant-bed trucks and look inside and see that battleship gray interior, absolutely everything stripped out of it, and to realize that I was actually going to drive one of these things was really a shock to me. Getting entrusted with driving this car made me realize that maybe I really was a driver."

While confessing to being somewhat in awe of Roger and Mark, Posey describes an air of secretiveness to the Penske operation. He ascribes much of this to the mystery surrounding the actual relationship between the team and General Motors, which was still officially espousing a "no-racing" stance.

"I was very unsure of myself in the presence of Penske or

Donohue," Posey says, adding that he felt like an outsider on the team. His experience was not unique. The Roger/Mark tandem was a powerful one, and a great deal of their success may have come from a shared sense of purpose and a common approach to achieving goals. This was a hard partnership to penetrate, and mutual loyalty was integral to the relationship. Sue Donohue said, "They had a bond and they had the racing together—that was theirs. You could not split that bond no matter what."

"I guess I've always considered Mark like a brother," Roger later told *Road & Track*'s Mike Knepper. "We both realized we were after the same goal and never allowed . . . disagreements to get in the way." Mark told Knepper, "We bent over backward for each other many times. It has been, I guess, a perfect partnership."

Charlie Hayes observed a shared sensibility in Mark and Roger. "Mark had an essential humility in that he was able to acknowledge others, and that is also Roger Penske's greatest strength," says Hayes. "You never hear Roger say, 'I won the race.' It's always, 'We, the team, won the race.' The thing I would say about those two guys is that their identity wasn't 'I,' it was we. Their sense of egoic identity was much larger than a single individual ego."

Posey also comments on a "heavy emphasis on conformity" within the team, and believes team personnel subordinated their own personalities to mirror the image projected by Mark and Roger. Fred Marik, who was an integral member of the team present at virtually every race over a four-year period, saw the team differently. "All the guys on the team had so much respect for Mark. They were there because they wanted to be. They would get excited about ideas and challenges. You didn't see that spirit in other teams. There was very little grumbling at Penske Racing. They were a well-knit team with mutual respect."

Jerry Hansen believes that Mark and Roger's hands-on approach was at the heart of their success. "They were always there. Other people would go off to dinner and drinks and come back later to see how work on the car was progressing. Not Roger and Mark. They were there the whole time and there wasn't anything that either of them wasn't willing to do."

Hansen's comment reflects a basic credo of the Penske team, one consistently repeated by those who were part of it: There was no job that was beneath anyone. Mark set that standard by example. He was the first one there in the morn-

ing. "If there was nothing obvious to do Mark would begin polishing wheels or straightening things in the transporter," remembers Fred Marik. "Mark was ultimately responsible for making all the details work out and everyone responded to his energy."

Marik believes that Roger and Mark complemented one another in their inspiration to the team. He saw Mark as a leader in a completely different way than Roger. "Roger was extremely articulate and could verbalize his ideas precisely—what he wanted done and how and when. Mark led by example. Mark and Roger would talk over what they wanted and Mark would get it done. It was Mark's team—he was the leader—in the sense that it happened as he wanted it and to his standard. But his standard was remarkably in tune with Roger's."

The Penske team was now in the middle of a string of 22 races on 22 consecutive weekends. While the Trans-Am and Group 7 teams operated separately, some duties overlapped, and the strain on the small operation was enormous. This was particularly true for Mark, whose primary job as star race driver was just one part of the story. Mark's hands-on involvement even went beyond engineering the race car. As a typical example, he would specify the design of the car haulers down to the finest details. Gear ratios on the truck were changed for long hauls, and engines and rear ends were swapped around on a frequent basis. Mark was in the middle of it all, working out the logistics and vehicle maintenance. He often drove the transporter to the track.

"We were still a very small team," says Karl Kainhofer, describing the dedicated crew of Penske Racing in 1968. "As such I believe our record that year represents one of the greatest achievements in racing history."

CHAPTER 78:
Family Trip

The circuit at Kent, Washington, was next on the USRRC trail on June 30. The big news was the debut of Ford's aluminum 427ci engine, appearing in Peter Revson's Lola. Mark had shattered George Follmer's existing lap record of 1:18.3 with a strong 1:16.5 that looked set for pole position. He parked the McLaren in the paddock with half an hour left in final qualifying. With just four minutes to go Revson made a final run with three gallons of gas on board, beating

Mark for the pole by two-tenths of a second.

In the race, Revson's Lola lasted only one lap, and Mark dominated the first half, lapping the entire field except for Skip Scott, until the big Traco Chevy in the Sunoco McLaren failed. Mark was out, and Scott and Chuck Parsons gave Simoniz and Carl Haas another 1-2 finish in their Lolas. Jerry Entin had an exceptionally good drive and was running a solid third when his engine blew late in the race, turning the position over to Canadian John Cordts. Despite his dominance on the track, with three rounds of the USRRC series left, Mark was by no means certain of the championship. His 27 points were just 3 more than Scott, 8 more than Parsons, and 10 more than the very quick Lothar Motschenbacher.

Mark had last seen Meadowdale Raceway in 1961 when he towed his Elva Courier from New Jersey and won the race to capture points essential to his SCCA National Championship. Located in Carpentersville, Illinois, a suburb of Chicago, it was an unforgiving circuit. On July 7 it was hosting round seven of the 13-race Trans-Am series. A major point of interest was the Pontiac Firebird entered by Terry Godsall, with fellow Canadian Craig Fisher driving. Sam Posey had the bad fortune to get off-line during practice and lose the Camaro on the marbles, extensively damaging the right side of the car when he hit a guardrail. Sam was impressed with the crew's all-night repair job, right down to the pinstriping. He was even more impressed when Roger called the press together on Sunday and lined up the mechanics next to the car. "Here they are," Roger announced, "the men who have made it possible for Sam to be in the race today." Sam believes that Roger was among a very few team owners who understood the importance of recognition in motivating personnel.

Mark overcame early brake trouble to capture pole position. He won the race comfortably from Peter Revson in the Javelin. Revson's Javelin teammate George Follmer was disqualified after contact with Jerry Titus in the Mustang. Titus was not able to finish, and his teammate Horst Kwech had rear-axle trouble that dropped him to 10th at the finish. Despite starting near last after missing qualifying, Sam Posey was up to sixth position after six laps and finished third ahead of Craig Fisher in the Firebird.

The week after Meadowdale, Mark, Roy Gane, and the Camaro spent two days at the General Motors Proving Grounds. The first day was to introduce the new 1969 model Camaros to the media, with Mark there to give rides and interviews. The next day, with the press gone, they brought out the race car and conducted serious testing with advanced instrumentation. The car was run on two skid pads, one measuring 88 feet in diameter, plus a larger high-speed 240-foot unit. Mark was impressed with the data collected and the feedback from the GM engineers. He was less pleased to later discover that their findings were included in a booklet for private owners on how to prepare a Camaro to go racing.

Sam Posey points out how physically demanding the Trans-Am cars were to drive: "Those were tough races, three hours long. I would sweat so much my ear plugs would wash out, and I'd be deafened by half-distance and for two days afterward would be hearing bells ringing. After Bridgehampton we went to celebrate at Barron's Cove—it was a joyous occasion and everyone was happy with our success. I placed a call to my Mom, and Mark had to talk for me because I couldn't hear—apparently he was very amusing, but I couldn't hear a word."

Mark had come to terms the year before with the amount of strength and endurance the sedan cars required, and had embarked on a vigorous conditioning regimen. It was the beginning of what would become a lifelong pursuit of an overall commitment to healthy eating and exercise habits.

It is a fact of life in racing that number-two drivers do not get equal attention—in practice laps, testing, or access to the latest lightweight part. The situation was exacerbated on the Penske team because Mark was more than just the lead driver. He was the race engineer and an integral member of a team that was very loyal to him. "It was all about Mark," Sam recalls. "Mark would go out first, he would set up the cars, and everyone would swarm around him when he came in." Despite this, Posey says that "when I drove for that team my car was exactly as well prepared as Mark's—I also believe, though, that Mark took his car out and tested it relentlessly while I never got an extra lap outside of what I got on the track in regular practice." Posey emphasizes that he received terrific treatment and he understood his role on the team. "Roger would come up right before the start and say, 'Don't go berserk, don't get involved.' He just wanted me to run a steady race."

Mark understood the engineering that made the car the way it was, and he designed its handling characteristics to suit his style. Posey cites one example that reveals Mark's physical fitness: "There was so much caster on that car—you could not make the front end push—you just couldn't. You'd go into the corner and it was like the front end had a pin and the rear end slid out—it was very fast, oversteering like that, but heavier than anything to drive. Mark had done all these exercises to build himself up—I could stay with Mark for the first quarter of the race, or the first third, and then I would be just exhausted. It wasn't a question of driving skill, it was a question of not having the strength—my arms were like rubber bands by then."

At Watkins Glen on July 13, Mark seized the USRRC points lead. Although the lure of Watkins Glen attracted one of the strongest entries of the season, Mark completely dominated the race that he called the hardest he had run all year. Under a blazing sun with the track temperature at 120 degrees, Mark averaged 117.97 mph over the 200 miles, finishing a lap ahead of Chuck Parsons in the Simoniz Lola. In the victory circle, after Roger poured a bucket of cold water over his head, Mark told the reporters, "Penske wanted me to slow down after we got a lap on the second-place car. We tried to run as slow as possible so we wouldn't have to make a gas stop, because gas stops are so unpredictable."

Sam Posey had qualified the Caldwell DL7 second and raced hard for second place with John Cannon before both men fell out with no oil pressure. Skip Scott lost valuable championship points when he hit a car he was lapping and was out of the race with a broken radiator. Canadians George Eaton and John Cordts were third and fourth in their McLarens.

The USRRC race was part of a double-header weekend with the Glen's first International 6-Hours for the World Manufacturers Championship running on Sunday. The battle was between the works Porsche 908s and the John Wyer–managed Gulf Ford GT40s. The GT40 of Jacky Ickx / Lucien Bianchi won the race ahead of their team car, driven by Paul Hawkins and David Hobbs.

Mark's schedule was brutal and his time at home with his young family was limited. The same was true for Jerry Kroninger, who was attending virtually every race in his capacity for Sun Oil. Joan Kroninger and Sue Donohue had become friends and were the catalysts for a family trip between races. The ideal opportunity arose with a Trans-Am on July 21 at St. Jovite in the beautiful Laurentian Mountains district of Quebec, followed by a week's vacation along the way to Elkhart Lake, Wisconsin, for the USRRC.

After Watkins Glen, Mark, Sue, Michael, and David, joined by Mark's mother, Zilly, loaded the family station wagon and headed to Canada in tandem with the Kroninger family. The

Kroninger boys, David, 10, Robert, 7, and Jim, 5, were compatible with 4-year-old Michael Donohue and 18-month-old David. First stop was Montreal for a look at the World's Fair site. Jim picked up a metal splinter near the hotel swimming pool and his foot began to swell. He was advised to soak his foot at regular intervals in a bucket of water until the tiny splinter would present itself and could be removed.

At Mont Tremblant Mark and Sam had placed the Camaros on the front row, with Mark on pole with a 1:50.4 and Sam at 1:51.1. Between them on the three-car front row was the Javelin of Peter Revson. George Follmer had qualified his Javelin fourth, and it was he who chased Mark hard for the first 25 laps before Mark spun on oil and fell to second place. Mark's regularly scheduled pit stop followed soon after, and was perfectly executed. When Follmer pitted from the lead, the Javelin crew was unable to match the Penske team's performance, and Mark was back in front. Follmer was second, while Sam Posey set the fastest lap of the race, trying to catch him before settling for third.

Mark brought the handsome loving cup–style trophy to five-year-old Jim, who had been seen most of the weekend with his foot in a bucket. He presented it to him, saying, "Jim, now you can soak your foot in style." Jim still has that cup today.

Michael Donohue turned four on July 20, and his birthday, celebrated during the trip, was particularly joyous for Sue and Mark. He was just two weeks out of the hospital after a tough six weeks. In late May Michael had been admitted to Children's Hospital in Philadelphia with idiopathic thrombocytopenic purpura (ITP), a bleeding condition in which the blood doesn't clot due to a low number of platelets. Mark was at the hospital every evening to be with his older son, who was receiving regular transfusions. Sue recalls the day there was a crisis: "Michael was living on those platelets he was receiving and the supply ran low. It was announced over the hospital intercom that donors were needed immediately. Mark informed Roger of what was going on and Roger never hesitated. He cleared the floor of the dealership. Every salesman and other personnel were at that hospital donating their blood. Here I was fighting Roger for time with Mark, and he did this beautiful thing. Roger was a problem in my life because of the time he demanded of Mark, but he was a very compassionate man."

Summer is never more glorious or better appreciated than during July in Canada and the northern states of the American

Midwest. The Donohue/Kroninger safari was a great success, and brought the travelers to the beautiful Kettle Moraine region of Wisconsin for the Road America 500—the last stop on the journey before the long drive home. One night the combined families found accommodations in a college dormitory with a common bathroom for the floor. It was Mark's habit to spend at least a half-hour in the shower in the morning, shaving and allowing the hot water to gradually wake him up. Jerry Kroninger recalls, "This presented no problem for my sons and me, but my wife Joan had to wait patiently—or otherwise—until Mark was finished."

The 500-mile race on the 4.0-mile Road America circuit was the longest on the USRRC schedule, and one the Penske team had chosen not to run the two previous seasons. This year, with the championship still in doubt, it could not be avoided. Despite his win at Watkins Glen, Mark could still be caught in points by either of the Simoniz Lola teammates, Skip Scott and Chuck Parsons. Carl Haas ran both Lolas and nominated Sam Posey as co-driver in each car. Mark's co-driver was Minnesota businessman Jerry Hansen. Hansen had won the June Sprints at the track in the ex-Penske Lola T70 and could more than hold his own in professional racing.

The Penske strategy was for Mark to drive the first and last thirds of the race. By the time he finished his first stint, the Sunoco McLaren had lapped every one of its 33 competitors. Hansen comfortably maintained the lead until disaster struck on lap 56. The big Chevy engine in the beautiful blue McLaren broke its crankshaft, and Jerry coasted it off the track at turn five. Skip Scott's Lola had blown a piston after only 11 laps, and Carl Haas now put him in as co-driver to Parsons so both men could score maximum points. Scott and Parsons repeated their win in the previous year's 500, and had now made the battle for the championship a very near thing. For Parsons it was the third win in a row in the classic Midwestern endurance race. In the standings Mark still led with 36 points, trailed by Chuck with 34 and Skip with 33. The racing world would have to wait three weeks for the finale at Mid-Ohio.

CHAPTER 79:
"The meter is back to zero"

At Bryar Motorsports Park in New Hampshire on August 4, Mark won his eighth consecutive Trans-Am. The Penske Sunoco Camaro streak had started at Sebring in March, and its dominance appeared complete. The Mustangs and Javelins could run comparable times in qualifying, but in the races the combination of Mark's race craft, quick pit stops, and reliability were making the series a runaway. The Mustangs made it tough at Bryar. The SCCA permitted them to use a new Detroit-Automotive "locker" differential for the first time. It was a specialty part that was not homologated, but the SCCA decided to allow it. Jerry Titus and Horst Kwech led Mark for the first quarter of the race until the Mustangs began to develop mechanical trouble. Mark won by three laps from George Follmer in the Javelin. The race was sponsored by the *Boston Herald-Traveler.* When Mark accepted the Herald-Traveler Trophy, he said, "This race was won in the pits."

Mark's friend Jim Haas was at Bryar and was brought into the pit-stop routine. His assigned task was as jack man on the driver's side of the car, with the added responsibility of handing Mark a cup of Gatorade. His final task was to take the cup back and throw the remaining ice down Mark's back. The routine was practiced, and the big moment came in the race as Mark roared into the famously short and narrow pit lane with everyone crowded together. The car didn't need left-side tires, so Jim needed only to hand the cup to Mark through the window. "Suddenly with a roar and spinning tires, he was gone. I sort of bounced off the side of the car as he departed. They could get 21 gallons in that Camaro in about four seconds—and that was it! Mark won the race and when he came in the first thing he said to me was, 'Jim, you didn't get me my Gatorade!' "

Roy Gane, chief mechanic on Mark's Camaro, was a well-trusted member of the team, highly independent, and known for being methodical. After Bryar, Mark told the *Boston Globe*'s Arthur Kelley, "I think that my pit crew, led by Roy Gane, is as good as the famous Wood brothers." Gane and Roger had a long association, and it was Roy who had converted the wrecked Formula One Cooper Climax—purchased by Roger in the paddock at Watkins Glen after Walt Hansgen's crash in the 1961 U.S. Grand Prix—into the original Zerex Special. Al Holbert was the mechanic on the Posey car. Sam recalls the tremendous influence Mark unknowingly had on the young man. "Al so much wanted to model himself after Mark that he actually patterned his handwriting after Mark's."

By the August 11 Trans-Am at Watkins Glen, the strain and pace of the racing season was taking its toll on Mark. Stress and fatigue had caught up with him, and he had developed a full-blown case of strep throat. Although it was still raging at Watkins Glen it did not stop him from capturing pole position with Sam Posey second. As he did so often in his career, Mark was able to subordinate physical distress when he was in the race car. The Watkins Glen Trans-Am was a long 114 laps over the very fast 2.3-mile circuit, and the heavy cars demanded great physical input. Mark had overcome all this on a less-than-perfect day until he lost his lead on the 91st lap when the Camaro ran out of brakes. Jerry Titus had been pursuing hard and now took the lead. Sam Posey took up the chase, and in the final pit-stop sequence came out on the track in the lead. Although Titus was pressing hard, Sam appeared set to bring the Camaro home a winner when he fell victim to tough racing luck.

Sam was about to lap the Camaro of Wilton "Rusty" Jowett when Jowett crashed violently in front of him. Sam had to brake drastically to avoid being involved, and the loss of momentum turned the lead over to Titus. Worse yet, he had flat-spotted his tires in avoiding Jowett's wreck, and despite his best efforts was unable to catch the Mustang. Titus won with Sam second and Mark third, a lap down but ahead of fourth-place Peter Revson's Javelin. Mark did set the fastest race lap, and that gave him the Onyx Trophy and the cash that went with it. Lentheric, a toiletries company, was a Watkins Glen sponsor—they rebuilt the Paddock Club which became the Onyx Club—and their Onyx Trophy was presented for the fastest lap in each professional race at the Glen. Mark had also won it in the USRRC race earlier in the summer.

Mid-Ohio was the showdown race to see who would be the United States Road Racing Champion for 1968. For Sue Donohue it was a last chance before the school year to organize a family trip. Although less ambitious than the two-week-plus jaunt in July, the Donohues and Kroningers again drove in tandem with their young sons in the backseats of their respective station wagons. Mark was feeling better, and the trip was a success, welcomed particularly by Sue for the chance for Mark to spend time with the family.

On Friday evening a Western Union telegram was received at the Downtown Motor Lodge in Mansfield, Ohio, addressed to Roger Penske:

6Mark6Roger6Karl6Peter6Jerry6John6Scotty6And6Friends

Sending	Sunoco	Team's
U	Penske	Efforts
Now	Establishing	Always
Our	Championship	Merit
Confidence	1968	
Of	At	VICTORY!
	Lexington	

E. R. Bradley, Bob Finucane, George Keegan, John Gottlieb, Marylou & Chick Clipsham

The loyal friends back at Sun Oil Company carried the team's success on their sleeve.

Lothar Motschenbacher remained the only USRRC regular who could run as fast as Mark, and he proved it again by capturing pole position in his McLaren with a 1:30.8 to Mark's 1:31.2. Chuck Parsons and Skip Scott, on the other hand, were the only drivers who could beat Mark for the championship. Lola designer Eric Broadley arrived from England to join Carl Haas and the Simoniz team for the big race. Parsons chose the team's brand-new Lola T160 as his mount. The untried car was fitted with an Al Bartz–tuned aluminum 427ci Chevy. Parsons wanted to win the championship by beating Mark instead of hoping for the Sunoco McLaren to break. Charlie Hayes in his McKee-Olds was fast in qualifying and was third, alongside Parsons on the second row.

Mark took an immediate lead that he never lost, gradually pulling clear of Lothar and setting the fastest lap. Parsons ran a steady third until the new 427 lost all its oil. Skip Scott persevered in the older Simoniz team car to finish third after an early race battle with Sam Posey, who finished fourth in the Caldwell. Scott's third made him second in the final points standing. On the last lap Sue showed Mark the pit board, which read sock it to 'em! Mark was the United States Road Racing Champion for the second year running.

With the end of the 1968 season, the SCCA's USRRC was being retired after serving American road racing well for six seasons. The series had encouraged development of sports-racing cars, and its success paved the way for the Can-Am. Now the SCCA announced that in 1969, the Can-Am would expand from an autumn-only series to take over some of the earlier USRRC dates. Mark had been the only repeat champion, having won the title in its last two years. The previous champions had been Bob Holbert (1963); Jim Hall (1964); George Follmer (1965); and Chuck Parsons (1966).

Now Penske Racing, along with all the Group 7 teams, looked forward to the Can-Am, which opened in just two weeks. Mark's comment to John Radosta of the *New York Times* expressed it perfectly: "Now, as we say in Philadelphia, the meter is back to zero, and we'll have to start all over again for the Can-Am."

Before that Mark and the Trans-Am team were headed to Colorado for the 11th round in the series on August 25, at the high-altitude Continental Divide Raceway. Mark won in another great race against Jerry Titus with the Mustang, which again failed late in the race. Dan Gurney was in the other factory Mustang and his engine blew up. The Javelins had a terrible race, with Follmer suffering rocker-arm trouble and Revson being disqualified for a push-start. Craig Fisher in the Pontiac Firebird was second. The SCCA permitted the Firebird to run with a Chevy Z28-based engine because Pontiac had no engine that conformed to the series rules. Although not a factory car, Malcolm Starr's Mustang had the latest tunnel-port engine from Ford. Anxious to know how it compared to the Camaro in straight-line speed, Malcolm decided to experiment as he saw Mark coming up to lap him. "I intentionally blocked him so we could run up the straight together—we started the straightaway at the same speed. I had the tunnel port engine, but Mark had several car lengths on me by the next corner."

CHAPTER 80:
Road America for the Can-Am Opener

Roger sold the well-proven but hard-used McLaren M6A to Jerry Hansen. A fresh car was needed for the Can-Am, and it was developed from the spare M6A chassis that had been included in Roger's purchase of Bruce McLaren's personal M6A the previous year. Everything the team had learned was put into the new car, including an updated suspension to accommodate the 427ci engine and the larger Goodyear tires. The team had developed special lightweight bodywork, and the paint job featured beautifully intricate pinstriping. Beyond new bodywork the car was fitted with a Ron Fournier–fabricated rear wing designed

with a hydraulic lever that would allow Mark to adjust it on the straightaway for low drag. Before heading west for the opening round of the Can-Am, the team went to test at Bridgehampton. The car was fast but the adjustable wing proved impractical.

In the paddock at Road America were the exciting new McLaren M8As for reigning world champion Denny Hulme and team principal Bruce McLaren. The pair had dominated the previous year's Can-Am, and the new cars took the game up another notch. Their design followed contemporary Formula One practice—as pioneered on the 1967 Lotus 49—by using the engine as a stressed frame member. McLaren's primary competition would come from the American contingent that had just completed the USRRC series, and the most notable representative of that group was Mark. Jim Hall had run only two early-season USRRC races in the Chaparral 2G, as his hopes were focused on the new 2H being developed in Midland. The 2H never appeared in 1968, and Hall later announced that final tests had resulted in a suspension failure that was believed to be integral to the design. Hall supported the series with the now-venerable 2G, but was still very competitive.

The media had hyped the 1968 Can-Am series, and there had been suggestions of interesting new cars and drivers. The actual entry at Road America, while large, featured few new teams or new cars. Missing among the serious teams were those of Dan Gurney and John Surtees, though both would appear as the series moved forward. The Swiss-domiciled Swede Jo Bonnier added international flavor with his McLaren M6B-Chevy, although at Road America he was well off the pace in qualifying. Mexican star Pedro Rodríguez was more competitive in a NART-prepared Ferrari 330 P4.

The McLarens were as good as they looked, qualifying three seconds faster than they had the previous year. Bruce was on pole with a 2:09.8 and Denny was only a tenth slower. Only Jim Hall and Mark approached their times, with Hall third at 2:10.8 and Mark at 2:11.0. The third row of Motschenbacher's McLaren and Parsons's still-new Carl Haas Lola T160 was another three seconds down, closely followed by the fastest Fords—Peter Revson in a Shelby-entered McLaren, with the experimental 427ci all-alloy engine, and Mario Andretti in a George Bignotti–entered Lola T70 Mk III. Charlie Hayes in the McKee and Rodríguez in the Ferrari rounded out the top 10, albeit six seconds off the McLaren/Hulme pace. Just behind them came Ronnie Bucknum in a Lola-Ford and

Jerry Hansen in the ex-Penske McLaren. Tom Swindell had a serious crash on Friday on the exit of the extremely fast kink when his McLaren sailed high into the surrounding trees and bushes. Sam Posey stopped to help pull him from the burning race car. Swindell remained on the critical list all weekend with burn injuries.

Twenty-nine cars took the green flag on Sunday, September 1. The generally good weather of the weekend had changed to a cold morning drizzle, and a hard rain began to fall on the pace lap. Mark had a near-disastrous start. Following the orange McLarens from the second row, the airbox on the Sunoco McLaren picked up track material that jammed the throttle butterflies open. "My car had a scoop, or ram airbox, on the injector stacks, and it collected a rock or something," Mark remembered. "Finally I discovered that all I had to do was give the throttle a hard blip to let the rock fall into the engine and get digested, and there was no more problem."

Before clearing the jammed throttle, Mark drove off the track at the bottom of the hill in turn three and again in the Carousel, dropping all the way to 23rd position as most of the field stormed by. Once he had successfully cleared the throttle, he spent the rest of the race catching up. By lap 8 Mark was up to 8th place, which he improved to 5th by the 11th lap and 4th on lap 16 of the 50-lap race. Hulme was in the lead with McLaren second, and the driver chasing them hardest in the rain was Mario Andretti. As the track began to dry, Andretti had dropped back from McLaren, and at the halfway point in the race—25 laps—Mark trailed Mario by 58 seconds and was gaining. The crowd was riveted and stood to cheer as the Sunoco McLaren passed, each lap a little closer. With just two laps to go Mark had caught Mario and was directly behind when the DOHC Ford blew up in turn 13. Mark saw a connecting rod fly directly into his radiator. Andretti was out while Mark made it to the finish in third place—with coolant all over the pedals and floor pan and the front of the Sunoco McLaren bathed in oil from the blown Ford. Peter Revson was fourth, Jim Hall fifth, and Lothar Motschenbacher sixth and setting fastest race lap. Two drivers who impressed in the rain were Bonnier and Canadian George Eaton, though both encountered trouble later in the race.

CHAPTER 81:

A Can-Am Win and a Trans-Am Title

The Manufacturers Championship had been clinched for Chevrolet by virtue of Mark's 9 wins in the 11 races run to date, with 2 more to come. With the racing program in the forefront of the marketing effort, Chevrolet dealers had experienced tremendous sales of the Camaro Z28. It was widely believed by consumers that the Z28 was close to being a race car as it sat in the dealer's showroom. The West Coast market was too important to miss, and on September 8 the team was at Riverside for round 12.

Al Bochroch would later say of the Mission Bell 250 at Riverside that "Donohue made more news by failing to win, than Horst Kwech did in winning." Mark had qualified fastest and had a tremendous race with Jerry Titus's Mustang. Both men fell out with engine trouble, and Kwech won in the second works Mustang. Kwech was a 30-year-old Australian who, after settling in Waukegan, Illinois, made his name in SCCA amateur racing beginning in 1963. He won two National Championships and was awarded the club's President's Cup in 1966. He had been racing an Alfa Romeo GTA in the Trans-Am, and as a frequent winner in the under-2.0-liter division, was brought into the Shelby team for 1968. In practice before his Riverside win, Kwech had been off the pace, prompting a spirited discussion with Ford racing boss Fran Hernandez. Hernandez was said to have pointed to the Armco barriers on the outside of Riverside's fast turn nine and told Kwech, "The next time you come back in, I want to see yellow paint on these barriers and the marks all along the left side of your car." Hernandez later confirmed this to Al Bochroch, adding, "That's just about what I said. But what you don't know is that the next time Horst went out he took two seconds off the lap record."

The competitiveness of the Can-Am was enhanced by the return of John Surtees and Dan Gurney at Bridgehampton on September 15, although neither man played a central role in the great race that unfolded. Surtees had been developing the latest Lola T160 at his own Team Surtees base in England. He was no longer associated with the Lola works, and entered the car as a TS-Chevrolet. Gurney had a highly modified McLaren M6B which he named the McLeagle to indicate the extensive engineering changes by the AAR shop in Santa Ana, California. It was fitted with a 325ci Ford. He also entered a new Lola T160 with a 305ci engine for protégé Swede Savage. The rest of the field was much the same as the one seen at Road America two weeks earlier.

Mark posted the fastest time on Friday at 1:28.53, with Peter Revson next, followed by McLaren, Hulme, and Gurney. On Saturday Mark did not improve his time and was left fourth on the grid as the McLarens took the front row—Denny was fastest with a 1:27.77—and Revson had moved up to third. At the start Mark was initially fourth before Revson had trouble and Mark drove around him. Mark began to close on the McLarens as Hulme went by his teammate to take the lead. Jim Hall was flying in the Chaparral, and after 30 laps the first four cars were covered by just four seconds. Hall now asserted himself: On lap 32 he passed Mark, on lap 34 he passed Bruce, and on lap 36 of the 70-lap race he took the lead when he went by Denny Hulme in traffic. Suddenly on the 42nd lap the Chaparral began to suffer fuel-injection trouble and dropped back. Mark was now pressing the works McLarens hard. Hulme's engine failed on lap 53, then McLaren's on lap 62. Mark ran out the race a winner with a comfortable lead over Hall. Motschenbacher was third, Savage fourth, Richard Brown fifth, and Dan Gurney, struggling with handling problems, sixth in the McLeagle.

It was a great win for Mark and the Sunoco McLaren. With characteristic modesty, he downplayed its significance because he had inherited the lead when the McLaren duo broke. His view ignored the fact that he had been part of the battle at the front all day and richly deserved the victory. Most close observers considered it the most exciting and competitive Can-Am race in the three year history of the series. Mark's respect for this most challenging of circuits was evident in his post-race answer to the question, "How did he drive the Bridgehampton track?" Joel Finn was present to hear Mark reply, "Carefully. Very carefully." He was now leading the Can-Am with 13 points, compared to 9 for second-place Hulme.

For the first time since June, Mark had no race the following weekend. Penske Racing had maintained a flat-out pace since early spring. The 13-race Trans-Am schedule and the combined USRRC and Can-Am schedules of 15 more races left little margin for error. Mark personally organized and generally took responsibility for much of the logistics of getting to the races and the test days. Travel alone ate up time, and Mark was hands-on involved with preparation work in

the small Newtown Square race shop. The Trans-Am cars and Group 7 cars each had their own dedicated crew, but Mark was involved with both. Although Roger was busy running his dealership and other businesses, he remained intimately involved in what was going on in the race shop. His own demanding schedule dictated that meetings with Mark were typically held early in the morning or late in the day—often late in the evening.

These activities left little time for a life at home with Sue and the boys. Sue recalls the all-too-familiar routine: "Mark would go to the race shop at seven in the morning and he would be there all day. He would come home for dinner. And Roger would call the minute he sat down for a hot dinner. He would talk to him the whole time he was eating. And then Mark would go back to the race shop." Roger pushed Mark no harder than he did himself. His personal ethic in this regard was reflected in a comment he made to AutoWeek's Leon Mandel: "I try to eat dinner at home with my family a minimum of one night a week."

Edmonton, Canada, was a new venue for the Can-Am, and its inclusion meant that the last four races in the 1968 series would be in the far western regions of North America. It was also the only race keeping the "Can" in Can-Am: St. Jovite's fall race had become the Formula One Canadian Grand Prix, and the organizers at Mosport had not been able to satisfy purse demands for the growing series. The 2.53-mile, 14-turn Edmonton International Speedway was brand-new in 1968, having been developed from a facility previously known as Speedway Park. The city of Edmonton is enormous in its geographic sprawl even though it is home to well less than a million residents. It is the provincial capital of Alberta and the center of Canada's oil industry.

From the last stop at Bridgehampton it was more than a 2,500-mile tow for the Can-Am teams. Karl Kainhofer loved the long drives, and on this occasion his companion in the transporter was Peter Law. "That trip to Edmonton was a challenge because the roads were very different then," Karl recalls. "But I never minded them; it was part of the job." Peter Reinhart had also rejoined the team for the Can-Am after a successful season racing in Europe. Reinhart had purchased the 1967 Trans-Am Sunoco Camaro at the end of the season and taken it to his home in Germany, where he won five of the seven races he entered. He had maintained the car in Sunoco colors and received some sponsorship assistance from the Belgian subsidiary of Sun Oil.

At Edmonton Mark qualified a strong fourth with a 1:26.5 on the new and still-dusty circuit, just a tenth slower than Jim Hall, with whom he shared the second row. The Chaparral had been the fastest car throughout qualifying until the McLaren duo of Denny and Bruce achieved identical times of 1:26.0 to capture the front row. The rest of the 24-car field was essentially the same as at Bridgehampton. Peter Revson and Dan Gurney occupied the row right behind Mark. Jim Hall made the race interesting when he mixed it up aggressively with the McLarens, only to pit later with brake problems. On the pace lap the Sunoco-McLaren's radiator air intakes had collected leaves and other debris and the engine began to overheat, seriously compromising Mark's ability to put pressure on the orange cars. He pitted just long enough to have the leaves removed, but that slight overheating had taken the edge off the engine. Mark did well to finish third, and was the only car on the lead lap with winner Hulme and second-place McLaren. Mark was 30 seconds down at the finish—the same amount of time he'd lost in the pits clearing the radiator. Fourth-place Sam Posey, driving teammate Brett Lunger's Lola T160, was four laps down. Two more laps behind came the final point scorers: Chuck Parsons in the Simoniz Lola T160 and Charlie Hayes in the McKee-Olds.

With the Can-Am series half over, Hulme was now the leader with 18 points to Mark's 17. Mark crisscrossed the country, first heading east for three days at home and in the race shop, then flying even farther west for the season-ending Trans-Am at Kent, Washington.

Before the race at Kent, Jerry Titus severed his long relationship with Ford and Shelby American to move into a Pontiac Firebird in partnership with Canadian Terry Godsall. TG Racing ran Firebirds for Titus and Craig Fisher. Replacing Titus in the lead Mustang was Peter Revson, who had in turn left the American Motors Javelin to take the seat. Also in factory Mustangs for this final race were Horst Kwech and Ronnie Bucknum. Ford was taking no chances. They wanted to win the race, and even more important, to prevent AMC from taking second place from them in the final championship points. Despite the loss of Revson, AMC still had George Follmer, and now put Lothar Motschenbacher in the vacant seat.

Titus outqualified Mark by a tenth of a second, but it was Mark who led into the first turn and held the lead until he pitted before Titus. Mark controlled the race, and Titus's brave effort in the Firebird ended with a blown engine after 43 laps. The Firebirds were fast using the Z28 engine, and Craig Fisher finished second, with Ronnie Bucknum third for Mustang. Follmer and Kwech tangled, knocking Horst out of the race and George out of contention.

With another victory Mark and the Penske-Hilton racing team had completed a remarkable season. The Sunoco Camaro won 10 of the 13 races in the most intense road-racing series in America. The Can-Am was for purists, but the Trans-Am was the title the auto industry cared about. These were the glory years for the series, and the manufacturers would remain committed for the next several seasons. Ford had been the dominant team in the series and had won the first two years. Now Ford was smarting from losing the title to Chevrolet, and partisanship was fierce. The company went away mad and ready to return with renewed effort. AMC could only feel good about their first year in the series. Despite not winning a single race, they were competitive, and had come within a whisker of taking second from Ford. Pontiac had much to overcome, as the SCCA wasn't certain to let them continue using a Chevrolet engine in the Firebird. Their best hope came from the considerable force and driving talent represented by Jerry Titus.

Roger and Mark had decided that for 1969 they would need to run two cars on a regular basis in order to defend the Trans-Am championship. After the last race at Kent, several drivers—including Charlie Gibson, Tony Adamowicz, Skip Scott, and Ronnie Bucknum—were tested in Mark's winning car. Roger also took the opportunity to try the race car, the first time he had driven since his retirement at the end of 1964. The Sunoco-Camaro was fairly tired from the previous day's race, and all the drivers complained that this made it impossible to approach Mark's times. Mark gave the best possible response by getting into the car himself and going two seconds faster than their best. Skip Scott and Ronnie Bucknum were the fastest, and Bucknum was chosen for the drive because of his consistency. According to Mark, "Skippy and Ronnie were the only ones there who understood the way those cars had to be driven. They need to be manhandled, driven really, really hard. That does not mean they had to be abused. You had to be pushing them into a drift all the time. It was all about braking and turning and inducing a slide."

CHAPTER 82:

Foggy Goggles and Other Disappointments

At Laguna Seca for round four of the Can-Am on October 13, the Sunoco McLaren had engine trouble that hampered Mark in qualifying. He was fifth fastest, and the third-row spot alongside Chuck Parsons was his poorest qualifying position in the entire series. Jim Hall had the Chaparral on the front row with pole sitter Bruce McLaren, and row two was occupied by Denny Hulme and Peter Revson. Two contenders were scratched from the 30-car grid moments before the start. Charlie Hayes in the McKee-Olds had an injector go bad, while the starter failed on the Chaparral, forcing Jim Hall to vacate his front-row spot. It had rained all morning and never let up all day.

For Mark it was a dismal day. He was running fourth when his goggles became so fogged that he could not see at all. Although Roger and Karl were waiting in pit lane with a replacement pair, Mark was reluctant to stop. As he later recounted, his mind was stuck on a conversation from earlier in the weekend. Karl Kainhofer had casually mentioned that he admired the way Mark pressed on in races while many Grand Prix stars were inclined to stop in the pits with the least problem. "I had it in my mind that I wasn't going to pit for something as inconsequential as that," Mark remembered. "Because of what Karl had said, and because I was too proud, I wasn't going to come in." He had two pairs of spare goggles taped inside the cockpit and finally pulled alongside the road to put one of them on. They, too, proved useless and Mark soldiered on, a victim, in this case, of his own obstinacy. "My pride really cost me on that day," Mark later said. "Coming in for the goggles would have been the smart thing."

The sensation of the race was John Cannon. Driving an outdated McLaren 1B, he moved from 15th on the grid to 5th by the end of the second lap. He picked off the top runners one lap at a time, and by lap seven was in the lead and motoring away. Eventually Cannon lapped the entire field for an overwhelming win in an obsolete car. Cannon was on the right Firestone tires for the conditions, and the wet track meant that his less-powerful 365 Traco Chevy and older chassis were not a disadvantage. It was a great display of his considerable talent. The usually dominant orange

McLarens were second (Denny) and fifth (Bruce). George Eaton also sparkled in an older car, and finished third ahead of Motschenbacher. Jerry Titus was sixth, Skip Scott seventh, and Mark a very unhappy eighth.

Riverside on October 27 attracted a large field of 35 cars for the Los Angeles Times Grand Prix. Mark was third on the grid alongside Bruce and Denny. Jim Hall, Peter Revson, and Dan Gurney were next. Gurney had fitted his McLeagle with a 427ci engine for the long Riverside straights. The McLarens showed their superiority and dominated the race. McLaren won, but Hulme had an off-course excursion while lapping a backmarker, and subsequent pit stops dropped him to fifth at the finish. Mark finished second, 37 seconds behind McLaren, with Hall third and Motschenbacher fourth. Laguna Seca race winner John Cannon again qualified 15th and produced another good result, bringing the tube-frame-chassis McLaren home for the final point position in sixth.

Mark was happy with his result on a hot day that saw many cars struggle with overheating. He had insisted on fitting an oversize oil cooler that protruded from the bodywork. It was ugly, but Mark had insisted that he needed it, and afterward felt vindicated. There was one race to go, and the championship would be decided at Las Vegas. Mark was very much in the hunt—tied for second at 23 points with Bruce McLaren, with the pair only three points behind Denny Hulme.

Before the last round of the Can-Am, Mark, Roger, and Karl headed east to take part in a Goodyear test day with the Eagle at the Indianapolis Motor Speedway. It was Mark's first time at the Speedway, and although he gained a feel for the storied track, it was ultimately a frustrating experience. As a "rookie" who hadn't taken the USAC driver test, he was limited to lapping at a maximum average of 150 mph. A fast time was 170 mph, so Mark was unable to gain a full sense of the limits of the car or the track.

The Stardust Grand Prix on November 10 started with a disaster for the Sunoco McLaren and ended with a bigger one for Jim Hall and the Chaparral. The grid assumed a familiar pattern, with Hulme and McLaren in the first two spots and Jim Hall third, just ahead of Mark. Sam Posey was quick all weekend and sat alongside Mario Andretti in the third row. They were both driving Lola T160s with 427ci engines, although Sam's was a Chevy and Mario's a Ford. Gurney and Revson were next in their regular cars, and in ninth alongside Jerry Titus was Chris Amon in the works Ferrari 612. The car was making its first appearance after being touted all year. The debut of the V12, 6.2-liter Ferrari, the first dedicated Can-Am effort from Maranello, was a shot in the arm to the series even at this late date. It was a tight field and a great race was expected.

It all fell apart for Mark on the grid. The big Chevy engine in the Sunoco McLaren would not start. The culprit was the condenser within the distributor. Although the battery would turn the engine over, it would not fire. The start was delayed long enough for the crew to change batteries, but the car still wouldn't start. Karl Kainhofer had never seen Mark so completely frustrated and upset. "I took it so hard that I was actually crying under the visor," Mark admitted later. "Karl was the only one who saw it." Karl told Mark he shouldn't take it so hard, and Mark later reflected, "That's a problem I've always had in racing—taking it too hard. . . . Maybe winning was too important to me."

The McLaren was pushed to the side and Mario moved up to Mark's slot on the second row. He made a great start that placed him among the orange McLarens in the first turn. Mario and Bruce tangled, and the following cars were mostly off the road trying to avoid the accident. The incident had a profound impact on the race. Amon's Ferrari was eliminated immediately, and numerous other cars were involved sufficiently to affect their final result. McLaren and Andretti both pitted, Mario eventually finishing ninth and Bruce struggling up to a sixth-place finish that proved important when the prizes were awarded. Sam Posey looked as though he would finish second, but had to stop for a last-minute fuel splash and finished fifth. Denny Hulme won, while George Follmer was a richly deserved second ahead of Jerry Titus, third, and Chuck Parsons, fourth.

Far worse than Mark's bad luck was the calamity that befell Jim Hall. He had been among the cars victimized in the turn-one mess, and had fallen to 22nd place before battling back to fourth. Another stop on lap 43 of 70 dropped him to ninth, and he had moved back to eighth when he came up to un-lap himself from second-place Lothar Motschenbacher in the high-speed first turn. At that moment Motschenbacher's McLaren broke a suspension upright and slowed dramatically. The Chaparral rode over the left rear of the McLaren and was launched high in the air to land upside down. Both of Jim Hall's legs were broken, his jaw was dislocated, and he was burned. Motschenbacher suffered minor burns and bruises.

The day had been an enormous disappointment for the Penske team. Roger had a contingent of business associates in attendance, and the failure to even start must have been a great letdown. He handled it well, showing his strength of leadership by remaining calm in the face of adversity. The season had started in Mexico City with a failure to make the starting grid, and now the Can-Am had ended with a similar experience. Otherwise, Mark and the Sunoco McLaren had been not only fast but consistent. And the Penske reputation for preparedness continued to grow. In a story for *Road & Track*, Bruce McLaren expressed his surprise at the generally poor preparation among the Can-Am teams compared to Formula One. But he added, "There is no standard of preparation other than in the Penske area."

In the motoring press there was a general view of the Penske/Donohue operation as Teutonic in its efficiency and precision. Before and after World War II, the Mercedes-Benz racing team had set the standard under the firm and absolute direction of team manager Alfred Neubauer. Now a popular tongue-in-cheek reference to Roger was as "Herr Neubauer." Roger's reputation for infallibility also inspired a joke that asked, "Did you hear that Roger had a close call while taking his morning walk? He was almost run over by a speedboat."

The mood at the traditional end-of-season party at the Stardust Hotel brightened considerably when news came that Jim Hall was out of danger. Mark had regained his composure and gave an amusing speech, opening by saying, "We came, and we saw, and we lost." It brought down the house. Mark's success as a speaker often owed more to his natural sense of comedic timing and emphasis than to his material. Fellow Can-Am driver Bobby Brown remembers how much fun Mark could be in these settings. "Mark would write a menu out and send it over to you; it might be birds' beaks for appetizer, cow's gizzards for an entrée, and bull's balls for dessert. He was a great character that way—a fun guy who would play practical jokes. He also had a dry sense of humor. He would tell you outrageous things with a straight face. But you knew he was kidding."

Mark congratulated the McLaren team as Denny Hulme received the Johnson Wax Trophy. The single point that Bruce McLaren had scored for finishing sixth was worth almost $10,000, as it elevated him to second place in the final standings—one point ahead of Mark. The payout from the $126,000 end-of-season points fund gave $40,000 to Denny, $26,450 to Bruce, and $16,700 to Mark. These payouts were exclusive of the purse posted for each race, and helped make the Can-Am experience a financial success for the top teams.

A sportsmanship award of $1,000, posted by Triangle Productions, was particularly popular. The selection was made by the drivers, who gave the award to John Cannon.

CHAPTER 83:

Naked on Mount Fuji

The SCCA had arranged a post-Can-Am race at the Mount Fuji circuit near Tokyo, Japan. It was dubbed the World Challenge Cup and enjoyed enormous support from the Nippon Auto Club. The organizers originally hoped that the entire top tier of Can-Am teams would be transported en masse to Tokyo for the November 23 race. But lack of interest from the European teams and the devastation at Las Vegas thinned the field. Nonetheless, Roger Penske supported the event, as did Carroll Shelby, who entered a car for Peter Revson. Five Japanese Group 7 cars helped fill out the field that included Can-Am regulars John Cannon, Jerry Titus, George Follmer, Jo Bonnier, Sam Posey, Chuck Parsons, Al Unser, and Pedro Rodríguez.

Karl Kainhofer, Jerry Kroninger, and Jim Travers flew to Japan on a specially chartered plane carrying SCCA officials and most of the American drivers and team personnel. At the airport in Tokyo the reception from the press and the sponsoring clubs was terrific. The Penske team was greeted with banners and great enthusiasm by Sun Oil's Japanese subsidiary. Mr. Iguchi, the company president, formally greeted them and offered the Penske team a ride to the Mount Fuji circuit some 45 miles distant. They later regretted turning down the offer. The bus that was to take everyone to the track never arrived, and after several hours of waiting, the exhausted group drifted off to find their own accommodations. Mark and Roger arrived together the next day and joined the team at the circuit. Mark was suffering from flu symptoms and was under the weather all weekend.

Toyota had a team of Group 7 cars entered in the race, and their presence at the track made a lasting impression on Travers, Kroninger, and Kainhofer. Each morning before they began working on the race cars, the mechanics and other team personnel assembled for group calisthenics. Observing the vigorous exercises, Karl remarked to Jim and Jerry how fortunate they were that Roger wasn't present to see the exhibition. "He would have us out there doing jumping jacks, for sure."

Mount Fuji race circuit is a magnificent venue that included a 1.25-mile straightaway. USAC had run a race on the circuit two years earlier, and Jackie Stewart held the lap record at 1:22.0 in a Mecom Lola-Ford. The Can-Am cars were substantially faster, and Mark took the pole with a 1:16.8, sharing the front row with Peter Revson at 1:17.7. Mark and Peter ran away with the race and battled wheel to wheel throughout. The struggle between the two rivals was memorable, and with five laps to go Peter and Mark were two laps ahead of Sam Posey in the next car. Sam was also sick that weekend but drove well to eventually finish second. Then suddenly the Sunoco McLaren was starving for gas. There was sufficient fuel in the tank, but the Japanese circuit ran counterclockwise and the fuel pickup was on the wrong side. Mark rushed into the pit to find the crew unprepared. The Group 7 McLaren was not set up for rapid fueling, and the seat had to be moved slightly to gain access to the filler cap. Karl resourcefully grabbed a pit-lane pylon and inverted it to create an impromptu funnel as Jerry Kroninger poured in the Sunoco 260 gasoline.

Under the circumstances, a fast pit stop was not of utmost importance. Mark was not going to catch Revson in the time remaining, and his lead over the third-place car was sufficient to do the refueling without rushing. Roger, for once, failed to grasp the situation and yelled repeatedly for Karl to pull the funnel out, finally grabbing it himself and yanking it out. The result was that the substantial amount of fuel still in the pylon/funnel poured onto Mark. He exited still in second place but now soaked through with fuel. He made it just out of the pits before being overcome by the burning pain of raw gasoline. Karl recalls that Mark actually thought he might have been on fire. "I think the fire at Watkins Glen always stayed in his mind," says Karl, "and, of course, that raw fuel can burn terribly." Mark stopped the race car on the circuit and began to remove his fuel-drenched clothes as fast as he could. He ended his Japanese experience huddled out on the circuit, in front of the crowd of 30,000-plus and a live nationwide television audience. "There I was, crouched down in the bushes, naked, while Peter went on to win," Mark recalled. "Finally someone came around with some woolen towels and rescued me, but it was a very embarrassing end to my year with the McLaren."

CHAPTER 84:

"Charge it to Roger Penske"

It was only a week after the adventure in Japan that Mark had the chance to race the Indy Eagle in the final round of the USAC championship, the Rex Mays 300 at Riverside. Peter Reinhart and Peter Law had brought the Eagle to Riverside while Mark and Karl were in Japan, and the team met up to test early in the week. It had been more than five months since the race at Mosport, and the Riverside round was eagerly anticipated by the Penske team. The combined Trans-Am / USRRC / Can-Am schedules had been so intense that they had not been able to run in an earlier race. From the perspective of the USAC regulars, Mark was one of the "road-racing specialists" now appearing as potential spoilers in their championship series. In fact, Riverside would prove to be the deciding race that gave the championship to Bobby Unser over Mario Andretti. The 1968 USAC championship trail had encompassed 28 races that included the Indy 500, dirt and asphalt ovals, road courses, and the Pikes Peak hillclimb.

But the ultimate spoiler on road courses was Dan Gurney, who placed his Olsonite-sponsored Eagle on pole position with a time of 1:18.95. Andretti was second at 1:19.2 in the Brawner-Ford. Mark showed he would be competitive by qualifying fifth—barely a second slower than Dan at 1:20.01, and alongside Jack Brabham on the third row. Third and fourth were Joe Leonard and Al Unser.

Karl Kainhofer had set up the Traco Chevy to run on the methanol fuel used in USAC Champ car races. Sun Oil did not manufacture methanol, so Jerry Kroninger carefully researched the literature and ran comparative tests on the dynamometer in the company's laboratories. He immediately discovered that methanol produced 10 percent more power and roughly twice the fuel consumption of gasoline, and began to carefully evaluate power gains obtained by the addition of nitromethane. While nitromethane is extremely effective in increasing engine power because of its high concentration of oxygen, it also has low antiknock qualities that are harmful to engines. Armed with his charts, a thermometer, and a hydrometer, Kroninger worked with Mark and Karl at Riverside to determine the amount of nitromethane to be used. They went with 15 percent for qualifying but conservatively decided not to use any during the race.

Mark was soon running a strong second behind Dan and ahead of Mario. The great run ended abruptly when Mark crashed at turn six on lap 35 of the 116-lap race. Exiting the previous turn Mark had slipped slightly into the dirt on the right side of the track. As he eased back onto the track, he grazed a tire marker and the right front suspension broke, taking out the wheel, hub, and brakes. Karl and Mark later discovered the reason for the breakage. Peter Law and Peter Reinhart had unknowingly fitted a front upright that had been previously broken and had a hairline crack. After overcoming his initial upset, Mark decided not to mention it to Roger or either of the Peters, concluding that it was not worth a confrontation with people he otherwise had a high regard for. "I didn't want the guys to feel like I had 'caught' them at something," Mark recalled. "Roger never did that to me, or anybody else, and they certainly hadn't done it on purpose. That broken upright sat in my drawer for four years as a reminder, and those guys never knew about it."

Despite the disappointing result, Mark, Roger, and Karl were encouraged that they could run competitively in the USAC series. The Riverside race would play an important part in their thinking as plans unfolded for the new year ahead.

The morning after the race Martini & Rossi hosted a commemorative breakfast at which they honored Mark as recipient of their Driver of the Year award. Mark received a check for $7,500 and a dramatic bronze-sculpted trophy depicting three eagles in flight. Runners-up were David Pearson, Denny Hulme, and Bobby Unser.

A combined Christmas and end-of-season party was always looked forward to by the Penske Racing Enterprises family. At the party in December 1968, Joan Kroninger read a poem she had composed. Joan had an interesting literary history. Before becoming editor of the *The Chatterbox*, the paper at Shillington High School in Pennsylvania, she was the assistant to then editor John Updike. Her enthusiasm illustrates the close identity felt between Sun Oil's people and the Penske organization.

Ode to the Sunoco Racing Team—1968
Here's to the team that won the Trans-Am,
And the cars that are yellow and blue,
Here's to the hours of sleep that were lost
Making racing dreams come true.
Here's to the United States Road Racing champ,

A driver who's won quite a few,
May next season bring even more success
To "nice guy," Mark Donohue.
Here's to Can-Am and McLaren and Hulme,
They're due at least one small cheer,
Especially since they'll be second and third
To "Sunoco Special" next year.
Here's to the bills for motels and food,
For no matter what the expense be,
Here is the phrase that takes care of it all,
"Charge it to Roger Penske."
Here's to engine changes at midnight,
And to time spent in search of a part,
Here's to fogged goggles, blown engines, and gas
fumes,
And the times when the car would not start.
Here's to the races of '68,
The dull ones and the rousers,
And here's to the beauty one cannot forget
The beauty of Roger's trousers.
Here's to next season, and the team, and the cars
That will make racing history,
By winning the Can-Am, Trans-Am, Indianapolis,
Not one, not two, but all three.

Professional Race-Car Driver

A hero cannot be a hero unless in an heroic world

—NATHANIEL HAWTHORNE

CHAPTER 85:

Change in Direction

Roger and Mark's priorities continued to grow for 1969. The first was to defend the Trans-Am championship for Chevrolet with the Sunoco Camaro. They also wanted to increase the team's involvement in USAC racing, with a debut at the Indianapolis 500 as the principal target. And they planned to continue in the Can-Am and to enter as many World Championship prototype races as possible. With the exception of the Camaro program, the equipment to do all this would come from Eric Broadley's Lola factory in Slough, England. The Indy car was a completely new design, the four-wheel-drive T152. To make way for the new Lola, the Eagle was sold to the Weinberger Homes team for their driver, Ronnie Bucknum. The Can-Am Group 7 Lola was the latest T163, while the car for endurance racing was the Lola T70 Mk IIIB. There was also talk over the winter of running a Lola T142 in the SCCA's single-seater Continental Championship for Formula A cars. That idea was abandoned when it became apparent that the demands of Indy, Trans-Am, Can-Am, and prototype racing made it impossible.

The decision to commit to Lola for the new season resulted from Penske's inability to obtain the very latest in competitive equipment from the dominant McLaren team. McLaren would sell last year's race cars, or new versions of the cars, through their arrangement with Trojan. But when the new Can-Am season opened, the "works" team was certain to appear with something newer and more special than last year's car. They were running a very professional operation against customer teams using equipment that was at best slightly outdated. The only logical alternative to McLaren was Lola, which built cars but did not have its own team. (Chaparral, in contrast, built and raced its own race cars, but was not in the business of selling them.) Lola was also strongly supported by their aggressive American importer, Carl Haas, who was eager to forge relationships with customers.

The big news at the SCCA National Convention in Denver, Colorado, was the departure of executive director John Bishop, who had been forced out in a power struggle with members of the organization's governing board. It was "with great regret" that the SCCA board of governors accepted the forced resignation of Bishop, who had been executive director since 1962 and a member of the professional staff

since 1956. With his departure came the end of the greatest era in the club's history. During the 1960s it had seen unprecedented growth as it evolved from a strictly amateur racing organization into a major force in international and professional racing. Under Bishop's leadership the board of governors had been content to allow the professional staff to run the operation with minimal interference. Bishop had nurtured professional racing, and under his careful guidance it burst into glory with the USRRC, the Trans-Am, and the Can-Am. At the same time, Bishop was always mindful of the importance of the amateur voice within the club. While the pro races brought greater glory to the SCCA, he nurtured the much-larger amateur constituency and made the two elements work in concert.

Tracy Bird, who was not one of the conspirators in Bishop's removal, was named the new executive director. Jim Kaser continued for a period as director of professional racing. It was Kaser's appointment to the post several months earlier that had driven a great deal of the turmoil. He had worked closely with Bishop as director of competition—Bishop's job before becoming executive director—and deserves credit for the emergence of the pro series. His new title and position, reporting to a newly formed Professional Competition Board, was represented as a means of improving efficiency and administration. The new three-man pro board immediately sought greater control, and its members were frustrated by their man Kaser having to report through Bishop. The three influential members, convinced they were acting in the best interests of the club, came to the annual meeting with the intention of ousting Bishop. The result would be a rapid decline in SCCA's importance and influence in international and professional racing. Bishop's ouster also led to great distrust among rank-and-file members regarding the board of governors' leadership and the relationship between professional and amateur racing within the SCCA. These tensions would continue to affect the group for decades to come.

Close observers at the time knew that the SCCA had taken a step that portended little good for the future. In his *Road & Track* column, Al Bochroch quoted a statement by Alex Keller, the new chairman of the SCCA's board of governors, that the board accepted Bishop's resignation with regret, and that "SCCA's 25-year-old policy of complete dedication to the membership needs and wishes remains unchanged." Bochroch concluded by saying, "I doubt the accuracy of both statements."

The decline in the quality and importance of SCCA pro racing was important to Mark Donohue's future as a race driver. He had prospered within the SCCA, first as a dominant driver in the amateur ranks, and then as a champion of the new professional series. Over the next few years Mark and Roger would look to the SCCA less and less as the place they wanted to be.

Convinced that an increased level of personal fitness was essential to his continued growth as a driver, Mark became serious about losing weight and increasing his stamina. He had embarked upon a serious fitness regimen during the Trans-Am season the year before. Now he rose at 5:00 a.m. to fit in a run and exercise routine that would allow him to be at the shop by 7:00. He was inevitably the first there and the last to leave. He later said, "I knew that working all day in the shop and eating poorly and never finding the time to exercise was not helping me on the track. It was hard to stay with it, though. I hate to be laughed at and the neighbors would laugh at me and Sue would laugh at me. But I kept a mental picture of those orange McLarens pulling away from me—and that kept me going." Mark's complete commitment to his profession continued to affect his home life. Sue and Mark had a five-year-old and a two-year-old, and most of the parenting was on her shoulders.

There were also changes at Newtown Square. The success in the early years of Penske Racing had been achieved by a very small team of dedicated individuals. Plans for 1969 required more personnel and in specialized areas. Chuck Cantwell was hired away from Shelby American where he had been co-manager with Lew Spencer of the Shelby Mustang team. Chuck had also helped Phil Remington with preparation of the Cobras and GT40s. He had known Mark from the days of the B Production program with the Shelby GT350R, and had come to know Roger through his role with the Shelby Trans-Am teams. Chuck had a substantial background in racing as a driver and as a board member of the Detroit Region of the SCCA. He had moved to California with his wife Joanne to help engineer and produce the GT350 and 350R for Shelby.

"I knew Shelby had funding from Ford for one more year through 1969—Carroll had lost his enthusiasm for Trans-Am halfway through the '68 season—I knew after '69 that was it. I had this offer to go to Penske and I knew they would be going on. It was the right time for us—we liked California but we wanted to raise our family in the East," Cantwell says. At Penske, Chuck became shop manager and team manager of the road-racing teams. Chuck started with Penske at the end of October but didn't move east until after the New Year. In the interim he was at Traco, developing headers and getting to know Frank Coon and Jim Travers. Coon and Travers, although highly independent, were an essential part of the Penske operation. "They were top guys," Chuck remembers. "They had experience with Offys from their days with Bill Vukovich and were a big part of our success."

Mark was now general manager of Penske Racing Enterprises. The appointment fulfilled Mark's gradual assumption of control over the racing program. "Because of this, I believe we have been able to do a better job," Mark told a *Copley News* reporter. "I have a better idea of what's happening and am just not a weekend warrior." Mark explained the evolution of his role, saying that when he first joined Penske he had been "itchy" to become more involved. "So, I went down to the garage to see if I could help." Since then Mark had become integral to the operation and achieved the control of his environment that he sought.

Sue provided an insight on their income during this period in an interview for the *Newark Sunday News*. "Yes, racing has been good to us. Last year, Mark won $130,000 in purses alone (he doesn't keep all of it, some of it goes to Mr. Penske and to the pit crew, etc.). That could drop down to $1 next year—like the rodeo people say, chicken one week, feathers the next—but Mark is doing what he loves best, and I love having him do it." Although Mark probably kept only about 40 percent of his prize money, Sue did not mention that Mark was also on a monthly salary.

While Roger maintained a near-daily involvement with the racing team, he was increasingly occupied with his expanding businesses. In addition to his Chevrolet dealership, his interests at the time included an insurance agency, a General Tire dealership, National Car Rental franchises in Philadelphia and Atlantic City, and the Goodyear racing tire distributorship for the eastern states and Canada. He was also president of Atlantic City Dragway and on the board of directors of the Atlantic City Raceway for Thoroughbreds.

The line of support between Penske Racing and General Motors took on greater focus. John DeLorean, a close personal friend of Roger Penske's, had just been named general manager of the Chevrolet division. More important than his relationship with Penske was the fact that DeLorean was a firm believer in the value of racing in marketing cars. In March, DeLorean personally assigned Don Cox, one of the brightest young engineers in GM's Research and Development area, as liaison between Penske and the giant auto builder. Up to this time the relationship between Penske Racing and General Motors had been through the Product Performance group, headed by Vince Piggins, but Penske saw R&D as offering the leading edge of GM's engineering.

An important part of Penske's future success arrived at Newtown Square just a few days after Christmas 1968 in the person of John Woodard. Woody had learned his racing in George Alderman's race shop and was ready for greater challenges. Mark and Roger interviewed Woody and his first day on the job was January 14. Mark, not expecting much from the newest member of the team, asked him to install a gas tank in the bare chassis of one of the new Camaros while the rest of the team was away. When they returned Woody had the entire car together. According to Mark, "It was gorgeous! It was as if he had been building race cars all his life." Mark later said that as the years went by, "Woody just got better and better, and we came to realize that no matter how bad the circumstances he could, and would, do anything." Chuck Cantwell believes that Woody represented the increasing professionalism of the Penske organization. "Woody was a top-notch guy and a great asset as a methodical and intelligent mechanic. He was focused and intense."

At the Winding Way shop in Newtown Square, the new cadre soon found a working rhythm in the small space. Cantwell recalls the environment: "It was Roger who was the head shot-caller and set the program. He was in and out of there all the time. Mark and I had this little office we shared—it was about four feet wide and ten feet long—we had a pay phone and a dish full of dimes—if we wanted to call anybody we had to put a dime in. Mark had a mechanical adding machine and I would keep track of all the petty cash and other expenses on that thing—which was a trick, because it didn't have a tape or anything. Roger would give us two or three hundred dollars and we would put it in the kitty and buy stuff out of that. Leroy Gane was crew chief for the Trans-Am cars. Leroy wasn't happy at first with me being there and he could be pretty difficult, but eventually we worked it out and became friends."

Ron Fournier was shop fabricator and worked on all the cars. He recalls, "I would work with Karl on the Indy car program, earlier the Can-Am program, and with the Trans-Am cars too. I covered all bases. My assistant was Don Kean, a great guy and very capable. We worked on whatever was needed."

CHAPTER 86

"No fire ever is dead while the ashes are still red"

Daytona and Sebring did not have a category for Trans-Am cars in 1969, so the Penske team initially entered the Camaro in the Group 2 category. But when Mark and Roger became intrigued by the latest Group 4 Lola, a car was ordered and they abandoned the idea of running the Camaro in the 24-hour race. "Roy Gane and I were down at U.S. customs on January 1, 1969, when the Lola T70 Mk IIIB arrived," Mark remembered.

The FIA's World Championship for Manufacturers continued to evolve as the international governing body sought to provide categories that would entice manufacturers of sports and specialty performance cars to enter the major endurance races. Along with the needs of the constructors, the rules makers also felt pressure from race organizers and the paying public, who wanted exciting and fast cars. Since 1968 the rules limited pure prototype cars—Group 6—to 3.0-liter engine capacity. The Sports class—Group 4—had been established to "grandfather in" the many existing sports cars that were essential to creating a field. While a minimum production of 50 cars was initially required for Group 4, for 1969 that number had been reduced to 25, and the FIA was liberal in its method of counting cars produced. Lola had met the 50-car minimum by counting every T70 chassis ever built.

The new Group 4 Lola, the T70 Mk IIIB, differed in important respects from its predecessor, the T70 Mk III. Its lighter monocoque chassis was derived from the T162 Can-Am car, and the use of spruce-wood strengthening strips in the body panels further lightened the car. The gullwing doors of the earlier cars were replaced by forward-hinged doors.

Mark and Roy Gane took the Lola to Daytona for an early test, and after various spring-rate changes, made the car handle very well. Mark thought the car was great and had high hopes for the race despite the poor reputation Lola enjoyed in endurance racing. No Lola had previously completed more than eight hours in an endurance race. Mark liked the coupe, saying it was more comfortable than an open car. "It is a little hotter, but you don't get the wind buffeting and you don't get crudded up with dirt and rubber dust," he told a reporter.

At Daytona on February 1–2 for the 24-hour race, the Group 6 Porsche 908s were expected to dominate with competition primarily from the Group 4 John Wyer Gulf-Ford GT40s. The works Porsche team had won the race the year previous with the 907, and the new 908 was a significant advance in the evolution of Porsche racing cars. Swedes Jo Bonnier and Ulf Norinder had the latest Lola coupe, like the Penske car, and there were two of the earlier version of the car entered by James Garner's American International Racing (AIR) team.

James Garner in 1969 was a film star of international fame. He had fallen in love with motor racing when he headed an all-star cast in John Frankenheimer's movie *Grand Prix*. The MGM production was unprecedented in its attention to detail in recording accurately the Formula One world of 1966. The production enjoyed extensive access and the cooperation of the majority of Grand Prix teams, drivers, and circuits. The movie that emerged was a triumph. Garner had taken his driving role in the film to heart, and through his serious approach and obvious enthusiasm had gained the respect and friendship of the racing fraternity. Limited by studio and insurance restrictions on his own racing, Garner later became a serious entrant and fielded race cars in professional series including Formula A and international endurance racing. For Daytona he entered two Lola T70 Mk III coupes for Scooter Patrick / Dave Jordan and Lothar Motschenbacher / Ed Leslie.

Ronnie Bucknum, Penske team driver for the second Trans-Am Camaro, was the choice to co-drive the Lola with Mark. It wasn't until practice began that Bucknum realized that his finger—badly broken in a recent motorcycle accident and now in a special brace—made it impossible for him to drive effectively. Roger made a quick phone call to Chuck Parsons, who flew in from California. Although Parsons had never raced at Daytona, he was a logical choice: He drove for Lola importer Carl Haas and had previously driven for John Hilton, who remained a close associate of the Penske team. Parson's late arrival allowed only enough time for him to complete nine laps in practice in the new car on the unfamiliar circuit. But Parsons was fortunate to have arrived at all. He missed his originally scheduled flight, which was subsequently hijacked and diverted to Cuba.

Mark qualified second at 1:52.7, just behind the lead Porsche 908 of Vic Elford / Brian Redman at 1:52.2. The first hour hardly seemed like an endurance race as Mark diced hard for the lead with Elford and Jo Siffert in the 908 Porsches and Bonnier in the other new Lola. Mark was the

first to falter, pitting to complain of fuel starvation. The Sunoco Lola would pick up only 21 gallons of its 37-gallon fuel load, and for the remainder of the race was handicapped by needing to pit for fuel nearly twice as often as scheduled. Mark took full blame, telling the media, "I engineered the fuel system on the car. We were having trouble with it when we got here and made a couple changes. Then, the night before the race started, we made a third change. It made things worse." Ron Fournier recalls that it was an indication of the respect Mark had for Eric Broadley, and the importance he placed on the relationship with Lola, that he chose to place the blame on himself.

The Porsches were dominating, with only the GT40 of David Hobbs / Mike Hailwood providing early pressure. Bonnier dropped out and the Garner Lolas were well off the lead pace. The Sunoco-Lola was fourth, three laps down, when Mark pitted with flames coming from the exhaust. The problem was serious, and the Lola went behind the wall to make repairs. The exhaust system had to be removed, cracks welded, and patches applied. It was Ron Fournier who fabricated the repair. Ron later discovered that the exhaust had failed at a 90-degree bend because the supplier had placed the seams incorrectly. When the car returned to the track it had been in the pits for 1 hour and 19 minutes and had fallen to 11th place—40 laps behind the leading Porsche. Still, the Penske team never gave up. Roger told the *Daytona Beach Morning Journal*, "I knew there were 15 hours to go, and any endurance race takes its toll on the faster cars." Mark stressed the same point to *AutoWeek*'s Dennis J. Cipnic. "Roger would have done anything to keep us going, short of putting an entire new engine in the car. We were out to last and win."

Remarkably, the seemingly indestructible Porsches all faltered, initially with exhaust problems that overwhelmed the drivers with fumes. Ultimately, however, all five cars were eliminated by the same problem, as an intermediate driveshaft between the crankshaft and camshaft failed on each car. The Wyer Ford GT40s led until dawn on Sunday morning, when they too failed or crashed. When the last Porsche finally retired for good, the Sunoco Lola was the leading car still running—but ranked only third in distance run. When the Lola wouldn't restart after a pit stop, it took a further 20 minutes to replace the starter. Finally, Mark made on-track contact with another car that extensively damaged the left front fender. The Lola finished the race looking like a severely wounded battlefront veteran, so extensively was the dark blue car held together with gray racer's tape. The car had spent so much time in the pits—by race end they had pitted 31 times and spent a combined 2 hours, 10 minutes, and 12 seconds in the pits—that it took more than two hours circulating the track to match the distance run by the now-retired Porsche.

Around 10:00 a.m. the Sunoco Lola finally completed enough laps to be the official leader. As Mark told Cipnic, "We were something like 50 laps down there at one point, but we thought the time we had left would let us make it." They did indeed make it: Mark and Chuck won the race a full 30 laps ahead of the second-place AIR Lola driven by Lothar Motschenbacher and Ed Leslie. Ronnie Bucknum also had a share in the victory. Splint on his finger notwithstanding, Bucknum drove a stint in the Lola in the early-morning hours. Ev Gardner in the *Washington Star* led a later account of the Penske team victory by quoting author Edna Ferber: "No fire ever is dead while the ashes are still red."

In the victory circle, Mark and Chuck were presented the Prestolite International Challenge Trophy by Miss Universe, Martha Vasconcellos of Brazil. Although he had driven three-quarters of the race distance himself, Mark insisted that Parsons deserved the lion's share of credit for the victory, having adapted to a new car and a new track on such short notice. Daytona Speedway founder Bill France was impressed. It was a remarkable effort, he told the Associated Press. "Most other crews would have quit. They didn't."

It had been a long two days. The team, including Chuck Cantwell, Roy Gane, Ron Fournier, Bill Mayberry, Peter Reinhart, and Jerry Kroninger from Sunoco, had been at the track to set up their pit and paddock at 8:00 a.m. on Saturday. The race began at 3:00 p.m. and ran all night and into the next afternoon. Beyond an occasional catnap, there are few opportunities for sleep during a 24-hour race. This one had been particularly demanding on the crew. At race's end they began the job of packing everything up and preparing to leave. That evening Mark and Roger greeted the mechanics in a private room at a top local restaurant for a victory celebration, arranged especially for them by Roger. The beautiful meal notwithstanding, the men soon found themselves nodding off to sleep in the midst of conversations.

CHAPTER 87:

"The best-ever Sebring"

Despite the travails of Daytona, a victory is sure to inspire optimism and further expectations. With Sebring ahead on March 22, development on the Lola included switching from Lucas fuel injection to Weber carburetors on the 305ci Traco Chevy engine. At an open test day at Sebring on March 9, Jo Siffert broke the lap record in the Porsche 908 Spyder at 114.77 mph, but Mark promptly smashed that speed with a 115.91 in the Lola.

Ronnie Bucknum's finger had healed, and he co-drove with Mark, who qualified second fastest with a lap time of 2:40.92. Chris Amon—who was co-driving with Mario Andretti—put the new factory-entered Ferrari 312 P on the pole with a 2:40.14. When Chris and Mark, along with the 70 other race starters, sprinted across the track to their cars, it marked the last time the Le Mans–type start was used at Sebring. FIA regulations soon outlawed the colorful tradition on safety grounds. Seat belts were now mandated—the FIA had been among the last regulating body to demand their use—and the fear was that drivers were not taking the time to buckle up before charging into the race. It was true. Most drivers waited until the race pace had settled down to go through the process of attaching belts and harnesses. Another tie with the past would soon be gone.

Jo Siffert in the Porsche 908 made the best start, but Mark chased him down to take the lead, the two racing hard throughout the first hour. After the first driver change, Bucknum remained in the lead until being passed under braking by Chris Amon in the Ferrari. It was a tremendous race, with the Sunoco Lola battling with the factory teams from Ferrari and Porsche, as well as the John Wyer-run Gulf-Ford GT40s. Al Bochroch, reporting for *Road & Track*, said it was "the best-ever Sebring, perhaps one of the best-ever sports car races anywhere."

"Mark and Ronnie had an outstanding chance of winning that Sebring race outright without any Porsches breaking or any other help," recalls team manager Chuck Cantwell. "The upper trailing arms of the rear suspension were mounted to the chassis on a post—they didn't look right, but we didn't change it because it kept working. In hindsight we should have—we had done a lot of testing—it was such a rough circuit and those things broke. Bonnier's Lola broke in the same way." When Ronnie Bucknum pitted around the five-hour mark, he described a peculiarity in the handling. Mark took the Lola out and returned to the pits almost immediately. The radius rods had indeed pulled away from the chassis at the mounting point.

Before the Lola retired the Penske team had been making the fastest pit stops, and their apparent attention to enabling details made an impression. It wasn't just the well-choreographed and carefully practiced pit-stop routine; close observers also noted fine touches, such as the tapered hubs, painted with aligning marks on the hub itself and the center nut lock, making cross-threading almost impossible.

The appearance of the Group 6 Ferraris brought a serious challenge to Porsche. Their battle was waged throughout the European season. On this day, however, it was the John Wyer–entered Group 4 Ford GT40 driven by Jacky Ickx and Jackie Oliver that beat them both. The Amon/Andretti Ferrari was second, a lap down, and the Porsche 908 for Rolf Stommelen / Joe Buzzetta / Kurt Ahrens was third.

Despite the disappointment of not finishing at Sebring, Mark and Roger had developed an appetite for endurance racing, and now determined to take the Lola to the test days at Le Mans on March 29–30. Time was of the essence. There were plans to use GM's Black Lake testing facility to refine the Lola further before leaving for Europe. Although General Motors was not providing financial support, they were providing technical assistance with engines and sending personnel. Bill Mayberry and Peter Reinhart left Sebring with the Lola in the transporter. Their route home took them directly past Daytona International Speedway, where they stopped to watch the motorcycle races. The next morning they came out of their motel to discover that the transporter was gone. It was Peter who called Mark with the bad news.

"I figured we had to find that stuff in a hurry or we were out of business," Mark remembered. "I called everyone I knew in Daytona." Roger was also involved, according to Ron Fournier. "Roger's Chevrolet dealership serviced FBI cars in Philadelphia and he knew who to call. They called their counterparts in Florida as there was the possibility the stolen material had crossed state lines. They got a helicopter up, and it didn't take them long once they got up above the tree line making circles around the area. The rig was too big to hide very easily."

Although the truck was found abandoned in a marsh within 24 hours, it was a total loss. The Lola chassis was there, a virtual shell stripped of its engine, gearbox, and instrumentation. The spare engine, too, along with all other spares, wheels, and toolboxes had vanished. Mark threw himself into the recovery effort, reluctant to abandon plans for racing the car in Europe. Although the thieves were eventually apprehended and much of the stolen property recovered, the loss proved too great a setback. It was a matter of time and commitment to other programs. The plans for Le Mans were scrapped. There was insufficient time to obtain a new Lola and prepare it for the test days at the Sarthe circuit, coming up just a week after Sebring. The great adventure for Mark and the Penske team with the Lola coupe in endurance racing was over.

The loss of tools was a practical setback. Ron Fournier remembers asking Mark on a daily basis when the insurance claim was coming through so he could go out and buy the replacement tools he needed. "Mark got tired of me bugging him," recalls Ron. "One day I walked into the office and before I could say anything, he handed me his own personal check for $800, which was the amount of my claim. He said, 'Ron, here. Don't ask me about those tools anymore.' The next day they found the tools and we got them all back. I was able to give Mark his check back."

The test days brought another tragedy. Belgian driver Lucien Bianchi, winner of the 1968 24 Hours at Le Mans and a frequent competitor with Mark, died when his 3.0-liter Alfa Romeo T33/2 crashed and burned.

CHAPTER 88:
Boyhood Dreams Realized

The Indianapolis 500 occupied the time and attention of the racing world throughout the month of May. Of the 84 entries, the Sunoco-Simoniz Special (Lola T152) was one of a small number of cars ready to go when the track opened on Thursday, May 1. The Simoniz name appeared on the car through the involvement of Carl Haas, the Lola importer. "Both Carl and I felt a combined effort on the part of our teams would produce better results than if we each tried to go it alone," Roger said in a prepared statement. "So we decided to wave the white flag of truce until after Memorial Day. June 1, we will be back at each other's throats at Mosport Park, the Can-Am season opener." The official entrant, an amalgam of the two teams, was U.S. Racing. According to Carl Haas, he had a 15 percent interest in the operation. One of Haas's contributions to the joined team was to bring Lola mechanic Jim Chapman from England to work on the car with Karl Kainhofer.

Bobby Unser, with sponsorship from Bardahl, was running a four-wheel-drive Lola identical to Mark's. Bobby, in his seventh appearance at Indy, was the defending race champion, having won the 500 in 1968. In March, Unser and his mechanic Jud Phillips had joined Mark, Roger, Karl, and Goodyear's Larry Truesdale on a trip to the Lola factory in England. While there Mark phoned Paul Hawkins, who had lived in London since 1960, and Hawkeye met Mark and Karl for a night out at a club in London's East End. It was the last time Mark and Paul were together, and Karl recalls that the two friends had a great evening. Jud Phillips and Karl stayed in England to build up the cars for the 500. Mark's car arrived in America first. As soon as the Offenhauser engine was fitted, Roger rented the one-mile oval track at Hanford, California, for testing. Bobby Unser also drove the car and shared insights with Mark on oval racing techniques.

"We were both Goodyear drivers and they brought us together," remembers Unser. "We agreed to do a development program on the four-wheel-drive Lola. It was during that time that Mark and I became friends, because you never really get to know a person until you work closely together, as we did. There were no secrets and we worked well, it was a good experience. Mark and I were opposites—he was an educated engineer and I was a self-educated engineer. Mark had the ability to put things we did onto paper and into numbers, and good sound reasoning. I would put it into terms of 'feel' and what I knew was right from my racing experience. Karl Kainhofer was similar to myself in terms of savvy, and putting it all together as a group we got results because we all got on well and cooperated well. My mechanics were outstanding too—Jud Phillips and 'Little Red' [Tom Herrmann].

"You have to understand that the Penske operation wasn't as we know it today," continues Bobby. "But Roger was a good car owner, and they had very good people. That team was motivated by Mark."

The Indianapolis 500 on Memorial Day is ingrained in the American culture. Racers and non-racers alike remember the 500 as an integral part of the holiday, typically father and son sitting by the radio or listening while washing the family car. As the biggest race in America the 500 loomed large, not only in the dreams of young boys but for all race drivers irrespective of their origins, be that dirt-track ovals

or sports-car road races. And it was so for Mark Donohue and Roger Penske.

Roger was anxious to make a good impression on the regulars in his first year at the Speedway. Mark completed the first phases of his rookie test, controlled runs at an average of 140, 145, and then 150 mph under the watchful eye of chief steward Harlan Fengler. The first days of May featured beautiful weather, and Mark was on the track each day, receiving his final rookie approval on Saturday. It was not lost on veteran observers that the car had been one of the first on the track on May 1 when the Speedway opened, and that now Mark was the first of the five rookies in the race to complete the test.

"We could tell that he was a very smooth and thinking driver," recalls Al Unser. "He knew what he was doing out there."

"To be a rookie again, after almost 10 years racing, is an interesting situation. But after some practicing and passing a driver's test, I can see the point," Mark told syndicated columnist Bob Cochnar. "The track is much more complicated than it appears. Drivers accustomed to road courses often like to belittle Indy. You've heard the cliché 'All you have to do is turn left four times.' There's more to it than that."

Official opening-day ceremonies on Saturday, May 3, included exhibition laps by historic Indy-type race cars. Mark was invited to drive the famous Leader Card Special, a John Zink–owned, A. J. Watson–built roadster that Jim Rathmann had driven to victory at Monza, Italy, in 1958 in the "Race of Two Worlds." Mark ran three careful laps in the roadster around the 2.5-mile circuit, saying, "It was an experience. I didn't get into any trouble, but I almost stalled the engine. I really have a lot of respect for the guys who drove those machines."

Herb Porter was the established Offenhauser expert—known as "Herby Horsepower" to insiders at the Brickyard—and he prepared the engine from his garage in Gasoline Alley. Initially the oil pressure was low. When Porter learned that the team was using multi-viscosity oil, he was certain that was the problem. Sunoco engineer Jerry Kroninger was convinced it had nothing to do with it, as they had tested extensively and used it successfully in other racing applications. To prove the point Jerry obtained Valvoline SAE 50, and they ran it for a practice session. Mark came in and reported that pressure was still low. Kroninger breathed a sigh of relief. They returned to the Sunoco SAE 20W/50, which was officially certified by USAC. The low oil pressure was traced to another cause and corrected.

Mark explained some of the technical aspects of the Lola T152 in an interview with syndicated motorsports writer Bob Cochnar: "The transmission and gearbox is especially interesting. Manufactured by Hewland, it incorporates four-wheel drive in conjunction with a four-speed gearbox. The torque split between the front and rear wheels is adjustable, allowing a power differential variance between the front and rear wheels. This offers a good deal of control and a lot of power out of the turns where at Indy, the power is especially needed."

The first week featured excellent weather, and Mark easily had the Lola—or, in Indy speak, the Sunoco-Simoniz Special—over the 160-mph milestone speed. By Thursday, May 8, the weather took a turn for the worse, and the track was closed entirely on Friday and Saturday because of heavy rain. It worked out fine for Penske Racing, since Mark and Roger were needed at Michigan International Speedway (MIS) for the opening round of the 1969 Trans-Am.

CHAPTER 89:
"No, no, no . . . That can't happen"

When SCCA director of professional racing Jim Kaser arrived at Michigan International Speedway on Sunday, May 11, he encountered Chuck Cantwell at the corner of the pits. The two men exchanged pleasantries, and then Kaser turned to walk around the pit wall. That was when he came upon the ultimate manifestation of the Mark Donohue–inspired, Jerry Kroninger–designed and –executed fueling rig. The tower rose 20 feet above the Penske pit, and to Mark and Jerry it was a thing of beauty.

"No, no, no. We can't do that. That can't happen," Kaser exclaimed. He told the team they could use the rig that day, but that a new rule would immediately ban any such structure in the future. "He instantly made up his mind that it wouldn't be at the next race," says Cantwell.

Sure enough, a directive from the Westport, Connecticut, SCCA headquarters, titled "Trans-Am Fueling Rule," arrived at Penske Racing headquarters and was forwarded to the R&D lubricant section of Sun Oil Company, where it was stamped received on May 21. Among other things the new

rule specified a maximum height of "no more than six (6) ft. from the ground to the base of the container."

The Penske organization was angered by the ruling, since the tower conformed to the existing rules. Mark was adamant that considerable expense had gone into the rig and that banning it was equivalent to changing car eligibility rules during the season. At the next race, SCCA executive director Tracy Bird made a joke of the matter, saying, "Ha—you guys thought you were so clever. I guess we fixed that up." Mark exploded, expressing his disgust at the cavalier manner in which the rule was changed: "It's ridiculous. To ignore the substantial financial commitment we have made to that rig and then to laugh about it is unconscionable." The ban stuck, however. The SCCA responded by admitting that the rig was technically legal, but argued that its overall height "was not to the spirit of the rule."

While the Penske refueling tower was causing a great deal of official concern, there was also a rustle of unhappiness over the appearance of the Sunoco Camaros. The cars appeared with vinyl (or Landau) tops, and had the entire paddock talking. "We were running Landau roofs because the roofs were too thin," says Woody Woodard. Soon after Woody came to work at Newtown Square, he flew with Mark to Los Angeles where the new bodies were acid-dipped. "The raw steel uni-body is called a body-in-white. Just before it goes into the primer tank they grab it off the assembly line. We got three and they were trucked to a chemical company in Long Beach, California, that would dip them in acid," he explains. "They pretty much knew how many seconds would take a thousandth off all the body surfaces. They did the work at about 10:00 p.m.—they would only do it at night because it would put a huge cloud of blackish gray smoke in the air. The whole body was put on a hook and submerged in the acid where it just sat and bubbled and stank. When they came out they were hosed down, sprayed with neutralizer, and shipped to Newtown Square. The process chemically removed—it was probably tens of thousandths—uniformly off of every steel surface. And of course it was lighter. The only problem was that on this occasion Mark convinced the guy to do it a little bit too long—and the roofs on all three cars were just a little bit different."

So different that even the craftsmen at Molin Auto Body could not get them to look right. Molin Auto Body was a small, prestigious shop in Wayne, Pennsylvania, that did the painting and bodywork on all Penske race cars from 1966 through

1973. Molin's master body and fender man Harry Tidmarsh is remembered as an artist who, according to John Woodard, "could take an aluminum fender and put it back in shape so you wouldn't ever know it was scratched." Mark came up with the idea of putting vinyl roofs on the cars, calculating that the weight of the vinyl plus the glue used would be less than putting on a new metal roof. "Mark convinced Roger it was the way to go," says Woodard. "Mark's attitude was 'I don't care what—I want a light race car.' "

Before the season-opener at MIS, Mark had visited Black Lake, an immense area of asphalt used for testing at the General Motors proving ground. A week of testing with a fully instrumented car and the presence of GM engineers Don Gates and Don Cox produced some progress, but convinced Mark that the 1969 car would be a challenge. Cox, the official liaison between Penske Racing and GM Engineering, already knew the 1969 Trans-Am season would be a struggle. Before being asked by John DeLorean to take on the job, he had by chance shared a ferry ride across Lake Michigan with Lee Dykstra, a longtime friend and ex-schoolmate. Dykstra, then a top engineer at Ford, had confided to Don the extent of his company's preparations to recapture the Trans-Am. Cox was impressed, and realized that GM would be hard-pressed to match Ford with its own comparatively modest commitment.

Consulting engineer William F. Milliken was also present at the Black Lake test and introduced Mark to his "friction circle" concept of driving. Mark and Don Cox later visited Milliken at Cornell Aeronautical Laboratories in Buffalo, New York, where they further discussed the theory, as later explained by Mark in *The Unfair Advantage*:

> . . . the car—or its tires—has relatively equal traction capabilities in any direction, whether accelerating, braking or cornering. The theory is that you get maximum performance when you pass from one condition to the other without going through the center of the circle. In other words, the fastest way into a corner is to gradually trade off braking traction versus cornering traction, until all traction is being used in cornering.

This technique became integral to Mark's driving philosophy and the technical approach that he encouraged other drivers to follow.

Appraising the team's chances for 1969, Mark told *AutoWeek*, "Our dependability was pretty good last year. Now it's a question of making the cars quick enough to be competitive with how fast we think the other teams are going to go . . . the Trans-Am series is going to be competitive."

Michigan International Speedway had burst upon the motor-racing scene with great fanfare. Lawrence "Larry" LoPatin, president of American Raceways, Inc., the track's owner, presented his company as the new wave in motor-sports and himself as a virtual savior. MIS—with a two-mile oval and a road course encompassed in a modern stadium setting—was his model for tracks of the future.

The first race at MIS on the oval was a USAC 250-miler won by Ronnie Bucknum the previous October. Texas World Speedway near College Station, Texas, was soon opened by the company as a near replica of MIS. LoPatin's company had also acquired Atlanta International Raceway and a majority position in Riverside International Raceway, bringing in the California track's promoter, Les Richter, as director of racing. LoPatin was the loudest among the voices declaring automobile racing the "sport of the '70s." He promised to revolutionize and bring new direction to the sport. The tremendous growth in the sport in the 1960s led many people to believe LoPatin was right. It was the same optimism that fueled construction of Ontario Motor Speedway in California that opened in 1970—at $25.5 million, the most expensive racing venue built to that time.

When Les Richter, in his new role with American Raceways, arrived at MIS to oversee preparations for the Trans-Am, he found serious problems with the 3.18-mile road circuit. An SCCA Regional held at the brand-new facility two weeks earlier had revealed rough pavement and dangerous transitions from the oval to the road course, resulting in serious bottoming. Repairs were attempted, and the circuit was rerouted in one area, resulting in a revised circuit length of 3.31 miles.

Ford, determined to regain the Trans-Am championship, backed two separate teams to make it happen. Bud Moore, who had run the Cougar team two years earlier for Ford's Lincoln-Mercury division, now fielded Mustangs for Parnelli Jones and George Follmer. Shelby continued as a major Ford team with Peter Revson and Horst Kwech as lead drivers in their Mustangs. AMC had John Martin and Ron Grable in the Javelin. Jerry Titus was the driving force behind the Pontiac effort in partnership with Terry Godsall. Pontiac had been unable to produce the new 303ci engine that the team was pinning their hopes on to gain homologation approval. As a result, Godsall and Titus were running 1968 cars for Titus, Craig Fisher, and Milt Minter. The Penske team's 1969 Sunoco Camaro was all new, and it wasn't just the vinyl tops. The engine had a stronger bottom end and visually featured a new hood with a rearward-facing scoop.

Along with the car makers, the other major industrial rivalry in Trans-Am racing was between Firestone and Goodyear. "The tire companies were as competitive with one another as Ford was with Chevrolet—maybe even more," says George Follmer. "They were competing in all forms of racing, of course, and at the beginning of 1969 Trans-Am wasn't Firestone's main focus. We were in trouble with the tires. They would be fast for a few laps and then they would go away. We were making far more pit stops than were the Penske team and other Goodyear runners." Follmer and Parnelli Jones were long since committed to Firestone, and the Bud Moore team ran exclusively on their tires. The Shelby Mustang team was on Goodyears. "The importance of the tire companies and the competitiveness of that end of the racing spectrum cannot be overstated," emphasizes Follmer. "Tire companies were big. They were spending a lot of money. Development, servicing, driver contracts, support—they were big."

The Wolverine Trans-Am race proved an organizational disaster and a black eye for the MIS facility, as well as for the new SCCA administration. Even the weather was horrible, with steady rain culminating in snow on race morning. On a wet and cold qualifying day, Jones and Follmer qualified on the front row, with Mark and Titus on row three behind Kwech and Titus's Pontiac teammate, Milt Minter. Mark had little track time as the Penske team was busy changing differentials through most of the qualifying session.

After the start, Mark moved quickly to the front, and he and Parnelli finished the first lap side by side. On the eighth lap Horst Kwech crashed on the infield section of the track, and his Mustang landed in a spectator area. He had been making a pass at the spot where the road circuit crosses the oval and found himself suddenly transitioned from dry to wet track. Although Kwech attempted to spin the Mustang to reduce speed at impact, the wet grass provided no traction, and the car headed toward the snow fencing at virtually full speed.

Durward Fletcher, an AMC dealer from Lansing, Michigan, and his wife Lorna were seated in their car to get out of the rain. The Mustang tore through the snow fencing and

struck Fletcher's car at more than 100 mph. Although Kwech was uninjured, Fletcher later died of head injuries at Foote Hospital in nearby Jackson. Twelve other spectators were injured, including Mrs. Fletcher, who suffered head injuries, rib fractures, and leg lacerations. Don Cox, now officially attached to the Penske team as liaison to General Motors, had left the viewing area moments before. "It just came to me that I was viewing the race from a very vulnerable spot," he remembered.

Mark and Parnelli Jones battled through the rain-plagued race, and at the finish Mark was declared winner, with Pontiac Firebird driver Jerry Titus second. But Penske timing and scoring whiz Judy Stropus—and her counterparts in Bud Moore's pit—knew better. Mark had pitted on the 80th lap for rear tires, and the SCCA scorers had missed the stop. After Mark received the trophy and a kiss from Miss MIS, Candy Kaiser, Roger sent him and the rest of the team back to the motel. Roger had Judy hide in the bathroom of a motor home until they left, so she and her charts were unavailable to the SCCA. Mark explained it this way in *The Unfair Advantage*: "We figured the SCCA could find any mistakes on their own, so we didn't make any noise. . . . Who knows—we could have been wrong." By the time it was sorted out and Parnelli correctly named winner, five hours had elapsed, and most people had gone home. On an unhappy day Mark was officially second and Jerry Titus third. Ronnie Bucknum in the second Penske Camaro had dropped out early with problems from an experimental power steering unit.

Judy Stropus was such an asset as a timer and scorer that her services were sought after by a number of teams. She had worked the 1968 Trans-Am for Jim Jeffords and his Javelin team, and with Roger and Mark on the Can-Am. When she agreed to join the Penske team on an exclusive basis for 1969, it was considered a major coup for Roger and Mark. Such was her reputation that when conflicts arose, it was Judy's records that were considered the final authority. Her introduction to timing on a professional basis had come at the Marlboro Trans-Am in 1967, when Fran Hernandez and Bud Moore asked her to work for the Mercury Cougar team. At the time it was a revelation to her that she could be paid for doing something she loved to do. And she did it extraordinarily well.

The following week at Indianapolis, Mark gave *Los Angeles Times* reporter Shav Glick his slightly disingenuous perspective on what had happened. "My crew kept giving me the No. 1 sign and I thought all I had to do was keep an interval between me and Jerry Titus. I wasn't trying to prove anything else as I thought he was the one I had to beat. I went home thinking I had won and it was quite a shock to hear about the change."

Privately Mark and Roger believed the race had been lost in the pits. On one stop lug nuts were stripped, and throughout the race, tire changes were slow. Mark made the point that it mattered little how fast the fuel stops went if they couldn't execute tire changes. Roger, who later dressed the crew down for their performance, left Mark on rain tires late in the race on a drying track, reasoning that Mark would lose less time on the wrong tires than he would changing them.

Roger had stayed alone at the track to hear the final outcome. Bud Moore, Parnelli Jones, and Homer Perry from Ford became antagonistic and the insults turned ugly and were directed at Roger on a personal level. When Roger returned to the motel to address the team, he was furious—Mark said he'd never seen him so mad. Ford had made it personal, and he now vowed to beat them at whatever cost. The Trans-Am took on such importance to Roger as a result of the MIS confrontation that he was prepared to subordinate any of the other racing programs to the goal of winning the series. If necessary, he would have withdrawn from the Indianapolis 500.

Uneasiness and paranoia had developed in both camps. Roger and Mark became convinced that the strength of numbers represented by the two Ford teams would result in one of their cars being designated to literally take Mark out of a race. To prepare for this possibility, Roger purchased back the team car that he had sold to Sam Posey at the end of 1968. Sam had stored the car in a garage, leaving it basically untouched since then. The car was now converted to 1969 specs and even had a vinyl roof installed. It was maintained race-ready in Newtown Square throughout the season, although it was never actually used or brought to the track.

CHAPTER 90:
Rookie of the Year

When Mark and Roger returned to Indianapolis the rains had stopped and the good weather held until the end of the week. Mark and 45 other hopefuls were able to practice each day leading up to the first weekend of qualifying. Traditional qualifying for the 500 was spread over four days on two consecutive weekends. Qualifying on the first day was important because the fastest cars that day maintained their positions irrespective of how fast other qualifiers went on subsequent days. The exception to this rule came after the complete field of 33 cars was filled. Then, a faster qualifier could "bump" from the field the car with the slowest qualifying speed. If you were that slowest car, you were "on the bubble."

Indianapolis drew crowds for qualifying that exceeded what any other track saw even on race day. With 150,000 people in attendance, the first weekend of qualifying—May 17–18—was rained out. One car made an attempt on Saturday afternoon. Rookie driver Jigger Sirois registered a four-lap average of 161.486 that would by rule have captured pole position for his Quaker State–sponsored Caves Buick Company Special, a Gerhardt-Offy. But on the last of the four laps owner Myron Caves signaled he was not accepting the attempt. Minutes after his run the rains came down and no one else was able to make an attempt on either day. Pole position at Indy goes to the car that qualifies fastest on the first day irrespective of faster speeds on subsequent days. Sirois attempted to qualify for the 500 in the years ahead but never made the race. The rain never let up and the big crowd went home disappointed.

Mark was anything but disappointed, as he admitted to Associated Press writer Eric Prewitt. "I woke up that first morning and looked out the motel window. The stands were full and it was only eight o'clock. It kind of shook me up." On Monday the rain was gone and practice resumed as the teams made ready for qualifying—now to be compressed into just two days. Mark ran every day, and while he was fast, remained below the radar, seldom cracking the much-publicized "ten fastest" ranks on any day of practice.

On May 20 Roger announced to the press that his team would not contest the early rounds of the Can-Am, and indeed might not run the series at all. He emphasized that his priorities were the Trans-Am and the Indy 500. "The Can-Am, we have realized, is not what it's cracked up to be," he said.

Mark told Shav Glick that the Trans-Am was also more important to the team than the other races on the USAC Championship Trail. "We are more interested in keeping our Camaro competitive in the Trans-Am. It's too early to tell exactly what the opposition will do, but it is apparent that Ford will spend all the money they need and get all the drivers they need to try and beat us." In the same conversation he shared his view on the Indy mystique with the veteran reporter. "If you stop and talk with everyone in the garage area who has an idea, you'll begin to think it takes some sort of 'black magic' to go fast here, and I don't believe it. I try not to listen. I just want to do a good job with no fanfare, and I know getting the car ready takes more than another tweak here and a twist there."

On Wednesday, Mario Andretti, one of the fastest drivers all month, had a huge, fiery wreck that destroyed the STP Lotus-Ford. Mario's Type 64 Lotus four-wheel-drive (chassis #64/4) was part of the three-car Team Lotus with teammates Graham Hill and Jochen Rindt. The turbocharged Ford in the Lotus team cars was turning out more than 1,000 horsepower with a three-second lag on the throttle. Mario was fortunate to get out of the massively destroyed car with only facial burns to show for it. The accident was traced to a faulty right rear hub. When it proved impossible to manufacture substitute hubs on time, Team Lotus withdrew all three cars. With his primary car gone, Mario switched to an older Clint Brawner–built Hawk. He went from race favorite to being considered a likely also-ran. But on Saturday, May 24, Mario put the supposedly slower car in the middle of the front row. A. J. Foyt captured pole position with a speed of 170.568 mph. Filling out the front row was Bobby Unser.

Mark qualified fourth—inside of the second row—at 168.903, the best qualifying position for a rookie since Andretti in 1965. Peter Revson qualified 33rd and last in Jack Brabham's backup Repco Brabham. Brabham was in the row ahead. The field was sprinkled with many of Mark's road-racing compatriots. George Follmer and Denis Hulme were on row nine, Ronnie Bucknum on row six, and Dan Gurney was tenth fastest on the inside of row four.

That same Saturday morning Dave Lawton was working in his garage at home in Rhode Island sorting out some problems on a friend's Formula A race car. Confused with the time difference in Indianapolis, he hadn't yet turned on his garage radio to follow the qualifying results. Judy came outside and announced that Mark was on the phone. "Dave," said Mark. "I did it—I'm qualified. I'm on the front row. It won't stand up, but for right now I'm on the front row." Mark had gotten out of the race car and gone straight to the garages to call the friend who had been party to his earliest dreams of racing. It was a meaningful moment for both men.

On Tuesday morning of race week Mark received the unhappy news that Paul Hawkins had died the day before in an accident during the Tourist Trophy International at Oulton Park in England. Hawkins was driving a Lola-Chevrolet T70 Mk IIIB, the same model Mark had won with at Daytona. Paul and Mark were the same age, and Sue remembers that their friendship was important to her husband. "I believe that after Paul died Mark became less inclined to form strong bonds with other race drivers."

The Lawtons came to Indianapolis for the race weekend, and the day before the race Dave walked with Mark from the driver's parking area to the garage-area gate. They worked their way through the large crowd of race fans seeking autographs. When they were inside the gate Mark said to Dave, "Can you believe this? Would you ever have thought that this would happen when we used to lie on the beach at Martha's Vineyard?"

Judy and Dave Lawton sat with Mark's mother Zilly during the race in the second deck with an excellent view of the pits. Sue told a reporter, "I'm the loudest fan my husband has, except for his mother."

The Penske team decided to cool the fuel for Indy just as they had been doing successfully in Trans-Am. There was just one approved fuel rig at the Speedway—a 500-gallon tank laid on its side. Jerry Kroninger had it painted in Sunoco colors for race day. To cool the fuel on race day Jerry designed a canvas cover for the tank with two rows of pockets to hold the dry ice. Noticing immediately that the cover obscured the Sunoco blue paint job, Jerry found a blue thermal blanket at a local Sears store. The blanket helped keep the dry ice from dissipating in the direct sun. Jerry then personally sewed Sunoco decals and patches onto the blanket to give the appropriate corporate identification. After the race USAC banned cooling fuel.

At the Indy 500 cars and drivers are placed on the starting grid early as part of the traditional pre-race excitement. With the grid packed with team personnel, officials, and well-wishers, Mark quietly said to Ron Fournier, "Ronnie, follow me." Mark led Ron to a small room tucked under the infield grandstand. It was the back room of the Firestone garage, and Mark had found a cubbyhole he could squeeze into. "Mark wanted to be alone," remembers Ron. "He told me to come and get him when the drivers were told to get into their cars and not before. Back on the grid everyone wanted to know where he was but I never said a word. When the time came to get him, I found him in the same spot on that tire, with his head in his arms. He had managed to clear his mind of distractions."

"Once I had the helmet on and was in the car it was a feeling of incredible relief after all the pressure and all the pageantry and buildup," Mark said.

After the start he initially dropped back as he adapted to running in traffic. As he came to terms with the pace Mark was smooth and fast and always in contention. He had run as high as second place, and with 176 of the 200-lap race run, the Sunoco-Simoniz Special was a solid third. Other than some blistering on his Goodyear tires Mark had steered clear of trouble. So the disappointment was great as Mark drove into the pits with ignition trouble. Karl Kainhofer maintained his legendary calm as he quickly identified the culprit. While Mark sat patiently, albeit somewhat disconsolately, on the pit wall, Karl replaced the magneto in 10 minutes, 32 seconds. Magneto failure was extremely rare, although Karl recalls with justifiable pride that he was prepared for the eventuality. "The magneto on the front of the engine got hot and failed," says Karl. "This is something that never happened before or again. But we were ready."

Back on the track Mark brought the Lola home in seventh place. During the long stay in the pits one of the cars to pass him was the Repco Brabham of Peter Revson. Revson had driven a terrific race, coming all the way from 33rd and last on the grid to a fifth-place finish driving one of the three naturally aspirated cars in the race. (Jack Brabham and Dan Gurney were in the others.) Peter later told Eoin Young, "I was so far back on the grid that I couldn't hear when Tony Hulman said 'Gentlemen, start your engines.' I had to wait until the guy in front of me started his!"

Mark was ultimately disappointed in his Indy debut despite his tremendous showing. "I suppose you shouldn't complain when you finish in the top ten, but you always drive to win, not just to finish high," he told *AutoWeek*. "I had a good car but we went with a richer fuel mixture and I ended up with a little less throttle response coming off the turns. It was quite an experience. This is a different race course than the road courses, there's no doubt about that. Oval racing experience still pays off at Indianapolis. I think the reason why the sports car drivers made a good showing today was because we all had good cars."

Mark's seventh place was worth $20,512.04, plus an extra $1,000 for the Stark & Wetzel Rookie of the Year award. Rookie-of-the-year honors at Indy typically, but not necessarily, go to the highest-placed rookie. On this occasion, though, Mark had been so impressive all month that the award went to him. While Mark had done a great job and deserved the honor, it bothered Peter Revson for years after. Jennifer Revson confirms that her brother remained bitter about what he considered a slight, and believed that politics had come into play in the decision. Five years earlier the decision had gone differently when Mark's friend Walt Hansgen was easily the most impressive rookie throughout the month. He, too, had run as high as second place when a late pit stop dropped him to thirteenth. But in 1964 the award went to the higher-finishing rookie. USAC regular Johnny White was never as fast as Walt but persevered to finish fourth. Although there was considerable outcry against the decision, Hansgen never commented. Later the same year the racing community was glad White had received the accolade when he was left paralyzed after a flip over the wall at Terre Haute in a sprint car.

The 1969 award bothered Revson, in part, because he believed he was not taken seriously as a committed race driver. As a son of well-known Charles Revson and alleged heir to the Revlon company fortunes, it was always assumed that Peter had ample funding. He told the Associated Press: "Look, I'm on my own, I make my own living. And I make it in racing. I get no help from my family. I am a race driver period. I have no other income." After the 500, influential syndicated West Coast writer Jim Murray referred to Peter as "the Park Avenue A. J. Foyt."

When Mark learned of Peter's reaction he wondered, "Who is Peter upset with? Surely not with me—I didn't vote on it. If it had gone the other way I would have understood."

Mario Andretti was an enormously popular winner, completing a great comeback from his crash in practice. His record speed for the race was 156.867. He received a famous smooch on the cheek in Victory Lane from STP's Andy Granatelli, and at the award ceremony the next day received a record payout of $205,727.06, from a total purse of $804,627.57. It was a great day for Granatelli too. He had been trying to win the race for 23 years, and his tremendous talent for publicity had made him one of the most recognizable figures in racing. Indy was his greatest stage, and he had gained particular notoriety when he introduced the turbine-powered cars that had nearly won the race the two previous years. Granatelli's penchant for innovation was integral to his public persona, so to finally win the 500 in such a conventional car as the Brawner-Hawk was ironic. Dan Gurney drove a great race to match his second-place finish of the previous year.

Mark Donohue in an undated photograph from his early teens.
(Donohue family collection)

ABOVE: At a college party during his junior year at Brown University, Mark is seated in front of the fireplace. Standing next to him is lifetime friend Phil Burrows. (Phil Burrows collection)

RIGHT: Ready to depart for the SCCA drivers' school, Mark's Elva Courier is on the trailer behind his 1954 Chevrolet station wagon. With characteristic irony Mark dubbed the station wagon "the Scaglietti" after the celebrated Italian coachbuilder who designed beautiful, elegant bodies for Ferrari. (Donohue family collection)

LEFT: Mark and Burge Hulett prepare to leave for their first SCCA drivers' school. Mark adjusts the front tie-down straps on Burge's Bandini while Burge works on the rear. (Donohue family collection)

BELOW: In a paddock scene at Marlboro Raceway in 1960, Mark is sitting on his Elva Courier. Burge Hulett's Bandini and Jay Signore's Courier can be partially seen on the right. (Signore family collection)

LEFT: Mark's first international race was the Sebring 12 Hours in 1962 for the factory TVR team. The cars are gridded for the Le Mans–style start. Mark is in the center wearing a red driver's suit with Jay Signore next to him in the blue driver's suit. (Donohue family collection)

BELOW LEFT: On April 20, 1963, Mark married Sue Warren in Fairhaven, New Jersey. Sue's sister Renee Rost was matron of honor and is to her left. At the top of the stairs is Mark's best man, Burge Hulett. (Donohue family collection)

RIGHT: Mark at Lime Rock Park in September 1963 in a winning drive in Jack Griffith's Cobra. (Donohue family collection)

LEFT: At the Sebring 12 Hours in 1965, Mark (shown in the car) co-drove John Mecom's Ferrari 250 LM with Walt Hansgen. (Donohue family collection)

BELOW: On the grid at Lime Rock in the Malcolm Starr–owned Lotus 20, Mark smiles for a photo. Mark won the 1965 SCCA Formula C Northeast National Championship driving this car. (Donohue family collection)

TOP LEFT: This is the crucial moment when Mark lost the 1965 SCCA National Championship Runoffs at Daytona. The left rear wheel of the Malcolm Starr–owned Shelby GT350R has just come off while Mark was leading the race. It can be seen to the right along the guardrail. (Lawton family collection)

ABOVE: Mark co-drove again with Walt Hansgen in the 1966 Daytona 24 Hours in the Holman-Moody–entered factory Ford GT40 Mark II. (Donohue family collection)

LEFT: At Daytona in 1966, Mark chats with Bob Grossman (left) and Walt Hansgen. Grossman was a popular driver based in the Northeast who had had success racing at Le Mans as well as in national competitions. He and Walt had been on Briggs Cunningham's team together, and both men had served as president of the Road Racing Drivers Club (RRDC)—a position Mark would later assume. (Donohue family collection)

Mark raced at Mount Fuji in Japan carrying the name of Sunoco's local distributor on the Penske McLaren M6A. He qualified on the pole and had a dramatic wheel-to-wheel battle with Peter Revson before encountering fuel problems that eventually caused his retirement. (Jerry Kroninger)

TOP LEFT: This is the crucial moment when Mark lost the 1965 SCCA National Championship Runoffs at Daytona. The left rear wheel of the Malcolm Starr–owned Shelby GT350R has just come off while Mark was leading the race. It can be seen to the right along the guardrail. (Lawton family collection)

ABOVE: Mark co-drove again with Walt Hansgen in the 1966 Daytona 24 Hours in the Holman-Moody–entered factory Ford GT40 Mark II. (Donohue family collection)

LEFT: At Daytona in 1966, Mark chats with Bob Grossman (left) and Walt Hansgen. Grossman was a popular driver based in the Northeast who had had success racing at Le Mans as well as in national competitions. He and Walt had been on Briggs Cunningham's team together, and both men had served as president of the Road Racing Drivers Club (RRDC)—a position Mark would later assume. (Donohue family collection)

LEFT: The dramatic Le Mans–style start began the 1966 Nassau Trophy race. Mark won the race in the No. 7 Lola T70 for Roger Penske. (Donohue family collection)

BELOW LEFT: Mark has just won the 1967 Watkins Glen round of the United States Road Racing Championship (USRRC). Sue is beside him in the Sunoco Lola T70, while Roger Penske (in the red shirt) kneels to the left of the car. (Barry M. Tenin)

RIGHT: Mark and his two sons, Michael (left) and David (right), in 1968. (Donohue family collection)

FAR RIGHT: Frost can be seen forming on the outer barrel as Mark proudly shows off the latest Penske Racing innovation—iced fuel. It is the 1968 Trans-Am at War Bonnet Raceway, where Mark and the team went on to win the race. (Jerry Kroninger)

BELOW: Smiling, and at the center of activity, Mark celebrates winning the Trans-Am category and finishing third overall in the 1968 Sebring 12 Hours. Co-driver of the Sunoco Camaro, Craig Fisher is on the far right in a white Goodyear driving suit. (Barry M. Tenin)

Mark raced at Mount Fuji in Japan carrying the name of
Sunoco's local distributor on the Penske McLaren M6A.
He qualified on the pole and had a dramatic wheel-to-
wheel battle with Peter Revson before encountering
fuel problems that eventually caused his retirement.
(Jerry Kroninger)

LEFT: In his USAC debut in the Rex Mays 300 at Riverside, Mark qualified fifth driving the Eagle-Offy. He ran a close second to Dan Gurney until he suffered a suspension failure, ultimately not finishing the race. (Barry M. Tenin)

BELOW LEFT: Chuck Parsons co-drove this Lola T70 Mk IIIB with Mark to victory in the 1969 Daytona 24 Hours. A few weeks later Mark teamed with Ronnie Bucknum at Sebring where this photo was taken. The car developed suspension problems around the fourth hour and was withdrawn from the race. (Barry M. Tenin)

ABOVE: Mark was rookie of the year at the Indianapolis 500 in 1969. This post-qualifying photo depicts the Lola T152-Offy and, from left to right, Jerry Kroninger, Roger Penske, Bill Galbraith, Carl Haas, Karl Kainhofer, Bill "Scotty" Scott, Mark Donohue, and John Woody. Jim Chapman is present in the photo but obscured from view. (Donohue family collection)

LEFT: Action at the 1969 Mid-Ohio Trans-Am encapsulates the season-long rivalry between Parnelli Jones in the Bud Moore–run Ford Mustang and Mark Donohue in the Penske Sunoco Camaro. Here Parnelli slides to the outside while Mark aims for the inside of the corner. Also evident is the controversial vinyl roof that graced the team Camaros for much of the season. (Pete Luongo)

RIGHT: Penske Racing switched to the AMC Javelin for the 1970 Trans-Am, and Mark gave the manufacturer its first victory at Bridgehampton in the rain. (Barry M. Tenin)

BELOW: Porsche 917s, Alfa Romeo T33-3s, and a Ferrari 312 PB occupy the grid behind Mark in the immaculate blue Penske Racing Ferrari 512 M on the pace lap for the 1971 Watkins Glen 6-hour race. Mark started from pole position and took a dominant lead, but steering failure ended his race early. (Barry M. Tenin)

ABOVE: The Questor Grand Prix at Ontario Motor Speedway pitted the international Formula One cars and drivers against the best American Formula 5000 teams. Mark in the Lola T192-Chevy was fastest of the Formula 5000 entries and ran as high as third overall. (Barry M. Tenin)

RIGHT: At the 1971 Canadian Grand Prix, Mark made an impressive Formula One debut with a third-place finish driving the Penske-run McLaren M19 in the rain at Mosport. (Barry M. Tenin)

RIGHT: Winner of the 1972 Indianapolis 500, Mark rides in the pace car on a lap of honor. Hall of Fame crew chief Karl Kainhofer is seated in front of Mark, and Roger Penske waves from the far right. Goodyear's Larry Truesdale is seated between Mark and Roger. (Karl Kainhofer collection)

FAR RIGHT: Through the first turn of the opening round of the 1972 Can-Am at Mosport, Mark has taken the lead in the Porsche 917-10, ahead of the McLarens of No. 4, Peter Revson, and No. 5, Denis Hulme. The black UOP Shadow of Jackie Oliver is next. (Barry M. Tenin)

LEFT: Mark has just won the 1973 NASCAR Winston Cup Western 500 in the AMC Matador and celebrates with the crew and trophy girls. Linda Vaughn is on the top step with Mark. Crew chief Chuck Cantwell is at bottom left. (Cantwell family collection)

ABOVE: In 1973 Mark won the Canadian-American Challenge Cup (Can-Am) in dominant fashion driving the Porsche 917-30. Here at Mid-Ohio, he leads David Hobbs, McLaren M20; Hurley Haywood, Porsche 917-10; Derek Bell, McLaren M8F; and Scooter Patrick, McLaren M8F. (Larry Neuzel)

TOP: Mark was the inaugural winner of the International Race of Champions (IROC). The six finalists wave from the podium before the final round at Daytona Speedway in 1974. From left to right: Mark Donohue, Peter Revson, Bobby Unser, George Follmer, David Pearson, and A. J. Foyt. (Dresang family collection)

ABOVE RIGHT: Mark and Eden White relax on the pit wall during a break in testing. They were married in 1974. (Dale von Trebra)

ABOVE: The challenge of Formula One lured Mark out of retirement. This is the maiden race for the Penske PC1 at the 1974 Canadian Grand Prix at Mosport Park. (Adrian Ketchum)

RIGHT: This photo of Mark and Eden was taken in the paddock at the Österreichring on race day for the Austrian Grand Prix—August 17, 1975. (The woman on the right is unidentified.) Mark's fatal crash occurred later the same morning in the pre-race warm-up. (Paul Powell collection)

CHAPTER 91:

The Dimple Effect

Mark Donohue and Ronnie Bucknum missed round two of the Trans-Am at Lime Rock Park because it was held the same day as the Indianapolis 500. Bob Johnson and Ed Leslie were brought into the team for the race. Bud Moore replaced Jones and Follmer with Swede Savage and John Cannon. Carroll Shelby had the best idea of all, replacing Revson with Sam Posey, who lived within earshot of the track and was dubbed "Lime Rock's driver in residence" by Al Bochroch. Sam won, with Savage making it a Mustang 1-2. Bob Johnson brought the Penske Camaro home third, while Ed Leslie dropped out early in the second team car. Posey would doubtless have been at Indy, too, if USAC/SCCA rivalry hadn't raised its ugly head. USAC refused to allow Sam to take the rookie test, claiming he was too inexperienced. The real reason, as confirmed by Indy insider Bob Wilkie, was that Sam was a star in the rival SCCA's single-seat series, the Continental series for Formula A cars (latterly to be known as Formula 5000). Sam was outspoken in his preference for road racing over oval tracks, and committed Indy heresy by publicly proclaiming Formula One as the ultimate goal for a serious driver.

Reflecting a growing rift between Penske Racing and GM Engineering, Vince Piggins complained when Mark was not in the Camaro at Lime Rock. Roger handled the matter in his usual straightforward manner, asking Piggins if he was prepared to make up the financial losses that Penske would incur by withdrawing from the 500. The issue was dropped.

The Penske team was still without a win when round three of the Tran-Am took place on June 8, at Mid-Ohio. The vinyl roofs were continuing to cause a stir among rival teams. Woody Woodard remembers SCCA tech inspectors taking every opportunity to ask, "Why is this on there? Why do you have this?" He and Mark were in tech inspection at Mid-Ohio when John Timanus—who Mark considered a "straight shooter" and among the very best SCCA officials—approached them. He demanded, "Hey. Everyone is on me about your roofs. They are too light and you had to cover them up with this stuff. What's the real scoop?"

Mark responded in a serious tone. "John, come on. Have you ever played golf? You've seen those little dimples on golf balls?" Timanus said he had. "Well," said Mark, "what do

you think they're there for?" Mark explained that when the golf ball is spinning, the dimple creates a negative pressure, which makes it lift like an aircraft wing. "That dimple on that golf ball is not that dissimilar to my vinyl roof on my race car—it provides lift at speed, and that's why it's there." Timanus walked away, shaking his head.

Mark was fastest of the 35 qualifiers at Mid-Ohio. The early stages of the race featured a great Mark/Parnelli duel. After a long pit stop to replace a wheel bearing, Mark was out of contention for the win, although he would finish seventh. Meanwhile, Ronnie Bucknum in the No. 9 Sunoco Camaro picked up the pace, and when Parnelli made a late stop it was Ronnie who gave the Penske team its first win of the season. The Trans-Am was a manufacturer's championship, not a driver's championship, and Bucknum's win was a shot in the arm to the team. Bucknum, who had raced at Indianapolis the weekend before, commented that 240 miles at Mid-Ohio was much tougher than 500 miles at Indy. After Saturday qualifying, Roger, with the disappointing result at MIS still in his mind, had kept the crew at the track late into the evening practicing pit stops. In the race Ronnie Bucknum's car needed only 19 seconds for his two pit stops—25.5 seconds less than Parnelli Jones took for his two stops. Bucknum won the race by 13 seconds.

Although the Trans-Am as a spectacle would have been greatly diminished without their presence, the under-2.0-liter category suffered both on and off the track. The lion's share of media attention and the biggest slice of the purse went to the big 5.0-liter "pony" cars. On the track, the hard-nosed professionals in the heavier and faster Mustangs, Camaros, and Javelins were not averse to making body contact when it suited their needs. Mark's friend Bob Bailey and his Porsche 911 co-driver, Jim Locke, had an experience at Mid-Ohio that was typical. With just a half-hour to go, and leading the under-2.0-liter class, Locke was on the proper line in a corner when Parnelli Jones thumped him soundly from behind with the Mustang. Along with an earlier hit from Peter Revson's Mustang, it was enough to collapse the Porsche's rear axle.

Bad blood between the Penske team and the Ford operation was already evident in a season that would see the rivalry escalate to a new level. Roger and Mark were furious at a tactic Ford had employed to shut their team out of pre-race practice. Talking to Hal McCoy in the Dayton *Daily News* (who described Roger as "the mod, mod car owner who works in the pits in clothes most guys reserve for the golf course"), he complained: "Ford has bought out every track we'll run a Trans-American race on. They've bought time the whole week before each race to practice. None of the other guys can get on. I told them we wouldn't race unless we got some practice time. It's not fair and I'll make the same demands at every track."

Roger's demands were heard and some time was allotted on Friday at MIS to test the Camaros. At Mid-Ohio Mark was still mad, telling McCoy, "Ford's trying to buy their way in racing. We just want to show that the small operators like us can beat them."

"Roger and Mark played that card of being the little guys pitted against the massive Ford juggernaut until it became more than a little tiresome," remembers George Follmer. "Our view was that they had resources at least the equal of ours."

The superficial—and sometimes genuine—cordiality that characterizes racing rivals along pit lane was fast disappearing. When Roger entered the Ford pit to discuss a point of contention, Homer Perry told him to leave, saying, "If we want you, we'll call."

Back at Newtown Square in the two weeks before the next race, both Camaros were completely stripped. The engines went to Traco and new gearboxes, rear ends, and driveshafts went on. Molin Auto Body worked their magic, including completely new paint jobs on both cars. Mark's No. 6 car now sported a red chin spoiler and red lights. Bucknum's car was similarly trimmed in yellow. According to Greg Pierson, red was Mark's favorite color; in addition to the famous socks, his first driver's suit was red, and later in his career he often used a red helmet. Pierson and Jim Russell had been close friends with Mark since their boyhood days in New Jersey. Now they attended every race they could to support him. To Mark's delight they bought red baseball caps and wore them at the races, allowing him to identify them in the crowd.

Penske Racing knew it was up against a serious effort by Ford to recapture the Trans-Am. It wasn't just that Ford's two independent—but fully supported—professional teams provided strength in numbers. The early-season races made it clear that the work Ford had been doing since the previous year, engineering parts and homologating them, had given them a significant edge. The Mustangs were outright faster early in the season, proving it with wins in four of the first five races.

To get the most out of the Camaros, Roger wanted Don Cox at every race. "It got to where I refused to be at every race because I already had a list three feet long of problems that I knew about, that needed to get solved," Cox says. "I needed the time back at the office in Warren, Michigan, to solve these things. Roger didn't agree with my approach on this at first, but it proved the right strategy in the long run." Cox concentrated first on improving the brake system. At Mid-Ohio he phoned Roger and told him of a breakthrough he had developed and suggested they implement the system immediately. It worked, and Roger now saw the wisdom in Don's approach to sorting the problems.

Ford now became serious about closing the tire gap. "We had the best cars and the best engines," says George Follmer. "We were really getting hurt because the tires would go off after 10 or 12 laps, and as a result we were making more pit stops than the Goodyear runners. The call to Akron came from the highest possible level at Ford to an equivalent top level at Firestone. There was a family relationship between the two companies and a history that went back to the earliest days. Within two weeks we were testing new tires and were working with a whole different staff of engineers—the top guys from their Indy program."

Trouble with the SCCA staff started on Friday of the Bridgehampton race weekend when Mark presented the Camaros for technical inspection. Series chief steward Dave Tallaksen—known then and now throughout racing as "the mouth of the south"—refused to pass the Sunoco cars because of the holes in the door sills for rear brake ventilation. When Mark asked, "Well, can you show me the rule?" Tallaksen replied, "I don't care about the rules—when I see something like that, a little red light goes off in my head, and I am not permitting your car to participate in the race. You can practice that way, but you can't be in the race until you cover them."

Faced with what he called "typical SCCA Neanderthal thinking," and unimpressed with the "little red light" reference, Mark protested the chief steward's decision to the stewards of the meeting. The stewards heard Tallaksen's explanation of the "little red light" and then Mark's exposition on the relevant rule. The stewards overturned Tallaksen's decision and allowed the cars to race. To Mark the favorable ruling was no surprise, since he knew the stewards were "straight shooters" who understood racing, had read the rule book, and were strong enough not to be bulldozed by the National office. What infuriated Mark and Roger most was that Roger had received pre-approval for the door vents from the SCCA. Now the club was vacillating and apparently giving in to Ford lobbying.

It was a tiring weekend, especially for the crew, as the team struggled with a vibration problem. Mark worked late into the night with Woody and Earle Macmullan to find it. Woody was now crew chief on Mark's car, and Earle had been promoted to crew chief of Bucknum's car. Commenting on the workload, Roger said, "The days of the guys who are winning races going to parties are over."

Mark's 1:42.96 lap was the fastest qualifying time, and made the Sunoco Camaro the first sedan to lap the 2.85-mile circuit at more than 100 mph. The Mustangs of Jones and Follmer were a second slower in second and third, and prospects appeared good for Mark to score his first win of the season. Disaster struck on race morning when the engine in Mark's car blew up in the pre-race warm-up. Roger switched Mark to the car that Ronnie Bucknum had qualified fourth, quickly swapping Mark's seat and harness from his No. 6 car to the No. 9. Because of the change the New York Region stewards of the meeting ruled that Mark would have to start from the back of the field. Although Roger protested vehemently the decision stuck.

Mark knew that the stewards' decision was correct, but by now he was tired, angry, and frustrated enough to argue the point anyway. When the race started he stormed through the field from his 31st starting position. Joel Finn was an eyewitness to the drama and described it in his book, *Bridgehampton Racing: From the Streets to the Bridge*: "All eyes were glued to Donohue's rapid progress through the field. He moved forward from 31st to 12th on the first lap alone, weaving his way through and around slower cars with abandon."

By lap 15 Mark had brought the Sunoco Camaro up to third place and was now trailing race leader George Follmer by 17 seconds and Peter Revson by just 13 seconds. When Revson's gear lever stuck in fourth, Mark soon flashed by into second place and continued to gain on Follmer. Just past half distance Mark was nine seconds off the pace when the Camaro broke a rocker arm, forcing him to slow in order to bring the car home. Follmer won, a full 86 seconds ahead of Mark in second. Jerry Titus drove a strong race in the Firebird to finish third, and would have caught Mark's fading Camaro had the race gone a few laps more. Follmer told *Newsday* writer Charles Clark, "I didn't get the ease-off sign until the end was in sight. Mark is still dangerous as long as he is on the course."

CHAPTER 92:
Showdown on the Roof

It was at Donnybrooke Raceway on July 5 that the great vinyl-roof dispute came to a showdown. The team arrived early in the week at the beautiful 3.0-mile road circuit near Brainerd, Minnesota, in the northern woods, nearly two hours north of Minneapolis. The name of the circuit derived from the first names of popular local drivers, Donny Skogmo and Brooke Kinnard, who had died in racing accidents.

A complication developed when Ronnie Bucknum suffered fractured ribs when his rental car was hit in an intersection in St. Cloud, Minnesota, on his way to the race. It was the second time in the year that Bucknum's services had been lost to the team because of a non-racing accident. Ed Leslie, who had driven the Sunoco Camaro at Lime Rock, was brought in on short notice. Leslie was an outstanding road racer from Monterey, California. He had been a key driver for Shelby in the Cobra and Cooper-King Cobra programs and was fast, dependable, and highly experienced.

Mark was at the track early in the week to test when he again encountered Dave Tallaksen—or, as Mark now liked to think of him, "the Red Light Kid." They exchanged pleasantries, and Mark had every reason to believe that it would be a relatively noncontroversial weekend. Roger had reached an agreement with the SCCA over the phone to remove the vinyl tops after Donnybrooke but before the next race at Bryar. When Mark returned to the track on Friday he received a very different reception. Dave Tallaksen had apparently not forgotten being overturned by the stewards of the meeting at Bridgehampton.

Tallaksen and Walter Hane—now SCCA technical administrator in charge of car eligibility and rules enforcement—declared that the Sunoco Camaros could not race until the vinyl roofs were removed and the holes in the door sills patched. Woody, crew chief on Mark's car, remembers well what happened next. "Roger said, 'Boys, load 'em up. We're out of here.' While the politics commenced between Ford, GM, the Donnybrooke owners, and the SCCA, we were back at the motel just lying around in the sun."

Roger told the press he was ready to withdraw entirely from the Trans-Am and all SCCA racing over the issue of the vinyl roofs. Saturday sports sections in newspapers across America carried some version of the headline that appeared in the Chicago *Daily News*: "Penske may pull out of SCCA, Trans-Am." Roger told the reporters, "Forty-four percent of all Camaros made have this kind of styling. This is what the public wants to see. The SCCA says that we could run them. Then they change their minds. If they don't give their approval before race time, and it isn't likely, we're pulling out of all SCCA events, and that includes the Can-Am series."

While the Penske crew lounged at the motel pool, the SCCA was conducting meetings, with owner George Montgomery in the middle attempting to broker a compromise. SCCA officials told Roger they knew he was bluffing and that Chevrolet would never allow him to pull out. Roger made it clear that they were very mistaken. Mark emphasized the point, saying, "We were very serious. Roger and I discussed it and decided to make a stand. If the ruling had gone against us we would have liquidated all the Trans-Am equipment and concentrated on USAC."

With no senior Sunoco executives easily accessible, Roger discussed the company's position with Jerry Kroninger. "I provided the approval to withdraw if necessary," remembers Jerry. "I was confident that I could explain the situation to top management."

On Saturday morning a statement was released: "The SCCA stewards have not declared the Penske modifications legal, but because of the time considerations, they are permitting the cars to run under the assumption that the cars will be brought to specifications for the next Trans-Am."

Now it was the turn of the Ford players to bluster. Bud Moore, Carroll Shelby, and Lew Spencer were among those weighing in with indignation that the Penske team seemed to be getting a free pass. Jerry Titus added his voice, and Ford's Homer Perry threatened to withdraw his team—but in the end, everyone raced.

The race itself featured a battle for the lead between Mark and Horst Kwech, with Parnelli running third. According to Mark, "The Mustangs really ganged up on me. Kwech hit me several times but eventually it came down to Parnelli and me and we were equally matched." Mark appeared set to win when with just 5 laps to go in the 84-lap event, the Traco engine exploded. Jones was now in the lead and won the race as Kwech spun off the road. Ed Leslie did a great job to salvage second place, and the points that went with it, for Chevrolet.

The Penske Camaro effort had hit rock bottom at Donnybrooke. The team was well down in points, trailing the combined Mustang teams of Shelby and Moore by 42 to 30, and acrimony was at an all-time high in Trans-Am racing. The abuse that Roger suffered, and the general attitude displayed by their competitors toward the Penske operation, proved to be the rallying point that the team needed. Roger told them that he was taking this personally, and that they would win the championship whatever it took.

The Penske team stayed over until Monday to test. Donnybrooke was a very fast track with one particularly long straightaway—perfect to evaluate front-end lift. Don Cox installed instrumentation to measure aerodynamic lift. Don remembers serving as a "living telemetry recorder," strapped in the back of the Camaro to read the instruments: "We had manometers strung up in the car, little pressure taps run all over the car—I'm trying to read these things the best I can—every once in a while I look up to see if there is a corner coming up. At one point a corner loomed up and I couldn't understand why Mark wasn't slowing. It flashed through my mind that he must have died—he's frozen at the wheel. It was impossible that we're going to make this corner as he was still on the throttle—but just about then he tapped the brake and made a wheel adjustment and we were through the corner. I couldn't imagine we were doing what we were doing."

On July 19 at Bryar the SCCA conducted a tough technical inspection as they grasped for credibility. The Penske Camaros no longer had vinyl roofs and the holes in the door sills were closed. Mark won his first Trans-Am of the season—his first race win since the Daytona 24 Hours in the Lola—but not without controversy. He captured pole position with a 1:13.0 and shared the front row with Parnelli in the Bud Moore Mustang, who turned a 1:13.4. Ed Leslie was again a super sub, qualifying third with a 1:13.6 alongside Peter Revson in the Shelby Mustang. Parnelli charged into an early lead and Mark did fierce battle with all four Mustangs. The Mustangs fell by the wayside one by one, and when Parnelli spun out Mark was in the lead with Leslie some distance behind. "When Parnelli spun it gave me a chance to open up," Mark told John Kelso of the Manchester *Union Leader*. "And after that it seemed like the competition just fell apart."

Mark had pushed hard taking the battle to the Mustangs, and although now in the lead, his Sunoco Camaro was suffering. Teammate Leslie closed rapidly and was soon on Mark's bumper. Roger gave Leslie the hold position sign, and the two ran out the race, comfortable 1-2 winners. They finished well ahead of the Mustangs of Revson and Follmer in third and fourth, and the Firebirds of Bob Tullius and Dick Brown, fifth and sixth. Bryar proved the Penske Sunoco Camaro team was back.

People still found reason to be mad at Roger and Mark. It was clear that teammate Ed Leslie could have won the race, as he paraded behind Mark's crippled car, which Mark described as "very used up with the rear end cookin' and smokin'." Leslie was disappointed at Roger's team orders but said nothing. Others said plenty. Mustang driver Horst Kwech approached Roger after the race to speak his mind, saying, "Roger, if I was driving for you, I would have gone by that Donohue no matter what you said. Leslie deserved to win that race and I think you are a real son-of-a-bitch for not letting him win." The response was calm and measured. "Well, Horst, that is why you are not driving for me. And, if you want further information, you never will drive for me."

It wasn't any easier being the second driver to Mark on the Penske Racing team than it ever was to be second to Jim Clark at Team Lotus. Woody explains: "Mark's car came first—Mark did all the testing. The two cars were not purposefully tiered—you wanted as strong a two-car team as possible—but in reality there probably was some difference. The best crew was on Mark's car, and it just worked out because of the priorities involved."

The team's loyalty to Mark was intense. He was the man who met the crew at the door when they came to work in the morning and was still in the shop when they went home in the evening. A hired driver who came in for the weekend could not compete with that. Mark appreciated Roger's gesture at Bryar and ignored the cynics, saying to the press after the race that "the best thing to do is to win at the slowest possible time." He sensed that giving him the win was Roger's way of acknowledging the struggles and sacrifices he had made to get the team to where it now was.

CHAPTER 93:
"That next level"

July 27 was an open weekend between Trans-Am dates. Roger and Mark chose to run a USAC race at Indianapolis Raceway Park (IRP) rather than debuting the Group 7 Lola T163 at the Edmonton Can-Am. Mark explained to Bill Simmons of the *Philadelphia Inquirer*, "We simply haven't had enough time to properly set up the Can-Am car. We didn't get

the chassis until late May; our new 430ci Chevrolet engine didn't arrive until early this week. We conceivably could have made Edmonton but we wouldn't have been competitive."

After the Indy 500, Eric Broadley had prepared a special short-wheelbase version of the four-wheel-drive Lola for road racing. The chassis was unchanged, although the wheelbase was shortened from 104 to 98 inches. The biggest difference was that the road-racing Lola was fitted with a Traco-prepared 5.0-liter Chevrolet in place of the Offenhauser.

IRP in Clermont, just a few miles down the road from the Indianapolis Motor Speedway, was decidedly anticlimactic after Mark's great result in the 500 two months earlier. The weekend got off to a bad start when the tow vehicle was involved in an accident. When the car did arrive at the IRP road course, Mark found the Lola's handling diabolical. After struggling to qualify 12th, Mark reluctantly decided it would be a mistake to race the car. Chuck Cantwell announced to the press, "We don't think it is wise or safe for Mark to drive because the car is not handling right."

The Indy 200 at IRP comprised two separate 100-mile races. Dan Gurney won the first 100 in his stock-block Ford-powered Eagle, chased hard throughout by Al Unser. Gurney was unable to start the second race when his fuel tank disintegrated. Peter Revson, driving for Jack Brabham, won the race, with Mario Andretti second.

A week later the Trans-Am resumed at St. Jovite, the beautiful circuit in the Laurentian Mountains of Quebec. Momentum had shifted away from the Mustang domination when Mark won at Bryar. Now the Ford juggernaut was dealt a very tough setback. An eight-car crash midway through the race eliminated all of the Mustang threat.

"It all started with bad valve springs," remembers George Follmer. "We were changing them between practice sessions. They were flying springs in by the hour—it wasn't a good situation. I had a big lead when a valve hung open and it blew oil out the exhaust port and all over the track. I pulled the car off the track alongside the Armco barrier and ran back up the track to warn the flagger to put the oil flag out. He wouldn't do it—he insisted on just putting out a yellow. I finally took the oil flag away from him and started waving it, but by that time it was too late."

The race was stopped for more than an hour. Flag marshal Bruce Fowler suffered shock and a fractured arm as race cars stacked one on top of another after hitting the oil spill. The Mont Tremblant circuit was unforgiving, as Mark told *Sports*

Car Graphic's Jack Brady: "I really hated to see all those cars go out at once, but the competition is getting rougher and rougher. When you have Parnelli and Follmer working you over, you have to be careful. There's only one penalty for a mistake on a course like this, and that's total destruction."

"The real blow to Ford at St. Jovite was that we scored no points at all to offset the nine earned by the Camaro," says George Follmer. "From then on we were playing catch-up." Suddenly Chevrolet led the series 49–46 from Ford. Mark was winning races at a speed, in his words, "just fast enough to win." At St. Jovite Mark told Brady, "At the end of the race I was running near half-throttle. I had a 30-second lead at Brainerd and blew an engine with five laps to go, and I didn't want that to happen again."

Practice for the next round at Watkins Glen on August 10 began just four days later. Ford gathered all available resources—including Kar Kraft working alongside Bud Moore and Shelby crew members—to have the extensively damaged race cars replaced or repaired in time for the race. The rapid turnabout in fortunes had tensions running higher than ever. Mark and Parnelli were the primary flag carriers in their respective camps, and their personal rivalry was reaching a breaking point. On the very fast circuit, Mark captured pole position with a 1:14.13, and Parnelli was alongside on the front row with a 1:14.40.

The start line at Watkins Glen was at the bottom of a hill and required an almost immediate turn to the right as the cars climbed through the esses. Mark and Parnelli bumped fenders all the way up the hill and beyond, neither man willing to yield his position. Jones told Jack Brady, writing for *Competition Press*, "Yeah, we went through there huggin' each other a bit." Mark's equally understated comment was, "When that many cars pile into a corner at one time, there's bound to be a little bumping." The two men were well matched, as were their cars. At 153.85 mph, Parnelli's Bud Moore Mustang was the fastest car that day through the Watkins Glen speed trap. Mark's Sunoco Camaro was next fastest at 152.54.

It was an eventful race. When Parnelli pitted from the lead for fuel he was on his way in a fast 11.7 seconds. When Mark stopped soon after, the Penske crew had the fuel in and the Sunoco Camaro away in a head-turning 5.2 seconds. Jerry Kroninger had calculated that using a four-inch-diameter nozzle could cut fueling time by half compared to the standard three-inch piece. To accommodate it, Don Cox engi-

neered a slide valve, and the setup debuted at Watkins Glen. "One guy had to pull the slide open and the other guy inserts the hose," said Mark. "The first time we used it we came in and went out so fast no one could believe we had filled the entire tank. The two or three seconds we saved may not have helped us that much on the track, but it demoralized the other team and created tremendous publicity. It was spectacular. There would be so much wasted fuel splashing all over, it was unbelievable."

Parnelli made an unscheduled stop with a shredded tire and Mark held the lead until the race's lavender-suited, cigar-chewing starter, "Tex" Hopkins, showed him the black flag for passing under a yellow flag. It evened out when Parnelli was also shown the black flag for the same incident. A black flag requires a driver to call at the start/finish line to discuss the infraction with the chief steward. Neither man was happy with the move, although after the race, Mark praised the flag marshals, saying that it was a job that was becoming increasingly dangerous as speeds escalated. Mark won by over a minute from Parnelli: The score was now 58–52, Chevy over Ford, with just four races to go.

To Mark, Parnelli Jones represented another benchmark as a driver. Just as he had with John Cannon early in his career, Mark needed to ratchet up his competitiveness and adjust his driving skills. Sam Posey comments: "Mark was aware that people thought Parnelli was faster. This was the kind of fear that Mark had—that there was a class of driver that he wasn't as good as—that he could compete with only because of how he could set up the car. But he kept hauling himself up to that next level, and I believe in the end he was as good as any of those guys."

Sam believes that Parnelli was the quickest of the Trans-Am guys. "Definitely—Parnelli adapted his style to what was needed in Trans-Am—of using curbs and expanding the line by driving off the road. He did this for the situation. At Indy he was a clean, neat, and tidy driver, certainly. Trans-Am cars just seemed to need to be driven a different way and seemed to go faster if you didn't worry about driving the perfect lap."

Mark, in turn, adopted Parnelli's style of driving. Posey points out that it was at Mark's core to do whatever was needed to compete. "He didn't accept that he wasn't as good, and he would keep trying things. Mark eventually achieved within the racing community what Parnelli had, and that was that when you saw him coming you tended to get out of the way. Also, like Jim Clark and later Jackie Stewart, Mark could get out front and set the pace—they could back off and people would accept the pecking order. Mark was like that. Very few drivers ever achieve that degree of recognition among fellow drivers."

CHAPTER 94:
"Can-Am is McLaren's business"

After the Watkins Glen Trans-Am, Mark went straight to Mid-Ohio raceway near Mansfield, Ohio, where Karl Kainhofer was waiting with the new Group 7 Lola T163. On Monday, August 11, Mark tested the new car all day in preparation for the Can-Am there the following weekend. The Lola had been delivered to Newtown Square in late May, and the Traco-built 427ci Chevy had been fitted just a week before leaving for Ohio. The only benchmark was Lothar Motschenbacher's lap record of 1:30.8, set the previous year in the USRRC. Despite breaking in a completely new car on two hours' sleep, Mark was comfortably in the 1:27 range within 10 laps. Mark was tired, and the pressure of the season was just beginning. He told Andy Stern for the Mansfield *News-Journal*, "I've been running almost every other weekend, and now we go every weekend until October 19."

Chuck Parsons was also there with the Simoniz Lola T163, and he and Mark worked together on setups and other sorting issues. The Simoniz Lola headed west that evening to Carl Haas's race shop in Highland Park, just outside Chicago. Parsons was now living in the Chicago area and working full-time for Haas. The Sunoco Lola returned east to Newtown Square.

Mid-Ohio was hosting its first Can-Am and road-racing fans responded, with a long line of cars backed up outside the track on race day. When Les Griebling, owner and manager of Mid-Ohio, opened the gates 40 minutes early at 5:20 a.m., to alleviate traffic, cars and people on foot poured into the circuit. For 1969 the series had increased from a tight 6-race schedule in the late summer and autumn to 11 races beginning June 1. Mid-Ohio was round five.

Roger Penske had attended the Can-Am race at Edmonton in late July, where he told John Radosta of *The New York Times* that his team and driver were as good as McLaren's, but he saw no point in pursuing McLaren futilely. He made

clear where his priorities lay. "It's only good business to decide where you're going and to make your plans. Can-Am is McLaren's business, and he can concentrate on it. Trans-American is my business, and that's why we are concentrating on it."

To the close observer, the decline of the Can-Am—now in its fourth year—was apparent. The size of the starting fields continued to diminish, and, more critically, the competitiveness at the front end was now very different. Long gone were the early days of Group 7 racing, with fields of 40 and more cars that demanded a qualifying race to determine a starting field. Now organizers courted every entry and hoped for a starting field of 20 cars. The Penske team entry had been sorely missed, and Mark's appearance at Mid-Ohio in the blue Sunoco Lola was heartening to the SCCA and other boosters of the series. More telling was the complete dominance of the McLaren team. Bruce McLaren and Denny Hulme occupied the front row of every grid, and the margin to the second row was typically two seconds or more. It became even worse as one looked down beyond the third row.

It wasn't all bad. The cars were still exciting to watch. A well-driven Can-Am car, applying full power and using the entire road and more on the exit of a turn, was breathtaking. Even with the decline in competitiveness, Can-Am racing remained popular with race fans for the pure spectacle. The appeal came from the visible challenge the cars presented to drivers. Technology in the form of tires, aerodynamics, chassis tuning, and brakes had not yet caught up with the enormous power in the light cars. It took a fuel load of 80 gallons to get most cars through a 200-mile Can-Am race without a pit stop. The difference in handling from early to late race, as nearly 500 pounds of raw gasoline was burned up, required tremendous finesse and adaptability. Jack Deren contrasts the difference between early Can-Am racing and the computer-driven technology of 21st-century race cars: "Can-Am cars were 800-horsepowered, flat-bottomed, 1,800-pound, no-brakes monsters that had only a couple of wires in it. A battery and a cable to start it, a brake light to let the guy behind know you were trying to slow down and a mag kill wire to stop it!!"

There were plenty of great drivers in the races; they just lacked equipment up to the McLaren standard as represented by the Mk 8B, a refined and well-tested development of the previous year's dominant car.

One of the best of the competing drivers was John Surtees,

a World Champion and winner of the 1966 Can-Am. Surtees was now driving for Jim Hall and the Chaparral team. The latest Chaparral, the 2H, was not ready to start the season, and had just debuted at the previous race at Edmonton. To provide a car for Surtees to race in the early rounds of the series, Hall had purchased a McLaren M12, the latest customer McLaren available through Trojan Engineering. The pairing of Surtees with the Midland, Texas, Chaparral team seemed, in theory, a dream arrangement. The reality proved different. The 2H was the least successful of all Chaparral designs. Chaparral performance also suffered as it became apparent that Hall and Surtees did not click on a personal level. Although each was brilliant in his own sphere, they did not find a winning chemistry.

Adding interest to the Mid-Ohio race was the first Can-Am entry by a Porsche 917. Swiss driver and Formula One star Josef Siffert, with support from Porsche-Audi, entered a 4.5-liter, 12-cylinder version of the model prepared to Group 7 specifications. Retrospectively, the Porsche entry is interesting given the eventual importance of the 917 in Can-Am racing with Mark and the Penske team. But at the time the Porsche was somewhat overweight and down on power compared to the McLarens, though Siffert's extraordinary talent made it a reasonably competitive proposition. He finished fourth.

An indication of the McLarens' edge is that Siffert qualified seventh, a full five seconds off the pole-position time of Denny Hulme. Just as revealing is that Mark, considered the great hope to bring competitiveness to the series, qualified the Lola third, 3.6 seconds off Hulme's pace. Admittedly Mark had been faster in testing, and qualifying was cut short by bad weather. The Sunoco Lola gave trouble in practice with a broken halfshaft and engine problems. Chuck Parsons was fourth on the grid, and the third row comprised Surtees in the Chaparral and George Eaton in a McLaren M12. Well down the grid in 12th after mechanical trouble was Chris Amon in the Ferrari 612 P. Since rejoining the series in round three at Watkins Glen, Amon had provided the closest competition to the McLarens.

Hot summer days at a rural track like Mid-Ohio were a recipe for Mark's worst symptoms of hay fever. This day was particularly bad, and although his face was swollen and nasal passages clogged, Mark would not take medication when he raced. "I was taking medication during the week," he told Andy Stern. "But I can't do anything while I'm driving." Sue recalls that no matter how badly he suffered, Mark was able

to overcome the discomfort once he put on his helmet.

Amon provided the greatest interest in the race as he tore through the field in the Ferrari to come up on Mark in the Sunoco-Lola. Mark had been running in fourth place behind Chuck Parsons, and now Mark and Amon went by the Simoniz car. What might have been an entertaining duel between Mark and Chris ended soon after when the Lola broke another halfshaft. Mark was out of the race on lap eight, and Hulme and McLaren went on to win decisively from the Ferrari.

CHAPTER 95:

"Looks like a choirboy, drives like a demon"

The Trans-Am now shifted to the West Coast for the final four rounds. The sudden reversal of fortunes found Ford trailing in the point standings. Hatred and discontent were at an all-time high. At Laguna Seca on August 24, Shelby's team manager Lew Spencer seemed to be grasping at straws when minutes before the pre-race protest deadline, he alleged the Penske Camaros were underweight. The minute Roger got word of the protest he filed one of his own against the height of the new Ford refueling rigs. At the scales Mark's car was found legal at 71 pounds over the 2,900-pound minimum, with Leslie's 80 pounds over. After measurement of the Ford rigs, Roger's protest was upheld. The illegal Ford refueling rigs sat idle behind the pits all day.

At the post-race press conference Mark characterized Ford tactics as "if you can't win, protest," saying that their approach could wreck the series. He went on to note that it had been obvious to him when he first saw the Ford rigs that they were over the height limit, but he had no intention of saying anything. Only when Ford lodged the nuisance protest on weight were he and Roger moved to take action.

After qualifying, the Bud Moore Mustangs occupied the front row of the grid, with George Follmer on pole with a 1:12.14 and Parnelli Jones at 1:12.28. Ford was pulling out all the stops as they brought Dan Gurney in to drive one of the Shelby Mustangs. Mark was officially third fastest only after Roger protested the time assigned to Dan, prompting Bruce Johnson in the *San Jose Mercury-News* to observe, " 'Captain Nice' proved he isn't all that pleasant." On the other hand, Jack Woodard of the *Sacramento Union* was moved to say that Mark "looks like a choirboy and drives like a demon." Gurney was making his first Trans-Am start in more than a year, and the adjusted times dropped him from 3rd to 10th. The same detailed review of the timing logs moved Ed Leslie up from 9th to 5th on the grid.

It was Judy Stropus who calmly sorted out the timing problem. Roger knew the official times were wrong and was ready to argue his point on logic and the sequence of events. Judy counseled him that this was the wrong approach, arguing that timers and scorers were focused on numbers and data. Roger smiled as he walked away to let her handle it. Judy recalls that one of Roger Penske's strengths was to trust the people in his organization to handle their own areas of expertise. She met with the chief timer, and upon careful review of their data the error was discovered and corrected.

Jones led the early laps of the race until he was passed by his teammate, Follmer. Mark was holding a steady third. On lap 44 Parnelli entered the pits with the transmission on fire. It spread to the differential and the Mustang was retired. George led until lap 50 of the 119-lap race, when a brake line failed on the right front wheel. Mark won his fourth consecutive Trans-Am race, with Ed Leslie second. Shelby teammates Gurney and Peter Revson were third and fourth. After the race Mark shared his winning formula with Dinah Chapman of *Competition Press*, emphasizing how hard the crew had worked and claiming that the famous Penske reliability was owed to their efforts. "The idea is to go the whole distance and have a car underneath you at the end of the race," Mark told Chapman. "We wait until the first pit stop, hanging back and not straining the car, and then decide how fast we have to go."

Ford had counted on a 1-2 finish to close the points gap. Only the lead car for a given manufacturer could earn points, but by occupying second, for example, it meant the opposition could only score the lower number of points for the position they thus occupied. The result at Laguna Seca was the opposite of Ford's hopes. The Chevrolet lead over Ford was now 11 points, with only three races to run.

The next day Mark was at nearby Sears Point Raceway in the California Wine Country testing for the Trans-Am there in late September. Actor James Garner and a film crew were there shooting background for Garner's racing movie, *On the Scene*. Mark accommodated them by running with the Sunoco Camaro rigged for in-car shots of a fast lap.

Ford made its strongest possible effort to turn the tide when the series resumed at Kent, Washington, on September

7. Despite fielding the same driver lineup that had appeared at Laguna, the fates seemed to conspire against Ford. Nearly the entire team was hit by food poisoning. Among the drivers Dan Gurney was hit the hardest, although all were suffering.

Mark captured pole position by just a tenth of a second from Parnelli. Ronnie Bucknum's injuries had healed, and he returned to the team to put the second car seventh on the grid, 2.3 seconds slower than Mark. Parnelli once again leapt to the front on the green flag, with Mark following. The complexion of the 135-lap race changed suddenly when Mark pitted early with a flat tire. Six laps later he was back in the pits with a broken engine. Bucknum, in a strong third, carried the battle to the Mustangs of Jones and Gurney, passing and re-passing both during pit stops and on the track. When Dan had to stop to replace the differential on his car, Ronnie kept the pressure on Parnelli. The climactic moment came on lap 73 when the cars stopped in the pits simultaneously. A six-second Penske pit stop left Parnelli now doing the chasing. Ronnie pulled steadily away as Parnelli struggled with various problems, concluding when a tire blew 150 yards from the checkered flag. Parnelli finished on the rim, but Ronnie had already captured the victory. It was a great win for Bucknum—his second of the season in the Sunoco Camaro—and a satisfying result for the team, which, even with Mark watching from the pits, had increased its lead on Ford for the championship.

That evening Mark was asked to address the crowd at a dinner in Seattle. He later remembered the occasion as the first time he felt confident entertaining an audience. He was relating an incident from earlier in the day on pit lane when he was being interviewed for a television series on the Trans-Am. Jerry Titus had run up with a sign that said your fly is open. It had amused Mark greatly, and as he related the story, he discovered what he called a phenomenon: "If you can say something funny and convey to the crowd that you think it is funny yourself, it's almost like a stampede and suddenly you can take them wherever you want."

After the unsuccessful USAC race at IRP in July, Karl Kainhofer had converted the Lola T150 from four-wheel-drive to the more conventional two-wheel-drive form. A two-week break in the Trans-Am schedule after Kent provided the chance to rejoin USAC's Championship Trail at Brainerd, Minnesota, on September 14. At the Donnybrooke circuit Mark was again a visitor, inserting himself into the busy USAC season. Although Dan Gurney's Eagle-Ford was dominant in both 100-mile-heat races, he lost the first one when he ran out of fuel on the last lap and was passed for the lead by Gordon Johncock, just 600 yards from the finish. Dan coasted home second, with Al Unser and Mario Andretti third and fourth. Mark finished seventh. Mark ran a strong second heat to finish fourth—he was also fourth on aggregate—behind Gurney, Johncock, and Andretti.

The week after the race at Brainerd, Mark made a trip back to Hillside, New Jersey, to be the head speaker at the Pingry Alumni Association Dinner. It was one of many times that Mark showed his loyalty to his school. He frequently addressed student assemblies where he was immensely popular. His consistent advice to students was to pursue their studies seriously to build a bright future.

CHAPTER 96:

Champions Again

Although Ford's Trans-Am situation was now desperate, they were unwilling to concede the championship in this most bitterly fought season. At Sears Point on September 21, Parnelli Jones captured pole position, and the Bud Moore plan was to run the entire 80-lap, 201-mile distance on one pit stop. The 2.523-mile Sears Point circuit in the vineyard country north of San Francisco had opened only the previous year.

It was all decided in the last few laps. Mark's strategic drive, allied with brilliant pit work, made Chevrolet the Trans-Am champion for the second year running. Parnelli's one-stop strategy fell apart when he pitted from an eight-second lead on lap 69, having signaled his crew for a fresh left rear tire. The Bud Moore crew replaced the right rear by mistake, and in the confusion that followed it was 51 seconds before Jones left the pit—although now on four fresh tires. It left Mark with a lead sufficient for Roger to bring him in for a fresh left front tire on lap 73. Unlike today, there were no speed limits on pit lane, making the action dramatic and violent.

David Bean watched Mark's last stop and described it in *Car Life*:

The pit marshal sounds a claxon when he sees a car approaching . . . warning everyone to run for cover, for most drivers take it [the last corner] in a full, power-on drift, then fishtail down the pit lane scattering

pedestrians like chickens in a farm yard. Donohue's pit was the very last one and by the time he got there he was flat out in second gear, sliding to a stop just short of running over Penske. Car up, Donohue looks straight ahead, expressionless, ignoring the activity around him. Zip, zip, zip, zip, zip, lug nuts off. Wheel off. New wheel on. Star cluster of nuts on in one motion. Zip, zip, zip, zip, zip. Car down and tires lit, boiling back onto the track. 23 seconds. Everybody could breathe again.

At the finish Mark was 2.17 seconds ahead of a hard-charging Parnelli Jones. The championship was won. "It's a gamble," said Mark. "We gambled, they gambled, and it could have gone either way." Acknowledging Parnelli's late challenge on fresh tires, Mark said, "One more lap and the outcome could have been quite different. He goes out and drives his heart out and the crew blows it all for him." Jim Gilmartin of *The Marin County Independent Journal* called Mark, ". . . the boyish-looking 32-year-old golden boy of road racing."

There was a beer party for the Sunoco Penske team at the motel after the race, replete with water fights and other frivolity. Judy Stropus remembers that Ronnie Bucknum was as big a prankster as Mark, and they enjoyed nothing better than one-upping one another. That day Mark managed to set up a bucket of water over Ronnie's motel door that doused him thoroughly. It was the time to let off steam. Woody Woodard as crew chief on Mark's car and Earle Macmullan on Bucknum's had worked miracles all year. So had Don Cox, who as engineering liaison at GM for the team had stayed away from many races to solve the huge problems the 1969 car had presented.

Cox remembers the challenge: "Ford did have a big jump on us at the beginning of the year. We did some things right and we had some luck come our way. It was a fairy tale story, really." Cox says that the brake problems were fairly easy for him to fix once he figured out what was wrong. "We did a good job on team strategy and race management and conducting ourselves in the race. Ford had their problems—the St. Jovite setback really hurt them." Traco had also worked to overcome engine problems.

It was a great team achievement. Penske Racing had overcome the hurdle of winning only one of the first five races. They reengineered the car and beat a powerful and determined Ford team. To do it Roger had made the commitment that the Trans-Am program was more important than the

Can-Am, and would have even withdrawn from Indy had it been necessary.

With the championship over, Ford was determined to gain some solace by winning the season-ending race at Riverside. Equally, Penske Racing was out to add a final decisive stamp to their championship year. Up to this time, Mark and Parnelli, while fierce rivals, had enjoyed mutual respect. That relationship ended at the Mission Bell 250 at Riverside on October 5.

Bud Moore brought a third team car for Al Unser. Along with the Shelby cars for Peter Revson and Horst Kwech, factory Mustangs outnumbered the Penske Sunoco Camaros five to two. The big news was Carroll Shelby's announcement that he would end his long relationship as the public face of Ford road racing after the race. It was generally known, too, that AMC was looking elsewhere for 1970, making Riverside the swan song for Ronnie Kaplan's Javelin race operation.

Parnelli and Mark qualified on the front row with Parnelli on the pole. Although Mark led off the line, Parnelli was in front by the end of the first lap. They ran close together until the first pit-stop cycle, when Parnelli came in six laps earlier than Mark. When Mark exited pit lane, Parnelli was right on his bumper. Parnelli's fresh tires were now fully warmed up and he was carrying a lighter fuel load. On cold tires and a full tank, Mark was slow on his out lap and braked earlier than normal for the slippery turn six. Parnelli was caught by surprise and hit the rear of the Camaro hard. Mark described it this way: "I was fresh out of the pits with a full load of fuel, the tires cold and squirrelly, and when Parnelli came up and hammered me I thought, oh Christ, what did you do that for?"

Respect ended at that moment—at least on Parnelli's part. Convinced that Mark had braked early with the intent of breaking the Mustang's radiator, Parnelli—with a crippled car—stayed on the track, circulating slowly, until Mark came up to lap him. Mark was chasing Parnelli's teammate George Follmer, who had taken the lead. Parnelli now blocked Mark for a couple of corners until they again reached turn six, where he drove into the Camaro's left front fender, sending Mark spinning off the track. It took Mark 30 seconds to restart the engine, and he was now third behind Follmer and Jerry Titus.

Titus later hit an apex marker tire that had been kicked onto the track by another car, and he eventually finished third with the Firebird. Mark, a lap down on George but now on

fresh tires, was in hot pursuit. When he passed Follmer to go back on the lead lap, he held up one finger, indicating he needed to gain back just one lap. Moments later the left front wheel on the Mustang collapsed. Follmer displayed great car control, attempting to slow the car by grazing the pit wall; but when the wall ended, he hit a cinder-block abutment hard enough to take out the Mustang's right front corner.

Post-race, Parnelli and Mark each had a point of view on what had happened in the crucial turn six collision. Parnelli told *Motor Trend*'s John Lamm that Mark had shut the door on him. Mark said he had been taking a cautious approach to the turn and that Parnelli "came roaring up behind me and bumped me from the rear." Mark expressed his disappointment over the subsequent incident: "The whole thing upsets me. Parnelli and I have driven a lot of races against each other and I would never pull a dirty trick on him."

After the award ceremony Mark tried to talk to Parnelli in the race paddock, but found he had already left the track. "While I was out on the track Parnelli was bad-mouthing me to the press and claiming I had purposefully short-braked him and had broken his radiator. I later learned from someone on the Bud Moore team that there was nothing wrong with the Mustang and that Parnelli was just mad, and it was all just an excuse for taking me out."

Mark was confident Parnelli would understand the circumstances if they just could talk it out. They never did. Parnelli made himself unavailable for Mark's phone calls, and according to Mark, they never communicated in future years beyond a nod and a hello.

There was recent history that hardened Parnelli's view. Mark, showing what he later admitted was poor judgment, had semi-clandestinely obtained a set of the latest Firestones for comparison testing and analysis. It was generally viewed as an unsportsmanlike and even unethical action. He succeeded in annoying not only Parnelli and the Firestone people, but also Roger and the Goodyear bosses. It was an embarrassing incident. Mark realized his error and regretted it. When he attempted to talk it out with Parnelli at Kent, he was given the cold shoulder. Later, when someone mentioned the Captain Nice appellation, Parnelli commented, "I don't care what people think, Donohue is no angel out there." Mark realized that Parnelli thought he had "knifed him in the back."

Jones was not the only contemporary figure to challenge the generally accepted view of Mark as a kind and easily approachable figure. Jack Brady, one of the more insightful motorsports writers of the time, questioned Mark's easygoing image in an article for *Our Sun*:

> Donohue, like most champions, has a streak in him that belies his nickname and like most athletes in the solitary sports, he has a very tough and ribald sense of humor at times. . . . This same introspective existence makes many professional sportsmen extremely sensitive to failure in any degree and Donohue seems to be one of these. Jubilant in victory, he can be almost morose when he feels his error contributed to losing a race.

At Riverside, with Parnelli not available for a frank talk, Mark endured chastisement from the Ford people. All the frustration from the championship that had slipped away was vented on Mark. It was unfair and unwarranted—he was convinced of his innocence in the incident and believed it was Parnelli who had taken him out—but Mark took it.

On October 22, American Motors Company and Roger Penske dropped a bombshell on the racing industry when at a press conference in Los Angeles, they jointly announced they had entered into a three-year agreement to pursue the Trans-Am Championship with a two-car team of AMC Javelins. Sun Oil was also involved, and the cars were to be painted "Red, White and SUNOCO Blue." When asked who would drive the second car, Roger replied, "I'd like to have Mark drive both cars, but I haven't figured a way to do that yet."

The news was a sensation, coming so soon after the team had dramatically won the 1969 championship for Chevrolet. Roger explained his decision in a statement to the Associated Press: "Racing is something General Motors is not involved in and we have relied heavily on the other sponsors in the Trans-Am area." Roger also made a statement that would be thrown up by his rivals in the year ahead. "Our Javelin team will take seven victories in next year's Trans-Am. This is a lot to say but we're going to back it up with results." AMC marketing vice president Bill McNealy echoed the promise, saying, ". . . there's going to be a hand-to-hand struggle between the behemoths of Detroit . . . and AMC is going to be a top dog with a proven winner."

Mark knew that Roger's optimism would be hard to live up to. His comment to the press was cautious: "If we do our homework right, Javelin has a good chance, perhaps the best chance, of being a winner." Prior to the announcement he had tested one of the existing Javelin team cars after the last race at Riverside and was not impressed. In *The Unfair Advantage* Mark had few good things to say about the equipment inherited from Ronnie Kaplan's operation, but Kaplan and his team were not the disaster he suggests. In 1968 the team had performed superbly and had finished third in the championship, nearly beating Ford out of second, but 1969 had not been a good year. As success eluded the team, AMC became disenchanted, and it became common knowledge that the company was looking elsewhere. Painting the predecessor team with a dark brush in order to justify the difficulties his own team experienced in making the Javelin a winner was not one of Mark's more admirable traits.

Roger made his first move toward making the Javelin a winner by offering the position of chief engineer of Penske Racing to GM's Don Cox. Cox left Chevrolet in November and moved to Philadelphia. It was a difficult step for him to leave the big corporation. "Roger offered me a great opportunity," says Cox. "When I first arrived, though, I remember—I had been used to ten thousand other cars in the parking lot—at Newtown Square there might be seven cars. I wondered what I had done, but it was the greatest decision I ever made." Cox was helping to remake racing. "There weren't many real engineers in racing at the time—you had a few people—but most race teams were 'engineered' by racers through instinct and savvy."

To the outside world Penske's move from Chevrolet to AMC seemed inexplicable. Roger was, after all, a major Chevrolet dealer, and on the racing side had just won the Trans-Am for the second consecutive year. The answer lay in the fundamental relationship between Penske and General Motors Research and Development. Unlike Ford's Mustang program, racing the Camaro was not funded by Chevrolet. Most of the budget was derived through sponsorship from Sun Oil, as well as from Goodyear, Sears, and Champion spark plugs.

Don Cox stresses this point: "It should be remembered that Roger Penske never got a nickel from GM in terms of cash input. He got some help on parts and had a great deal of access to engineering input—witness my involvement in 1969. But he was up against teams that had all that, plus they were being totally funded." The time had come for Roger to take a pragmatic view. AMC offered substantial direct funding that would put the Penske Trans-Am team on a better business model. There was also the challenge. The Javelin had never won a race, yet Roger and Mark believed they could bring AMC a championship.

It was shaping up to be a classic year for Trans-Am in 1970. The week before the Penske/AMC story broke, Dan Gurney announced that he had signed an agreement with Plymouth to develop, build, and race Barracudas with his company, All American Racers, running the team. His protégé Swede Savage would be the second team driver. Chrysler Corporation was also supporting a team through its Dodge division. The deal to race the Dodge Challenger went to Sam Posey and Caldwell, who had been close to making the deal for the AMC program before Penske entered the picture. GM turned to Jim Hall to continue their representation in the series.

CHAPTER 97:

"Most underrated driver in the country"

Such was Dan Gurney's stature that a race was named for him while he was still an active driver. At Kent, Washington, on October 19, USAC presented the Dan Gurney 200. Mark and Karl were there with the Lola T150-Chevy in almost the same form as it had appeared the month before at Brainerd. It was a disappointing result after the long haul to the Northwest. Mark qualified ninth—four seconds off Gurney's pole time. The race was run in two 45-lap heats, and Mark only made nine laps of the first heat before being involved in a crash with Bobby Unser and George Follmer. The Sunoco-Simoniz Lola was the only car damaged badly enough not to continue, and it could not be made ready to run the second heat. The race winner was Mario Andretti, with Al Unser second and Dan Gurney third. Sam Posey drove a brilliant race to finish fourth in Andy Granatelli's STP Lotus 56–based four-wheel-drive car, powered by a stock-block Plymouth.

Bucknell University in Lewisburg, Pennsylvania, had a noted engineering college, and Mark was there in November to address the university's chapter of the Society of Automotive Engineers (SAE). Bucknell student Chris Ellison attended the lecture, where she met Mark and interviewed him for *The Bucknellian*. Growing up in Norwich, New York, the U.S. base for the McLaren racing team, Chris had made friends with the McLaren team members and later married Greg Syfert, a prominent mechanic with Penske Racing.

The final race on the USAC circuit was the Rex Mays 300 at Riverside on December 7. Mark tested the Lola on the track in mid-November and ran two seconds faster than Gurney's lap record. Dan had been even quicker when he tested. Although Mark remained something of an interloper with his occasional USAC appearances, his speed was no longer a surprise, and along with Dan Gurney and Mario Andretti, he was named one of the pre-race favorites to win. Still, Penske Racing remained an enigma to some. John Lamm in *Motor Trend* described the team as "resplendent in chrome wheels and plaid pants."

Before the race Mark told San Bernardino *Sun-Telegram* racing editor Ryan Rees, "We'd really like to win this race. The investment we have in this car is monumental compared to the financial rewards of winning. But I've never won a Championship Trail race before and I want to very badly."

The Riverside track was in turmoil. Larry LoPatin was attempting to oust the hugely respected Les Richter as its race director. Richter had resigned his position in LoPatin's American Raceways, Inc., and the rift between the two men was said to have undermined the event's promotion, with attendance down from traditional levels. A larger threat for the circuit was the new and soon-to-open Ontario Motor Speedway. The Riverside event made some positive news as the first USAC race to admit female news correspondents in the pits for a Championship Trail race.

Mark qualified on the front row with Dan's Olsonite Eagle on pole. At the start Mario Andretti passed Mark. Dan, Mario, and Mark were soon locked in a duel that pulled them clear of the rest of the field. On the 13th lap Mario pitted with a loose wheel. Mark now hounded Dan closely and passed him for the lead. Mark relinquished his lead on lap 48 when he pitted for fuel, but was back in front when it was Dan's turn to stop on lap 61. Mark seemed to have the race well in hand until lap 67, when he rolled into his pit to retire with a cracked cylinder head. Mark was terribly disappointed, and as he climbed from the Lola, immediately instructed the crew to load the car on the transporter. The Penske team was gone from the track before the race was over.

It was a race Mark might have won. His performance was impressive, prompting Dan Gurney to suggest "[Donohue] may be the most underrated driver in the country." Mario battled back the entire race. His perseverance was rewarded when Dan's Eagle broke a halfshaft with just four laps to go, depriving him of a third consecutive win in the event. For Mario it was his ninth win on the Champ Car Trail in his championship year.

There was still one more race in 1969 for Mark. The demands of the season had made it impossible for the Penske team to run a car in the SCCA's Formula A Continental series. An opportunity was now presented by Lola importer Carl Haas, who offered the loan of the latest Lola chassis, the T190. Haas entered the car in the series finale at Sebring on December 28, and Eric Broadley came from England to see how his newest creation fared. Penske Racing provided race preparation, including fitting a Traco Chevy engine.

Formula A—later known as Formula 5000—was another example of the exciting things that came out of the SCCA in the 1960s. The club's first professional series dedicated to single-seat race cars had debuted in 1967. The original categories—A for up to 3.0-liter engines, B for up to 1600cc, and C for up to 1100cc—closely paralleled the European classes that were the source of most chassis and engines. The five-race series in 1967 was won by Gus Hutchinson in his Formula B Lotus 41C. For 1968, the club responded to a groundswell of interest in racing homegrown powerplants by expanding Formula A to include production-based engines up to 5.0 liters (305ci). Three-liter, Formula One–type, pure racing engines were also still eligible. The response was tremendous, and a great racing series was born.

The Continental Championship for Formula A featured a cadre of professional teams and was producing exciting races. Most of the players were well known to Mark and Roger. George Wintersteen had been runner-up to series champion Lou Sell in 1968, and finished fourth in points in 1969. Malcolm Starr, now retired from driving, was running a very successful team in partnership with Carl Hogan, with John Cannon as driver. Starr's team used an Eagle chassis all season, though for Sebring had a McLaren Mk 10. Tony Adamowicz, Sam Posey, and David Hobbs had waged a season-long battle at the top of the points battle, and going into the 13th and final round of the series at Sebring on December 28, Adamowicz and Posey each retained a chance at the championship. Adamowicz had an Eagle and Englishman Hobbs was driving a factory-supported Surtees. Posey had replaced his Eagle midway through the season with the latest McLaren Mk 10, the Eagle having been destroyed in a towing crash on Route 66 outside of Flagstaff, Arizona.

The race at Sebring had an international listing and an increased purse thanks to sponsorship from L&M cigarettes—the first foray into racing sponsorship by the Liggett & Myers Company. The Traco engine and the Lola chassis—painted Penske Sunoco blue—arrived late at Newtown Square. By the time Mark and the Lola, attended by Roy Gane and Bill Mayberry, arrived at the track in central Florida, they had missed the first day of practice. Roy, and Mayberry on loan from George Wintersteen's team, were not getting along well. The two men had known each other for a long time, but they were both renowned for their independence and stubbornness.

Most top cars in Formula A in 1969 were running the 305ci Chevy. There were exceptions, and Swede Savage put a Plymouth-powered Eagle on pole position. Despite typical new-car sorting trouble, Mark qualified third in the 28-car field with a 1:05.0 behind Savage's 1:04.2 and Mario Andretti's 1:04.6. The international listing and large purse had attracted Andretti—in his first Formula A race—in a Ford-powered Lotus 70 prepared by John Dunn in the Shelby race shop. Sweden's Joakim Bonnier drove a Lola T190 like Mark's.

The race was run in two 100-mile heats. Mark was fast in both. He immediately grabbed second place behind Andretti after the first start. Mark's strong run was over after only six laps when the fuel filter clogged. Andretti dropped out of the lead on lap 12 when a gasket failed. David Hobbs—supported for this race by a second Team Surtees car for ex-Team Lotus Formula One driver Trevor Taylor—won the heat, with Taylor second and American Gus Hutchinson third in an ex-works Formula One Brabham BT26-Cosworth. The championship was settled in the first heat. Adamowicz blew his engine, but Posey's chance to become champion was lost when a car in front of him crashed through the pylons. One of the pylons lodged in the suspension of Posey's McLaren, causing damage that put him out of the race. Despite his own DNF, the Continental champion for 1969 was Tony Adamowicz.

Mark started the second heat from the back of the grid and created most of the race's excitement as he charged through the field. Hobbs and Taylor in the Surtees TS5s were out front, but Mark caught them and drove away to a 38-second lead before the fuel-filter problem repeated itself. He was out after 31 of the scheduled 45 laps. Taylor fell out and Bonnier caught and overtook Hobbs, but Hobbs responded by making a pass in the last corner to win by two-tenths of a second. The aggregate results had Hobbs the winner, with Hutchinson second and Bonnier third.

It was an exciting race but not a success for Sebring promoter Alec Ulmann. It was the first race he had organized at the track outside March's traditional 12-hour endurance event, with the exception of the 1959 United States Grand Prix. As had been the case 10 years before, the crowd was sparse.

For Mark, being fast was never enough—he never accepted anything short of victory as a success. It was a disappointing end of the season, with the car not finishing either heat. Mark believed that acrimony between Bill Mayberry and Roy Gane had resulted in a car that was not up to Penske Racing standards. Roy Gane left Penske Racing not long afterward, despite his long history with Roger. It was a difficult parting for Mark, who recognized Gane's great contributions and valued Roy as a friend. From Gane's perspective it was time to move on. Penske Racing had evolved over the previous year into a more structured and hierarchical organization than Gane had experienced in the early years. His departure was symbolic of the new era.

CHAPTER 98:

Zilly's Javelin

At American Motors, the racing team fell under the Performance Activities Department, which was in turn under the umbrella of the Marketing Department. In contrast, Ford, Chevrolet, and Chrysler all supported their Trans-Am programs, at whatever level, out of their engineering divisions. Bill McNealy, AMC's director of marketing, had convinced management that racing had to come under Marketing if they were going to change the image of the company from the staid old days of the Rambler. Walter Czarnecki had joined the department in 1968 as assistant manager, and by 1969 had been promoted to manager. As Roger Penske's interest in running the Camaro waned, he and Bill McNealy began to have serious private discussions about the 1970 season. McNealy and Czarnecki knew they needed to continue in the Trans-Am and that they needed to win. "The Trans-Am had star power," says Czarnecki. "It was, in the 1960s, what NASCAR is today in terms of manufacturer involvement, top drivers and fan interest.

"One of the first things I did after the contract signing was to invite Mark to Detroit. We flew together to the AMC plant in Kenosha, Wisconsin, where the Javelins were built," recalls Czarnecki. "Mark wanted to understand this new animal. We had the full cooperation of the management of the plant—we went onto the assembly line—and Mark selected some 'bodies in white.' "

He points out that AMC was not culturally prepared for much of what Mark needed to approach the project. *We can't do that* was often the response from department heads. But Mark's determination and Walt's inside persuasion and finesse usually got it done. "I learned something that day," Walt recalls of that first trip with Mark. "This is where Mark wanted to start—he wanted to engineer the rest of the car. I remember coming back on the plane that day and thinking, 'I'm glad we're on the same team.' He made that kind of an impression on me with his approach."

Walt Czarnecki had grown up in Detroit with an early interest in racing. A friend of his father's had a midget that he ran at Motor City Speedway, and at age 10 Walt saw his first Indy 500. Mark and Walt hit it off as friends right away. "Mark was a great practical joker and loved nothing better than to pull a trick. He could be almost childish in many ways, but he so enjoyed it when he'd pulled one on you," recalls Czarnecki. "On my first visit to the race shop, Mark said, 'Follow me.' We had to go from Roger's dealership out to Winding Way in Newtown Square—it was dark, no streetlights. Mark took off and it was a wild drive with me trying to keep up. He would pull this on many people. Mark would be laughing and really enjoying himself."

When Don Cox came to Newtown Square he knew what the expectations were. "One hundred percent, my job was to make the Javelin a competitive car," he says. Don's first step was to look for his counterpart at American Motors. Walt Czarnecki gave him a name to call in Engineering, and Don phoned to introduce himself and make an initial technical inquiry. It was a frustrating conversation, after which Don understood there would be no help forthcoming from the engineering department. "It wasn't a wasted call," Don remembers. "If you know you don't have any help, you're way better off than if you think you have help, because then you know what you've got to do."

Traco had built the Javelin engines in their debut season of 1968, but in 1969 Ronnie Kaplan had built his motors in-house. Roger now secured an agreement with Jim Travers and Frank Coon to be their exclusive customer in Trans-Am, and for Traco to immediately begin developing the Javelin engine.

Though not a round in the Trans-Am, the Daytona 24 Hours was an opportunity to evaluate where they stood. Peter Revson had been selected as the team's second driver—Roger promised him a car equal to Mark's—and co-drove the number 0, red, white, and blue Sunoco Javelin. Before the

24-hour race, both Mark and Peter had tested the new car on January 17 on the Daytona circuit. Mark wasn't giving much away when asked about the test day by Nick Nagurny for the Philadelphia *Sunday Bulletin*. "Testing is just that," Mark replied. "We try to eliminate problems before a race."

"Mark was a problem solver," says Ron Fournier. "And that was the spirit of the team. It started at the top with Roger and Mark. There wasn't any time lost pointing fingers when something went wrong. The thing was to overcome adversity and to a find a solution that wouldn't allow it to happen again."

The "Daytona Javelin," as it was known within the team, was the only Penske Trans-Am car since 1967 that had not been acid-dipped for lightness. It did start its life as a body in white and was built as a race car by Ron Fournier at Newtown Square. The Javelin was something new to the team, and they wanted to assess the car at Daytona and Sebring without going to extreme measures. The next two cars built were acid-dipped.

At technical inspection for the January 31–February 1, 1970, 24-hour race, the SCCA refused to allow the Javelin to run on the grounds that sufficient quantities of the eligible car—a limited-edition Mark Donohue signature version— had not been produced. Daytona owner and promoter Bill France wanted the car in the race, and pointed out that the Javelin complied with NASCAR's Grand American Challenge Cars, which were also eligible to participate. NASCAR technical inspectors approved the car and the Javelin was in the race.

The Javelin qualified fastest of the Trans-Am cars entered, although none of the other factory-supported teams had appeared. Mark opened an impressive class lead in the race until, unable to read his pit signals, he ran out of gas on the backstretch and had to walk back to the pits for a can of Sunoco. Mark and Peter overcame the delay to build an impressive lead in the Touring car class before the engine lost oil pressure. After seven hours and 205 laps the Javelin was retired. Roger noted to Joe Dowdall of the *Detroit News* that the 24-hour race was "the equivalent of four Trans-Am races and that's what were preparing for. We're pleased with the way things went." The race was won by the impressive Porsche 917 prototype driven by Pedro Rodríguez and Leo Kinnunen.

Further tests on the Javelin were conducted at Sebring on February 28 and March 1 in anticipation of the 12-hour race there on March 21. Both Mark and Peter turned laps in the 2:59s, three seconds faster than the existing Trans-Am record.

But on March 11 Roger Penske announced that they would not be in the race. The SCCA had disallowed the Javelin for failing to meet its homologation rules, which required that at least 2,500 production models be built by the end of the month. AMC had not yet produced sufficient quantities of the Mark Donohue Javelin.

The Mark Donohue "signature" Javelin came from the need to homologate a car with some of the engineering changes that Mark and Don Cox were developing. "Weaving in and amongst the regulations is always a challenge," says Cox. "We had fabricated front uprights. We did a spoiler and a splitter which showed up on the Mark Donohue signature cars." Though Mark had initially feared that Cox would prove difficult to communicate with and too oriented toward advanced technologies to develop a car as basic as the Javelin, he soon came to appreciate Don's problem-solving skills.

Mark had gone to AMC in Detroit and pleaded for a spoiler. "I just wasn't going to take no for an answer," he later said, adding, "If they had said no, we would have been in serious trouble." Ron Fournier recalls that creating the prototype for the spoiler was an example of what he and Mark called "arm wave" design, involving only the most basic specifications. Mark showed Ron what he had in mind, described the angle and height, and then asked Ron to fabricate it. "When I was done Mark had me make a few more tweaks to it and we put it in a box and sent it to AMC," recalls Ron. "What they produced for the signature car was identical to what we sent them with a small change to the trunk key area."

The signature car was Bill McNealy's way to make marketing sense of the need for a special production run embodying the aerodynamics and other performance items that racing demanded. In addition to the rear spoiler and Mark's signature just above the right rear taillight, the "Mark Donohue Special Javelin SST" as available in AMC dealerships was equipped with either a 360ci or 390ci V8 engine, four-barrel carburetor, "Ram-Air" hood scoop, heavy-duty suspension, power front disc brakes, dual exhausts, and six-inch rims fitted with E70x14 wide-profile Goodyear Polyglass tires. For 1970 SCCA rules did not require the 305ci engine to be homologated in production, as long as a crank for the 305 could be purchased over the counter.

When asked by the Philadelphia *Evening Bulletin*'s Nick Nagurny how he felt about having his signature on a production car, Mark confessed to being "quite thrilled," and "slightly embarrassed."

"Why would anyone want to drive a car with my signature on the back?" Mark asked Nagurny. "American Motors thought it would be a great idea to have the name there, but I don't know. Anyway, it's there. I just don't want to sound like I'm blowing my own horn."

When the first Javelins bearing his signature became available in February, Mark bought one and gave it to his mother. Zilly was thrilled, and she and Mark Sr. drove the car with great pride. It was also exciting for some acquaintances who did not understand that Zilly's car was part of a production series. When they saw another Javelin with Mark's signature on the back, they would phone the Donohues to report spotting a stranger driving their car.

Mark always spoke of his parents with tremendous warmth. Zilly, possessed of great charm and an outgoing and exuberant style, was a constant and vocal booster for her son. Mark said of his parents, "The only problem with my mother is she will tell you I'm the greatest, and of course that's not true. My father is a serious man, calm and analytical—not a great race fan like my mother, but he enjoys seeing me compete. They are at many of my East Coast races."

Mark also recognized his parents' influence on the diverse careers pursued by him and his siblings. Nancy was an actress with a sideline as a greeting card designer, and Mary Ellen ran a riding school and stable. In a cover story for *Family Weekly*, Mark told Larry Bortstein, "We had the kind of parents that let us do what we liked for the most part. There were no objections to my racing, but this is not the kind of profession you go into lightly. I think my parents wanted to make sure I knew exactly what I was getting into. I haven't been sorry and I'm sure they're not sorry either."

Mark Sr. was in Salt Lake City, Utah, when he suffered a heart attack in the courtroom in the middle of a trial. "My father was alone and he wouldn't let anyone come out," said Mark. "My mother was frantic, and I stayed closely in touch with his doctors. They wouldn't release him because they feared the stress of commercial air travel. Knowing he was always most comfortable and relaxed in his own home, I came up with the idea of chartering Roger's Learjet. Once I persuaded the physicians of the medical capabilities and the ability to make him comfortable on a private flight, I was able to get him home three weeks earlier than he would have been otherwise. It meant a lot to me to be able to do that for him after all he has done for me."

Mark made all the arrangements—including paying for the flight—and was happy in his belief that it speeded his father's recovery. Mr. Donohue quit smoking, lost weight, and resumed as active a life as he'd enjoyed before the incident.

Mark was extremely conscious of the importance of fitness and a healthy lifestyle. He had despaired that his father worked too hard, and in common with his close friend Burge Hulett, manifested all of the worst behaviors: overeating, particularly high-cholesterol foods; smoking and drinking to excess; and failing to exercise. Mark had become very knowledgeable about an appropriate diet and was in better physical condition than he had ever been. He maintained his commitment to health and fitness for the remainder of his life.

CHAPTER 99:
Designing a Race Track

While the new race track at Ontario Motor Speedway was about to open in southern California, Mark was deeply involved in plans for a modern road-racing circuit on the East Coast. Chesapeake International Raceway (CIR) near Elkton, Maryland, was planned as a 3.0-mile circuit. Mark worked hard on detailed plans to create a challenging circuit with amenities for both participants and spectators. Through his influence the SCCA promised the track a full calendar of events in 1971, including a Trans-Am and a Can-Am. The arrangement also gave CIR exclusive rights to SCCA races within 125 miles of Elkton. Bill Smyth, president of USAC and a close friend of Mark's, was said to be considering a race on the track. At the same time, Larry LoPatin's American Raceways, Inc. had purchased land to build Eastern International Raceway, a multipurpose race facility, at Cherry Hill, New Jersey. The exclusive arrangement between the SCCA and CIR was seen as an effort to preempt the LoPatin project, at least for top-level road races.

Mark, who was named to the CIR board and also carried the title of safety consultant, was designing the course, and was certainly attracting most of the publicity for the venture. His earnest approach was reflected in a statement to the press: "I've raced on virtually every road course in North America and on several European circuits. I can honestly say there are problems with every one of them."

The location, just two miles off Interstate 95, an hour's drive from Philadelphia, Baltimore, or Washington D.C., was ideal for drawing spectators. Mark spent a great deal of time designing the circuit and was said to be using a computer. Computers in 1970 remained a mystery to most people, and using one was considered to be working on the cutting edge of technology and beyond. One reporter rhetorically asked if the machine's name was "Hal," referring to the computer in the popular movie *2001: A Space Odyssey*, the most familiar frame of reference on the subject. The reality, as Mark told Karl Ludvigsen for *Sports Car Graphic*, was that he was using Roger Penske's telephone tie-in to a central GE computer. He added that Don Cox was using the same technology to design springs and sway bars for the Javelin program.

The circuit Mark designed incorporated his most idealistic views of what a road-race track should be. It was to be 40 feet wide all the way around, and its 3,000-foot straightaway would be 60 feet wide. Mark decried decreasing radius turns, telling Karl Ludvigsen for *Sports Car Graphic*, "Some drivers like the decreasing-radius situation because they think it is very challenging. And it is, but it's accident-prone too. If you can start with a clean sheet of paper it's not worth the risk. If you make a mistake early on, it doesn't show up until it's too late, and then you're off in a spectacular way." Mark seemed to be having a great time creating his version of the perfect road-racing circuit.

Groundbreaking scheduled for January 1970 was delayed, and in May the corporation registered a public offering of common stock with the Securities and Exchange Commission.

Mark was also working with his racing friend Bob Bailey to develop a line of driving suits and accessories. They formed a company, Mark Donohue Performance Products in Ballston Lake, New York, to market the products. That spring the new company announced 12 distributors in the U.S. and Canada. The signature driving suit, the Mark Donohue Durette, was the first single-layer race suit approved by the SCCA for use without Nomex underwear. A 44-page catalog offered everything from driving shoes to steering wheels and racing gloves.

CHAPTER 100:

"Not a business for little boys in short pants"

Mark made headlines by putting the Sunoco Lola-Chevy on pole position for the USAC race at Sears Point, California, on April 3. He did it in style, qualifying the Lola more than a second faster than Mario Andretti in the STP Hawk-Ford. Dan Gurney and Al Unser occupied the second row, and John Cannon was fifth fastest. Mark and John were the only drivers among the 32 qualifiers with previous experience at the two-year-old road-race track. Mark had clinched the 1969 Trans-Am by winning at the Sonoma circuit the previous September. Much was made of Mark's advantage—although the converse was seldom mentioned when he appeared at an oval for the first time.

There was also grumbling in some quarters because Mark had tested on Thursday. Although it was standard Penske Racing protocol to test whenever possible before a race, the United Press International wire service reported that several unnamed drivers "were surprised and angered when they heard of Donohue's early warm-up. They said they were unaware the course was available for such an early practice." The incident shows how even in the highly professional world of USAC, the regulars still had much to learn from Penske Racing. It was another case in which Roger's familiar quote certainly applied: "This isn't a business for little boys in short pants."

The race was a less-glorious experience, as Mark failed to complete the first race lap. The best he could manage was a dramatic pace lap that turned into two. Mario's car wasn't ready when the field departed behind the pace car, and he hadn't caught up when the first pace lap was completed. The cars went around a second time as Mario slotted into the front row. Mark, already aware he had a problem, moved over and ceded the inside pole to Mario. When the start was given the Lola faltered, and Mark immediately raised his hand to warn other cars. He rapidly dropped back through the field, driving into the pits at the end of the lap. The team reported that "some foreign matter" had entered the engine at the end of qualifying. It appeared to have been cleared up, but in morning warm-up the problem persisted. It was Dan Gurney in the Olsonite Eagle-Ford who used his brilliant road-racing technique to pass first Unser and then Andretti, holding

Mario off throughout to win the Golden Gate 150.

Mark's qualifying time of 1:36.34 on Friday not only brought him pole position but also broke the existing Sears Point lap record of 1:36.9. That mark had been set by Sam Posey in taking the pole for the SCCA Continental in his Formula A Eagle the previous year. The 5.0-liter Chevy-powered Continental cars were clearly as quick or quicker than most USAC cars around a road course. This troubled USAC, as the long-standing feud between the two sanctioning bodies continued. There was resentment of the road-racing set by the traditional oval racers and teams, and this feeling would be displayed more openly during the month of May at Indianapolis. The 500 was exactly what Mark and Karl Kainhofer were focusing on now, with the Speedway opening in less than a month. In the meantime, the first round of the Trans-Am would occupy Mark's attention and that of the Javelin crew.

CHAPTER 101:

Timanus Cracks Down

The 1970 Trans-Am is remembered as the year that all the manufacturers were committed on a big scale with factory-supported teams. The support came in different ways and at varying levels. Chevrolet had Camaros run by Jim Hall's Chaparral team, including a 1969 car purchased from Penske. Chrysler was supporting teams from two divisions: Dodge had Sam Posey and Ray Caldwell's Autodynamics team developing and running Challengers, while Dan Gurney's All American Racers ran Barracudas for Plymouth. Despite losing the Shelby team, Ford had never been better prepared to start the season than with Bud Moore's operation. Finally, American Motors had taken a big step forward by backing Penske Racing for their Javelin.

Sam Posey later observed, "It was really the peak year for Trans-Am. It was the peak year for Roger too. The Javelin team had been around a couple of years and had never been able to get the job done—and Penske took the engine that was never very good and made it good, and they brought all their pit stop tricks and Mark drove the hell out of it. It's not that Ford weakened; they just made that car competitive. It was [Penske Racing's] crowning achievement I think."

The season opened on April 19 at Laguna Seca to many changes. For the first time in the five-year history of the series, the under-2.0-liter cars and the big 5.0-liter pony cars no longer raced together. The smaller-displacement cars had their own race. The SCCA had changed some rules. To gain homologation, 2,500 cars of a given model had to be produced. Minimum weights were increased to 3,200 pounds dry, or 3,400 with fuel. Other new rules banned dual carburetors and replaced the tall, gravity-fed fueling tanks with NASCAR-style dump cans. Burdette "Burdie" Martin was about to replace Dave Tallaksen as series chief steward; he would commence his duties at Lime Rock while Merle Stanfield filled in at Laguna Seca and in Texas. Martin's people skills and race savvy contributed to improved harmony in the pits and paddock. John Timanus was now well established as technical administrator, and in 1970 the SCCA did a better job of keeping peace and evenly enforcing rules than it had in 1969.

After the team's exclusion from Sebring for having insufficient cars built, Javelin was now the only competing car at Laguna Seca to meet the minimum production run and receive the SCCA "OK stamp." But less than a week before the California race the organization reversed its position and extended the period for verification until Lime Rock in May. Without the extension, the Barracuda, Challenger, Mustang, Firebird, and Camaro would have all been excluded. The principal problem was insufficient manpower at the SCCA and within the Automobile Competition Committee for the United States (ACCUS) for verifying production quantities through visits to marshalling yards and dealers.

Timanus ran a tough tech at Laguna Seca. Large rear-deck spoilers on the Jim Hall–prepared Camaros and the Titus Firebirds were disallowed for not having been produced in sufficient quantity. The Firebird also had to remove its hood air scoop. The Mustangs were made to remove the front brake air ducting that ran from where the headlights had been to be reducted through the front spoilers. And Bud Moore was particularly unhappy not to be allowed to run the dual carburetor setup they had developed.

In the most colorful Trans-Am paddock yet, the Javelins were red, white, and blue; the Challengers, lime green with black numbers and a black roof; the Camaros were white with a wide black stripe down the middle; the Mustangs, school-bus yellow with black hockey-stick stripes; and the Barracudas, dark blue with red, yellow, and orange stripes.

At Laguna Seca the Javelin was still a work in progress. Parnelli Jones dominated, with updated bodywork on the same well-developed and engineered Mustang that he had used at the end of the previous season. Nominally a Boss 302 model for homologation purposes, the car was one of the special Mustangs built by Ford's Kar Kraft racing shop in 1969. According to Ted West in *Vintage Motorsport*, "It was acid-dipped to a fare-thee-well and also received ultra-lightweight sheet metal." West reports that the car had a fully revised front and rear suspension, its nose was channeled and dropped an inch, and it incorporated a roll cage that was far more a chassis stiffener than any real driver protection. The 1969/70 "Boss 302" engineered by Lee Dykstra, built at Kar Kraft, race-prepared by Bud Moore, and driven by Parnelli Jones may have carried the art of Trans-Am rule bending to its ultimate manifestation. It all resulted in a great race car.

At this point in their development, the Penske Javelins were substantially underpowered compared to their competitors. Mark did well to qualify second with a 1:12.36 to Parnelli's 1:11.90. Dan Gurney in the Barracuda and George Follmer in the second Bud Moore Mustang were the third- and fourth-fastest qualifiers. Javelin teammate Peter Revson suffered a blown engine before he could turn a fast qualifying time and was down in 18th position at the start. Parnelli built an immediate lead in the race and Mark was able to pass him only when the Mustang pitted. Three laps later, Mark made his fueling stop and also took on a rear tire. When he rejoined the race he was third behind Parnelli and Swede Savage's Barracuda. Meanwhile, Revson had charged through the field in his Javelin and reached seventh place before a severed brake line created an undriveable car. After a couple of off-course excursions he retired.

At this early stage of the season Mark and Peter were already both unhappy with the driving arrangement. Peter was convinced that his car was not as good as Mark's, which Mark adamantly denied. Mark was also annoyed at what he considered Peter's total lack of sensitivity to the machinery. He believed engines had been unnecessarily destroyed because Peter would keep driving an obviously broken machine. "The trouble with Peter on the team was that he had his own personal problems with guys like Posey and Follmer and he would take that out on the track," Mark later said. "That, along with his lack of feel for the mechanical side, really made me mad."

Mark was second again when Savage made his pit stop, and, with the Javelin unable to match the power of the Mustang, stayed there to the end, finishing 40 seconds behind Parnelli.

Follmer was third, a lap down, Savage fourth, Milt Minter in a Camaro from the American Racing Associates team fifth, and Sam Posey scored a point for his Dodge Challenger team by finishing sixth. John Thawley summed it up for *Hot Rod* magazine: "In short, Ford was ready. They had possibly 35 to 50 more horsepower than any other team, no handling problems, no braking problems and the right drivers."

Mark knew how far off the pace they were. "I was destroyed," he said. "Second place may have looked good on paper, but we were so far back that we may as well have been last."

The teams immediately headed south for round two at Dallas Raceway in Lewisville, Texas, the following week-end. It never happened. Massive rainstorms that dumped 8.25 inches of rain in the Dallas area left most of the track underwater. The team hung around the track all day Friday waiting for a bridge to be repaired before Mark and Peter finally got in a few laps late in the afternoon. On Saturday the track was again hit by torrents of rain and the qualifying sessions were canceled. Some of the Trans-Am cars practiced briefly, but the Javelins never got on the track. When the rains became even worse on Sunday, April 26, the entire event was canceled. Mark said that the cancellation cost Penske Racing about $15,000 in unrecoverable expenses. Dan Gurney estimated an even higher number for his team.

Opening Day for the Indy 500 was coming up in just six days on Saturday, May 2. Mark and the Trans-Am crew now embarked on a back-breaking schedule to test the Javelins at both Lime Rock and Bryar. When it was official that the Dallas race was canceled, the crew immediately loaded up the transporter and began the long drive northeast to Philadelphia. Mark flew back Sunday afternoon and put in a full day's work on Monday in the Newtown Square race shop. Early Tuesday morning he got in the team transporter that had arrived from Texas the night before and personally drove it to Lime Rock Park. Arriving at noon, Mark tested all Tuesday afternoon, spending as much time under the car making adjustments as he did on the track. It was a frustrating and exhausting day, but when it was over Mark loaded the transporter and drove to Laconia, New Hampshire, for more testing on Wednesday at Bryar. Just three days later it all began at Indy.

CHAPTER 102:

First Million-Dollar Purse

The 1970 Indianapolis 500 marked the 25th anniversary of the historic track's ownership by Anton "Tony" Hulman Jr. The 69-year-old Hulman had saved the 500 after World War II when he purchased it from Captain Eddie Rickenbacker. Rickenbacker—a driver in the inaugural 500 in 1911—had performed a similar renaissance for the Speedway when he took it over in 1927, at a time when the future of the facility and the race were threatened. After lying fallow during World War II, the Speedway was in bad shape before Hulman injected new energy and capital that preserved its great history while substantially enhancing the facility and organization. His modernization included paving the brick track surface with asphalt, adding new grandstands, building the Speedway Museum, the infield golf course, and an up-to-date adjacent motel. Indianapolis celebrated the anniversary by posting their first race purse to exceed one million dollars.

Penske Racing was relying on the familiar Lola T152 but was making a big change in the engine department by moving to Ford. Ford had broken Offenhauser's long-held domination in the victory circle when Jim Clark won the 1965 race. The Associated Press asked Roger if he felt there was a conflict because of his Chevrolet dealership. He replied, "This is business. I don't feel funny about it. . . . It's been reliable, and we've gotten lots of help from the factory people and from Foyt." A. J. Foyt had recently taken over the Ford engine preparation program.

The Vel's Parnelli Jones Racing team had a Lola of a different sort. George Bignotti, master mechanic and crew chief on the "Johnny Lightning Special," called the car a Colt LTD, with LTD standing for Lola Type Design. It was a 1969 Lola chassis with Bignotti-created suspension. It worked wonderfully well, and Al Unser was one of the hottest drivers in USAC.

On May 7 all attention was on Mark as he turned the fastest time of the month at 168.9 mph. It was a fast day, with Al Unser, Foyt, and Dan Gurney all exceeding 168. Dan—long a proponent of the stock-block engine alternative—was now running an Offenhauser, while the others joined the Sunoco Lola in using Fords.

The next day, Mark, Roger, and Peter Revson were among a number of top teams and drivers abandoning the Speedway

for the Saturday race at Lime Rock on May 9. Mark broke the Trans-Am lap record with a 58.8-second lap to capture pole position. It made the huge effort devoted to testing the week before seem worthwhile. Roger was delighted with all Mark was accomplishing. "With our team we could have about any driver we wanted here or at Indianapolis," Roger told Nick Nagurny. "I wouldn't want anyone else. Mark is the best."

The Sunoco Javelin shared the front row with Dan Gurney in the Barracuda. Parnelli was on row two next to Ed Leslie, driving with Jim Hall in the Chaparral Camaro program. A review of the grid reveals the competitiveness between the manufacturer-backed teams: Swede Savage in the Barracuda and Peter Revson in the Javelin were on row three; George Follmer (Mustang) and Jerry Titus (Pontiac) on row four; and Jim Hall (Camaro) and Sam Posey (Challenger) on row five. Sam was having a tough weekend on his home track after the Challenger had fallen off the trailer on the way back from Texas. Although Mark and Parnelli raced hard for the lead for the first 30 laps, it was not a good day for Penske Racing. Mark's Sunoco Javelin lost oil pressure, and he parked the car alongside the No Name straightway. On lap 76, Revson's Javelin blew in spectacular fashion—Peter spun in his own oil, which then liberally coated the entrance to the pit lane. There was great attrition throughout, and despite a broken pushrod in the Mustang, Parnelli won by a lap ahead of Ed Leslie in the Camaro. Sam Posey salvaged his weekend with a third-place finish.

Back at the Speedway on Sunday, Mark had the Lola up to 168.8, although Al Unser became the first driver officially over 170 mph. John Cannon, in his rookie year at Indy, sprained his wrist when he hit the wall. The crash extensively damaged his Rolla Vollstedt–entered, turbo-Ford-powered, and Bryant Heating & Cooling–sponsored Vollstedt.

On Tuesday, May 12, Bruce McLaren and his team suffered a setback as Denny Hulme was burned when the quick-open fuel cap opened at speed. Hulme managed to steer the car through the turn and slow sufficiently to bail out with the car still in motion. First- and second-degree burns on both feet and second- and third-degree burns to his hands sidelined him. Peter Revson was brought into the team the next day, and by Thursday had turned laps in both team cars—McLaren M15 Offys—at over 165.5. None of the drivers who had appeared on Opening Day in the three McLaren M15s were in the cars for qualifying. Team owner McLaren was concentrating on running the team, and Chris Amon declined to continue when he felt uncomfortable on the track.

"Our strategy is to take whatever respectable speed we can get and be in the field at the end of the opening day of time trials," Mark told United Press International. "Making the race on the first day of qualifications means a lot more than being quickest any of the other three days." He emphasized that the team's focus was on the race, saying, "Our car is capable of what it will take to finish fastest."

For the opening day of Indy qualifying on Saturday, May 16, Penske crew chief Karl Kainhofer had drawn the 12th spot in the qualifying line for the Sunoco Lola. Al Unser went out immediately ahead of Mark and put the Johnny Lightning car on pole, beating Foyt's earlier speed with a sensational four-lap average of 170.221. Mark followed with a 168.911—third fastest at the time—that wound up as the fifth-fastest speed and placed him squarely in the middle of the second row for the race. The front row was Al Unser, Johnny Rutherford, and A. J. On row two with Mark were Roger McCluskey in fourth and Art Pollard sixth. Seventeen cars qualified on pole day, and when Peter Revson had his chance in the McLaren on Sunday, he turned in a 167.942 average for the four laps. Peter earned a $1,200 prize as fastest driver on day two and was 18th on the grid. Carl Williams also joined the McLaren team and qualified during the second weekend.

Even the fiercest rivalries seldom altered the respect maintained between drivers at Indy. It was part of the code, but the concern for, and interest in, one another was genuine. Nick Nagurny for the Philadelphia *Sunday Bulletin* was talking to Mark after his qualifying run when Al Unser came up to congratulate Mark. "Have any troubles?" Al asked. "Of course," Mark replied. "You have to have some sort of excuse." Both drivers laughed. Al wanted to know what Mark thought about Johnny Rutherford nearly taking pole position. "He must have been holding his breath," said Mark.

"I never have been a good qualifier and my record shows that, but I don't worry about it too much," Mark told Robin Miller for the *Indianapolis Star*. Miller asked Mark what he thought about those who said he didn't drive close enough to the wall in the short chutes. "I don't know, I might not have but I couldn't say for sure," said a less than amused Mark. "I think I drive up there, but it's pretty easy for someone else to say I don't."

Rain showers on race day, May 30, delayed the start a half-hour. With the pageantry complete, the cars appeared ready to take the green flag as they exited turn four on the final pace lap. Suddenly a car was in the wall and spinning through the middle of the field. The lower right radius arm on Jim Malloy's car had pulled out of the chassis, and somehow the 24 cars behind him all missed hitting him. The start was not given and the cars were brought back to the pits where they were permitted to add two gallons of fuel. After a delay of another half-hour, Tony Hulman repeated his famous refrain, this time with a slight variation: "Gentlemen, restart your engines!"

Al Unser jumped into an immediate lead that he held for the first 120 miles. Mark kept the Sunoco Lola close enough to occasionally lead the race during pit-stop sequences. Lloyd Ruby was a big story, coming from 25th on the grid to second place in 10 laps. He took the lead briefly after 40 laps before developing an oil leak and being black-flagged. A. J. Foyt pursued Unser hard but destroyed his clutch when he had to drive into the grass to avoid a wall of fire from a six-car crash in front of him.

Mark drove a strong race although he never was in a position to seriously threaten Unser's lead. He finished second, 31.8 seconds behind, and summed the day up this way: "We were neither too good nor too bad."

Two great drivers made their final Indy 500 appearances. Jack Brabham, who had led the rear-engine revolution when he raced a Cooper-Climax in 1961, finished 13th. Dan Gurney, an even more active catalyst for change at the Speedway, who had come so close on several occasions to winning the race, finished third. Both men retired at the end of the year.

CHAPTER 103:

"Another fine mess Roger has gotten us into"

The day after the 500, Mark was racing on a track that could not differ more from the fast and wide-open Speedway. Bryar Motorsports Park, with its twists and turns, ups and downs, and not much of a straightaway in its 1.6 miles was the very antithesis of Indy. Initial qualifying for the race had been on the same day as the 500, and Roger had taken the precaution of having Bob Johnson and Rusty Jowett qualify the Sunoco Javelins. In final qualifying on race-day morning, Mark equaled Sam Posey's time in the Challenger. They occupied the second row behind Swede Savage, on the pole in the Barracuda, and Parnelli Jones.

Bryar was hard on even well-developed race cars, but on this day the oil stayed in the Javelin engine. Mark and Peter finished second and third—the exact order was disputed—behind George Follmer, who won in Bud Moore's Mustang. Penske lap charts had Mark in second place, while the official charts gave the spot to Peter. The discrepancy was thought to have occurred when J. Guy Roy's Camaro burst into flames during a pit stop. Roy and crew man Caron Ivon were injured and taken to the hospital. Only a prompt response by everyone in the area, led by the Chaparral and Autodynamics crews, saved the incident from having far worse consequences. Ace Penske lap charter Judy Stropus was confident she had it right and believed the SCCA scoring crew had missed a lap for Mark during the confusion of the fire. Team manager Chuck Cantwell declined to protest the results, although Judy told writer Ray Marquette, "Our Mark would like his second."

Meanwhile, Mark and Peter joined Roger on his Learjet as they rushed back to Indianapolis for the traditional victory dinner. Mark's share of the record million-dollar purse was $86,427.

Just two days later racing lost one of its great figures when Bruce McLaren died in a testing accident. McLaren was a consummate tester, and the overwhelming superiority of his team in the Can-Am was owed in significant measure to his insistence on being prepared and fully sorted when the season began. He was shaking down the new M8D at the Goodwood circuit in England on June 2 when he crashed. The accident was caused by the rear deck of the car coming loose. Along with being acknowledged driver-engineers of particular talent, Bruce and Mark shared many experiences—including accidents caused by loose bodywork. As Mark's teammate in the Ford Mark IV at Le Mans in 1967, Bruce had survived the frightening experience of losing the car's bodywork on the Mulsanne straight. The same thing had happened to Mark the year before at Le Mans, and would recur again later in Mark's career with severe consequences. McLaren's death left a great void in the sport. Though only 32, he had enjoyed a long tenure at the top level of road racing. Bruce was the paradigm for the successful driver-engineer and had created a company that was developing and applying race technology at a level matched by few others. His friend, Dr. Frank Falkner, in a tribute that appeared in *Road & Track*, asked, "Can there have been in the history of the sport a more universally loved figure?"

While the bulk and additional bodywork of Group 7 cars was thought to add a degree of safety compared to single-seat Formula cars, the reality was that this was only a marginal difference. Two weeks later, the Can-Am suffered its first event fatality when Dick Brown from Birmingham, Michigan, got on oil in a high-speed part of the Mosport circuit and crashed in his McLaren M6B.

McLaren's death was also felt in the Trans-Am. Dan Gurney left his Challenger team in the hands of Swede Savage and crew as he took a seat alongside Denny Hulme on the McLaren team for Formula One and Can-Am. Dan had been out of Formula One racing since the end of the 1968 season.

Just a week after Bryar, Mark showed again that the Javelin was fast by capturing pole position at Mid-Ohio for the June 7 Trans-Am. Moments later, Ed Leslie in the Chaparral-Camaro and then Parnelli Jones in the Mustang equaled Mark's 1:41.0. The competitiveness of the Trans-Am was never more evident, with the first three cars on the grid scoring identical times, and the next three within an additional half-second. The race, however, was all Mustang, with Parnelli winning ahead of teammate Follmer. Mark held on to finish third, but he was more than a minute behind the Ford parade. After his great run at Bryar, Revson's weekend was a disaster. After only one lap of qualifying his transmission failed and he was 24th on the grid. In Sunday warm-up his oil pressure was low and he pitted. Mark took the car out to diagnose the problem and blew the engine up when the oil pump failed completely. Roger called for a new engine. While the change was accomplished in a remarkable two and a half hours, allowing Peter to start the parade lap, the electrics failed before he and the Javelin made it to the green flag. Ford was beginning to pull away in points and Penske Racing had yet to score a win for AMC in the Javelin.

Penske Racing had not figured out how to keep the oil in the Javelin engine. It wasn't for want of trying. The mystery was why instruments would indicate sufficient oil pressure yet suddenly there would be a failure. "We had huge, huge problems with the engine—the distributor drive gears for the spark distribution would fail under heavy use—we couldn't keep the bottom end in the engine," says Don Cox. Don and Mark set up a test-bed at Newtown Square and ran a wide variety of different distributor gears and coatings to find something that would hold up. It took time to find the right product from which to create the gears. "The high cornering forces we were achieving in the car plus the extreme braking we were able to achieve manifested itself in the oil not staying at the pickup points," Mark later concluded.

Because the Javelin race program was being run from American Motors Marketing, there was little help coming from engineering. Walt Czarnecki partially solved the problem by retaining the services of Dave Potter, the former chief engine engineer at AMC. Potter consulted with Traco Engineering on development of the small-block engine. Czarnecki recalls, "We paid Potter out-of-budget to be the outside development person because we couldn't get anything done inside the company—in fact, at the time there was some pushback from engineering. Their attitude was 'We're not interested—if you guys are going to do it, spend the money out of your marketing budget.' Some of the people in engineering felt they should have had responsibility for racing, so we didn't get anything from them. We did everything on the outside—the engineering of the engine on that team was done by Dave Potter, Jim Travers, Frank Coon, and Don Cox."

"Mark and I were lying on our backs under the car in a pool of oil. In racing we call it an oil pan failure—the oil pan had failed to keep all the bits inside the engine that had blown up!" recalls Don Cox. "I looked at Mark, and looking back with a smile on his face he said 'This is another fine mess Roger has gotten us into.' I told him, 'Just remember Mark, these are going to be the good old days that we are going to be laughing about some day.' "

As Cox told the story he became visibly saddened, realizing that he and Mark never reached those good old days together.

CHAPTER 104:
Triumph and Tragedy

Sue Woodard was expecting her husband John home for lunch. She heard a very loud rumble coming down the road and looked out as Mark and John pulled in the driveway in an orange Camaro with black stripes. "He had brought Mark home for lunch without warning me. I had nothing in the house but some macaroni and cheese." Mark told Sue that it was his absolutely favorite food. "I knew he was lying through his teeth, but that was just the sweet guy Mark was." The friendship between the Donohues and the Woodards was strong. When Adrienne Woodard, Sue and

John's first child, was born on June 12, 1970, Sue and Mark were at the hospital with the Woodards.

Testing the Javelin on the skid pad at Marcus Hook could only reveal so much. "The oil problem was so subtle," said Mark. "It would show 45 pounds' pressure all the time and then, just for an instant it would go away. It was so brief I couldn't even see it." With the Camaro program a great deal of testing had been done at Black Lake on GM's testing ground. This year was different; the team did not have access to AMC's testing facility. Instead they tested at Bridgehampton before the upcoming June 21 race there. "The engine would starve for oil in certain types of corners," Jerry Kroninger remembers. "It was a little bit of a mystery, and we wanted to see if oil temperature or oil pressure was going away when the driver was busiest and hence unable to read the gauge."

In the meantime, a variety of baffle and oil flow systems and pickups had been devised. To determine which, if any, system would work, Jerry braced himself in the back of the race car against the roll cage and read the gauges over Mark's shoulders. Three consecutive laps were the most Jerry could stand before being made ill by the violent g-forces. That was enough to get the desired readings, and by the time a new oil pan was fitted, he was ready for his next ride. "Mark had to run flat out or it wouldn't have had any relevancy, and he bettered the Trans-Am lap record," says Jerry. "We figured out that my weight in the back had stabilized the rear end enough to overcome the weight disadvantage." Jerry had total confidence in Mark on the race track—although he continued to avoid being a passenger with Mark on the highway.

Swede Savage was quick in the Barracuda at Bridgehampton, qualifying on pole position and leading the early laps with Mark and Parnelli fighting for second. When it began to rain on the 10th lap, Mark's great talent came to the fore—as did the brilliant Penske pit work. Mark told *Newsday*'s George Clark, ". . . it was very slippery out there and if you didn't come close to losing it, then you just weren't trying." The leading cars pitted roughly together and all three crews made quick work of it. But Mark emerged in the lead and began to draw away. Parnelli ran wide chasing Mark and punctured two tires. Savage had dropped 36 seconds behind Mark when the differential failed in the Barracuda. George Follmer was now second but had the extreme misfortune of being called in on a mistakenly given black flag that was intended for his teammate Parnelli. Follmer charged back to second, finishing two laps behind Mark. Parnelli was third, ahead of Jim Hall.

It was an emotional win with the crew leaping in the air and embracing all around as Mark flashed under the checkered flag. Roger Penske later told Al Bochroch that the win at Bridgehampton was the single incident he remembered most vividly from the five years his team competed in Trans-Am racing. Roger had set himself and the team up for some serious razzing by predicting before the season began that they would win seven races with the Javelin. At AMC it was a time of jubilation and vindication for the money and effort expended.

In the victory circle Mark credited the crew for making the breakthrough win possible. The gearbox had broken in the pre-race warm-up, only an hour before the race start. "I never saw guys work so fast and so well," said Mark. "That's the kind of pit work that can make the difference." The win closed the point gap to Ford from 41 to 25. Mark and Roger both believed they could still make a run at the championship, with Mark saying, "We're on our way now. We're going to win a few more."

Mark and the team went early to Brainerd, Minnesota, to test in private on the Thursday prior to the July 5 race at Donnybrooke. This time it was Woody Woodard who braced himself in the back of the Javelin and rode 10 hot laps staring over Mark's shoulder at the oil pressure gauge. It ran steadily between 80 and 60 psi, and while Woody was on board Mark turned laps less than a second slower than his fastest of the day. Mark did 93 laps, 20 more than the race distance.

On race weekend, although he had not seen the track before Friday practice, Swede Savage captured pole alongside Parnelli. Sam Posey said Swede could learn a new track faster than anyone he had ever seen. In the first qualifying session Mark was third with a 1:45.9—six-tenths of a second slower than his best in testing and half a second slower than Swede and Parnelli—but blew up his engine. Sam Posey in the Challenger and Peter Revson in the Javelin were next with 1:46.3 and 1:46.4. For the second qualifying Mark took over Peter's car and turned a 1:45.9. He was fifth fastest, irrespective of which car he drove, and shared the third row with Posey. Ed Leslie in the Chaparral-run Camaro and George Follmer's Mustang were on row two.

In the warm-up session on race morning the new engine in Mark's Javelin blew up. Without time to fit a new engine, Roger moved Mark into Peter's car. Mark remembered, "Peter really got mad at me that day when I took over his car. He was upset and I don't blame him." Revson was frustrated. It was

the third consecutive race he would not start. At Mid-Ohio his engine had failed on the pace lap, and at Bridgehampton it blew up in warm-up.

It was not a year that would produce closeness in what was already a tenuous and difficult Donohue-Revson relationship. The team was struggling to make the Javelin a winner. It was hard to make even the lead car work, and not always possible to get the second car to the same level. As team timer and a confidant to both men, Judy Stropus observed them as teammates: "They were strong rivals. Mark may have been a little jealous of Peter in some ways. Peter resented that Mark was setting up cars—he never believed his car was as good." Judy believes that because the cars were set up to one person's preference, it was difficult for the other driver.

At the start at Donnybrooke the six leading qualifiers broke away to run at the front in the early laps. Sam Posey, writing for *Auto Racing* magazine, described Mark as he battled for fifth position:

I pulled out of the draft and moved alongside him on the right. Only inches apart, we rushed toward the first turn at 160 mph. At this moment I looked over at Mark with a big grin on my face and waved, partly to psyche him out but mostly out of sheer exhilaration. Smiling cherubically, he waved back, as if we were having a tea party out there. I had the inside line as we swept into the right-hander, but Donohue hung in there grimly on my left. Suddenly he cranked the wheel hard right, deliberately broadsiding me. Captain Nice, huh? The Challenger rocketed off the road but I kept my foot in it and rejoined the track in a shower of gravel. The impact of the collision had sent the Javelin hurtling toward the guardrail. For an instant I had the pleasure of seeing Mark struggling on the ragged edge, and then he tucked in behind me.

On lap 15 the Javelin engine failed Mark again. Parnelli and Sam fell out of the race at about the same time. Ed Leslie and Joe Leonard (driving in place of Jim Hall) were giving the white Camaros their best race of the season, and Leslie took the lead over George Follmer and Swede Savage. It was a short-lived renaissance for the Chaparral-run cars, as Leslie's gearbox failed and Leonard was slowed by tire punctures. Excitement continued right to the end with Milt Minter's winning Camaro and Follmer's Mustang battling mightily. Both cars finished with body damage, and Follmer was ready to fight Minter in the victory circle, but Burdie Martin calmed everyone down and avoided an embarrassing scene. George was fined $100 for precipitating the post-race action. It was a brilliant and well-earned victory for Minter, particularly as his American Racing Associates (ARA) was considered a "private" or non-factory-backed team. Team owner Roy Woods sweetened the victory by finishing third in the team's second Camaro. Chevrolet finally had a winner in the 1970 Trans-Am series. With 6 of the 11 races now run, Ford led with 48 points, followed by Chevy at 26, AMC at 25, Dodge, 7, and Plymouth, 5.

Oil pressure remained the weak point in the Javelin, and the car wasn't going to be a consistent winner until it was sorted. After the debacle at Donnybrooke, Mark, Woody, and Jerry Kroninger went straight from Minnesota to Wisconsin to test at Road America in advance of the next round. "We were trying to find an oil pan that would work," says Woody. "We had at least four pans to try from different people—all trying to find the right combination. Traco, Geri Stahl from York, Pennsylvania, who built all of our headers, someone from AMC, Sun Oil—each had built a different oil pan configuration to test. All of the pony cars had a cross member under the engine. I cut the cross member out of one of the Javelins so I could unbolt the pans. Otherwise you had to remove the engine to get the oil pans off."

They tested at Elkhart Lake for three days. Again Woody was the human telemetry recorder as he braced himself in the back of the Javelin to read the gauges over Mark's shoulder. "We would test a pan—I would pull the cross member out— pull the pan down—stick a new one up," says Woody. "I was black and blue after three days of that. We came up with an oil pan that lived and we never blew another engine. I can't remember whose oil pan we used."

After sorting oil pans and before the Road America race weekend, Mark was in southern California for initial testing in the turbocharged Ford-engined Lola at the new Ontario Motor Speedway. Mark and A. J. Foyt were testing tires for Goodyear. Mark turned the fastest lap to date at the new facility at 173.5. Promotion for the September opening was intense, and the new Speedway was clearly the biggest news story in motor racing in 1970.

Mark bought Sue a gold-colored dune buggy. It was her "fun" town car, and Mark loved to give the boys adventuresome rides in it around the grounds of the new house he and Sue purchased that summer in Media. The Colonial-style tan-brick house was situated on a hill with extensive grounds that gave six-year-old Michael and three-year-old David tremendous freedom to roam. It would have been an ideal family scene if the hectic testing, racing, and more testing weren't keeping Mark increasingly away from home. Sue was devoted to Mark and was an attentive and loving mother. In a later *Sports Illustrated* story, Robert F. Jones said, "Sue is an equally tidy blonde who runs the house and the two Donohue sons with Penske-style precision." In her spare time she liked to garden and occasionally found time to play tennis. She did not have a maid or housecleaner as she liked doing her own housekeeping. Sue attended as many races as family circumstances allowed, and attempted to maintain an equilibrium within the family to balance Mark's increasing stardom.

Elkhart Lake's Road America circuit was hosting its first Trans-Am race on July 19. It was running as a "double-header" promotion with the L&M Continental Championship for Formula A. After their exploratory venture into race sponsorship at Sebring the previous December, L&M was now firmly established in road racing as the title sponsor of a series. They were also in the Can-Am as the primary sponsor for the L&M Lola entered by Carl Haas and driven by Peter Revson.

When Mark arrived at Road America he was impressed to see a large number of Javelin people present as the cars were unloaded from the transporter. Their ranks tripled the next day as more AMC personnel arrived to support their team in a race in the company's home state.

The long Road America straightaways seemed to favor the Mustangs. They qualified first and second. Mark was on the third row, again with Sam Posey, and in the row ahead were Ed Leslie and Swede Savage. Jim Hall was back in the Camaro alongside Revson in the fourth row of the 36-car starting field.

After qualifying, Jerry Titus took his car on track to try a new power-steering system. Something inexplicable happened in the difficult left bend under the Billy Mitchell Bridge, which was usually taken nearly flat out. Titus encountered a slower car and either experienced brake or steering failure, crashing the Pontiac Firebird into the bridge abutment at turn 13. The accident was clearly serious and cast a gloom over the paddock. However, before the weekend was over the news seemed good. Although Titus was in critical condition, the word as people left the circuit was that he would recover. It was false hope. The enormously popular Jerry Titus died of his injuries on August 5, 1970, two weeks after the accident. Sam Posey wrote a beautiful tribute that appeared in *Auto Racing*. It concluded with these words: "He was the first real master of the Trans-Am. He had several close friends, a devoted crew, a loyal backer and a young wife that dreams are made of. He was a keen guy."

Road America removed the bridge in 2007 and built an access tunnel some feet up the road. Describing the easier and more-direct access provided by the tunnel, a track spokesman, with an apparently straight face, also mentioned improved driver safety, citing the Titus fatality 37 years earlier as compelling evidence of the need for it.

The Road America race was a triumph for Donohue/Penske race craft. A new pit-stop strategy designed to separate Mark from traffic proved decisive, as Don Cox remembers: "We timed Mark's pit stops to give him a clear track—so instead of giving him a full fuel load we ran our short fuel stop first, so we wouldn't be in amongst them." The strategy worked beautifully, as competitors were surprised to see Mark peel off from second place to pit after only 10 of the race's 50 laps. It was assumed that he had trouble and when he returned at the back he was largely ignored. But Mark made only one more stop, on lap 30, and returned to the track second behind Swede Savage. The Javelin was running strong, and Mark passed Savage before the Challenger made its pit stop. Mark won the race in front of a large crowd that included 400 AMC dealers. Savage was second, Posey third, Hall fourth, Jones fifth, and Milt Minter sixth—all on the lead lap. It was the kind of experience that delighted Mark Donohue. "We never saw anyone, we never passed anyone, and we won the race and they all couldn't figure out how we did it," he later said.

While Mark and Roger had played their roles perfectly in the pit-stop subterfuge, they failed to coordinate their post-race stories. Mark maintained the fiction in his disingenuous comments to the Associated Press's Bob Greene: "We wanted to run high on oil. But, if you smoke early in the race they usually black-flag you. So we purposely started low. Only we started a little too low by mistake." Roger, meanwhile, was being totally candid regarding his strategy. A non-bylined story in the Newark *Star-Ledger* quoted him thus: "Mark pointed to the hood every time he came around. I kept flashing the oil? sign at him and he nodded back. So I waved him in. But

it was all planned. The other teams thought we were having trouble. We didn't add a drop."

It was the second win for Mark, AMC, Sunoco, and the Penske team in three races. Best of all, the oil pressure problem had been solved.

CHAPTER 105:

Another Indy Second to Al

Just five miles down the road from the Indianapolis Motor Speedway, the less-famous Indianapolis Raceway Park (IRP) hosted the Indy 150 on July 27. This was Penske Racing's first appearance in a USAC race since the Indy 500, and for the race on the IRP road circuit, the team used the Lola T150 fitted with a Chevy engine. The turbo-Ford used in the 500 was unsuited to road racing because of the throttle lag that occurred before the power of the turbocharger kicked in. Unlike previous USAC races at IRP, which had run as two 100-mile heats, the format was a single race of 150 miles.

The 15-turn, 2.5-mile road circuit was part of the multi-purpose concept pioneered by IRP when the facility was first built in 1960. The main straightaway and start/finish line were on the drag strip. Leaving the drag strip, the circuit makes two fast right-hand bends; then a series of corners carries the track around the outside of the free-standing, three-quarter-mile oval track. The track works its way through the drag-strip staging area and, after squeezing between the main grandstands in a tight left-hand hairpin turn, returns to the drag strip and the finish line.

Although flat, IRP is fast with challenging turns that deliver good value for spectators and drivers alike. When first built, the IRP road course was expected to bring Formula One racing to Indianapolis. Amid great publicity the 1963 United States Grand Prix was announced for the track. It never happened, but many years later Formula One did come to Indianapolis at the Speedway itself. IRP achieved, and maintains, its greatest glory as the site of the premier NHRA drag race (the Summer Nationals), although the three-quarter-mile oval and the road circuit remain active.

Mario Andretti qualified fastest with a 1:29.65, sharing the front row with Al Unser at 1:29.76. Mark equaled Unser's time but was on the second row alongside Swede Savage with a 1:29.82. Andretti's McNamara chassis was fitted with a Gurney-prepared stock-block Ford. Savage was in Dan

Gurney's own car since Dan had been expected to race for McLaren at Edmonton in the Can-Am the same weekend. But Dan was at IRP, because his drive with McLaren had ended. He declined, however, to ask Savage to give up his seat for the race. Instead, Dan drove the pace car.

After Bruce McLaren's death, Gurney had driven for the McLaren team in both Formula One and Can-Am, winning the first two Can-Am races at Mosport and St. Jovite. The relationship ended in part because of conflicting oil sponsors, but equally because the culture of the British team didn't fit Dan Gurney's persona. Dan was an acknowledged engineer-driver in his own right, with strong feelings on car setup and team management. Dan told Peter Manso in a *Road & Track* story, "I didn't have free run of their place in Europe, wasn't invited into their engineering offices and so on, and I thought, 'Okay, fair enough.' But at the same time I realized I didn't want to be in a position where I couldn't be on intimate terms with my team, not after having run a Formula One team of my own, and knowing, as I did, what such an arrangement could mean, just how important it is." It was too soon after Bruce's death for the close-knit McLaren team to want to hear input from any outside source. Dan later recalled for Tim Considine in *American Grand Prix Racing*, "Once you've had your own team, it's very difficult to go and drive for someone else."

The early race action featured Mario, Al, and Swede, with Mark just behind but not mixing in the battle. Savage pushed into an early lead and Mario crashed out of the race on the 15th lap. A. J. Foyt moved up to challenge Savage and took the lead on lap 34 of 60. It started raining midway through the race, and A. J. was slowed with misted goggles. He faded from the front group and ultimately ran out of fuel and did not finish. Unser and Savage battled through the rain, exchanging the lead in a series of off-course excursions. Savage finally crashed in the fast turn two, and Al had a sufficient lead on Mark to make a "stop-and-go" fuel stop. Just as he had at the 500 in May, Mark finished second to Al Unser. Although he was the only other car on the lead lap, he was never a competitive factor for the lead. Gordon Johncock and John Cannon were third and fourth.

Vic Elford Blues

The Trans-Am series had tightened up. With Mark's victories in the Javelin and Minter's in the Camaro, Ford had been out of the winner's circle for nearly two months. A third car for A. J. Foyt was added for the St. Jovite-Mont Tremblant round on August 2. A. J. didn't like the way the Mustang handled, and Parnelli Jones was sent out in the car to ascertain if it had a problem. Within a few laps Parnelli crashed the car backwards into a dirt bank, and it could not be made ready for A. J. on race day. Parnelli and Mark qualified 1-2, with George Follmer and Ed Leslie in the row behind at the start. A new addition to the series was Vic Elford, who placed the second Chaparral-Camaro on the fourth row alongside Peter Revson. Elford had joined Chaparral to drive the team's latest Can-Am car, the 2J. Jim Hall, still not recovered from his injuries at Stardust in 1968, now turned his seat in the second Camaro over to the English driver.

"Mark was all business on a race day—he would get himself mentally prepared," recalls Walt Czarnecki. "He would sit in the back of the trailer—in those days it was a car carrier with a box on the back—in the dark, preparing for the race through what is now called visualization. That is what Mark was doing. When it came time for him to go into the zone, it was my impression that his personality changed to the point where you couldn't communicate with him."

In the early laps at the Mont Tremblant circuit, the Javelin appeared very strong, and Mark ran second between the Mustangs of Jones and Follmer. The strategy from Road America was again employed and Mark pitted early. When the Fords completed their stops Mark held a commanding lead. Toward the end of the race, unexpected tire wear seemed to dictate fitting a fresh set of Goodyears when the Sunoco Javelin made its final stop for fuel. Mark had a good lead on Follmer in second, but likely not enough to make a tire change and hold the lead. The issue was resolved five laps from race end when Follmer pitted with his left rear fender contacting the tire. With that Roger called Mark in, and as right side tires were replaced, the last can of Sunoco was added. Mark won the race by more than a minute from Follmer. A lap down in third and fourth were Jones and Posey. Overcoming tire trouble that dropped him all the way to the back of the field, Peter Revson drove a fine race to finish fifth.

In the week between the Canadian Trans-Am and the round at Watkins Glen, Mark was one of the featured drivers at a Pro-Am race at Ontario Motor Speedway in southern California. The much anticipated facility was just two weeks away from opening day for its inaugural 500 on Labor Day. The publicity-driven Pro-Am event featured a variety of celebrities, including Kirk Douglas, Paul Newman, Steve McQueen, Robert Wagner, Pancho Gonzales, Pete Conrad, and Wilt Chamberlain, with each one driving in tandem with a top race driver. Mark was partnered with Hugh Downs, host of NBC television's the *Today* show, with whom he finished fourth. The erudite Downs was a consummate gentleman and a genuine race enthusiast. Downs explained to syndicated racing columnist Bob Cochnar why he and Mark were chosen to race together. "We were paired because of compatible size and emotional temperament, which is quite a compliment to me." The winners were Bobby Unser and comedian Dick Smothers, who might have qualified in either category. Smothers was a better than average race driver, experienced in powerful cars.

The great momentum of three wins in the past four races brought the Penske Team to Watkins Glen on August 16 with hopes to repeat their come-from-behind championship year of 1969. The strongest entry of the season—45 cars attempted to gain the 35 starting positions—produced the most exciting race of the year. On an overcast day the race started with all the top cars on dry tires. Mark and Parnelli were on the front row followed by Elford, Posey; Savage, Revson; Leslie, Follmer. Mark was running second, ten seconds behind Parnelli and due for a pit stop when the rain started. It was the last series of pit stops that cost Mark the race. The rain had stopped, and with the track now dry, Roger decided to go with a full set of dry tires, as did Bud Moore in the Mustang pit. Jim Hall made the brave call of fitting Vic Elford's Camaro with dry tires only on the left side, leaving wet-weather tires on the right. The strategy saved 25 seconds and Elford's brilliance did the rest, bringing Chaparral its only victory in the series. Mark trailed by 10 seconds at the finish, passing Follmer on the last lap when the Mustang had momentary fuel starvation.

In the hills surrounding Watkins Glen there are guitar pickers who know the "Vic Elford Blues," even if they have never seen a race outside of Dundee Speedway, the nearest dirt track. The tune is a riff taught by Vic to a local guitar player who was serving as a crewman that weekend on the Chaparral-Camaro.

CHAPTER 107:
"It was just plain rotten"

Mark was one of seven Champ Car drivers on the track on Saturday, August 22, 1970, for Opening Day of the inaugural race at Ontario Motor Speedway. He was joined by Swede Savage, Al Loquasto, John Cannon, Jim Hurtubise, Les Scott, and Kevin Bartlett. Mark turned the fastest speed of the day at 165.14 mph. The public was admitted for free to view the magnificent facility, and 27,582 passed through the turnstiles. (On race day, admission fees would range from $8 to $25 for regular seating; a $250 seat would place you in the Victory Circle Club.) It was a hot day, and fifteen people were treated for heat prostration. It was also a day of ceremony befitting a facility that modeled itself on the Indianapolis Motor Speedway. A parade of dignitaries was followed by the Mayor's Breakfast, presided over by Ontario mayor, Howard Snider.

Ontario Motor Speedway (OMS) had loomed large in the American motor-racing picture since its earliest announcement. It enjoyed national press coverage that equaled and perhaps exceeded the annual media frenzy for the Indianapolis 500. Construction costs alone made the facility big-league: $25.5 million in the late 1960s was a breathtaking figure. The location in southern California alongside the San Bernardino Freeway, just 25 miles east of Los Angeles, the supposed mecca of the car culture, seemed a sure bet for success.

The track promoters sought to emulate Indy in every possible way, matching not only its track size and appearance, but even its traditional pomp and self-conscious ceremony. The Indy 500 was on Memorial Day; Ontario's California 500 would be on Labor Day. Clarence Cagle, the longtime superintendent of IMS, was hired as a consultant. But even as Ontario imitated Indy, no opportunity was missed to say that it was also an improvement. The track was almost an exact copy, except wider—70 feet on the front chute and 55 feet on the back straight—and the short chutes were banked to make it faster. Another difference was that the back straight was elevated 10 feet higher than the front to give the grandstands better sight lines over the infield buildings. The design was intended to provide maximum comfort for spectators at all levels. It was the first track or outdoor stadium to have skyboxes, penthouses leased at $33,000 a year.

OMS also presented itself as a model of business like

nothing seen before. Indianapolis attorney David Lockton, a 33-year-old Yale graduate, was the driving force. Financing was put together by Dan Lufkin, a Harvard Business School graduate considered a real up-and-comer on Wall Street. Lufkin was pioneering the expansion of the concept of what municipal financing could be used for.

Though beautiful and "cutting-edge" in many respects, Ontario was doomed even before it opened, and seasoned racing people knew it at the time. The bond issue guaranteed by the City of Ontario carried a debt service of proportions that demanded peak crowds at every event. OMS had promised the city of Ontario 1.5 million paying spectators a year. In addition to the core USAC event on Labor Day, the multi-purpose circuit needed to attract the United States Grand Prix for Formula One, a Can-Am, a Trans-Am, a NASCAR Grand National, a top National Hot Rod Association (NHRA) event, and an American Motorcycle Association (AMA) race. More critically, the business model essentially called for each event to fill the 140,000-plus seats every time. There was also the expectation of substantial television revenues.

On Sunday, August 23, Mark was fastest again at 169.81 mph. Mark had tested on the track for Goodyear in July when he turned a 173.50, the fastest speed at OMS up to that time. Since then Al Unser had tested at 174.8. On Monday Mark was fastest again, but when asked if he was the race favorite, said, "When everybody gets here at the same time, same place, then we'll know who's fastest." On Tuesday his speed of 171.76 was eclipsed by Joe Leonard at 172.41. Leonard was driving for Vel's Parnelli and was teammate to Al Unser. The team principals were Mark's Trans-Am adversary Parnelli Jones and California businessman and longtime race supporter Vel Miletich. Joe Leonard had enjoyed a legendary career in motorcycle racing before becoming a success racing cars.

Mark had drawn 10th in the qualifying line and, along with Karl, the crew, and the turbocharged Ford-powered Lola, was ready when his turn came. Trouble began when starter Shim Malone missed Mark's signal that he was ready to begin his timed laps. It was a fast lap, and Mark now pitted as Roger protested vehemently. He was allowed to go out again, but neither the driver nor the car was quite as primed as they had been the first time. "It's only a guess what difference it made," Mark told the Los Angeles Times's Shav Glick. "But it didn't do me any good. When you get prepared mentally, it hurts to get jacked around like that. As to how much the hot engine affected my time we'll never know." Roger was

upset, telling the press, "It was just plain rotten. This starter just plain blew it. Mark had his hand plainly raised when he went by the start/finish line. Plenty of people saw it."

Starter Malone had a difficult situation to deal with. Smog was lying thick on the track, and he was having trouble seeing the drivers' signals even through binoculars. The beautiful OMS facility suffered from difficulties attendant to its physical location. Smog was an even greater problem in the industrial area around the track than it was in the city of Los Angeles. Dirt was constantly blowing from nearby agricultural fields, and the prevailing eastward wind was hot and swirled within the track. Although it was difficult to see Mark's signal from the starter's stand, Ray Marquette of the Indianapolis Star said that ". . . more than 40,000 watchers did and showed that California race fans know how to boo."

Roger acknowledged to Marquette that Mark probably wasn't in contention for pole position, but said, "Mark had a 174.5 on what should have been his first lap of qualifying. Then he had to come in and sit in the heat while they decided what to do. When he went back out, the temperatures were all out of whack and I'm sure he wasn't keyed as high as he had been on his first run."

Mark's disappointing 173.019 on his four-lap run qualified him 13th fastest, on the inside of the fifth row. The front row comprised Lloyd Ruby at 177.567; Dan Gurney, with a turbocharged Ford in his Eagle at 176.401; and Johnny Rutherford, 176.375.

On the race track the wind and heat were a big problem. Jerry Grant said, "It's hot and miserable here. The heat will make it a tremendous fatigue battle. The track is faster than Indy, and sometimes heat waves distort a driver's vision going into the turns."

The race started on time in front of an enormous crowd. It was a near thing: The smog was so bad that as late as 30 minutes before the 11:00 a.m. start, USAC was planning to delay the event. The tie between OMS and Indy was underscored with a guest appearance by Tony Hulman, who intoned the words that he made famous at his Indianapolis Motor Speedway: "Gentlemen, start your engines."

The wind that blew the smog away brought other trouble. The race was plagued with multiple burned-out engines, blamed on dirt blowing into intake manifolds. Mark was out of the race after 10 laps with a burned piston. "I was over-whelmingly disappointed," he said. Peter Revson drove a great race in the Offenhauser-powered McLaren and might have won. He finished fifth when his car vapor-locked, causing him to stall exiting the pits. Jim McElreath driving A. J. Foyt's backup car took the lead for the first time three laps from the end and won his greatest victory. Art Pollard was second, Dick Simon third, and Gordon Johncock fourth. None of the favored and highly publicized teams and drivers finished.

The strain of competing in so many intense race programs was taking its toll on Mark. Johnny McDonald, a motorsports writer for the San Diego *Union*, was among many to comment on Mark's changed persona, noting that "[a] scowl has replaced that boyish smile."

It was a great day for the OMS staff, however, who had worked so hard to prepare the magnificent facility. Racing had never seen anything quite like it, and OMS would never again have a day quite as grand and successful.

On this same weekend racing lost one of its greatest drivers and personalities. Jochen Rindt died in a Lotus-Ford in an accident during qualifying for the Italian Grand Prix at the Monza circuit near Milan. Later in the year, Rindt became racing's only posthumously awarded World Champion when, in the remaining three races, no one was able to overcome his lead in the point standings. Rindt was superbly talented, loyal to his friends, devoted to his family, and altogether one of the world's most delightful human beings in or out of racing.

CHAPTER 108:
"The cheers of the fans"

Mark and Penske Racing had last participated in the SCCA's professional series for Formula A the previous December at Sebring. The L&M Continental for the up-to-5.0-liter single-seat class was a competitive success, and the cars were fast and exciting. On a road circuit, Formula A cars were faster than USAC Champ cars. After their experience sponsoring the December race at Sebring, L&M had taken on the entire race series, and marketing director Cope Robinson was fast creating the art of product promotion within the racing environment. The series included both U.S. and Canadian circuits. The races in Canada were run under FIA rules that banned tall wings. Most of the same teams that had featured in 1969 were still running, although Sam Posey had abandoned the category to concentrate on his Trans-Am program with Dodge. Malcolm Starr's racing team

had merged with Carl Hogan to form Hogan/Starr Racing Ltd., and their driver John Cannon was leading the series in points in a McLaren Mk 10B. Gus Hutchinson, Ron Grable, John Gunn, David Hobbs, George Follmer, Eppie Wietzes, Dick Smothers, Davey Jordan, and Bill Brack were among the top runners contesting all or a significant number of the races. Mark's appearance at Mosport Park on September 13 was the 11th race in the 13-race L&M series.

The T192 Mark was driving was Lola's prototype for the next season, which Eric Broadley had made available to Penske Racing for development. The car arrived at Newtown Square just 10 days before the race, and there was insufficient time to paint it. It appeared in white carrying the Penske No. 6.

David Hobbs in the Surtees TS5A qualified on pole position, with Mark second. On the row behind them were familiar faces: George Follmer in a Lotus 70-Ford and John Cannon in the McLaren. On race day it rained, and at Mosport the rain can be torrential and persistent. Mark made a great start off the line, but to his horror realized he was carrying too much speed for the first right-hand turn. "Oh Christ! Fifty feet off the start and I'm going to crash," he remembered thinking. He attempted to place the Lola parallel with the guardrail to lessen the inevitable impact. It worked: Mark and the Lola glanced off the guardrail almost as if it was a planned move and motored away from Hobbs and the rest of the field. Mark—always a master of a wet track—won the race from Eppie Wietzes's McLaren M10B by more than 80 seconds. Hobbs was third.

The weekend after Mosport was the next-to-the-last round of the Trans-Am at Kent, Washington's, Seattle International Raceway on September 20. With the strong results of recent races, there was still hope that the Penske team might pull off winning the championship from Ford as they had so dramatically the previous year. Ford's lead in points was 60 to 49, and Mark would not only have to win both races, but Ford would also need to finish worse than second place. The team had the Kent track on Tuesday before the race for testing. On race weekend Parnelli Jones was dominant, qualifying the Mustang on pole position with Mark again second fastest. Parnelli won the race with Mark 20 seconds behind in second place and Sam Posey third. The Trans-Am championship was Ford's again, for the first time since 1967.

Penske Racing's determination and Mark Donohue's never-say-die attitude were at their best the following weekend for the L&M Continental race at Mid-Ohio on September 27. In private testing on Thursday, Mark went off the road, damaging the suspension and the tub, and splitting the fuel cell. While the Lola went straight back to Newtown Square, phone lines were already burning as the needed replacement parts were lined up. Bill Scott came in from Sun Oil to repair the tub, and all hands were involved finishing the car. The truck left the race shop late Saturday evening and arrived at Mid-Ohio Sunday morning in time for Mark to run the warm-up session. He was placed 25th in the 28-car field.

Reporter Mel McKeachie for the Ashland *Times-Gazette* said, "George Follmer won the race, John Cannon won the series, and Mark Donohue won the cheers of the fans." Mark's white No. 6 Lola was up to 13th place by lap three and 8th by lap eight. Halfway through the race he was 4th and battling with Gus Hutchinson. Once by Hutchinson's Lola, Mark chased Cannon and Follmer hard, but their lead was too great and he finished 3rd. David Hobbs had qualified on the front row, but was knocked off the road and out of the race in a wheel-to-wheel incident as he attempted to pass John Cannon. Cannon's second place made him the 1970 L&M Continental Champion. Follmer was a happy winner from pole position, a full minute clear of Cannon.

Mark was enthusiastic about the series and the cars, telling UPI, "There were no factory teams and everyone can buy the same equipment, so everyone can enter the series and expect to be competitive." While Mark was no doubt sincere—and technically correct that there no factory teams in Formula A—there were clearly advantages to having a preferred relationship with a major constructor. Penske Racing's relationship with Lola's Eric Broadley and Lola importer Carl Haas provided exactly that edge. This illustrated a simple fact of life common to all forms of racing. The best teams attract the best drivers, and the best team/driver combinations receive the best support within the industry.

Follmer's average speed for the entire race was faster than any race previously run at Mid-Ohio. Despite giving away more than 2.0 liters in engine size, Follmer's qualifying time of 1:27.6 was identical to the Can-Am pole time set by Denny Hulme in the McLaren M8D. Mid-Ohio was a tight track that favored the lighter, better-handling single-seat Formula A cars. In making the comparison it is important to note that Hulme's pole time had been 1.7 seconds quicker the year before, and that the difference was greater between the two types of cars on faster tracks. Still, only the McLarens

were that fast, with just one or two others in Can-Am able to approach their times. The rest of the Can-Am field was substantially slower than the top 10 or so Continental cars. The Can-Am continued to decline in competitiveness while delighting a diminishing number of paying spectators with the appeal of technological innovation and big, noisy cars. However, people weren't turning out in any great numbers to see the Continental either.

CHAPTER 109:

Farewell to Dan and the Factory Teams

Five races in five weeks now had Mark rejoining the Trans-Am team for the season finale at Riverside, California. Parnelli Jones qualified on pole with teammate Follmer second. Dan Gurney had rejoined his Barracuda team for the last race of his career and showed he had not lost his speed by qualifying third. Mark was fourth and Javelin teammate Revson sixth.

Parnelli opened a lead from the start of the race but on lap five was knocked off the track and into the desert surrounding it. He kept his foot on the throttle and returned to the track with a battered car, now in ninth place and 30 seconds behind the leaders. Mark had the Javelin in fourth place behind Follmer, Gurney, and Savage. Revson and Posey had been battling for position, and when Sam tried an aggressive outbraking move the cars made contact and were off the road. Both cars returned to the race only to retire midway through the race. Sam was out first and was sitting on the pit wall when Peter returned to the pits after the engine blew on the Javelin. "Peter handed me his helmet and gloves and walked straight to where Sam was sitting and knocked him over the wall," recalls Walt Czarnecki. From Sam's perspective, "[I] didn't see Peter until he was almost on top of me. His eyes burning with fury, he seized my throat. I lost my balance and fell off the wall into the pit lane."

The encounter was quickly broken up but it made headlines everywhere. Perhaps Peter had been carrying a grudge against Sam since the first round of the series when their cars got together at Laguna Seca. It is equally likely that the extremely difficult year he had experienced in the Javelin had brought him to a boiling point, and that Sam was the unfortunate victim of Revson's pent-up frustrations. Much of Peter's unhappiness at Penske Racing was his conviction that he wasn't getting a fair shake. The following month when he was honored by the SCCA as grand marshal for the Runoffs at Road Atlanta, Georgia, he told the Atlanta *Constitution*'s Pat Zier, "Donohue gets the most attention and the second car isn't always as good. I'm not going to drive for them unless I know my car is getting the same consideration."

Back on the track Parnelli was driving one of his greatest races. He charged through the entire field to bring the battered and bruised Mustang home the winner. It was his final stamp on a championship season. George Follmer finished second and Mark was third, more than 20 seconds behind.

The big story was Dan Gurney's retirement announcement after finishing fifth in the Barracuda, a position behind his protégé Swede Savage. "I have always felt that part of being a successful driver is in knowing when to quit," said Dan. "And in one piece. So this is it." Dan led two laps in his final race and was fast and competitive right to the end. He had been third at Indy in May and still had the enormous stores of talent that made him America's most popular road racer and an international legend. His exploits in Formula One had begun in the late 1950s and his record was remarkable. He gave Porsche their first and only Grand Prix win, and two years later gave Brabham their first. His most famous and historically important "first" was winning the 1967 Belgian Grand Prix in his Eagle—still the only example of an American driver winning a major European Grand Prix in an American car of his own manufacture. Dan had also been an innovator at Indy, and was as responsible as any single person for the successful adaptation of rear-engine race cars there. Dan deserved a win in the Indy 500 and came close, with two seconds and a third. It was appropriate that he called it quits at Riverside. It was a circuit he dominated in every category, be it USAC Champ cars, sports cars, NASCAR, or anything else he raced there.

It was a farewell race, too, for most of the teams. Chrysler had told the Gurney-run Plymouth Barracuda team and the Sam Posey–run Dodge Challenger team that they were leaving racing. It was the beginning of the end of factory-backed teams in Trans-Am. Ford soon shocked the industry by announcing their pullout from all forms of racing. The Chaparral team would not return in 1971, and AMC was left alone among manufacturers directly supporting teams in the series. The reasons differ for each of the big three manufacturers withdrawing direct support to teams in the Trans-Am. The evolution in design and concept of the pony car itself and the attendant changing market needs are part of the story. Neither Chrysler division was prepared to spend the amount of money needed to win, and to therefore justify the exercise from a marketing standpoint. Ford's withdrawal was part of an overall move away from performance marketing that affected all forms of racing. GM's position had not changed. They had never supported the series from a marketing budget, and while private teams could obtain technical support, they were on their own to fund team operations.

The final 1970 Trans-Am tally had Ford with six wins and 72 points, AMC with three wins and 59 points, Chevrolet with two wins, 40 points. Winless, but scoring points and enlivening the season with their competitiveness, were Dodge (18) and Plymouth (15). Penske team manager Chuck Cantwell summed up the year: "If we hadn't had the engine problems at the beginning we would have won that first year; 1970 was one of the greatest years with all the teams. We never felt we were inferior to any of them. Ford was obviously the biggest competition because they had the most money and the most factory support. Our big focus was Ford."

Despite the disappointment of not winning the championship, Penske Racing had every reason to feel good about their first year with the Javelins. They had taken a car that had never won a race and won three times with it. Though short of the seven victories predicted by Roger when the AMC program was first announced, this was still a significant accomplishment. They had started from scratch, and the entire organization had pulled together to make the car competitive enough to capture second place in points behind the well-honed and highly developed Mustang team of Bud Moore. Mark had smarted under false media assertions that Penske's success in the Camaro program was owed to GM engineering. He called the Javelin the "ultimate challenge" and proof that Penske Racing could build, develop, and race a winner. It had been done through commitment, race craft and strategy, and the brilliant driving of Mark Donohue.

While privately Mark was immensely proud of what the team had accomplished in making the Javelin a winner, he would never admit to being satisfied with anything short of victory. "I wouldn't say finishing second was successful no matter what people think," he told United Press International.

"We hoped to win it and we didn't. We didn't enter this series with the idea of coming in second."

Along with understating his own achievements, Mark increasingly projected a frank, no-nonsense persona to the media, and seemed to strive for a harder personal image than that known to those close to him. Before Riverside, he told a UPI reporter, "I never believed that Captain Nice stuff. I always was told that nice guys finish last."

Mark was still a nice guy and retained his instinct for kindness to strangers and essential good manners. But he had changed. Far rarer were the glimpses of pure joy that he derived from the very experience of competing. Even winning often was no longer enough. Too frequently there was something that diminished the experience. He may have won the race, but he didn't win the series. Particularly during the 1970 Trans-Am season, if the result had been something as embarrassing as a mere second place, Mark would sit unhappy and unapproachable in the race car for a long time after the race. Friends thought it had stopped being fun for him. He had accepted the mantle of pure professional at a very literal level.

The season ended on an upbeat note. A full month after the L&M round at Mid-Ohio that had decided the championship, the Continental series concluded at Sebring on October 25. After Mid-Ohio, Mark had detected chassis fatigue in the Lola during testing at Summit Point Raceway in West Virginia, The two races and the damage to the tub had been hard on the car, and it would never again be perfect. Lola agreed to provide a fresh chassis that would incorporate Eric Broadley's latest thinking as well as some of the ideas Mark and Don Cox had identified.

The car they took to Sebring was very good. It had the European-style low wing unlike most of the U.S.-run cars that ran a very high wing. Testing on the skid pad and at Summit Point convinced Mark that the low wing was, in fact, the way to go. At the race Mark qualified on the pole, with David Hobbs in the Surtees second. In front of a disappointingly small crowd, Hobbs and George Follmer brought the race to Mark, who led the first lap. Hobbs was ahead on laps two and three and George took over through lap seven before Mark forged into a lead he never lost again.

A week later, Mark and Roger were prominent observers at Riverside of the last round in the 1970 Can-Am series. Speculation always surrounded Roger's next moves, and the media had Penske Racing planning a return to the series in 1971 in the latest Lola, or a McLaren identical in specifications to whatever the works team ran. Most interesting was a report in *Road & Track* by Eoin Young that Roger was in discussions with Porsche over plans to run a 16-cylinder, 7.0-liter supercharged spyder with backing from Porsche-Audi.

CHAPTER 110:
Music by the Scott Singers

Kirk F. White was an entrepreneurial dealer in European classic sports cars, particularly Ferraris. In 1970 White was said to be the largest-volume exotic car dealer in America, with a main office in Philadelphia and stores in Miami, Indianapolis, and Berkeley, California. Through his friendship with Roger Penske's brother David, Kirk had come to know Roger. Kirk F. White Motor Cars was in the west Philadelphia suburb of Overbrook near Roger's Chevrolet dealership. Both men were in the habit of coming to work early, and one day at 7:00 a.m., Roger paid a brief call at Kirk's office. "I've got a good idea," Roger told Kirk. "Why don't you get some of your customers and investors together and we'll round up a 512 Ferrari and run for the World Manufacturers Championship. Let me know—I've got to go."

With that Roger was back in his car and gone, but the simply expressed idea appealed to Kirk. He brought in friends Roberts "Bobs" Harrison, Richard "Jerry" Riegel, and three others. Kirk wrote Roger a three-paragraph letter agreeing to buy the car and parts with the understanding that Penske Racing would prepare the car and race it.

While Kirk was looking for the right Ferrari, he had another call from Roger, who now said that buying a Porsche 917 might be the way to go instead. Kirk said if that was the case then he was out, since his friends and investors were pro-Ferrari guys and not at all interested in Porsches. "The 512 S we isolated was chassis 1040, which was owned by Steve Earle and Chris Cord and being raced in the Can-Am by Jim Adams, with legendary hot-rodder Doane Spencer as mechanic," recalls White. "It was the available car that had been the least abused. They were coming to Mid-Ohio to run the Can-Am on August 23 and agreed to sell us the car after the race for $28,000 if we thought it looked good."

At Mid-Ohio on August 23 Bob Bondurant, whose Lola had dropped out early in the race, finished the race in the Ferrari in seventh place when Adams was overwhelmed by the sweltering heat. After Mid-Ohio, Doane Spencer delivered the Ferrari 512 S spyder to Kirk White Motor Cars. "The car was on our premises for two or three hours before the Penske transporter arrived and took it away," recalls White. "It was the last time we saw it for quite a while." When the Ferrari arrived at Newtown Square, John Woodard recalls that "it was really beat." Mark told Woody, "We're going to rebuild this thing and turn it into a coupe and race it at Daytona."

Mark immediately began setting up the car. He was experimenting on the skid pad at Marcus Hook with a locked differential on the Ferrari and wanted to find out how it worked on a track. Winter was closing in, but he returned to Summit Point Raceway because he could "get on for $5.00 a day." He and Woody arrived unannounced to find the track booked for the day by a go-kart club. Mark waited patiently, sitting on the pit-lane guardrail and visiting with track manager Pat Goodman, waiting for a break in the action. He told Goodman, "I don't need much time to find out what I need to know." According to Goodman, when Mark did go out on the track he lapped the two-mile course at 1:09, the fastest time that had ever been seen there. Goodman remembered the spectacle: "You could actually see dust rise from the bridge planking when he went under." What impressed Goodman most was Mark's complete lack of pretentiousness. "That was the type of man Mark was; he would tell bad jokes and laugh while [the go-karters] used the track instead of insisting that he be allowed to practice with his Ferrari."

The week after Thanksgiving, Roger and Mark went to the Ferrari factory in Modena, Italy, where they were warmly received. The 512 M was the factory's updated version of the 512 S. Ferrari was offering a parts package that allowed private owners to make the update. Penske/White bought most of the package, so although Penske's modifications went far beyond the factory's, the White/Penske car is generally considered a 512 M. When they came to settle up they realized the enthusiasm at Ferrari for their project did not extend to any discounts.

Back home they waited for the parts, which were slow in coming. Mark later noted that "Ordering the parts and getting them was two different things—some never arrived until after the first race at Daytona." The new engine arrived first, and along with the original motor in the car, it was sent to Traco in California to be gone through. Traco's careful preparation to the all-aluminum, four-cam, four-valve, 4993cc, Lucas-injected V12 included modifications to the cylinder heads that significantly increased horsepower.

Kirk White recalls that they started with about 590 horsepower on their dyno. Although Mark says in *The Unfair Advantage* that the critical adjustments to find additional power were made on the Champion dyno, White is clear that it happened at Traco, and that it was Mark who found the extra power when he asked, "What kind of oil pressure are you running?" The answer was 125 pounds. "Mark said, 'Shut the motor down,'" remembers White. "He took the oil relief valve and lowered the oil pressure from 125 pounds to 60. That adjustment increased the horsepower output to 614, and it came from Mark."

Meanwhile, the Ferrari was being completely transformed in the hands of John Woodard, Don Kean, and Lujie Lesovsky. Lesovsky, already a legendary figure from his California racing days and as the builder of a winning Indy car, was on loan from Holman-Moody on a short-term basis. Woody describes Lesovsky as a master metal fabricator: "Lujie was better than anyone. He could build anything out of metal—headers, he could do it all." Mark recalled that unlike many specialists who were typically arrogant and could upset the working relationships within a team, "Lujie was very soft-spoken, an easygoing guy who did a tremendous job and ultimately gained more respect from the guys for being that way. The whole shop came to love Lujie and still does."

Ron Fournier, who had been the team's chief fabricator since 1967, was gone to Texas. "I had a tremendous desire to build an Indy car," remembers Ron. "A. J. Foyt was after me to come to work for him to do just that. When I told Roger what I was thinking he urged me to reconsider. He said he had a commitment to Lola for Indy in 1971, but after that it was possible we could do it. But A. J. was really pestering me to come so I made my move."

Woody and Lujie stripped the Ferrari down to the bare steel frame, even removing the riveted epoxied aluminum panels. They made suspension pickup changes based on direction from Mark and Don Cox. There were already subtle changes to the car that had been performed by Doane Spencer, who had lowered the center of gravity of the tub. The entire center section including cab, doors, windows, and fuel system were fabricated new by Kean and Lesovsky in the Penske Racing shop, with input from Harry Tidmarsh, and a completely new electrical system was designed. "We built the car back up from scratch with all new aluminum panels which Lesovsky made, and we even used special rivets," say Woodard. "It was one of the neatest cars we ever did." It was stunning in the deep blue associated with Sunoco and Penske, drawing a crowd wherever it appeared.

Early in December Mark was back at Ontario Motor Speedway testing the 1971 Javelin on the track's road circuit. They also tested at Riverside where Roger also drove the car. It was strictly a test car, and from the lessons learned they went home and built a new car from scratch. Roger had already sold the 1970 cars and equipment to Roy Woods, who had campaigned Camaros in the season just completed. Woods announced that Milt Minter would again join him in the team. Woods had taken the Javelin to Road Atlanta in November where the SCCA's amateur American Road Racing Championship, the Runoffs, was making its first appearance on the still-new track. Woods won his race in the Javelin and was crowned SCCA A Sedan National Champion.

Mark was a fine public speaker and was happy to share his thoughts with a diverse range of organizations in varied settings. On December 15 he was the featured speaker at the annual Father-Son, Father-Daughter Dinner of the Industrial Management Club of Coatesville, Pennsylvania, at the West End Fire Hall. The Christmas music, provided by the Scott Singers from the Scott Intermediate High School, under the direction of Miss Lois Wamsher, vocal music director, no doubt helped put Mark in the mood of the season.

Two days later Mark was present at a downtown hotel in Philadelphia when Jack Morris, executive vice president of public relations for the Schaefer Brewing Company, announced that Schaefer would be the title sponsor for the first Pocono 500, a new USAC race scheduled for 1971's Fourth of July weekend. Dr. Joseph Mattioli was chairman of the board and the driving force behind the super speedway that was still under construction among the pines of the Pocono Mountains. Other prominent drivers at the lunch were Peter Revson, Wally Dallenbach, and Mario Andretti. Mario lived in nearby Nazareth, Pennsylvania, and was named technical adviser for the new track. Despite being a banked tri-oval, the new track, like Ontario, identified closely with the Indianapolis Motor Speedway, naming its access roads Andretti Road, Clarence Cagle Corners, and Hulman Road. Tony Hulman was at the luncheon and welcomed the new track. "Some ask me if Ontario and Pocono are in competition—they don't know what they're talking about. They [the new tracks] add a little to us and we add a little to them."

The proposed new Chesapeake International Raceway that Mark had labored so devotedly to design now languished. A tight money market was blamed for the suspension of its development. The exclusive agreement with the SCCA for "protected area" status also backfired, as the race track at Summit Point, West Virginia, sued for restraint of trade.

As the year ended, the American Auto Racing Writers and Broadcasters Association named their first "Auto Racing All American Team," and Mark was one of the 10 drivers selected. Al Unser was the top vote getter and recipient of the Jerry Titus Memorial Trophy. The 10 drivers named represented different disciplines within the sport: Mark, Parnelli Jones, and Dan Gurney represented road racing; Richard Petty, Mario Andretti, and Unser were named for oval racing; and Don Garlits and Don Prudhomme for drag racing. Completing the team in the at-large category were Gary Gabelich, who set the Land Speed Record at 622.407 mph, and Ronnie Sox, who was drag racing's biggest winner.

CHAPTER 111:
Transitions

The Penske Racing McLaren M16 for the 1971 Indianapolis 500 came about almost by accident. In December 1970 Mark and Roger went to England to discuss their ideas for the new season with Lola's Eric Broadley. Mark and Don Cox had done a great deal of work on wing technology, and Mark had a pretty good idea of what he wanted. They were also contemplating a possible return to Can-Am and decided to call at McLaren headquarters in Colnbrook. They knew they had no chance of obtaining anything like what McLaren had in the works for the 1971 Can-Am, but it so happened that Teddy Mayer was interested in talking to them about Indy. When Mark saw the Gordon Coppuck–designed McLaren M16 he immediately knew it would be better than anything he had envisioned Lola producing. Drawing upon the team's Formula One experience, the new car incorporated a wing as an integral part of the body. "I quietly marveled at their guts to come up with such a new concept," Mark later reflected. It took some push and pull between Penske and Mayer to make the deal—Roger, Teddy, and Mark went way back, and the rivalries went just as far. Mark pushed Roger a little at his end, as he had tremendous confidence that the car would be a winner.

In January the first M16 arrived at Ontario Motor Speedway for testing by Mark and McLaren team drivers Denny Hulme and Peter Revson. After Ontario the car went to Penske Racing, and Mark, Karl Kainhofer, and Don Cox took it to Phoenix where they tested for an entire week. USAC did not permit wings on race cars, and the McLaren M16 was a breakthrough because the wings were integral to the body. Frank DelRoy, technical chairman of USAC, came to Newtown Square at Roger's request and gave his seal of approval to the design. Mark later believed that it was the careful and thorough understanding gained of the car that week that gave them the speed advantage they enjoyed in the month of May at Indy. Gordon Coppuck recalls the testing experience with Mark: "He was very good right from the start in finding just the right set-up to take advantage of the significantly higher downforces we were generating."

On January 8 in Rochester, New York, Mark and Roger McCluskey signed autographs at the Marine Midland Bank booth at the Rochester Auto Show. In a joint interview with *AutoWeek*'s eastern editor, Jack Williams, they agreed that a vacuum-type car like the Chaparral 2J should be banned from Indy. The 2J had shaken racing to the roots with its technological breakthrough in ground effects, and had been banned from the Can-Am. Mark revealed to Williams that when the 2J was first developed in mid-1969 at Chevrolet Engineering, Mark had proposed to GM that he drive the car.

"The car was ready to race in August 1969," Mark said. "I suggested we take it to the Riverside Can-Am two years ago in a big van which would say 'Chevrolet Engineering' on the side. We would get the pole then withdraw from the race and call a press conference." At this press conference, Mark proposed that General Motors make the following announcement: Even though GM doesn't race, they still have the best automobile engineers in the world. Mark went on to make the point that Don Cox, one of the key engineers on the car, was now with Penske Racing, and "has the ability to do it all over."

On the first day of 1971 a national ban on cigarette advertising on radio and TV went into effect. Cigarette companies suddenly had budget money available and unmet marketing needs. Motor racing was one of the venues seen as an opportunity to reach a mass market. L&M had chosen to ally with the SCCA in 1970. Marketing director Cope Robinson's research data showed that the sports-car group had the best demographics: 18- to 40-year-olds, predominantly college graduates, above median income, and an equal male-to-female ratio. Marlboro became the title sponsor of the USAC Championship Trail and added $300,000 to the point fund. R. J. Reynolds and their Winston brand chose NASCAR.

Just when Penske Racing was beginning to solve their oil problems on the Javelin, their innovations became a moot point. A major rule change from the SCCA now allowed a dry-sump oil system for Trans-Am racing. Racers had been lobbying for the change for years. It is incalculable how many engines were destroyed because of the inability of a wet sump to meet the harsh demands of racing. "If you were very careful in building the pan, and if you were very close in the tolerances, and if you had a very good pump in the front, and a very good oil cooler, you could just make it work," said Mark. "But the ultimate answer was the dry sump."

As the year began there was a key loss in the AMC/Penske chain of command that ultimately became a huge net gain in the Penske business structure. As performance activities manager for AMC, Walt Czarnecki had been the direct contact for Penske Racing with the sponsoring automaker. Walt was in Philadelphia to meet with Roger at his Chevrolet dealership at 48th and Chestnut streets. Walt recalls, "When business was concluded, Roger reached under the desk and pulled out the plans for a new Chevrolet dealership he was building in suburban Detroit. Roger said, 'Chevrolet has approached me with this and I'm looking for a guy to run the business.' " In addition to his motorsports responsibilities, at AMC Walt also had worked in dealer marketing activities and programs, and had become fascinated with the retail side of the car business.

Roger Penske had already developed a reputation for only being associated with the very best people, and Walt felt honored that Roger thought about him in that way. It was a big step for a young man who seemed to have a great future with the carmaker. Walt discussed it with his wife, who was expecting their second child. They agreed that at age 26, Walt was young enough to be flexible even if things didn't work out. "I told Roger yes, and went back to my boss at AMC. I told him I'd be leaving in a couple of weeks," recalls Czarnecki. "I got fired on the spot and was told to leave immediately and come back Saturday to clean out my desk."

Walt called Roger in Philadelphia, who asked, "Did you let them know?" Walt replied, "Yes—they fired me." Walt never forgot Roger's response. "You're on the payroll effective eight o'clock tomorrow morning. Your first assignment is, I want you to take the rest of the week off." The move took Walt out of the racing side of the business for a time as he started working immediately on developing the Detroit dealership.

At Newtown Square all focus was on the Ferrari and the 24-hour race at Daytona at the end of January. Two weeks before the race they tested at the track and Mark was impressed with the car, although he didn't immediately try for a fast lap. Roger was concerned that the lap times were slow. When Mark, completely certain that all systems were functioning, turned up the pace, everyone was impressed. The Ferrari was fast, and the next day they did more testing for wing angles and gear ratios. Don Cox designed new springs based on the test, and when they came back on race weekend the team was ready.

There was a new face at Newtown Square as the small office space was squeezed further to make room for Dan Luginbuhl. Dan had been associated with the team since 1969 when he joined Fred Marik's Professionals in Motion public relations firm. Marik's company had performed outstandingly with Penske Enterprises, but Roger's growing business required an internal marketing services capability. Luginbuhl had left the prestigious advertising firm of Batten, Barton, Durstine & Osborn to join Marik, and now he moved to Philadelphia to become the in-house public relations and communications director for Penske Racing. It was a struggle at first for the engineers and craftsmen to understand why a marketing person would be housed with them. Roger, however, knew the importance of making Dan an integral part of the team. His representation of the entire Penske operation and support to sponsors would require an intimate relationship and understanding of the race team.

The office building—really a converted house—at Newtown Square was right on Winding Way Road. It was separated from the workshop by roughly 100 feet of wide, paved courtyard on a relatively steep slope. In the race shop Karl Kainhofer looked after the two Indy cars with help from Bill Blankenship. Don Kean was on board full-time as a fabricator, along with Lujie Lesovsky, who had joined the team on a full-time basis after previously being "on loan" from Holman-Moody. John Woodard was in charge of the Ferrari 512 M and the Formula A car. The new Javelins were still being developed, and Earle Macmullan now had responsibility for that program. Blaine Ferguson assisted on both the Trans-Am car and the Ferrari with Woody. The office secretary was Mary Ann O'Donnell; there was an office for Mark, one for Don Cox and his engineering table, one for general manager Chuck Cantwell, and now one for Luginbuhl. There was a small dormer room above the office, and increasingly the long days at the shop found Mark sleeping there instead of making the five-mile drive to his home in Media. Mark was growing his hair longer now—gone was the college-boy brush-cut look—and the cherubic round face had become leaner, developing into a more handsome profile.

Sue was happiest on the days Mark was home. She told a reporter, "I like to cook for Mark. He's easy to please, and would never fuss about anything. His favorite food really is meatloaf." There were other distractions from the family time Sue longed for. Mark's favorite relaxation was on the water. He enjoyed sailing, but his greatest passion was for powerboats. That year he obtained a 28-foot Donzi racing boat, a gift from his friend, John Mecom.

When David Belden accompanied Charlie Rainville on a trip to Philadelphia for a meeting of the Road Racing Drivers Club (RRDC), the two of them were Mark and Sue's houseguests for the weekend. After the meeting the entire membership was invited for a tour of the Penske race shop. When the others had gone home Charlie and Dave returned to the Donohue home for the evening.

"Mark's passion for racing was as strong as ever but it was apparent that it was no longer the lark for him that it had been," says Dave. "He talked about the pressures and the importance of testing—he had just completed tests with the Ferrari 512 and the Lola Formula 5000—but his enthusiasm returned when he talked about the testing he had just completed with the McLaren M16 at Indy. He believed that the Ferrari and Lola would be competitive cars in their respective forms of racing, but he saw the McLaren as a breakthrough car at the Speedway. He was that excited about it." The three men talked late into the evening and then returned to the race shop for a meeting at 1:00 a.m. with Roger Penske and Chuck Cantwell. "They were that tightly scheduled—it was the only time they could meet. They discussed lap times and set-ups. Roger was preoccupied with correct placement of sponsor decals and overall car presentation."

The 1:00 a.m. meeting was nothing out of the ordinary. Even when Mark was at home he was tightly scheduled and preoccupied. And he wasn't home a great deal. Dave Lawton recalls a celebratory victory dinner at Bridgehampton. Roger leaned in and reminded Mark that he had to be on an 8:30 a.m. flight to Los Angeles for testing at Riverside. "Sue's face fell. She had anticipated a drive home together and Mark being home for a few days. She drove to Philadelphia alone."

CHAPTER 112:
Hobbs on Board

On a dark winter evening at his home in Upper Boddington, England, David Hobbs received a phone call from Dan Luginbuhl, who delivered the unexpected but welcome news that Roger Penske wished to talk to him about a drive with his team. When David first came to Philadelphia to meet with Mark and Roger, he stayed at the Donohue home in Media. "David was a prince of a guy and an immediate hit with everyone on the team," remembers Kirk White, who recalls that the team gathered at Newtown Square on a Sunday afternoon to meet David.

"The interview with Roger, Mark, and myself went smoothly until the very end when Roger said something like, 'Well, what about your hair?' " Hobbs remembers. " 'Well, what about it?' I replied. Roger suggested I may want to get it cut and I said, 'Not a chance.' That was the end of it."

It was agreed that he would join Penske Racing as Mark's co-driver in the Ferrari and would also drive the Lola-Ford at Indianapolis, Pocono, and Ontario. The long-haired driver already had an enthusiastic following in America from his drives for John Surtees' team in the Formula A Continental series. Hobbs had been second and third in points in 1969 and 1970, despite only running half of each season. Roger also wanted David to be a Goodyear driver—John Surtees and his teams were committed to Firestone—and arranged a drive for him with Carl Hogan's team in Formula A/5000. David stayed with Hogan for five years.

Possessed of a quick wit and a well-earned reputation as one of the best storytellers in racing, Hobbs was a favorite of the media. Mark thought David was a great teammate, but worried at first that Hobbs would prove to be the faster driver. He came to appreciate that Hobbs was fast while maintaining a great sensitivity to the car. David's optimism and sunny disposition were good for the team. Mark's intensity could verge on dourness, and with Peter Revson on the team, the atmosphere had always been tense because of the lack of ease between the two men. Mark was not secure in his own talent and remained uneasy that someone like Peter or David would show him up as not fast enough to do the job. That insecurity, in the face of all indications to the contrary, drove Mark, both on and off the track.

Hobbs, unlike many other drivers who had driven alongside Mark, had a strong technical and mechanical background. He grew up in a family with a bent for invention and engineering advancements. His father Howard Hobbs was a pioneer of the automatic transmission, and David's earliest races had been in development cars using the Hobbs Mechamatic transmission. It was David's understanding of the engineering side without the attendant need to usurp Mark as the resident genius driver-engineer that likely endeared him to Mark and the rest of what was always "Mark's team." John Woodard says, "David Hobbs was a class guy—a super guy—one of the nicest people I have known." Hobbs was as hungry as the next driver, but his integrity spoke for itself, and Mark appreciated their relationship. Mark noted Hobbs's "strong, personable image," and summed up the impact David made on the team: "He always did a great job for us . . . I liked him, the mechanics liked him. I think it was because his attitude was so positive. He was always smiling and he always had something good to say about the car—a real pleasant optimist."

For once Daytona was not round one of the FIA Manufacturers Championship—that honor went to the 1000 Kilometer race at Buenos Aires. An accident in the Argentine race claimed the life of Ferrari driver Ignazio Giunti, and influenced Ferrari and Matra to skip Daytona. Jean-Pierre Beltoise had run out of fuel and was pushing his works-entered Matra to the pits when the car veered onto the racing surface. Giunti's 312 PB struck the Matra and he died immediately from his injuries in the fiery collision. The race was won by the Gulf-Porsche 917 driven by Jo Siffert and Derek Bell.

Two weeks before the 24-hour race the team rented the track at Daytona for testing. It was the first time the car had been seen in public, and Kirk White remembers standing next to veteran Associated Press racing correspondent Bloys Britt when the transporter doors opened and the gleaming Sunoco-blue Ferrari emerged. "Britt, who was a giant of a man and had seen everything in racing, was thunderstruck," recalls White. "He told me, 'That is the single most beautiful racing car I have ever seen.' " The car was also startlingly fast. "It was partially lettered up," recalls White. "My name was on the car in white and in Times Roman upper and lower case. I remember standing out at the Horseshoe corner and thinking, 'It's nothing but a white streak.' That's how the 'F.' got in my name on the car. I told Roger I needed the same size lettering as Sunoco, and by making it 'Kirk F. White,' it gave it more length and recognition. If that isn't a towering ego at work, I don't know what is!"

John Wyer's Gulf-Porsche team, which had 917s for Pedro Rodríguez / Jackie Oliver and for Jo Siffert / Derek Bell, was the major factory effort for the 24-hour race. Hans-Dieter Dechent's Martini & Rossi team had 917s for Vic Elford / Gijs van Lennep and Rudy Lins / Helmut Marko. Ferrari was represented by NART with a 512 M for Sam Posey / Peter Revson and a 512 S for Ronnie Bucknum / Tony Adamowicz. There was another 512 M entered by the Young American team and driven by Gregg Young / Masten Gregory.

Mark found a band at Daytona Beach that week that he couldn't get enough of. The two-person Frothing Schloss Fandango Band was playing at the Sheraton Hotel in Ormond Beach, and Mark went every evening he could. Nick Nagurny was covering the race for the *Philadelphia Bulletin* and remembers Mark dragging him and others along to hear the music, saying, "You've got to hear these people, they are amazing." Nagurny remembers the incident as an example of Mark's unorthodox taste and his ability to find pleasure in the unusual.

During practice the quickest car/driver combinations were Mark in the Ferrari and Pedro Rodríguez in the Porsche 917. On Wednesday Pedro turned a 1:45.2, and Mark waited until night practice to top it with a 1:44.4. Qualifying for the top 10 grid positions was limited to Thursday practice. "The fast time was going back and forth between Mark and the two Wyer Porsches with Siffert and Rodríguez," recalls Kirk White.

Mark was initially fastest with a 1:43.7, then Pedro came back with an all-out lap at 1:43.68, but Mark wasn't done. He did laps of 1:42.57 and then a 42.42. "Mark said to Roger, 'You know this engine is redlined at 8,400 rpm and it's really too low; let's give it a push,'" White continues. "They pushed it up to 9,000 on the next run and picked the pole back up, but Rodríguez went back out and went faster still. After that they went to 9,500, recaptured fast time, and again either Siffert or Rodriguez eclipsed it. So they decided to go for it and took it up to a dime, 10,000 rpm." Mark got pole position with a time that was a full nine seconds faster than Mario Andretti's pole time the previous year.

"When the car rolled into the pits after qualifying there was great excitement, and the press and others were running after it," recalls White. "Mark drove straight into the garage, the doors came down and the door was locked. During the session Roger had the windows painted out so no one could see in. There was a great buzz, 'What's happening? What's going on?' And then, with perfect Penske timing, Dan Luginbuhl emerged from a side door and the press descended on him, wanting to know what was going on. 'Oh,' said Dan, 'that was the practice engine; we're just switching over to the race engine.' It was a masterful piece of drama and one-upmanship."

John Wyer was approached by the media for his thoughts on this amazing blue Ferrari. The legendary team manager is said to have replied, "Well, it's a marvelous car, very fast, very well done. But you must remember, there are four of us, and one of them."

Mark took an immediate lead in the race from Rodríguez, and although Pedro passed him on lap 13, Mark was ahead again the next lap and pitted in the lead. The Sunoco Ferrari had been set up with everything needed for a Penske special pit stop, and Mark was away still in the lead. Trouble came on the third pit stop when four and a half minutes were lost, repairing a fuel-pump belt. A few laps later the beautiful blue Ferrari was back for more attention to the fuel pump, and a further eight minutes was lost. Porsche now had a clear lead with the Penske Ferrari third at the four-hour mark.

It was at midnight that near disaster struck. "The right rear tire on the Porsche 917 came off on the banking at more that 200 mph and I had a monster spin," Vic Elford recalls. "When it finally stopped down on the infield grass I got out with the intention of running away, except I had no idea in which direction to run. There were no lights around Daytona in those days, unlike today when it is a bit like a Sunday picnic."

The yellow caution light came on for the accident as Mark was coming up to lap a 911 Porsche. Mark slowed, and in the darkness the 911 swerved into the side of the Ferrari. Mark slid through the grass, coming to rest with the left side suspension and most of the bodywork wrecked. The 911 came down the banking to hit the 917 that Elford had just exited, then flipped end over end. Mark blamed himself for the accident, maintaining that he should have somehow better anticipated the situation. He managed to bring the car into the pit lane for a major rebuild, taking one hour and ten minutes. Team manager Chuck Cantwell and the crew headed by Woody Woodard and supported by Blaine Ferguson did great work to get the now-battered Ferrari back on track. "People speculate about how many rolls of duct tape we used on that car," says Cantwell. Luigi Chinetti heard that the Penske team was missing critical suspension pieces and immediately provided what was needed from the NART parts bin.

Now the leading Porsche was forced into the pits for a lengthy stop to fix the gearbox. During the long stop the NART Bucknum/Adamowicz 512 S continued to circulate despite broken valve springs and eventually made up its lost time. It had a lead over the Porsche of a lap and a half when Pedro left the pits to chase it. Mark and Pedro were again on the track together, and diced furiously until Mark was forced to pit to replace the fuel-pump belt. Pedro caught the NART Ferrari to win the race, with Bucknum/Adamowicz only a lap behind. The Kirk F. White 512 M was third, although 14 laps down.

Back in Newtown Square Mark was putting in incredible hours. This was nothing new. He had always driven himself relentlessly, and as he and Roger took on new projects, the pace increased, forcing Mark to increase his commitment of time and energy commensurately. Pingry friend Jim Haas would frequently drop by the workshop to visit. He knew it was never too late in the evening to catch Mark in the shop. "I remember coming by one night at 11:00 p.m. and there was Mark with the Formula 5000 car on the scales—the weight bag in the seat, setting the suspension himself. He worked on the set-up of that car until well past midnight. That had become typical." On such occasions it was becoming common for Mark to spend the night in the small apartment above the office on Winding Way.

It would be easy to ascribe Mark's long days and nights in the shop to working for Roger Penske, a famous perfectionist who demanded a complete commitment from anyone who worked for him. Certainly Roger's influence added to the existing workload. However, those closest to Mark believe he created his own work environment and schedule. The fact is that Mark and Roger were both "Type-A" personalities— each personally committed to excellence and imbued with a "whatever it takes" work ethic when it came to completing a task to their mutual high standards.

CHAPTER 113:
"Extreme fatigue and undiluted adrenaline . . ."

When the Ferrari's body was rebuilt in preparation for Sebring, Don Cox was able to act on an instinct he'd had the first time he saw it. The day the car arrived at Newtown Square the previous summer, Roger had asked him what he thought it needed. Don's near-immediate response was, "It needs a bigger rear wing." Now he set to designing one, and Lujie Lesovsky built it. On March 6 the team was at Sebring for a pre-race test day.

After Mark tested on Saturday it rained all night, and the track didn't dry enough to go out until 10:00 a.m. When Mark immediately came in to report a large puddle at the end of the long straight, Roger sent the crew out with brooms to disperse the water. David Hobbs also drove the Ferrari and received most of his technical information on the car and its setup from Don Cox. Hobbs was taller than Mark, and like most co-drivers he had to adapt to the lead driver's preferences in chassis setup and seat position. "I don't think the seat had any adjustment," says David. "I was pretty tightly cramped in there and my head was bouncing off the roof. But it was really a nice car and I was able to adapt." Mark spent some time driving the Ferrari behind a camera crew shooting action for a Sunoco promotional film. He also gave Kirk White the ride of a lifetime on the circuit. When Mark gave people a lap in a race car he held little back. For a non-racer the violence of a lap at or even near the limit is an experience never forgotten. White recorded his impression: "My initial reaction was, this guy hates me. He's going to kill me. I'm going to tell Roger the man drives like a lunatic."

After the testing session there was great enthusiasm and confidence for the upcoming race. The race car was expected in Sebring on Wednesday before the March 20 race. Mark was supposed to fly to the race, but the night before they were to leave he had to fire the transporter driver. He decided to solve the manpower shortage by driving the transporter to Florida himself. On Tuesday morning at 2:00 a.m. Mark was at the race shop helping to load when he stepped in a drain grate and severely sprained his left ankle. They got under way at 5:00 a.m., and Mark drove through the day and following night with the throbbing pain in his foot. Then, 100 miles north of Sebring, the engine in the transporter failed. Their arrival was further delayed as arrangements were made for the entire rig to be towed the remaining distance. At the circuit, with news of Mark's injury, Roger Penske had updated his license and taken his physical and was prepared to race the car. When the transporter limped in on Thursday at 2:00 p.m., Mark—sleep-deprived and with a throbbing ankle—went to bed for the balance of the day.

Roger confined his stint in the Ferrari to driving it from tech inspection in downtown Sebring to the track. "Roger jumped into the car and offered me a ride," remembers Kirk White. "He was hot, he was so angry at what had transpired and with Mark showing up with an ankle the size of a football, but he drove the car beautifully, taking it through the gears on the drive out of town. When we pulled into the pits the press was sure Roger and Hobbs were going to race the car."

David Hobbs was quick in Thursday afternoon practice and later the same day in night practice. Mark practiced on Friday morning, and on Friday afternoon he qualified the car on the pole. It was a brave effort. Once again Mark had overcome extreme discomfort to perform brilliantly. Describing the travails of political campaigning in *The New Yorker*, Hendrik Hertzberg once noted, "Extreme fatigue and undiluted adrenaline make a powerful cocktail." He could well have been describing Mark's Sebring experience.

Alongside Mark on the front row was a Ferrari 312 PB for Mario Andretti and Jacky Ickx. The 312 PB had a 3.0-liter, flat-12-cylinder Formula One engine (versus the 5.0-liter V12 of the 512 M) and was the only factory-entered car of the numerous Ferraris in the race. Factory-supported Porsche 917s and Alfa Romeos were expected to provide the greatest competition.

"Ferrari had entered that 312 fairly quietly and intended to come over and dust off all the 512s—and they did except for ours," recalls White. "After qualifying, Mauro Forghieri, who was Ferrari's chief engineer, walked down with a number of people from the Ferrari team and examined our car. Mark went out to visit with him and as they walked around the car, Forghieri said to Mark, 'They'll never let you run that wing at Le Mans.' Mark never skipped a beat. He looked him in the eye and said, 'Well, I wouldn't want to run this wing at Le Mans, would I?'" Forghieri instructed the Ferrari mechanics to observe the workmanship and preparation of the Sunoco car, saying to Mark, "It is the finest-prepared Ferrari I have seen." John Woodard and Kirk White both heard him, and White remembered having a sinking feeling of concern for the great Ferrari engineer, wondering how he would explain the remark if it got back to Maranello.

Mark took an immediate lead at the start and held it until he made his pit stop on lap 20. Bob Lundy, trainer for the Atlanta Falcons football team, was helping out in the medical trailer, and whenever Mark was out of the car Lundy would come to the Penske pit to tape his injured ankle. Lundy, who had first taped the ankle prior to Friday qualifying, said, "It's a very light taping job. That's nowhere near what I would do to a football player. But the problem is that he needs so much flexibility."

The leading cars were now the Porsche 917s, the Penske/White 512 M, and the 312 PB, which enjoyed the advantage of fewer fuel stops. Around the four-hour point, the wheel-to-wheel racing between Mark and Pedro Rodríguez that had enlivened the Daytona race was renewed in a battle for second place behind the leading 312 PB Ferrari of Andretti/Ickx.

"I tried to pass Pedro in this little kink after Webster Turn," said Mark. "I think he was a little surprised that I got underneath him there, then I had to slow down because there was a slower car we were lapping and he turned into me and then again and again. I was straight off the road." The blue Ferrari came out the worse in the incident with a ruptured fuel tank filler pipe. Mark and Pedro each blamed the other and Pedro and Roger had a heated exchange in pit lane, with Pedro calling Mark a "loco gringo." Roger's anger was equal to Pedro's and he lodged a protest against the Porsche driver. John Wyer trumped the protest by sending a message to Race Control that if the protest was upheld, he would withdraw both his cars.

Each driver had a reasonable point of view, as is often the case in a racing incident when two top drivers seek the same piece of road. And both Mark and Pedro shared blame for allowing the situation to happen in an endurance race with more than seven hours still to run. Mark precipitated the problem when he went inside Pedro on the entrance to a high-speed right-hand kink. The move, in itself, was not outrageous, although Mark admitted he could just as easily have made the pass on the straightaway. When Mark lifted slightly for the slower car they were lapping, Pedro hit the Ferrari's outside rear tire, and then turned into and bumped the Ferrari twice more.

As Mark told Gary Long of the *Miami Herald*, "I had just passed the No. 2 Porsche on the inside. Then he rammed me from behind not once, not twice, but three times." The last two hits did the damage, and on the way back to the pits the wrecked tire flailing on the rim tore the filler pipe apart. Few race drivers will acknowledge blame for an accident if the issue is in doubt. While Mark, in hindsight, admitted he should not have forced the issue at that point in the race, Pedro clearly should have resisted the urge to retaliate. Each man made an error in judgment that affected their chance to win the race.

It is also a fact that, in general, Mark had little good to say about Pedro. His reasons are unknown, but it may have been nothing more than what David Hobbs calls, "A clash between Mark's Irish temperament and the equally fiery Mexican." Pedro, a star on the international circuit since the age of 16, possessed an urbane and sophisticated style that clashed with Mark's down-to-earth personal aesthetic.

Damage to the Porsche was slight, and the car was soon back in the race. The Ferrari was severely damaged, and the crew's first instinct was to call it a day. Roger and Mark wanted to try to fix it, and the Penske crew worked hard and long to get the Ferrari back on the track. When it returned after 50 minutes and the loss of 20 laps, it was the fastest car on the track. Mark and David drove flat out and brought the car home sixth. Ahead of them were three Porsche 917s, including the winning car of Vic Elford / Gerard Larrousse, and two Alfa Romeo T33s which finished second and third.

At the victory breakfast the next day, Mark's great drive was recognized when he received the trophy for the "Old Forester Driver of the Race." Sebring was important to Mark, as it was the first important race he had ever run when he raced the TVR there in 1962. "It was almost like Indianapolis to me," Mark said. "As a road racer it was one I really wanted to win."

Mark still had a duty to perform. Sunoco had asked him to shoot a commercial at a new service station in Orlando, Florida, and were anxious that the car used by Mark in the spot be his actual family car. Sue and Mark had a Chevrolet station wagon—the family garage also included Sue's dune buggy, a Javelin, and a black Chevrolet sedan with red pinstriping—but neither had the time to drive it to Florida. Mark asked George Alderman, who wasn't racing in the 12 Hours that year, to do it as a favor. George and his wife Marilyn, along with four-year-old Paul and two-year-old Laura, drove the car to Florida and met Mark and the Sunoco people for the shoot.

Two days after Sebring, on March 22, Penske Racing took the fully restored blue Ferrari to Daytona to make a quiet attempt at breaking the closed-course speed record. John Oliveau, executive director of the Automobile Competition Committee for the United States (ACCUS) was scheduled to be present to set up the official timing devices that would verify the speed. The current record, set at Talladega Speedway, had been set by Bobby Isaac in a modified NASCAR Dodge at over 201 mph. The day before the record run attempt, the tragic news came to Oliveau that his son and two grandchildren had died in a fire. He left immediately for New York.

Although the Monday run at Daytona could now not be verified as an official record, the team still made the attempt. Using the same engine that had run the 12 Hours at Sebring just two days previous, Mark lapped the Ferrari at over 199 mph. It fell just short of Isaac's speed on the steeper banking of Talladega, but eclipsed the Daytona Speedway record of 194.015, set by Cale Yarborough in qualifying for that year's 500. Mark told Bob Smith for the Tampa *Tribune*, "We ran 199.5 miles per hour at the first try but to get higher we would have had to jack things around quite a bit and with no official clocks to record a record there wasn't much use in it so we gave up." Mark believed an average speed of 210 mph was possible in the car.

CHAPTER 114:

Respect and Appreciation

On March 27–28 Mark faced the challenge of a double race weekend with the Lola-Ford Indy car at Phoenix and the Formula 5000 Lola at Ontario. To pull it off Mark, joined Mario Andretti, who was doing the same two races, flying back and forth from Arizona to southern California.

The Questor Grand Prix at Ontario Motor Speedway was a one-time event designed to showcase the facility as a venue for the United States Grand Prix for Formula One. After failing to obtain the Grand Prix in the track's second year of existence, the organizers posted a purse of $278,400 and invited selected Formula One teams and drivers to compete against American Formula 5000 cars (the SCCA had now adopted the international class name for its Formula A class). The race was billed as a shoot-out between the European drivers and their technology versus the American version of single-seat road racers. While it took a great deal of innocence to believe that the comparatively unsophisticated F-5000 cars could compete with a Formula One car, the race had its own appeal as pure spectacle. Although the displacement for a Formula One engine was limited to three liters, these were pure race motors compared to the heavier, stock-block based 5-liter units in the F-5000 cars.

Whether it was innocence or pure enthusiasm, Mark Donohue was ready to have a run at winning, saying, "I didn't come here to lose." Mark's early view on the competitive comparison between the two types of cars was that while the Formula One cars would be faster through the road section of the 3.194-mile combined road and oval circuit, the power of the 5.0-liter engines would even things out on the straightaway. The white Lola T192 was now painted Sunoco Penske blue and given the ultimate in "show" finish. "We 'Penske-ized' it with Molin paintwork and chrome and the latest Traco engine," remembers John Woodard. Woody trucked the car to southern California and waited while Mark crisscrossed between the two races.

In Phoenix, Karl Kainhofer had the Lola-Ford—the team wasn't ready to show their hand with the McLaren M16— ready for the Jimmy Bryan 150. It was the first race for Mark on a 1.0-mile oval. He qualified ninth on Friday for the Saturday race before hitching a ride with Mario Andretti on the STP jet to practice for the Questor GP. Back at Phoenix on Saturday morning, Mark ran an uneventful race to finish sixth, a lap down to winner Al Unser, who fought a race-long duel with his brother Bobby. Swede Savage was third. Immediately after the race Mark and Mario were on a helicopter to the Phoenix airport, and the STP de Havilland jet again delivered them to Ontario Motor Speedway.

At Ontario Mark was impressive, qualifying seventh—by far the fastest of the Formula A cars. The Questor company— a corporate giant with subsidiary companies encompassing products from sporting goods to children's toys and furniture—spent a great deal of money air-freighting most of the Formula One "circus" from Europe and paying the necessary starting money and inducements to obtain the marquee names. This included finding rides for A. J. Foyt, Al Unser, and Bobby Unser. Unfortunately these American stars were not positioned to shine. They were driving unfamiliar and uncompetitive cars on a circuit they'd had no time on. But their presence was essential, since this race was all about hype and the pretense of a showdown. By race time Mark had reevaluated his earlier optimism on the relative merits of the two types of cars. "What the hell do they expect?" Mark asked Brock Yates. "This thing cost $20,000. The Europeans are driving around in cars that cost $120,000 and we're supposed to keep up?"

Mark was still ready to try. The race was run in two 100-mile heats. Charging through the field, Mark was in a strong third place until the last lap, when he appeared to run out of gas and headed for the pits. His third place became ninth. Jackie Stewart in the Tyrrell-Ford had passed the Ferrari of Jacky Ickx to take an early lead, but Mario Andretti in a Ferrari came up from a spot well back in the middle of the grid to catch and pass Jackie to win at the line. It was great theater and played well before an excellent crowd. The problem with a massive stadium like Ontario was that even 60,000 people—a fine crowd—looks small among 144,000 seats.

The second heat featured more brilliance from Mark, who again moved into third place, ahead of all the Formula One drivers except Stewart and Andretti. But once again the Chevy engine in the Lola faltered with no fuel pressure. Mark was out of the race. "I don't think we were embarrassed out there today, but it doesn't do much good if you don't finish the race," Mark told the *Los Angeles Times*'s Pat Ray. It was later discovered that he hadn't run out of gas at all. Scale from the chromed rollbar had broken off and clogged the fuel-tank vent. Mark realized that if they had skipped the chrome the result would have been very different. His comment on the failure is a thoughtful reflection on the racing life. "The interactions on a race car are so complex that you never know where your mistakes are going to come back and haunt you."

The day was marred by a terrible crash suffered by Swede Savage in the first heat. He went off the road in a 100-mph bend when his throttle-return spring broke, and in the violent crash his head hit the concrete wall. His convalescence would be long and difficult. Savage was an attractive and promising new face on the American racing scene; fans and those within the industry were pulling for his full recovery. He grew up in the San Bernardino area where he was a high school football star. He got his racing start in quarter midgets at age 10, and moved on to go-karts and then motorcycles, where he won 40 professional races. John Holman had given him a chance to drive in NASCAR in 1967 and he had performed brilliantly. His big break came when Dan Gurney took him under his wing at AAR.

Despite the disappointment of not finishing, the race brought Mark Donohue great respect and appreciation for his exceptional talent. This was particularly true among the international set and foreign journalists who had known him only as a name in the results from America, or in international endurance races. Single-seat racing at the top level was considered the only measure of great talent, and Mark's drive at Questor could not be denied. In one of his greatest performances Mark had made Formula 5000 a great deal more glamorous and appealing than it had ever been.

The private dining rooms and sumptuous penthouse suites joined with the sophistication of the international set of Grand Prix drivers to make OMS glitter. And even those most convinced that the venture would fail wished that it would succeed because American racing glittered along with it.

On Friday, April 2, Mark was back in the Lola-Ford Indy car for testing at Trenton Speedway in preparation for the USAC race later in the month. The Lola appeared there without numbers or stickers. Mark was candid in his assessment of the learning curve for driving the tight ovals. He told Bill Simmons of the Philadelphia *Inquirer*, "I ran as hard as I could at Phoenix and still came in sixth. There's no doubt in my mind that the car was as quick as any out there. The problem was that I wasn't." Mark went on to explain the difference in style between road and oval racing. "Boy, did those guys show me a thing or two," he told Simmons. "It's as different as night and day. In road racing we pass on the inside of turns. On the shorter ovals in championship racing you pass on the outside, coming off the turns." On the same day Mark told New Brunswick, New Jersey, *Home News* reporter Ed Albin, "I don't expect much in the early races with this Lola-Ford car. Phoenix and Trenton will be a prelude for us before the Indianapolis race. I definitely want to run a Ford at Trenton as I feel I can get around the turns easier and I can run faster in the straightaway." Left unspoken was Mark's growing confidence that at Indy the Offenhauser-powered McLaren M16 would be a sensation.

"We should be thinking more of a safer driver than a safer car," was Mark's message to the Detroit Sports Broadcasters Association. Mark Donohue was never a man afraid to express an unpopular view if he believed in it. On Wednesday, April 7, Mark was the featured speaker at the Association's luncheon meeting where he aired controversial views regarding safe driving and vehicle safety. Mark had a consistent message on the subject, and told the Detroit group that the government should concentrate on training motorists to be better drivers rather than mandating auto companies to develop expensive

safety features. Air bags were the issue of the day, and Mark branded them "ridiculous." His view was that drivers did not use anywhere near the evasive ability already built into cars. What was needed, he maintained, was dramatically improved driver training. Mark warned that continued government interference at the wrong end of the problem would only result in more expensive cars and would hurt the consumer. When asked about the safety of the innocent occupants of a car struck by an incompetent driver, UPI reported his response: "There are some dangers we are unable to avoid. It's a free country, and we have the choice of driving or not driving on the highways."

CHAPTER 115:

"Superman has descended"

Before Opening Day at Indy, Mark raced the Lola-Ford in the Trentonian 200 on April 25. Trenton, New Jersey, was just a 45-minute drive from the Donohue home in Media, Pennsylvania. Sue and Mark loaded Michael and David in the big black Chevrolet and went to the race together. On a cold and blustery day at the 1.5-mile oval, Mark qualified seventh in the 26-car field. During the early race action he dueled with eventual race winner Mike Mosley for fourth place until suddenly raising his hand and moving to the top of the track to give the racing line to his competitors. The clutch had failed on lap 33 of the 134-lap event. Mosley won ahead of Wally Dallenbach and Lee Roy Yarbrough, second and third.

At Indianapolis, Mark and the McLaren M16 became the topics on everyone's mind from the first day. Motorsports writer Ray Marquette said, "Superman has descended on Indianapolis Motor Speedway in a dark blue cape with a big 66 stenciled on it."

Penske Racing was for the first time running two cars in the month of May at Indianapolis, with David Hobbs driving the Lola. On Opening Day, May 1, Mark was immediately on the track in the Lola-Ford. When he switched to the McLaren, Hobbs took over the Lola and was the first rookie on the track. Karl Kainhofer was the overall crew chief, and he had an excellent team working with him. The Offenhauser engine specialist on loan from Traco was George Howell—known by all in the pits and garages as Davy Crockett. Although the origin of the appellation has been obscured by time, veterans of the period recall Howell's rough-and-ready appearance and persona. John Woodard had moved from Trans-Am to the single-seat cars, and Lujie Lesovsky was again a part of the team. Despite his understated style, Lujie was already a legend. He had come out of the California racing environment of the 1940s and '50s and was responsible for Lee Wallard's 1951 Indy 500–winning "Belanger 99." Lesovsky liked being part of the Penske operation, and told *Sports Illustrated*'s Robert F. Jones, "This is the most businesslike operation I've ever been involved with. Roger is an excellent administrator . . . Mark is the catalyst. He's a driver and an engineer. . . ." Lesovsky compared Mark to legendary three-time Indy 500 winner Rex Mays, and said of Mark, "You'd do anything for him."

With time in both the Lola-Ford and the McLaren-Offy, Mark had a good sense of the characteristics of each engine. He told Clare Wise, senior editor of *Machine Design*, that at speed there wasn't much to choose between the two. It was in low end performance that the Offenhauser excelled. According to Mark, the Ford was a bit slower exiting the pits. "It floods and it's very easy to stall. You have to learn how to handle it." When cold the Offenhauser had a distinctive characteristic. "It vibrates something terrible when you're warming it up," Mark told Wise. "Half the brackets will fall off the car if they're not mounted right. It's incredible . . . It gives you a massage if you're in the car. After it warms up, though, it's reasonably smooth."

On May 3 Mark separated himself from the pack. His speed of 174.757 was a record that shook the establishment—and earned a reprimand from Harlan Fengler for exceeding the speed limit imposed by the Speedway for the first few days of the month. Two days later Mark impressed one and all by running 18 laps faster than 172.5, with a best of 174.622. Before leaving for the weekend to race the Javelin at Lime Rock, he further emphasized his advantage with a startling lap of 177.901.

An unknown wire service reporter sought the reaction of the competition. Johnny Rutherford was candid: "We have upped our goal a little, I guess." When asked why the Penske McLaren was so fast, Art Pollard was willing to give Mark credit as a driver, saying, "He's a real fine race driver, first of all." When asked the same question, Mark responded with a smile, saying, "If you had a million dollars stashed away in a cave someplace, I don't think you'd tell me where it is. I don't want to tell you either."

McLaren designer Gordon Coppuck has a straightforward answer to why Mark had such a dramatic advantage over even the cars from the McLaren factory team. "I think it is fair to say that Mark and Don Cox got to an optimum set-up very quickly and that we, along with our drivers, simply took longer to get there."

"I learned early on that Mark never told lies," says Bobby Unser. "He was always a straight shooter and would not deceive you. He wouldn't offer help at times, but that shouldn't be anyway, but if you asked him a direct question he would tell you the truth. That was very rare for race drivers, myself included. Maybe he wouldn't answer a question—but he never would lie to you. Most often he would tell you even to his own detriment."

"He was a super guy," says Johnny Rutherford. "If you had any problems with your car and talked to him about it, he would get a concerned look on his face, as only Mark could, and he would think about it seriously and give you what he thought about it and several ideas to try."

"Mark also had a hell of a sense of humor," continues Rutherford. "I can remember one time I had just bought a really supple leather jacket from Neiman Marcus here in Fort Worth and wore it at Daytona on one of those cool evenings. We went to a little restaurant where there were other drivers, including Mark. When Mark saw me he slapped me on the back and we talked for several minutes. When I got back to the hotel that night I took my jacket off and discovered that Mark had slapped a Penske Racing sticker right on the back of the jacket. I peeled it off and it took the surface leather off and left a mark exactly where the Penske sticker had been. It was typical of the type of tricks and sense of humor among drivers back then."

The comparison between the defending champion Al Unser and his Vel's Parnelli team with the Penske team and Mark was striking. It was a head-to-head matchup on several fronts: the Penske Offenhauser versus Ford in the engine compartment; the Penske McLaren chassis versus the revamped Lola chassis used by the Johnny Lightning car; team managers Roger Penske versus longtime Trans-Am adversary Parnelli Jones; Penske Goodyear tires versus Firestone; and Penske crew chief Karl Kainhofer versus equally legendary George Bignotti. Despite the great rivalry there was mutual respect, particularly between the two drivers. "We're just trying to catch him," said Al Unser. "They've just got a good-engineered car, that's about all I can say."

Mark recalled: "Al Unser came into our garage one day, and said, 'We're on different teams and we compete against each other, but I just want to say that anybody that can run that fast—I don't care what the car is—I've got to tip my hat to you.' That meant a great deal to me that Al would say that, and it showed his sportsmanship."

"There are just not enough words to say how much I respected Mark Donohue," Al Unser says today. "He had a natural talent as a driver and he was a good person—a real gentleman. He knew what to do to make a car work, and he could get it around the track very fast, so as a race-car driver he was the whole package."

CHAPTER 116:
New Look Trans-Am

When the 1971 Trans-Am series opened at Lime Rock on May 8, it had a different look. Penske was the only team with serious factory backing. The loss of manufacturer support to the series was causing race promoters to panic. A Trans-Am date had previously been much sought after by road-racing tracks. Now the series was contracting, and Laguna Seca was one of the first circuits to announce it would not host a race in 1971. The SCCA did persuade the tracks to increase minimum prize money from $25,000 to $30,000.

Bud Moore Racing continued with the Mustangs even though Ford had drastically cut all racing budgets. Moore's operation was backed by Ford dealers in Connecticut and New York for the Lime Rock race only, and they also paid Parnelli's driver fee. The Penske strategy was to put all of its effort into a single Sunoco Javelin. Mark had talked to Roger over the winter and argued, "If we concentrate on just one car we can win this series." Earle Macmullan was promoted to crew chief, with John Woodard moving on to take responsibility for the Ferrari 512 M and also joining the Indy car team.

The Sunoco Javelin had some changed bodywork in the front end of the car along with suspension improvements. The Penske Javelins from 1970 had been sold to Roy Woods, who painted them yellow and entered the cars for his ARA team for Peter Revson and Tony Adamowicz. Revson was standing in for this race for Woods, who had been injured two weeks earlier in the opening round of the Continental

5000 series at Riverside. Traco was building engines for both the Penske team and Woods's operation. The Trans-Am's new dry-sump rule was welcomed by all.

The front row at Lime Rock had a familiar look with Parnelli and Mark, but this time it was Mark on pole position. The Javelins of Revson and Adamowicz were on row two. Mark ran side by side with Parnelli through turns one and two and emerged in the lead. It was a day of heavy rain and Mark, in his element, drove away from the 30-car field, winning by five laps from second-place Tony DeLorenzo in a Mustang. Parnelli was off the road early and thought one of the yellow Javelins had pushed him. Mark said he drove a conservative race—"I had to concentrate on not putting myself in a vulnerable position," he told Jack Warren for *Competition Press*—but emphasized how important the victory was in vindicating the decision to concentrate on one car.

The race's most dramatic drive came from Bob Tullius in a 1964 Pontiac Tempest GTO. Tullius started dead last after not recording a qualifying lap, and created a great deal of excitement by coming all the way through the 31-car field to second place before retiring with overheating just 10 laps from the end. "Art Peck of CBS was the track announcer," remembers Tullius. "Later he said, 'Bob, I didn't even know you were in the race until I announced you were fifth and moving up.'" The car was developed by a group of Pontiac engineers who took the project on as a personal challenge. Though low-key, their effort had been a very professional one. In fact, the Pontiac had not even started life as a GTO. Until pressed into service as a race car, it had been a garden-variety Tempest, the personal daily driver of project head Herb Adams's wife.

CHAPTER 117:
Dominance Unrewarded

The Indianapolis 500 was an incredible publicity machine. Just being in the race could make you famous, and once you were perceived as a top driver, you were guaranteed celebrity from coast to coast. Boys in the sophomore class at Richmond High in Richmond, Indiana, were talking excitedly about prospects for the 500 when one remarked that this guy Mark Donohue was sure a sensation. Paul Powell couldn't resist replying, "Mark is a friend of mine." This brought hoots of derision and complete disbelief at the likelihood of any one of them actually knowing one of the "gods" of the Speedway. When Paul defended his position, the boys decided they would all skip school and go to the Speedway to prove the lie.

The Richmond High boys did take off from school to go to the Speedway for a practice day during the week before qualifying. Standing behind the fence as the drivers walked by on the way to the garages, Paul called out, "Mark, I'm over here!" Mark immediately recognized him and walked over to talk. Paul introduced him to each of his awestruck companions. Mark was friendly and greeted each in turn. Then he said, "Paul, why are you here? Why aren't you in school?" Paul had to admit that he'd ditched school to come to the track. Mark said that he wanted to meet them all in the Speedway cafeteria in half an hour.

At the cafeteria he spoke warmly but firmly to all the boys. School was far more important than anything that could be going on at the Speedway—they needed to focus on getting the best education. Then he turned to Paul and said, "I want you to tell your father you skipped school. I am calling him tonight to make sure you do." Paul did confess his truancy to his dad that evening, and it wasn't many minutes later that the phone rang with Mark's call. His school friends were fairly unimpressed by the experience, but for Paul it was a lesson of a lifetime.

Paul had known Mark since he was 12 years old. His parents, Enola and John Powell, were active in SCCA, and John had introduced his son to Mark at a Mid-Ohio Trans-Am race in 1969. Mark and young Paul had a lively conversation that day, and when they got to the next race at Elkhart Lake, Paul could hardly contain his excitement at the prospect of picking up where they had left off. John Powell felt he had to forestall a likely disappointment for his son, and explained that Mark met many people and probably wouldn't remember Paul when he saw him. More than slightly chastened, Paul did not approach Mark as he had planned. But later in the day he turned a corner in the paddock to encounter Mark coming in the opposite direction. "Paul," exclaimed Mark. "Where have you been? I've wanted to talk to you."

During the weekend, while Mark had been away at Lime Rock, Al Unser in the Johnny Lightning Special and Bobby Unser in the Olsonite Eagle-Offy had upped their speeds into the 174-mph range. On Monday, May 10, Mark's first day back, he waited until minutes before the track closed at 6:00 p.m. to turn a 177.340. Almost every day Mark would turn the fastest time, and he and David Hobbs literally dined out on the accomplishment. "There was a little restaurant/café in a strip mall on 16th street that was offering dinner for the fastest man of the day and a guest," recalls David. "So, basically, Mark and I ate every day down there for nothing. It was fantastic!"

According to a feature article by Robert F. Jones in *Sports Illustrated*, a sign above the telephone in the Penske garage in Gasoline Alley read "Those of you who think you know it all are particularly annoying to those of us who do." Dan Luginbuhl remembers Jones as a brilliant writer who found unique perspectives on a story. Jones spent a great deal of time with the team, as well as visiting Mark and Sue's home in Media. As the quote on the wall suggested, his story emphasized the "Prussian efficiency" of the team, and the technical and serious bent of Mark. Roger is described as having ". . . not a hair out of place on his charcoal graying head, not the least fleck of lint on his Sunoco-blue cashmere sweater, nor a wrinkle in the creases of his Sunoco-yellow slacks." And David Hobbs told Jones that Roger reminded him a little of John Wyer, who was ". . . also a master of meticulous preparation. . . . Roger rules with an iron rod but it's not really a rule of fear—rather a rule of tension."

Jones made the following comparison between Mark and Roger: "Penske is pure, uncut, 100-proof methyl enthusiasm all the time. Donohue suffers moments of doubt, though he rarely mentions them out loud."

Jones's story contributed greatly to the popular perception of Mark Donohue as the engineer who also raced. While an insightful profile, the story belied the fact that Mark was much more a driving talent than he ever was a race engineer. He did understand the race engineering principles and applied them better than most race drivers—but his success came more from his driving skill than what he did to help prepare the cars.

In the *SI* article Mark provides insight on race-car design and aerodynamics as they were understood at the time. "The wing is only a partial solution to the road holding problem. If you ran a ground effects vehicle—a vacuum cleaner job like Jim Hall's new Chaparral—at Indy, you'd never have to take your foot off the throttle. You could go around the course flat out. Lap speeds would be 195 mph or so." When asked by another reporter what the maximum possible speed was at Indy, Mark replied, "There's no maximum on speed. It just depends on technology."

Leading up to the first weekend of qualifying, Mark's advantage was further emphasized on Wednesday when he was timed officially at 179.6 mph; unofficially the Penske crew caught a lap at 181.090. The next day Mark made it official as the first man to lap the Speedway at more than 180 mph—officially, 180.977. There were 45 cars on the track during the day, and the second fastest was Peter Revson in the team McLaren at 177.100.

Mark would phone home every evening to talk to his sons and share news from the Speedway. Michael was now just a month shy of seven and David was four. Sue told Donna Snodgrass of the *Indianapolis Star*, "They ask for his speeds for the day and are excited about it, and all, and they're very proud of him, of course, but I try not to let them know if he is on television or making big headlines." Sue was trying to maintain a family equilibrium amid Mark's superstar status. She was sometimes reluctant to bring the boys to the track, fearing they could become spoiled by people who wanted to please Mark.

After the virtually unprecedented dominance by Mark and the Penske Sunoco McLaren during practice, qualifying was an enormous letdown. Qualifying opened at 11:00 a.m., with Mark fifth in line and next to go out after A. J. Foyt. A. J. captured provisional pole at 174.317—3 mph faster than the existing qualifying record. At 11:38 a.m. Mark responded by adding almost 3 mph more to the record, with an average of 177.087 for his four laps. Impressive as the speed was, it was an anticlimax to Mark and the crowd, who both had expected more. The very hot conditions had created oversteer, and each lap was progressively slower: 178.607, 177.130, 176.540, and 176.091. A disappointed Mark told John Radosta of *The New York Times*, "I hope the speed is good enough for the pole, but if it is not, we will take our lumps like anyone else."

It wasn't. More than an hour later, Peter Revson was on the track. David Hobbs remembers the atmosphere around Mark and the Penske team: "The garage was full of people and press—he was being slapped on the back 'Congratulations, first pole at Indy, etc.' At the height of the celebration, as Mark was crediting the team effort and hard work, came the distinctive voice of Tom Carnegie over the loudspeakers. 'Annnnd—a neeewww pole record, Peter Revson at 178.696.' Mark's face went white. He was absolutely stunned and mortified."

Johnny Rutherford also remembers that it was a difficult moment for Mark. "It was heartbreaking to see," he says "His face wilted like a balloon with a slow leak."

Peter still couldn't let go the resentment from his Rookie of the Year disappointment two years earlier, telling United Press International, "You might say winning the pole from Mark was sweet revenge." Mark took the high road. Although he admitted his disappointment at losing the pole, after his run he had walked down pit lane to talk to Revson and Teddy Mayer and share setup tips based on his experience in the hot conditions. Those tips gave the factory team the chance to finally catch up.

"Everything had gone so fantastically all month only to have it snatched away from us by a guy who had badmouthed us so much," Mark said later. "Nobody could speak. I didn't know what to say to the guys and they didn't know what to say to me. Finally Roger got everyone together and said, 'Look, what's done is done. Let's go get some sleep and come back here fresh and concentrate on winning this race.'"

Bobby Unser has a different perspective on the qualifying issue. "The thing is, that I don't think Mark was a great qualifier, because qualifying wasn't what was important to him," says Bobby. "I was a fast qualifier and enjoyed that status, but I couldn't sustain that speed in the race. Mark, what he turned in qualifying I knew he could run in the race. Whatever Mark did, that's what you saw all the time. You don't see that in many other drivers. He was a hell of a lot better driver than he ever got credit for being. Don't look for him to slow down because he wasn't going to do it."

Although Mark was seldom interested or involved in the political world, he did lend his name to a group seeking attention for the plight of POWs and MIAs. On May 22 America's Sports Stars for POWs-MIAs announced its formation to bring help "to U.S. citizens who are either being held captive in Indochina or are missing in action." Mark joined his name with Joe DiMaggio, Althea Gibson, Joe Louis, Jesse Owens, Arnold Palmer, Ted Williams, Arthur Ashe, Peggy Fleming, Joe Frazier, Billy Kidd, Bobby Orr, Bill Muncey, John Petraglia, Richard Petty, Brooks Robinson, Don Schollander, Willie Shoemaker, Bill Toomey, Johnny Unitas, and Jerry West. The organization was nonpolitical and its members were not criticizing the U.S. administration. They just wanted to lend their names to put pressure on Hanoi to discuss the welfare and repatriation of prisoners.

Sue spent the last week of May at the Speedway and wore a pink knit pantsuit on race day. She was comfortable in the company of the other USAC wives. When Donna Snodgrass asked her if the fast speeds Mark was recording concerned her, Sue replied, "I know Mark wouldn't be going that fast unless he felt comfortable in the car." Commenting further on Mark's commitment to racing, she added, "He's done very well and it makes him happy. He spends virtually all his time with the cars."

Despite the upset in missing pole position, Mark was widely touted to win the race. On the second weekend of qualifying he turned a practice lap at 179.354. The Union 76 Racing Panel of Experts gave Mark 30 votes as the driver favored to win. A. J. Foyt received 21, Al Unser 10, and pole sitter Revson just one.

Race day was on Saturday, May 29, the first time since 1915 that the traditional Memorial Day race had not been held on May 30 or 31. Congress had changed the holiday observance from May 30 to the last Monday of May. The race organizers had decided to run the 500 on the first day of the holiday weekend to allow rain dates for Sunday and Monday. It was also the debut for the Speedway's new Victory Lane, which had been built near the tower. Another first was same-day television coverage provided by ABC TV.

Mark was in the middle of the front row with Revson to his left on pole position and Bobby Unser in the Eagle to his right. The pace car was a Dodge Challenger, and local Dodge dealer Eldon Palmer—with astronaut John Glenn, ABC sportscaster Chris Schenkel, and track owner Tony Hulman as passengers—had the honor of leading the 33 cars on their pace laps. As Palmer peeled off into the pit lane the field waited for the green flag. Just about the time the start flag fell, Palmer realized he was carrying far too much speed down pit lane. As the race cars charged into turn one, the Challenger—brakes now locked—crashed into the photographers' stand at the exit of the pits. Twenty-nine people were injured, two seriously. A sprained ankle for Hulman was the only injury in the Challenger.

Mark and Bobby Unser made a great start. Revson later said, "I was first across the starting line all right, but those two were right behind me going 20 mph faster. They beat me fair and square and I just got snookered." Mark immediately took the lead and completed lap one at a record first-lap speed of 169.651. Mark controlled the race and led every lap—he lapped Peter on lap 45—until he pitted for fuel on lap 51. The stop consumed 29 seconds, and the Sunoco McLaren regained the lead when Bobby Unser made his pit stop on lap 65. On the next lap Mark set the race speed record with

a lap of 174.961. "But I was worried it was going too easy," Mark later wrote in *The Boys of Indy.* "I was right." On lap 67 Mark slowed on the backstretch, and while exiting turn three, pulled the McLaren off the track—neatly controlling a slide through the grass. He parked along the inside wall of turn four at the head of the main stretch. The gears had broken in the transmission.

Unlike current practice, when every opportunity is embraced to use a full-course caution flag and bring out the pace car to bunch up the field, the disabled car sat there as the race roared on. Steve Krisiloff's car was already there after being parked with a blown engine on lap 10. He had spun in his own oil and set up an accident that eliminated Mario Andretti and Gordon Johncock. Ten laps after Mark stopped, Bentley Warren also suffered a broken transmission, and he too parked along the fence close to the Sunoco McLaren.

On lap 113 the gears in the Penske Lola-Ford driven by David Hobbs broke on the front straight. David picks up the story: "I had just been in the pits and taken on a full fuel load, so with almost 500 extra pounds on board, I was running slower. Rick Muther was right close behind me, and when I came out of turn four there was this god-awful clattering behind me. The Lola slowed dramatically and I shut it off. Now I'm freewheeling up by the wall where I had come off the corner. I look in my mirror and wonder where has Rick gone? He had swerved left to avoid running up my back and hit the wall on the left side—just before the pit entrance."

When Muther came off the wall he hit the Penske Lola and his car turned upside down before landing on its wheels. Neither driver was injured but it was a near thing. "My car spun down the road and I was completely doused in oil from the oil tank being ripped open," Hobbs remembers. "When the car stopped I stood up in the seat, as I knew it was full of 75 gallons of fuel and I was ready to get off. I had to lift the visor—it was covered in oil—to see, and I jumped out and ran for the pit wall—it's hard to judge how fast cars are coming when they're at 175 mph or thereabouts. I just made it—A. J. Foyt missed my back foot by inches as I leaped up on the wall." It was an unfortunate result for David who was blameless in the accident. He had been on his way to a finish likely good enough to be named Rookie of the Year.

The reason for the gears breaking in both cars was a mystery. David Hobbs points out that he had run more than 2,000 miles at Indy during the month without trouble. John Woodard adds that the gears had never been tested for continuous running at the distance involved in the race. Testing each day was done in shorter segments. Karl Kainhofer, who was responsible for the transmissions on both cars, recalls that the material in the gears supplied for use on race day was inferior. This is confirmed by McLaren designer Gordon Coppuck, who remembers that some of the gears supplied by Hewland were indeed made from the wrong-grade steel. "We were horrified to find that some of the gears supplied by Hewland were made from mild steel instead of the proper En36 steel. It would run for a while but didn't have the underlying strength. As a consequence of the experience we changed to an aircraft specification, S82, and had our own forgings done."

With both team cars now out of the race, Karl Kainhofer and John Woodard walked down to turn four to look at the M16 parked alongside the fence. Karl returned to the garage, but Woody was there to witness Mike Mosley hit the turn-four wall and then spin to the inside of the track, barely missing Peter Revson as he did. Mosley crashed violently into the parked Penske McLaren after first hitting the Warren and Steve Krisiloff cars. The Sunoco McLaren bounced high in the air and incurred massive damage. Bobby Unser was also caught up in the accident and hit the wall in the Olsonite Eagle. Gary Bettenhausen stopped his race car to assist, and Mosley suffered serious burns, along with a broken leg and broken elbow.

Al Unser became a back-to-back winner of the 500, and Peter Revson—despite never leading a lap—drove a steady race to capture second place. Although Teddy Mayer and Roger Penske were out on the pit wall urging him to close the gap, Peter was unable to respond from pure exhaustion. For the last 100 miles he was holding his head up on the straights with one hand. Total prize money earned by Mark for officially finishing 25th was $26,697.24.

Despite all the travails and ultimate disappointment of the race, few drivers had ever dominated a month at Indy as did Mark in 1971. Race winner Al Unser remembers: "If Mark Donohue had finished the race I would have never beat him," says Al. "He was gone. He had the car, he had the team, and he had the ability."

Karl Kainhofer was one of the biggest reasons for the team's success. His contribution was acknowledged when he was honored with the respected Mechanical Achievement Award presented by D-A Lubricant Company and membership in the Mechanics Hall of Fame. Karl was always the epitome of

calm, even in the tensest situations. He expressed his state of mind to an unnamed reporter this way: "You actually live with the race car. I may look like I'm relaxin', but I think of the car every minute. Even when you're completely ready, you're thinking, listening and worrying about it." It was Karl who now helped bring confidence to the team. He flatly told Mark and Roger that he and the crew would fix the seriously damaged McLaren, and they would win the next race.

John Woodard recalls the importance of Roger's leadership at the time: "Roger was at his greatest. 'We'll get another tub' was his upbeat attitude. We had to work hard, but Roger didn't get down; he pumped everyone up in those situations. He was always focused on going forward."

CHAPTER 118:
Sobering Moment

After the 500 on Saturday, Mark and Roger were on the jet to New Hampshire for Sunday qualifying for the second round of the Trans-Am at Bryar Motorsports Park. Mark in the red, white, and blue Sunoco Javelin, George Follmer in the orange Bud Moore Mustang, and Tony Adamowicz in the yellow Roy Woods Javelin were all officially credited with identical times of 1:12.0 on handheld stopwatches that recorded only to the nearest tenth of a second. The problem of which two cars would occupy the front row for the start was resolved by chief steward Charlie Rainville, who had the drivers draw straws. Mark got the short straw and started on row two. After the drawing Mark calmly said that it was a fair process that he could agree to. Tony Adamowicz remembers the incident as an example of Mark's characteristic graciousness. In this instance, Mark's good nature was helped by his knowledge that Penske team timer Judy Stropus had recorded the laps to a finer resolution than had the officials, and indeed, both Tony and George had been faster. With qualifying over Mark and Roger headed back to Indianapolis for the Sunday evening victory dinner. They left Indianapolis at 5:00 a.m. on Monday morning for the return to Bryar and the Memorial Day Trans-Am.

When Charlie Rainville steered the Maserati pace car down pit lane, the 33 Trans-Am sedans made an impressive sight as they thundered into the first corner. Mark passed Adamowicz's yellow Javelin on lap five, and in pursuit of

Follmer's Mustang the pair pulled clear of the pack. Mark tried repeatedly to outbrake George on the tight track's numerous corners, and finally made the pass on lap 30. It was an exciting race with George close on Mark's bumper—so close that when the Javelin engine suddenly failed on lap 35, George and Mark were both off the road. Follmer quickly regained the track without losing the lead but Mark was out. A sticking float in the carburetor had flooded the engine and Mark was unable to restart. Follmer and Peter Gregg finished 1-2 for Bud Moore's Mustang team, with Peter Revson third in the ARA Javelin. Bob Tullius showed that the speed of the Tempest at Lime Rock had been no fluke, bringing the seven-year-old car home in fourth.

It was likely the same weekend that Hurley Haywood first met Mark. He was crewing for Peter Gregg, who told him to stroll down to the Penske pit and see what Goodyear compounds Mark was using. "Peter told me where to look for the numbers and said to be casual, not to look like I was doing anything," recalls Hurley. "Judy Stropus spotted me doing this and told Mark. Mark approached me and said, 'You look like Peter Gregg's brother. What are you doing?'"

Bryar had been on Monday, so it was less than a week before the series resumed at Mid-Ohio. Follmer qualified a second faster than Mark. The race started in the rain and Mark opened a big lead. When the track dried Follmer closed up as the Javelin brakes went away. The problem was a leak between the engine and the vacuum brake booster, and it set up an incident that could have been disastrous. For pit stops Roger always positioned himself exactly where the nose of the car should stop. It reflected Roger's confidence in Mark and was the key to the precise teamwork that normally followed. On this occasion the brake problem prevented the car from stopping properly. Roger was thrown onto the hood of the Javelin and carried 15 feet into the next pit stall, which fortunately was not occupied by another car. Roger was unhurt, but it was a sobering moment for all concerned.

George won the race with Mark second. On the victory podium Mark showed his sportsmanship and spirit of fun as he showered George and high-booted, short-skirted Miss Mid-Ohio with champagne. After sharing George's champagne Mark rushed to the airport to begin his trip to France and the challenge of Le Mans.

Mark in His Element

Entering the 512 M at Le Mans had been difficult, with the organizers rejecting the team for filing too late. Finally Luigi Chinetti allowed Roger one of his entries, and the car carried a small NART logo. Penske's expenses between the Daytona and Sebring accidents and the Indianapolis debacle were staggering, and Kirk F. White Enterprises already had a six-figure investment in the Ferrari. It was Mark who went to White to negotiate for more money to go to Le Mans, and White agreed to foot the bill.

It was a small team at Le Mans, with Mark, Roger, Woody, Blaine Ferguson, and Judy Stropus. As at the earlier races, 19-year-old Bobs Harrison Jr. was also along, and is remembered as a tremendous and enthusiastic helper. Adding to the Penske presence was Fred Marik as head of Professionals in Motion—the public relations firm that had, through their representation of Sun Oil, effectively been the Penske Racing communications arm since 1968. The mechanical strength was augmented by Peter Reinhart, who took leave of his job at McNamara Racing in Lenggries, Germany, to help out. Peter and a helper saw the car and spares through customs at Orly Airport in Paris and trucked everything to Le Mans. According to Bernard Cahier, to avoid posting a large temporary import bond, the blue Ferrari was brought into France as a registered street car complete with a Pennsylvania license plate mounted on the back.

Cahier, through his relationship with Goodyear, was also part of the team. Cahier had contacts at the highest levels, and his ability to organize everything from a press conference to race passes or hotel rooms was a further asset. Cahier perfected the European motorsports tradition of combining an active career as a journalist with public relations services for one or more of the principals he covered. At Le Mans the Penske/White Ferrari would carry the hopes of Goodyear in the race against the Firestone-shod Porsche 917s.

Mark had been a big star at Indy the whole month of May, but Fred Marik never saw him happier and more relaxed than at Le Mans in 1971. "For Mark, this was his element. He was a road racer and this was what he considered to truly be the greatest race in the world," recalls Marik. "Le Mans was more important to him than Indy." Although Cahier had made all the arrangements for the team, including a hotel and a place to work on the race car, Mark saw himself as "the team manager, the driver, the parts guy, and the interpreter—it was a low-budget deal." Actually, the interpreting was done by Georges Goudchaud, who had provided the same service for the Ford team when Mark raced at Le Mans in 1967. Mark loved that he was flying in the face of tradition and laughed at some boos elicited by the blue color on the Ferrari. It all played into his sense of humor and adventure. There was tremendous interest in the small American team. "We were the red, white, and blue team, no doubt about it," said Mark. He and Roger felt they were representing their country.

The opposition was strong from Porsche, who were loaded with 917s from John Wyer's Gulf team and Hans-Dieter Dechent's Martini & Rossi teams. They were supported by a number of 908s. There were no fewer than nine 512 Ferraris from various privateers.

The first practice session went poorly. Mark had relied on Ferrari's recommendation for gear ratios and found himself geared too low. The Ferrari only reached 205 mph on the Mulsanne straight while the Porsche 917s were 30 miles an hour faster. At the end of the session Mark was 15 seconds off the pace. A higher gear was fitted, but the Sunoco Ferrari would still only reach 212 mph. Mark now realized that the terminal velocity of the 512 M was limited more by its aerodynamics than by power or revs. On Thursday evening in final qualifying Mark picked up 11.5 seconds to become fourth fastest overall and the fastest Ferrari.

Kirk White appreciated a good turn of phrase and wasn't averse to telling a story at his own expense. When the French newspaper *France-Soir* made him out to be extremely wealthy and generally painted him as the quintessential "ugly American," he was besieged at his hotel by messages and telegrams from "crackpots and inventors." Mark listened to White complain about the unwanted attention and said, "Anybody who wears Gucci loafers with no socks to night practice deserves anything he gets."

There was no track time on Friday, and that afternoon Georges Goudchaud invited the small team to his home, complete with a vineyard, where he hosted a party that Mark remembered as "an interesting and wonderful experience. I met a lot of great people." That evening, the night before the race, Roger informed Mark and Woody that the engine would have to be changed. He had made an arrangement with Ferrari for the loan of their latest engine, and believed it was the way to go. Mark and Woody were opposed to

changing the engine without a chance to try it before the race, but Roger was adamant, saying, "They convinced me it's the right thing to do."

The Penske Ferrari was housed in a Shell station with minimal facilities and no engine lift of any sort. Mark told Woody, "Get it ready to take out—I'll be back." About an hour later, Mark, with a huge grin on his face, came down the road driving an enormous crane. Woody recalls, "I heard this diesel noise—in the driveway comes Mark Donohue driving an absolutely huge four-axle crane that could lift the Empire State Building. It had a huge telescoping boom that goes out 50 feet—cables, steel ball. The hook underneath the ball weighed more than the entire race car. That's what we changed the engine with. Mark had gone out and found some contractor and got them to let him use it. He personally drove it back and he operated it."

It was quintessential Mark. Co-driver David Hobbs saw the operation and said, "Crikey! Probably have the least damage if you just let them pick the car up and bang it against the wall a few times till the engine falls out."

Kirk White recalls, "As the first major American team to come to Le Mans since the factory Ford GT effort, we were of great interest and were well received. When we brought the car out on the grid and they played 'The Star-Spangled Banner,' it was the single most emotional moment I have experienced in motorsports. The emotion caught all of us. None of us could say a word."

It was the first year the race was started with a rolling start behind a pace car. Mark was fifth at the end of lap one, and a solid third when he pitted for the first fuel stop after 16 laps of the 8.36-mile Sarthe circuit. Each pit had its own steward—the *commissaire de stade*—who observed the stop for possible rule infractions. Only with this official's clearance could a car leave the pit. With Mark staying in the blue Ferrari for a second stint, the stop was typically smooth and quick. Permission to depart was granted, but as Mark made ready to pull out, the *commissaire* in the next pit box leaped in front of the Ferrari, maintaining he had observed an infraction.

"An elderly man in a blazer with many armbands jumped in front of the Ferrari with his flag and stopped Mark from leaving the pit," remembers Kirk White. "Roger, thinking this was some lunatic and wanting his car back on the track, angrily elbowed him out of the way." In the confusion Mark returned to the race. Other officials rushed to the aid of their comrade. "Down the pit road came a platoon of officials with multiple armbands and clipboards to descend on the Penske pit," says White. "One actually whacked Roger on top of his head with the handle of his flag. It took everything in Georges Goudchaud's considerable arsenal of diplomacy to keep us in the race."

Mark and David were running a conservative race strategy and were a strong third when the engine failed at the end of the Mulsanne straight. A piece of dirt had clogged an oil passage to the cam bearings. Mark nursed the blue Ferrari back to the pits where they worked on it for 40 minutes before officially retiring. They were out of the race before nightfall.

Woody and Blaine Ferguson had worked straight through the night before to install the engine. After the retirement Woody remembers Mark telling the pair, "Look, I'm going to finish getting this stuff packed up. You guys go back to the hotel. Whenever you wake up, go to the desk—there will be two tickets to fly home on. I'll take care of everything here." According to Woody this was entirely on Mark's own initiative because he recognized how hard they had worked. Woody finishes the story: "The next morning there were two Air France first-class tickets—which Mark had paid for from his own pocket."

Porsche 917s achieved a 1-2 finish, with the Martini & Rossi car driven by Helmut Marko and Gijs van Lennep leading the Gulf car driven by Richard Attwood and Herbert Müller. Americans Sam Posey and Tony Adamowicz were third in a NART Ferrari 512 M.

After the race Mark and Judy and Sam Posey were among a group of Americans who repaired to the German beer garden on the Le Mans circuit grounds. "We had been so conscious of representing America in a foreign country," Mark said. "Now we just cut loose and got drunk."

At Le Mans Roger was invited to lunch with Mrs. Louise Porsche Piëch, the wife of Dr. Anton Piëch. Mrs. Piëch was Dr. Ferry Porsche's sister and a principal in the Porsche firm, who, along with her sons Ferdinand, Ernst, and Michael, were key decision makers in the company. Over lunch at the Moderne Hotel in Le Mans she expressed interest in Penske running the Can-Am program for them. Although this was not Porsche's first overture to Penske Racing, it was a serious approach. Porsche had been considering other teams for the task, including Wyer's J. W. Automotive Engineering. The 917 was in its final year of FIA eligibility, and Porsche had a tremendous investment in its development and engineering, so the Can-Am was an attractive next step for their racing program.

"Roger told me about the meeting that same day, and we were both very interested," Mark recalled. "I thought it was too good to be true, that a major company like Porsche would seek us out. But Roger in his unique way followed up on it. He had no ideas about the car—whether it would be competitive or not—or what the details were of what they had planned." From the outset, Mark and Roger were interested in a joint development arrangement with Porsche.

CHAPTER 120:
Winning Streak

After Le Mans it was time to concentrate on the Trans-Am, where after winning the opening round at Lime Rock, the team had encountered trouble at each of the next two races. Javelin now trailed Ford in the point standings despite Ford's providing little or no support to Bud Moore's team. The long tow to Edmonton, Alberta, for round four on June 20 discouraged many teams from participating. Mark won with George Follmer second. Mark and George so dominated the small field that the third-place Camaro of Joe Chamberlain finished six laps behind. The Penske Javelin had now equaled Mustang with two wins, and had closed the points gap to 30–28.

In Indy car racing, the two-week buildup for the inaugural Pocono 500 began when the track opened for practice on June 19. The Indy 500 had traditionally been USAC's (earlier the AAA's) sole long-distance Championship Trail race. Now Pocono brought the super-speedway concept to the East Coast and joined Indy and Ontario to create a Triple Crown. Unlike Ontario, Pocono did not copy the Indy layout. The fast 2.5-mile circuit was a tri-oval with three turns, each with its own distinct characteristics. While the conflicting Trans-Am date at Edmonton made it impossible for Mark to appear on opening day, the team was, in any case, still working at a feverish pace to repair the extensively damaged McLaren. The M16 and Karl Kainhofer had gone to England immediately after Indy. At the McLaren works in Colnbrook it was put on the assembly jigs, and Karl had helped with the rebuild and assembly. It was now back in Newtown Square, and with Pocono qualifying the weekend of June 26–27, all energy was devoted to having the M16 ready. The plan to run David Hobbs in the second car was abandoned. Although helpful in repairing the wrecked car, McLaren's Teddy Mayer was unwilling to sell Penske a second car. With the Lola badly damaged, Roger decided there was no point in preparing it, as the car had been overtaken by McLaren's newer technology.

On Wednesday, June 23, the team took up residence at the new super speedway and put in a full day of testing. They used the same settings as at Indy. Late in the afternoon Mark took the McLaren out for a serious run and turned a lap at 172.2 mph, easily the fastest speed recorded to date. Peter Revson in the works M16 had previously been fastest at 170.325. Mark tested again on Thursday, the last day the track was open until Saturday's qualifying, and pronounced the McLaren—and himself—ready.

Mark was in line early on Saturday to qualify, but didn't like the feel of the car in the day's intense heat. He pulled in after one lap and the team put the car in the garage and rested. At 5:10 p.m. Mark drove the McLaren to the starting line. "The car felt good when I ran my practice lap, and we didn't want to take the chance of someone dumping some oil on the track, so we got right in line," Mark told *AutoWeek*'s Ray Marquette. "We agreed there would be no signals—they were to give me the green flag the first time around." Mark's four-lap average speed of 172.393 mph knocked Bobby Unser, who had qualified at 171.847 in the Olsonite Eagle, off the pole. The front row was completed by his brother Al in the Vel's Parnelli Jones Racing Johnny Lightning Special. Joe Leonard, Mario Andretti, and Gordon Johncock formed row two, with Peter Revson in the McLaren team M16 sharing the third row with A. J. Foyt and George Snider.

On the Fourth of July holiday weekend Mark was attempting to win races in two different types of cars at race tracks more than 1,200 miles apart. Early in the week Mark was at Donnybrooke in Minnesota, testing for the Trans-Am on Sunday the fourth. On Friday, July 2, Mark instructed at an RRDC advanced driving clinic at Lime Rock, Connecticut. The clinics were always fully subscribed and were only open to SCCA drivers holding a full National license. At one such clinic, Peter Revson was approached by someone wishing to engage him in conversation while Mark was talking. Revson shushed the individual, saying, "When Mark Donohue talks, even Peter Revson listens."

"The RRDC clinics were really respected and appreciated by the experienced drivers who participated," remembers Skip Barber. "Mark did a terrific job, and I admire what he put into them because he was a busy guy. I took over the clinic when Mark couldn't do it anymore, and it eventually led me to found the Skip Barber Racing School. Mark's influence was a big part in our curriculum from day one. He was the guy who thought about and explained the friction circle—the whole concept of moving from straight-line braking to braking and turning as you rotate the car. It was a cornerstone of our school."

That evening Mark drove to Pocono, Pennsylvania, for the inaugural Schaefer 500 on Saturday, July 3. Sam Hanks, winner of the 1957 Indy 500, drove the pace car, a very special Camaro prepared for the job by Penske Racing. Mark completely dominated the race and scored the victory he should have had at Indianapolis. There were six restarts, and on each occasion Mark smoothly pulled away from the field. It was the first event on a big track where USAC used their new yellow-flag procedure of bringing the pace car out to bunch the cars up, though this was common at short tracks. Under the old rules, a yellow flag only required drivers to slow down and refrain from passing, maintaining roughly the same interval between cars as before the flag. Aimed at improving safety, the new procedure dramatically changed racing tactics. The presence of a pace car made yellow flags an advantageous time to make pit stops.

The race's chief drama came when the last yellow was displayed with just 18 laps to go. When the lights flashed green again, Joe Leonard in the Vel's Parnelli Colt challenged Mark hard, passing him for the lead when the McLaren got loose in oil in turn two. Mark calmly stayed in Leonard's draft for two laps before re-passing for the victory. "I had a bit of trouble in the second turn earlier," Mark told *AutoWeek*'s Ray Marquette. "And when I saw the oil there, I slowed, and Joe took advantage of me with a faster throttle response. I followed him for a while to see how he handled it and then got my bravery back." Behind Mark's winning McLaren were Leonard, A. J. Foyt, and Mario Andretti.

Dave Mueller was living in Philadelphia in 1971 and gives his account of the race on Paul Powell's Web site (www.unfairadvantageracing.com):

Mark was a sort of hometown hero. My greatest memory is the 1971 Pocono 500, the first race held at that track. I had just graduated from high school. I bought tickets early, pit road seats, next to top row. Donohue started

on the pole and dominated nearly the entire race. He lost the lead on lap 191 briefly but stormed back to the lead in front of a huge crowd on the front straight. I have never experienced a more electric moment in racing, the entire crowd was cheering for him and there was no way they would let him lose!

When it was over Mark told Brock Yates that it was "heart-breaking" every time he built up a lead only to lose it when the yellow lights came on. "I was going as hard as I could," Mark said. "I had no cushion at all." Mark was happy to have the McLaren back in dominant form, saying, "I have to give Karl Kainhofer a lot of the credit for this victory. He and his crew worked day and night to get my car back in shape after it was wrecked at Indianapolis."

As race winner, Mark was presented the Camaro pace car. "I drove it home and Sue drove it for a while and she let the neighbors drive it. Everyone had fun with it," Mark remembered. "When I got ready to sell it I made the mistake of having all the pace car lettering taken off—it would have been worth more with it on. In the end a local radio station bought it from me and gave it away in a promotional drawing."

The evening after winning at Pocono, Mark and Roger cut short their post-race celebrations and boarded the Learjet to return to Brainerd, Minnesota, arriving at 2:00 a.m. Final qualifying was Sunday morning with the race in the afternoon. Concerned that rain at Pocono could force a postponement to Sunday and leave Mark unavailable for the Trans-Am, Roger had covered his bets by flying David Hobbs in on Friday to practice the Sunoco Javelin. David had a Formula 5000 race the same weekend at Mid-Ohio, but would have been available on Sunday since that event was on the holiday, Monday, July 5. Despite never having previously driven the Javelin, David was fastest in Friday's practice.

On Sunday morning, Mark's best lap of 1:43.855 placed him on pole position. Peter Revson had also arrived after racing at Pocono and qualified the yellow Roy Woods Javelin on the outside of the two-car front row with a 1:45.040. The underbudgeted Bud Moore team did not race. They were now negotiating with each promoter on a race-to-race basis for starting money to field the team. Race sponsor Grain Belt Breweries and the Twin Cities Ford Dealers Association were unable to match the money needed to bring the Mustang team, which they hoped would include Parnelli Jones. Despite the absence of Jones and George Follmer, Trans-Am racing

had not lost its popularity; the Donnybrooke track drew its largest crowd to date. Parnelli never appeared again in the series after the first race at Lime Rock. It was George Follmer who led the Bud Moore driving strength, with Peter Gregg in the second car.

Revson chased Mark hard in the early laps and took the lead when the Sunoco Javelin made an early pit stop on lap 17. When Peter made his stop on lap 22, Mark soon had a 30-second lead. The second round of stops briefly brought the leading cars together again until Peter stopped, leaving Mark with a lead of over a minute, an advantage he held to the finish of the 70-lap, 210-mile race. Mark looked tired in the victory circle and admitted that he was. Roger pointed out that Mark's wins on consecutive days had encompassed 710 miles of race action, and estimated that practice and qualifying for the two events had involved another 1,000 track miles. Mark made a telling point to *AutoWeek*'s Jerry Gilbert: "Yesterday I won $100,000 at Pocono, and today I won $4,000. The effort was about the same. I came up through SCCA and I have great loyalty to them, but the success of a series depends on the prize money. I guess it comes down to how smart SCCA is, if they want to get the top competitive drivers."

A week later, on July 11, Pedro Rodríguez crashed at the Norisring in Germany and died of a skull fracture and severe burns. A top Formula One driver for BRM and a key member of the Gulf-Porsche 917 team in endurance racing, Pedro was at the German race driving a Ferrari 512 M for Swiss private entrant Herbert Müller.

Just two weeks after the dramatic double-win weekend at Pocono and Brainerd, Penske Racing was ready to attempt a repeat on July 17–18. Again the races were a SCCA Trans-Am and a USAC Champ car race. This time the Trans-Am race was on Saturday at Road America—the Elkhart Lake, Wisconsin, circuit was presenting their own doubleheader with a Formula 5000 race on Sunday—and the USAC race was the Michigan 200 at the high-speed Michigan International Speedway on Sunday.

With its parent company American Raceways, Inc. (ARI) overextended, Michigan International Speedway was in bankruptcy hearings. ARI had been as much as $13.5 million in debt. Larry LoPatin was gone from the company, and Les Richter, now in control of ARI, was liquidating the properties that included Riverside, Texas World Speedway, Atlanta International, and an 800-acre tract of land in New

PROFESSIONAL RACE-CAR DRIVER

Jersey that had been intended for development as a race track. Richter successfully sold an 80 percent interest in Riverside to Sunnymeade Land Investors while maintaining control of the race-track operations.

Bobby Unser beat Mark for pole position on the high banks of Michigan with a speed of 193.444 mph—the fastest lap ever turned on a closed circuit in an open-wheel car. After Mark had qualified at 190.476, he told Ray Marquette, "I haven't won it [the pole] yet. Bobby was running faster than me in practice and he might blow me right off the pole." Mark later blamed himself for missing pole position, saying he had not really anticipated Bobby being that fast and hadn't tried hard enough.

The next morning Mark was at Road America in time for the final Trans-Am qualifying session. While the rolling 4.0-mile road circuit in Wisconsin could not have contrasted more with the high banks of Michigan, Mark moved from one venue to the other and back again with the confidence of the true professional. The competition was stronger at Road America than in the previous round at Donnybrooke. Bud Moore Racing was back, and George Follmer had been fastest in the previous day's session. Roy Woods had strengthened his driver roster by putting Vic Elford in one of his Javelins alongside Peter Revson.

It was Elford who gave Mark the strongest competition for pole position although Mark prevailed, breaking the Trans-Am lap record by four seconds with a 2:29.827. Elford was close with a 2:30.189 and Follmer two seconds slower in third. Peter Revson had been in the 2:31 range before his engine seized and he was unable to race. Filling out the second row was the Mustang of Tony DeLorenzo with a time nearly five seconds slower than Mark's. Peter Gregg in the second Bud Moore Mustang went through three engines and started next to last in the 35-car field. Although the Trans-Am was still filling the grid on popular tracks like Road America, the competition at the front had declined with the departure of the factory teams.

Mark won the race decisively. The matter was settled early when the left rear tire on George Follmer's Mustang went flat just after passing the pits on the 14th lap, forcing him to run an entire four-mile lap with the disintegrating tire. The only remaining threat was Elford, but the Englishman had begun to drop off the pace after four laps. Mark told *AutoWeek*'s Mike Kupper, "Elford was surprising in qualifying, but once the race started I didn't know he was there. I didn't see him

at all." By lap 30 Vic was gone from the race with a failed oil pump. Follmer overcame his early bad luck to charge back for a second-place finish although a lap down. Jerry Thompson in a Mustang was third, and Peter Gregg came all the way from the back to finish fourth.

Mark and Roger rejoined Karl Kainhofer and their USAC crew at Michigan on Sunday. Mark took an immediate lead, but fearful he had jumped the start, he let Unser by. Afterward he told Ray Marquette, "I knew I'd jumped him but I backed off and let him by me going into the first turn. I didn't want any question coming up that would lead to a restart because that wouldn't be fair to the rest of the guys." Bobby led the early laps, with Mark telling Marquette, "Bobby was running awfully fast and I wanted to see what he could do and what I could do." On lap 16 Mark drove around Bobby and dominated the remainder of the race, only dropping out of the lead briefly on the pit-stop sequences. Toward the end Mark could hear the engine detonating and backed off the throttle as much as possible. Only second- and third-place Bill Vukovich and Roger McCluskey finished on the same lap.

Mark had completed a string of five wins in consecutive races. The victories in the USAC Champ car races at Pocono and Michigan helped offset the disappointment of Indy. The three Trans-Am wins in the streak gave Mark four out of six in the series, and AMC a 46–40 lead over Ford for the championship.

CHAPTER 121:

"Mark, will you sign an autograph?"

There was a final opportunity to race the Ferrari 512 M. Along with Daytona and Sebring, Watkins Glen was one of three American circuits that annually hosted a round in the FIA World Championship for Manufacturers, and in 1971 it would be the final round in the championship. The six-hour race was on Saturday, July 24, paired with a Can-Am race on Sunday. It had become a tradition for the prototypes and their European drivers, on hand for the Saturday race, to also enter the Can-Am. The Penske Racing / Kirk F. White Sunoco-Ferrari 512 M was entered in both races.

There was a strong entry for the six-hour endurance race. Porsche was represented by two Gulf-Porsche 917s driven by Jo Siffert / Gijs van Lennep and Derek Bell / Richard Attwood. The successful collaboration between Porsche and John Wyer's Gulf Oil–backed operation ended with this race. There was also David Piper's 917 with Tony Adamowicz / Mario Cabral driving. Autodelta entered two factory-backed Group 6 Alfa Romeo T33/3s for Ronnie Peterson / Andrea de Adamich and Vic Elford / Nanni Galli. The sole works Ferrari, a Group 6 312 PB, was driven by Mario Andretti and Jacky Ickx. There were five privately entered Ferrari 512s, with the Sunoco Ferrari for Mark and David Hobbs the most prominent. NART entered a car for Sam Posey / Ronnie Bucknum. Other 512 entries were Alain De Cadenet / Lothar Motschenbacher, Herbert Müller / George Eaton, and Gregg Young / Jim Adams.

The Watkins Glen facility was in the midst of a massive rebuild, and the circuit used for this race was something of a hybrid. The entire circuit had been widened to 36 feet with a new pit straight 50 feet in width. The new pits and race tower were under construction and relocated to the newly configured straight preceding The Ninety. That corner had been the last turn on the old course and would become turn one when the changes were complete. An entirely new one-mile extension was being completed for the Formula One Grand Prix in the fall. Most noticeable was the placement of blue guardrails and catch fencing on both sides of the road all around the circuit.

New Watkins Glen executive director Mal Currie announced that the recommendations of the CSI (the sporting commission of the FIA) were followed in placement of the guardrails and in other safety issues. The reason, he explained, for placing the guardrail so close to the edge of the circuit was so that a car leaving the track surface would hit the railing with a glancing blow rather than head-on. Mark pronounced himself impressed with the new guardrail, which he believed would protect the spectators. He joined other drivers, though, in criticizing the bumpy pavement, later telling the *Elmira Star-Gazette*'s Garth Wade, "It seems a pity that you repave a new track and it ends up so bloody bumpy. They must have had a bunch of driveway contractors out there putting it down patch by patch. People have been building roads now for about 50 years and they ought to be able to do a better job than they did at this place."

In qualifying on Friday Mark placed the blue Ferrari on pole position with a 1:07.74, a full 1.3 seconds faster than the Porsche Siffert was sharing with van Lennep. The six-hour race started at 1:00 p.m. on Saturday, but Mark had the Ferrari out for Can-Am qualifying at 10:00 a.m. that morning.

Mark did not match his enduro qualifying speed, but his 1:08.32 was good enough for sixth on the Can-Am grid for the next day. It was not a good indicator for the state of the Can-Am, for a 5.0-liter Group 5 car to be that far up on the grid. Other Group 5 cars showing up near the front of the grid were van Lennep's Porsche 917K in 8th, Sam Posey 10th in the Ferrari 512 M, and Richard Attwood 11th in the second Gulf-Wyer 917. Ferrari thought it sounded like a good idea to get in on the rich Can-Am purse and sent Jacky Ickx out during qualifying in the Group 6, 3.0-liter 312 PB Ferrari. Ickx turned a lap fast enough for 10th on the grid before being called in and disqualified for a cockpit and a windshield that did not meet regulations, proving that the Can-Am was never the totally wide-open, unrestricted series that many believe it was.

Although the Can-Am continued to suffer from declining entries and lack of competitiveness, it had a seemingly endless stream of interesting technology and fascinating cars. The series was fortunate in 1971 to produce a challenge to the dominant orange McLaren team. Carl Haas, with sponsorship from L&M, had Jackie Stewart on his team in a Lola T260. Stewart had won at St. Jovite, with the Mosport and Road Atlanta rounds going to McLaren team drivers Denny Hulme and Peter Revson. Stewart captured pole position at Watkins Glen, just ahead of Revson. A factory-prepared and -entered Ferrari 712 for Mario Andretti made its first appearance at Watkins Glen. The V12, 7.0-liter engine was fitted to a 512 chassis. Another car new to the series was the Porsche 917-10 Spyder for Jo Siffert. The car had been developed by Porsche at their test facilities in Weissach, Germany, and was sponsored by Porsche-Audi and STP. Siffert qualified it ninth. Mark told John Woodard to take a careful, but discreet, look at the car—telling Woody for the first time about the plans for Penske Racing and Porsche for the 1972 Can-Am.

When the flag dropped to start the six-hour race, Mark took an immediate lead from the Porsches, Alfa Romeos, and other Ferraris. Mark was controlling the race and held a comfortable lead of nine seconds over Jacky Ickx in the Ferrari 312 PB. Ickx took the lead on lap 50 when Mark stopped for fuel, but within two laps Mark was back in front. "This was the only other race where the 24-foot fueling rig from the 1969 Michigan Trans-Am race was used," recalls John Woodard. "Our first pit stop was for fuel only, and the stop took two-point-something seconds. Certainly less than three seconds to fuel the car."

Two laps later, and still in the lead, Mark suddenly went straight off at The Ninety. He immediately returned to the track but pulled over within a few yards at the start/finish line. Mark told Jack Williams for *AutoWeek*, "The stud which holds the steering arm to the upright broke and I sailed right off." Ickx led for just two more laps before stopping for fuel and to turn the car over to Andretti. Mario never got on the track as the car would not restart; the starter motor had seized. The race was won by the Group 6 Alfa Romeo of De Adamich and Peterson, by two laps over the Gulf-Porsche of Jo Siffert and Gijs van Lennep. The Bell/Attwood 917 was third, while De Cadenet and Motschenbacher brought the Jacques Swaters–entered 512 M Ferrari home fourth.

It was the end of an exciting era for the FIA Manufacturers Championship. The Group 5 cars like the Porsche 917 and the Ferrari 512 M would not be eligible in 1972. Going forward, the championship would be contested by Group 6 race cars (limited to 3.0 liters). It was in anticipation of this that Porsche had turned to the Can-Am as a new outlet for the 917 series.

The Ferrari was ready the next day for the Can-Am, where its only hope was to outlast the powerful Group 7 cars. Mark was frustrated on the high-speed Watkins Glen circuit at being unable to hold the Can-Am cars on acceleration. On top speed the Ferrari was holding its own, recording 188.5 mph through the speed trap; Jackie Stewart in the Lola was fastest at 194.6. Mark was running in a strong top-10 position when the engine blew up from a hole through a piston.

The Penske/White saga with the famous blue Ferrari was over. It was always fast but never won a race. While Mark blamed himself for the accidents at Daytona and Sebring that had kept the team from winning, he was proud of the team for having developed the car and preparing it so beautifully. He also blamed Ferrari's unwillingness or inability to provide parts that would not break. Co-driver David Hobbs believes it was racing luck, which in this instance did not shine upon Penske Racing. "We had a great car, great technical assistance, and top drivers," David recalls. "I know they say you make your own luck, but you do need some good fortune in racing, which is what we didn't have with the Ferrari."

With the Ferrari out of the race Woody walked out to the back of the track where he found Mark sitting on the car under a tree. "It was a beautiful day but very hot," recalls Woody. "Mark said, 'Boy, I'd like to have a beer.' I walked up to the fence and asked, 'Would anybody like to give Mark and his mechanic a beer?' Several six-packs were immediately proffered. We sat there and watched the race and enjoyed a couple of beers.

"When the race was over the snow fence came down and we were instantly surrounded by a couple hundred people. Up comes a babe with big boobs wearing a sweatshirt, asking, 'Mark, will you sign an autograph?' He says, 'Sure, do you have a pen?' She lifts her sweatshirt and shows all. Mark turns beet red—tons of people were watching all this. But Mark did sign. He was a nervous wreck for weeks after that. He didn't want that image and didn't want Roger or Sue to know about it. In retrospect he thought, 'I shouldn't have done that, it wasn't the right thing to do.' But at the time he was in the spirit of the moment, interacting with the crowd."

Jackie Stewart fell out of the race lead with a flat tire on the Lola and eventually had his transmission break. With Stewart gone, there was no one to match the McLarens, and Peter Revson won with Denny Hulme second. Jo Siffert brought the new Porsche 917-10 home third, although two laps down on the leaders. Mario Andretti was fourth in the V12 Ferrari.

Bobs Harrison Jr., a popular member of the team all season, returned to college in the fall. He later died in an automobile accident and was mourned by the entire team, all of whom attended the funeral. "I had a call from Roberts, Senior, who wanted to keep the 512 M as a memorial to his son," remembers Kirk White. "Hours before I had sold the car back to Steve Earle and Chris Cord for precisely what we bought the car for—of course, that says nothing about what we spent on it as a race car. Because of the circumstances Steve and Chris were willing to unwind the deal and the Ferrari resided for many years in the Harrison family garage."

CHAPTER 122:
Crucial Wins

At St. Jovite for the fifth round of the Trans-Am on August 1, the important qualifying proved to be the Friday session. Mark was fastest with George Follmer second—race sponsor Player's cigarettes had paid the starting money to bring Bud Moore's Mustang team to the race. On Saturday it rained and the Friday times stood. Mark dominated the race, although Follmer stayed close enough that an uncharacteristically poor pit stop by the Penske team gave him the lead. Back on the track, Mark began to whittle into George's lead, but he knew the Mustang still needed to make a pit stop. "I wasn't giving it the white knuckles treatment to catch him," Mark told *AutoWeek*'s Jack Williams. When asked about the fumbled pit stop, Mark replied, "I've made mistakes in racing and the crew went along. I'll go along with them." In praising the hard work of the crew Mark singled out crew chief Earle Macmullan, who he claimed "hasn't spent 24 hours at a time with his family for five months." The same might have been said of Mark, who wasn't doing a great deal better himself.

During the St. Jovite post-race interview Mark made an oblique reference that wasn't clear to his audience at the time. "This race meant a lot to us to win. You will see later why winning this one meant so much to us." When pressed to elaborate Mark refused. But inside Penske Racing the reason was clear: The team needed every race win to clinch the Trans-Am championship early enough to be able to forgo the West Coast races at Kent and Riverside, which conflicted with the grands prix of Canada and the United States. Penske Racing had plans to be in Formula One.

After the Questor Grand Prix in March, Roger and Mark had first discussed the possibility of running a Formula One car in the fall rounds of the World Championship in North America. A drive in the third Tyrrell alongside Jackie Stewart and François Cevert was considered. Ken Tyrrell's team was having great success, with Stewart on his way to winning his second World Championship. Ultimately they decided their increasingly close relationship with Team McLaren made it sensible to run one of the team's M19s. It had not been a successful year in Formula One for McLaren, but Teddy Mayer believed the Penske team might be able to help sort the M19 out, and Mark and Roger had a feeling the car was basically good. Although Mark characterized McLaren team leader Denny Hulme as a "pure racer and a great driver and character," he considered himself the better chassis developer, and thought the combination could benefit both parties. Finally, the Penske organization was very keen to cement the relationship with McLaren to be assured of getting their Indy car for the next year. Mark later admitted to Brock Yates: "I told Teddy I'd drive their Formula One car free if we could continue to get their Indianapolis cars."

Kirk F. White was again a participant in the financial arrangements, and his name appeared on the car. "Roger called and asked me if I wanted to be part of the deal, and I thought,

no, I don't think so," remembers White. "Then I asked him how much it would be and he said $5,000. I decided at that price I would do it after all."

Now Mark went to England for six days and tested the Formula One car on a skid pad and at the Silverstone and Goodwood race circuits. It was the car that Peter Gethin had been driving alongside team leader Denny Hulme. Despite damp weather that infringed somewhat on the testing, Mark came away convinced the car could be improved. He worked with McLaren designer Ralph Bellamy, and suggested some new suspension pieces be prepared for further testing when the car came to America. Gordon Coppuck recalls:

Mark came over to give us a different angle on the car than we were receiving from the works drivers. He identified the handling problem as basic to the rising rate suspension, and our inability to get the rate of the rising rate in the front to be compatible with the rear. The difficulty was that in a slow corner you obtained very little downforce and therefore wanted a softer spring. But in the faster corners you want a stiffer rate. But the rate at which the front and rear change is not necessarily linear, and as a result the handling was changing in the middle of the corner.

It was Mark who suggested the direction to go was to get the rear balanced in a conventional way—with a non-rising rate suspension—thus allowing us to play around with the front without confusing ourselves. It was his perception that if we were only dealing with the complications of one end of the car, we would be able to come to grips with it. As a result we made the car work massively better. Ralph Bellamy left us at just that time, and I had to do the necessary drawings to effect the changes. It was an all-night effort, and the boys did a yeoman's job getting it made before we shipped the cars off to Canada.

Back home briefly from England, Mark and the Trans-Am team were at Watkins Glen on August 15. George Follmer outqualified Mark and took the lead at the start. Mark, following closely, was frustrated at not being able to draft past the Mustang at the end of the straight. "We made a mistake in setting the car up," Mark told Jack Williams. "The gear ratio was too low and when I was slip streaming George the engine was over-revving, floating the valves and I wasn't able to sling-shot past. There was no way I could pass George on the straight." It was a faster pit-stop sequence that put Mark in the lead, and Follmer chased him all day. The lead changed briefly again on the second set of pit stops when Mark pitted first, but by the time George made his stop, Mark was safely ahead and stayed there to win.

After Watkins Glen, Mark and the Trans-Am crew headed to Michigan International Speedway to test. The circuit had undergone some changes, and there would be no other chance to practice for the Trans-Am round at the track on Labor Day weekend. Mark would be racing at Ontario on Sunday and would arrive at Michigan just in time for the final qualifying and race on Monday.

CHAPTER 123:
"I guess I ran out of gas"

The second running of the Ontario 500 was another chance for Mark and the Penske Racing team to underscore their dominance with the McLaren M16. Qualifying was August 29–30, the weekend before the race. Mark and the McLaren were fast during the early days of the week, but on Thursday, just two days before qualifying, Mark put the McLaren into the wall. He explained what happened to the *Los Angeles Herald Examiner*'s Bud Furillo: "It has been a rough week. We went through three engines and then I made my mistake in the third turn. I broke three corners of the car, the gearbox, and the engine."

Mark blamed himself for the crash on Thursday. "I talked to Roger by phone and told him we were looking good. We were running faster than anyone else on tires no one else was running, but Goodyear wanted me to try another size," Mark later recalled. "Roger said, 'You just put that car away now. You've done enough today.' But I felt I should help Goodyear out, so I did try the other size tire."

After trying and rejecting the recommended tires, Mark made his final runs back on the original tires. On a fresh set of rear tires he failed to compensate for warmer fronts and cold rears. He hit the third turn wall with the rear of the car at over 150 mph. The damage was extensive. Knowing Karl and Woody were already overworked, Roger flew in fabricator Don Kean and one other mechanic to assist, and they threw themselves into the task of repairing the car. Mark told the *Los Angeles Times*'s Shav Glick, "They worked straight

through, two nights and three days. When I arrived at the track this morning they were just about on their knees."

Saturday was an extremely hot day, and Mark passed up his first chance to qualify in favor of some final tuning. At 5:00 p.m. he went out, and his first lap at 186.7 was four miles per hour faster than anyone else had run. His four-lap average of 185.004 gave him pole position. Mark told Furillo, "I'm very sore and stiff. I had never hit the wall before so I had a mental block to conquer out there."

It was more than a psychological block that Mark had to overcome. His body had absorbed a severe impact, and he received no medical attention beyond a cursory visit to the track's medical center. By Thursday evening he had to hold his head up with one hand as he drove himself to his motel, the least acceleration causing his head to flop back on the headrest. He later recalled, "It was like my neck muscles were disconnected."

After qualifying at Ontario, and despite the still-painful back and neck, on Monday, August 30, Mark was back in the Formula One McLaren for testing at Mosport. He liked the changes Gordon Coppuck had made to the suspension based on the recommendations he had made after the testing in England earlier in the month. It rained on and off on Monday, but there were some encouraging fast laps. On Tuesday the weather was better and Mark improved by two and a half seconds. The test was shortened when he experienced a loss of brakes coming down the hill to turn five and crashed into an earth embankment. The M19 was only moderately damaged, but it ended the test day. Mark was uninjured, although the impact was felt on the muscles and ligaments he had damaged at Ontario just five days earlier.

On Sunday, September 5, an announced crowd of 168,420 watched the 33 starters at Ontario follow the pace car driven by Dan Gurney. Bobby Unser in Gurney's Eagle led the first three laps before Mark passed him and drove away from the field. By lap 50 Mark had a substantial lead, and it was coming close to time to stop for fuel.

Race engineer Don Cox had a sophisticated system for determining fuel consumption. He carefully charted every lap on a graph, factoring in the amount of fuel consumed on a full-throttle race lap, as well as the lesser amount expended behind the pace car on yellow-flag laps. Don typically would indicate to Roger when to put out the P3 signal indicating that Mark should prepare to stop in three laps. Each lap was counted down until Mark was given the in sign, meaning he should pit at the end of that lap. Roger, Mark, and Don knew it was always an advantage to stay out as long as possible. This was partly because they had observed that a high percentage of accidents creating full-course yellow flags happened after a flurry of pit stops, when cars would crash for reasons including cold or ill-fitted tires. If you were confident that your fuel would last an extra lap or two, you could benefit from pitting on a yellow flag, which was always preferable to doing so when the course was green.

Roger and Don did not always agree completely on these strategies, and on this occasion Roger may have thought Don was being too conservative. Observers differed as to when Roger gave Mark the signal to pit. The first sign Mark saw was in as he completed lap 51, but when he tried to pit at the end of lap 52, he was blocked by traffic from reaching the entrance to the pit lane. Don exited the pits in frustration, convinced Mark would not complete the next lap. The dark blue Sunoco McLaren coasted to a stop on the back straight, and Cox knew it from the reaction of the crowd. Mark later described himself as almost apoplectic over what had happened. He was towed to pit entrance and the crew pushed him down pit lane. When he returned to the track—14 laps down—he turned the fastest lap of the race at 179.7 mph. After 123 laps of the 200-lap distance he was out of the race. Running lean on fuel had damaged a valve. "If we had continued we could have scattered the engine all over the track and made it rough for the other guys," Mark told the *Los Angeles Herald-Examiner*'s Jack Disney. "So we didn't see much sense in going on."

Joe Leonard won the race for Vel's Parnelli Jones Racing, a lap ahead of second-place Art Pollard. Mark was officially credited with 18th, earning $16,334 in prize money.

Mark was bitterly disappointed, and within the team there was an obvious difference in interpretation of what had caused the crucial missed pit stop. The door to the Penske garage stayed closed long after the race. Once Mark had calmed down from the heat of the race, he realized that there was nothing to gain—and much to lose in terms of team cohesiveness—by placing blame. He recalled how the team had stayed behind him after his mistake that had wrecked the car on Thursday. When Mark was finally ready to talk, he told Disney, "I guess I ran out of gas." Disney said there was little conviction in Mark's voice. "I guess I deserved to run out of gas if I couldn't see the sign," Mark continued. "Apparently, it was a mistake on my part."

Winning pole position and dominating the race before running out of fuel was no comfort for Mark. As he later expressed to Charles Barnard, an editor at *True* magazine, "Who cares if you sit on the pole? Nobody gives a damn about those things. It's like landing an airplane. Nobody cares how the pilot does it so long as he doesn't crash."

The pace of Mark's life and his total immersion in running the race programs left his personal life in an unhappy state. It wasn't just that he was struggling to find time to be with his family. His personal finances were also disorganized. "Mark had no idea where he was financially," recalls Fred Marik. "My office in Cleveland was across the street from Mark McCormack's IMG, and I introduced him to Bud Stanner. It took six months to get Mark to go see him." McCormack's International Management Group represented prominent athletes in a variety of sports. H. Kent "Bud" Stanner headed the firm's motorsports group, which included Jackie Stewart as a client. IMG handled a client's business affairs and investments as well as pursuing new revenue streams through endorsements and public appearances.

CHAPTER 124:

Trans-Am Champion

The next day Mark was at Michigan International for the September 6 Trans-Am race. One of the first persons he encountered in the paddock was Brock Yates, who was racing a Camaro on Warren Agor's team. Yates thought Mark looked awful: "His eyes were red-rimmed from exhaustion, and his head was tilted to one side, as if in pain." Brock and Mark found refuge from the endless stream of autograph seekers and well-wishers in the back of Bob Tullius's camper. Mark told his friend that his back was badly bruised, saying, "I never hit anything that hard in my entire life . . . You don't want to try something like that too often." Mark was also still feeling the bruises from the testing crash at Mosport earlier in the week. Brock asked Mark if he shouldn't consider not racing that day. Mark explained that he had no choice. He had to wrap up the Trans-Am championship at this race or he would be forced to run the last two rounds at Kent and Riverside. That would mean scrapping the plan to race the Formula One car.

At MIS the teams had already been practicing and qualifying for two days when Mark arrived just in time for the final qualifying on race-day morning. The testing in August paid off, as Mark turned a lap at 1:49.934, more than a second faster than George Follmer who had provisional pole. No more than five minutes after Mark turned his fast time it began to rain. Follmer's Mustang remained on row one with Mark while Peter Revson and Milt Minter occupied row two. Mark's friend Brock had a solid run to qualify 20th in the 40-car field. Paul Van Valkenburgh, who would later co-author *The Unfair Advantage* with Mark, was directly in front of Yates on the grid in the 18th starting position.

The rain stopped in time for the race to start on a dry track, although the sky was dark. Follmer took the lead in turn one and held the spot until lap eight, when Mark passed him. Mark later explained that he had started the race on unscuffed tires and waited to make his move until the tires came in. After passing Follmer's Mustang, the Sunoco Javelin was never headed. The Penske team's pit stops were perfect, and Mark lapped every car in the field except Follmer's. The victory clinched the 1971 Trans-Am Championship. Mark and Roger had given AMC what they had promised, winning seven of the nine races they participated in and the last six in a row. It was a classic win for Mark and the Penske team, and it was Mark's last Trans-Am event.

Although the Trans-Am was a manufacturer's series, for 1971 the SCCA had created a driver's championship, and Mark was the first to win it. Later, the club retroactively proclaimed a driver champion for the years prior to 1971. As a result, today Mark is heralded as a three-time driver champion of the Trans-Am. But what he really was responsible for was the Manufacturers Championship going to Chevrolet in 1968 and 1969 and to AMC in 1971, when he was also driver champion. What is more impressive is his record of winning 29 of the 54 Trans-Am races he started.

AMC and Penske had already decided to shift their focus to NASCAR, using AMC's intermediate-sized two-door hardtop, the Matador. Roy Woods picked up the remaining AMC pieces in the Trans-Am and some budget from the manufacturer. But AMC's departure effectively marked the end of the manufacturer-supported era for the series, and many predicted its rapid demise. Mark believed that the series would endure, saying that the Trans-Am had been a success before the manufacturers entered and would be a success without. He was largely correct: The Trans-Am continued as a series for another 30 years, although it never again commanded the respect from the media that it had enjoyed in the halcyon days from 1966 through 1971.

CHAPTER 125:

Courage, Determination, Know-How, and Competitive Spirit

After Michigan, Mark returned to Mosport for more testing with the Formula One McLaren. Afterward, the McLaren came to the shop at Newtown Square where Mark tested on the Marcus Hook skid pad. It was checked over physically and sent to Molin Auto Body to be painted and detailed. Woody accompanied the car to Canada and Watkins Glen.

Sitting in back of the Penske car hauler at Mosport to avoid the crush of fans, Mark told Brock Yates that he was generally impressed with Formula One racing without being in awe of it. "They are good, I'll agree that there are a lot of top-flight drivers here, and there's no question that it's not easy to be competitive." Mark considered Yates, a fellow race driver, to be as much a friend and confidant as he was a journalist. He went on to say that although they would be hard to beat, that did not mean the Formula One drivers were unbeatable. Mark also believed that the light and responsive Formula One cars, while not tremendously fast in his view, generated enormous cornering speeds and forces, and thus helped sharpen one's ability as a developer and tester.

Before the race Yates had a private moment with Jackie Stewart, who was on the way to the second of his eventual three World Championships. Brock asked Jackie how he rated Mark in comparison to the regular Formula One drivers. "We've known for a long time that he's among the very best," answered Jackie. "Anything he does here won't surprise me."

Qualifying was in the dry and Mark was extremely competitive. He qualified on the third row, eighth fastest with a time of 1:16.3. Jackie Stewart had pole position with a 1:15.3 in the Tyrrell-Ford, and his teammate François Cevert was on the outside of the front row with a 1:15.7. Splitting them in the middle of the front row was Jo Siffert at 1:15.5 in a V12 BRM. The two-car second row featured Emerson Fittipaldi in a Lotus-Ford and Chris Amon's Matra-Simca, both at 1:16.1. Ronnie Peterson in a March-Ford was on the inside of the third row with a 1:16.2, while Reine Wisell (Lotus-Ford) and Mark completed the row with identical times of 1:16.3.

The three rows behind Mark featured, in order: Howden Ganley, BRM; Denis Hulme, McLaren; Jean-Pierre Beltoise, Matra; Jacky Ickx, Ferrari; Mario Andretti, Ferrari; John Surtees, Surtees; and, Graham Hill, Brabham. Twenty-four cars started the race.

The Grand Prix was delayed by a fatal accident in the supporting Formula Ford race. Canadian Wayne Kelly died when his race car struck an ambulance that was on course for another incident. The accident investigation delayed the start of the Grand Prix for an hour, and a heavy rain began. Mark went out in the 10-minute warm-up session and decided to make changes to compensate for the changed track conditions. Using his best instincts, based on experience in wet conditions and previous testing, Mark had more camber put into the rear wheels, adjusted the wing for greater downforce, rebalanced the brakes to put more bias to the rear, and completely disconnected the rear sway bar.

On the first lap Mark moved from eighth to fourth position behind Stewart, Peterson, and Beltoise. Mark was close behind Beltoise until lap 15. Hoping to avoid a repeat of his mistake in the fog at Laguna Seca in 1968, he stopped in the pits for a fresh set of goggles. He was in the pits for only 12 seconds and was already so far ahead of the next-placed car—Emerson Fittipaldi's Lotus 72—that he was able to resume the race without losing his position. On the same lap Beltoise spun off the track while attempting to lap another car, and Mark was now third. He later had a quick spin in turn 10, but recovered quickly without losing position. Stewart won the race with Peterson second and Mark third on the lead lap. Fourth, a lap down, was Denny Hulme, and Wisell and Cevert were fifth and sixth.

British private entrant and *Road & Track* correspondent Rob Walker thought Mark had "put up a superb performance for his first Formula One race." When Walker congratulated Mark, asking if he was happy to be third in his first Grand Prix, Mark's response was predictable. "I am never happy to be third," he told racing's consummate gentleman.

Despite Mark's modesty, it was a remarkable achievement that is seldom acknowledged today. Without checking carefully, many latter-day pundits have concluded that Mark was lucky to inherit his position in the inclement weather. The facts reveal that the opposite is true. He moved into fourth on the opening lap and never ran lower, taking over third position on lap 15 and staying there to the lap-64 finish. For any close observer, this showing put his enormous talent in

perspective. It was also not a good year to be in a McLaren in Formula One. Mark was the only driver to put the team in the top three all year. Team leader Denny Hulme managed only two fourths, a fifth, and a sixth in the 11-race series.

Two days later Mark and Roger were at the White House in Washington, D.C., as two of 200 invited guests from the motorsports world to be honored by President Richard Nixon. The 5:00 p.m. reception on October 21 was in the State Dining Room, and four examples of American racing cars were on display in the White House driveway. In his remarks the president said that the qualities possessed by the race drivers in the room were those that had made America great—courage, determination, know-how, and competitive spirit.

CHAPTER 126:
Conflicting Schedules

The USAC race at Trenton, New Jersey, was scheduled for September 26, and when it rained there, too, it created a major difficulty. USAC does not run in the rain and spectators held rain-check tickets for Sunday, October 3—the same day as the United States Grand Prix at Watkins Glen. Both Mark and Mario Andretti had the same problem. Mario's contract with STP required him to be in all the races on the Marlboro Championship Trail. In Mark's case, Roger believed that the Trenton race would be more important to Sunoco because of its proximity to company headquarters. But after his great run at Mosport, Mark wanted to be in the Formula One race. USAC, ABC broadcasting, and Marlboro all pressured Trenton promoter Sam Nunnis to hold the race on Saturday, October 2. Nunnis wouldn't budge, maintaining that the tickets were printed with October 3 as the rain date and that ticket holders would demand a refund if they showed up on Sunday to find the race had been run the day before.

Mark was testing at the Watkins Glen circuit all week, along with David Hobbs and Denny Hulme. There was hope to the very end that some accommodation could be made with Nunnis. There was also the possibility of more rain at Trenton on Sunday, in which case Roger planned to jet Mark and Mario to Watkins Glen. Since it was uncertain who would drive in the GP, David Hobbs and Mark shared time in the McLaren right through qualifying. As a result, neither had significant time in the car and neither made an optimum time. "On Saturday we both drove but, of course, the car was set up for Mark so it was less than ideal," remembers David. Mark's 1:45.2 would have placed him only 18th on the 29-car grid. Hobbs recorded a 1:46.270 that gave him 22nd starting position. Jackie Stewart was on pole with a 1:42.642.

The Watkins Glen facility had completed their major renovation that included relocation of the pits and tower and extension of the 2.3-mile circuit to 3.4 miles. Cameron Argetsinger—who had founded the races at Watkins Glen in 1948 and brought Formula One to the circuit in 1961—had resigned as executive director of the Watkins Glen Grand Prix Corporation the previous year when his offer to purchase the circuit was not accepted. Argetsinger's package had come with sufficient cash to pay for the much-needed updates without incurring debt. With Argetsinger's offer off the table, the corporation still faced the need to update the facility. The capital required was raised by floating a bond issue and simultaneously incurring a cash deficit of nearly a million dollars. Combined with the debt on the bond issue, Watkins Glen was headed down the same slippery slope of financing that had doomed Ontario Motor Speedway. Both tracks were bankrupt by the end of the decade. While the magnificent Ontario facility disappeared entirely, Watkins Glen continued to host Formula One and World Sports Car races until 1981. The track was purchased out of bankruptcy by the Corning Glass Company in 1983. In the process, Formula One racing was lost to the circuit, but the track survived to remain an important economic factor in the region as a NASCAR venue, and is now owned by International Speedway Corporation (ISC).

During the busy week Mark was also at Riverside making public relations appearances on behalf of AMC and testing the Javelin—even though the team had no plans for Mark to race in the upcoming Trans-Am. The Trans-Am at Kent on September 19 had been canceled, leaving only Riverside. Penske's contract with AMC allowed the team to miss any two of the season's races, but Roger still sent the team to Riverside to support West Coast AMC dealers and the SCCA. With Mark at Trenton and David Hobbs at Watkins Glen, Swede Savage was offered the drive. When Savage had to refuse—he was a USAC-licensed driver and committed to Trenton—NASCAR's Donnie Allison was brought into the team but cracked his wrist during practice. Ex–Team Lotus Formula One veteran Jackie Oliver, who was racing in the Can-Am with the Shadow team, wound up with the drive.

Oliver closed the Penske Racing chapter in the Trans-Am by coming from 12th on the Riverside grid to finish third behind winner George Follmer and second-place Vic Elford, both in Javelins.

That same day Mark was in Trenton, New Jersey, instead of where he wanted to be—at Watkins Glen in the Formula One car. The 1.5-mile Trenton oval on the New Jersey State Fairgrounds had the unusual feature of a dogleg left bend on the back straight. On his first qualifying attempt Mark was one of several drivers who slid off the track at this point, with Lloyd Ruby landing his car in the infield lake. Mark explained his error simply: "I guess you call this pilot error in the airplane business. I simply made a mistake."

Mark did not have a happy day in the M16 at the Marlboro 300, first missing out on pole position to Bobby Unser and then struggling home sixth in the race with faulty throttle response. Although Mark could not run with either of the Unser brothers, he did participate in a spirited battle for most of the race with Mario Andretti, Swede Savage, Gary Bettenhausen, and Bill Vukovich.

Meanwhile, at Watkins Glen, David Hobbs gave a solid performance in the M19 McLaren to finish 10th. The race was won by François Cevert in a Tyrrell. Although Mark was unable to participate, he had been in on the buildup to the race and present at the Watkins Glen circuit through Saturday. He saw firsthand the tremendous enthusiasm among Americans for Formula One, and particularly the desire to see an American driver in Grand Prix racing. Mark, who had proven in Canada that he could more than hold his own in Formula One, was the man fans most wanted to see carrying the American banner in Europe.

The Championship Trail moved on to Phoenix. Forty cars attempted to qualify for a 24-car starting grid as the USAC season ended with the Bobby Ball 150 on October 23. Mark was on the front row in the McLaren M16, his lap of 26.70 seconds just missing the pole as Bobby Unser turned a 26.68 in the Olsonite Eagle. Mark and Bobby's cars were Offenhauser-powered, but it was the Ford-powered Coyote of A. J. Foyt that won the race. Mark engaged Unser and Foyt in an early race battle but his Offy engine overheated and he was out of the race on lap 48.

The next day, October 24, Josef Siffert was killed in a Formula One race in England. The great Swiss driver, one of the fastest and most fearless in the world, was also one of the most popular. His drives in the Porsche 917s in endurance races were the stuff of legend, and he was one of a small number of drivers who could extract the maximum performance from that difficult car. He had a long career in Formula One driving for private teams, including Rob Walker's. Siffert won the 1968 British Grand Prix at Brands Hatch for the Walker team. It was also at Brands Hatch in an end-of-season non-championship race that he inexplicably crashed on the straightaway in a Formula One BRM. He was team leader for BRM and had been fastest in both practice sessions. He had also broken the lap record by three seconds the day he died.

CHAPTER 127:

Three Weeks in Weissach

By the time the 917 made its dramatic entry in the racing world in 1969, Porsche was already well established as a formidable presence at the top level of the sport. Porsche was a small company, located in the Zuffenhausen district of Stuttgart in southern Germany, with a worldwide reputation for engineering. While the primary focus in development of the 917 was as a Group 5 car to compete in the FIA Manufacturers Championship and to achieve an overall win at Le Mans, participation in the Can-Am was part of the program from the first year.

Under the Porsche-Audi banner a 917 had been campaigned by Jo Siffert in 1969. Despite appearing for the first time with the series already half over, Siffert finished fourth in point standings by the end of the season. Siffert campaigned the first 917-10 in the 1971 series, and through his excellent driving and the inherent reliability of the car, had produced reasonable finishes, although never approaching the cutting-edge performance exemplified by the McLaren team. Porsche's decision to focus on the Can-Am in 1972 was partly because Group 5 had been dropped by the FIA as a category eligible for the Manufacturers Championship. But it also reflected the firm's desire to support marketing in North America for the recently formed Porsche-Audi dealership network. Jo Hoppen, director of racing for Porsche-Audi in America, understood the impact racing success could have on creating a brand image among car enthusiasts.

Roger had made several trips to Stuttgart to hammer out an agreement that was settled in August 1971. Integral to the relationship was that Penske Racing would not accept a car that they had not tested and helped develop, as Roger and Mark had agreed earlier. Mark and the team were busy finishing their season, and in the meantime, development continued at Porsche on the prototype car, with Willy Kauhsen doing the testing.

On October 26, just three days after the final USAC race at Phoenix, Mark, Roger, and Don Cox were in Stuttgart to discuss the development program. After introductions and initial meetings at Zuffenhausen with key Porsche people, beginning with the Piech brothers, Michael and Ferdinand, the three Americans were taken to Porsche's engineering center at Weissach, 25 kilometers from Zuffenhausen. There the Piechs introduced them to Helmut Flegl, the engineer who would have complete control of the program and be Penske Racing's contact at Porsche. Mark and Don Cox were hugely impressed with the Weissach facilities, and realized that Porsche had the laboratories, test track, and state-of-the-art machinery needed to develop an advanced race car. "Don immediately saw the potential represented by the facility, and the engineering capabilities," Mark recalled. "I think it was because he was able to relate it to what he had worked with at General Motors."

At Weissach the media was present, along with a number of senior Porsche executives and their families. It was a picnic atmosphere and Mark, Roger, and Don joined in the convivial lunch of beer and wurst. After lunch Mark was asked to drive the prototype race car, something he had not anticipated. "I expected to do nothing more that day than to stand beside the car in my race suit and have my picture taken," Mark later said. "I had no desire to drive because of the time change, the long flight the previous day, and the drinks that had followed late into the evening."

Mark went out on the unfamiliar track and turned some laps at a less than fully committed level, assuming that "some motion" was all that was expected for the photographers. In an article by Pat Bedard in *Car and Driver*, Mark recalled his thoughts while driving the 917 for the first time: "Boy, this car is not the way I would do it. I won't say it is bad, but it isn't good either. It just doesn't feel good to me."

Thinking that an exhibition run was all that was required, Mark was startled when Helmut Flegl asked him what was wrong—Mark had lapped at 56 seconds, well above the car's record of 51.5. It suddenly came to Mark that despite the circumstances—his first look at the car and the track—he was still expected to produce a lap record. One factor working in his favor was that the Weissach test track wasn't completely unfamiliar. Mark later noted that "in terms of layout and length as well as the straightaway and nature of the corners, [Weissach] is very like Lime Rock Park in Connecticut."

Needing to refocus his approach, Mark bought time by asking for a minor adjustment to the throttle cable. When he returned to the track he went much harder and paid careful attention to what the car was doing. He came close to the record and was again asked what he thought. Mark, still with only a cursory sense of the car, enumerated several setting changes—specifying rollbar and wing-angle changes, as well as toe-in adjustment. Now it was Flegl's turn to be disconcerted. He complained to Mark that his role as engineer was being usurped. At Porsche it was not the custom for a mere driver to give specific instructions for changes. In Flegl's view, the driver's job was to convey to the engineer what the car was doing and the role of the engineer to specify changes. Despite the upset, the changes were made as Mark requested, and he returned to the track, where he immediately was faster than the previous lap record, turning a 49.7. Now the party was over and the dignitaries went home or back to their offices satisfied. It was only then that Mark fully realized what the day had been all about. He had confirmed that Porsche had chosen the correct partner in Penske Racing.

At the heart of the 917's success story was the fabulous 12-cylinder engine developed by Porsche engineer Hans Metzger. Now Porsche decided to continue to develop the car with the normally aspirated motor before fitting the turbo motor, which had always been envisioned for the car.

During this period Mark and Flegl overcame their initial misapprehensions and developed a mutual trust and respect. "I began to realize that he was a very valuable guy to work with and that I would be able to concentrate on driving and let him be the engineer," Mark later said. "It was matter of two guys with a shared view of how to develop a race car. It made things much easier for me." Mark believed that Flegl's confidence in Penske Racing owed a great deal to the impression Don Cox made on him and others in Porsche's engineering department. "You could almost see the twinkle in Flegl's eye as he began to realize that we were unlike other race teams he had previously worked with," said Mark.

John Woodard also came to Weissach while Mark was there to learn the car. He had expected to stay a month but he was ready to go home after two weeks. Mark said that Woody had a great capacity for learning quickly and

impressed the German engineers with his proactive, hands-on approach to the task.

Mark had come to Germany with the expectation of being there for three days. He ended up staying for almost three full weeks (with the exception of two short side trips to Indianapolis to test the McLaren), working every day with Flegl and the mechanics. Mark would later say, "To be successful, it seems to me it's a question of how much effort you want to put [into] it."

CHAPTER 128:
Life Change

It was mid-November when Mark returned home. Sue was thrilled to see him, as were the boys. Michael was now seven, and David was two months short of five. While Mark being away was a constant, this had been a particularly long separation. "I'm away from home about half the time," he had told Charles Barnard earlier in the year. "But you've got to realize that in this world you've got to make a living. There are salesmen who are on the road a lot more than I am."

The weeks in Germany and the flights back and forth across the Atlantic had taken a physical and emotional toll. Lack of regular sleep and exercise compounded with stress caused Mark to lose weight and focus. He was on edge.

Soon after Mark's return the family attended a hockey game. When they came home Mark had a surprise announcement for Sue. He said, "I'm leaving." Sue was stunned. There was no explanation—he was just leaving. They had never even discussed separation or divorce. Although Mark's career had put strains on the marriage, Sue had never contemplated or anticipated a separation. She was in a state of disbelief and shock.

There is ample evidence from friends and relatives that in the early months of the separation—Sue and Mark were not divorced until September 1974—Mark believed he had made a serious mistake and wanted to return to his life with Sue and the boys. He never did. They did remain friendly when they saw each other.

The question of how Mark was able to reconcile his devout Catholicism with the separation and eventual divorce goes unanswered. And beyond his religion, Mark also had the example of a strong family background formed by loving parents. What began as a passion for his sport had gradually become an obsession that overcame the grounding of his upbringing and his instinct for traditional values.

When a man leaves a stable family environment there is always the question: Why? Often it surfaces that there is another woman involved. This was not the case with Mark Donohue. Few marriages are perfect, and it is not unusual for a spouse to apply some pressure, subtle or otherwise, for more family time—particularly in a situation where one party or the other has a demanding career that involves constant travel and being away for extended periods of time.

The answer would appear to lie within Mark and the multiple influences he was experiencing at the time. Rather than addressing, and making adjustments to, the pressures in his career—Mark was fully engaged in every facet of the Penske Racing operation—he chose the lesser line of resistance and removed his family life from the equation. Could he have made adjustments at Newtown Square that would have preserved his principal role as driver, and made his hands-on involvement less essential? It is likely he could have, but his own personal insecurity may have made this alternative something he was unwilling to face. Roger Penske asked for a great deal from his associates and employees, and Mark exemplified the loyal response that made the operation what it was. But Mark always underestimated his personal worth. Roger Penske was pragmatic and demonstratively capable of adjusting to changing circumstances. Mark never asked for the adjustments in the workplace that may have given him the time he needed with his family. It was Mark who had created his environment, and he was unable, or unwilling, to change it.

The 17th-century French philosopher Réne Descartes said, "The greatest spirits are capable of the greatest vices as well as the greatest virtues." Obsession with his sport may have been the vice that lived within Mark's great spirit.

Charlie Hayes makes the point that an obsession with racing was a common experience of race drivers. "Racing was such an intense experience that it was very much like what Karl Wallenda said of the high wire, 'Life is being on the wire—everything else is just waiting.' It was much the same for many race drivers, and Mark was among those. For this reason we often made bad choices in other parts of our lives."

"Mark was about the only driver I knew at the time who was working full-time at it," observes Sam Posey. "After the race the rest of us would go home. Mark would go back to the shop. The reality for Mark became the shop—eventually he was sleeping in the shop."

Mark had created a disconnect between his career and his life at home. When asked earlier in the year if the pace of his work was causing him to miss anything, he had told Charles Barnard, "No, I don't miss anything. If I missed anything, I probably wouldn't race."

Now he missed his family, he confided to those closest to him. He did not know how to find his way back, and succumbed to the alternative of throwing himself ever deeper into his preoccupation with racing, immersing himself even more in the challenges of the moment. There was the Porsche program, and now the Matador to develop for NASCAR racing. He lived in the small apartment above the office in Newtown Square and frequently stayed in the guest room of his friends, Barb and Jay Signore in New Jersey.

CHAPTER 129:
"I've never seen a stock-car race"

On November 16 Roger Penske Enterprises and Volkswagen of America officially revealed that Penske Racing would field a car for the 1972 Can-Am with sponsorship by the Porsche-Audi Division of Volkswagen of America. Although the arrangement had been widely rumored, the joint announcement was the first official confirmation. It was a great shot in the arm for the SCCA, who hoped for a more-competitive Can-Am in 1972. "There's a great deal at stake for us," Mark told Parton Keese for The New York Times. "Our reputation is on the line."

Earlier in the month McLaren had announced that 1971 Can-Am champion Peter Revson was moving to their Formula One team, and that World Champion Jackie Stewart would drive for them in the Can-Am series alongside Denny Hulme. Stewart had contested the 1971 Can-Am for Carl Haas's Lola team.

Mark remained active in the RRDC and drove the pace car at the 1971 SCCA Runoffs—officially the American Road Race of Champions—which were held for the first time at Road Atlanta the week of November 26–29. When the RRDC named F Production champion Larry Campbell as recipient of their Outstanding Driver award, Campbell received his prize directly from Mark's hands. It was a coffee table made from a magnesium wheel that had been on the McLaren M16 when it hit the wall at Ontario. The prize is still given annually and is now known as the Mark Donohue Award.

At a press luncheon at Daytona International Speedway on December 18, more news was made official: AMC and Penske Racing were taking the Matador into NASCAR. After lunch Mark drove journalists around the 2.5 mile tri-oval, holding engine revs to 6,500, which limited the top speed to 170 mph. "The first impression one gets sitting beside Donohue is his utter cool," wrote John Radosta in *The New York Times*. "He is as relaxed as a tourist in a rent-a-car. He is absolutely precise."

The red, white, and blue Matador was handsome, with the number 16 on the door and—in keeping with NASCAR custom—a large 366 on each side of the hood. At 366ci—achieved by stroking the well-developed 304ci engine the team had used in the Trans-Am—the Matador was substantially down in displacement to the Fords, Plymouths, and Chevrolets that dominated the series. Bill McNealy, AMC's vice president of marketing, said the Matador "moves around the track like it belongs there."

"I've never seen a stock-car race," Mark told Radosta as he took him on the fast lap. He later told Radosta that one of the things he had already learned was that the word "tires" is pronounced *tars*. He also told Radosta what he had learned from an unintelligible answer given by a crewman. "I found out not to ask any more questions."

Because of their lack of experience building and preparing a NASCAR racer, Mark and Roger had contracted with Holman-Moody to build the car. "It would have been foolish of us to build that first Matador," said Mark. "We didn't know the culture and what could be gotten away with and all the established tricks." Dick Hutcherson and Eddie Pagan from Holman-Moody were in the process of establishing their own shop—Hutcherson-Pagan Enterprises in Charlotte, North Carolina—and after the first car was built, it went to them for further development.

After the media day at Daytona, Mark flew straight to Atlanta. The 917-10 test car had arrived in early December, and at Newtown Square the team created larger rear wings. On December 18 and 19 the team was at Road Atlanta, and Mark tried variable-rate springs and experimented with different-size wings. Although the engine was still normally aspirated, the Porsche was fast. Expectations were high for the new turbocharged engine.

CHAPTER 130

NASCAR Debutant

On January 4, 1972, the American Auto Racing Writers and Broadcasters Association announced Mark Donohue as their 1971 "Auto Racing All American." Mark was named on 152 of the 169 first-place ballots cast. Others honored, in order of votes received, were Don Garlits, George Follmer, Peter Revson, Richard Petty, Joe Leonard, Ronnie Sox, Parnelli Jones, Bobby Allison, and Ray Elder. As the leader of the top 10 drivers selected, Mark won the Jerry Titus Memorial Trophy—a beat-up portable typewriter and a battle-worn helmet symbolizing Titus's twin careers as a driver and magazine editor.

Plans for the 1972 season included the SCCA's Can-Am with the Porsche 917, NASCAR with the still-nascent AMC Matador program, and USAC's Championship Trail, including the Indy 500 with a two-car team of new McLaren M16Bs for Mark and Gary Bettenhausen. USAC had lost their title sponsorship from the Marlboro cigarette brand. The company abruptly dropped the series from its marketing mix when the Vel's Parnelli Jones Racing team announced sponsorship from Viceroy Cigarettes. The distinct possibility that a car bearing a competitor's name could win the series made Marlboro's position untenable.

Work continued over the winter on the Matador, and in early January Mark tested the car at Charlotte Motor Speedway in North Carolina. Hutcherson and J. C. Elder along with Port Thompson were there, attending to the Matador and explaining the NASCAR way of setting up a car. Dick Hutcherson was well known to Mark from their time racing together on the Ford team in 1966 and 1967. Elder, who had been with Petty Racing before joining Holman-Moody, was chief mechanic.

After Charlotte the Matador came to Newtown Square for more work, and Elder and Thompson came with it. They worked alongside the Penske regulars doing final preparations that included fitting four-wheel disc brakes. Don Cox engineered and produced the necessary hardware to fit the calipers. Although some NASCAR teams had experimented previously with disc brakes on the front, Dick Hutcherson said, "As far as we know, they have not been used all around." Mark ran the car on the Marcus Hook skid pad and the team loaded up and headed west for the first race.

Development of the Matador, the Porsche 917-10 Can-Am car, and the new McLaren M16B was being carried out concurrently. Mark was flying across the country and was in all three cars. The new McLaren M16Bs replaced the successful 1971 M16 McLaren. Initial testing on the M16B was conducted in January at Ontario Motor Speedway.

McLaren designer Gordon Coppuck and race engineer Tyler Alexander had been at Ontario the previous day for the National Hot Rod Association Winternational Drag Races. "One of the competitors blew his gearbox and free-wheeled through turns one and two and then down the back straight, eventually pulling into his garage somewhere between three and four, having left a trail of really thick gearbox oil," recalls Coppuck. "The next day was our test and the oil was still there. Mark went out and tried it a couple of times but came in and said, 'It's impossible; we can't learn anything this way.'"

But Mark wasn't ready to give up. "He had this fantastic technique in a road car of being able to spin just the inside back wheel," continues Coppuck. "He set the car up by looking out the driver's window back at the left rear wheel and placing it precisely on the mark of the oil trail and, on full-throttle, spun that inside rear wheel all the way around the track until it eventually wore away the oil. Tyler, myself, and Don Cox walked alongside to help keep him on the oil and it was a spectacle. We were able, therefore, to resume our testing."

At Road Atlanta, testing continued on the Porsche, and on January 5, Mark had turned a lap at 1:16.4—a full second under the lap record. The test car was still running the normally aspirated motor, and the team was feeling good about being so fast without benefit of the turbo, still under development in Stuttgart. Over the phone Roger warned Mark that the twisty Road Atlanta circuit might be masking the engine's lack of power. He told Mark to pack up and head for Riverside where the long straights might tell a different story. On January 17 at Riverside Roger's instinct proved correct, as the high speeds of the California track gave a more accurate representation of the power deficit. Mark's best lap was five seconds down on the times recorded there by McLarens. Having dominated the series for the past five years, the orange cars from Colnbrook were the benchmark for the Can-Am. The Riverside test confirmed Mark's suspicion that the Porsche needed a more aerodynamic nose. Even more they needed the turbocharged engine.

At Riverside on January 23 Penske Racing debuted as a NASCAR entrant with the AMC Matador. Although it was the NASCAR debut for both Mark and the car, Roger was not a stranger to racing stock cars on the famous track in the Southern California desert. He had won the NASCAR-sanctioned Riverside 250 in 1963 driving a Ray Nichels Pontiac. Darrell Dieringer finished second and Joe Weatherly third.

Eddie Pagan said, "Mark has come up with a lot of ideas and most of those ideas are on the car now. It's a different race car, I can assure you that!" A. J. Foyt in the Wood Brothers Mercury shared the front row with Richard Petty's Plymouth. Mark was third fastest, his time of 1:26.985 comparing to A. J.'s pole time of 1:25.710. Qualifying third on the starting grid in his first NASCAR race in an untried car would have delighted anyone but the famously hard-to-please Mark Donohue, who never seemed to appreciate a personal accomplishment. Perhaps he feared that even justifiable pride in a given result would lower his standards and lead to complacency. He was hard on himself and seldom considered a job well done unless it came with a win.

There was respect for Mark from the NASCAR regulars. "About anything he does, he does real good," Richard Petty told John Radosta for *The New York Times*. "He should do as well with us." Mark diced for the race lead in the early laps with Petty—the eventual race winner—Foyt, and David Pearson until the rear axle pulled out of the frame and he retired the Matador on lap 13. After that disappointing result Roger and Mark decided to build a new car and to do it themselves.

On February 8 Mark was the guest speaker at Pingry School. As a favored alum he was a popular speaker, although he offered the attentive audience in the packed auditorium no encouragement to become race drivers. Dressed handsomely in an Ivy League–cut suit, Mark radiated warmth and interest in his audience as he emphasized the importance of education and the opportunities that life would present to those who excelled in their studies. In the question-and-answer session one teenage boy asked, "Are you afraid of dying in a crash?" Mark's answer startled some in the audience. "Not at all; it might be a relief. If you die in a race car, you are dying in something you wanted to do." Mark was remarkably forthcoming, and also admitted to the Pingry audience that although he preferred road racing, the large prize money at Indy made it the race to be at.

Another student asked how his wife felt about his racing. "If you're going into the racing business don't figure on getting married" was Mark's candid reply. What remained unsaid was the fact that their marriage had virtually dissolved—they had been separated for three months. Mark was still living in the small apartment above the office on Winding Lane. His visits with Sue and the boys were infrequent, and his focus on the race team became even narrower.

CHAPTER 131:

Racing the Box

The Daytona 500 on February 20 was a bigger challenge for the still-green NASCAR team. At Riverside, Mark had enjoyed the advantage of being a seasoned road racer. On the high banks of the 2.5-mile Daytona International Speedway, he faced a steep learning curve in the very heart of NASCAR. "They've never seen anything quite like me," Mark told Bill Verigan for a local newspaper. "They laugh at my shoes, my gold driving suit, the steering wheel. But if we had come out and blown them off the track they probably wouldn't laugh."

As NASCAR's premier race the Daytona 500 rates a buildup not unlike the tradition of Indy. The starting grid for the 500 was determined on Thursday, in two 125-mile races. Mark made progress with the Matador but was still down on top speed—all important on the near flat-out high-banked oval. The essential problem with the Matador was not its undersized engine—according to J. C. Elder it was turning out a competitive 514 horsepower—it was the car's poor aerodynamic shape that caused NASCAR veterans to dub it "The Box." Elder explained to *AutoWeek*'s Randy Laney, "The Matador has a higher roof line than the other top cars, the front end's kinda square and the windshield stands almost straight up-and-down instead of slanting back like the others. The car's just boxy and it won't break the wind, which you have to do to run fast here."

NASCAR rules, which included the use of a template by inspectors to ensure that the cars were shaped like their street counterparts, made progress in this critical area extremely difficult. Elder told Laney that initially handling had been a problem but credited Mark with solving it, saying, "Donohue reworked a lot of the suspension pieces himself, and he really did a fantastic job. The car's handling beautifully now." The other drivers were friendly and Mark was well known to them, as he told Verigan. "They're pretty good-natured. They think we're down here to add a little pizzazz and color to the scene. They don't even consider our chances of winning."

Mark had qualified 12th fastest at 173.808—a full 13 mph off Bobby Isaac's pole-position speed. He started seventh in his 125-mile qualifying race and ran well to finish fifth, although never in contention at the front. This put him on the fifth row for the start of the 500. Still running the original car, Mark had the disappointment of the engine losing power and he ran off the pace until retiring with another DNF. Mark was willing to take his lumps. "American Motors has made this effort and I can't be a prima donna and give up," Mark told Verigan. "We have a reputation that everything the Penske team touches turns to gold. All the joking is unimportant at this point while we're 13 miles an hour slower than the pole-sitter."

On February 27 the team took the Porsche to Road Atlanta for the first tests with the turbocharged motor fitted. Despite adding 300 more horsepower, the car was two seconds slower than during their tests on the circuit the previous month. This was also the beginning of a series of engine failures. Mark was shifting on the rev limiter, set by Porsche at 8,500 rpm. After blowing four engines the factory was certain Mark must be over-revving, but Mark decided on his own to lower the rev limit to 8,000. It worked, and in the entire Porsche project Mark never exceeded 8,000 rpm.

Still waiting for the new Matador to be finished, the team returned to the West Coast with the original car for the NASCAR race at Ontario Motor Speedway on March 5. The Matador still wasn't competitive on speed, although Mark qualified a decent seventh and in the race ran as high as third. While running nose to tail with Bobby Isaac, Mark braked lightly for a slower car ahead. Isaac was unable to avoid hitting the Matador from behind in turn one. Both cars were wrecked. "It was just one of those things that happen," Mark said later. "Not anything either one of us wanted." Although Mark was beaten up and sore, he suffered no serious injury.

The new Matador was ready to be tested at Atlanta Motor Speedway on March 14–15 in preparation for the race there later in the month. Mark was now trying to apply everything in his experience logically and intuitively to set the car up to go faster. "You end up with entirely different circumstances from road racing," Mark later said. "I had been on the banks at Daytona in sports cars, but that wasn't the same experience at all." He came to the realization that the high-speed ovals in the heavy stock cars required a different finesse than the light, single-seat Champ cars or the sport prototypes.

The stock cars were a different beast and needed a different approach.

Atlanta Motor Speedway is near Hampton, Georgia, on Route 19, south of the city of Atlanta. The day after testing the Matador, Thursday, March 16, it was a short drive north for Mark through Atlanta and northeast to the Road Atlanta circuit, where he met Woody and the crew to test the Porsche. That same evening he flew to Phoenix for the season's first race for the USAC Marlboro Championship Trail.

CHAPTER 132:

A Welcome Vote of Confidence

Mark was in top form for USAC's season-opener at the fast 1.0-mile oval in Phoenix on March 17–18. Debuting the new McLaren M16B with Mark was his new teammate, Gary Bettenhausen. A veteran USAC driver, Bettenhausen, from Tinley Park, Illinois, was a member of a well-known racing family. His father Tony, one of the most popular and successful Indy car drivers of the roadster era, had died at the Speedway in 1961 practicing the car of his friend, Paul Russo. Gary and his brothers Merle and Tony Jr. carried on the family legacy, and all were outstanding drivers.

Mark at 26.47 seconds and Gary at 26.68 were together on the fourth row. The Unser brothers were on the front row with Bobby fastest at 25.36 (141.996 mph) in the Olsonite Eagle-Offy. On lap 52 of the race Mark took the lead and held it until he pitted on lap 75—halfway through the 150-mile event. In an extremely rare Penske team pit-stop error, the cotter pin that secured the nut on the right front hub was improperly seated, allowing the wheel to loosen. After completing one lap at reduced speed under a yellow flag, Mark noticed wheel wobble and attempted to nurse the car back to the pits. He didn't make it. The right front wheel came off in turn four, with Mark managing to hold the car in a 90-degree slide. His race was over. Teammate Bettenhausen finished fourth behind winner Bobby Unser, with Mario Andretti and Mike Mosley second and third.

"I was really surprised how well Mark and I got along, considering our different backgrounds," says Gary. "He was from sports cars and that was something I had never done. But we hit it off, right off the bat—he always called me 'mate.'

He was so interesting to talk to about chassis setup and what made cars work. I knew what made things work on a race car, but I didn't know why. It helped me a lot as my career went on—I learned a lot from Mark." Gary Bettenhausen competed 21 times at the Indianapolis 500 before retiring in 1993.

It was back to Georgia on Monday morning for more testing with the Porsche at Road Atlanta on March 20. The obstacle now was that the engine would run strong on full throttle but was unresponsive in corners where a steadily increasing throttle feed was required.

The next NASCAR race was held the weekend of March 26 on the 1.5-mile Atlanta Motor Speedway. Mark qualified 11th in the 40-car field and the Matador finished the 500-mile race in 15th position without mechanical incident. The result would have been better had Mark not had a lap-five collision with the pit-lane barrier, despite what *AutoWeek*'s NASCAR editor Randy Laney described as "a beautifully controlled skid." No caution flag was needed and Mark drove to the pits where sheet-metal repairs delayed progress for several laps. Despite the incident Roger Penske was encouraged, saying, "Mark said he simply lost control on his wreck early in the race. But I thought he did a great job saving the car . . . we didn't have a good finish, but the car ran pretty good the rest of the way. The best thing is that we were able to run the full 500 miles for the first time this year and we'll be able to learn a lot when we get home and study the car." Bobby Allison drove a Junior Johnson Chevrolet to a close victory over A. J. Foyt in the Wood Brothers Mercury.

In early April Mark and Roger decided there were too many engine problems with the 917 to solve via transatlantic telexes. "I decided that it was foolish to waste any more time in the States," Mark later recounted. "I told Flegl that I'd have to go to Germany and work with their engine men personally." It was a critical time in the development of the Porsche Can-Am program, and Mark stayed in Germany for three weeks.

One interruption in the work at Weissach was Mark's brief visit back for the USAC Trenton 200 race on April 23. Mark had trouble all weekend with the McLaren's turbocharger and was in the middle of the grid with only the 12th-fastest qualifying time. Teammate Gary Bettenhausen was half a second quicker than Mark, placing him fifth for the start. The turbo problems persisted for Mark, and he was out of the race on lap nine. Bettenhausen, who drove a fine race to win for Penske Racing, told Dan Luginbuhl that thanks to

Mark, it was the easiest Champ car race he had driven: "Mark set the cars up since he had tested here and is familiar with the McLaren. The race setup was perfect; my car handled like it was riding on rails." That evening Mark drove back alone to the simple apartment above the office. Although happy for the team win, he was feeling down about his own unproductive season, and, most likely, not a little lonely. His family was only five miles down the road but for Mark, it was an impossible drive to make.

When the team returned to the shop they saw his light on and brought him down to take part in the victory celebration. Mark remembered the night as one when his teammates reached out to him to let him know they appreciated his part in the day's success: "Of course, everybody always congratulates me when I win, but they were expressing it then when I really needed a vote of confidence."

Back in Weissach on April 28 there were still problems to overcome. Mark endured days of frustration, and not speaking German added to his stress. He would discuss a given problem with Helmut Flegl or Valentin Schäffer, Porsche's head engineer for the V12, and explain what he wanted to do. Flegl would talk to the mechanics, who would then discuss it among themselves. Mark would have no idea what they were saying. As a result, learning patience and restraint was not the least of his challenges in developing the car. Mark was used to being the unquestioned leader, working with a crew who would throw themselves into the task, irrespective of hours. At Newtown Square the prevailing attitude was, "Whatever it takes." The German system was different, and Mark was not calling all the shots.

There was still no solution to the problem of the engine making great power on full throttle but little at partial throttle and lower engine speeds. It was the classic conflict between an engineer analyzing dynamometer readings that appeared ideal on the test bed, while the driver knew that it just wasn't working when it came to the real-life application on the track. The challenge, in part, was adjusting fuel flow to appropriately match different rpm levels and throttle openings. The day finally came when a new Bosch fuel-injection metering pump arrived, which correctly matched the part-throttle / minimum-boost airflow. Now the 917 was fast. When Mark went well under the lap record at Weissach he was able to tell Porsche that he was happy with the car.

CHAPTER 133:

"Just like he always was. Strong-minded. Stubborn. Brave. He hangs on."

For the 1972 running of the Indianapolis 500 the increase in speed was even more pronounced than it had been in 1971. USAC rule changes allowed much larger wings, which meant more downforce. Now the new McLaren M16B was merely a contender. Although the Penske team continued to sparkle, they did not have the jump on the opposition they had enjoyed the year before. The new Eagle from Dan Gurney's All American Racers was the car to beat. As much superior to the field as the McLaren had been in 1971, in 1972 the Eagle was that much better again.

Mark was at the Speedway for opening day on May 1. The plan was to qualify the first weekend, May 13–14, and then go back to Stuttgart for final aerodynamic tests on the Porsche. The big story in the Penske garage at Indy was Mark's incredible run of bad luck with the Offenhauser engines in his McLaren. One after another blew up, so Mark wasn't getting a great deal of track time. Meanwhile, teammate Bettenhausen never had an engine problem all month. Mark's engine woes were for a different reason each time—one day a rod bearing, another day a valve, a piston, a turbo—and the month was becoming a nightmare. "Whatever we did, it was trouble," Mark later recalled. "I never had any chance to work on my car because the engine kept failing. I could hardly get any practice at all." Instead of his dominance of the previous year, Mark seldom figured in the daily reports of fast times.

In the week before qualifying, Bettenhausen set a record on Tuesday in the No. 7 Sunoco McLaren at 191.315 mph. Peter Revson in the works-entered McLaren M16B was next fastest at 188.442. Jim Malloy in an Eagle, who had been the fastest up to that point, was third with a 184.275. Mark, meanwhile, was struggling in the No. 66 team car and posted only a 178.713. The next day Bobby Unser turned a 194.721 as the Eagle team showed their hand for the first time. Bettenhausen lapped in the 191 range. Mark, now on his fourth engine, had his best run to date with a 186.412. For the first time in the month he was cautiously optimistic, saying, "I'm about a week behind." But the following day that engine, too, blew up as Mark's frustrating month continued. Gordon

Johncock also lost his engine in the second McLaren team car after running a 187.227.

With the distraction of developing the Porsche, Mark did not have his usual control over the Indy operation. Don Cox was managing the team and Mark was reluctant to interfere. Mark later related his circumstances: "I had an investment in an apartment building in Indianapolis through IMG. The people who managed the building called me to say they could fix up one of the apartments and I could stay there during the month of May. At first I didn't want to do it because it was across town and I thought I should stay at the Speedway Motel like I always did and be closer to the team. But it was really a good way to keep sanity. I lived there; it was definitely a way to be away from racing. The team may have thought I was ignoring them slightly but I hate to stand around and do nothing, and at Indianapolis there is a lot of that. Don Cox had such good control of the situation—and I was constantly back and forth to Germany—that there wasn't much I could do unless I threw myself totally into the middle of it, and the circumstances weren't appropriate for that."

Gary Bettenhausen remembers that the team ran with great discipline and organization. "It was a very tight ship—everything had to be just so, even the way I combed my hair," he says. "One day I was 10 minutes late getting to the race track. Roger had told me to be there at 9:00 a.m. every morning even if we weren't going to practice. This one morning I got there about 10 or 15 minutes late, and when I got to the garage my car was gone. I ran out to the line figuring they were waiting on me and just as I got out there my car was going out of the pits with Mark driving it. It was Roger's way of making his point.

"Mark liked to party and he liked to have fun," Gary continues, "but when it was time to work it was all business. During the month of May he didn't party with the guys and would never go to the bar. He would take his notes and go to his room. If he had a drink, he had it in private."

Friday, May 12, was the last day before qualifying. Mark, now on his fifth engine, turned an encouraging 188.363, but wasn't even close to Bobby Unser, who did another lap in the 194 range. Bobby was heavily favored for the pole while Mark was still off the pace. Pole day on Saturday was a letdown for the enormous crowd and for the teams. It rained all day and the track wasn't open until 4:30 p.m. No one made an official run, so for the second day on Sunday, everything was still wide open.

It rained off and on again on Sunday. When Jim Malloy's car hit the wall exiting turn three during the morning practice, both of his arms and legs were broken, and he suffered severe burns. Malloy's Thermo King Eagle-Offy had been one of the fastest cars all month. He was rushed by helicopter to Methodist Hospital in Indianapolis where he died on May 18. Twelve cars had made the field before the rain came, and Bobby Unser was fastest at 195.940 mph. Gary Bettenhausen was second fastest at 188.877. Mark and Peter Revson were among the five cars in line that didn't get to make a run before the rain. Because they had been in line before the session was ended, they were considered first-day qualifiers and would still have a chance for the pole the following weekend.

Not being able to make a qualifying run the first weekend cut sharply into the time Mark had intended to devote to final preparations at Weissach. Mark flew to Stuttgart on Monday and managed two days of testing before returning to Indy. When Mark left Germany on May 18 he told Helmut Flegl, "At some point you have to say testing is over and racing starts. That day is today." It was time to race-prepare the Porsche 917-10 for the first round of the Can-Am in June.

Back in Indianapolis, Mark had his sixth engine failure on Friday, May 19, in the final practice session before qualifying resumed on Saturday. It was the last engine left in the Penske garage except for one that Gary Bettenhausen had rejected because it was 100 horsepower down. Roger scoured Gasoline Alley in search of a replacement. The price for the engine he found in the garage of Dick Jones was $35,000 cash, and Roger and Mark thought long and hard about the expenditure. Mark was willing to accept the lesser engine because he hadn't shown much speed all month. Mark later described Roger pacing the garage before making the decision to spend the money. The fresh engine went into the McLaren, and on May 20, Mark did his part, qualifying at 191.408 to place the McLaren on the outside of row one. Peter Revson was faster at 192.885 and occupied the middle of the front row. Bobby Unser's speed of 195.940 from the previous week had held up to give him the pole. Mark told Ray Marquette, "In the back of our minds we thought we could go as fast as Bobby did. But it was hot and the conditions were just not right for it."

The fast times of Mark and Peter pushed Bettenhausen to fourth and Mario Andretti and Joe Leonard to fifth and sixth. Sam Posey in an Eagle-Offy occupied the inside of the third row, placing seventh fastest in his rookie year at Indy. The fastest of the second-day qualifiers—gridded 15th behind all the first-day qualifiers—was Jerry Grant at 189.294 in a new Eagle-Offy from Dan Gurney's team.

Judy Stropus, as timer and scorer for Penske Racing, was one of several women to break down the longtime barrier prohibiting women in the pits at the 500. The *Indianapolis News* called it "One of the last exclusive male bastions on the face of the earth." Ruth Nixon and Gretchen Wintersteen were scoring for the Eagle team, making it a strong showing for women with a road-racing background.

The race start was controversial. Chief steward Harlan Fengler called for the green flag after two pace laps, but the drivers had been told there would be three pace laps. Chaos ensued as many drivers were unprepared for the start, although once the field settled down a great race developed. Bobby Unser took a commanding lead with Gary Bettenhausen second, Revson third, and Mark fourth. Unser dominated the early laps, and Revson's McLaren fell out of second place with a broken gearbox on lap 23. Just eight laps later Unser was out of the race with a broken distributor rotor. Gary Bettenhausen now took the lead, and Mike Mosley moved into second place ahead of Mark. Mosley briefly took the lead from Gary before losing a wheel and crashing into the turn-four wall, suffering burns to his feet, hands, and face. Bettenhausen now had a firm grip on first place while Mark had dropped to third behind Jerry Grant, who was driving an inspired race in the Eagle.

Mark now upped his game and on lap 150 ran the race's fastest lap at 187.539 mph in pursuit of Bettenhausen and Grant. Bettenhausen's hopes to win the race were dashed when his engine faltered on lap 176 and Jerry Grant charged into the lead. "I was driving easy to save the engine," remembers Gary. "I was driving it on the water temperature gauge. I had been smelling steam—we were using antifreeze, which was legal then, to help cool the engine, and that is why I could smell it—so I knew we had a water leak. There was a little pinhole in the swirl pot. The temperature was getting warmer and warmer and for about 20 laps before it blew up I was shutting the ignition switch off—we had a kill switch on the steering wheel—at the end of the straightaway and coasting through the corners with the throttle wide open to run all that cool air and methanol across the pistons. It was a trick I had learned from running Sprint Cars on dirt tracks when the radiators would get all clogged with mud. Then a yellow came out and we had to run 80 mph and I couldn't

do anything about it. When the green came out the engine was just welded together."

Roger radioed Mark that he had to catch Grant. Mark was driving with abandon, enjoying the chance to push the car for all it had and reveling in the pursuit. The race turned when Grant was forced to make a pit stop on lap 188, having picked up metal in one of his tires. Mark sailed by into a lead that he never lost. His winning average speed was 162.962 mph—a record that held up for 12 years.

After receiving the checkered flag, Mark remembered becoming emotional and excited, saying, "I just couldn't believe that after all our trouble during the month we had won the darn thing." When he pulled into victory lane to accept the Borg Warner Trophy and drink from the traditional jug of milk, he thought it was "about the happiest moment of my life." He received a victory kiss from the 500 Festival queen, Purdue sophomore Elaine Scher, and another from Zilly. Always his most outspoken advocate, his mother hugged and kissed him, saying, "This is wonderful . . . so wonderful."

If driving into victory lane at Indianapolis was the happiest moment of Mark's life, the most memorable in Karl Kainhofer's was the ride that followed. A lap of honor was an Indy tradition, and Karl joined Mark, Roger, and Goodyear's Larry Truesdale in the Oldsmobile pace car. Mark shared Karl's feeling. "The most thrilling thing of all was to be in the pace car for the lap of honor with Roger and Karl," he said. "Back in 1966 when we started together I don't think we ever anticipated—well, maybe Roger did—that the day would ever come that the three of us would be in the same car as winners of the Indianapolis 500."

"In the garage area after the race it was hard to keep my composure," Mark remembered. "So many people were congratulating us, and I was amazed and overwhelmed. Our secretary Mary Ann O'Donnell had arranged a party at Elmo Steak House, so I went back to the apartment building to change clothes. The people in that building—there were four or five couples who lived there—had tied sheets together and draped them from one window to another, and created a huge sign that said "Welcome home Mark Donohue, winner of the Indianapolis 500." I didn't really know any of those people except to say hello, and they had gotten together to do that. I had this Porsche that Roger had gotten for me to use for the month of May, and it was one of the highlights of the whole thing to drive back in that really super car and to see what these people had done."

After the race two protests were filed. Dan Gurney thought Grant was ahead of Mark and posted the required $100 fee to have the official scoring tapes reviewed. After examining the data Gurney was satisfied that Mark had won the race by 43 seconds over his driver. Then came a protest from George Bignotti against Grant and the AAR team. Bignotti had been refused permission to fuel Mario Andretti's car from his teammate's tank. As a result Mario spent the last laps of the race in pit lane and dropped to ninth. Bignotti now maintained that during Grant's late stop for a tire, he had received fuel from Bobby Unser's supply. The protest was upheld and Grant's penalty was to have all 12 of his final laps deleted from the scoring.

Grant, who believes he was the rightful winner of the race and that the scorers got it wrong, remembers the circumstances clearly. "They were slowing me down from the pits because I was so far ahead," Jerry recalls. "Bobby Unser walked out on the track with a cigarette to make sure I got the message. It's tough to slow down once you've been going for the whole race. I finally did slow, and in doing so I picked up a bunch of stuff on my tires. Then they wanted me to speed up and when I did, the right front tire was washing out—it wouldn't go through the turns. I calculated that I had enough time to go in and get a tire change and still keep the lead. I was positive of that or I never would have stopped. Our radios had broken down, so I surprised the crew, and Dan motioned me into Bobby's pit because they were a faster crew. I was pointing at the right front tire—well, it was the left front tire, but Dan got that squared away pretty quick—and they changed the tire and I was out of there. But what happened was that the fueler is programmed to get the hose in the car and he hooked me up—I believe it was for less than a second before Dan stopped him. Donohue passed me while I was in the pit, but I re-passed him when I got back on the track."

The penalty dropped Jerry from a hard-earned 2nd place to 12th. "Prior to that the biggest penalty they had ever given for taking fuel out of the wrong tank was $500," Jerry recalls. Al Unser was now scored second—three laps behind Mark—and his Vel's Parnelli teammate Joe Leonard was third. Sam Sessions was fourth in a Gene White Firestone-entered Lola-Ford, and the first rookie home was Sam Posey in fifth. For Sam, coming fifth at Indy in 1972 seemed like "Business as usual—Mark would win and I would be somewhere behind."

Although Mark's win had not been achieved with the dominance he had displayed the year before, it was richly deserved. His race was well judged and brilliantly driven. The accomplishment is all the more impressive considering how Mark's time and attention throughout May had been split between Indianapolis and Germany. Pressure notwithstanding, winning the Indianapolis 500 can fairly be seen as the high point of the Penske/Donohue collaboration that had begun in 1966. "It was the biggest one of our career together," Mark told Ray Marquette. The bond between Mark and Roger remained inseparable.

"Mark and Roger had tremendous respect for one another and a working ability that was unbelievable," says Steve Beizer, a friend of Mark's since his earliest days in racing. "They talked all the time and completely understood one another. No one could ever say anything bad about Roger to Mark, because he would stand up for him. And I believe it went both ways. It was a wonderful friendship."

The winning share of the $1 million-plus purse was $218,767.90. Mario Andretti remembers Mark as happy and relaxed the next day at the victory banquet. Mario believes the public's perception of Mark was not in line with his real nature. "There was a great misconception about Mark's personality; people thought he was just totally focused and always proper. Very few people saw the lighter side of Mark, which was very likeable. He had a tremendous sense of humor. I remember Mark at the podium at the banquet—he was having a great time and he was so funny and his talk was very well done. It was so good to see him let go, as it was so unlike how most people saw him. He was so entertaining and it just wasn't the public perception of him."

At the victory ceremony it came as a surprise when Mike Hiss, who finished seventh, was named Rookie of the Year. Although Hiss had done well to come from 25th on the grid to finish just behind veteran Lloyd Ruby, Posey had been the more impressive rookie by any impartial gauge. ABC broadcaster Chris Economaki and numerous others had already congratulated Sam on the honor—no one doubted it was his. Some believed Posey's misstep was having said in a prominent pre-race interview that his racing goal was to be in Formula One. That was heresy at Indy, where the faithful believed that even F1 World Champions were only complete as professionals after they had qualified for the 500. At the ceremony Hiss said, "This is the biggest thrill of my life. I am really surprised and it means so much to me." Sam was gracious in accepting the disappointment, publicly congratulating Hiss from the podium, saying, "I know Mike did an outstanding job. He obviously didn't have a 'super' car. Next year, maybe I'll win the race."

Posey believes that Mark did a great deal to offset the road-racing versus oval-guys rivalry at the Speedway: "Mark was a huge factor in breaking that down—much more so, for example, than Revson. Peter was very fast and always in contention, but wasn't a guy who was approachable. Peter was an accessory to the McLaren team. Mark was fundamental to the Penske team and respected instantly by guys like the Unsers and Andretti. People who really knew their business saw that Mark knew his business—he wasn't just a guy here today, gone tomorrow—he earned respect right away."

Mark had attracted admirers across the broad spectrum of American racing—he was no longer considered one-dimensional in terms of being a road-course specialist—but his win particularly thrilled road-racing people. He was the first driver to emerge from SCCA racing to win the 500. He had come up through the club in the most classic sense: starting with an SCCA driver's school, racing his own production-class sports car, winning an amateur National Championship, and eventually earning a professional drive on merit. It had been the SCCA's professional series that had promoted Mark's career and created his reputation. The outpouring of appreciation and respect showered on Mark came from even a deeper source. Many drivers have passed through the club on their path to professional racing without much notice or acknowledgment of their local SCCA region. Mark knew the race organizers, the stewards of the meeting, the pit workers, the flagging and communications people— most of them by name. Mark Donohue held a special place in the hearts of American road-racing supporters and fans at all levels.

Later that evening in New York City, Nancy Donohue was on the Lexington Avenue bus with a copy of the Sunday *Times* under her arm. Nancy was now an actress in Manhattan with a sideline as a recognized greeting-card artist. She had intended to watch the 500 on television but thought the race was on Sunday. She found a seat and opened the paper to the drama section, "When I had a flash of suspicion that set me trembling," she told *Motor Trend*. "Was the race Saturday? I found the sports section." There she saw a headline proclaiming "Mark Donohue wins Indianapolis 500, sets record." Nancy read the words over and over to make them real.

"I was shaking all over now as I jubilantly announced to the startled passengers on the bus, in a loud and unsteady voice, 'My brother just won the Indianapolis 500!' " Along with the enormous pride she took in her brother's achievement, Nancy also understood that this was a confirmation of his lifetime's work. She remembered the oft-repeated advice to Mark: "Think twice about spending all your hard-earned money on such a dangerous and expensive hobby as amateur racing." And then, "For the dear Lord's sake, don't go racing professionally." Mark would listen patiently and just go on perfecting his skills.

Perhaps only a sister in the theater could understand the motivation that drove a brother to pursue such an unforgiving vocation. Like the theater, racing is intensely competitive and heartbreaking, with far fewer chances to perform your craft in a professional setting than there are talented and deserving performers. As she sat on the bus Nancy Donohue knew what she would say when people asked, "What is Mark really like?" She would say, "Just like he always was. Strong-minded. Stubborn. Brave. He hangs on."

Porsche president Dr. Ernst Fuhrmann was a guest of Penske Racing at the 500. Fuhrmann loaned Mark a Porsche 911, and on Tuesday morning after the race Mark drove the car from Indianapolis to Media, Pennsylvania. On the Pennsylvania Turnpike Mark ran out of gas. He hitchhiked to the nearest filling station, leaving the 911 alongside the road with his attaché case on the rear seat. In the case was $140,000 of the $218,000 he had won at Indy. According to his friend Burge Hulett, writing later in *Automobile Quarterly*, "Donohue's winning luck continued. . . . it was still there when he returned."

CHAPTER 134:
Mark Saves the Can-Am

During the New York Auto Show at the Coliseum, the RRDC provided a forum on safety in racing with Mark as the featured speaker. John Connell remembers Mark as an outspoken advocate for safety-belt use. "Mark emphasized that if we were washing our car in our own driveway and needed to move the car ten feet that we should attach the belts before doing so," Connell recalls. "He was adamant that the act of attaching the safety belt should become automatic and completely second nature."

Mark had been appointed by President Richard Nixon to the National Highway Safety Advisory Committee—the first race driver to be named to the committee, chaired by Secretary of Transportation John Volpe—where he advocated for safety-belt use and careful driving on the highway. That in his personal driving habits Mark did not practice these virtues is a seeming contradiction. While at first blush appearing remarkably disingenuous, it reveals the disconnect that existed between Mark's public and private life. Those close to him believe that his espousal of driving safety was entirely sincere. He never flaunted his disregard of the safety principles he endorsed—he was simply too caught up in living his life to connect with how far removed he was in practice from what he preached.

While American race drivers on both oval and road courses had a tradition of using some form of restraint system, Europeans resisted the idea well into the 1960s. Race drivers had traditionally been concerned about being trapped in a burning car. Fire was a major issue before the advent of fuel cells and other means of containment. As fuel cells came into vogue, race-car constructors were also beginning to understand and apply principles of construction that emphasized driver protection within the car and applied energy-absorbing techniques inherent in the design of the car. These advances in car construction, somewhat simultaneous with improved standards for driver's suits, helmets, and other safety gear, ultimately convinced people that the best place to be in a big crash was contained within the driver cockpit.

Road-going performance-car drivers held to the negative view on seat belts even longer than did their racing counterparts. The enthusiast point of view is embodied in a delightful comment by *Motorsport* editor William Boddy—written in 1968 in response to a new law in England requiring the use of seat belts:

> To comply with the requirements of the Farewell State, the Editorial Rover was fitted the other day with safety-belts. Never mind whether or not they will ever be used! As they had to be fitted, we used the very best possible, in the form of Britax Auto-Lok reel-type belts (12 gns. a pair). They afford maximum protection for those who are too timid to travel in a motor unless they are securely attached to it. . . . We still consider the ruling a ridiculous one and another step towards bidding farewell to freedom of choice and fun of one's own making . . .

American road racing had mandated seat belts in race cars since the first-ever SCCA race in 1948 at Watkins Glen. They were specifically required in the Rules and Regulations for that race, and no car was approved for competition without having them fitted—a world first. Those regulations were written by race founder and organizer Cameron Argetsinger, with considerable assistance from William F. Milliken Jr., technical chairman for the event. In his autobiography, *Equations in Motion*, Milliken remembers: "Cam and I used Indy and Pikes Peak entry blanks as models, but expanded the supplementary information. For the first time (to my knowledge) we mandated the use of seat belts in racing. This was Cam's idea, one I endorsed wholeheartedly. . . . It would save my neck on at least two occasions at the Glen."

More than 20 years later Argetsinger found in Mark Donohue a major ally in resolving a crisis related to circuit safety issues. Having recently been appointed director of professional racing for the SCCA in early 1972, Argetsinger was confronted with a problem that threatened virtually all professional SCCA races with an international listing from the FIA. The Circuits and Safety Commission of the CSI—the CSI being the governing body within the FIA that regulated worldwide motorsports—announced an edict declaring six American road courses as unsuitable for competition on grounds of safety.

Donnybrooke, Road Atlanta, Mid-Ohio, Road America, Laguna Seca, and Riverside were the tracks named—the very heart of the Can-Am! The international status of the Can-Am was integral to its appeal, as it traditionally attracted teams and drivers from Europe and other parts of the world. Under the CSI edict the Can-Am would have become a series limited to drivers holding American licenses.

Argetsinger developed a rebuttal strategy, with Mark Donohue in the leading role. He asked Mark for his help, and Mark responded immediately, saying that he was willing to do whatever was required to resolve the problem. "Mark was vital," Argetsinger recalled. "If there was any chance of the plan working it rested on Mark's shoulders. His international stature allied with his ability to express himself and the energy he brought to the task were the deciding factors."

"Cam knew I wasn't a fanatic on making people do things that were going to put them out of business—I wasn't a Jackie Stewart who would suggest everyone put double guardrail around their track and go broke doing it," Mark said later. "But Cam thought there should be a driver involved, and knew I had a good sense of safety issues for drivers. It was really a courtesy thing. I did it for the good of the sport."

Mark personally wrote detailed rebuttals to the CSI edict. Dean Delamont—British representative to the CSI as head of the Royal Automobile Club, and a member of the Circuits and Safety Committee—joined Argetsinger on an inspection tour. Cameron Argetsinger recalled one portion of the tour: "I met Dean Delamont in Cleveland from his international flight. We had chartered a private plane, and our first stop was Mid-Ohio, where we were met by track owner Les Griebling. The following day we flew on to Sheboygan, Wisconsin, and Clif Tufte whisked us to Elkhart Lake for the inspection of Road America. Our final stop that day was in Brainerd, Minnesota, where Donnybrooke track owner George Montgomery met us. [The inspections of Road Atlanta, Laguna Seca, and Riverside were accomplished in separate trips.]

"It was Mark's careful and constructive analysis, along with his impeccable credentials and considerable professional reputation that carried the day," says Argetsinger. "The result was a complete overturn of the edict and a return to full international status of all the dates and races affected."

CHAPTER 135:
Everything on the Line

Final testing for the 917-10 was at Mosport on May 29. The first round of the Can-Am was coming up at the circuit in just two weeks, and the test day gave most of the race media its first look at the car. The Porsche was striking in white and red livery featuring L&M sponsorship. The joint venture between Porsche and Penske Racing had produced a great car. Horsepower was more than 900 and the handling was superb. Mark held nothing back in the test at Mosport, and the proof was a lap at 1:13.4, 3 seconds faster than the Group 7 record set by Dan Gurney in a McLaren. It was also a second and a half faster than the Formula One lap record. The performance of the 917-10 was breathtaking. According to Porsche, the car would go 0 to 60 mph in 2.1 seconds, 0 to 100 in 3.9, and 0 to 200 mph in 13.4 seconds.

Mark and Helmut Flegl had developed a relationship based on trust and mutual respect. Like Don Cox on other projects, Flegl was the race engineer who could apply Mark's practical approach to a problem and translate it into an engineering solution. Mark's genius was in understanding how to develop a theoretically fast car into one that actually could be driven fast on the race track. Mark was far more than a test driver

and something less than a true race-car engineer. "I've got a unique relationship in this project," he told Pete Lyons for *Road & Track*, "a kind of relationship I've never had before. Helmut Flegl is, oh, sort of 'the boss of the 917' and he's a man who is capable in every respect. I can say things to him and he to me and we understand each other perfectly."

Their relationship had come a long way since the rough start at Weissach in October when Flegl had seen Mark as usurping his role. They had learned to accommodate one another and Flegl had come to understand that Mark was something well beyond the typical test driver. On a rare free day in early June, Mark and Jay Signore took Helmut out in Mark's brand-new 28-foot cigarette boat. It was fitted with two bunks, a head, and dual 350ci Chris-Craft Chevrolet engines. They had a great day on the water off Sandy Hook, New Jersey. It was the first time Mark had been able to use the new boat and they ran it hard. Mark later said of the boat, "It was terribly expensive, but it was my first extravagance, my first diversion, since I began racing professionally." He also told Harvey Duck for *Auto Racing Digest* that at 65 mph, the boat was so comfortable that it was hard to believe it was going that fast, adding: "You've really got to have a fast boat to have fun. There's no kick in puttering around in just any old kind of boat and motor and then have some fresh young kid pull alongside and take off leaving you chugging along in his wake."

When Mark bought the boat Jay had gone to Miami with him for the launch. They brought it north and it stayed at Jay's house. "When he needed the boat Mark would call me and say, 'I'm coming down—can you get the boat ready for me?' recalls Jay. "So I would take it over to the marina and have it all set."

The month of June was a high point for Mark, who was feeling on top of the world. He was confident now that the Porsche program would be a success, and there remained a fresh glow from winning the Indy 500. Mark stressed his role as the prime developer of the 917-10 in a comment to Patrick Bedard for *Car and Driver*: "I like to drive this car for the same reason I liked the Trans-Am Javelin. It's exactly the way I want it—no compromises."

The Milwaukee Mile at the Wisconsin State Fairgrounds traditionally hosts the stars who had appeared at the Indy 500 the preceding week. "I don't think I realized what a big deal it was to win Indianapolis until we got to Milwaukee and I saw the reception we got," Mark remembered. "Everyone seemed really happy for us." Mark qualified the Sunoco McLaren fourth for the June 4 Rex Mays 150 with a 28.917-second lap; his teammate Bettenhausen was fifth at 28.992. It was Mark's first time at the historic 1.0-mile oval. Bobby Unser had pole position with 28.557, and his teammate Jerry Grant shared the front row. Alongside Mark on row two was Billy Vukovich. Bobby Unser dominated the race in the Eagle. Mark passed Gary five laps from the finish to take second place, but trailed race winner Unser by 4.2 seconds at the checkered flag.

Qualifying for the first round of the Can-Am was held June 10 at Mosport. The McLaren team's new design for 1972 was the M20 for drivers Denny Hulme and 1971 Can-Am winner Peter Revson. Revson returned to the team after world champion Jackie Stewart had been forced to take a month off from any kind of racing to heal a duodenal ulcer, and later decided to skip the Can-Am entirely. Revson had moved to McLaren's Formula One team and planned to enter just three USAC 500-mile races. Now Revson was back in the Can-Am.

The McLaren team had dominated the series for the past five years, in no small part because they did more testing and developing of their cars, so they were always the best prepared at the beginning of the season. At Mosport it was apparent that Penske Racing had usurped this advantage. The new M20—fitted with a 494ci Chevy—was the first departure from McLaren's earlier series of M6 and M8 derivatives, and had not had the benefit of the team's famous level of preparation.

The best of the remaining competition came from the one-car Shadow entry for Jackie Oliver and customer Porsche 917-10s—with normally aspirated engines—for Milt Minter and Peter Gregg. The fast times were turned in Friday's qualifying as the Saturday session was spoiled by cold, windy weather and a greasy track from a preliminary race. Mark qualified on pole with a 1:14.2. He privately claimed to have held something back, in order not to show his full hand to the McLarens. He was joined on row one by Revson at 1:15.0. Hulme at 1:15.2 was on row two with Jackie Oliver, who did a 1:15.6 in the Shadow. After that the times dropped off dramatically, with the sixth-fastest qualifier a full six seconds slower than Mark. There were only 18 starters, and the cars on the last row were 19 seconds off Mark's pole-setting time. In *The New York Times* John Radosta described it as "a handful of strong cars and a procession of jalopies."

Mark timed the turbo lag perfectly on the rolling start and pulled through turn one ahead of Revson. By the end of the first lap he was two seconds clear, and by lap 10 had six seconds in hand over Revson in second and Hulme third. Though the L&M Porsche was clearly powerful, the careful observer saw that Mark gained his greatest advantage in handling and speed through the corners. Pete Lyons compared segment times through turn one and later reported in his book *Can-Am* that Mark and the Porsche were not only the smoothest through the bend, they were also measurably the fastest.

On lap 18 Mark noticed a loss of power as he passed the pits. By the time he had completed a full lap to enter the pits, the McLarens had swept by in the lead. The problem was diagnosed quickly as a stuck intake turbo valve, and the stop took only four and a half minutes. Quick though the stop was, it meant Mark reentered the race ninth, three laps down, positioned between leader Revson and second-place Hulme. With the Shadow already out, it was a three-car race as Mark unlapped himself from the rest in his pursuit of Revson. By the 43rd of the 80-lap distance the Porsche was third. Denny Hulme in second was struggling with severe vibration and a sticky throttle; meanwhile, Mark was taking eight or more seconds off his lead with each lap. By late in the race he was on the same lap as Hulme and appeared to have a shot at second place. Suddenly it became a charge for the victory as race leader Peter Revson's Chevy engine failed with only two laps to go. Despite Hulme's problems there wasn't time to catch him, so the finish was another McLaren victory, with Mark second.

Though the result for the Porsche was only second place, the media was already decrying an upset in the balance of the series, with some calling for a ban on the turbo motor. The truth was that without the Penske Porsche, there would have been no balance in the Can-Am at all—it would have been complete McLaren domination. Mark declared himself happy that despite the unplanned pit stop, the car had run the full 80-lap, 200-mile distance. He reacted to criticism of the turbos and calls for their ban by noting that he and Roger had said in 1968 that the Can-Am should impose technical limits to keep costs from escalating. He wondered why now that they had a great car, they were suddenly the bad guys. "All we did is read the rules and front up with the best car," said Mark.

Mark believed his reputation had been at stake, and he considered the result a success and a vindication of his effort. He had invested a tremendous amount of energy in the program and later wrote that had he been off the pace at Mosport, he determined that he would have quietly retired from the sport. "Everything I'd been working on in racing since 1966 was on the line. It really meant that much to me." Whether Mark would have actually retired had the program not succeeded is a matter of conjecture. He had just won the Indianapolis 500 and was at a peak in earning potential and prestige. The remark does, however, illustrate the emotional commitment he had made. He believed the Penske effort with Porsche to be one of the best joint efforts ever in racing.

At Le Mans on Saturday, June 11—the same weekend as the Mosport Can-Am—Swedish driver Joakim Bonnier died during the 24-hour race when his Lola hit a slower car and was catapulted over the guardrail into the woods. Bonnier had a great career in Formula One and sports cars and had served as president of the Grand Prix Drivers' Association, where he was a leading advocate for circuit safety.

CHAPTER 136:
"This is going to be bad"

There was unprecedented rain and flooding in the Northeast throughout the month of June, and no area was harder hit than Pennsylvania, where a state of emergency was declared. Although Pocono International Raceway was in the middle of it, they attempted to maintain the original schedule for their 500-mile race, with practice on Saturday, June 17, qualifying the following weekend, and the race on Sunday, July 2. The track did open on the 17th, but bad weather kept most cars off the circuit until Tuesday. Bobby Unser underscored the dominance of the Eagle by turning the fastest lap at 185.518 mph—13 mph faster than Mark's lap record of the previous year. Unser was having a season similar to what Mark had experienced in 1971—he was dramatically faster than anyone else at every track, but often failed to win through bad luck of one sort or another. Today Bobby philosophically remarks, "Speed often causes a lack of success," reflecting that the absolute pursuit of speed can result in breakdowns and DNFs. That same day Mark recorded a lap of over 180. It rained the rest of the week, and the organizers reluctantly canceled the qualifying scheduled for the weekend of June 24–25. The new plan was to hold qualifying the following Thursday and Friday and maintain

the race date of Sunday, July 2.

The rains continued and the state suffered billions of dollars' worth of property damage. Nearby Wilkes-Barre was one of the cities hardest hit in flooding that was said to be the worst in Pennsylvania history. Under pressure from state officials, and lacking the emergency and contingency services needed for their large-scale event, Pocono officials postponed the race. Despite the track being dry and minimally affected by the storms, the teams were locked out of the facility on Thursday. USAC executive director Bill Smyth initially took a hard line in his negotiations with track owner Dr. Joseph Mattioli and demanded the race be held or he would distribute to entrants the $275,000 purse the organizers had posted. Smyth's stance brought Roger Penske into play as an outspoken supporter of Pocono's position. The exchange became so heated that Roger threatened to withdraw from USAC and form his own sanctioning body if USAC did not relent.

Eventually, through compromise, the race was rescheduled for July 29, and a financial accommodation was made to buffer the expenses of teams that had been shut out. The near-term result was a public relations blunder for motorsports because all the parties involved in the dispute appeared callous in their disregard for the suffering going on around them. A longer-term impact was Roger Penske's growing disenchantment with USAC's ability to represent the sport and the individual team owners. Within a few years Penske and other team owners would break away from USAC to form their own sanctioning body, Championship Auto Racing Teams (CART).

After the rainout was official, Mark persuaded Roger to come out on the boat with him. They met Jay Signore and the boat at Point Pleasant, New Jersey, and Mark gave his friends an offshore ride at up to 65 mph. "It scared the hell out of Roger," Mark told Bob Cutter for *National Speed Sport News*. "He said, 'Jeez, this is the greatest. I'm glad you've got one, but I wish you hadn't shown it to me because now I've got to get one.' "

Mark now turned his attention to preparing for round two of the Can-Am at Road Atlanta on July 9. John Woodard and the two race cars arrived at the circuit for testing on Monday, July 3. Team manager Chuck Cantwell and the rest of the crew, including Greg Syfert and Heinz Hofer, were delayed en route by tire problems on the second Penske transporter.

As at Mosport, the team now had two identical-appearing 917-10s. The difference was that the newer car that had raced at Mosport had a lighter chassis built from magnesium. The team maintained an air of mystery as to just what the secret material was; when asked, Mark enjoyed referring to it as "unobtanium."

With Greg Syfert and Heinz Hofer still en route, Woody was shorthanded and busy preparing the new car. Mark took the original car out and when he finished his laps gave Woody a list of changes he wanted made. As Woodard turned his attention to the car, Mark said he would take the magnesium car out while the work was being done on the other car. According to Woody, he told Mark not to drive the car because it wasn't ready to go. Mark insisted, and Woody finally capitulated, saying, "Okay, then, but don't go hard because I need to finish putting the pins in the body." Chuck Cantwell explains that the car had an elaborate system for positioning and securing the body, with lots of attachments holding it in place.

It was out of character for Mark to have ignored Woody's warning regarding the body not being secured. He was not a risk-taker with equipment. He may well have misunderstood the issue regarding the pins. Mark later said he intended to go easy since they were running in a new engine. By the third lap he was still keeping the revs down but was now exiting the corners harder. The back straight at Road Atlanta is long and undulating. Even at slightly reduced revs the Porsche was exceeding 150 mph when Mark crested the rise before the downhill run. Mark felt the rear of the car come up and begin to rotate to the left. The rear bodywork had come entirely off and the car turned 180 degrees and struck an earth bank with great violence before spinning back on the track and beginning a series of cartwheels as it shed components. Mark was aware of the nose of the car striking the top of the guardrail and saw flashes of guardrail and road as the Porsche continued to flip. He recalled thinking, "This is going to be bad," and then, "This really is bad because I'm hurting a lot." When it all stopped Mark found himself sitting on the grass strapped into his seat. The engine was behind him and everything in front was gone.

Concerned with the possibility of fire, Mark unbuckled his harness. He assumed he had broken his left leg, which was bent at the knee at a 45-degree angle on top of his right leg. He managed to extricate himself from the car and painfully dragged himself by his hands away from the wreck.

Back in the pits Woody had heard the crash. He quickly mobilized the ambulance on duty. The driver/attendant ap-plied a pressure splint to the leg and Mark was taken to Hall County Hospital in Gainesville. Mark's leg was X-rayed and found to have suffered a terrible dislocation, but it was not broken. He was in tremendous pain and was given Demerol. Initially the hospital was prepared to release him with an ace bandage on the knee, but at Woody's urging—and Mark's concurrence—he was kept overnight. Mark immediately phoned Sue. Although they were separated he wanted to assure her that he was all right before she read about the accident in the papers. Mark also called Roger. The pain was overwhelming even for the famously stoic Mark, and he took more Demerol.

The next day David Hobbs received a phone call from Dan Luginbuhl saying Mark had injured his leg, followed by, "Would you like to drive our Porsche at Road Atlanta?" David had to reluctantly turn him down. He had a commitment to Carl Haas to drive the new Lola T310. David had tested the Lola and, although unimpressed with the new car, was being assured that all would be right. It would never be a top car and David regretted missing the chance to drive the Porsche.

Mark, hurting even more the day after the accident, was unable to navigate a wheelchair to the whirlpool in the hospital. He passed out in the hall. Meanwhile, Roger phoned George Follmer, tracking him down in his motel room in Brainerd, Minnesota, where he had just won the July 4 Donnybrooke Trans-Am. Roger still thought there was a chance Mark would recover by the end of the week, but he asked George to come to Road Atlanta and be ready to drive if Mark was unavailable. "I told him that he might get here, qualify the car, and then find out Mark could drive it after all and that he was out of a drive," Roger explained to Leon Mandel. "I didn't promise him anything. On the other hand, who would you rather have driving for you? George is a complete professional."

On Wednesday Mark did make it to the hospital whirlpool but it provided no relief. Mark still hoped he could drive that weekend. He was told to walk around the hospital corridors on a cane to gain strength. He had no idea how bad his injury was, although he knew the pain was intense with the Demerol having little effect. Convinced he needed better advice than he was getting in the regional hospital, Mark phoned Burge Hulett in New York and asked him to find out whatever he could on muscle injuries. The boyhood friends were still close and Mark had tremendous confidence in Burge's ability to get things done. "Burge is a guy who is able to find out anything about anything," he later observed. Within an hour Burge responded with the name and phone number of the best orthopedic man in New York. From his hospital bed Mark immediately called the doctor, who said, "Yes, I know who you are and that you won Indianapolis this year. I'm leaving for Europe, but if you can come and see me this week I will do what I can."

The crew was now preparing the second car at Mark's friend Steve Beizer's Northlake Porsche-Audi in Tucker, Georgia. Steve loaned them a courtesy car. Woody was in constant contact with Mark and told him that Roger had called his friend Eden White, who lived in Atlanta, for advice on the best orthopedic doctor in the area. Roger knew Eden through their mutual interest in downhill skiing, and had invited her to attend a practice day at Indianapolis. "We were looking at the race car at Indianapolis and Mark came by and visited with us for four or five minutes," Eden recalls. "There was something I liked about him immediately."

Eden knew and recommended Dr. James F. Funk Jr., who was team physician for the Atlanta Falcons football team. Mark was initially reluctant, telling Woody, "No. I don't want some Atlanta guy. I have this guy in New York." Mark called the New York doctor to ask what he knew about Funk. He was told, "Dr. Funk is as good a doctor, and as much an expert, as I am. I recommend you see him—he can do as much or more for you as I can, plus he's there and is the man you should go to."

Mark then called Dr. Funk who said he had heard about the accident, and if Mark would come to the emergency ward at Piedmont Hospital that evening he would look at him. It was Thursday of race weekend and Mark called Judy Stropus, asking her to take him to the hospital. He checked himself out of the Gainesville hospital and with Judy at the wheel arrived at Piedmont Hospital in Atlanta on Thursday evening. When Mark arrived he immediately bonded with the doctor, who he later described as "a very confident guy, very nice guy, a little bit loud, friendly, warm." Funk completely gained Mark's confidence, and after X-raying and manipulating the leg, told him he needed an operation immediately, and that he would be in a cast for eight weeks. Mark replied, "I can take a few days, I can take a week, but I can't take a couple months. This is my life, this is my year." Dr. Funk said, "You can do whatever you want. It is your life, I don't care if you do it or not. But this is what you need to do."

Mark was still reluctant. He wanted to go to New York to get the other orthopedist's opinion, and asked Funk if he could do the operation in a few days or a week. Dr. Funk said

no. He had people backed up for several weeks, although he was willing to fit Mark in that weekend. Finally he offered, "Tell you what. Call your doctor in New York and we'll talk." The two physicians knew each other well and chatted about the case with Mark in the room. Then Dr. Funk put Mark on the phone. The New York doctor told him, "Look, you've got a very good man there, and I think you need to do what he says. Let him take care of you."

Mark agreed to the operation and spent Friday night in a motel, pulling himself together to be at Road Atlanta the next day. He arrived at the circuit Saturday morning on crutches to do what he could to help George acclimate to the car and track. "I told George everything there was to tell him," Mark said. Follmer was taking on a huge challenge. The Porsche had more than 900 horsepower and the turbo's throttle lag added another degree of difficulty. And until he arrived at the track George had never even seen the fast and demanding Road Atlanta circuit. He would need to dig deep into his store of professionalism to meet the challenge.

Before Mark arrived George had driven around the circuit in a rental car with Chuck Cantwell. Later he did the same with Mark, who gave him the shift points, described the line he used in each corner, and showed him where he engaged the throttle early to anticipate the lag. "It was a challenging car to drive, probably the most difficult one I ever had to adapt to, especially under those circumstances," says George. "There was a throttle lag, and when the power came on, it came on all at once. You had to control the car with the throttle as much as with the steering. The 917-10 was a short-wheelbase car and did not have good manners when it came to high-speed corners."

It was hard on Mark to see George take over the race car. He now wanted to see the wrecked car, even though Woody and others initially attempted to dissuade him. Mark insisted, determined to find out why it had come apart. According to Mark's account in *The Unfair Advantage*, Woody now took the blame, revealing that all the pins had not been in the car's body at the time of the crash. Mark never acknowledged that Woody had warned him in advance that the pins were not all in place when he had insisted on driving the 917.

Although Mark said he could never be mad at Woody because he had accepted full responsibility for the oversight, he was still leaving him holding the bag. Mark apparently believed that no one had told him not to drive the car, and his later praise of Woody for taking the blame may have been a way of overcompensating. At some level Mark may have known he was wrong in placing the blame on Woody. The trauma of the incident likely made it difficult to acknowledge his personal responsibility.

Mark left the track and was admitted to Piedmont Hospital. On Saturday, while George Follmer qualified the Porsche at Road Atlanta, Dr. Funk operated on Mark. Back at the track George did a fine job to end up on the front row with pole-sitter Denny Hulme. In the race Follmer took an immediate lead in the L&M Porsche. On lap five Hulme's McLaren M20 pulled out of the Porsche's draft as the straightaway crested to begin its descent. At more than 170 mph the McLaren lifted from the front and went over backward near the spot where Mark had crashed. It was an enormous crash that Hulme fortunately walked away from. George Follmer drove on to a decisive victory. It was a great achievement for Follmer, who had stepped into a new car on a circuit he had not seen previously. For Penske Racing it was the first victory for the L&M Porsche 917-10.

CHAPTER 137:

"Okay, Captain, I'll pack my slide rule"

Because the accident at Road Atlanta had happened barely a month after Mark's win at the 500, Mark was denied the chance to savor the feeling of being on top of the world after his victory. "People would constantly ask me if winning Indianapolis had changed my life," Mark recalled. "It didn't. The accident came along right at the time IMG was lining up some speaking engagements and other good things that may have happened. But then I was removed from it and, while I was recuperating, other races had been run and won by other people, and when I came back it was yesterday's news. I think it did a lot of good for Roger and the morale of the team as a whole, but for me personally, very little happened."

After Dr. Funk's surgery Mark lay in Piedmont Hospital for two weeks. He continued to take Demerol, admitting later that he had become addicted to it. "I had a lot of Demerol for the pain," Mark said. "When I went off that I drank a little bit." Mark's friend Steve Beizer thinks Mark may have been overstating the extent to which he resorted to alcohol during this period. "I think talk of Mark as a heavy drinker is very much overstated," Steve says. "I never saw him inebriated."

While Mark was under care and recovering at Piedmont Hospital, Eden White was a frequent visitor. Eden was a 1962 debutante and a member of the Atlanta Junior League. Her education included The Westminster Schools, Hollins College, and a degree from the Sorbonne. She later studied at the New York School of Interior Design. The eldest of four children, she had three brothers, Larry, Richard, and Steven.

Once released from the hospital, Mark stayed in Atlanta at Steve Beizer's home. He would be in a cast from his hip to his instep for six weeks. It was Steve who took several pairs of Mark's trousers to a local tailor for alteration. For easy access to his cast for those who wished to sign, the left pants leg was fitted with a zipper from thigh to cuff.

Once he could walk with crutches Mark visited the White family home. He was driving a Porsche 911 loaned to him by Steve. Eden's brother Richard admired the car and was nearly dumbstruck when Mark tossed him the keys, saying, "Why don't you try it out?"

With George Follmer in the Porsche seat, the drive in the Penske Matador had gone to NASCAR regular Dave Marcis. By mid-season the arrangement with Hutcherson-Pagan was over and Penske Racing was running the car on its own. Chuck Cantwell was managing the operation. Dave Marcis, whose remarkable career continued into 2002, was already a NASCAR veteran when he joined Penske Racing at age 31, having started more than 100 races since his 1968 debut.

"Mark was a perfectionist who lived and breathed his racing," Marcis recalls. "He was also a very nice guy and fun to be with." Dave remembers visits with Mark in the small apartment above the office at Newtown Square. "He was a very educated man and I had only gone through ninth grade, but we understood each other well. He was a good listener, and together we could cipher out the good and the bad of what that car was doing." Dave says Mark was ahead of his time in recognizing the engineering principles that eventually became standard NASCAR practice. He cites Mark's emphasis on making the car lower, though he points out that they were stymied to an extent by the design of oil pans and other components of the time.

Penske carried on with Gary Bettenhausen as a one-man team in USAC with the McLaren M16B. At Michigan International Speedway on July 16, Gary was running fifth on the fourth lap when his brother Merle, driving a Kingfish-Offy in one of his first Championship car races, had a violent crash on the exit of turn two. The race was red-flagged and the cars not involved in the accident stopped in pit lane. Roger Penske was at the track hospital to provide whatever comfort he could. Merle's injuries were traumatic. He had suffered third-degree burns and his right arm had been severed. Roger took Gary out of the race car, telling him that there would be many other races and that he should be with his brother at the hospital.

Two weeks after Mark's operation and George Follmer's win in the Porsche at Road Atlanta, the Can-Am resumed at Watkins Glen on July 23. Encouraged by the Road Atlanta victory, Porsche brought a group of European journalists to the race along with senior members of the firm, including Dr. Ferry Porsche. It was a disappointing experience. The McLarens of Denny Hulme and Peter Revson captured the front row, with George Follmer on row two alongside François Cevert, who was a full second and a half slower than pole-sitter Revson. The race was no better. Struggling all weekend with handling problems, Follmer ran fourth for most of the race behind the McLarens and David Hobbs, who was driving the wheels off the ill-handling Lola T310. A late pit stop for another sticking turbo inlet valve and a new set of tires dropped the Porsche to a fifth-place finish. Hulme won ahead of Revson, Cevert, and a sweltering Hobbs, who lost third when he stopped to have a bucket of water dumped on his head.

Mark was still in Atlanta and felt removed from his team. "I was depressed," Mark revealed in a bylined column syndicated by a Catholic news service. "If you're not out there racing, and winning, you're out of the picture."

After the poor showing at Watkins Glen, Roger called Mark and asked him to take an active role in getting the Penske Porsche program back on track. "Mark," Roger said, "will you fly up to Ohio and help us find out what is wrong with the car?"

"I flinched," recalled Mark. "I was still recuperating. The cumbersome cast hung on me like concrete. What hurt even more was my pride." Mark revealed what went through his mind as he talked to Roger. " 'No,' I was about to say. And then, thinking about that Porsche and the mechanics who put their guts into her night after night . . . What was I doing in Atlanta? Simply nursing a grudge for not being able to sit in the 'honor seat,' which for me was the driver's seat. Meanwhile, a part of me that could help was being wasted."

It took only a flash for Mark to think past his first reaction. "Okay, Captain," Mark said. "I'll pack my slide rule." Roger also asked Mark if he thought George should be replaced. Porsche

was ready to bring in Belgian Formula One star Jacky Ickx, and other names were being discussed. "I had thought Roger had made the right decision going with George," Mark said. "I told Roger that George could do the job if anyone could."

On Wednesday of race week Mark and Steve Beizer flew into Mansfield, Ohio, where Woody was at the airport to meet them. "As we drove to the track he described some of the problems with the Porsche," Mark wrote in his column. "By the time we got to the shop, I had almost forgotten the pain in my leg." Still navigating on crutches, he worked with George, Helmut Flegl, Woody, and the rest of the team, identifying the handling problem that had plagued the car at Watkins Glen.

"Mark was a big help, no doubt about it," remembers George. "He knew that car; he had a lot of input in it and [had] done a lot of testing. That was his car, his baby."

George won decisively at Mid-Ohio—a perfect response to those who doubted him and redemption for the Penske team. Mark did not join the happy celebration in victory lane, as he explained in his column. "I swung myself on the crutches back to our trailer, with that letdown feeling that follows tension. I felt a little sorry for myself," he wrote. "And then I thought: For everyone there is a season. . . . This had been my time to help fix a car. The time to drive would come again."

After Mid-Ohio, Mark returned to Atlanta and continued to convalesce at Steve Beizer's home. The visits to the White home were more frequent, and Mark and Eden enjoyed one another's company. Through all of this Mark was still on crutches and always in pain. Not surprisingly, he again found diversion on the water. Steve had a friend with a houseboat and Mark spent long hours cruising Lake Lanier. "Mark had a favorite song that summer," Steve recalls. "He would play 'Alice's Restaurant' by Arlo Guthrie, over and over. He thought it was great." Mark, a lifetime devotee of jazz, may have just discovered the iconic, 18-minute-plus talking-blues song released by Guthrie in 1967.

On August 12, the night before the Milwaukee Champ car race—the Tony Bettenhausen 200—Gary Bettenhausen broke his arm in a sprint-car race in Toledo, Ohio. Gordon Johncock was brought into the team as a last-minute substitute. Bettenhausen was still unavailable for the Ontario 500, and the drive went to Mike Hiss, who had a tremendous race to finish second in the Sunoco McLaren behind Roger McCluskey.

"Mark and I talked on the phone several times before I raced the car," recalls Hiss. "I was a technical driver myself, so what he had to say was something I could relate to, and it helped me very much." Mike remembers that as a young driver he had admired Mark and hoped to meet him. On his way home from a race in 1970, he was passing near Philadelphia and stopped at the Penske shop in Newtown Square in hopes of meeting Mark. "It was the only time in my life that I had worn a beard, but I did then," says Mike. "Mark was very polite and we shook hands. Then he said something about a California boy and a beard and you can't trust those guys. It was just funny and I knew he was kidding, but I shaved that beard off the next day."

Mark was again present to help the team at the next Can-Am at Road America on August 27. The race was enlivened when George Follmer had to start 13th in the L&M Porsche. He had missed Friday's dry qualifying session because of a conflict with qualifying at Ontario. Peter Revson had the same problem and he, too, started well back. In the race George relentlessly marched through the field and was within two seconds of Denny Hulme's McLaren when the orange car pulled over with a dead engine, giving him the win.

Work was now proceeding at Newtown Square on preparing a second car for Mark to race. His strong personal drive made his recovery faster than Dr. Funk had predicted. He was now off crutches and working hard through physical therapy to rebuild strength in the injured leg. Mark had cured himself of the Demerol habit by substituting alcohol. Now, with a determination to be back in the race car, he quit that habit too. It had never been the intention to run a two-car team, but with George in a strong position to become Can-Am champion, replacing him was out of the question. This meant fielding a second car, and Karl Kainhofer helped prepared the spare for Mark. "Roger added one car, one driver, and one mechanic to the team," recalls Karl. The two-car team for George and Mark had John Woodard, Greg Syfert, Heinz Hofer, and Karl.

CHAPTER 138:
A Gutsy Performance

Mark returned to racing at Donnybrooke for the Can-Am on September 17. More than three months had passed since his last race at Mosport in June, and two and a half months since the testing accident at Road Atlanta. The field for the Can-Am was much stronger than

it had been in June. The addition of Gregg Young–entered McLaren M8Fs for himself and French Formula One star François Cevert provided greater depth at the front of the field. With turbo engines in their Porsche 917-10s, Milt Minter and Peter Gregg now had the same equipment as the Penske team.

Back in the cockpit Mark did not immediately feel at one with the car. Although he feared he had lost his touch, he had the satisfaction of capturing pole position with a 1:25.208, sharing the front row with teammate George Follmer, who turned a 1:25.647. Team McLaren with Hulme and Revson occupied row two—it was the first time since 1966 that no McLaren had been on the front row for a Can-Am race—with Minter alongside Cevert in row three. Jackie Oliver in the Shadow Mk III and David Hobbs in the Lola T310 were next, and the top 10 was completed by Young's McLaren and Carlos Pace in the second Shadow. The fast Donnybrooke circuit provided a showcase for Can-Am power. The long and slightly downhill straightaway ended with a fast, banked first turn, and the cars were able to sustain speeds of 200 mph for an extended run each lap.

Jackie Stewart drove the Porsche 911 Targa pace car, and when the field took the green flag, Mark made the best start to lead the race. Denny Hulme chased Mark hard in the early laps, but the 510ci Chevrolet in his McLaren broke from the strain. Mark and George now had only Revson within striking distance until he, too, fell out with a dropped valve. Penske Porsches now dominated the race, with George taking the lead on lap 25 and Mark resuming his position at the front on lap 30. Mark was becoming more comfortable as he "began to get the feel back."

On lap 44 of 70, Mark had a huge moment in the high-speed right turn one, when his left rear tire blew. George was close behind and described the action for *AutoWeek*'s John Gilbert. "I saw the tire start to go and I knew what he was in for—I've taken that ride myself, in a Trans-Am car here in 1969." The Porsche went over the banking and skidded to a stop. Mark described the 190-mph experience as, "a very scary ride," and was convinced at one point that the car would turn over. He exited the car safely and limped to the fence where he watched the remainder of the race.

George Follmer's apparent easy drive to a victory was stymied when the Porsche ran out of fuel in turn two on the last lap. George coasted to turn five and later told Gilbert, "I would have paid $100 for a nickel's worth of gas right then."

Despite not completing the last lap George was credited with fourth place, and the 10 points he earned added to his series lead. François Cevert came through to win in Gregg Young's blue McLaren M8F—the very car that had won the race the year before when painted orange.

A week later, Mark was back in the McLaren M16B for the Trenton 300 USAC race in New Jersey. It was his first race in the USAC series since finishing second at Milwaukee the week after his Indy 500 win. He had tested at the track to determine if his leg was strong enough to withstand the g-force loads experienced on a fast oval circuit.

Mark qualified fifth in the 28-car field behind Bobby Unser, whose pole time was a full second faster than Mario Andretti in second. Andretti had joined the now three-car Viceroy-sponsored Vel's Parnelli Jones Racing team alongside Al Unser and Joe Leonard. With legendary George Bignotti as chief mechanic, they were considered the "Super Team." Al and Joe were on row two and Billy Vukovich was alongside Mark on row three. Gordon Johncock in the works McLaren M16B and A. J. Foyt in his Ford-powered Coyote formed row four. Although Mark was among the leaders all day on the 1.5-mile Trenton oval, and led the race on two occasions, Bobby Unser in the Eagle had by far the fastest car in the race. Despite losing a wheel early in the race, which cost him a lap, Bobby overcame all obstacles for a decisive victory. Mark finished a strong second, and the only other finishers on the lead lap were Leonard and Vukovich. For Joe Leonard it clinched his second consecutive USAC Championship.

"I was getting into the swing of it and feeling pretty good about the progress I was making on learning the driving style you need for these short ovals," Mark remembered. To overcome the handicap of his still-weak left leg, Mark had made adjustments within the cockpit to maintain the pace. As the race went on the leg became so fatigued it was falling over on the brake and accelerator. Mark discovered he could solve the problem by wedging the leg under the clutch pedal. It was a gutsy performance and a fine drive. Second place had seldom felt so good.

CHAPTER 139:
A Drink with Dr. Fuhrmann

The final three rounds of the Can-Am were in October, with two-week gaps between them. At Edmonton for the October 1 race, Mark appeared on pit lane in a handsome full-length shearling coat. The normally plain-dressing Mark seemed to enjoy the new role as fashion plate and appeared relaxed and happy. He was beaten for the pole by George by just .046 of a second. The McLarens of Hulme and Revson again occupied the second row and there was just a three-second gap down to the ninth starter.

After a slow start, the Can-Am in 1972 had developed into one of the more interesting and competitive contests in the series' history. While the turbocharged cars were being decried as spoilers, they, in fact, provided the best competition at the front of the field for many years. The problem in the series was a lack of depth. After the first nine cars, times dropped off dramatically to a 16-second gap from the front row to the back of the 21-car grid. By comparison, the Formula One grid the week before at Mosport for the Canadian Grand Prix had a gap of less than two seconds from 1st to 10th, and the last car on the 24-car grid was only five seconds off the 1:13.06 pole time set by Peter Revson in the McLaren M19C—more than a second faster than the pole time Mark had set in the Can-Am in June.

Denny Hulme took the McLaren out to an early race lead with Mark comfortable to run fourth in the early going behind Hulme, Follmer, and Revson. Revson soon made a lengthy pit stop that dropped him out of contention, and Mark began to move forward, passing teammate Follmer and closing up behind Hulme at a rate of two seconds a lap. Mark followed Denny closely for a lap or two, and when the two leaders were lapping slower cars, made a decisive move to take first place. From there Mark controlled the race, although he was unaware that Follmer had made a pit stop to replace a deflating tire. When George came charging up from behind, Mark, thinking they were on the same lap, let him by into what he thought was the lead. Mark wanted George to score maximum points as he was in contention for the series championship. Roger, knowing that Follmer was still nearly a lap down, now signaled him to let Mark back ahead. Once again ahead of George, and still believing they were on the same lap, Mark now slowed and pointed George by so that he would be the winner. Mark was surprised to discover that he was in fact the winner after all. It was his first win since the Indy 500 in May, and his first Can-Am victory since Bridgehampton in 1968. More important, it was proof that he was back, and this made Mark noticeably happy and upbeat. Leon Mandel described Mark lingering late in the press room, drinking beer from race sponsor Molson and flirting with the Molson girls.

Mark was in top form at Laguna Seca for the October 15 Can-Am, and played a major role in bringing teammate George Follmer the 1972 crown. Mark and George occupied the front row with identical times of 58.66. The pole went to Mark based on a tiebreaker that showed him faster on aggregate of each man's three fastest laps. Peter Revson was on row two alongside Jackie Oliver in the Shadow, and Denny Hulme was back on the third row alongside Milt Minter's Porsche turbo.

Mark was dominant, leading from the outset with George trailing by as much as 20 seconds. At the end of the race they had lapped every other car in the race at least once. But Mark didn't win. With two laps to go Roger Penske gave the signal to change places, and in one lap, as Mark slowed drastically on the back part of the circuit, George made up 10 seconds and surged into the lead, the victory, and the 1972 Can-Am championship. Although second place would have been sufficient for Follmer to clinch the championship, Roger wanted George to be crowned champion in the victory circle as winner. "I guess Mark figured it would be nice for me to clinch the championship with a win," George told *AutoWeek*'s Mike Knepper. Mark, of course, hadn't made the decision, and worked hard to build up a sufficient lead to make Roger's choice difficult. He described himself as ". . . devastated. It was a very unpopular move with the crowd, and I think with the crew, too, as they had worked so hard on my car."

During the week between Laguna and the last race of the Can-Am season at Riverside, Mark was at Rockingham, North Carolina, for the 500-mile NASCAR race on October 22. Dave Marcis had been driving the Penske Matador since Mark had stepped out of the seat in March after the Atlanta 500. Although the car was still not a contender at the front of the field, further development had made it a consistent finisher, and Marcis finished seventh at Rockingham. As a spectator Mark moved from corner to corner on the 1.0-mile track, studying the line and the techniques used by the NASCAR regulars. Rule changes were expected that might make the Matador more competitive in the year ahead, and Mark was serious about winning in NASCAR.

The Can-Am season finale was at Riverside. While Mark admitted that he had had a stronger motor than George's at Laguna Seca, the opposite was true at Riverside. Mark's engine was now in George's car. Although Roger said nothing to him about an arranged finish, Mark discerned from remarks made by George before the race that he had been told to give the win to Mark. Such was the team's confidence and dominance that a victory was taken for granted by one car or the other. Mark had qualified third, slightly faster than the McLaren of Peter Revson alongside him on row two. Follmer was on pole position next to Denny Hulme, who had a special 565ci (9.26-liter) aluminum-block Chevy engine fitted in the McLaren M20 just for qualifying. The Can-Am cars were a great spectacle on the fast Riverside circuit, and top speed in the Porsche was more than 212 mph.

Mark followed Hulme after the start until the McLaren's engine failed. He then trailed his teammate George Follmer at a discreet distance until midway in the race. At that point Roger gave the signal for George to allow Mark to take the lead. In a maneuver the opposite of what had occurred at Laguna Seca, George pulled over to let Mark through for the lead. But Mark perceived a significant difference in how it was executed. At Laguna, he had discreetly slowed on the back part of the track to allow George through; now, in Mark's view, George made a point of slowing dramatically on the front pit straight, where everyone could clearly see that he was being made to give away his lead.

Follmer stayed close behind Mark until, with less than 10 laps to go, he pulled alongside and began weaving from side to side, as if to indicate he had detected a problem on the lead Porsche. "I didn't know what he was doing," Mark said. "I was having a hard time relating to George's actions." Fearing he had a deflating tire, and not wishing to repeat the experience of Donnybrooke, Mark headed for the pits. The tires were fine, but when Mark returned to the track he had dropped to third place, where he would finish behind Follmer and Peter Revson. Once out of the car Mark headed to the motor home for privacy, describing himself as sick with the outcome. Losing the race had caused him to drop from what would have been second in the championship to fourth. More important, he felt badly used. It had been a difficult year both physically and emotionally. After the commitment he had made to make the Porsche the outstanding car it was, he now experienced an enormous letdown.

Solace came from an unexpected source. Ernst Fuhrmann, Porsche's chief executive, sought Mark out to congratulate him and to commiserate, saying they all thought he should have won the race. Dr. Fuhrmann located some bourbon, and the two men sat drinking directly from the bottle, talking quietly. The thoughtful gesture from Fuhrmann made an enormous impression on Mark and was a form of consolation.

Dr. Fuhrmann wasn't the only person to understand the trials Mark had been through, and to have hoped he would cap the season with a win at Riverside. In a pre-race story in the *Los Angeles Times*, Sam Posey said, "I can't think of anyone more courageous or more deserving, and I hope he wins." Posey recently said that the irony of Mark's Indy win was that because of the subsequent accident, he wasn't able to celebrate for long.

Despite Mark's upset at the time over the Riverside outcome, he said that he and George Follmer never had a problem together on the track. Each man saw the incident differently, and when the heat of battle cooled, the issue evaporated. It is likely that no other driver was in as many races with Mark as was George, either as teammates or rivals. Mark praised his consistent sportsmanship, saying that George always raced cleanly and that he had nothing but the highest regard for him as a man and a driver. George gave Mark credit for developing the Porsche, saying, "The car stops better and it goes through the corners better than any of the rest of them. And you can thank Mark for that."

The Can-Am championship capped George Follmer's year—a banner one as he had also won the Trans-Am championship driving the Roy Woods Javelin. Follmer was one of the great American drivers of his era and at the age of 38 he still had some of his best years ahead of him. For 1973 he had signed to drive the Formula One UOP Shadow, contesting the World Championship in the international Grand Prix series.

Thanks to the turbo Porsches the Can-Am had enjoyed a resurgent year. Not since 1967 had the series been as varied and competitive. Small fields continued to pose a threat to the long-term future of SCCA's premier series, as only the best-financed teams could compete. Even then only a handful of cars were current enough to have any chance of winning. In *AutoWeek*, François Cevert observed that there were only two truly professional teams in the series: "With the exception of Porsche and McLaren, every driver, every team comes to have a nice weekend. They hope to do well, of course, but it just isn't professional."

There were other Porsche 917-10s in the series—driven by Milt Minter, Peter Gregg, and Willy Kauhsen—but the Penske cars were faster because they were better prepared and better driven. Roger and Mark had effectively left the Can-Am after 1968 because they could not obtain a state-of-the-art McLaren. They returned in 1972 when they found a true partner in Porsche, who made Mark an integral part of the race car's development. Although the customer Porsches had the same equipment, they could not match the body of knowledge that Mark and the rest of the team had amassed.

The pressure was always on Mark. Every time he went out on the track he felt a responsibility to Roger and all the sponsors. With multiple projects going on concurrently, it was always up to Mark to deliver the results. "Mark was tortured in a way that I, or Revson or others, never would have been—he was his work," Sam Posey says. "The cars were always so beautifully turned out that you expected them to be quick—and often Mark had to be the guy who made up for what they were lacking."

CHAPTER 140:

Developing the Porsche 917-30 and Fishing for Sharks

A week after the Can-Am finale at Riverside, the 1972 USAC Championship Trail series ended on November 4 with the Phoenix 150. In Mark's last race of the season he captured pole position with a 25.40-second lap and shared the front row with Mario Andretti, who turned a 25.59. Bobby and Al Unser made up the second row in the 24-car field. Mark jumped the start too blatantly and the cars were required to do another lap before seeing the green flag. Mark did not make a good start the second time either, and Bobby Unser and Andretti went by him. Mark ran a strong third and was in contention throughout until his turbocharger failed, putting him out of the race. Mark thought it had been his best effort on a short oval, and Don Cox agreed. He had come to terms with the specialized technique required for passing on the outside and was ready for more. As it happened, the Phoenix race proved to be his last short-oval start, and the last in the Sunoco McLaren M16B that had brought him victory at Indy. Despite failing to finish at Phoenix, and the many races he missed during his recovery, Mark finished fifth in the USAC championship.

After the Can-Am season Mark's 917-10 was sold to Georgia businessman Bobby Rinzler. Rinzler entered Charlie Kemp in the car for the SCCA American Road Racing Championship—the Runoffs—at Road Atlanta in November. Mark, George Follmer, and John Woodard were all on hand to help with the transition. Mark drove the car early in the week to make sure all systems were operating. Kemp crashed out of third place and slightly damaged the car. At the front Can-Am regular Steve Durst in his McLaren M8D battled Jerry Hansen in the Lola T310 just purchased from Carl Haas—the same car raced by David Hobbs in the Can-Am. Hansen won a close battle from Durst to become National Champion in the A Sports Racing class.

Penske Racing and Porsche were determined to take the 917's development to another level. The team announced late in the year that L&M would not be a sponsor on the 1973 Penske Porsche. The one-car effort would have Sunoco as the primary sponsor and run in their colors. Mark was already in Germany working on the car that would become the 917-30. Although Porsche was offering 917-10s as customer cars, the agreement with Porsche ensured that only Penske Racing would have the latest development.

When Sunoco agreed to sponsor the 917-30, Jerry Kroninger insisted that the fully formulated SAE 20W-50 engine oil be used as it had been in every Penske race car since 1969. Porsche initially resisted, preferring straight viscosity oil such as SAE 40 or SAE 50. Mark backed Jerry, and a drum of the SAE 20W-50 was shipped to Stuttgart. Porsche approved it. Sunoco-sponsored cars were the first to use multi-viscosity engine oil in Trans-Am, Can-Am, USAC, and NASCAR.

Like the 917-10, the 917-30 retained the space-frame chassis and extensive use of titanium. But the new car was much bigger—the wheelbase was six inches longer and the front track five inches wider—and even more powerful. The 12-cylinder engine was stretched to 5.4 liters and could develop as much as 1,100 horsepower. Mark was able to control the power output with an in-cockpit control knob that allowed him to adjust the amount of boost pressure depending upon the circumstance. As originally designed, the 917-30 could carry as much as 106 gallons of fuel. The body was all new

and had been designed by a French aeronautical company. The Porsche engineers referred to it as "the Paris body."

Porsche went to France's Circuit Paul Ricard for two weeks of testing. It was an enormous operation as the team was also testing the two new 2.7-liter Carreras that were entered for the Daytona 24-hour race, one for Penske Racing and one for Brumos. The 911 Carrera RS was painted in Sunoco blue at Stuttgart. Herbert Müller and Gijs van Lennep were doing most of the testing at Paul Ricard, as well as Brumos Porsche's Peter Gregg. Mark concentrated on the 917-30. One of the 917-10 Penske team cars that had not yet been turned over to Rinzler was used for baseline testing. The weather was bad, but enough was accomplished to establish the potential for greater top speed. Eventually Mark and Helmut Flegl devised a longer tail which was merged with the Paris body before the car was shipped to America.

Mark called Steve Beizer from Germany and asked him where he was going to be for New Year's. Steve said he had no firm plans and Mark told him, "Be at Islamorada." Steve headed for the Florida Keys, and when he answered the knock on his hotel room it was Mark and Eden with Jay and Barb Signore.

"We decided to go to Key West," remembers Steve. "It was a great ride down—Mark only knew full throttle or idle—until we hit a bow wave. We were almost submerged but Mark kept the engines running and we got there completely soaked." Eden recalls that they found someone to tow them in, and "porpoises followed us all the way in to the dock. It was magical. Then we found the nearest bar and had a lot of piña coladas." It was a great New Year's Eve despite hitting a sandbar on the way back to Islamorada. "It was pitch black and we were trying to get the boat loose," Steve remembers. "There were some fishermen close by and we asked them what they were doing. They were fishing for sharks."

CHAPTER 141:

NASCAR Victory at Riverside

Development of the Porsche 917-30 continued in early January in France at the Magny-Cours circuit as the team concentrated on running just one car in the Can-Am. In fact, the only series where Penske Racing intended to run two cars was USAC. New McLaren M16Cs were on order for Mark and Gary Bettenhausen. It would be a big year of single-seat racing for Mark, as the team planned to make their most ambitious effort yet in the L&M Continental F5000 series. Traco was preparing an AMC engine to go in the latest Lola, the T330. The team was also committed to run selected races in the FIA manufacturers' series in Porsche 911 Carreras prepared by the factory. Finally, the NASCAR program continued with the AMC Matador. Mark planned to do some of the races, with Dave Marcis continuing as the driver when Mark had other commitments.

Mark had not raced the Matador since the previous March. His first race of the season was the Winston Western 500 on January 21 at Riverside, where just a year before he had made his NASCAR debut. The Matador was still too boxy to provide good aerodynamics—it was known throughout NASCAR as "the Kelvinator"—and the engine was not as strong as the Fords, Chevrolets, and Plymouths. Traco had tried enlarging its displacement during the previous year but it hadn't worked and the car was back to 366ci. On the other hand, the car had been developed into a beautiful handler and featured disc brakes—still a novelty in NASCAR. Mark had been competitive at Riverside the year before and believed he could win.

David Pearson's Wood Brothers Mercury was fastest of the 66 cars attempting to qualify for the 40 starting positions. His lap of the 2.62-mile circuit at 1:25.083 put him on pole position alongside the Chevelle of Bobby Allison with a 1:25.665. Hershel McGriff in a Plymouth was third and Mark fourth with a 1:26.744. Mark was unperturbed by his qualifying time because he had recorded it with a badly slipping clutch and knew there was more speed in the Matador. He was unhappy with the state of preparation in which he had found the car and pushed the crew to bring it up to the standard he expected. They responded, and later in practice he did consistent 1:25s. On the rows behind him were Richard Petty, Bobby Isaac, Bobby Unser, Cale Yarborough, Buddy Baker, Benny Parsons, and 30 more.

Bobby Allison charged into an early lead with Mark following closely. By lap 11 Mark was in first place and dominated the rest of the race, leading 161 of the 191 laps. Allison and Petty both challenged at various points, but at the finish it was Mark giving AMC their first NASCAR win, a full two laps ahead of Bobby Allison in second. Allison told *AutoWeek*'s Mike Knepper that he knew from early in the race that Mark would be hard to beat. "If I could have gotten closer to him late in the race I might have driven harder," he said. "But the transmission wouldn't stay in third gear and some other minor things were going on, so I just hung back and hoped he would break. He didn't."

It was Mark's first NASCAR victory in only his sixth start. While elated to win, he did not believe it meant a great deal for the hopes of the car when the series returned to the oval tracks. "It's the same size as last year's car and the horsepower is about the same," Mark told Knepper. "Our better brakes made the difference here as well as getting some of the fine points in the chassis and suspension worked out."

Mark stayed at Riverside for the first tests of the new AMC-Lola T330. Fitting the AMC engine had presented a challenge, but Don Cox had managed to engineer a tidy package. Karl Kainhofer had completed the assembly at Eric Broadley's Lola factory. Round one of the L&M series was scheduled at the southern California race circuit on April 29. On Tuesday evening after a day of testing Mark left the track to rest. Crew chief Kainhofer and Haig Alltounian continued working in the Goodyear garage. "We had the car on wooden sawhorses and had the fuel system apart," remembers Karl. "It was dark and we had an electrical drop light. It fell and the heat from it ignited the raw fuel." Karl and Haig grabbed fire extinguishers but the blaze overwhelmed their best efforts to stop it. "It was pretty tough," recalls Karl. "There was tremendous heat and there were oxygen and nitrogen bottles we were afraid would explode, and of course the place was full of tires."

The fire spread to the driver's lounge, which was consumed in the flames along with Goodyear's tire-mounting shop and the 70 tires stored there. It took the Riverside Fire Department to bring the fire under control. The Lola was completely destroyed, along with three Formula Fords that were also stored in the building. "When it was all over Haig and I went to see Mark at the motel," says Karl. "He wanted to know how things were going and I said, 'They're not going so good; we burned down the car.'" Roger later announced that the team was withdrawing from the F5000 series, saying there was not sufficient time to replace and develop the car.

CHAPTER 142:
Most Courageous Athlete

On January 29 the Philadelphia Sports Writers Association held its annual banquet to honor the sports stars of 1972. Steve Carlton, the great left-handed pitcher for the Philadelphia Phillies, was named "Pro Athlete of the Year." For his seven goal medals in the Olympics, swimmer Mark Spitz was awarded the title "Amateur Athlete of the Year." Mark Donohue was proclaimed "Most Courageous Athlete of the Year." Previous winners of the award included Dizzy Dean, Jimmy Piersall, and Ben Hogan. The only other race driver to have been so honored by the group was Jim Hurtubise, who received the award in 1965.

Mark told *The Evening Bulletin*'s Jim Barniak, "I've never gotten an award of this type and I don't know how I qualify. There were months of tremendous pain after the accident. I was heavily drugged up. I had to get off that, so I switched to alcohol and I came pretty close to becoming an alcoholic. There were some tough moments and I kept wondering, geez, does anybody care about what I do, what I am going through? Now, at least, I feel like somebody does."

Eden, who saw a great deal of Mark during that period, believes Mark greatly overstated his use of alcohol during the recovery. "I never saw him drink to excess. I think by his standards he may have had more to drink than normal during that time, just to take the edge off the pain, but he never had a drinking problem."

More honors came to Mark in April when Drexel University in Philadelphia presented him their Engineering Award for "bringing professional engineering into auto racing." Previous recipients of the Drexel award included space exploration pioneer Wernher von Braun and Dr. Michael DeBakey, the father of modern open-heart surgery.

Since the previous fall Porsche had been developing the new 2.7-liter, 911 Carrera RSR for the Daytona 24 Hours on February 2–3. Despite the best efforts of Porsche, the car could not be homologated in time to run in the Group 4, GT category. Instead, the blue Penske Racing entry and the white with red and blue stripes Brumos Racing car ran in the Group 5 prototype category. George Follmer drove with Mark, and Hurley Haywood was teamed with Peter Gregg for the Jacksonville, Florida–based Brumos team.

The only European representation in the prototype class came from John Wyer's Gulf-Mirage team and Matra. Wyer fielded two cars for Derek Bell / Howden Ganley and Mike Hailwood / John Watson. Matra had a single entry for François Cevert / Henri Pescarolo. The works Ferrari team did not appear because Daytona's Bill France refused to meet Enzo Ferrari's extreme demand for starting money. It was standard practice for race organizers to pay appearance money combined with an allowance for transportation costs, with a generally agreed-upon fee for top-ranked teams. Ferrari was always the exception, and whether for Formula One or prototype races, negotiations with the team from Maranello could be excruciating. Enzo Ferrari claimed that no race could prosper or be considered important without the presence of his team. While the Matra and Wyer teams each received in the neighborhood of $2,500 to cover costs, Ferrari had demanded $30,000.

The Porsches for Penske and Brumos were nearly identical, both having been prepared at the factory. Mark told *Road & Track*'s Bill Warner, "We value our relationship with Porsche and if this is what they desire us to race, we will." During practice Mark asked Goodyear to fit a set of wide tires that he recognized as a type he had used successfully on the Trans-Am Camaro. When the tires didn't arrive at the garage he was upset and sought an answer. "I was told that the tires wouldn't fit," Mark recalled. "I said 'What do you mean they won't fit? We haven't tried them.' I wanted an answer and chased it all the way to the Goodyear fitting shop where I found out that while they were being mounted, Peter Gregg happened to come in and asked why they were fitting that tire. They told him they were fitting them for me. He said, 'Take them off. They won't fit.' So because Peter was God they took them off. I told them 'You let Peter Gregg have his car and do what he wants. I want these tires on.' It was obvious to me that Peter had never used those tires and he didn't want me trying them first. But they did fit and the car was faster and then immediately Peter had them on his car."

Before the race Mark made the decision to switch to Goodyear radial tires in place of the bias-plies being used on the Brumos car. He knew he was giving up lap time but believed it was in the best long-term interest of Penske in their relationship with Goodyear. The taller radial tire did provide an unexpected bonus of effectively giving the Porsche a higher gear ratio. "No matter what top gear you think is right in practice, you should always go up one for the race," said Mark. "Somehow, with all those cars out there on the track, you get a draft and the wind starts going around and you go faster. At least for the first six hours until the motor gets tired."

"Actually, over a long run the radials were just as fast," remembers Follmer. "I don't think they gave up as much as did the bias-ply tire. It was just in the early laps on a fresh set that we were at a disadvantage, and therefore they weren't as good a qualifying tire."

Just before the start Mark predicted to Warner that within two hours he would have the Carrera ahead of all the GT Corvettes. Mark made good on his forecast and by the end of the second hour was fifth overall behind the Brumos car, fourth. Twelve hours into the race all of the true prototypes—the quickest of which were more than 15 seconds a lap faster than the 911s—were either out or struggling. The Brumos Porsche was delayed when rocks broke their headlamps. Mark and George now were leading the race two laps ahead of Gregg and Haywood. By early morning the Brumos car had won back a lap but the Penske team continued to hold a comfortable lead. At 5:14 a.m the flywheel broke and the race was over for Mark and George.

"The ironic thing about that race was that Peter had found out that the flywheel was loose on our car when he had the engine torn down the week before the race," recalls Hurley Haywood. "We were down in the race shop when he found out and he immediately called Roger to suggest he check theirs. Peter was such a company guy that even though the rivalry between Peter and the Penske operation was intense, he wanted the playing field to be equal and he found out that the flywheel hadn't been tightened. Roger didn't credit it—I think he thought Peter was just pulling his leg."

The Brumos car ran on without incident and won the greatest victory to date for the team. It was also the first major overall circuit win for a 911-based race car—Vic Elford having won the 1968 Monte Carlo rally in a 911. Peter Gregg and Hurley Haywood became an extraordinarily successful pairing in endurance racing. Hurley recalls the rivalry that existed between Mark and Gregg. "Mark didn't like Peter, they didn't get along very well," remembers Hurley. "There was a professional rivalry—they would be friendly enough on the surface but they weren't likely to go to dinner together. Despite my friendship with Peter, Mark and I were very close and I had dinner with him frequently."

Mark rejoined the NASCAR series for the race at Atlanta International Raceway on April 1. Just as he had feared, the Matador was no more competitive on fast ovals than it had been the year before. On Friday, Mark was second fastest of the nine drivers who posted a qualifying time before rain halted the session. Continued rain canceled qualifying and the times were scratched. Starting positions for the race were determined by drawing race numbers out of a hat. Mark drew 12th and started on the outside of the sixth row. The Matador failed to run the distance and the race was won by David Pearson. Conflicting schedules made this the last opportunity for Mark to run a NASCAR race. Dave Marcis finished the season for Penske Racing in the Matador.

Mark purchased a new 28-foot cigarette boat from Don Aronow to replace his previous Donzi. On one of his first runs in the new boat Mark slipped and reinjured the leg that was damaged in his accident the previous summer. The pain was intense, but Mark applied his stoic approach and minimized the effect. Then the boat played into a potentially more serious accident. Mark was working on the boat late one April evening at the race shop at Newtown Square. While attaching the trailer to the ball hitch on his blue pickup truck, a jack slipped and Mark's right thumb was crushed against the truck bumper. Although he was briefly unconscious, he was able to yell loud enough to rouse Dan Luginbuhl who was working late in the office. Dan helped free Mark and drove him to nearby Riddle Memorial Hospital. Mark had suffered a double compound fracture.

"I am quite lucky, as the first diagnosis was that I would lose it," Mark told *National Speed Sport News* of his thumb injury. "But after one night in the hospital they decided they could repair it." Mark spent two nights in the hospital. "I can drive now but the pain is intense," he said. Undeterred, Mark left the next day for New York where he conducted an RRDC Advanced Driving Clinic. Afterward he left New York for Germany where he tested the 917-30 at Weissach.

Mark's accident featured in a *National Speed Sport News* headline that covered all the bases. Under a front-page banner that read "Indy winner quits USAC—Donohue returns license," the page-three headline followed with "Defending Indy car champ Mark Donohue's big week: 1) smashes thumb. 2) enters 500. 3) quits USAC."

The license story quoted Mark's April 4 letter to USAC president Dick King, saying in part, "I am doing this in the best interests of USAC and myself." Mark resigned his USAC license because of the hard line the sanctioning body was taking with respect to driver interchange. USAC considered single-seat racing their turf and greatly resented the SCCA's L&M Continental Formula 5000 series, which they saw drawing attention from their Champ car series. If Mark retained his USAC license he would be barred from the L&M series. The Can-Am was not an issue, as all of its dates carried an international listing. Likewise the Indy 500, Ontario, and Pocono all had international listings, allowing Mark to participate even as an SCCA driver. For Mark it was a simple business decision based upon the need to be eligible for races he wished to compete in. For USAC it was the loss of a star driver at a time when the political wrangling between sanctioning bodies was at its bitterest. The bad feeling culminated in USAC temporarily withdrawing from the Automobile Competition Committee of the United States (ACCUS), the American delegate body to the FIA.

CHAPTER 143:

Racing the Eagle

Penske Racing had their two new McLaren M16Cs ready to test at Indianapolis in March. Karl Kainhofer and Haig Alltounian had spent the winter in England building the cars at the McLaren works in Colnbrook. After working with the car Mark became convinced it would not be fast enough to beat the Eagles. He asked Roger to purchase an Eagle in kit form from Dan Gurney's All American Racers. Karl Kainhofer went to California and brought all the pieces to Newtown Square and spent April building it into a race car. Working in the shop with Karl on the single-seat race cars were Walter Gass and Nick Olilla. This would be the first time the team had run three cars at the Speedway. In the meantime, Bobby Allison joined the team to race the second McLaren alongside Gary Bettenhausen. Allison had tested for Roger the previous fall at Ontario with impressive results the first time he had ever sat in an Indy car. At the Speedway Roger worked with Allison and Don Cox worked with Bettenhausen on setups and race engineering. Mark was his own engineer and Karl Kainhofer was the chief mechanic on his car.

"Roger took a lot of static from the press for deserting McLaren and buying the Eagle, but he did it because he understood what it meant to me," Mark told *Road & Track*'s Mike Knepper. The Penske Sunoco-DX Eagle arrived at Indy without any previous testing. "We got the car just in time to get to the Speedway the first of May. I started having trouble right away: first oversteer, then understeer, everything. Gurney took me aside once and said that he would help me all he could, but that there was no way I could hope to make the car work in such a short time and against teams that had had Eagles for several weeks. He was right."

Looking back on this period of disillusionment and uncertainty, Mark was able to identify almost to the moment when he first thought seriously about giving up driving. "At the point I was most lost—which was half way through the development of the Eagle—I was sitting in the car thinking, 'What do I do next?'" he later remembered. "The crew was waiting for me to say 'Do this' or 'Do that'—and I really had no idea what to do next. I realized this was a situation I was frequently finding myself in, where I didn't know what to do next and I didn't have the energy or enthusiasm to figure it out—because it's the same old problem over and over again. The people change and the cars change, but the problem is always the same. I said to myself, 'I've had enough of this now. I'm starting to hate this. I should really stop. I can stop now.'"

Mark was finding satisfaction in the results of his efforts increasingly rare. "It's a lonely business you know, sorting out cars; you're on your own," he said later. "I'm not complaining. I wanted it that way. I brought it to that myself. But I often dug myself a hole I couldn't get out of. I didn't clearly say to myself at that point, 'I'm going to stop now,' but, I did say to myself, I should quit now because I'm beginning to hate it."

Mark said he still got the same degree of enjoyment out of driving, but he couldn't separate the responsibility of setting up the cars from the pure joy of driving them. He speculated about knowing the right time to retire. He didn't think he was getting any better as a driver and wondered how one recognized when one was on a downward slope. "I think Phil Hill did it right," Mark said. "He stopped when he was still at the top of his skills. On the other hand, Graham Hill is still doing it, and while he obviously still enjoys it, it's clear he has slipped. The unfortunate thing is that the memory of Graham will be somewhat clouded by the recollection people have of him in this last stage of his career as compared to the brilliance he had previously."

"I think Mark was going through a period of burnout," says Dave Lawton. "The last year at Indy was very, very difficult for him. The horrendous accident at Atlanta—he had a hard time getting over that. There were rumors that Mark's time had come and gone—that he didn't have it anymore. These things eventually get back to you—it's annoying as hell and adds to the pressure."

Mark was wistful about other drivers who just showed up and drove, while he had to worry about the logistics, the loading and unloading, the engineering, parts arriving on time, the latest this and that. Of course, he also reveled in all these added responsibilities and had largely wanted it this way. But on some level he envied the guys who didn't have to be concerned with other things—all they had to do was drive the car. He said, "When it's time for me to drive I have to shut all that out. But it's becoming increasingly difficult to do so."

For all the pressure and self-evaluation, Mark remained at his core a kind and thoughtful man. Dick Mittman was the motorsports editor for the *Indianapolis News*. The *News* ran a special section for the 500, and an interview with the previous year's winner was its center feature. Upon completing the rather lengthy interview with Mark, Dick was leaving the Penske garage when he discovered that his tape recorder had failed. More than somewhat dismayed, he returned to the garage to tell Dan Luginbuhl what had happened. Mark overheard the conversation and immediately suggested a solution. He was speaking that evening to the Indianapolis chapter of the Society of Automotive Engineers and suggested that Dick come along and they would redo the interview afterward.

The SAE event was at Ben Davis High School in Indianapolis, and Dick caught a ride there to hear the talk. When it was over, Dick suddenly realized he was stranded—he had forgotten to call his wife to arrange for her to pick him up. Mark again resolved the problem. Dick got the interview while Mark drove him home in his 1972 Cadillac. Dan Luginbuhl points out that a mechanical malfunction causing someone to not be able to do his job was something Mark could sympathize with.

Mark made an impression on many people. Nick Nagurny observed Mark over a number of years, and as a sportswriter for the *Philadelphia Bulletin* also encountered many other world-class athletes on a personal level. "Mark was the most unassuming person of all the top athletes I knew," says Nagurny. "He was soft-spoken and had a sensitive side. He would find time for you and always was insightful in his comments."

Racing insiders also saw this side of Mark. Charlie Hayes provides a racer's perspective on Mark's character. "Racing may have changed Mark a little. He had to put up some defenses against the constant media and fan intrusions. So there was sometimes a little vitriol, but the essence of Mark was an utterly charming, authentic, open guy—a pure, wonderful human being," he says. "To have all this and to have the type of resignation and despair that took him over was a very potent pointer to the immense frustration every race driver went through. After a good race you would feel whole and complete—for about two hours. Because then the conversation came back full force—when's the next race? Mark came full face with that after winning Indy. Mark was so authentic and had tremendous candor. He was willing to expose that. His humanness was, I think, the hallmark of his character."

Mark echoed Hayes's point about the need to defend against intrusions at inappropriate times. "It's true that I'm usually agreeable," he wrote in *The Boys of Indy*. "But if it's a couple of days before a big race like the Indy 500 and someone comes up to me and asks me something not directly connected with the race or wants to make small talk, he's going to walk away thinking I'm pretty awful. I'm not in a mood for small talk then."

Sam Posey remembers Mark's desperate efforts getting the Eagle up to speed. "I'll never forget Leon Mandel approaching me and saying, 'If I were you I'd get out of here as fast as you can. You are whistling past the graveyard.' I replied, 'No, it's not me. It's Mark.' I could see Mark struggling with his car—he had that look of blank determination—to have won Indy and then come back and not even be competitive—it was hard on him."

Mark later expressed it in another way to Mike Knepper. "I was so alone. You know Peggy Lee's song, 'Is That All There Is?' Well, I finally decided if this is what I had after all those years, if this is what it all came down to, I wanted out. That's when I decided to quit."

During the month a number of drivers approached the magic 200-mph average speed. The first weekend of qualifying brought the usual enormous crowd with the anticipation of seeing the speed achieved for the first time at Indianapolis. In morning practice on Saturday, May 12, prior to the opening qualifying runs, Eagle driver Art Pollard (driving for Robert Fletcher's Cobra Tire team) had a huge accident exiting turn one. The Eagle hit the outside wall and then flipped several times. Pollard, 46, was rushed to Methodist Hospital where he was pronounced dead.

Mark was in the middle of an intense battle for pole position and ended up placing the Sunoco-DX Eagle on the outside of row one with the third fastest speed of the day at 197.412. Pole went to Johnny Rutherford in the works Gulf McLaren with a 198.413. Bobby Unser was in the middle of the front row with a 198.183 in Dan Gurney's Olsonite Eagle. Row two had Swede Savage (Eagle), Gary Bettenhausen (Penske Sunoco McLaren), and Mario Andretti (Parnelli). Bobby Allison in the third Penske entry was the fastest rookie qualifier, placing his McLaren solidly on the outside of row four. "Mark had impressed me from day one," remembers Allison. "He impressed me behind the wheel of a race car. You wouldn't know by looking at him that he was one of the top race car drivers in the world—he was always calm and friendly, and he was the same way to all people. He was just a real good driver, and he helped me a lot with my road racing, too. He was all about being smooth and taking care of the car."

The Memorial Day race on Monday, May 28, began with heavy rain that delayed the start for four hours and five minutes. When the cars finally received the green flag there was a frightening accident in the middle of the pack. Just past the scoring pylon, David "Salt" Walther, who was in the middle of the sixth row, moved too far to the right (Walther believes he was hit from behind), and he tangled with Jerry Grant. Walther's car flew through the air, shedding parts and throwing flaming fuel into the spectator enclosure. Twelve cars were involved and the race was immediately red-flagged. Walther was severely injured with broken limbs and third-degree burns over 25 percent of his body; first- and second-degree burns covered another 15 percent of it. Thirteen spectators were treated for injuries. Mark, on the front row, was ahead of the accident and not involved.

By the time the debris and wreckage were cleared it began to rain again, and the race was delayed until the next day. On Tuesday the cars were on their pace lap at 10:15 a.m. when rain fell on the back straight. The race was red-flagged again and officials waited until mid-afternoon before giving up for the day. Wednesday morning it rained again and continued past 1:00 p.m. The officials finally had the track dry to restart the race at 2:10 p.m.

Mark ran near the front of the field with Bobby Unser. On the 59th lap the race was red-flagged yet again, this time for a crash that blocked the track. Swede Savage had lost control of his Eagle exiting turn four and had hit the inside wall with violent force. The crash tore the car in two and sent a ball of fire into the air. Savage was still in the burning car as rescue teams attempted to reach him and to douse the flames. An emergency truck, roaring up the pit lane in the wrong direction, struck and killed Armando Teran, a crew member on Graham McRae's team. Savage's injuries—including a broken arm, two broken legs, and severe burns over most of his body—would ultimately prove to be fatal.

When the race resumed Mark ran well until he burned a piston in the Offy motor and retired. He was officially classified 15th. The race ended after 133 laps—332.5 miles—when the rain began again. Savage's teammate and fellow Eagle driver Gordon Johncock learned of his victory while sitting in pit lane waiting to hear if the race would be restarted. There was no victory dinner. Everyone went home at the conclusion of one of the darkest and saddest Indy 500s.

Media reaction to the incident-plagued event was swift and virulent. Writers expressed outrage for the spectators' injuries and the deaths of Pollard and Teran, along with the devastating fire that consumed Swede Savage's car and left him fighting for his life in the burn unit of Methodist Hospital. Editorials in *The New York Times* and elsewhere railed with self-righteous indignation, grasping the high-profile incidents as an opportunity to declaim a sport they knew little or nothing about. The motorsports media joined in, and much of the finger-pointing was directed at veteran Indy chief steward Harlan Fengler.

With many in the sport scurrying for cover, it was Mark Donohue who provided sane perspective. Most admirable was Mark's strong support for Fengler, who had become everyone's favorite whipping-boy. Mark placed the blame for the lap one accident on his fellow drivers, not on Fengler. He told William Jeanes in *AutoWeek*, "[Fenger's] one of the best guys in racing and he takes all this so personally. He lives with that [criticism] all year long and it just tears him apart. He can't control the positions of all those guys by radar. He can't do it. If the drivers don't want to stay in line on the start, they aren't going to do it. He can't force them and neither can anyone else."

Mark went on to draw a finer distinction between what officialdom could reasonably control and the responsibility assumed by the driver. "We ran a race there last year under the exact same conditions and everything was fine," he told Jeanes. "If a driver makes a mistake, he's going to get in trouble. No matter who you are, you're going to make a mistake one of these days. Swede did; Pollard did. A lot of people have. When you put your helmet on and bolt on your clothes, you're accepting that possibility."

Mark debunked the talk that the month-long pageantry preceding the actual race set the drivers on edge. "Nobody's forcing us to come there. We come for the prize money like everyone else. Who else pays a million dollars? Nobody comes close. If they wanted us to come two months, we'd come two months. It's the greatest thing in America, really, and we shouldn't knock it."

CHAPTER 144:
Debut Race for AMC in Formula 5000

Despite the announcement in February that Penske Racing was withdrawing from F5000 because their car had burnt to the ground, Roger now told Mark that they needed to run the series. With the Matador not competitive in NASCAR, AMC needed a program they could publicize. Mark was unenthusiastic, believing they already had too many race series on their plate. A replacement Lola T330 arrived and Mark and the team tested at Road Atlanta.

Later Mark told *Road & Track*'s Mike Knepper: "Roger had promised American Motors we would race one of their engines in the series, but there wasn't the commitment, like with the Javelin, to pull all the stops and make it a winner . . . I don't like to work that way. I don't like to lose."

Three rounds of the L&M Continental series were already complete when the team made its first race start at Mid-Ohio on June 3. A number of teams were running the Lola T330 chassis and most found that it was difficult to handle. Brian Redman, driving for Carl Haas and Jim Hall, was doing the best job, and he won the opening round at Riverside. The other top car was the Sid Taylor–entered and Jerry Entin–run Trojan T101 for Jody Scheckter. Scheckter won rounds two and three at Laguna Seca and Michigan while Redman was busy racing in Europe. Virtually without exception, Chevrolet engines were the powerplant of choice. The Traco-developed AMC engine in the Penske Lola developed comparable power to that of the Chevy, but was significantly heavier, weighing 125 pounds more. Differences in the Penske Lola from other

T330s included a revised front suspension.

The series had a new system of heats to determine the grid for the feature race. The odd-positioned qualifiers (first, third, fifth, etc.) raced in heat one, the even positions in heat two. The two heat winners started on row one for the feature race, and each succeeding row had the next-placed finishers in their respective heats. Only the feature race scored points for the championship.

Because Indy had been delayed, the team did not arrive at Mid-Ohio until Saturday. Chuck Cantwell and John Woodard had flown direct from Indy on Wednesday evening to Newtown Square, where they worked straight through to be ready for Mid-Ohio. The transporter left the shop at 4:00 a.m. on Saturday morning, arriving in the paddock at 2:00 p.m. After bleeding the brakes there was just enough time to do three laps to check the car out, leaving Mark only two laps for qualifying. Consequently, Mark's time was 18th fastest, a full four seconds off the pole-position time achieved by Brian Redman. This placed Mark ninth on the grid for heat two. Jody Scheckter had won heat one, and Brett Lunger won Mark's heat ahead of Brian Redman. Mark came through to finish third, which placed him on the third row for the feature.

Mark drove through the rain in the feature race to finish third behind winner Scheckter, with Redman second. Tony Adamowicz, who finished fourth, wrote in his *AutoWeek* column, "The AMC-powered Lola didn't appear to have the steam down the straight, but Mark more than made up for any lack of power by negotiating the more difficult portions of the circuit with apparent ease."

CHAPTER 145:
917-30 Debuts at Mosport

The big letdown for the 1973 Can-Am was the absence of the McLaren team, which had been part of the series since the beginning in 1966 and had dominated from 1967 through 1971. But when the Porsche turbos beat them in 1972, they made the business decision to leave the Can-Am to concentrate on Formula One and Indy cars. The expense of developing a turbo engine—and the uncertainty of winning even if they did—was at the heart of their move. It illustrated the essential problem with the Can-Am as a professional series. To make money a truly professional team needed to win the preponderance of races; everyone else was losing money. McLaren had been the only genuinely professional team until 1972, when they came up against Penske Racing, who enjoyed a technical advantage and the manufacturing and engineering might of Porsche. It would have taken a very large infusion of sponsorship dollars to ensure a profit for McLaren, so when none was found, the team was gone from the series.

This left the remaining 917-10s from the previous year to provide competition for Penske Racing's new 917-30. Bobby Rinzler had purchased the Penske 917-10s from the previous year. He had George Follmer driving one and Charlie Kemp the other. During the spring the team had raced in several rounds of the Interserie—the European Group 7 series—with Follmer in one car and Willy Kauhsen in the car Kemp was to drive in the Can-Am. "Porsche told Rinzler and Vasek Polak and anyone else interested that they could have the cars they had, but we were going to have a new car," Mark recalled. "It was an exclusive deal between Porsche and Penske."

"Rinzler wanted a factory deal—and a better deal than ours. He spent a lot of time in Germany wining and dining the right people at Porsche," Mark continued. "We saw that as a possible thorn in the ointment with him trying to push us out. He would even try to hire Woody from time to time."

Follmer was having a big year in Europe, as he was also driving for Shadow in Formula One. Series boosters hoped that the UOP Shadow team would be a serious contender in Can-Am with their Chevrolet engines and driver Jackie Oliver. Roy Woods had purchased the ex-Revson McLaren M20 and entered it for David Hobbs.

Vasek Polak was running turbo 917-10s for Jody Scheckter and Swiss driver Hans Wiedmer, plus a normally aspirated 917-10 for Steve Durst. His crew chief was Alwin Springer. Polak grew up in Czechoslovakia and emigrated to America, bringing with him his great love for motorsports. A race driver and an expert engine tuner, Polak proved himself an astute businessman, becoming enormously successful after opening the first West Coast Porsche dealership in Manhattan Beach, California, in 1959. Scheckter was making his first Can-Am start at Mosport. Jerry Entin was helping Sid Taylor run Jody's Formula 5000 car, and went to Mosport to help ease Jody's transition to Can-Am. In the first practice session Jody was struggling with the car and well off the pace. He shared his frustration with Jerry, who approached Mark for advice.

"Mark agreed to help Jody on the condition that Jody didn't mess with him in the race," recalls Entin. "We were all staying at the Canadiana Inn, and Mark said he would talk to Jody at breakfast Saturday morning." They did talk and Mark shared the driving technique required by the Porsche's turbocharged engine. "I didn't know Jody Scheckter but I knew he was pretty fast," Mark recalled. "I was kind of nervous that he might damage the car. I just didn't know him that well at the time." Mark, who seemed to measure other drivers in terms of their threat to him within the sport, recognized Jody Scheckter as a great talent, later saying, "Along comes Scheckter and it was a new threat to deal with."

Hurley Haywood was another rising star who received help from Mark. He had purchased his 917-10 from Peter Gregg, and along with the deal came the crew and spares and maintenance. "Mark was really, really helpful in bringing me up to speed and explaining how to drive the car and what to look for," recalls Hurley. "He helped with the setup of the 917-10 and with tips on driving techniques peculiar to it. There was a whole mystique about those cars and Mark was a real mentor to me."

The 917-30 was particularly striking in its blue and yellow Sunoco colors. "I think the biggest thing we've done is to make it easier to drive," Mark told Nick Nagurny about the new improved Porsche. "The engine problem consisted of trying to further reduce the lag and make the engine more durable, and lighter." Mark also discussed the physical demands entailed. "It takes much more effort to drive Can-Am cars than Indy cars. You're exhausted much quicker. Indy cars are relatively easy to handle. In a road-racing car, you're doing many more things—going around slow turns, fast turns, right, left. Driving a road course with a powerful car requires that you coordinate brakes, steering, clutch, gears, and throttle. At Indianapolis you have basically the steering and the throttle."

Mark was slower than Scheckter and others in practice. It was his first time in the car since the right front suspension A-arm had broken in recent testing at Road Atlanta, almost causing a crash. The result was a final redesign, and Mark spent the practice session working out the changes. In qualifying Mark showed the car's superiority, lapping at 1:14.1, a second and a half faster than Scheckter. Kemp and Follmer were on row two in the RC Cola–sponsored

Rinzler cars, and row three had Haywood alongside the first non-Porsche, John Cordts in a McLaren M8D.

The first few laps of the race were exciting. Mark took an immediate lead only to see Scheckter slipstream by him at the end of the long straight. Mark followed for two laps and then passed for the lead in the same spot. On the next lap Mark came over the crest of the hill at the end of the straight to encounter Jim Butcher's McLaren M8C, the first of the cars to be lapped. The closing rate was fast, and as Mark moved first left and then right to pass, Butcher was doing the same in an attempt to provide room. Mark hit the McLaren with the Porsche's right front corner and was off the road at nearly 200 mph. He did a fine job of controlling the car in the grass but came to grief when he encountered the access road that met the track at a right angle. "The access road was about three feet higher than the grass I was on," Mark remembered. "When I hit that it was like hitting a launching pad." The Porsche hit the berm and flew through the air. Mark drove straight to the pits with the car's nose in the air. Butcher continued, although the contact had upset his suspension and he eventually retired.

It was four laps before repairs could be made, and even then the nose was still high, the bodywork ragged, and the steering dangerously compromised. It was impossible to replace the nose because all the supports were damaged. Mark returned to the track to make the best of the situation.

The race became a monotonous parade with Scheckter well in the lead. Goodyear tire engineer Gordon Calhoun came to the Polak pit and asked that Jody be brought in to check the tires. According to Jerry Entin, Calhoun said that Scheckter's aggressive driving style—he was reported smoking the tires off every turn—was more than the tire was engineered to tolerate. Polak refused to bring Jody in but agreed to give the slow down sign. On lap 27 a tire deflated and Jody hit the guardrail. Charlie Kemp won for Bobby Rinzler and RC Cola, with Hans Wiedmer second in a Porsche 917-10, two laps down. Mark and the battered Sunoco Porsche finished in seventh place, seven laps down.

CHAPTER 146:
Move to Wyomissing and an "irrevocable decision"

On June 14 Penske Enterprises took possession of Michigan International Speedway. Roger had purchased it out of bankruptcy after a protracted negotiation that had several other interested buyers in the mix. He ensured the financial viability of the facility by securing an agreement from AMC to lease the track for a minimum of 320 days a year for testing.

On June 16 and 17 Watkins Glen featured a double-header weekend with a Trans-Am race on Saturday and an L&M Continental on Sunday. Mark agreed to co-drive Al Holbert's Porsche 911 Carrera RSR in the Trans-Am. "Al came to me and asked if I would drive with him," Mark remembered. "I didn't really want to but said I would be glad to do it. Al had been a friend of mine for years and his father Bob went way back with Roger." It was the same car Mark and George Follmer had raced at Daytona, but it was now owned and entered by Holbert's Porsche-Audi of Warrington, Pennsylvania.

Future star Al Holbert had made his professional debut at Road Atlanta just two months earlier, and was thrilled to be racing with the man he had so looked up to when he'd worked for Roger Penske during summer breaks from college. Mark started the race, but because he hadn't qualified, the car started nearly last. The race began in heavy rain and, despite pitting for dry tires when it cleared, he brought the Porsche into the lead. When he turned the car over to Al the rain returned with a vengeance. "I no sooner got out of the car than it started to rain—I mean it really poured," said Mark. "I walked back to the pits and Al arrived with the whole front torn off the car. He had run into a puddle that he couldn't see—four or five cars crashed at the same time." The circuit had become engulfed in a fog so thick that drivers could not see beyond the front of their cars and literally did not know where they were on the circuit.

Two laps later the race was abandoned and the Carrerra was classified eighth. "Driving with Mark was a real thrill," Al told Al Bochroch. Race winner was Maurice Carter in a Camaro, with Peter Gregg second in his Porsche RSR.

The fog had disappeared for the L&M Formula 5000 race on Sunday. During qualifying the day before, Mark was in and out of the pits making adjustments to the AMC Lola and was only eighth fastest, placing him on row four for heat two. Tony Adamowicz recalls that Mark was using rear tires from a Formula B car as his front tires, hoping that adding grip on the front would cure a chronic understeer problem in the AMC Lola. "I encountered him in the paddock and asked, 'Mark, are you really trying out there?' " recalls Tony. "He looked at me and said, 'I've never tried so effin' hard in my life.' "

Mark was indeed trying hard: His fastest lap of 1:42.761 in the heat race was a full second faster than the lap record set by Jody Scheckter in winning heat one. Brian Redman won the heat, with Mark second. After Scheckter had crashed his Trojan T101 beyond repair on Friday, his car owner Sid Taylor rented Bob Lazier's Lola T330. Scheckter dominated the feature race and Redman finished second. Mark had a race-long battle with Brett Lunger, who beat him to the finish line by inches, leaving Mark and the AMC Lola fourth.

On June 29, 1973, Mark was elected to membership in the Society of Automotive Engineers. The SAE promoted the Arts, Sciences, Standards, and Engineering connected with the design, construction, and utilization of self-propelled mechanisms, prime movers, components thereof, and related equipment.

Nick Nagurny remembers Mark's fitness regimen that summer. "Mark would perform countless sit-ups at various times during the day," Nagurny says. "He was also into healthy eating and extremely aware of different food values."

Mark had missed qualifying the first weekend at Pocono for the USAC Schaefer 500 because he was racing at Watkins Glen. Twenty-one cars had qualified the first weekend, leaving Mark with a best hope of being 22nd on the grid in the Eagle-Offy even if he was fastest. When he appeared on June 24, his speed of 185.510 was the day's second fastest after Gordon Johncock, earning the 23rd starting position. In the July 1 race Mark and the Eagle made steady progress through the field to take the lead for eight laps until the engine failed on lap 104.

Pocono was the first race to be run under USAC's new fuel rules, enacted in response to the furor over the fiery accidents at the Indy 500. On-board fuel could now only be carried in the left-side tanks and was reduced to 40 gallons from the previous 75. Total fuel permitted for a 500-mile race was down from 375 gallons to 340. Additionally, rear wing width was cut from a maximum of 64 inches to 55 inches. These changes were an attempt by the sanctioning body to slow the cars and to lessen the fire risk.

At Pocono Mark told Roger for the first time that he intended to retire at the end of the season. The idea of retirement had first come to Mark during the difficult month of May at Indianapolis. "It suddenly seemed that all of the problems were so big although I knew that all of them could be solved in time," Mark said later. "It was an irrevocable decision."

A great part of Mark's frustration and ultimate disillusionment came from being involved in too many projects. In a *Road & Track* article by Peter Manso, Mark later explained, "Much of the problem all along was that I didn't have the balls to stand up to Roger and say, 'Hey, I'm just not going to get involved in that.' It wasn't Roger's fault. It was mine."

"I burned myself out," Mark later reflected. "I tried so hard for so long to do more than I should have done in terms of working on the car, getting the car right, doing the driving, doing the sorting, and so forth. I just didn't have anything left—I couldn't cope with all that anymore."

Roger Penske never lost faith in Mark, telling *Road & Track*'s Mike Knepper, "Mark is the ultimate manager and actually manages the race team. He tends to be pessimistic so I try to balance things out with some optimism. I also try to get him to enjoy things more. . . . All things considered, all types of racing, there is only one other driver in the world as good as Mark and that's A. J. Foyt."

While Roger's appreciation was genuine, apparently Mark needed a great deal more positive reinforcement from the entire team than he was receiving. "If my guys and Roger had boosted my ego a little bit it would have meant a lot," Mark later said. "Any time I would drive really well Roger wouldn't say a word, no one would say a word. It was a combination of a lot of things, problems I had personally as well as the way I was treated as a driver. I only see it now, I didn't see it then. Now that I have retired I can see how important it is that the driver's morale and ego gets boosted."

Mark and Roger were intensely loyal to one another and neither would brook hearing criticism of the other. The famous communication between the two men, which often seemed to border on the intuitive, was not operative in this instance. Roger took Mark literally, believing that he had had enough of driving. Mark was unable to admit that what he really wanted was to be the team's driver without the enormous responsibility he had acquired for running the operation. He had created his own environment and now it was finally too much. His inability to convey his true feelings to Roger put in motion a retirement that he wasn't ready for.

Many people close to Mark didn't believe he was ready to stop racing. His evident fatigue with the multiple race programs for which he was responsible was exacerbated by difficult issues in his personal life. Mark and Sue had now been separated for a year and a half and were working toward an eventual divorce settlement. A combination of stressful forces had pushed Mark to a decision.

The team had loaded for Pocono at the race shop on Winding Way in Newtown Square, and after the race went directly to their new home in Reading. The new headquarters for Penske Enterprises brought Roger's racing and truck leasing operations under one roof. The 13.8-acre property also encompassed a skid pad just a few feet from the door of the race shop. Roger had assigned planning of the long envisioned step to Norman Ahn, who also supervised construction of the entire complex. Mark bought a condominium in the nearby suburb of Wyomissing. "It was a very simple two-bedroom apartment," remembers Eden. "One bedroom was for the boys. Up to that time he hadn't had a place where they could stay with him. There was a trundle bed in the boy's room and each bedroom had its own bath."

On July 2, Swede Savage died from the terrible burns he had suffered in his Indianapolis crash. A popular driver and a great talent who was expected to become a major figure in American racing was gone. He was survived by his wife Sharyl, and a seven-year-old daughter, Shelly. "I knew Swede and I liked him," Mark told Ron Hudspeth of the *Atlanta Journal*. "But I never went to dinner with him and I'm not really sure what his wife looks like. That's how close I was to him. A lot of guys I've known have died doing this, and I suppose that's why race drivers tend not to be friendly with each other. If someone is killed, you don't feel so badly about it."

CHAPTER 147:

Fantastic beyond Words— But No Win

After the Mosport season-opener in June, the SCCA created a new format for the Can-Am series. Henceforth the Can-Am races would be run in two parts, with the first part essentially setting the grid for the continuation of the race in part two. The change was dictated by the need to provide more entertainment value. The small fields and lack of real competition was producing boring races. The new format at least provided spectators with the excitement of two race starts. The rule permitted the organizers of each race to decide whether to run both heats the same day or on consecutive days.

Road Atlanta chose the latter approach and held races on July 7 and 8. It was not a true heat system, but rather a single race of 90 laps in which the first 40 were run one day and the remaining 50 the next. But it was also not a true continuation race because all cars remaining on the lead lap at the end of part one would resume on equal terms with the leader on the start of part two. Lapped cars started the second race down the number of laps recorded in the first race. Mark dominated the Saturday portion of the race and finished 70 seconds ahead of George Follmer in the Rinzler RC Cola 917-10. "The car is fantastic beyond words," Mark told the Associated Press. Mark said he didn't like the split-race format but concluded, "It does make better races for the spectator and they're the ones who should decide it."

On Sunday the race began in similar pattern to the day before, with Mark opening a lead over Follmer. Jody Scheckter in the Vasek Polak 917-10 was next, although a lap down from the previous day's event. On the warm-up laps Mark noticed something leaking in the cockpit but thought it was only the water bottle. Once the race started, however, he realized it was the fuel cap. He was soon covered in gasoline and stopped briefly at the pits to have water poured over him to dilute the fuel. Later he stopped again to have the problem fixed. When Mark returned to the action he was third, two laps down to Follmer and behind Scheckter, who had regained his lap when Mark was in the pits. "It was an incredibly painful race after the water evaporated," said Mark. He overcame the discomfort and soon caught Scheckter for second place and unlapped himself twice from George to regain the lead lap. But time ran out, and at the finish Mark was 50 seconds behind. Losing the 70-second lead from the day before rankled. Two rounds of the Can-Am were complete and the Sunoco 917-30 had been beaten each time by one of Bobby Rinzler's 917-10s.

Although Eden did not attend all of Mark's races they were frequently together as their romance continued to grow. When Mark raced in her hometown of Atlanta it was a special time for the White family, all of whom had grown fond of him. Steve Beizer, who usually loaned Mark a Porsche when he was in town, this time had handed him the keys to a 365 GT4 Ferrari for the weekend. After the race, Steve asked Eden's brother Richard White if he would deliver the car back to the dealership the next day. "As he handed me the keys, he winked and said, 'We don't close until 5:30, so just get it there by then,'" remembers Richard. Richard made the most of the day and, accompanied by a series of friends, made repeated efforts to get the Ferrari over 150 mph. "It would do it easily but whenever I got close I would come flying up on traffic and have to back off."

Mark's fatigue and the strain of carrying so many of the team's responsibilities were apparent to his fellow competitors. "I bumped into Mark at Detroit Metropolitan Airport that summer," recalls Bob Tullius. "I was appalled at how exhausted he looked. We decided to share a room while waiting for our flight connections. We talked a little about the pressure he was under, and when we got to the room he fell asleep immediately, like he hadn't slept in weeks."

"The thing was that Mark was spreading himself too thin," says Bobby Unser. "Roger kept coming up with new projects and Mark would do whatever Roger wanted him to do. Roger could motivate and Mark would tirelessly do it. But remember, it wasn't all Roger's fault—Mark wanted to do it."

CHAPTER 148:

First Win for the 917-30— and Mark Strikes Again

Mark and George Follmer were teamed again in a 911 RSR Carrera for the six-hour endurance race at Watkins Glen on July 21, the day before the third round of the Can-Am. With its 3.0-liter motor, wide tires, and big spoiler on the back, the Carrera RSR was more sophisticated than the car they had driven at Daytona in February, but they had little hope of beating the Group 5 prototype cars.

"The only reason we were there was that Jackie Stewart was supposed to be entered in a Ford Capri," Mark remembered. "Porsche wanted someone there to beat him." The Porsche factory had built two of the cars on an experimental basis, and they were raced at Le Mans and in Austria by Martini Racing. The cars were then shipped to America for the use of Penske Racing and Brumos Porsche. Mark said, "All we did with ours was paint it blue."

On the way to the circuit on race-day morning, Hurley Haywood's rental car would not make the climb up the hill outside of Watkins Glen. "The car started up without trouble outside my room at the Glen Motor Inn and drove fine down the hill and through town," recalls Hurley. "As it sputtered to a stop with a full tank of gas on the climb up out of the Glen, I realized Mark had struck again." Mark had cleverly switched the plug leads in a manner that would allow the car to drive downhill but render it powerless to climb the steep grade.

"The planning that would go into his mischief was beyond belief," says Hurley. "Mark was a great prankster, playing tricks on everyone. He was good at it and devious to an extreme. One time he had engineered these wooden blocks that went under my rental car—this was also at Watkins Glen. He had gotten some help, and the crew had lifted up the back of the car; he put the blocks under the axle and they lowered the car back down. When I got in the car to head to the driver's meeting—at that time in the Can-Am you were fined if you didn't get there on time—I put the car in gear and boom—it wouldn't go anywhere—just spin the tires. He had made the cradle in such a way that you couldn't just rock the car off it. I had to get a bunch of guys to come over and help lift the car off the block. Of course, I was way late for the meeting and got fined."

Watkins Glen was the final race in the 1973 World Championship for Manufacturers, which was still in play between Matra-Simca and Ferrari. Ferrari brought three 312 PBs for Jacky Ickx / Brian Redman, Arturo Merzario / Carlos Pace, and Carlos Reutemann / Tim Schenken. Matra had a two-car team for Jean-Pierre Beltoise / François Cevert in an MS670B and for Gérard Larrousse / Henri Pescarolo in an MS670. The other European prototype team present was John Wyer's, which fielded Mirage-Fords for Derek Bell / Howden Ganley and Mike Hailwood / John Watson. The anticipated entry of Jackie Stewart in a factory-backed Ford Capri never materialized.

The Beltoise/Cevert Matra captured pole position with a 1:42.273. Mark was 10th with a 1:57.880 in the Penske Porsche, just ahead of Peter Gregg's sister Brumos car at 1:58.042. By comparison, Al Holbert in the Porsche RSR Mark had shared with him in the Trans-Am the previous month (and Penske Racing's Daytona car) qualified with a 2:04.555. Mark and Gregg ran nose to tail for the first 90 minutes before the Brumos car pitted to replace a halfshaft. Mark and George finished sixth with Gregg and Haywood seventh—10 laps behind the Penske Porsche. The Pescarolo/Larrousse Matra won, with the Ickx/Redman Ferrari second. Matra's win earned them the Manufacturers Championship when the last round scheduled for Argentina was canceled.

Losses in the first two Can-Am races to Bobby Rinzler's team had not made the start of the season a happy experience for Mark and Roger. "We worried more than we should have," Mark recalled. "I told Roger that. I said 'Don't worry about Rinzler being at the factory. Just do your thing and let the record on the track speak for itself. There's no way he can have the team we have.' I think the ultimate performance of the car is very dependent upon minor details in the suspension and chassis," Mark continued. "Everything has to be just right. I don't think Rinzler's crew had the expertise among the mechanics and others involved with the car."

At Watkins Glen on July 22, the weekend began on another down note. On Wednesday in pre-race testing, the crankshaft had broken, necessitating an engine change. On Friday, the first day of official practice, the new engine would not run on all 12 cylinders in the morning session. The problem was a throttle-slide on the right cylinder bank. Mark went on the track in the afternoon session expecting to put up a fast time. On only his second lap the suspension's left rear A-arm broke in the middle of the high-speed esses. The Porsche went backwards at more than 150 mph and hit the guardrail on both sides. The car was damaged and morale was at a low ebb.

But it was always in the face of adversity that Mark and Penske Racing shone most brilliantly. The reserve car (chassis 002) was taken off the back of the transporter and Woody and the crew made it ready for qualifying while Mark rested in the back of the transporter. Mark set a new lap record while putting the car on pole by a full second over George Follmer.

Mark's allergies were severe and he took the start with a swollen face, red eyes, and a very runny nose. He later said, "I was trying so hard and it was so hot, that I thought I was going to pass out." Fred Marik recalls that Mark would never take medication on a race weekend. "His eyes would often be watering and he would be sniffling, but he feared medication would affect performance," Marik says. "Once he put the helmet on the adrenaline kicked in and he was oblivious to the discomfort."

Mark dominated both 30-lap heats to win, with David Hobbs second in a McLaren M20 and Jody Scheckter third in Vasek Polak's Porsche 917-10. Mark told Leon Mandel that the Porsche 917-30 was the best car he had ever driven. "There isn't a single thing that's extreme about it," said Mark. "No extreme boost, nothing. We can go just about any way we want with it."

Again, much was made of the Can-Am cars being faster than those of Formula One. Indeed, the pole position for October's United States Grand Prix was slower than Mark's pole time—albeit by less than a second. But there was only one Can-Am car that was that fast: the Sunoco Porsche 917-30 of Penske Racing. The difference between the two forms of racing is revealed by noting that the seventh fastest qualifier for the Can-Am was seven seconds slower than Mark. In the Formula One race the seventh-fastest qualifier was just 1.2 seconds off Ronnie Peterson's pole-position time. And even at the very tail end of the Formula One field in 27th starting position, Rikky von Opel was less than six seconds off the pole. The last row of the Can-Am grid was a full 20 seconds slower than Mark. It is little wonder that Mark and Roger had been considering Formula One as the place they wanted to go. The experience at Mosport in 1971 had convinced both men that they could succeed in Grand Prix racing. That idea now dimmed with Mark's determination to retire at the end of the season.

Dan Gurney was considering a return to building Formula One cars, and there was talk of Mark racing an Eagle in 1974. And there was never a great deal of doubt that Mark and Roger had seen Formula One racing as a relatively near-term goal. "We want to build our own race cars as soon as it's feasible," Roger had told *Road & Track*'s Mike Knepper over the previous winter. "It would be great to tackle Formula One with Mark driving an all-American-designed and -built race car."

CHAPTER 149:
"Finally, I turned it way up"

The Road America L&M Formula 5000 race on July 29 showed the Lola T330-AMC to be way down in top-end speed from its competitors. The long straightaways of the Elkhart Lake, Wisconsin, circuit underlined the penalty presented by the 125-pounds-heavier AMC engine. Mark qualified ninth fastest and was sixth in his heat race on Saturday. In a strong performance in Sunday's feature race he was fifth on the last lap and in hot pursuit of David Hobbs in fourth when the car ran out of gas. Mark was officially classified sixth in the race that was decisively won by Brian Redman over Jody Scheckter.

On August 4, Roger Penske married Katherine Hulbert in Salt Lake City and did not attend the Can-Am at Mid-Ohio on August 8. Although Mark qualified two and a half seconds faster than Jody Scheckter and three seconds faster than George Follmer, both men blasted by him going into the fast left-hand turn one—George giving Mark a good bump on the left side as he went by. Follmer grabbed the lead and Scheckter was second. It took Mark two laps to pass Jody, and on lap six he outbraked George to regain the lead. Once in front he pulled away at two seconds a lap.

Scheckter failed to start the second heat but Follmer repeated his pass into turn one and led the race for 37 laps. The crowd was finally seeing a good Can-Am race as George kept the door shut for lap after lap on the tight and twisty circuit. Cynics thought Mark was playing with George to put on a show for the crowd, but Mark later insisted he had made every effort to find a way by. Mark made his move on lap 38 by turning the adjustable turbocharger boost screw up to the full 1,150-horsepower notch, and passing Follmer on the straightaway. Mark later described responding to the pit signals that said boost! "I turned it up a little—and nothing happened. I turned it up some more, and nothing happened. Finally, I turned it way up."

Although the Can-Am program was satisfying, Mark had not shaken off the general disillusionment he had first identified at Indianapolis. His decision to retire at the end of the season still rested uneasily, and he suffered doubts as to where his future lay. Mark clearly needed time to think his life through, but the stress of the multiple race programs left little time to do so. Those who knew him remember his introspection during this period, and many believe that after his return from the accident at Road Atlanta, he was never again the same open spirit. At the same time, he retained his essential goodwill and was capable of spontaneous gestures, large and small.

David Saville Peck remembers a classic moment at Mid-Ohio: "Mark was about to lap me for the umpteenth time, but for perhaps as much as two laps or more he just stayed behind me. After the race he came over to our pit, looked at the car and then said to me 'David, you need to change the rear roll center and stiffen up the front roll bar and move the front splitter forward a bit.' He had stayed behind me to see how my car was behaving so he could point me in the right set-up direction. This would seem remarkable but not if you knew Mark."

David and his wife Felicity lived the classic racer's dream during the summers of 1973 and 1974. Traveling from race to race and sleeping in the tow vehicle, they relied on whatever David had earned at the previous event. As an innovator, David represented the very essence of the Can-Am. He had immigrated to Canada from England where he had designed and engineered cars in the smaller-displacement classes. The new car that he took with him to Canada to make his living as a race-car driver became the Costello SP7 when his friend Brian Costello fronted the costs to the tune of 10,000 pounds sterling. After a heavy crash at Laguna Seca, a completely new car—the SP8—was built around a fresh chassis, incorporating Saville Peck's latest design changes.

"Mark had the ability to translate his engineering instincts into what he was doing inside the cockpit," recalls Saville Peck. "He had amazing hands—he would allow the race car to drift, he didn't fight the car, making small inputs to the wheel with incredible smoothness."

Mark was back in the Formula 5000 AMC Lola T330 at Road Atlanta on August 19. The fast, difficult, and intimidating circuit was a place where Mark's talent could shine, and he posted the fastest qualifying time. The first heat featured a good battle between Brian Redman and Jody Scheckter in team owner Sid Taylor's new Lola T330—until Jody damaged his engine. Redman won easily. Mark dominated the second heat and joined Brian on row one for the finale. It was not a close race. Redman pulled out an early lead that he extended throughout the race. Mark in second place was opening a similar gap back to the rest of the field. At the finish it was Redman, Donohue, Peter Gethin third, and Jody Scheckter fourth. It was the most competitive show of the season for the AMC-Lola.

CHAPTER 150:
Dominance

Qualifying for the USAC Ontario 500 was held the same weekend as the Can-Am at Road America. Ontario Motor Speedway was now under the management of the Vel's Parnelli Jones Racing organization, and Parnelli Jones had come up with an idea to make qualifying more interesting. Essentially adopting the SCCA F5000 format, he instituted qualifying races while maintaining the traditional qualifying system to set pole position. Mark and David Hobbs as Can-Am drivers were allowed to qualify on Friday but were not eligible for pole position. Mark put the Eagle-Offy in the race with a 194.817 and immediately left for Road America. On Saturday Peter Revson was the fast man at Ontario with a 200.089-mph lap in the works McLaren.

The lack of competitiveness in the Can-Am was producing boring races. The cars quickly became spread out on the track and rarely battled for the lead. Early in the season the SCCA had made an effort to provide better entertainment value by splitting the races in half. This had at least provided the opportunity to see two race starts with the excitement of the entire field running into the first corner together. Now another attempt was made at improving the format. The split heats were each made an independent race with their own purse. The first race, the Can-Am Sprint, set the grid for the Can-Am Cup, which paid points. One-third of the race purse was allocated for the Sprint and the remainder for the finale.

At the race tracks Eden remained in the background. "Mark was highly focused on his job and intent on his racing," says Hurley Haywood. "He wasn't really very good at knowing how to bring Eden into the mix." At the same time she made lasting impressions within the team. John Woodard's wife Sue remembers Eden as a warm and gracious presence. "Eden was a very nice and very attractive woman," recalls Sue. "She was an interior decorator, and after the first time she came to our new home with Mark, she called and offered to get furniture at her decorator's discount."

At Road America Mark demonstrated the superiority of the Sunoco Porsche by qualifying at 1:57.518—the first time the 4.0-mile track had been lapped in under two minutes. According to track historian Tom Schultz, no one else got under two minutes until 1982. Mark's lap record held up until 1984. Jody Scheckter was three seconds slower than Mark in qualifying and finished second in the 100-mile Sprint heat with Follmer, Haywood, and Kemp all in Porsches filling the top five positions. James Hunt was making his Can-Am debut for UOP Shadow and finished seventh behind Scooter Patrick, sixth in a McLaren M8F.

Attrition in the 100-mile Sprint reduced the original starting field of 23 cars to just 16 for the finale. Mark and Jody enjoyed informal and good-natured banter between the two races. The men had a friendly relationship, and Jody was capable of appealing to Mark's sense of humor. At a recent race the drivers had been paraded around the track in Porsches in order of qualifying position. Mark, sitting up high on the lead car's rollbar, looked back to spot Jody sitting low in the seat of his car. While Mark motioned for him to sit up high in the seat of the Porsche Targa, Jody responded the entire lap by motioning at his head. Finally he called out to Mark that he didn't want to mess up his hair. Mark was so convulsed with laughter he nearly fell out of the car.

At the start of the first race Jody jumped Mark and led through the first two corners. Mark had no intention of letting Jody repeat the performance in the finale. He made a very aggressive start that was deemed too aggressive by the starter, who refused to throw the green flag. A second pace lap was needed, and Mark had no problem taking an immediate lead. He again dominated a less-than-exciting race, with Scheckter finishing second and Follmer third.

The USAC Ontario 500 on September 2 was a disappointment. Mark started 18th in the 33-car field because he had not qualified with the rest of the field and had missed the qualifying races. Mark managed only 22 laps in the race before the crankshaft broke in the Offenhauser engine. Wally Dallenbach won the race with Andretti second. It was Mark's last time in the Eagle and his last USAC race. The DNF ended a strong summer for Mark. Since July 1 he had run 14 races—including heats—and had won 8 of the 13 he had completed, with two seconds and three sixths.

Mark was doing a "double" on Labor Day weekend and immediately after the 500 left for round eight of the L&M Continental for Formula 5000 at Pocono. The Pocono road course used the fast tri-oval in reverse of its normal direction. The cars exited the main circuit into an infield section that featured a difficult right-hand turn—actually turns one and two (in reverse) of the half-mile oval inside the larger circuit. The infield section continued through a series of first-gear hairpin turns before returning to the extremely fast oval section. The AMC-Lola was still down in top-end power and Mark qualified only eighth fastest. He finished second to Tony Adamowicz in his heat, placing him on the second row of the grid for the feature race. Brian Redman, who had won his heat, also won the feature race, with Brett Lunger second and Jody Scheckter third. Adamowicz in fourth, Eppie Wietzes fifth, and Mark in sixth place were the only cars to finish on the lead lap.

On September 16 a slim starting field of 17 cars appeared in Edmonton, Canada, for the Can-Am. Mark dominated qualifying, but with spark plugs fouling on the pace lap for the preliminary Can-Am Sprint, he was beaten off the starting line by both George Follmer and Jody Scheckter. Follmer's lead in the Bobby Rinzler RC Cola Porsche 917-10 lasted only to the end of the first lap, when he spun. Scheckter kept the Vasek Polak 917-10 in first place for two more laps until he ran wide on the exit of turn two and ended in the grass. With the plugs cleared and the Sunoco Porsche now in full song, Mark won the race, 30 seconds clear of Scheckter.

During the race Hurley Haywood had a potentially serious accident. "I went off the track and hit the embankment," he recalls. "The 917-10 fell over on its top and trapped me under it. It looked like a bad wreck. Mark saw it and freaked out. The next lap he saw me standing there. After the race he told me, 'I've never been so close to stopping and throwing the race away because I saw my friend in a position where he could have been hurt. The next time I came by, if you hadn't been out of the car I was going to drive my car over there and help.'"

For the Can-Am Cup finale on Sunday, Mark made an aggressive start and immediately pulled away from the field at a rate of a second a lap. He won the race by 47 seconds from George Follmer, whose Porsche was the only other car on the lead lap. Jackie Oliver was third in the UOP Shadow. Only 8 of the 15 starters were circulating at the finish.

For the final round of the Formula 5000 series at Kent, Washington, on September 30, Mark fitted taller front tires to the AMC Lola. The result was a better-handling car, with Mark telling *AutoWeek*'s Dee Norton that the increased height

"makes it easier to set up the car the way I think it should be balanced. I think we are as fast as any of them in the corners." He was fast in qualifying, with only pole-sitter Brian Redman outpacing him. Swiss driver Clay Regazzoni qualified third in his first appearance in the series. But power-to-weight ratio was still a problem for the AMC engine. Mark told Norton, "When we get out on the straightaway, I just can't stay with them. The car will just not accelerate with the others."

Peter Gethin beat Mark in the heat race, and both profited from David Hobbs's bad luck when his engine failed on the last lap after a dominating run. Starting from row two Mark ran a strong race in the feature and finished second behind winner Brian Redman. Jody Scheckter became the L&M Continental series champion, with Redman second and Mark third. Despite finishing third in the series even after missing the first three races, Mark was disconsolate about the effort. The car was never competitive at the front of the pack and achieved only a single heat win and no feature victories.

On October 6, François Cevert died at Watkins Glen when his Tyrrell-Ford Formula One car crashed in the esses. The Frenchman was tremendously popular, possessed of natural charm and movie-star good looks. The accident happened on the final day of practice. His teammates Jackie Stewart and Chris Amon withdrew from the race in respect, and Stewart announced his immediate retirement. He had planned to break the news after the race, which would have been his 100th Grand Prix start. Jackie Stewart had already clinched the 1973 World Championship, and his great career ended with a then-record 27 Grand Prix wins in 99 starts.

Laguna Seca on October 14 was the penultimate round of the 1973 Can-Am, and dominance by Mark and the Sunoco Porsche 917-30 had become the expected order. At 57.374, Mark qualified a full two seconds faster than Jody Scheckter in the Vasek Polak 917-10 at 59.404. George Follmer was third at 59.478. The graceful handling characteristics of the 917-30 were evident on this twisty circuit. The 917-10s now had the same 5.4-liter motor as the 917-30 and were its equal, if not faster, on the straightaway. The additional six inches of chassis length built into the 917-30 provided a beautiful balance and was the reason for its superiority. Alongside George on row two was another Vasek Polak entry—ostensibly another 917-10 that Brian Redman had qualified with a competitive time of 59.833. Redman was only to discover later that this was not an authentic 917-10; Polak had converted the original 917 PA that Jo Siffert had first campaigned in the Can-Am in 1969. "Vasek had done the engine and the bodywork and it looked in every respect like Scheckter's genuine 917-10," recalls Brian. "Before Laguna we tested at Willow Springs and I drove both cars. I said to Vasek, 'It's okay, but it doesn't feel solid on the road like the other car.' He said, 'Eet's the same, the same.' "

Mark qualified both the 917-30s, each at a speed fast enough to capture pole position. He elected to race his regular car and the spare went back in the transporter. At the start of the Can-Am Sprint he pulled away to a comfortable lead over George and Brian, until lap 22 when the engine began smoking; then Mark was in the pits and out of the race with a broken cam-cover stud. The team's first thought was to roll out the spare 917-30, but this was against the rules. Only cars that had participated in the Sprint were eligible for the feature Cup race. The Penske team, led by John Woodard and assisted by Greg Syfert and Heinz Hofer, made the engine change in record time. Under normal circumstances Woody figured five hours of concentrated work to change the turbo engine. On this occasion they accomplished it within the three hours between the races and had the car ready for the finale. "During the engine change, Roger Penske pulled some wrenches and assisted in removing the hot turbochargers, burning his hands in the process," recalls Woody. "During my 20 years of racing, this was the only time I witnessed Roger using tools on one of his cars."

Mark and the Sunoco Porsche were on the eighth row in 16th position at the start. By the end of the third lap Mark was fourth and trailing race leader George Follmer by only 13.3 seconds. On lap four an incident that ultimately involved six cars brought out the pace car—which was believed to be the first time in Can-Am history that a pace car had been deployed. After six laps the field was released and four laps later Mark passed Jackie Oliver in the UOP Shadow to capture third place, and one lap later passed Redman for second. Mark, now pursuing race leader George Follmer, came up to lap George's teammate Charlie Kemp. Kemp appeared to be blocking Mark, although he claimed he wasn't. He did admit to *AutoWeek*'s Jim MacQueen that, "After Penske made an obscene gesture [from the pits] the second time around, I sure wasn't about to just take my hand off the wheel and wave him by!"

Once by Kemp, Mark closed up to within half a second of Follmer, where he remained for a number of laps. George never faltered under the pressure, but on lap 45 of the 66,

his turbocharger failed and he was out of the race. "Mark looked totally effortless—very little hand movement—it was great to see the way he drove that car," recalls Bobby Brown, who finished fourth in his McLaren M8F behind Jackie Oliver second, and Hurley Haywood third. Mark ran out the remaining laps an easy winner—although he was nursing a broken valve spring and a broken rear rollbar—and became the 1973 Can-Am champion with still one race to run at Riverside.

CHAPTER 151:

IROC—"The finest idea ever"

The inaugural International Race of Champions (IROC) was an early and impressive example of Roger Penske's ability to bring a major event and promotion to fruition. As with all Penske motorsports activities at the time, Mark Donohue played an important role.

The idea was brilliant in its essential simplicity and appeal: bringing the world's best drivers together in a single series to compete in identical cars spoke to one of the core curiosities of race fans. Are the oval-track guys from the Indy world as fast as the road racers? Can the road racers keep up with the hardened professionals from stock-car racing? The topic was a staple of bench-racer debate, and the idea for an event that would address it had long been mooted. The genius of Roger Penske was to make it happen in a first-class and credible manner. The organization Roger formed for the purpose was called Penske Productions, and the other primary players were race promoter Les Richter and television packaging agent Michael Phelps.

The format for IROC's first year called for three races over two days at Riverside during the weekend of the Can-Am's season finale, the Times Grand Prix. The 12 invited drivers would compete to become one of six finalists invited to Daytona in February for a one-race shootout to determine the champion. The original 12 nominated drivers came, three each, from NASCAR (Richard Petty, Bobby Allison, and David Pearson), the SCCA (Mark Donohue, George Follmer, and Peter Revson), USAC (A. J. Foyt, Mario Andretti, and Bobby Unser), and Formula One (Jackie Stewart, Emerson Fittipaldi, and Denny Hulme). When Mario Andretti could not resolve the conflict with Firestone, his tire sponsor (all the

IROC cars were fitted with Goodyears), and Jackie Stewart announced his retirement from racing, Gordon Johncock and Roger McCluskey filled their open spots. "A big effort was made to bring Firestone-contracted drivers into the series—especially Mario," said Mark. "Goodyear made a strong pitch to Firestone that their drivers could run with no lettering on the car—no Firestone or Goodyear. I think Firestone made a big mistake not letting their drivers run."

Penske Productions bought 15 1974 3.0-liter Porsche Carrera RSRs from Porsche, insuring them for a total value of $375,000. The premium was $25,000. It was Mark who suggested that Roger use Porsches, pointing out that although the cars were expensive, they were essentially race-ready, and anything else would require far more expense to prepare. ABC television would broadcast each of the four races on consecutive Sundays in January and February. Keith Jackson and Jackie Stewart were the commentators.

Practice began on Wednesday, October 25, with a qualifying session on Friday. The first two races were Saturday and the third on Sunday between the Can-Am Sprint and Can-Am Cup. Fittipaldi captured pole position but started last in the first race on Saturday. A strict rule required every driver to be present for the pre-race briefing or else be relegated to the back of the grid. Emerson apparently didn't get the message and started on the last row with George Follmer, who missed the meeting with better cause. Can-Am qualifying ended right before the meeting, and George was still fully engaged in the RC Cola Porsche 917-10. No exceptions were made.

The penalties placed Mark, who had qualified second fastest, on the front row with Peter Revson. Mark made a strong start and immediately pulled away from the field, winning the race decisively. George was impressive, coming from 12th to 7th on the first lap and finishing 4th. Second and third were Bobby Unser and Revson. The next four were Hulme, Foyt, Petty, and McCluskey. Johncock, Pearson, Fittipaldi, and Allison had all ended their race in the pits. For winning round one, Mark received a Porsche 914-6.

Between IROC races one and two on Saturday came Can-Am qualifying. Mark placed the Sunoco Porsche on pole position with a lap at 1:10.290—an average speed of 130.089 mph. For all of the dominance of the Sunoco Porsche and the largely processional races it helped produce, the race fans loved it. The blue and yellow 917-30, seen as the ultimate manifestation of the wide-open Can-Am concept, captured the hearts of race enthusiasts. The crowds had been excellent all year, coming for the pure spectacle despite complaints from both the general and racing press that the series was boring and undersupported.

The format for race two of the IROC was to invert the field. Drivers who finished at the back of the field moved to the front, and switched cars. This placed Mark last on the grid. He retired on the eighth lap of 30 laps with a stuck throttle linkage. Follmer, Pearson, and Fittipaldi had a great race for the lead, and the final result had George the winner followed by Pearson, Fittipaldi, Foyt, Revson, Allison, Unser, Hulme, Johncock, Petty, McCluskey, and Donohue. Mark was now tied for sixth in points with Denny Hulme. The final race was set for Sunday, and only the six top point scorers would go forward to Daytona in February for a shot at the championship.

Mark remembered an exchange with A. J. Foyt, who said, "Well, I just hope an American can win this thing." Mark replied that he thought an American could, noting that A. J. was doing well, he was doing all right himself, and George and Peter were both doing well. At that point A. J. interrupted him to say, "Peter I don't reckon is an American." Mark asked, "Why don't you feel Peter is an American?" "Well," A. J. replied, "he's a good driver and all, but somehow he just gives you a feeling he's above it all."

On Sunday the third IROC race was sandwiched between the two parts of the Can-Am. Mark easily won the Can-Am Sprint, with George Follmer and Jody Scheckter encountering problems. Mario Andretti ran a distant second in the Commander Motor Homes–entered McLaren M20 before his tires went off. Brian Redman finished second and David Hobbs third in a McLaren M20.

It was time now to switch back to the IROC Porsche and another blind draw to see which car he would race. Mark's bad luck in the second IROC race now played in his favor. The rule was to again flip the field in the order of the previous race's results. This placed Mark on the pole alongside Roger McCluskey. Mark made a decisive move at the start and established a lead he never lost. Denny Hulme was the only driver to press Mark at all, and he spun out of contention with seven laps remaining. The finishers in order behind Mark were Unser, Fittipaldi, Pearson, Follmer, Foyt, Revson, Hulme, Allison, Petty, Johncock, and McCluskey. The six top point leaders who would go forward to Daytona were Follmer and Unser with 29, Mark and Peter Revson with 25, Pearson 24, and Foyt 21. Just missing making the final six were Formula One champions Fittipaldi and Hulme.

The IROC races had been a success. All three featured good battles and hard-nosed racing despite Mark's dominance of races one and three. It made great television, and the media attention was tremendous. Pete Lyons wrote in *AutoWeek*, "If history doesn't look back on the International Race of Champions as the finest idea ever . . . then the whole sport had better just quit now and be done with it."

CHAPTER 152:
"It's time to quit"

At Riverside Bobby Allison was standing near the Porsche 917-30 while a tire was being changed and quietly told Mark he thought a balancing weight was just about to fall off the wheel. Jody Scheckter walked by in time to hear Mark tell a mechanic, "There's a wheel weight about to fall off that wheel—let's take it off and fix it." Jody exclaimed in astonishment, "Jesus Christ! Not only do you know all about engines and aerodynamics and setting up the cars, but you're not even in the car yet and you can feel that the wheel weight is about to come off." In telling the story Mark said that he didn't do anything to set Scheckter straight. When Jody left, Mark went over to Allison and told him what happened, saying, "Us old guys have to stick together."

Mark had now won the Can-Am Sprint and the IROC race, and only he and Roger knew that the Can-Am Cup was to be his last race. Although he was committed to the final round of the IROC in February at Daytona, he regarded the Can-Am as his last real race. Mark didn't think it would be professional to announce his retirement before the last race. "If you did, there would be all kinds of people wanting to talk to you about it and it would be a distraction," he said. So he waited. He wanted to make a clean cut at the end of the year.

Mark had a lot of trouble not telling his friends. "At Riverside I had to tell Woody and Heinz—they had already figured it out, I think," said Mark. "Dr. Fuhrmann approached me and said, 'What am I hearing? Do you not like Porsche?' How could I not like Porsche—I love Porsche. I couldn't stand to have my friends think I didn't appreciate their car and all they had done for me. I felt very close to them. I didn't seem to be good at expressing that." So Mark told the engineers Helmut Flegl and Helmut Bott. "They were surprised but they understood," remembered Mark. "They both shook my hand

and said, 'We're really happy for you.' I hope my relationship with them remains good."

Mark had been tempted to surprise everyone—including Roger—but refrained from doing so because of their professional relationship. But Roger was talking to other drivers and Mark was sure he was tipping his hand about Mark quitting. "It was hard on me in the last few races when Roger was going around talking to drivers about the next season," Mark said. "I was fairly certain he had told Peter Revson as it became clear to me that the McLaren team knew."

Mark now concentrated on his last race in the magnificent Sunoco Porsche. He easily pulled away from the field and won from Hurley Haywood second and Charlie Kemp third. The other top runners fell out but had never threatened for the lead. While Brian Redman was running second he had a huge moment in Vasek Polak's 917 when a chassis tube broke in a 200-mph bend. A similar incident had happened in practice. Brian managed not to wreck the car, later noting, "I didn't spin but I missed that outside wall by nothing." He brought it to the pits where Polak asked what the matter was. "This time it had broken at the uni-ball attachment to the chassis on the bottom right rear wishbone," recalls Brian. "It was only then I saw that it did not have parallel links. I asked why there wasn't another ball joint there. Vasek said, 'This is the original PA car.' It was the first I knew it."

In the 917-30 Mark was making a conscious effort to savor the moment. "I was enjoying every minute of it," he said. "I was enjoying it more than I have in a long, long time." He was playing with "the adjustable sway bar that the Germans had come up with." Mark thought it was very clever and was enjoying ratcheting it up to add more and more oversteer as the race went on. "I was practicing driving the car on the throttle—maybe not Jody Scheckter style, but a real precision technique—letting the throttle bring the tail of the car around," he said. "It was a very satisfying thing to do. That was so enjoyable having all that power—I was letting it hang out but I wasn't going to take any chances." Being so far ahead he was keeping the revs down, but coming out of the turns he was trying to maximize the oversteer and experience the balance. "It was an exercise in control," said Mark. "I really enjoyed it tremendously."

Mark did a checkered-flag lap of the Riverside circuit and Woody, Heinz, and Greg climbed on board for a final lap of honor in the 917-30 they had worked on so hard. Their efforts and Mark's driving had added another chapter to the car's legendary story. "I think riding with me on the victory lap at Riverside was an expression of their rapport," said Mark. "I believe it was their way of saying farewell—all unspoken."

Then the Sunoco Porsche rolled into victory circle. After accepting the trophy and kiss from the race queen, surrounded by a crush of reporters, Mark made his announcement: "I'm 36 years old and not getting any younger. And I don't think I'm getting any better. It's time to quit. I've accomplished all I had hoped to. I want to quit while I'm on top. Except for the last race in the Champions Series at Daytona, I will not compete again in a racing machine. I have always said that I was a better engineer than I was a driver. Now I'll have a chance to prove my theory."

That evening Mark spoke again at a more formal ceremony that Dan Luginbuhl had arranged at the Mission Inn. He had already given a lot of thought to what he would say. "Then I decided to just speak from the heart, as that is how I've always done it," he said. "That's the only time I've really not worried about what Roger may say. Always before Roger was contriving it: 'Don't say this, don't say that.' On that occasion I didn't worry about it, I just said what I felt. It was a unique experience. I didn't even know if Roger was in the room. Usually if I know Roger is in the room I feel intimidated."

At the Mission Inn Mark repeated his post-race comments and then said that the turning point in his career had been "when I made an agreement with Roger Penske to drive for him." Later Mark could not remember all he had said but felt it had been well received.

Roger followed up with his own statement: "With Mark announcing his retirement we are making the necessary changes on our team in preparation. I am very happy to say that Mark will continue as president and general manager of the Penske Racing part of the Penske Corporation—at our new complex in Reading, Pennsylvania." Roger said that Chuck Cantwell would leave his position as general manager of Penske Racing to assume an administrative position with Penske Leasing. Don Cox, who had been director of engineering since 1969, was named a vice president.

Roger also announced that Peter Revson would replace Mark on the USAC team and would drive with Gary Bettenhausen at Indy. Bobby Allison had been slated to drive at Indy but decided instead to concentrate on NASCAR's World 600 in Charlotte. Finally Roger announced the purchase of the McRae Cars shop in Dorset, England, as "an extension of our headquarters in Reading. The Dorset shop will be the center

for developing and constructing a Formula One car."

The response to Mark's announcement was warm and generous. In a tribute to Mark in *Road & Track*, Mike Knepper said, "We may well have been privileged this season to witness the ultimate man-machine combination in the history of the sport."

Knepper was prescient in identifying the moment for which Mark would be most remembered:

> **The 1973 season and the elegant, blindingly fast Porsche 917-30 have become the most universal image and frame of reference for Mark Donohue. The fact that the car was so obviously advanced and powerful is the dominant part of this equation. Lost is the pure talent as a driver that was Mark Donohue and replaced by an image of the consummate tester and developer who made a car fast through his engineering ability. It is not the true picture. Mark Donohue was a giant talent as a driver, among the very quickest of his era.**

Roger told Knepper: "I guess I've always considered Mark like a brother. There have been many disagreements, but we both realized we were after the same goal and never allowed those disagreements to get in the way." Discussing Roger, Mark later told Knepper, "We bent over backward for each other many times. It has been, I guess, a perfect pairing."

Roger made the same point to *AutoWeek*'s Jim MacQueen: "Like two brothers growing up together we didn't always agree. But we were willing to take each other's ideas for what they were worth and make use of the best from each. He is the most versatile of all the people I have known in the racing business and has set the stage for all who follow, both as an engineer and as a driver."

"Donohue is a man who engenders not only respect and admiration, but affection as well," wrote Ted West in *Motor Trend*. "As a driver he will be missed. As a man, however, we all have the good fortune that Mark Donohue is still very much with us."

Brock Yates said of Mark, "His ranking among the most skilled and courageous drivers of all time is beyond dispute."

After the Mission Inn press event Mark and Eden were emotionally exhausted. They were also hungry, and said to their friends, "Let's go to the Cask 'n Cleaver for dinner." The year before at the NASCAR race Mark had gone there every night by himself and really loved the place. He knew the people and they knew him—he liked the way he was treated, the service, the food. But when they arrived that night in a group of eight or ten, the restaurant had just closed. They went next door to Bob's Big Boy, a sandwich place, and had just sat down when staff from the Cask 'n Cleaver came in and invited them to come back. "We've talked to the boss and we can open up and you can come and eat," Mark remembered them saying. "We went back and they opened up a long table—they brought out a very special salad—they brought out wine—took our orders—the staff said, 'We would like to join you.' All of the waiters and cooks sat at one end of the table—must have been 25 people—I got up and gave all the same speeches I had given at the Mission Inn. They got up and gave speeches. They brought out champagne and all kinds of things to drink." Mark felt they were showing their appreciation of who he was and what an important day it was in his life.

CHAPTER 153:
"Never too much horsepower"

Mark reflected on his position in the sport and how he would be seen by others. "Any driver of my generation is going to be glad I'm gone—George, Peter, and I grew up together in this," he said. "For George it's a way of life. He doesn't need the money—he just really likes to race.

"Maybe I burned myself out because I was doing all the testing," Mark continued. "For drivers who are just involved three or four days a week—it's a better life for them. For me it's seven days a week. I'm not complaining—I chose that route myself—but maybe now I'll have three lives."

Mark also spoke with great feeling about his old teammate David Hobbs. "The only current driver who has spoken to me about my retirement is David Hobbs. He is really a super guy, down to earth. He's a squared-away professional with a really good perspective on life."

With a worldwide fuel crisis dominating the news, the racing industry took steps to conserve resources and show themselves as good citizens. Races were shortened and other public relations moves were made to counter the naysayers who identified racing as a conspicuous consumer of resources.

Most significant, both USAC and SCCA announced fuel limitations for their races. Mark felt he was getting out when things were changing for the worse. "It is the end of the era of powerful cars and the end of 'knife-fight' rules where anything goes," he said. "By cutting the fuel down and adding pit stops—taking aerodynamics off—all these engineering freedoms are gone. My leaving at the same time as the end of this era is really good.

"I was never hung up on Formula One," Mark continued. "For me it was always the high horsepower cars that were the most interesting." Mark recalled being asked by Porsche engineers when he would consider he had too much horsepower. "Never too much horsepower, I told them," Mark remembered. "My definition of too much horsepower may be when all four wheels are spinning in every gear. I guess too much would be when the tires are spinning in top gear at the end of the straightaway. We were far away from having too much horsepower."

Much of Mark's sense of self-worth was tied to his image of himself as a race driver. He didn't think the press would be interested in talking to him now that he was retired. "When I say press I really mean people," he said. "It will now be my responsibility to reach out to people—I'm not sure they will be interested in me anymore."

Characterizing himself in past interactions with others, Mark said, "When I would open the faucet to speak to someone, I would speak at length and from my heart. But I tried to avoid that—being in that position. Roger was more comfortable with that—that was his role. I was not one to run to the press."

Mark wondered how much he would miss the limelight and thought it may be nice to be away from center stage. He likened driving a race car to being a concert pianist. "You receive the tremendous response from the crowd when you appear, and the applause, and you can sustain all of that up to the point when you raise your hands above the keyboard. And then at that point you have to perform."

In late November, Mark, in his new role as president of Penske Racing, looked on as Gary Bettenhausen did 510 miles of testing at Daytona in the team's new Matador. The Matador had more aerodynamic lines for the new season and laps were consistently run at 176 mph, with some in the 181-mph range. A pole-position time for a recent NASCAR race had been 179 mph.

As Roger had mentioned during the Mission Hill announcement, he had purchased the Dorset, England, race shop of Graham McRae as a European base for building and racing a Formula One car. Geoffrey Ferris was engaged to design the car, and work commenced immediately. It was a major step for Penske Racing. All the cars they had previously raced had been designed and built by outside manufacturers or constructors before receiving the "Penske treatment" as they were developed into race cars. Roger had attended at least one of the European grands prix in 1973 to evaluate the scene.

As focus turned to preparations for a new season, Mark was experiencing the first feelings of withdrawal from his traditional role. He was putting his best face on it. "Nobody's forcing me to do this: Nobody held a gun to my head to get in the cars, nobody is holding a gun to my head to get out of them," he said. "Now I'm trying very hard to be happy with the new role, which is very difficult."

Return

Show me a hero and I will write you a tragedy.

—F. SCOTT FITZGERALD

CHAPTER 154:

"I miss racing already"

We take pleasure in announcing these new appointments:" read the formal announcement card from Penske Racing Inc. of Reading, Pennsylvania, dated January 1, 1974. At the top of the card was listed Mark N. Donohue Jr., President. On the lines below him were: Donald O. Cox, Vice President and Director of Engineering, and Jay J. Signore, General Manager. Chuck Cantwell, who had been general manager of the racing operation and team manager for road races since 1969, left the racing side of the business to join Penske Leasing in a management position.

Mark's initial plan for the new season was to oversee four major racing divisions. The team would contest the USAC Championship, including the Indy 500; the Can-Am; Formula 5000; and NASCAR, with Gary Bettenhausen driving the AMC Matador in the season-opener at Riverside. Bettenhausen was also the lead driver for the USAC series, although Peter Revson would drive a second Penske car at Indianapolis. Penske Racing's participation in the Can-Am was still under consideration pending rule changes as the SCCA attempted to find a way to save the dying series.

Additionally, Mark was making occasional visits to England to oversee development of the Penske Formula One car being designed by Geoffrey Ferris at the 4,800-square-foot former McRae Cars racing shop in the Dorset village of Poole.

Mark said the car would "reflect the thinking of Penske Racing." According to Mark, the car was being designed as a group effort. "There's this fellow named Geoff Ferris. . . . He's kind of coordinating with Don Cox, Roger, and myself, as well as doing the actual drawing of the lines on paper," he told Bob Cutter for *National Speed Sport News*. "We're checking each step, adding and subtracting, and trying to make sure that the car reflects the things we've learned over the years."

The decision to retire from driving had not made Mark relaxed or content. He told the Associated Press: "You don't really appreciate how much racing means until you leave it. Strangely, I don't exactly relish the idea of running a racing team, and letting someone else do the driving. But that's the way it will be."

In a bylined column in the *Philadelphia Inquirer*, Mark expanded on his feelings. "It is like a person never appreciating his parents until he moves away from home. For me,

I never appreciated myself as a driver until I saw myself as not being one."

On January 20 Mark was the featured speaker opening the fifth annual lecture series sponsored by the Friends of the Muhlenberg Township Community Library (Laureldale, Pennsylvania). Mark gave a talk and showed the film, *Four Years to Victory*. The Sun Oil–produced film detailed the first four years of the Penske Racing team experience at the Indianapolis 500, culminating in the 1972 victory.

Mark was also busy disposing of the Porsche 914-6 he had received for winning an IROC race at Riverside. Mark organized an auction attended by more than 100 enthusiasts at Heinrich's Porsche dealership, which was near his apartment in Wyomissing. The winning bid of $5,700 came from Richard Larrick, a Heinrich's service adviser.

On January 20 Gary Bettenhausen drove the Matador to a seventh-place finish in NASCAR's Winston Western 500 at Riverside. At Daytona for the 500 the car continued to struggle and Mark was despondent. "I just don't know what's wrong," he told Michael Katz for *The New York Times*. "I don't think I'm contributing. American Motors is very important to us. I want to produce for them." Mark went on to contrast what he had previously been able to provide as a driver with his frustrations running the operation. "I'm not getting paid to drive cars anymore," he told Katz. "Winning as head of the team, that's my job now. And if a man doesn't do his job, he loses it. I'm not independently wealthy. This is a life and death deal for me."

CHAPTER 155:

IROC Champion

When the IROC resumed at Daytona on February 14, Mark could hardly wait to be back in a race car. "I want to get behind the wheel of a race car so bad it hurts," he told Bloys Britt for the Associated Press. Mark not only wanted to be behind the wheel—he wanted to win. Very conscious that this was his last race, he was already regretting his decision to quit. "That's a tough bunch to work against," he told Britt. "But the urge is so great to compete again that I don't care if I crash, run off the course, or anything. I can't wait to get going."

The IROC format had eliminated 6 of the 12 original drivers at the first three rounds at Riverside in November. Now it was down to one race at Daytona for the six remaining drivers to decide the champion. Two of the eight Porsches were designated for qualifying. Mark was fastest with a 2:00.82, to share the front row with Peter Revson at 2:01.75. The next fastest were David Pearson, George Follmer, Bobby Unser, and A. J. Foyt. The Porsche that each driver would use for the race was decided by luck of the draw. As pole-sitter Mark was last to draw and came up with the orange Carrera.

In the early stages of the 25-lap race on the combined oval and road circuit, it was all Mark and George Follmer. Follmer, despite wearing an eye patch to cover a scratched cornea, stayed close behind Mark as the two pulled away from the field. Mark was certain that George was biding his time for a last-lap pass. "George seemed to have me pretty well set up and didn't seem to want to show his hand," Mark told Michael Katz for *The New York Times*. "So I showed my hand. I pretended to make a couple of mistakes—like letting the car slip on a couple of turns—and hoped to throw off his rhythm."

Mark explained to United Press International that he wasn't necessarily trying to induce George to make the same mistakes. "When you follow a guy around the track like George was, you have a tendency to start watching what the other guy is doing without realizing it," Mark said. "When you do that you get mesmerized. That means you lose a little concentration. I was trying to work on George without endangering his safety, or my car. As it turned out, it worked out all right."

George spun on lap on lap 10, leaving Mark with a 12-second lead. On the last lap Peter Revson passed Bobby Unser for second as Mark won by a comfortable eight seconds. "That last lap I didn't really want it to end. I wanted it to go on and on. After I took the flag and was making my victory lap and got onto the road course, there was a big banner from the SCCA workers. They'd shown it on the pace lap before the race and then they all were out there showing it on the cool down lap," Mark told Ray Marquette in the *Indianapolis Star*. "I don't cry, believe me. But there I was with tears coming out of my eyes. I was surprised at myself." Mark later wrote in his *Inquirer* column: "It was a tremendous emotional experience of racing, of leading and of winning. I tried to implant every scene in my mind forever."

"It was a great day," Mark remembered later. "Eden and I went out that night to the Boot Hill Saloon on Dan Luginbuhl's recommendation. We really had a good time. It was

a great relief—finally it was over." He rejected the idea that winning the IROC made him the greatest driver in the world, as some people were saying: "I would never say that; I would never think that. It's never so cut and dry. On a given day—everybody has a good day and a bad day. Or you make one mistake and you're history."

"I know retiring is the right thing for me to do and I won't change my mind and come back," he told Joe Biddle in the *Daytona Beach News-Journal*. "Although it is tempting."

Nevertheless, Mark continued to express his doubts regarding his retirement. "I miss racing already," he told *Daytona Beach News-Journal* sportswriter Brad Wilson. "I suppose the game plan could have been to move to Formula One cars . . . but I'd have to learn a new team, new cars, new tracks . . . and accept the possibility that I wouldn't excel in Formula One . . . which would have been devastating."

There were many who doubted Mark would remain in retirement. "You're not going to be retired too long," Bobby Brown remembers telling Mark. "Mark looked at me in a funny way," continues Bobby. "He was too damn young to retire and he was too good."

At the SCCA National Convention in San Francisco on February 21–24, Mark was awarded the 1973 Woolf Barnato Trophy for outstanding contributions to the SCCA. The Trophy is the club's premier award and honors the memory of Englishman Woolf Barnato, who as a Bentley driver won the Le Mans 24-hour race in 1928, 1929, and 1930. Barnato also financed Bentley and was chairman of the company. Early SCCA members Helen and John Stack were friends of Barnato's and donated the original trophy because they believed he embodied the finest tradition of sportsmanship. Mark received the trophy from the hands of Burdette Martin, the 1972 recipient. Mark was recognized for his leadership as a member of the SCCA's Circuit Safety Committee, and as a member of the National Highway Safety Advisory committee and the Motor Racing Safety Society. He was also serving his fifth year as president of the Road Racing Drivers Club (RRDC) and continued to champion driver training through the Advanced Driver Clinic he put on for the club.

"Mark really kept the RRDC alive during that period," remembers Bob Tullius. "The club was going though a precarious time, and it was Mark's reputation and stature, as well as his ability to draw people to the driver clinic, that kept it all together."

Reflecting to *National Speed Sport News*'s Bob Cutter on the major influences in his racing career, Mark named Walter Hansgen, Roger Penske, and Karl Kainhofer. The names of Hansgen and Penske were expected, but including Karl came as a surprise to Cutter. "He was a fabulous bloke," Mark explained. "He taught me an awful lot about self-control, and neatness and cleanliness in the operation, and sensibility when it comes to mechanics and all that sort of thing."

On March 9 at a breakfast at Ontario Motor Speedway— OMS had abandoned their traditional Labor Day date for the California 500—Mark was honored by the American Racing Writers and Broadcasters Association. As the top vote-getter of the 10 drivers honored as members of the All American Racing Team, he was named Driver of the Year for 1973, and also received the Jerry Titus Memorial Award. It was his fourth selection to the team and the second time he had been the top vote-winner. Others named to the team were drag racer Gary Beck, George Follmer, Don Garlits, Peter Gregg, Parnelli Jones, Roger McCluskey, David Pearson, Richard Petty, and Peter Revson.

More honors and recognition followed. A formal invitation advised the recipient that: "Martini & Rossi cordially invites you to a luncheon on March 19 in honor of Mark Donohue upon retirement from a brilliant driving career. Gallagher's Steak House, 228 West 52nd Street, New York, New York— cocktails at noon."

The event was organized by Frank Blunk, now retained by Martini & Rossi after retiring from a long and distinguished career with *The New York Times*. At the head table with Mark were Josef Hoppen, special vehicle director for Volkswagen / Porsche-Audi; Tom Binford, who had recently been appointed chief steward for the Indianapolis 500; International Motor Sports Association (IMSA) president John Bishop; and former USAC vice president, Bill Smyth. Chris Economaki was master of ceremonies. Mark Sr. and Zilly were also present. Roger had to miss the luncheon, and Mark joked, "Well, I didn't go to his wedding last year, so he told me he wouldn't come to this luncheon, but he sent his wife instead. Besides, she's a lot prettier!"

In his remarks Mark said, "I don't plan to get back in a race car at all. If I wanted to, I never would have stopped." Mark added, "Nobody in racing has come back successfully after being retired. And I don't think I'm going to be the exception to that rule. Drivers can't go on forever."

CHAPTER 156:
Mark and Peter

On March 22 Peter Revson was fatally injured when his UOP Shadow Formula One car crashed at the Kyalami circuit during practice for the Grand Prix of South Africa. He had enjoyed great success in Formula One the two previous seasons for McLaren, winning the British and Canadian grands prix in 1973, and established himself as a premier driver. Peter and Mark never reconciled the long-held uneasiness of their relationship. They had each succeeded in related but slightly different spheres of racing. From a purely American perspective Mark would be longer remembered and regarded as the more successful. This would not be true from a more international view, where Grand Prix victories are the stamp of greatness. For an American driver to have accomplished what Peter Revson did in the brutally cutthroat world of Formula One was a brilliant thing.

Their seemingly parallel careers had followed very different roads, intersecting occasionally over the years. Mark had found a home with Penske Racing, where he was able to create an environment he largely controlled. Peter moved from team to team, seeking the best situation to demonstrate his talent but always at the mercy of the given team's resources and approach.

In *The Unfair Advantage* Mark said of Revson's death, "I was terribly upset, but it wasn't such a personal thing." This rather sad comment is an indicator of the complicated feelings the men had toward each other. Revson's book, *Speed With Style*, written with Leon Mandel, was in the publication process at the time of his death. Revson and Mandel treated Mark poorly in the book, with Mandel dismissing Mark as "one-dimensional" while laboring to portray Peter as a sophisticated man of multiple interests and worldviews. Peter furthered the characterization, while acknowledging that Mark had achieved greater success. "I certainly want to be as successful in racing as Mark has been. But to be well balanced, to be accepted as a man of many interests and thoughts beyond the race track is more important to me." Peter also revisited the origins of their rivalry in the 1961 race season with a slightly revisionist angle. Ignoring the multiple teardowns that always resulted in Mark's Courier being proven legal—something Peter earnestly acknowledged at the time—he now suggested that Mark had probably found a way to cheat without being caught.

Mark's treatment of Peter was hardly anything to be proud of. Even Mark's strongest supporters believe that Mark felt some jealousy toward his rival. He criticized Peter for his lack of mechanical sympathy, although he did somewhat grudgingly say, "Peter may have been a better driver, while I was a better developer." Their year together as teammates in the Javelin had hardened Peter's feelings, although the circumstances were not all Mark's fault. The Javelin was being developed on a race-to-race basis, and it was physically impossible for the team to produce equal cars for both drivers at every event.

Had Revson survived he and Mark would have been thrown together again in a new context. Peter had signed to drive the Penske entry in the USAC championship races, and Mark would have been managing the program. Perhaps they would have found a means to reconcile past differences. It is nice to think so. They were both great drivers of comparable talent, each a more interesting human being than the other had ever bothered to discover.

CHAPTER 157:

New Challenges

When Jay Signore joined Penske Racing it reunited longtime friends. Jay had been helping Roger with his offshore racing boat and Roger offered him a position. "At first I was reluctant because I didn't want anything to spoil my friendship with Mark," Signore says. "Chuck Cantwell had left the race operation and I basically replaced him. Mark was the boss and together we ran the shop and the relationship was good.

"There were serious times—it was now a business—but outside of that we all stayed the same," remembers Signore. "One day Mark was racing home in his bright red Cadillac convertible. He was indulging in curb walking, where you get the right front wheel up on the curb and try to stay up on it. He missed a turn in slushy ice and banged up the front of the car pretty bad—ripped the front end off. He took it back to the shop. Roger walked in, shook his head, and said, 'What the hell are you guys doing?'"

Mark had made frequent appearances at Pingry School, his alma mater, to address the student body. On May 17 he was commended by the Pingry School Alumni Association

at their annual dinner for "distinguished alumnus service." His responsibilities at Indy made it impossible for him to attend, so Mark Sr. and Zilly were there to accept the honor for him. Later Mark was inducted into the Brown University Sports Hall of Fame.

Mark and Don Cox faced new challenges in engineering the Penske entry for the 1974 500. Rule changes stemming from the accident-plagued 1973 race were aimed at reducing speed. The new regulations reduced rear wing span by a third, with the maximum set at 43 inches. Fuel capacity was reduced by almost half, with the new maximum being 40 gallons, and the tanks now had to be carried on the left side of the car. Turbocharger boost pressure for qualifying was limited to 80 inches, although it was unlimited during the race. The most dramatic change was that each car's fuel supply for the entire race was reduced from 375 gallons to 280 gallons.

Engine efficiency was now crucial in achieving the needed fuel economy at peak performance levels. "Because of the new fuel limitation, we're concentrating almost all our efforts right now on fuel efficiency," Mark told *Machine Design*'s Clare E. Wise. "We have never been required to do this before with racing engines, and quite frankly it's somewhat of a gray area for us. We've always looked for maximum horsepower; now we're studying bsfc [brake-specific fuel consumption in lbs per bhp per hour]. . . . So we have to find a way to keep the engine happy at the lowest possible bsfc. The margin for error is very thin; the minute you run too lean, you burn through a piston. It's just like you were using a cutting torch . . . it only takes a second."

While Mark continued to apply his engineering talent effectively, he was less successful when it came to managing the race operation. "Mark was a lousy team manager. He was terrible at it—and he knew it," says Judy Stropus. "He just didn't know how to do it. He was miserable."

Judy observed Mark primarily at the race track, but Dan Luginbuhl and others who worked with him every day thought he was adjusting well to his new role. "Mark worked so well with each individual on the team," says Dan. "It was really an extension of the finely tuned operation from before. The difference was that Mark was no longer the driver."

Mark described himself as impatient with other people's work habits. He wanted things done immediately, and was critical when someone would spend time on the phone on what he considered irrelevant small talk. He also couldn't understand why someone would go about a task in a way other than the way he would do it.

However, Mark recognized his mistakes and believed he was growing in the job. There were things that he didn't like about the way the race operation had been run before he assumed responsibility, and he hoped to at least correct those things. Mark realized that his intolerance of other people was an issue, and he was able to admit to his mistakes. Ultimately, he believed he was growing in the job.

Meanwhile, Mark continued to appear uneasy at the track, where *AutoWeek* columnist Eoin Young saw him "prowling the pits like a lion on a leash." Mike Hiss, who had joined the team to drive the McLaren, thought Mark was coming to terms with his new role. "He was very helpful because of his technical knowledge," says Mike. "His presence was extremely beneficial to me." Hiss placed the McLaren M16C on the outside of the front row at Indianapolis, the only race of the season in which the team ran two cars. Neither he nor teammate Gary Bettenhausen finished the race. The Penske USAC program was not a great success in 1974. Bettenhausen's second-place finish in the Milwaukee 150 the week after Indy was the best result. In July, Gary crashed his dirt car at Syracuse, New York, causing extensive nerve damage to his left arm. Mike Hiss returned to the team to complete the season.

The NASCAR season brought only slightly better results for the AMC Matador, with a number of different drivers in the seat. Gary Bettenhausen started the season but was replaced by Bobby Allison after his injury. Dave Marcis and George Follmer had also done a race in the car. Allison brought his experience and great talent to the program and capped the season in November with a win in the Ontario 500.

"I was running my own car the first half of the season," recalls Allison. "After Michigan Mark called and said, 'Gary got hurt in a Sprint car, and we need you to run the Matador at Daytona Fourth of July.' I told him I needed to have Coca-Cola on the car, and he made arrangements for that to happen. Mark said I could go to Reading and set the car up to my own liking. He said, 'We've been going fast but we've not been doing good.' "

At Daytona Bobby put the Matador on the front row. "Three cars got rained out of regular qualifying and were allowed to make their run at 7:00 a.m. on race day when things were a lot cooler than when we had run in the heat the day before," remembers Allison. "One of those cars was David

Pearson, and he beat me for the pole by one ten-thousandth of a second. The car was fast and I led a lot of laps before it went to seven cylinders with 15 laps to go. They told me to keep going and I was able to finish fifth." By the end of the season Allison brought the Matador its first oval win with the victory at the Ontario 500.

Mark was conscious of the frustrations inherent in his new managerial role. "As a racing driver—at least when I'm in the car—I don't have to think about those things," he said privately. "But now I have to on an everyday basis." In these previously unpublished comments from his own tapes, Mark is introspective and candid. He was intimidated by Roger and couldn't really control the operation; he questioned whether he was doing the right thing. The hardest thing was to decide what to do with the rest of his life. His heart was telling him that perhaps it was time to break away from Roger and do something else. Mark was conflicted, and he was having trouble coming to terms with the realities of the business world. He said, "I'm really trying to do the best I can in this new era of my life. The biggest conflict I'm having with myself is not the fact that I'm retired, as is the question, what do I do? What is the right thing to do? Something inside me tells me to get away from Roger and make a new start. Is success really worth the stress?" Mark also worried that as time went by his ability to go somewhere else would only be diminished.

Mark was showing how unhappy he was with the job. Those close to him observed that he was tense—uneasy. "I had strongly supported Mark when he announced his retirement," says Jerry Kroninger. "But I had second thoughts in 1974, as I witnessed how unhappy he seemed to be."

"I tried so hard for so long to do more than I should have really done in terms of organizing everything and sorting the car out and driving the car," Mark said. "If things don't work out as manager, I'm going to try to arrange to get a car dealership—through Roger or someone else. If none of those things work out I'll be forced back into driving—I don't want to forsake the kids."

When he told Roger of his interest in obtaining an automobile dealership, Penske replied, "No, you don't want to have a dealership. It's just the same old thing over and over, looking at numbers month after month."

Money was an issue. Although Roger was paying him a handsome $100,000 annual salary, it was half of what he had earned as a driver. In his unpublished tapes Mark lamented that he had to send a minimum of $30,000 to Sue, and his personal expenses were $40,000. "It sounds like a lot of money, but when you put it all down on paper, it's not that much," said Mark. "I'm not going to be rolling in dough." IMG got 25 percent of anything he earned in endorsements or other fees. His agreement with Roger was that he could do anything on the side that didn't interfere with what Penske Racing was doing.

Mark recalled Bud Stanner of IMG saying, "You could be making more working for anyone else." Mark wasn't sure that this was true, and in any case explained, "I'd never do that because of my loyalty to Roger." Stanner advised him that he needed to have a contract with Penske and promptly drew one up for him. According to Mark, Roger took one look at it, "threw up his hands, and said, 'I can't agree with this.' "

"We took out various things," said Mark, "and eventually I said, 'Then let's not have a contract.' So now I'm on a month-to-month basis."

One place Mark continued to find relaxation was out on the open water in his boat. Hurley Haywood recalls: "I had a 28-foot cigarette [boat] similar to Mark's, and we would race together from Miami down to the Keys. Mark loved the machinery aspect of the boats, but I believe he most enjoyed the feeling of privacy with no one bothering you out on the ocean. Mostly it was just you and the boat. It was very peaceful."

CHAPTER 158:
Return of the Turbo Porsche

At the announcement and unveiling of the Formula One car at Penske Plaza in Reading on June 28, Roger said, "About the only thing I can say is that I'm not going to drive it and neither is Mark." He added, "Mark will conduct comprehensive vehicular capability tests . . . . on our skid pad in Reading." Geoffrey Ferris was introduced as the car's designer, and it was said that Mark and Don Cox "collaborated with Ferris on the initial design theory of the car."

When asked by *Road & Track*'s Mike Knepper if he would race the car, Mark said he would confine his involvement to skid-pad testing. "Once you say you're going to retire, I think you have to retire," Mark told Knepper.

On a visit to Eden's family in Atlanta, Mark, as always, had the use of a car from his friend Steve Beizer. On this occasion it was a Ferrari 330 GT. Mark liked the car a great deal and was pulled over going 90 mph on his way to take Eden to dinner. He had none of his identification with him, having thoughtlessly left everything at Eden's house. Mark remembered the deputy saying, "You have no license or registration. If you stole this car, what are we going to do?" He wanted to know if Eden could drive the car but she couldn't drive a stick shift. Eden had to stay with the car while Mark was taken to the station. He phoned Eden's mother who, thoroughly amused, soon arrived with the identification and license. Mark was issued a ticket.

Penske Racing and Porsche had decided not to return to Can-Am racing in 1974 with the famous turbocharged 917-30 Sunoco Porsche. The new fuel restrictions instituted by the SCCA certainly reduced some of their advantage, but they clearly remained eligible and would have been odds-on favorites had they returned. It is likely that Porsche and Penske Racing had achieved their goals in Can-Am and were ready to move on. The rule change provided a good excuse to leave. Roger Penske often said that the 917-30 had been "banned," and this theme was repeated by Porsche. To this day people choose to believe and remember that the SCCA banned the cars. It isn't so.

Can-Am racing in 1974 was dominated by the Universal Oil Products (UOP) team and their Shadow DN4s. They were beautifully engineered race cars that were professionally run to a high standard by team owner Don Nichols for drivers George Follmer and Jackie Oliver. The problem was that there was little competition.

On August 11, the so-called Turbo-Panzer, the 917-30 with which Mark had dominated the 1973 Can-Am, did return to the race track. It was at Mid-Ohio for round four of the Can-Am, and Brian Redman was the invited driver. "Around June I had a call from Roger Penske asking me if I would like to drive the Sunoco Porsche at Mid-Ohio," recalls Brian. "I answered that I thought the car couldn't run because of the fuel restrictions. Roger said, 'It can run.' "

Redman came to Penske headquarters in Reading. "I sat across from Roger at his desk—not a paper on it—and he said, 'How much do you want?' I said, 'I don't know—five thousand dollars.' He said, 'Brian, you're the most reasonable racing driver I ever met.' "

Brian recalls that Mark didn't have a great deal to say on the race weekend and was obviously unhappy in his new role. "It was raining for the first heat, and I, of course, had never driven the car before in the rain. I was careful with it and we won the heat. For the final it looked like it may rain again and I asked Mark, 'What happens to the handling if we groove the slicks and then the track dries out?' He said it would have no effect."

The race started on a damp track. "We hand-grooved the tires because we thought it would dry out and didn't want to be on full wets," says Brian. "As soon as the track dried the handling went to hell. The throttle was very sensitive because of the turbo lag, and on one of the tight corners I opened it just a fraction early and the car went sideways. I caught the slide but Follmer and Oliver had got by. I caught up behind them and watched them. George hit Jackie in the door in a place where you can't pass and George was out of the race. I tried my hardest to get by Jackie. I gave it more boost but nothing happened. I don't think the car had had a lot of preparation for the race. I was really struggling with the handling as the tires were creating an enormous push.

"What Mark had managed to do with that car that was fantastic in the handling department, is that when he turned into a fast-ish corner, let's say 120 mph, as you turned in with the power off, the back end immediately started to very gently come around," continues Redman. "That meant you could open the throttle so that when it was straight, the 1,100 horsepower came in and you shot off like from a gun. By grooving the tires we wrecked this fine balance. Now it just understeered like crazy, unbelievable. If we hadn't grooved the tires we would have won, I think. Having said that, the Shadows were extremely quick—it was a very good car."

Meanwhile, Mark and Jay Signore were preparing 15 Camaros for the 1974 IROC. The plan had been to run Porsches again, but Roger had not been able to complete a satisfactory deal with the German company. "The whole idea is an incredible challenge," Mark told Mike Knepper. "Because this thing was jacked around for so long there isn't time to do all the things we'd like to. Where it would normally take six months to design and build a Trans-Am race car, we're having to build 15 in two months. Obviously it's not going to be the ultimate racer, but it's going to be very good."

Mark explained to *Autosport*'s Gordon Kirby: "I told Roger I would build the Camaros if I could have a completely free hand and didn't have to conform to any set of regulations." The design and engineering was a joint effort by Mark, Don Cox, and Jay Signore. Signore later took an ownership position along with Roger in IROC and eventually owned the company.

The decision to go with Camaros instead of the Porsches wasn't made until mid-July. A crew of 16 men was assembled to get the job done. The challenge in building the IROC Camaros was to make them raceable at a reasonable cost and to make them as equal as possible. There was no acid-dipping or other radical modifications made to the cars. They were lightened by removing dashboard, seats, upholstery, and windows, and replacing parts such as brakes and brake lines, springs, and fuel tanks with racing parts. Traco built the 350ci engine to produce a consistent 420 horsepower. Mark said the resulting car would be approximately 70 percent of the performance of a fully prepared Trans-Am Camaro.

IROC II had a slightly different format than the original. The first year had been all road races—three at Riverside, and the finale on the road course at Daytona. Now the series opened with a 50-lap race at the 2.0-mile oval track at Michigan International Speedway on September 14. Two rounds would be run at the Riverside road course on October 26 and 27, and the finale would again be at Daytona, but this time on the oval. The 12 drivers selected included 7 returnees from the previous year: George Follmer, A. J. Foyt, Bobby Unser, Richard Petty, Bobby Allison, David Pearson, and Emerson Fittipaldi. New to the series were Graham Hill, Cale Yarborough, Ronnie Peterson, Johnny Rutherford, and Jody Scheckter.

At MIS Ronnie Peterson pulled off a big surprise by qualifying on the pole ahead of the seasoned oval drivers. In the race, however, experienced oval racers dominated and it was Unser who won ahead of Yarborough, Pearson, Allison, Follmer, and Fittipaldi. Peterson was seventh, followed by Rutherford, Foyt, Petty, Hill, and Scheckter.

For Mark and Jay it was a more-than-satisfactory result. The Camaros had held up as race cars, and the racing was close and exciting. It was also a success for Roger. The series was again broadcast on ABC's *Wide World of Sports*. Interest in the IROC was tremendous.

Rounds two and three were held at Riverside on the 2.54-mile road course, the same weekend as the F5000 L&M Continental Challenge. On Saturday the IROC race was won by Fittipaldi, with Follmer and Foyt second and third. The next day the winner was Bobby Allison, driving with a cracked vertebra. Behind him came Unser, Fittipaldi, and Foyt. This time only three drivers were eliminated from the Daytona finale in February: Hill, Scheckter, and Petty.

CHAPTER 159:

"Formula One is the ultimate challenge"

Mark began to test the new Penske PC1 only six weeks before the Canadian Grand Prix, the first race scheduled for the team. "Roger, of course, was looking around for a driver," Mark told Knepper. "I called him and told him to hold off on hiring anyone, that I would drive it if a couple of problems could be worked out."

Speaking to Peter Manso, Mark expanded on the evolution of his thinking. "I had the thing running on the skid pad and it started to work on me. My gut was telling me that pretty soon Roger would be getting a driver, that he'd have no trouble at all, and I started thinking I'd consider it if I could be back as Number One, if he'd take me over others like Peterson or Reutemann, say. I wanted to see where I stood, if I could do it, and of course whether the money would be good. . . . And when I made this clear to him all he said was, 'Christ, if you're considering coming back, I'll stop talking to these other people right now,' which of course was the kind of vote of confidence I'd been looking for."

Mark believed that his relationship with Roger was unique among driver / car-owner arrangements. He doubted that many other drivers would last with Roger because they were unlikely to give him the respect he deserved in the operation, or interact with the same intuitive sensibility. He talked about drivers who would typically get out of a race car after practice and say, "It's no good—make it right," and go to the motel. He didn't believe that kind of driver would last with Roger. Mark believed that the core of his successful relationship with Roger was his willingness and ability to be much more than just a driver.

"I don't need to race anymore," Mark wrote in *The Boys of Indy*. "I think I've proved I'm one of the best. But it's actually much more than that. People think we do this to prove our manliness or whatever. But that's crazy. You do it because you like it. You don't ask anyone's permission, and you don't need it. You're driven to it."

The team went quietly to Mosport on August 29 and 30 for Mark to test. There was no name on the car, and Mark wore an unmarked helmet. On Penske Racing letterhead Mark had written a formal letter of agreement to Mosport management, saying in part, "Under no circumstances will any photographers, media representatives, or any other individuals be permitted to enter onto the grounds during the two-day period of time that Penske Racing Inc. is renting the track."

Despite the strong attempt to keep the tests secret, Canadian journalist F. David Stone was among the media who found their way to the circuit. He reported for *The Globe and Mail* of Toronto: ". . . the Mosport gates were locked, the no trespassing signs up and Penske's public relations man Dan Luginbuhl fruitlessly tried to patrol the 500-acre race track to keep out the intruders." Some journalists resorted to masquerading as flag marshals, and one television cameraman was described by Toronto *Star* sports editor Len Coates as crawling, "commando-style through the bushes, aggravating a severe case of hay fever. When he was spotted the crew moved a passenger car into his line of fire. He crawled 100 yards to get his shot from another angle."

On September 13 Mark announced he was coming out of retirement to race The First National City Travelers Checks Special. "Formula One is the ultimate challenge," said Mark. "This was the one missing link in my career as a driver."

"After a year in the 'real world,'" Mark later told Mike Knepper, "I found it wasn't for me. I'm a race-car driver. That's what I do best, and that's what I want to do more of." He said that the dissolution of his marriage had played a part in his decision. Sue and Mark had been separated since November 1971, and their divorce became final in September of 1974. Mark told his friend Greg Pierson that he decided to drive the car because "the money is too big to walk away from."

Jay Signore believes that it was the specific challenge of Formula One that brought Mark back. "If he did the testing, why not drive the car? Being a driver and then having to be on the other side of the fence are two different stories. I think Mark liked both sides—but the racing side was what he enjoyed the most. Way back in the days racing Couriers—Mark and myself, Timmy Mayer and Peter Revson and just about everyone else—that's what we talked about. Formula One, that was your goal."

Why did Mark return to racing after having successfully retired at—from an American perspective—the very pinnacle of his profession? People will say with conviction that he did it for the money, or that he was restless, or even that he was pressured into it from one source or another. Eden probably comes closest to the truth, observing, "If you are a great artist and for some reason denied your art—you will do anything to take it up again. It was that way with Mark and racing. He had a great talent and he missed it very much. When the opportunity came to return, I think he did it in the spirit of an artist returning to his craft. Mark was very, very focused about his racing," says Eden. "When you have a talent for something you have to be doing it."

It is unsurprising that of all the people who professed not to understand why Mark returned to driving, few were race drivers. There is an intuitive understanding among drivers about why they race that was perhaps best expressed by Duncan Hamilton. The great British sportsman was one of the finest drivers of the postwar era and raced with great style and success. His many wins include the 1953 Le Mans 24 Hours, co-driving the works D-type Jaguar with Tony Rolt. In his autobiography *Touch Wood*, Hamilton says, "There was no answer I could give those who questioned the wisdom of what I did; for our incompatibility of spirit prevented understanding; while those who understood had no reason to ask any questions."

George Follmer understood, but he still urged Mark not to race in Formula One. "I told Mark not to do it," remembers George. "As a friend, I said 'Mark, don't go there. You're going to be frustrated.' I thought he had too much going for him without having to get back behind the wheel."

When he entered Formula One Mark gave up his job as president of Penske Racing. He would be a full-time Formula One driver and live in Europe. Mark told Peter Manso, "I made it clear to Roger that I didn't want to stay in racing forever, that I'd work at it for two years and I meant it. I still mean it."

Mark was pragmatic about his decision to return to the cockpit, and the risks that it entailed. "If you're going to be in a racing car and you're going to drive mile after mile after mile, sooner or later the odds are that either you'll make a mistake or somebody working on the car will make a mistake," Mark said to Nick Nagurny. "That's why you get paid a lot of money. That's part of the risk you assume when you say you'll get in the car and drive it. If I get wiped out and they carry me away in a box, I wouldn't expect anybody to feel sorry for me. It's something I know is a possibility. I'm not complaining."

CHAPTER 160:
Grand Prix Racing in the Penske

The Penske entry was not the only Formula One debut in Canada for an American team, as Mario Andretti made his first appearance in the new Parnelli VPJ4 for Vel's Parnelli Jones Racing. The two teams joined UOP Shadow on the Grand Prix circuit, giving America a nearly unprecedented presence in the top league of international racing. Shadow had debuted the previous year with George Follmer driving alongside Jackie Oliver. Although Follmer distinguished himself in his single year in Formula One, he was not part of the team in 1974. Inevitably, the results for the two new American teams were closely compared everywhere they went. The Parnelli was designed by Maurice Philippe, who had previously designed the highly successful Lotus 72. It had debuted in 1970 and was still a frontline car in 1974. Mario had far more Formula One experience than Mark, having been on the Grand Prix tour for parts of each season since 1968, when he had made his F1 debut with a pole position for Lotus at Watkins Glen. Mario had won the 1971 South African Grand Prix; Mosport was his 19th Grand Prix start. Mark was making his second Grand Prix start on the same circuit where he had debuted three years earlier with a third-place finish in a McLaren.

The official entry form was dated August 30 and signed by Mark. He listed the crew as Heinz Hofer, Karl Kainhofer, Bruce McTavish, Bill Woodland, Geoffrey Ferris, Max Egli, and John Woodard. Also named was the commercial identification that would be exhibited on the car: First National City Travelers Checks, Goodyear Tire & Rubber Co., Norton Company, Sun Oil Company (Sunoco-DX), Sears Roebuck and Co., and Ford Motor Company.

Although Mark's personal best on Friday of 1:15.731 was just two seconds slower than Niki Lauda's fastest time in the Ferrari 312 B3, he was the 17th fastest. Mark's time was not helped by the Penske's gear ratios being too high. Formula One was a new level of competition for the Penske team. After the session, Mark told Rob Walker, reporting for *Road & Track*, "We feel that we are in kindergarten and everybody else is in the 12th grade."

In the qualifying session on Saturday, when conditions were ideal for fast times, the mechanical fuel pump on the

Penske failed. Mark's Ford-Cosworth could not pull more than 8,000 rpm, and he recorded a disappointing 1:17.071. His time from Friday just got him into the 26-car field in 24th position.

Mark was never in contention during the race, but he also never put a wheel wrong on a blustery, cold day with occasional rain showers. He brought the red, white, and blue No. 66 Penske home 12th, with his fastest lap a 1:15.067. It was a physically difficult race for Mark as he struggled with a severe front tire vibration. The Parnelli was more competitive, and Mario battled up from a 16th starting position to finish 7th. He just missed scoring one of the World Championship points awarded to the first six finishers. Emerson Fittipaldi won the race in a McLaren M23-Ford ahead of Clay Regazzoni in a Ferrari 312 B3 and third-place Ronnie Peterson in a JPS Lotus 72E-Ford.

Two weeks later on October 6, the World Championship was on the line at the final race of the season at Watkins Glen for the United States Grand Prix. Fittipaldi and Regazzoni were tied in points, and Jody Scheckter, driving for Tyrrell, still had an outside chance.

Mark took part in the open test day on Wednesday along with most of the teams. Official practice began at 11:30 a.m. on Friday. The Ford engine immediately suffered a persistent misfire. It took 45 minutes to discover the cause—a loose battery terminal. "We're where we should be," Mark told Mike Knepper after Friday practice. "I just don't have enough laps in the car to know what to do to make it work right. It's the same science as with any race car, but with the Formula One car there just isn't the power I'm used to. With the Porsche Can-Am car, or even our Trans-Am cars, there was always enough power there to make up for minor faults in setting up the suspension. With an F1 car everything has to be perfect, not almost perfect." Mark also admitted that he was still regaining his touch after the layoff. "You do get rusty: I'm starting to get it back, but I still have to tell myself to do things I would have done automatically a year ago."

In Saturday's final practice Mark made a determined effort and placed the Penske PC1 14th on the grid with a time of 1:40.834. Pole position went to Carlos Reutemann in a Brabham BT44-Ford at 1:38.978, just ahead of James Hunt's Hesketh 308-Ford, whose time was 1:38.995.

Mark ran mid-pack until the 27th lap, when the right rear suspension bracket broke. He was in 13th place when he retired. Andretti's Parnelli had failed to start at the green flag.

It was a great disappointment to the team and the American fans, as Mario had been fastest in the first practice session and had qualified third.

The day was marred by a fatal accident. Austrian Helmuth Koinigg, driving a Surtees TS16-Ford, went off at the exit of turn seven, "the toe of the Boot," and crashed through the catch fencing, hitting the Armco barrier head-on. The bottom layer of the guardrail broke on impact and the race car speared underneath the upper two rows, killing Koinigg instantly. He was 25 and had married just two months earlier.

Reutemann won the race and Pace made it a 1-2 for Brabham. James Hunt was third. With Regazzoni 11th, four laps down, and Scheckter not finishing, Emerson Fittipaldi's fourth-place finish was enough to make him the 1974 World Champion. The McLaren team also captured the Constructors championship.

CHAPTER 161:
A Small Family Wedding

Mark managed to fit in tire testing for the IROC Camaros at Daytona in early December. The final round of the championship was set for February 14 at Daytona, but unlike the previous year, the road course would not be used. During the tests Mark turned laps at 162 mph.

Back in London, First National City Bank threw a gala party and press conference to honor Roger and Mark. Held at the famous Dorchester Hotel, a favorite of the racing set, it attracted virtually everyone in the sport. Roger outlined plans for the 1975 season and confirmed that Mark would continue as sole driver of the Penske PC1 Formula One car. He also announced that Mark and team manager Heinz Hofer were now living in Bournemouth near the race shop at Poole in Dorset. Questioned about circuit safety, Roger responded that if drivers didn't like a given circuit they didn't have to race there. "Drivers ought to look at some of the Grand Prix cars they've been driving before they look at the circuit." Mark agreed strongly with Roger's statements.

A more important event was in the final planning stages in Atlanta, Georgia. Eden and Mark had decided that summer to be married. "Mark had to work it out on his schedule," remembers Eden. He was able to give her a date in December that worked for both of them.

The small wedding, held on December 14, 1974, at St. Luke's Episcopal Church in Atlanta, was unpretentious but elegant. It was a family wedding with a few close friends including Barb and Jay Signore and Kathy and Roger Penske. Mark's boyhood friend Burge Hulett joined them from New York. Mark Sr. and Zilly were there along with Eden's mother Carmen. Eden's father, Robert White, was deceased. Mrs. White gave a reception the night before the wedding at the Piedmont Driving Club. After the ceremony the wedding party adjourned to the home of Mrs. Robert Hugh White Sr., Eden's grandmother, for a luncheon. Mark and Eden left immediately for a honeymoon in Jamaica. They returned to Atlanta for Christmas and New Year's. During the holiday they were also in New Jersey at Mark's sister Mary Ellen's home to be with Michael and David, now 10 and 7 years old. Mark invited his sons to visit them in England in the new year.

After the first of the year, Eden's brother Richard helped move her from Atlanta to the couple's new home in Reading. Richard had graduated earlier that month from the University of Georgia. In Reading Mark offered him a job. "Mark wanted me to help set up the southeast division of Racemark. At first I didn't think I would like it, but Mark took me to lunch and convinced me that it would be interesting and not just sitting in an office moving inventory."

Mark may well have reflected on a year of great change. The emotional ending of his racing career among tremendous accolades as IROC champion had been followed by a clearly unhappy period as he struggled with diminished income and a self-perceived loss of prestige. Before the year was out he was in the seat of a Formula One car, now freed of the responsibility of managing the entire Penske racing operation. All this had happened during an emotional divorce and a new marriage. Now he could look forward to a fresh approach to his racing as he concentrated on just being a race driver and facing the challenge of the Grand Prix circuit.

"I've got a fresh attitude," Mark said. "Roger sees to it that the pressures on me are reduced, and I think I can cope with it mentally."

CHAPTER 162:
"Any improvement must be good"

The opening Grand Prix of the 1975 season was at the Almirante Brown Circuit in Buenos Aires on January 12. Argentina had a great history in Formula One as the home country of five-time World Champion Juan Manuel Fangio. Following the death of President Juan Perón in 1974, the country was politically unstable and lawlessness prevailed. Kidnappings were rampant, and law enforcement was ill prepared to prevent them. For these reasons Eden declined to attend the race with Mark, as did Roger Penske.

The small Penske team that arrived in Argentina included Heinz Hofer, team manager; chief mechanic, Karl Kainhofer; and crew members Greg Syfert and Bill Woodland. "Heinz was ideally suited as a team manager," says Karl. "He spoke at least five languages and was a very good organizer who could get things done." Syfert had been part of the 917-30 team in 1973 with John Woodard and Hofer. He had started work at the shop in Poole the week before. The team hoped a new tub and a new suspension they had created over the winter would result in a much-improved car. Other changes included a wider front track and changes to the cockpit and airbox. Before leaving for South America, Mark tested the new Penske PC1/02 setup at Riverside.

To ship the Penske to Buenos Aires, Karl and the crew at Reading had to construct a special wooden crate that would hold the race car as well as all the spares, including an extra engine and gearbox. The crate was designed to be reused for shipping the car to Brazil and eventually on to England. "It traveled pretty well," recalls Karl. "After we unloaded it in Argentina, we just leaned the pieces up against the side of the garage."

The sponsor-preferred name for the Penske PC1 was The First National City Travelers Checks Special. This prompted Denis Jenkinson, the revered correspondent for Britain's *Motor Sport* magazine, to provide a classic Jenks appraisal. "The Penske car has a long and complicated name which is that of its major financial backer, but the name is too long to get on a badge, almost too long to get on the side of the car, and certainly too long to put in any historical table of results, always assuming it gets results."

The fearless, brilliant, and original Jenkinson was deservedly a legend, but he had little or no interest in American racing and tended to dismiss it as irrelevant. As the season progressed, Jenks never missed a chance to devalue the modest successes Mark and the team achieved. In this regard he generally reflected the British take on Mark as not up to Formula One standards. Ignored were the odds the small team was facing in its first foray into Formula One—developing a new car in a new environment, with the driver seeing all of the circuits for the first time. There may have been resentment that the Penske operation represented itself as an American team despite having a British designer and several British personnel.

Not all were unkind. Dan Luginbuhl recalls that veteran motorsports reporters including Gérard "Jabby" Crombac, Alan Henry, Pete Lyons, and Eoin Young expressed a genuine appreciation for the challenges faced by the new team.

Mark had resumed his fitness regimen with new purpose. In *Autosport* Pete Lyons reported that Mark was "looking tougher and leaner and browner than ever before in his 38 years." Mark told Nick Nagurny that Formula One had pushed him to increase his already-intense fitness routine. "He said that he was on a vigorous exercise program, running every day despite an often achy leg," said Nagurny. "He was doing 300 push-ups a day and special neck exercises and choosing his foods very carefully." The Penske press kit provided Mark's particulars as 5 feet 10 inches in height and 166 pounds. Mark, who would actually not turn 38 until March 18, was the oldest man in Formula One.

Formula One was in a particularly strong state in 1975. The easy availability of the relatively inexpensive Ford-Cosworth engine and Hewland gearbox made it possible for many small teams to become Formula One constructors. Ferrari and BRM (recently renamed Stanley-BRM) were the only teams producing their own complete car from chassis to engine to gearbox. The multitude of teams produced a healthy situation, with more cars typically vying to qualify for each race than there were starting positions. The racing was close and exciting. To be a Grand Prix driver meant you were at the top of the sport.

Despite improving his time by a second in each of the three practice sessions in Argentina, Mark qualified a disappointing 16th at 1:52.36 in the 23-car field. It was clear that Mark was facing a major challenge between developing an untried chassis and mastering the steep learning curve of new circuits

and new circumstances. Pole position was captured by the third American team, UOP Shadow, with Jean-Pierre Jarier turning a 1:49.21. Jarier had the bad fortune to have a ring and pinion gear strip on the warm-up lap, and was unable to make the start. Mark drove a steady and determined race, improving his position both through attrition and on merit. Rob Walker wrote in *Road & Track* that "he went faster and stronger as the race progressed." The seventh-place finish was encouraging, although Mark was lapped by race winner Emerson Fittipaldi's McLaren.

After the race Mark told Walker, "I was not happy with seventh place, but it is an improvement and any improvement must be good." Walker commented that Mark looked particularly fit and drove an excellent race. Pete Lyons concluded that "One driver did stay impressive right to the end, and this was Mark Donohue, who drove as hard he knew how for the whole distance and suffered not so much as an oil leak from his superbly prepared Penske."

Defending World Champion Fittipaldi won the race for McLaren with James Hunt second in the Hesketh. Formula One awarded points for the first six finishers on a 9-6-4-3-2-1 scale. The remaining point earners were Carlos Reutemann, Brabham; Clay Regazzoni, Ferrari; Patrick Depailler, Tyrrell; and Niki Lauda, Ferrari. Mark missed the points by one position. Rounding out the top 10 behind him were Jacky Ickx, Lotus; Vittorio Brambilla, March; and Graham Hill, Lola. Mario Andretti failed to finish in the Parnelli.

São Paolo hosted the Brazilian Grand Prix on January 26. "We got a late start in testing," recalls Karl Kainhofer. "We had flown from Argentina to Brazil where we waited for the box with our race car to arrive. It got held up in customs, although Heinz Hofer did a good job of finally getting the problems sorted out."

In unofficial testing on the 4.95-mile circuit, Mark was fast in the improving Penske, but further adjustments were made that produced a slower time in official practice. Mark was 11th fastest in the first practice session, and after the second session was in the top 10. Roger told Rob Walker, "Mark is never happy until he gets up with the big boys, but he is doing all right."

Encouraged by the progress, changes were made for the last two sessions, but they resulted in a loss of speed and Mark qualified 15th alongside Ronnie Peterson in the JPS-Lotus 72 on row eight. Mario was on the row behind him.

Midway through the race Mark was running 13th and

just holding off Andretti when the Penske developed vicious oversteer. Mark pitted for fresh Goodyears but they didn't help. When Mark pitted again Roger decided to retire the car. It was later discovered that the rear wing tab had gone out of adjustment.

Brazilian Carlos Pace scored a popular win for Brabham. It was his first Grand Prix victory and he was followed home by countryman Fittipaldi. The remaining point scorers were Mass, McLaren; Regazzoni, Ferrari; Lauda, Ferrari; and Hunt, Hesketh. This time it was Mario Andretti's turn to miss scoring points by one position in seventh.

Mark flew from Brazil to upstate New York to fulfill a speaking engagement at the annual sports banquet in Elmira on Monday evening. Mike Semel, a local high school senior, was interested in racing, so his principal arranged for Mike to ride with the banquet committee members to pick up Mark in Rochester, two hours away. "When we got there it was snowing, but Mark got off the plane with just a lightweight summer suit on, because he had just flown up from Brazil, where it was summertime," remembers Semel. "I let him wear my overcoat and rode with him to Elmira. Instead of driving him back to Rochester that night I approached NBA basketball player Bob Weiss on the dais and asked him if he was driving home to Buffalo that evening. He said he was and I asked if he would consider detouring to Rochester to give Mark a lift to the airport. Bob said, 'You mean Mark Donohue would ride with me?' A few minutes after Mark left with Bob he came back with a sheepish grin on his face, and handed me my London Fog overcoat. Mark said 'I wouldn't want you to think I would steal your coat.' That was the last time I saw him."

Mark told Peter Manso, "A lot has changed for me—my divorce is final, I've remarried, and I've got a better idea of what it's like in the business world. I also know what to expect when I finally get out, and I know I'd better start planning for that."

One of the businesses that Mark was making a commitment to was an expansion of his longtime relationship with Bob Bailey's B & B Auto-Sport, Ltd. Mark was vice president of new product development and a director of B & B, the parent company of Racemark, Inc., which distributed products designed by Mark, such as the Fypro race suits and other safety and performance products. Burge Hulett was busy getting Racemark's Southeast division set up in Fort Lauderdale with considerable assistance from Mark's brother-in-law,

Richard White. Mark gave Richard his pickup truck with a camper to use to drive to Florida. Before he left, Richard accompanied Mark to the race shop in Reading to load up many of Mark's personal items and tools.

"Mark was uneasy, and glad that Roger wasn't there that day," says Richard. "It was all Mark's stuff, but he knew Roger wasn't happy about the new venture." Before heading south, Richard worked for six weeks at B & B in Ballston Spa, New York, learning the business. Richard drove to Fort Lauderdale and remembers, "I stayed with Burge for the first month while I looked for a place to stay. Burge had located a warehouse, and it was my job to get it up and running." The warehouse was south of Fort Lauderdale in Hallandale.

CHAPTER 163:
Try for the Record

Early in the year Mark and Roger decided not to include the Indianapolis 500 in Mark's schedule. Mark would concentrate solely on Formula One. In a letter postmarked February 3, Mark answered a letter from Malcolm Starr with a handwritten note on letterhead bearing his Reading address and phone numbers on the left side, and the Bournemouth, England, address on the right.

> Dear Malcolm,
> Thanks for your letter. Congratulations are in order for your daughter, I understand. I'm glad to hear everything is going so well for you. I'll not be going to Indy this year from the looks of things. The Formula 1 effort is so difficult the captain reckons I should spend all of my time over there—hence this new stationery with new addresses!
> I still can't imagine your new lawyer status. It must be a real challenge and something super to do once you're out. I trust this will be the last school for you!!! Hmmmm.
>
> Sincerely,
> Mark

Mark and Roger had long been fascinated with closed-circuit record speeds. Now Roger had the idea to reunite Mark and the 917-30 Porsche in a final dramatic quest. By establishing the closed-course speed record in 1974 at Talladega with his Coyote Indy car at 217.835 mph, A. J. Foyt had provided a target and a challenge. The 917-30 was brought out of retirement and prepared for the attempt. Roger was providing color commentary for ABC television and made a deal with Bill France to attempt the official record between the Twin 125 qualifying races at Daytona International Speedway during Speed Weeks, on the Thursday before the 500.

The famous blue and yellow Sunoco Special colors did not have the honor of being on the record car. The car appeared in red and black as the CAM2 Special. During the height of the oil crisis in 1974, Sunoco management decided that it was not the time for their logo to appear on a race car. The 1974 Indy car had appeared as the Score Special because Score was the name chosen for the mass-merchandised product planned by Sun Oil. It was not in stores at the time because of a federal ban on introducing new oil products during the crisis. Sun decided to run Indy with the Score name in expectation of product being available later in the year. But entrepreneur Mickey Thompson objected to the name—SCORE was the acronym for his racing operation, Southern California Off Road Enterprises. Rather than negotiate with Thompson, Sun changed the product name to CAM2. The first year the new product could legally be marketed was 1975, so the name and its colors were on the 917-30 for the record runs.

According to Jerry Kroninger, Mark had not been consulted by Roger before making the commitment for the record run. "The car was not designed for this kind of performance," Mark told Jerry, saying the turbos were not designed for sustained wide-open running and would overheat. During preliminary runs on Sunday, February 9, two engines were lost, but not before Mark turned a lap at 201.734 mph. Mark believed that even if the car worked reliably they would fall short of the necessary speed. "Daytona has very little margin for drifting, that is, letting the car drift upwards on the banking, and the turns are awfully narrow," Mark told an Associated Press reporter. Mark estimated that he would only be able reach a speed in the 208-mph range.

Asked why he wanted to break the record Mark seemed to struggle for a rationale: "Sometimes, I even have trouble explaining it to myself. Having an honor no one else has . . . seeking that mysterious quality . . . going into the unknown. Some people go to the moon; some go to the bottom of the sea. To go faster than anyone else, that's an honor I'd really like to have." The runs were postponed until later in the summer and the engines went back to Porsche to be reworked for the specific purpose of sustained high-speed runs.

Although Jay Signore now had primary responsibility for preparing the IROC cars, Mark remained the public face of the series. The series finale was on February 14 at Daytona, the Friday before the 500. Mark had tested all the cars at Daytona, found them within a half-second of one another, and was pleased with the performance equality they had achieved. The cars were also nicer to drive than they had been at Michigan. Mark told *Autosport*'s Gordon Kirby, "I know what the guys wanted of the cars, but we just didn't have enough time before Michigan. Since then we've been able to listen to everybody." The race was a great success and made excellent television. Bobby Unser won the 40-lap finale and with that succeeded Mark as IROC champion.

Boating continued to be a big part of Mark's life, and whenever he could be in south Florida he would immediately go out on his cigarette boat to unwind. Richard White would meet his plane, and often they would go directly to the marina. Mark's idea of relaxation on the boat was just to go as fast as it would run, Richard recalls. "We would cruise around and if we encountered another cigarette boat—which we typically would—it would be a few minutes of looking one another's boat over and then a race."

The new boat was a sensation when it was launched at North Miami Beach in February. The topsides were dark blue and the deck was gel-coated in yellow—a familiar color for Mark. The custom fittings and detail work were to an extraordinarily high standard. The designer-builder Don Aronow was a close friend of Mark's, and as much a legend in his sport of offshore boat racing as Mark was in motor racing. Aronow had won the world offshore driving championship in 1967, and again in 1969, and had been the American champion in 1967, 1968, and 1969. He had built or designed offshore race boats that had won more than 250 races, 9 world championships, and 20 U.S. championships. "Some guys run these things for years and never get the hang of it," Aronow told Brock Yates. "Mark's different. With a week of practice he could be as good as there is."

Mel Crook of *Yachting* magazine noticed that Mark's new 35-foot custom-built cigarette boat had no name on the stern, so he asked him what he planned to name her. "Why have a name painted on her?" Mark replied. "I don't name my cars." Aronow had designed the new boat exactly to Mark's specifications and said it was the fastest non-race boat in the world. Mark had no desire to race it. He told Crook, "I want to have the fastest offshore boat possible with a high degree of reliability—plus enough comfort to lure my wife along on our trips."

"Mark spent a lot of time getting that boat just the way he wanted it," recalls Eden. "He became very close to Don Aronow. It was very important to him to get all the details just right. It was his world away from racing."

The custom-built boat was based on a standard fiberglass cigarette "Awesome" model with special engines from Traco Engineering. The twin 454ci V8 Chevrolets were tuned to produce slightly more than 500 horsepower. Richard White recalls picking up the Traco engines at the airport and delivering them to Don Aronow's shop for installation. "They had been dynoed at 502 hp and 504 hp and were set up to run on regular gas. Mark didn't want to get caught out somewhere obscure that didn't have the high-octane stuff." Richard was sent to Mercury's maximum security "Lake X" in central Florida to pick up some very special out-drives that were being made available only to Mark. "The place was impossible to get into and unknown to most people. There were armed guards—the whole deal."

Net weight of the boat was 7,000 pounds, with the twin engines close to the stern drives. The gas tanks held 225 gallons. There were two shock-absorbing bucket seats, one of which faced the steering wheel and gauges. The wheel was unusually small for a boat and was supplied by Racemark. Forward of the bucket seats was the entrance to a surprisingly comfortable cabin, custom-trimmed in teak, with ample seating, a concealed head, and a king-sized double berth. Large skylights provided excellent light and ventilation.

Mark's love of high-performance boating went way back—to the regattas when Mark Sr. held him on his shoulders so he could see the action above the crowd. Later on Martha's Vineyard, Mark and Dave Lawton modified their outboards. Later still, Phil Burrows remembers Mark at age 15 borrowing his new outboard and disappearing for an entire afternoon. He had raced every boat on the lake and was oblivious to how long he had been gone.

Mark and Eden moved to England after returning from Brazil, although they continued to maintain the apartment in Reading, Pennsylvania. In Bournemouth they lived at Wimborne Road 28, The Gables. Eden was discovering the perils and attendant worries of the racing lifestyle along the way. "In the beginning I used to worry about getting involved with Mark," she told *People* magazine. "But after a while I decided that if you want something badly enough in life you

just have to take the chance and grab it. I stopped thinking that anything could happen to him. And now if somebody told me that Mark had been hurt, I wouldn't believe it until I had actually seen him myself in the hospital."

"Eden's too gentle for racing," Mark told *People*. "She doesn't even like to hear the sound of tires squealing."

CHAPTER 164:
"The unwieldy and erratic handling Penske"

The next round in the Grand Prix series was at the 2.55-mile long Kyalami circuit in South Africa on Saturday, March 1. The Penske PC1/02 had been modified since the South American races by making the rear suspension wider and lengthening the wheelbase by adding a five-inch spacer between the engine and gearbox. "The formula has stayed the same for so long that everybody has perfected their designs," Mark told Patrick Bedard in *Car & Driver*. "They know all the quirks, what works and what doesn't. The long-wheelbase cars were quickest in Brazil and Argentina, so we went back to England and lengthened ours." With the bad weather in England and Mark's responsibilities in Florida, there had been no opportunity to test since the last race at Brazil.

"We went out for testing at Kyalami in South Africa more than a week before the race," recalls Nick Goozèe. Goozèe, who later became president of Penske Cars in the United Kingdom, had joined the team from Brabham the previous year to help build the first car. "I was primarily involved in the race shop operation," he says. "South Africa was the only race meeting I joined the team for outside of the British Isles." The small Penske team that flew to South Africa included crew chief Karl Kainhofer, designer Geoff Ferris, and mechanics Greg Syfert and Goozèe. "Mark seemed very relaxed and in his element while we were testing," remembers Goozèe. "He was more intense at the actual race."

Early in practice Mark told Pete Lyons that the Penske PC1 was handling fine—it just wasn't quick. As the sessions progressed Lyons described Mark as "in a low mood," complaining that the chassis was "unforgiving." This was apparent to onlookers such as Andrew Hedges, who in *Motor Sport* called it "the unwieldy and erratic handling Penske."

Formula One was competitive and tough. Although Mark's qualifying time was less than two seconds off the pole time, he was 18th on the grid. In the race Mark made a steady drive to finish eighth, but he was a lap down on race winner Jody Scheckter's Tyrrell 007-Ford. Scheckter, winning in front of his home crowd, fought a race-long battle with second-place Carlos Reutemann. Next in order were Depailler, Pace, Lauda, Mass, and Stommelen, with Mark next ahead of Pryce and Peterson.

At South Africa the team had gained a lesson in what it would take to learn the ropes in their first season on the circuit. The long-wheelbase cars were not the hot setup for Kyalami. "We asked why," Mark told Bedard. "They said they didn't know but to leave it long for Brands Hatch because it would be good there. They know this stuff and we're a race late." Mark was referring to the collective knowledge of seasoned teams in the paddock.

CHAPTER 165:

"The wet is a great equalizer"

Non-championship Formula One races were still part of the racing scene in 1975, particularly in England, which was the center of the Grand Prix racing industry. The Race of Champions at Brands Hatch in Kent was a traditional spring event that opened the European Formula One season. First National City Bank Checks was an active sponsor. They promoted their product with a centerfold ad in *Autosport* the week before the race featuring Mark at speed in the Penske PC1. First National also threw another elegant party for the racing fraternity at the Dorchester Hotel. Eden accompanied Mark along with Kathy and Roger Penske. In conversation with Nick Brittan, Mark was typically candid. "In USAC and NASCAR racing there are probably only six guys running really competitively. So with a decent car you can get yourself into the first few rows of the grid. Here in F1 everyone is competitive and the going is real tough for a newcomer." Although the car was slow, it was extremely handsome in its red, white, and blue livery, with "First National" emblazoned on the body and the Sunoco logo on the front wing endplates.

The race on April 5 attracted most of the U.K.-based Grand Prix teams. The 16 Formula One cars were augmented by half a dozen Formula 5000 cars to make a full field. Friday practice was wet and cold, and Mark made the most of the conditions. Rob Walker wrote in *Road & Track*, "The person who impressed me most was Donohue, who had never been around Brands Hatch before and had not driven in the rain since Mosport in 1971. In spite of a few spins, he was really trying and hurling his Citibank Penske around to such good effect that he was 7th." When congratulated by Walker on his qualifying performance, Mark said, "The wet is a great equalizer."

On race day it snowed before the start and the track was a mixture of wet and dry. Reveling in the conditions, Mark ran a strong sixth place before spinning. He was further delayed when he made a pit stop for overheating, but returned to the race and continued to impress. Near the end he had another spin and hit the guardrail, putting him out of the race. Tom Pryce scored his first Formula One win, also the first for UOP Shadow.

Jody Scheckter in his *Autosport* column observed that Mark had been trying really hard. "He was driving just like he told me not to in the Can-Am a couple of years ago, riding up on the outside kerbs."

Just a week later on April 13 the second of the traditional British non-championship Formula One races, the Daily Express Trophy, was run at Silverstone. For the first time Mark had two Penske PC1s to choose from. PC1/3 was a brand-new car with the original short-wheelbase setup. Mark—needing every possible lap—got a late start in Friday practice in PC1/2 because of a slipping scavenge pump clutch in the oil system. He still managed a decent 1:19.0 compared to fastest man Niki Lauda in the Ferrari at 1:17.4. Mario was a tenth of a second slower than Mark. The day ended ingloriously for Mark when a tire abruptly went flat as he was receiving the checkered flag to end the session. The Penske spun down the pit straight and damaged the nose on the guardrail.

On Saturday Mark concentrated on the new car and achieved the same time he had on Friday in the long-wheelbase car. Mario improved to a 1:18.7 and started 10th, with Mark 11th. Mark chose to race the long-wheelbase PC1/2 on Sunday, telling Pete Lyons it was more "comfortable and felt quicker." Mark had an excellent result, finishing sixth in a race won by Niki Lauda in the Ferrari ahead of Emerson Fittipaldi's McLaren. Mario Andretti was third in the Parnelli, with John Watson fourth for Surtees and Patrick Depailler fifth in a Tyrrell. Just two seconds back in sixth was Mark, ahead of Alan Jones in a Hesketh and Carlos Reutemann in a Brabham.

Mark and Eden's flat in Bournemouth was near Poole where the cars were built and headquartered. Eden's brother Steven remembers their residence. "Mark and Eden lived in a wonderful old half-timber house which had been split into a number of apartments." Eden loved being in Europe. She would drive into London to Portobello Road where a friend was an antiques dealer. On non-race weekends Mark would be home. But Nick Goozèe recalls that Mark never really totally adapted to living in England: "It was simple things like getting his laundry done and not being able to eat or drink at all hours as he was accustomed to." Goozèe adds, "Although Mark was very quiet when he was in the workshop, he was very nice nonetheless. It was a very small facility. Mark liked to come and work on a project—some detail thing he wanted on the car. He was very good company although he didn't have a great deal to say. I think he was shy."

On several occasions Mark and Eden drove Mark's black Porsche 911 to races on the continent. They also flew to many races. Nick Goozèe memorably rode with Mark to Heathrow Airport in the 911 and then brought it back to keep in the shop at Poole until Mark returned. "Those trips were not for the fainthearted," recalls Nick. "Mark had no respect for the U.K. laws of the road. He would do some really outrageous things on the road but he found it great fun. It was a Wall of Death thing most of the time." Nick recalls that Mark's Porsche was distinctive, "with fat wheels and a big spoiler on the back. It was a really special vehicle."

Eden's brother Steven, who had graduated that year from the University of Virginia and spent part of his summer with Mark and Eden, remembers the car fondly. "Mark drove the most beautiful black Porsche 911 with flared rear wheel fenders and black leather with red piping (or the other way around). He washed and waxed it sometimes several times a week. I questioned the need to wax the car so often, to which Mark, in his usual calm and gentle manner, yet ever the perfectionist, responded that if one coat of wax is good, many must be better. When Mark was away from Bournemouth for a few days, he gave me the keys to the Porsche. What a dream; I was 23 years old and driving along the English coast in a Porsche 911."

CHAPTER 166:

A True Road Course

Mark had picked up a bad cold and was suffering from a sore throat when the team went to Barcelona for the Spanish Grand Prix on April 27. The gracious and sophisticated Rob Walker—who had been a privateer owner in Formula One, entering cars for Stirling Moss and others, and then later a correspondent for *Road & Track*—had befriended Mark and Eden. On Thursday while Mark familiarized himself with the circuit, Eden and Rob explored Barcelona. "Rob was the consummate gentleman," remembers Eden, "and great fun."

Barcelona's Montjuich circuit was a true road circuit, magnificently laid out on a system of roads that went through city parks and other areas of great beauty and spectacle. With the advent of guardrails, preparing the circuit had become a challenge for the organizers because most of the Armco barriers had to go up just before the race weekend and then be dismantled afterward. On Friday the teams discovered that the majority of the temporary guardrails around the 2.35-mile circuit were not properly bolted and secured. All were mindful of the accident at Watkins Glen the previous October where a bolt had failed and a lower Armco piece had collapsed, contributing to Helmuth Koinigg's fatal accident. Meetings between the Grand Prix Drivers' Association (GPDA), the Constructors Association, the CSI, and the race organizers resulted in a promise that all of the more than 3,000 guardrails would be properly secured by Saturday. Until then, drivers loyal to the GPDA refused to participate in Friday practice. The exceptions were Jacky Ickx and Vittorio Brambilla, and theirs were the only cars on the track. Missing Friday practice was particularly difficult for Mark who desperately needed track time.

"I haven't seen any of the tracks," Mark told Patrick Bedard. "If on the first day of practice you are just trying to figure out which way the track goes and what gear ratios you should have, you can't be as competitive as the guy who has all of that stuff sorted out and is just tuning himself up." Mark again had the choice of PC1/2 and PC1/3, but only used the long-wheelbase PC1/2.

The guardrail controversy continued on Saturday because the work was deemed incomplete. The CSI gave the go-ahead for practice to begin, but the GPDA was not satisfied.

Wrenches were picked up by team owners Bernie Ecclestone, Ken Tyrrell, Colin Chapman, Frank Williams, and along with some of their mechanics they threw themselves into the overwhelming task of tightening bolts and adding safety washers. Emotions were high as drivers came to terms with whether they would compete on the circuit. Jacky Ickx was again on track, this time joined by Roelof Wunderink and Bob Evans. Mark and Mario Andretti maintained solidarity with their GPDA brethren, but were among those who felt a responsibility to the crowd to race. "We are here to race and we should make the best of it and race," said Mario. "The organizers have made some effort to put things right so we should help them. I am here to race and that is what I want to do."

Emerson Fittipaldi decided on principle not to participate. The remaining cars and drivers finally began practice and qualifying at 4:00 p.m. on Saturday. Mark's best lap was a 1:26.3, which placed him 17th on the 26-car grid. His lack of track time was exacerbated by time lost making a major suspension change to cure a pulling condition. Pole position went to the Ferrari of Niki Lauda at 1:23.4.

The race was spoiled by accidents that began in the first turn of the first lap. Mark was running in midfield when on lap four he came into a blind entrance to a turn and found cars blocking the track. Moments before, Jody Scheckter's engine had massively blown up, leaving an enormous amount of oil on the track and causing several cars to spin. Mark was one of them: He had nowhere to go, and hit the guardrail and then the Hesketh of Alan Jones. He was out of the race.

Accidents continued. Perhaps the most disappointing was Mario's, which occurred when the front suspension of his Parnelli collapsed and he crashed while in first place with a 20-second lead. The accident that the race is best remembered for came on lap 25 when the rear wing mounting on the race-leading Embassy Hill of Rolf Stommelen suddenly snapped off on the entry to a high-speed bend. Stommelen hit the left-side guardrail, then bounced across the track to straddle the guardrail on the right side. He crashed through the catch fencing where the car came to rest. It was not a spectator area, but official observers and photographers were there watching the race. Four people died in the crash, and 12 were injured. Stommelen suffered two broken legs, a broken wrist, and fractured ribs.

It took four laps for the organizers to realize the severity of the accident and to decide to stop the race. Only then were ambulances and rescue vehicles dispatched to the accident scene. The race was not restarted. The guardrails had not been to blame in the accident; they held up, with the section impacted being among the ones worked on by the teams the day before.

Jochen Mass in the McLaren was the winner, and all point scorers were awarded half points because the race had not gone sufficient distance to be classified complete. Lella Lombardi, sixth in a March 741, became the first woman to score points in a World Championship Formula One Grand Prix. The Montjuich circuit was never used again for F1 racing, although it continued to host motorcycle events into the 1980s.

CHAPTER 167:
The Glamour of Monte Carlo

The Grand Prix of Monaco in the charming small city of Monte Carlo on the Côte d'Azur is a great deal more than another stop on the Formula One circuit. The circuit is unique and difficult, and its tradition rich and deep. The glamour associated with Monaco attracts racing aficionados and the glitterati alike. For Mark and Eden it was their first visit, and they participated fully in the great fun of the weekend. Fred Stecker of Citibank, the Penske Team's primary sponsor, had a yacht moored in the harbor in the middle of the social scene that annually makes Monaco unlike any other stop on the Grand Prix calendar. Mark and Eden met Princess Grace and Prince Rainier at a reception and dinner at the palace. They were seated with Princess Grace's brother, John Kelly Jr., a friend of Roger's from Philadelphia.

It was unseasonably cold on Thursday for the first day of practice. Because of the tight nature of the 2.037-mile circuit, the field was limited to 18 starters. This made qualifying all the more tense and important, with 26 cars attempting to make the field. The entry was essentially the same as at Barcelona, with Graham Hill replacing the injured Rolf Stommelen for the Embassy Hill team. For Monaco the original PC1/1 was extensively modified to create a shorter wheelbase and a narrower track both front and rear. Although Mark was pleased with the handling—telling Pete Lyons, "It's almost as good as my Porsche was"—he was puzzled by the car's overall lack of speed. Lyons also noted that "many observers were enthralled by its spectacular oversteer."

Friday was pleasant, sunny, and warm for qualifying. Mark was going well, having turned a lap at 1:28.81 (he had recorded a 28.38 in practice) which placed him safely on the grid. Trouble came when he ran wide exiting St. Devote corner and hit the barrier. "He felt the back come around, and elected to help it, Indy-style, so as to go into the wall backwards," Pete Lyons wrote. The Penske could have been repaired in time for the race. The real damage was done when the mobile crane used to lift the car off the track swung it into a lamppost. Now PC1/1 was beyond repair at the track and PC1/3 had to be readied for the race.

Mark's time placed him 16th fastest of the 26 cars attempting to qualify for the 18 available starting places. Mario was 15th with a 1:28.11, while Niki Lauda was on pole in the Ferrari with a 1:26.40.

Saturday was a day off for most teams at Monte Carlo, but the Penske crew worked all day to prepare the backup PC1/3 for the race. Sunday, May 18, dawned to a persistent rain. "Monaco was a disaster, really," remembers Karl Kainhofer. "It was raining and the paddock area was a joke. It amounted to a tarp strung off the end of the transporter. The road bed was uneven and made setting the car up impossible. We had thirteen wheels for two cars and all of them wound up bent and so did both cars."

Peter Parrott, an English mechanic who had joined the team at Brands Hatch, remembers it well. "Water was running through our area. It was a mess—a complete mess. But you work through it and around it. Mark was going quite well in the race, actually."

The rain stopped before the race, but everyone started on rain tires and changed to drys as the track improved. Although he reached as high as sixth place in the first half of the race, the spare car was not a match for the crashed car, so Mark was struggling. The front A-arms were bending and became progressively worse until one broke, pitching Mark into the guardrail. Despite his race-long struggle with PC1/3, he completed 66 laps of the 75-lap distance—the race was scheduled for 78 laps, or two hours, and with the rain the time ran out on lap 75—and was classified 10th. Niki Lauda won the race with Emerson Fittipaldi second.

After the race a special dinner was arranged on the First National City Bank yacht for the Penske team mechanics who had struggled so mightily in the difficult circumstances. Crew chief Karl Kainhofer was joined by Greg Syfert, Peter Parrott, and truck driver George Burns. While they appreciated the sentiment, the experience was not unlike a similar dinner after the Daytona 24 Hours victory in 1969. "We couldn't keep our eyes open," remembers Karl. "We were so exhausted our heads were almost dropping into the soup."

Chris Ellison had arrived in Europe to join her then-boyfriend Greg Syfert (the two were married later the same year). On Monday she was on the flight back to England with Mark and Eden. "I took the train with them from London to Bournemouth where we loaded the Porsche with piles of luggage and Mark drove Eden home. I waited at the station until Mark returned to drive me to the duplex Greg was renting. Mark said, 'I think I know where it is.' I didn't, as I had never been there, and, of course, I got back well before Greg did."

It was just a week until the Belgian Grand Prix on May 25. Formula One had abandoned the magnificent Spa-Francorchamps circuit because of safety issues and now ran on the 2.648-mile Zolder circuit. Zolder was a decent track with some challenging corners, but suffered in comparison with the majesty, breadth, and history of the fast 8.9 miles of Spa. Mark and Eden drove to the race in the 911 and Karl rode with Heinz Hofer in Heinz's new BMW.

Roger Penske was not at Zolder because the Indianapolis 500 was run the same day. Mario Andretti and the Vel's Parnelli Jones Racing team were also absent from Zolder in favor of Indy. During the 500 Tom Sneva had a horrific crash that he survived with only minor injuries in the Penske McLaren M16C. Bobby Allison was driving the team's second M16C. Bobby Unser in Dan Gurney's Eagle won the race.

At Zolder Mark was running the repaired PC1/01 that he had crashed in practice at Monte Carlo. Karl and the crew had done a great job making it race-worthy, although a leaking brake line hampered progress in the first practice session on Friday. Mark had only a few laps at speed on the track when he went off in the high-speed left-hand bend after the pits, significantly damaging the car. With only a week between Monaco and Zolder the spare car was not yet repaired and available. Work was concentrated on making the PC1/01 raceable, and Mark missed the final practice session Friday afternoon.

The reality of being a race mechanic in the 1970s—even in the exalted world of Formula One—was one of hard work and little glamour. Karl Kainhofer and Peter Parrott, after working late into the night repairing the crashed race car, ended their day by smuggling the Varley batteries into their hotel room in order to charge them for the next day's activities. In the morning they had to smuggle them back out. While the scene was a familiar one to Formula Ford and Formula Three drivers of the period, it wasn't a great deal different at the top of the ladder.

The consequence was that Mark had minimal track time, resulting in his poorest qualifying result of the season, gridded 21st of the 24 starters. The race went slightly better. Pete Lyons wrote, "Donohue, whose handling was visibly difficult—tail snapping out exiting corners—did have a race-long dice with a couple of other cars." Mark persevered to finish 11th but was three laps down to winner Niki Lauda in a Ferrari 312T. The Penske PC1 was not competitive despite all the effort Mark and the team were exerting.

"Roger is ready to build a new car right now, but I'm not sure exactly how it should be different," Mark told *Car & Driver*'s Patrick Bedard. "So we're going to stick with this one for a while and try a few things. Maybe that will slip us a clue. Like every other new kind of racing we've ever tried, I think we have to pay our dues. You can't unload a brand-new car and sit on the pole."

CHAPTER 168:
Roger Takes Stock

At Anderstorp for the Swedish Grand Prix on June 8, Mark qualified alongside Mario Andretti, on the eighth row of the grid—16th of the 26 starters. On the row in front of Mario and Mark were James Hunt in the Hesketh and Jochen Mass in the McLaren M23. On the row behind sat Tony Brise in the Embassy Hill and Jacky Ickx in the JPS Lotus 72. At the front of the grid on pole was Vittorio Brambilla in a March 751.

Eden remembers the race weekend for its easy sociability. Carl Gustaf, the Crown Prince of Sweden, attended a reception for the drivers, and Eden recalls a warm conversation with him.

Although he was never in contention for the race lead, Mark was a solid runner near the front of the field. He finished fifth on the same lap as race winner Niki Lauda after a long battle with Ronnie Peterson, Emerson Fittipaldi, Tony Brise, and Jochen Mass. Mario Andretti finished one position ahead

of Mark in fourth. Niki Lauda won for Ferrari, with Carlos Reutemann second in the Brabham and Clay Regazzoni third. Brambilla's March had dominated practice and qualifying, but in the race its handling deteriorated and he ultimately retired with a broken U-joint. For Mark and the Citibank Penske it was a highlight in the season as they scored two World Championship points. He earned his position as he battled on track to first pass Ronnie Peterson and then to chase down and pass Emerson Fittipaldi.

Once back at home base in Poole, the team readied for a Goodyear test at Silverstone on June 11 and 12. On the way to Silverstone on Tuesday, June 10, Mark stopped at Heathrow Airport to meet his son Michael, who had arrived that morning for a three-week visit. Michael, still a month short of 11 years old, made the trip unaccompanied. Plans for the visit had been decided over Christmas at Mary Ellen and Dan Wulff's home near Warren, New Jersey, when Mark and Eden came to visit for the holiday. Both boys had been invited, but eight-year-old David did not make the trip. "I think it was because I was too young to fly alone with just my brother," recalls David. "But to be honest, as I remember it, my dad had taken me to the movie *Airport 75*, and it scared me out of flying."

Father and son drove in the black Porsche 911 directly to Silverstone. With the British Grand Prix just a month away it was a chance for Mark to gain more track time. His best time of 1:18.53 was still two seconds off the fastest runners. On the other hand, many established teams and drivers fared no better or were a second, or more, slower. Ronnie Peterson in the Lotus 72 managed a 1:18.52. As a new chassis the Penske PC1 was never going to be on equal terms with well-developed cars. Mark took particular notice that, once again, Vittorio Brambilla in the March 751 was among the fastest. Mark was constantly evaluating other cars, and had already discussed with Roger the possibility of buying a proven chassis from another team. Only Tom Pryce in the Shadow was quicker than the March on the test day.

Back at the flat in Bournemouth Michael and his father had meaningful time together. "It was just great and, obviously, something I will never forget," remembers Michael. "It was a time for getting closer to my father, getting to know Eden. It was the most time I'd spent with my father since he had lived with us." A day at the beach together is especially vivid in Michael's mind, made memorable by an unexpected detour. Attempting to cut through the sand dunes for a more direct route to where the car was parked, 10-year-old Michael stumbled upon the nude section of the beach. "I couldn't get through there fast enough," recalls Michael.

At Poole in the race shop Michael busied himself polishing wheels and waxing the race car. "I also flew from London to Italy with my father," says Michael. "It was for his Racemark business, and we spent the day in Turin at the Momo steering wheel factory. The owner also made mini-bikes and he said he would send me one. I didn't think much about it, but sure enough, one day a large wooden crate arrived at our home in Pennsylvania with the red 50cc mini-bike. Between that and a 75cc Kawasaki my father had won for winning pole position at a race, David and I were set."

A week later the team left southern England for another Grand Prix on the continent. The trip to Zandvoort was made by overnight ferry from Harwich to Hoek van Holland. Eden's brother Steven recalls the passage. "Mark went ahead to the Dutch Grand Prix, and Eden, Michael, and I drove in Heinz Hofer's BMW Bavaria via ferry to Holland. One memorable moment was sharing a cabin with Michael and his falling out of the top bunk in the rough seas."

Zandvoort, on the Dutch coast of the North Sea, was a traditional Grand Prix venue with an atmosphere very much its own. The town exuded the boisterous atmosphere of a second-tier resort, featuring cabanas filled with stout Germans in a holiday party mood, all perched on what must be the windiest beach in Europe. At the raucous bumper-car arcade in the middle of town Michael and Steven played out their own races. The race paddock was an easy 5- to 10-minute walk from the center of town. The circuit ran through and around sand dunes, presenting one of the great driving challenges of the Grand Prix circuit. Fast and challenging bends were made all the more demanding by light sand blowing over the track. The close proximity to the sea virtually guaranteed at least some rain over any given race weekend. Altogether it promised one of the most delightful race weekends of the year. For those seeking more sophisticated nightlife, Amsterdam was barely an hour's drive down the road.

Much of this was likely lost upon Mark, who endured a frustrating and difficult Dutch Grand Prix. Sam Posey and Ellen Griesedieck encountered Mark and Eden having a quiet dinner together at a small restaurant in town. Ellen, who had created the cover art for Mark's book, *The Unfair Advantage*, published that summer, remembers that they had a good visit—although Mark couldn't mask his disappointment in the race car.

Driving PC1/03, Mark struggled in the early practice sessions with the wrong gear ratios. Once the gearing was corrected he gained more than a second, but remained frustrated with his time. "To make the car go well it needs a lot of wing, but even without any we are the slowest car," he told Rob Walker. "What chance have we?"

Mark qualified barely two seconds off the pole time posted by Niki Lauda in the Ferrari 312T, but it was only good for 18th position among the 24 starters. The race started on a wet track. As usual, Mark shone in these conditions, and soon had the Penske up to eighth place. "He says the wet is a great equalizer," Rob Walker wrote, "but I can't help thinking he is more equal than some."

Although Mark was driving superbly, the pit stop for dry tires did not go well, and using the Penske's wet setup on the drying track was a struggle. Mark said that oversteer in the high-speed bends was terrible. That, along with the slow pit stop, caused him to finish a lap down. Despite an excellent performance on his part, Mark finished eighth, two spots out of the points. James Hunt won his first Grand Prix in the Hesketh, ahead of the Ferraris of Niki Lauda and Carlos Reutemann.

At Zandvoort Mark had given Michael his credential badge, but getting on top of the pits to watch the race wasn't easy for Michael. After being turned away by the guard at the gate, he went to the transporter and obtained two First National promotional shirts which he effectively used as a bribe to gain admittance. "I was able to watch a little of the race from up there until the guard's boss noticed me and became incensed. I left and watched the rest of the race from inside the Tarzan Turn."

Roger was an infrequent visitor to the Formula One races but was very much on the scene at Zandvoort. "Roger always had the ability to take stock of a situation and make command decisions," recalls Karl Kainhofer. "He was under some pressure from Citibank to see better results, and on Monday when we came back from Holland, Roger, Mark, Heinz, and I met with Max Mosley and Robin Herd of March."

Michael Donohue was along for the visit to the March factory in Bicester, and recalls that Mark was impressed with the facility. "I remember him telling Heinz how well run he thought it was and that they had all the right equipment and personnel," says Michael. "He was really excited about getting that car."

Although the March was seen as clearly a faster car than

the Penske PC1, it was considered fragile. It was often fast in testing and qualifying but rarely maintained its pace to the end of the race. "Roger believed we could make the March a reliable car through our standard of preparation," recalls Karl. "He also believed it would be a good baseline car for us in the next development of the Penske chassis." On Wednesday, June 25, Mark tested a works-team March at Silverstone—the car normally raced by Lella Lombardi. Mark was quick, easily turning lap times he had struggled to attain in the Penske. The deal was done with Mosley for a new car and Karl went to the March facility in Bicester to complete the build.

"Despite all the development we had done on the Penske PC1, it was never going to be a very good car," says Nick Goozèe. "Once we had the March we began to develop the PC3, which was really a replica of that car, plus some of the modifications that Geoff Ferris wanted to do."

Before Michael Donohue returned to America on the last day of June his father taught him how to drive. The lessons began in Eden's blue Mini. "Eventually I drove the 911," remembers Michael.

Eden's brother Steven remembers the Mini was rather special in its own right. "Eden met me in Southampton (I crossed on the QE2) in the most wonderful little Mini that Mark had bought her. It was painted the same as the Penske 917, and he put a yellow pinstripe down the side with Eden's initials on the door. I was amused by the four-speed automatic transmission (to this day I don't think Eden can drive a stick), which, attached to the little Mini engine, constantly shifted up and down, causing the car to sound like a sewing machine."

CHAPTER 169:
Fast in March

On July 6 it was back to the French Riviera for the Grand Prix de France at the Circuit Paul Ricard, located between Toulon and Marseilles. Eden and a friend took the ferry and then drove to the south of France where they joined Mark, who had gone on ahead.

In Mark's last race in the Penske PC1/03, he qualified 18th on the 26-car grid with a time of 1:50.15, compared to Niki Lauda's pole-position time of 1:47.82. As Mark told Rob Walker, "It is the same position as usual—we are two seconds too slow." On a particularly tricky decreasing-radius U-bend, Pete Lyons called the Penske "clearly the most evil-handling

car on the circuit." Alongside Mark on the ninth row at 1:50.04 was Ronnie Peterson in the Lotus 72, while Mario Andretti was one row ahead with a 1:49.72. The Vel's Parnelli team, which at the beginning of the year had been seen as the best-funded in Formula One, was now consolidating downward. Team chief Andrew Ferguson and designer Maurice Philippe were among the personnel who had abruptly left, and the team was rumored to be existing on a race-to-race basis, with Jim Dilamarter now exerting management control. "We are definitely going to finish the season," Mario Andretti told *Autosport*. "The reason for all these guys saying we're in big financial trouble is because we let 'em go. We offered Philippe a month-by-month contract but he refused. . . . He's a good engineer but he's not a racer."

Goodyear assigned garage space and pit assignments, grouping together teams who worked with a given engineer. This typically placed Williams, Copersucar (Wilson Fittipaldi's team), and the Penske team in close proximity. At Paul Ricard it was Penske Racing that loaned Frank Williams an engine so his team could make the race.

Mark's own race was short. Making good progress in the early going, he was up to 12th place when on the seventh lap, he went wide on the exit of the last turn and struck the curb, resulting in a broken halfshaft. It was the last racing lap he would drive in the Penske Formula One car.

Once back in England, Karl and Peter Parrott prepared the new March for testing at Silverstone two days after Paul Ricard. "We worked all night to have it ready," recalls Peter. "I was driving from the shop in Poole to my aunt's home in Bournemouth where I was staying, to change clothes to go testing. I never made it home; I fell asleep at the wheel and crashed the car into a lamppost. I was in hospital for a couple of weeks."

At Silverstone Mark liked the new March 751 and easily turned a 1:16.6, nearly two seconds faster than his best efforts in the Penske PC1. He said he was confident there was more to come.

Mark took the opportunity during the 10 days before the British Grand Prix to make a quick trip back to Florida. *Sports Illustrated* was doing a special feature on Mark and the new cigarette boat. The photographer spent a day with Mark but finally said, "It just isn't working." He called his editors and requested a helicopter, which arrived the next morning. Richard White was part of the shoot, and had the choice of flying in the helicopter or riding in the boat with

Mark so his photo would appear in the magazine. "I had never been in a helicopter and I decided to go with them. It was the pilot and the photographer and me. Mark was blasting down the Intracoastal Waterway at 70 mph and more and the helicopter was swooping down and around. Sometimes the pilot would zoom up high to clear a bridge. It was great material but Mark died a month before publication and *SI* decided to scrap the feature."

That summer *The Unfair Advantage* came out, and the books would arrive in boxes at the Hallandale, Florida, warehouse where Mark had an office. Mark took time on this visit to sign a quantity of books. The book had been published by Dodd, Mead & Company of New York. Having the books in hand was the realization of a long project that Mark and coauthor Paul van Valkenburgh had worked hard on for more than two years. Destined to attain iconic status within the sport, the book was distilled by Van Valkenburgh from more than 60 hours of tapes created by the two men in recording sessions in restaurants, driving down the highway, at race tracks, in Mark's living room—wherever time could be carved out of Mark's life. In the foreword Mark pronounced himself satisfied with the book, noting that he had once again done the best he could. He concluded by saying, "That's the way things were—the way I saw them."

Mark's fast time testing in the March 751 convinced the team to put the Penske PC1 temporarily aside and race the March. "When you take a new car out of a box and run two and a half seconds quicker than your old car, then it's just got to make sense," team manager Heinz Hofer told *Autosport*. Mark described the advantages of the March over the Penske to Pete Lyons: "It's sensitive to tuning—when you do something, you can feel the difference; it's easy to drive; it's got the right aerodynamic properties; it's simple; and it's light." Mark said to Rob Walker, "If you gave them 1 to 10 points for racing cars, I would rate the March an 8 and the Penske a 3."

World Championship Points

Before the British Grand Prix at Silverstone, Pete Lyons had driven his Targa-red Corvette to Bournemouth to visit Mark and Eden. Mark drove Pete's Corvette, saying, "I've always liked Corvettes, they're such a good American car." Pete was pleased that Mark approved of his car. Mark took him out in a boat he'd rented in Bournemouth. It was not at all like his cigarette boat back in Florida. "It was like a trawler," recalls Lyons. "We went chugging out of the harbor into the English Channel. Mark just wanted to be on the water." The two men discussed the race season. "It really bothered Mark not to look good in Formula One," says Lyons. "Mark said it felt like 'We have our socks down around our ankles.' "

Lyons remembers Mark discussing the adjustment to Formula One culture. "In American racing we always seem to have plenty of time to set the car up, all day if we need it. Here we've got two and a half hours today and two and a half hours tomorrow and *that's it*," he told Lyons. "The other people seem to be able to cope with that; they know the circuits and they have a lot of experience with the cars and you can see them going fast right away."

At Silverstone for the Grand Prix on July 19, a Mark Donohue fan spotted Mark's black 911 Porsche in the paddock carrying Pennsylvania license plates. Visible on the rear shelf was Eden's copy of Robert M. Pirsig's popular philosophical novel, *Zen and the Art of Motorcycle Maintenance*. "It immediately made clear to me why people race," says Eden. "Mark then picked it up and he was about halfway through it when we got to Austria."

Just before the race weekend the famous Woodcote corner—the fast, challenging bend that brought the cars onto the Silverstone start/finish straight—had, in the name of safety, been given a chicane. The change made comparisons to lap times from the earlier configuration irrelevant. Although the new race car did not dramatically launch Mark forward on the starting grid, he was suddenly competitive. Even Denis Jenkinson described ". . . Donohue driving a brand-new [March] in Penske colours, and very quickly showing what has been wrong with their own car all season." In his first race appearance in the March 751 (751-4), he qualified 15th of the 26 starters, with a time of 1:20.50 against pole time of 1:19.36 for pole-sitter Tom Pryce in the UOP Shadow. He likely would have qualified faster had the Ford-Cosworth not been misfiring and down 500 rpm for most of qualifying. Karl changed everything on the engine and regained the power with just five minutes left in the session. All the same, the gap to the front was now just a tick over a second. Mark believed there was much more to come. Mario Andretti was 12th on the grid with a 1:20.36 in the Parnelli VPJ4.

After qualifying on Friday Graham Hill held an informal press conference to announce his retirement as a driver. Hill was immensely popular with both the public and his fellow drivers, and possessed of great personal charm and wit. He had the respect and admiration of people at all levels within the sport. Hill was twice World Champion (1962 and 1968), and won the Indianapolis 500 in 1966 and the Le Mans 24 Hours in 1972. He had truly done it all. He was now beginning to enjoy success as a constructor and team owner, and his driver Tony Brise was seen as the brightest new talent in racing.

At 2:00 p.m. on Saturday the green light came on—the first time lights were used to start a Formula One Grand Prix instead of the traditional flag. The track was dry under a sunny sky, although dark clouds surrounded the Silverstone circuit. The rain came around the 20th lap of the scheduled 67-lap race. Mark, running 12th until the track became wet, now came into his own. He made excellent progress to reach fifth place and was leading Vittorio Brambilla in the works March. The rain stopped and many cars stopped again for dry tires. When the cars completed the 55th lap Mark was in fifth place, and the light rain suddenly become a deluge. Mark, along with the rest of the field (except Fittipaldi), crashed off the track on lap 56. Confusion reigned as Emerson Fittipaldi in the McLaren M23 crossed the line at the end of the lap to eventually be declared winner as the race was red-flagged. Mark had come off the road at Stowe Corner in company with John Watson and Jochen Mass. The race was called complete as scored at the end of lap 55. Mark finished fifth, scoring two World Championship points as he trailed winner Fittipaldi; Carlos Pace, Brabham; Jody Scheckter, Tyrrell; and James Hunt, Hesketh. Behind Mark in sixth was Brambilla.

Despite ending in the catch fence it was a fine race for Mark, lifting his spirits and those of the team. Although the March required chassis repairs, including several new bulkheads, Mark had proven himself and the new car competitive. He now had four points in the World Championship table.

The next day Mark flew to Alabama for initial record trials with the 917-30 at Talladega Speedway; the official attempt would be made on August 9 during the weekend of the Talladega 500 NASCAR race. On Wednesday, July 23, Mark made a run of three laps. He pitted to check tire pressures and suddenly the rear body section caught on fire. It was caused by the body being forced onto the hot engine by air pressure at high speed. A plastic tie-wrap had ignited and spread to wiring and the body. The fire scattered the crowd of onlookers, but Mark waited coolly for adjustments and then drove the 1,100-plus horsepower Porsche on to the track, warming up with a lap at 218.600, then turning a lap at 220.645 mph. Although the speed was fast enough to break A. J. Foyt's existing record of 217.854, it was not an official run.

On the Wednesday prior to the German Grand Prix on August 3, Mark drove his Porsche 911 to the circuit in the Eifel Mountains to attempt to learn his way around the classic 14.2-mile Nürburgring. The degree of difficulty represented by the 176 corners and dramatic altitude changes of the circuit must be experienced to be fully comprehended. It is rightly considered the most demanding of all race tracks, and is considered by many to be God's gift to a race-car driver.

In his first practice session in the March, Mark's best lap was a 7:26.6. In the second session he improved to a 7:18.9. Although he was 19th on the grid of 26, his final qualifying time of 7:11.6 was a triumph for any driver racing for the first time on this circuit. By comparison, Mario was three rows ahead of Mark at 7:08.2, and Tony Brise and Ronnie Peterson were one row up with 7:10.9 and 11.6 respectively. Pole position was captured by Niki Lauda in a Ferrari at 6:58.6—the first man to ever officially lap the circuit in less than seven minutes.

On race-day morning before dawn, Mark and Eden were awakened in their hotel in Adenau to the sound of a roaring motor under their window. Mark rushed out to discover his Porsche had been stolen along with his briefcase, credit cards, and personal papers that had been left inside it. Eden's first reaction was that someone had done it to sabotage Mark's race. The police later found the Porsche abandoned in the woods and stripped of much of its equipment. "Mark's briefcase was finally returned after Austria," remembers Eden.

In the race Mark suffered a puncture to the left front tire at Wipperman, then slowly drove the remaining five miles to the pits. He had completed only the first lap. A new tire was quickly fitted and Mark was off again, only to have a tire explode within a few miles at Aremberg. Carlos Reutemann won the race in the Brabham, with Jacques Lafitte second for Williams and Niki Lauda third for Ferrari.

Despite the disappointment at the 'Ring, Mark told Harvey Duck for *Auto Racing Digest*, "We have discovered some things that will make us really competitive in Formula One racing; I'm really excited about the future."

Racing is brutal and judgment harsh. Nowhere is this more true than in the hustle and "man-of-the-moment" mentality of Formula One. Despite Mark's obvious speed and prowess in the wet, driving a clearly inferior car, many in the paddock remained unimpressed by the fledgling team's accomplishments. Mark's friend Dave Lawton had a sound perspective on the obstacles Mark was facing in Formula One. "You go to Europe—no one takes into account that it's your first year there. You're running against guys that have cut their teeth on these same circuits—in F3, etc. They already know these corners—they know the engineers. On top of this, for most of the season Mark was developing a completely new chassis with a new team."

Part of the problem is that Mark came to the Grand Prix circuit with a very big reputation, and everything he did was judged against high expectations. "It was a brand-new car that we were testing and developing as we went along," recalls Peter Parrott. "If you understand that, you have to say that our results were quite encouraging." Any fair assessment of Mark's performance in Formula One will conclude that he did very well in the circumstances and that there was every reason to expect a big step forward in a second season.

Parrott considered Mark an outstanding test driver. "The driver is always the key in a test situation because he conveys to the engineer what the car is doing and then a decision is made on what to change to make it work better," says Parrott. "In Mark's case, because of his engineering background, he was particularly attuned to what information was relevant. And Mark always drove ten-tenths in testing, which you must do to get the accurate readings you want. Mark knew that and did it extremely well."

"The team had a lot to learn from the new discipline of Formula One," says McLaren designer and race engineer Gordon Coppuck. "It was one thing for Mark to come into a well-organized Formula One team and make his contribution to an experienced group. I think it was a different kettle of fish when the response to his comments had to be reevaluated by a new team without the depth of Formula One experience enjoyed by competing teams. I don't think that anyone, certainly not ourselves, thought that Mark was out of his depth. It was just a new package that needed time to come together."

Mark had not lost his focus or his self-confidence. "I want to win a World Championship," he told Harvey Duck before leaving for Austria. "I think we can do it. It may take a couple of years, but we're learning something in every race and moving right along."

"I never saw Mark fail at anything, and I don't think he was about to fail at Formula One," says Sam Posey. "The trouble is . . . you've got this huge reputation, but you've got this car that just wasn't any good at all. People forget how very difficult it is the first year in any series—new tracks, setups, etc. Mark would have had a great season the second year."

Mark summed it up this way to Pete Lyons: "I wouldn't have come back and said I'd do this if I didn't believe I could get the job done."

CHAPTER 171:

Record Run Observed by the Great One

Six months after the failed record attempt at Daytona in February—and two and a half weeks after the preliminary test that had produced a lap at over 220 mph—it was time to try again. The 2.66-mile Talladega, Alabama, tri-oval with its high and wide-banked corners was the site. The official run was scheduled for Saturday, August 9, during a lull in the Talladega 500 NASCAR Winston Cup Grand National race activities. Earle Macmullan was crew chief on the car, assisted by Fred Muller. For the record run, a 5.0-liter engine was fitted in place of the 5.4. "Mark was just more comfortable with the 5.0-liter," remembers Macmullan. "He thought it had more torque."

The car weighed in at 1,729 pounds and carried 15 gallons of fuel for the run. Other minor modifications included a tonneau cover over the passenger seat and subtle changes to the nose for improved aerodynamics. Since the preliminary run two weeks earlier a new rear body section had replaced the one that had caught fire.

"When we were at Daytona in the spring and fell on our faces, I felt really terrible," Mark told Pete Lyons. "We'd said we were going to go fast and we weren't able to. So I went to the Porsche guys and said, 'Look, you've got to help us.'" He explained how Porsche had come up with an intercooler that would allow the engine to live at a sustained high speed. "The problem had been that, as a road-racing engine, it only had to develop its horsepower for about ten seconds or so," Mark continued, "but on the oval we needed it for a couple of minutes on end."

Mark arrived from England via a stop in Atlanta where he visited the White home and invited Steven to come to Talladega to see the record attempt. "I drove down with Burge Hulett to Montgomery, Alabama," recalls Steven. "The night before the racing events, we all went to the governor's mansion for a reception for the drivers. George Wallace was still governor; wheelchair-bound, and looking gravely ill. Mark was such a kind and gentle man, and went over to Wallace, kneeled down next to the wheelchair, and spoke to him quietly for some time. Mark later commented that Wallace couldn't possibly last much longer." Governor Wallace, paralyzed from a failed assassination attempt three years earlier, lived until 1998.

Saturday was dark with rain clouds close by. Mark was anxious to complete the official run. "Let's get it over with," he told Burge Hulett. "It's going to rain and we'll be here all day." In an *Automobile Quarterly* article Burge recounted what followed:

Provincial NASCAR mechanics don't look up from their sedans as the Porsche climbs onto the track's steep banking. The only people paying attention are the timer, the crew, and a few of Donohue's friends.

After passing the pits on a warm-up lap the big red car moves up a lane on the banking and you can hear the muffled whine of the turbos as they gain speed. Every other time Donohue has taken the Porsche out he lifted off the throttle slightly to let the engine cool. This time there is no let-up. . . . Donohue's foot is flat on the floor. A drop of rain falls and the now-black clouds are almost on the roof of the grandstands. The air is still and suddenly feels cold. . . . All you can hear is the sound of the engine straining against the redline.

Suddenly the bright red car bursts out of the fourth turn and slams onto Talladega's front straight at more than 250 mph, inches from the outer wall. . . . It takes a few seconds to register. Finally we realize Donohue has

the record and there's an audible sigh from several in the group. The Porsche enters the pit lane and coasts towards the small crowd collecting on the grass to form a makeshift victory lane. It's like old times as Donohue pulls off his helmet, and he's wearing one of his few smiles of the season.

Mark was indeed happy. Standing in the cockpit of the red Porsche he laughed and clowned. A can of CAM2 oil was handed to him for publicity purposes and he pretended to open it and drink it as if it was a can of beer.

"At 220 you're working pretty hard to keep the car on the track," he told Pete Lyons. "You come into the banking about in the middle, to avoid some bumps, and gradually let the car drift up to the top. It's wiggling around and sliding a lot; it's really very difficult. The engine would be about 100 rpm down coming out of the corner, and would build up again by the end of the straight; maybe it was dropping down more in the middle of the turn but I was too busy to look!"

Mark had set a new record for the fastest lap on a closed course. The speed was 221.120 mph. Jerry Kroninger was there for Sun Oil and gave Mark a lift to the press conference. "Mark could not have been a happier person when the run was over and a success," says Kroninger. "He had been embarrassed about the Daytona result, but he was all smiles when he got in my car for the ride over to the press area. It is wonderful to remember how carefree and happy he was when we parted."

The record run was sanctioned by IMSA, who were in charge of timing and maintaining protocol at the circuit. Lorna Fitts (who would later marry journalist Pete Lyons) worked for the sanctioning body, and recalls: "Howard Dougherty, technical inspector, was the enforcer for keeping people out of areas where they shouldn't be. An interested bystander was standing out on the edge of the first turn during Mark's record run, and Howard went to get him." "Who the hell do you think you are, Fangio?" demanded Dougherty. You can't stand there." When the man turned around to answer, Dougherty realized that it was indeed, the great one, Juan Manuel Fangio. According to Lorna, all he could say was "I am so sorry, sir—you can stand anywhere you want."

The press and other dignitaries had been served box lunches, but Mark hadn't had time to eat anything. When Associated Press motorsports editor Jerry Garrett asked for a private interview Mark agreed, but suggested a trade.

"He said I could interview him if he could eat my press box lunch," Garrett later wrote. "He ravenously stuffed himself with my cold fried chicken, potato chips, and an apple. . . . I got the better end of the deal; my lunch was forgettable; my interview with Donohue was anything but."

During his interview with Garrett, Mark said, "I can hardly wait to get back to work on our Formula One program. We think we've made a major discovery. If we're right, by next season we could be the dominant team in Formula One. I think we've really turned the corner." Mark believed that switching to the March had been a good strategic move. "We're going to combine the best features of the March and the Penske car this winter, and we should come up with a really hot concept by next season."

After the interview, Mark headed to a private plane that took him to southern Florida. Mark had not given up on the idea of owning an automobile dealership. He was working with his friend Hurley Haywood to make it happen. "Mark and I were very close to getting into business together with BMW," says Hurley. "Mark was going to be the racing director of BMW in the United States and we were going to own a dealership together and I was going to race for him. Mark was doing most of the negotiations. If that had happened it would have changed the face of my entire career. I wouldn't have won all the races I did, but I would have been a lot better off financially. Mark had a much more famous name in racing than I did. It was still at an early stage, but it was a serious endeavor. Mark was very serious about it, and by summer it had advanced fairly far along. I was involved with putting some of the financing together."

The plan was for the dealership to be located in Atlanta. Eden recalls that Mark was very fond of Hurley, and was "thrilled" at the prospect of their business venture together.

On Tuesday, August 12, Mark was on a flight from Miami to join Eden in England.

CHAPTER 172:
Goodbye, My Friend

On Wednesday, August 13, Mark and Eden flew to Austria for the Grand Prix. A Porsche representative loaned them a 911 for the weekend. The stunningly beautiful Österreichring near Knittelfeld in central Austria was fast and challenging, and yet another new circuit for Mark. The fast times were set on Friday, as Saturday proved partially wet and slippery all day. For Mark it was a setback, as his first Friday practice had been spoiled by a broken linkage rod on the fuel-metering unit. In the second practice on Friday he had to stop prematurely with a split driveshaft boot.

Mark and Eden were staying in the small village of Seckau in the Gasthaus Steinmühle, just five kilometers from the race paddock. On Friday evening Pete Lyons was among a small party of six who dined at the Gasthaus with Eden and Mark. Discussing the recent experience setting the closed-course record, Pete remembers Mark telling the group, "with a small grin, 'It's the only thing I've accomplished this year.' "

Saturday's weather was frustrating, as Mark was not able to realize the improvements he needed. As had happened so often during the season, the preliminary qualifying grid had Mark next to Mario Andretti. Both were disappointed to find themselves back on the 10th row.

"Mark and I had brief visits that season, but the most extensive conversation we had was Sunday morning before the Austrian Grand Prix," Mario recalled. "He was very lonely over there. We had a conversation just before the warm-up. 'I wish I was in your shoes,' Mark told me. 'After this race you get on the plane, you're home, you're with your family and you're racing in the States next week.' I was surprised at how much he wished he was doing it the way I was doing it."

On Sunday morning Mark left the Porsche in the parking lot of the Gasthaus and rode with Eden to the track on a motorcycle he had been loaned for the weekend. It was unseasonably cold on race morning for the special practice before the Austrian Grand Prix. Mark went out for pre-race warm-up to try the March on full tanks. He was determined to find the missing pace and pushed hard in the session. "Mark was in and out of the pits making adjustments," recalls Karl Kainhofer.

The pit straight culminated with an uphill run to the Hella-Licht corner, a high-speed right-hand bend at the brow of the hill. Thirty minutes into the 45-minute session it all went wrong. Pete Lyons was in the pits and described the sudden silence that fell upon the scene when it became apparent that someone was off the track: "Through the pits ran that chilling, almost psychic tremor. Someone had gone off. . . . as silence fell and one by one drivers came back or were otherwise accounted for, the luckless man was revealed. Mark Donohue was over the guardrail at the top of the hill beyond the pits and it looked bad."

The left front tire had failed—whether it was cut or burst remains forever in question—while Mark was turning into the bend. At more than 150 mph the March went immediately into the catch fencing on the left side of the track. There was very little distance from the edge of the track to the guardrail, and the four rows of catch fencing were tightly grouped. Catch fencing was designed to progressively retard the speed of a car before it struck the guardrail. In this instance the fencing was situated with so little space between each row that they rolled up on each other to create a virtual ramp that helped launch the car. Mark and the March catapulted over the guardrail, then knocked down the large signboards behind the railing. A metal bar supporting the signboards struck his helmet and knocked him unconscious. Marshals Manfred Schaller and Richard Huettner were seriously injured by the flying debris. Schaller died the next day.

James Hunt was one of the first drivers to come upon the accident scene. He told a wire service reporter, "I nearly crashed into the wreckage because there was nobody to warn us with a red flag." Emerson Fittipaldi, Hans Stuck, and Bob Evans all stopped their race cars to attempt to help. Seeing no fire marshals, Evans picked up a fire extinguisher and stood ready in the event the car caught fire. Fittipaldi later told Lyons that when he first approached the wrecked car, he was restrained by a marshal who told him the driver was dead.

Mark was still unconscious when taken from the car, but a track doctor administered a shot at the accident site that brought him around. Mark was sitting up on the litter chatting with Fittipaldi when he was loaded into the ambulance. Emerson reported that Mark could move his limbs and speak clearly, although he had no awareness of the accident. Mark was brought to the medical trailer in an ambulance. Formula One had inherited the medical trailer that Ford had developed for Le Mans, and it traveled to every European Grand Prix. It was well equipped as a trauma center with sophisticated equipment and staffed by a team of doctors and technicians.

There were no visible injuries or markings on Mark's head or body. Mario Andretti came to the medical trailer to check on Mark. "He was in obvious shock but was talking and I figured, 'Well, OK, he's going to have a headache but he has survived this,' " remembers Mario. "I gave him some words of encouragement and when I left him I felt pretty good. I thought, 'Mark, you'll be all right.' "

Eden ran as fast as she could to the trailer. She found him flat on his back and already beginning to experience pain. He was saying "Oh, I've got a headache. Is my wife here? Where is my wife?" The pain became so intense that soon, Mark could no longer communicate. The doctors decided take him as rapidly as possible to the hospital in Graz, and the fastest way to get there was by a military helicopter. Eden was told they didn't have room for her on board, so Karl took her on the motorcycle to the Gasthaus in Seckau. From there he drove her to the hospital—the Landeskrankenhaus—in the Porsche. Karl had grown up in Graz and knew the area well.

Back at the circuit the feeling was that Mark had gotten away with it. Andretti, Fittipaldi, and others who had seen or talked to him just after the accident were left with a sense of concern mitigated by a firm belief that medical attention would soon have Mark right. Their concern was genuine: Even in the tough world of Formula One, people cared about Mark. Chris Ellison was timing for the Williams team, who fared poorly in the rain-shortened race. When it was over she heard Frank Williams exclaim, "Well, that's over. Now we need to worry about Mark."

Mark's condition was deteriorating rapidly. What had not been initially detected was that the impact that rendered him unconscious had created an intracranial bleed. At the hospital they operated almost immediately. Dr. Fritz Heppner, a noted professor of neurosurgery, performed a four-hour operation to remove a blood clot. Eden asked Heppner, "Is my husband going to be all right?" His reply was, "I don't know if he is going to live or die." Eden recalls, "That was the first time it hit me how grave Mark's condition was. When I was with him in the medical trailer he was in great pain but he had no visible injury."

Later Heppner described Mark's condition as "extremely serious," and said that he expected the crisis to last four or five days. He emphasized that Mark's life was "in serious danger." Although the blood clot had been successfully removed, Mark remained in the intensive care unit because Heppner was concerned about life-threatening complications from brain swelling. Heinz Hofer contacted Roger in Talladega, where he was with Bobby Allison for a NASCAR race. When Roger arrived on Monday morning, he took over all dealings with the doctors and making other arrangements.

Mark never regained consciousness and continued to require life support. He was kept on life support until his father,

Mark Sr., arrived. "I think I was in such denial and shock that it wasn't until they told me Mark's father was coming that I was forced to accept what was happening," says Eden. Eden's mother, Carmen White, came to be with her.

Mark's heart and breathing stopped several times during his last hours. After the doctors removed life support, Roger and the family had the chance to say their good-byes. Karl then entered the room and sat with Mark for ten minutes or more. He said good-bye to his friend and left. Mark Donohue died minutes later. It was Tuesday, August 19, 1975, at midnight in Austria, 7:00 p.m. Eastern Standard Time.

CHAPTER 173:
"Farewell, Matey"

On a sunny day more than a thousand people attended St. Teresa's Church in Summit, New Jersey, for a Mass of the Resurrection held on Monday, August 25, at 1:00 p.m. The Pallbearers were Dave Lawton, Roger Penske, Don Aronow, Burge Hulett, Richard White, and Jay Signore. The altar boy was 14-year-old Paul Glessner from nearby Ridley Township. He had been corresponding with Mark since the age of six. Mark answered every letter, and in 1973 had sent Paul one of his used race suits. Eight-year-old David and 11-year-old Michael were there with their mother, Sue. The family requested that memorial donations be directed to the Auto Racing Fraternity Foundation.

Father Harold A. Murray remembered Mark as "a very human person. He did a lot of good on this earth besides being one of the greatest drivers in auto racing history." Father Murray recalled discussing a religious vocation with Mark but observed, "The lure of the engine was greater." He also remembered Mark as "a quiet man with a wonderful sense of humor."

Among those at the church were racing friends that included Mario Andretti, George Follmer, Gary Bettenhausen, A. J. Foyt, Tony Hulman, Bobby Allison, Tom Sneva, Bob Tullius, Sam Posey, and Brian Redman. Allison told an Associated Press reporter, "He was a hell of a driver, but more important he was just one great person." Redman said that Mark "was one of the nicest people, not just in racing but in the world."

Recently Redman talked again about Mark. "He was a very nice man, correctly known as Captain Nice. Of course, under that pleasant exterior there was a streak of steel. He was a great guy and will always be an American hero."

"There was every reason for him to go back to racing," says Sam Posey. "He got terribly unlucky—a tire went down. For all of us who raced in that era, you had to have a lot of luck on your side to make it through, and Mark had a lot of luck. It ran out on that occasion, and that is all there is to it. I don't think his decision was flawed when he decided to race again. There was every reason he would have had a different competitive result the next year and that he would have retired—after a very glorious comeback. He would have won the next year in Formula One."

Among the many tributes, Nick Nagurny remembered Mark Donohue as a "kind, charming, graceful, and intelligent man." Rob Walker wrote in *Road & Track*, "I felt sick at heart. I had grown very fond of Mark and Eden in the short time I had in getting to know them. All of F1, and indeed the whole motor racing world, will be deeply affected by the loss of well-loved Mark Donohue. I have had very many friends killed in racing but few to whom I felt closer than Mark. I feel totally inadequate to express my feelings for so great a person: I can only say, 'Farewell, Matey.'"

Mike Knepper expressed the American view this way:

Mark was dead. As possible as it had always been during those beautiful years of his driving career, it had always seemed impossible. He was too good. He meant too much to the sport, more than he ever realized. . . . When this happens we usually put together some well-chosen words that indicate the hurt is somewhat lessened by the knowledge the driver understood the risks, accepted them, and then followed the dictates of his own mind. Surely that was the case with Mark, and I guess it does hurt a little less knowing that. But it does hurt, and it will for a long time.

Epilogue

When nature removes a great man, people explore the horizon for a successor; but none comes and none will. His class is extinguished with him. In some other and quite different field, the next man will appear.

—RALPH WALDO EMERSON

Jim Travers took up cigarettes when he became involved in racing. "I made it all through school and the Army and being wounded on Iwo Jima, without ever touching the things," he remembers. "But when I became chief mechanic on a midget race car the responsibility of it was terrific, and I began smoking." The Hall of Fame mechanic was instrumental in Bill Vukovich's Indianapolis 500 victories, and later, as half of the Traco partnership that built most of the Penske Racing engines. As a close friend, Mark Donohue worried about smoking being harmful to Jim's health, and was continually after him to give it up. Jim never could, saying he was hooked.

Jim was sitting on the veranda of his home on Lake Mohave smoking a cigarette when word came to him that Mark had died. "I sat there and thought about Mark and said, 'Mark, there isn't a damn thing I can do for you now, but one.' I snuffed out the cigarette and wrote the date of Mark's death on it. I never smoked again. That cigarette is still on my mantel in my home."

It was difficult for people to accept Mark's death. His retirement at the peak of his success had seemed perfect, and he had been admired for it. Now he had returned in the sport's most challenging and dangerous arena and had died.

Sam Posey and his wife Ellen Griesedieck were in their apartment in Laurel Canyon when Tom Brokaw led the entire NBC evening news broadcast—not just the sports—with the story of Mark's death. "We looked at each other and I said, 'That's it, I'm through with open wheelers,'" recalls Sam. "It was a life-changing moment: If Mark can be killed—I can be killed."

"It is bittersweet to talk about him because it is a joy to remember him," says Posey. "Thinking about Mark really makes me sad—I think he missed so much—he so nearly got away with it. He needed to have the chance to see what life was like outside of the cockpit. Maybe, if he had just given himself six months more of retirement."

Dave Lawton recalls: "Mark called me and said, 'I've got to set up this trust thing—will you be trustee for the boys? They're going to send you the papers in the mail; just sign them and send them back.' We went on and talked racing. Nothing else was said.

"We were on the Vineyard when we heard about Mark's accident," continues Lawton. "He was still alive when we got back to Pawtucket. The phone rang on Monday after the accident—IMG calling from Cleveland. 'You know you are executor of the estate?' I replied, 'No, no. I am trustee for the boys. Go back and check your paperwork.' But I was. Mark had never told me. Now I knew I had the responsibility."

On behalf of the estate of Mark Donohue, Lawton brought a wrongful death suit in federal court against the Goodyear Tire & Rubber Company, Bell Helmets, and Penske Racing as a co-defendant. Penske and Bell settled with the estate, but Goodyear defended its position. After 10 years in the courts, this high-profile, and within racing circles much talked-about, case was decided in favor of the plaintiffs.

Roger Penske was so shaken by Mark's death that he considered withdrawing entirely from racing and focusing his attention on other areas of his business. "I realized after a time, though, that Mark would have wanted me to continue in racing," he told Harvey Duck. "He knew, like all good drivers, that racing is a risky thing, and things can happen over which you have no control. And Mark was always aware that you have an obligation to your sponsors to continue, no matter how badly you may feel. So, the decision was made to go ahead."

Penske Racing did continue in Formula One. They brought John Watson into the team as driver and finished the 1975 season. For 1976 a new Penske chassis—the PC3—was developed, based on the knowledge and experience gained in their first year. During the season the team became increasingly competitive with the introduction of the more-sophisticated PC4. At the Austrian Grand Prix in August, the team scored their first and only Grand Prix victory with Watson at the wheel—poignantly, just a year after Mark's death. At the end of the season Penske Racing withdrew from Formula One.

The team has remained a major force in American motorsports, participating in Indy car racing, NASCAR, and sports cars. Its achievements span more than 300 major race wins, including 14 victories in the Indianapolis 500. "I regard Mark as the catalyst for all that we have achieved," says Roger. "He set the standard."

Mark has been inducted into the International Motorsports Hall of Fame in Talladega, Alabama; the Motorsports Hall of Fame of America in Novi, Michigan; the Indianapolis Motor Speedway Hall of Fame; the Walk of Fame at Watkins Glen, New York; and the SCCA Hall of Fame.

The finest tributes to Mark's memory are his sons, Michael and David. Michael worked for many years in the Penske businesses and continues to have a career in the transportation industry. He now lives in Austin, Texas, and is the father of Madison and Michael. David lives in West

Chester, Pennsylvania, with his wife Jodi and children Mark and Anna. He is a professional race driver for Brumos Racing. His teammates include Darren Law, whose father Peter was a mechanic on the 1967 Can-Am team; J. C. France, grandson of Bill France Sr.; and Hurley Haywood.

Both Sue and Eden keep Mark's memory close to their hearts. Sue lives in Pennsylvania near her grandchildren. Eden remarried and resides in Washington, D.C.

Zilly remained Mark's greatest booster and missed him dearly. She died in 1993, 10 years after the death of Mark Sr. Mark's sister Mary Ellen died in 2004 of multiple sclerosis. She is survived by her husband Dan Wulff and their children, Mark and Hazel. Nancy, his only other sibling, died in New York in 1994 from complications of lupus.

As a young girl, Nancy Donohue wrote lovingly of her family. She ended by saying: "Every Sunday night, when we say the rosary together, I always add an intention—that our family may be together always, and that we will love each other as dearly till we die as we do now."

Acknowledgments

The experience of researching and writing Mark Donohue's biography has exceeded every expectation. The universally enthusiastic response I have received when asking for assistance from his family, friends, teammates, competitors, and loyal fans is a credit to the man himself. It may not be possible to recognize and thank each person who contributed to the preparation of this book, but it is my intention to try.

The Donohue families have been generous participants from the beginning, and the pleasure of getting to know them over the course of my research has been a particular delight. Sue Donohue and her sons Michael and David enthusiastically endorsed the idea of the book, and their encouragement was the final step in my decision to tell Mark's story. Sue's sister Renee Dalton helped greatly, as did Bob Rost on my visit to his home in the hills outside Pittsburgh. My lunch with Mark's brother-in-law Dan Wulff and his late wife Mary Ellen's friend Beth Boyle, along with numerous phone conversations, produced vital background on Mark's boyhood. Eden White Donohue Rafshoon has been equally gracious and thoughtful. This book is greatly enhanced by her insight and that of her brothers, Steven and Richard White.

The names Donohue and Penske became forever linked in the 1960s and 1970s. Roger Penske has been an important advocate in the preparation of this book. Although never asking for (or receiving) editorial oversight, he has made every possible effort to assist me in my research. The greatest impetus in this respect has come from Walter Czarnecki, who has proven his reputation as the consummate gentleman, and as the man who can make things happen. Dan Luginbuhl, now retired, has been a tremendous resource, as have Bernie King and Tammy Strait.

My travels to meet Mark Donohue's teammates from the Penske days have been a series of great adventures. Meeting Karl Kainhofer in his beautiful home in the hills of southern Pennsylvania was a revelation of insight and candor. Karl never appeared to tire of my many calls and provided important verification. I spent a day with Don Cox, observing his fascinating life and gaining perspective on the unique engineer/driver relationship he shared with Mark. Sue and John Woodard were gracious hosts in their spectacular home in southern Virginia, and Woody worked hard with me to make my telling of the story as accurate as possible. The same can be said for Chuck Cantwell and his wife Joanne on my visit to their lovely home. Norman Ahn, Fred Marik, Peter Parrott, Nick Goozèe, Earle Macmullan, Roger Bailey, and Ron Fournier are all former Penske Racing team members who I talked to at length by telephone, and each was generous in his recollections and perspective. Pete Luongo was attached to the team for many years as a photographer on assignment. Now living near my Chicago home, Pete became an invaluable resource, tirelessly providing accurate identification of people and places. His generosity extended to supplying numerous original photographs of his own. The genuineness of the admiration and loyalty that all these men and women still feel toward Mark was apparent with each meeting.

Two additional members of the extended Penske Racing family, as engineers for the Sun Oil Company attached to the team, are Bill Preston and Jerry Kroninger. Each has added detail and texture that could not have been found elsewhere. Similarly, Jim Travers of Traco Engineering was thoughtful in his recollections.

Kirk F. White was part of the story in one of the most colorful years in Mark's personal history, and he proved to be a generous and knowledgeable source for those days.

I was fortunate to have skilled readers of the early drafts of the manuscript whose editing comments added greatly to the process. Bill Siegfriedt's technical and literary perspective was invaluable. Sarah Smith brought her impressive editing skills to the task, as did others who read all or parts of the manuscript. They include Sita Green, Michael T. Lynch, Paul Medici, and the aforementioned Bill Preston and Jerry Kroninger. Each contributed greatly to the accurate telling of the story.

My own family participated enthusiastically. My parents, Jean and Cameron Argetsinger, brought perspective based on their unique knowledge of the era and their personal relationship with Mark and his parents. Each of my eight brothers and sisters were part of the process in many supportive ways. I especially thank Marya, an author and playwright, who was a constant source of advice.

One of my first research trips was to the Rhode Island home of Judy and Dave Lawton. As a friend of Mark's from boyhood, Dave remained close to Mark throughout his life. After Mark's death it was Dave, as executor of the estate and trustee for his young sons, who continued to look after his friend's interests. Dave was a constant source of good judgment and thoughtful perspective in telling this story. Also present for the sumptuous lunch served that day by Judy Lawton was Mark's boyhood friend, Jim Haas. It was Jim who helped me find many of Mark's friends from his earliest years, including Greg Pierson, David Belden, Phil Burrows, Link Eveleth, Linda Groves, John Holman, Jamie Weissenborn, and Charles Wynn. Each has added color and personality to the story.

On the same trip east I spent a wonderful day with Judy Stropus at her home in Connecticut. It was early in my research, and Judy's canny instincts and advice helped shape my research going forward. She generously opened her archives, and the book is richer for her advice and help.

Barb and Jay Signore may have been as close to Mark over a long period of time as anyone outside of his immediate family. The day I spent with them was memorable for their enthusiasm and undiminished affection for Mark. It was one of my earliest interviews, and they pointed me in the right direction.

Another early source in my research was Bob Bailey, who provided wonderful hospitality on my visit to Saratoga Springs. Bob was Mark's close friend and business partner in Racemark, as well as a respected Porsche driver in the Trans-Am.

Paul Powell may deserve the title of number one Mark Donohue fan. He is also an outstanding person who I am proud to count as a friend. Paul organized the Mark Donohue reunion at Watkins Glen in 2003, and is the creator of the UnfairAdvantageRacing.com website. He was a constant source of energy and provided contacts to many people who featured in Mark's life story.

Malcolm Starr was among the influential figures in Mark Donohue's career. On my visit to their home in Providence, Rhode Island, Malcolm and his wife Marty shared a candid and in-depth look at a crucial transitional period in Mark's life. They also provided a tour of the campus of Mark's alma mater, Brown University. Their kindness will be long remembered.

Particularly memorable were interviews with fellow race drivers, both teammates and competitors. On a visit to his home in Sharon, Connecticut, I spent the day with Sam Posey and his family, remembering Mark. His son John and his lovely and talented wife Ellen Griesedieck added greatly to the experience. Sam's insights are remarkable, and can be found throughout the pages of this book. Hurley Haywood was likewise generous and forthcoming with his observations

on Mark's career. Over lunch in Milwaukee with David Hobbs I gained a feel for Mark and Penske Racing during the time David was part of the team. On a visit to southern California I had a delightful lunch with Jerry Grant, who figured in some of Mark's greatest races. Jerry Entin and I met in the early days of my research and soon became friends. Jerry is an irrepressible spirit, and the depth of his knowledge and contacts is equaled only by his willingness to share them.

In Pennsylvania I met with Jack Deren and Oscar Koveleski, and their firsthand experience of Mark's early race days was priceless. In addition to these face-to-face meetings I had extensive phone interviews with many other race drivers, including John Surtees, John Heyer, George Alderman, Bob Tullius, David Saville Peck, Gary Bettenhausen, Johnny Rutherford, both Bobby and Al Unser, Brian Redman, Mario Andretti, Bobby Allison, Dave Marcis, Tony Adamowicz, Skip Barber, Frank Dominianni, Dave Marcis, Bill Claren, Bobby Brown, Larry Dent, George Follmer, Dave Helmick, Howden Ganley, Dick Guldstrand, Walt Hane, George Wintersteen, Jerry Hansen, Bob Sharp, Charlie Hayes, Charlie Kolb, Mike Hiss, Sir Stirling Moss, Michael O'Hara, and Lothar Motschenbacher. Without exception they were willing to share their thoughts, and all expressed their desire to see Mark's story told as accurately as possible. The contribution of each may be found among these pages.

The single most valuable institutional resource has been the International Motor Racing Research Center at Watkins Glen. Their impressive collections for the Donohue era include the Donohue family papers and records. This remarkable archive is staffed by knowledgeable and dedicated librarians, archivists, and historians: Mark Steigerwald, Bill Green, Glenda Gephart, Jon McKnight, and Samantha Hunter. Mark and Bill were particularly involved in this book and responded with admirable patience and promptness to my frequent calls for help and advice.

Augmenting the work of the staff at the Research Center was Kevin Hughey. While I wrote in Chicago, Kevin was delving deeply into the periodicals and original source materials available at the Center. He proved to be an insightful reader of the rough manuscript, and his personal knowledge and firsthand observations of the subject were critical to accuracy.

Another great source of archival information came from the Dresang family in Hartford, Wisconsin. Rick Dresang and his wife Alison are among the great collectors of American racing history, and their willingness to share their archival material was a tremendous boost to my work. Their son Jacques has gained an international reputation as a serious researcher and a devoted custodian of the precious archives of the sport. The Dresang collection includes the Eagle-Offenhauser that was Mark Donohue's last drive at the Indianapolis 500.

At the Indianapolis Motor Speedway I benefited from the legendary knowledge of Donald Davidson. Donald provided information that would have been available nowhere else. He also helped me to locate contact information for many people important to Mark's story.

In England Doug Nye was a valuable ally and a constant support through his encouragement and help in accessing other important figures.

I am fortunate to have the best and most supportive publisher any writer could hope for. David Bull Publishing has a justly earned reputation for consistently producing quality books. I am grateful to David Bull, James Penhune, and Melissa Hayes for pushing me in the editing process and demanding my best work. Their fine touch can be found throughout the book. Tracy Moore played an important role in production. The elegant presentation of the book is owed to Tom Morgan of Blue Design, who also designed my first book for David Bull.

Many other people deserve a paragraph of their own if space permitted. They include Dave Arnold, Randy Barnett, Steve Beizer, Ray Bell, Pat Billings, John Bishop, George Bloeser, Karen Bocsusis, Chuck Boone, Barry Boor, Brian Brown, Nick Brown, Robin Carroll-Mann, David Castelhano, Frank Cavanaugh, Marian Cerdeira, Roger Clark, John Clinard, John Connell, David Cooper, Gordon Coppuck, Alan Cox, Aaron Davis, Dan Davis, Wayne Davis, Roger Steven DeVore, Dick DiBiasse, Bob Dockery, Chris Economaki, Fred Egloff, Joel Finn, Joe Foering, Chris Franseze, Darren Galpin, Paul Glessner, Jack Griffith, Jim Grob, Carl Haas, Walt Hane, Bea Hansgen, Rusty Hansgen, Patrick Hogan, Lee Holman, Rick Hughey, Harry Hurst, Mike Kamm, David Kane, Adrian Ketchum, Michael Keyser, J. D. King, Kerstin Lane, Leo Levine, Burt Levy, Craig Libuse, Daniel Lipetz, Lorna Lyons, Pete Lyons, Bob Major, Ron Mann, Joe Marcinski, Burdette Martin, Simone McCarthy, Denise McCluggage, Rob McCullough, John Mecom, Bill Milliken, Doug Mockett, Mike Mooney, Ron Nelson, Larry Neuzel, Rob Neuzel, Dave Nicholas, Kerstin Nicholson, Mike Odell, J. J. O'Malley, Frank Opalka, Alan Patterson, Christina Petrigliano, Steve Potter, Jeff Price, Jennifer Revson, Bob Rogers, Craig Rust, Tom Schultz, Ted Schumacher, Ron Scoma, Dick Scott, Bill Seitz, Mike Semel, Syd Silverman, K.C. Stackawitz, Richard Stahler, John Starkey, Mark Staunton, Jill Stiles, R. Mark Stiles, Michael Stott, Doug Switz, Chris Syfert, Barry Tenin, Robert Tourville, Archie Urciuoli, Bruno Vagnotti, Ed Valpey, Bill Warner, John Welch, Richard Weldon, János Wimpffen, Werner Winter, Brock Yates, Yale Kneeland and Steve Zautke.

My closest collaborator has been my wife, Lee. This book would not exist without her love, patience, and support, combined with impeccable instinct and judgment.

MICHAEL REYNOLDS ARGETSINGER
CHICAGO, ILLINOIS
JANUARY 2009

Mark Donohue Race Results by Year

DATE	EVENT/SERIES	LOCATION	CAR	OWNER	RESULT
1960					
Mar 4-6	SCCA Drivers' School	Marlboro, MD	Elva Courier	MND	—
April 10	SCCA Regional	Vineland, NJ	Elva Courier	MND	1st
April 23	SCCA Regional	Lime Rock, CT	Elva Courier	MND	4th
June 5	SCCA Regional	Marlboro, MD	Elva Courier	MND	1st
June 12	SCCA Regional	Vineland, NJ	Elva Courier	MND	1st
June 18	SCCA Regional	Roosevelt Raceway, NY	Elva Courier	MND	1st
June 25	SCCA Regional	Watkins Glen, NY	Elva Courier	MND	1st
July 2	SCCA National	Lime Rock, CT	Elva Courier	MND	1st
July 24	SCCA Regional	Vineland, NJ	Elva Courier	MND	2nd
Aug 6	SCCA National	Montgomery, NY	Elva Courier	MND	2nd
Aug 21	SCCA Regional	Vineland, NJ	Elva Courier	MND	2nd
Aug 21	SCCA Regional	Vineland, NJ	Elva Courier	MND	1st
Aug 21	SCCA Regional	Vineland, NJ	Elva Courier	MND	14th
Sep 4	SCCA National	Thompson, CT	Elva Courier	MND	1st
Sep 5	SCCA National	Thompson, CT	Elva Courier	MND	1st
Sep 24	SCCA National	Watkins Glen, NY	Elva Courier	MND	5th
Nov 6	SCCA Regional	Vineland, NJ	Elva Courier	MND	1st
Nov 6	SCCA Regional	Vineland, NJ	Elva Courier	MND	1st
1961					
Jan 8	SCCA Regional	Marlboro, MD	Elva Courier	MND	1st
Jan 8	SCCA Regional	Marlboro, MD	Elva Courier	MND	2nd
Feb 4	SCCA National	Daytona, FL	Elva Courier	MND	4th
Apr 9	SCCA Regional	Vineland, NJ	Elva Courier	MND	1st
Apr 9	SCCA Regional	Vineland, NJ	Elva Courier	MND	1st
April 15	SCCA National	Marlboro, MD	Elva Courier	MND	1st
April 16	SCCA National	Marlboro, MD	Elva Courier	MND	1st
April 30	SCCA National	Va. Int'l. Raceway, VA	Elva Courier	MND	1st
May 7	SCCA Regional	Vineland, NJ	Elva Courier	MND	1st
May 14	SCCA National	Cumberland, MD	Elva Courier	MND	1st
May 28	SCCA National	Bridgehampton, NY	Elva Courier	MND	1st
June 3-4	SCCA Regional	Marlboro, MD	Elva Courier	Michael O'Hara	DNF
June 11	SCCA Regional	Vineland, NJ	Elva Courier	MND	1st
June 11	SCCA Regional	Vineland, NJ	Elva Courier	MND	DNF
June 24	SCCA Divisional	Watkins Glen, NY	Elva Courier	MND	DNF
July 1	SCCA National	Lime Rock, CT	Elva Courier	MND	1st

DATE	EVENT/SERIES	LOCATION	CAR	OWNER	RESULT
July 16	SCCA Divisional	Thompson, CT	Elva Courier	MND	1st
July 23	SCCA National	Meadowdale, IL	Elva Courier	MND	1st
Aug 6	SCCA National	Bridgehampton, NY	Elva Courier	MND	1st
Sep 3	SCCA National	Thompson, CT	Elva Courier	MND	DNF
Sep 4	SCCA National	Thompson, CT	Elva Courier	MND	DNF
Sep 10	SCCA Regional	Vineland, NJ	Elva Courier	MND	1st
Sep 10	SCCA Regional	Vineland, NJ	Elva Courier	MND	1st
Sep 16	SCCA Divisional	Lime Rock, CT	Elva Courier	MND	1st
Sep 23	SCCA National	Watkins Glen, NY	Elva Courier	MND	5th
Sep 23	SCCA National	Watkins Glen, NY	MGA	Herrymond. Maurer	12th
Dec 9	Nassau Prelim	Nassau, Bahamas	Elva F-Jr.	MND	4th
Dec 10	Nassau Trophy	Nassau, Bahamas	Elva F-Jr.	MND	4th

1962

DATE	EVENT/SERIES	LOCATION	CAR	OWNER	RESULT
Feb 10	Daytona F-Jr.	Daytona, FL	Elva F-Jr.	MND	1st
Feb 10	Daytona	Daytona, FL	Elva F-Jr.	MND	DNF
Mar 23	Sebring F-Jr.	Sebring, FL	Elva F-Jr.	MND	DNS
Mar 24	Sebring 12 Hours	Sebring, FL	TVR	TVR Cars Ltd.	25th
April 14	SCCA National	Marlboro, MD	Elva F-Jr.	MND	2nd
April 15	SCCA National	Marlboro, MD	Elva F-Jr.	MND	2nd
April 15	SCCA National	Marlboro, MD	TVR	R.M. Imports	13th
June 2	SCCA National	Bridgehampton, NY	TVR	R.M. Imports	DNF
July 8	SCCA Regional	Vineland, NJ	Daimler	MND	1st
Sep 3	SCCA National	Thompson, CT	Daimler	MND	2nd
Sep 15	Int'l. 400 Km	Bridgehampton, NY	TVR Mk2	R.M. Imports	DNF
Sep 22	SCCA National	Watkins Glen, NY	Daimler	MND	5th
Oct 14	SCCA Regional	Vineland, NJ	Lotus 22 F-Jr.	John Kalhoven	2nd
Dec 2	Tourist Trophy	Nassau, Bahamas	TVR Mk2	R.M. Imports	DNF
Dec 7	Governor's Trophy	Nassau, Bahamas	TVR Mk2	R.M. Imports	DNF

1963

DATE	EVENT/SERIES	LOCATION	CAR	OWNER	RESULT
Jan 5	SCCA Regional	Marlboro, MD	Elva F-Jr.	MND	1st
Jan 6	SCCA Regional	Marlboro, MD	Elva F-Jr.	MND	2nd
Mar 23	Sebring 12 Hours	Sebring, FL	TVR	R.M. Imports	DNF
July 27	ARDC Midget Race	Lime Rock, CT	Cooper-Offy	Ken Brenn	DNF
July 27	ARDC Midget/F-Libre	Lime Rock, CT	Cooper-Offy	Ken Brenn	1st
Aug 4	USAC Midget Race	Trenton, NJ	Cooper-Offy	Ken Brenn	8th
Aug 18	Marlboro 12 Hrs	Marlboro, MD	Renault 1093	Renault Imports	16th
Sep 28	SCCA Divisional	Lime Rock, CT	289 Cobra	Jack Griffith	1st
Nov 3	SCCA Regional	Vineland, NJ	289 Cobra	Jack Griffith	1st
Nov 3	SCCA Regional	Vineland, NJ	289 Cobra	Jack Griffith	DNF

DATE	EVENT/SERIES	LOCATION	CAR	OWNER	RESULT
1964					
Jan 5	SCCA Regional	Marlboro, MD	289 Cobra	Jack Griffith	2nd
Jan 5	SCCA Regional	Marlboro, MD	289 Cobra	Jack Griffith	1st
Jan 5	SCCA Regional	Marlboro, MD	289 Cobra	Jack Griffith	1st
April 19	SCCA National	Va. Int'l Raceway, VA	289 Cobra	Jack Griffith	1st
Aug 29	SCCA Regional	Lime Rock, CT	MGB	Walt Hansgen	5th
Sep 19	FIA 400 Km	Bridgehampton, NY	MGB	Walt Hansgen	8th
1965					
Mar 27	Sebring 12 Hours	Sebring, FL	Ferrari 250 LM	John Mecom	11th
April 24	SCCA National	Marlboro, MD	Lotus 20 FC	Malcolm Starr	1st
May 1	SCCA National	Vineland, NJ	Lotus 20 FC	Malcolm Starr	2nd
June 13	SCCA National	Vineland, NJ	Lotus 20 FC	Malcolm Starr	1st
July 5	SCCA National	Lime Rock, CT	Lotus 20 FC	Malcolm Starr	1st
July 5	SCCA National	Lime Rock, CT	Shelby Mustang	Malcolm Starr	2nd
Aug 8	SCCA National	Bryar, NH	Lotus 20 FC	Malcolm Starr	1st
Aug 8	SCCA National	Bryar, NH	Shelby Mustang	Malcolm Starr	1st
Aug 14	SCCA National	Bridgehampton, NY	Lotus 20 FC	Malcolm Starr	1st
Aug 14	SCCA National	Bridgehampton, NY	Shelby Mustang	Malcolm Starr	1st
Aug 21	SCCA National	Watkins Glen, NY	Lotus 20 FC	Malcolm Starr	1st
Aug 22	SCCA National	Watkins Glen, NY	Shelby Mustang	Malcolm Starr	3rd
Aug 29	SCCA National	Connellsville, Pa	Shelby Mustang	Malcolm Starr	DNF
Sept. 5	USRRC	Elkhart Lake, WI	Lola T70 Ford	John Mecom	DNF
Sep 26	SCCA National	Marlboro, MD	Shelby Mustang	Malcolm Starr	1st
Oct 3	SCCA National	Bainbridge, Georgia	Shelby Mustang	Malcolm Starr	1st
Nov. 28	SCCA Runoffs	Daytona, FL	Lotus 20 FC	Malcolm Starr	2nd
Nov. 28	SCCA Runoffs	Daytona, FL	Shelby Mustang	Malcolm Starr	DNF
1966					
Jan 9	SCCA Regional	Marlboro, MD	Shelby Mustang	Yale Kneeland	1st
Jan 9	SCCA Regional	Marlboro, MD	Shelby Mustang	Yale Kneeland	1st
Feb 5-6	Daytona 24 Hours	Daytona, FL	Ford GT Mk2	Holman-Moody	3rd
Mar 27	Sebring 12 Hours	Sebring, FL	Ford GT Mk2	Holman-Moody	2nd
April 3	SCCA National	Marlboro, MD	Shelby Mustang	Yale Kneeland	5th
May 29	Labatt 50	St. Jovite, Canada	Lola T70 -Chevy	Roger Penske	DNF
June 4	Player's 200	Mosport, Canada	Lola T70-Chevy	Roger Penske	DNF
June 18-19	Le Mans 24 Hours	Le Mans, France	Ford GT Mk2	Holman-Moody	DNF
June 26	USRRC	Watkins Glen, NY	Lola T70-Chevy	Roger Penske	DNF
July 17	SCCA National	Mid-Ohio, OH	Shelby Mustang	Yale Kneeland	2nd
July 24	SCCA National	Connellsville, PA	Shelby Mustang	Yale Kneeland	1st

DATE	EVENT/SERIES	LOCATION	CAR	OWNER	RESULT
July 30	USRRC	Kent, WA	Lola T70-Chevy	Roger Penske	1st
Aug. 7	SCCA National	Bryar, NH	Shelby Mustang	Yale Kneeland	5th
Aug. 21	SCCA National	Watkins Glen, NY	Shelby Mustang	Yale Kneeland	DNF
Aug 29	USRRC	Mid-Ohio, OH	Lola T70-Chevy	Roger Penske	DNF
Sep 4	SCCA National.	Thompson, CT	Shelby Mustang	Yale Kneeland	1st
Sep 11	Can Am	St. Jovite, Canada	Lola T70-Chevy	Roger Penske	DNF
Sep 18	Can Am	Bridgehampton, NY	Lola T70-Chevy	Roger Penske	5th
Sep 24	Can Am	Mosport, Canada	Lola T70-Chevy	Roger Penske	1st
Oct 16	Can Am Heat 1	Laguna Seca, CA	Lola T70-Chevy	Roger Penske	6th
Oct 16	Can Am Heat 2	Laguna Seca, CA	Lola T70-Chevy	Roger Penske	4th
Oct 30	Can Am	Riverside, CA	Lola T70-Chevy	Roger Penske	4th
Oct 16	Can Am	Stardust Raceway, NV	Lola T70-Chevy	Roger Penske	6th
Date	SCCA Runoffs	Riverside, CA	Shelby Mustang	Yale Kneeland	DQ
Dec 2	Governor's Trophy	Nassau, Bahamas	Lola T70-Chevy	Roger Penske	DNF
Dec 3	Nassau Classic	Nassau, Bahamas	Lola T70-Chevy	Roger Penske	2nd
Dec 3	Nassau Trophy	Nassau, Bahamas	Lola T70-Chevy	Roger Penske	1st

1967

DATE	EVENT/SERIES	LOCATION	CAR	OWNER	RESULT
Feb 3	Trans Am	Daytona, FL	Camaro	Roger Penske	DNF
Feb 4-5	Daytona 24 Hours	Daytona, FL	Ford GT Mk2	Holman-Moody	DNF
Mar 31	Trans Am	Sebring, FL	Camaro	Roger Penske	2nd
April 16	Trans Am	Green Valley, TX	Camaro	Roger Penske	4th
April 23	USRRC	Stardust Raceway, NV	Lola T70-Chevy	Roger Penske	1st
April 30	USRRC	Riverside, CA	Lola T70-Chevy	Roger Penske	1st
May 7	USRRC	Laguna Seca, CA	Lola T70-Chevy	Roger Penske	3rd
May 21	USRRC	Bridgehampton, NY	Lola T70-Chevy	Roger Penske	1st
May 30	Trans Am	Lime Rock, CT	Camaro	Roger Penske	2nd
Jun 10-11	Le Mans 24 Hours	Le Mans, France	Ford GT Mk4	Shelby American	4th
June 25	USRRC	Watkins Glen, NY	Lola T70-Chevy	Roger Penske	1st
July 18	USRRC	Kent, WA	Lola T70-Chevy	Roger Penske	1st
Aug 6	Trans Am	Bryar, NH	Camaro	Roger Penske	DNF
Aug 13	Trans Am	Marlboro, MD	Camaro	Roger Penske	1st
Aug 20	USRRC	Mid-Ohio, OH	Lola T70-Chevy	Roger Penske	1st
Aug 27	Trans Am	Castle Rock, CO	Camaro	Roger Penske	8th
Sep 3	Can Am	Elkhart Lake, WI	Lola T70-Chevy	Roger Penske	3rd
Sep 10	Trans Am	Modesto, CA	Camaro	Roger Penske	3rd
Sep 17	Can Am	Bridgehampton, NY	Lola T70-Chevy	Roger Penske	DNF
Sep 23	Can Am	Mosport, Canada	Lola T70-Chevy	Roger Penske	DNF
Oct 1	Trans Am	Stardust Raceway, NV	Camaro	Roger Penske	1st
Oct 8	Trans Am	Kent, WA	Camaro	Roger Penske	1st

DATE	EVENT/SERIES	LOCATION	CAR	OWNER	RESULT
Oct 15	Can Am	Laguna Seca, CA	Lola T70-Chevy	Roger Penske	DNF
Oct 29	Can Am	Riverside, CA	Lola T70-Chevy	Roger Penske	3rd
Nov 12	Can Am	Stardust Raceway, NV	Lola T70-Chevy	Roger Penske	2nd

1968

DATE	EVENT/SERIES	LOCATION	CAR	OWNER	RESULT
Feb 4	Daytona 24 Hours	Daytona, FL	Camaro	Roger Penske	12th
Mar 23	Sebring 12 Hours	Sebring, FL	Camaro	Roger Penske	3rd
Mar 31	USRRC	Mexico City, Mexico	McLaren M6A	Roger Penske	DNS
April 28	USRRC	Riverside, CA	McLaren M6A	Roger Penske	1st
May 5	USRRC	Laguna Seca, CA	McLaren M6A	Roger Penske	1st
May 12	Trans Am	War Bonnet, OK	Camaro	Roger Penske	1st
May 19	USRRC	Bridgehampton, NY	McLaren M6A	Roger Penske	DNF
May 30	Trans Am	Lime Rock, CT	Camaro	Roger Penske	1st
June 2	USRRC	St. Jovite, Canada	McLaren M6A	Roger Penske	1st
June 15	USAC	Mosport, Canada	Eagle Mk4-Chevy	Roger Penske	6th
June 15	USAC	Mosport, Canada	Eagle Mk4-Chevy	Roger Penske	4th
June 16	Trans Am	Mid-Ohio, OH	Camaro	Roger Penske	1st
June 23	Trans Am	Bridgehampton, NY	Camaro	Roger Penske	1st
June 30	USRRC	Kent, WA	McLaren M6A	Roger Penske	DNF
July 7	Trans Am	Meadowdale, IL	Camaro	Roger Penske	1st
July 13	USRRC	Watkins Glen, NY	McLaren M6A	Roger Penske	1st
July 21	Trans Am	Mt. Tremblant, Canada	Camaro	Roger Penske	1st
July 28	USRRC	Elkhart Lake, WI	McLaren M6A	Roger Penske	DNF
Aug 4	Trans Am	Bryar, NH	Camaro	Roger Penske	1st
Aug 11	Trans Am	Watkins Glen, NY	Camaro	Roger Penske	3rd
Aug 18	USRRC	Mid-Ohio, OH	McLaren M6A	Roger Penske	1st
Aug 25	Trans Am	Continental Divide, CO	Camaro	Roger Penske	1st
Sep 1	Can Am	Road America, WI	McLaren M6B	Roger Penske	3rd
Sep 8	Trans Am	Riverside, CA	Camaro	Roger Penske	DNF
Sep 15	Can Am	Bridgehampton, NY	McLaren M6B	Roger Penske	1st
Sep 29	Can Am	Edmonton, Canada	McLaren M6B	Roger Penske	3rd
Oct 6	Trans Am	Kent, WA	Camaro	Roger Penske	1st
Oct 13	Can Am	Laguna Seca, CA	McLaren M6B	Roger Penske	8th
Oct 27	Can Am	Riverside, CA	McLaren M6B	Roger Penske	2nd
Nov 10	Can Am	Stardust Raceway, NV	McLaren M6B	Roger Penske	DNS
Nov 23	World Challenge Cup	Mt. Fuji, Japan	McLaren M6B	Roger Penske	DNF
Dec 1	USAC	Riverside, CA	Eagle Mk4-Chevy	Roger Penske	DNF

1969

DATE	EVENT/SERIES	LOCATION	CAR	OWNER	RESULT
Feb 1	Daytona 24 Hours	Daytona, FL	Lola T70 Mk IIIB-Chevy	Roger Penske	1st

DATE	EVENT/SERIES	LOCATION	CAR	OWNER	RESULT
Mar 28	Sebring 12 Hours	Sebring, FL	Lola T70 Mk IIIB-Chevy	Roger Penske	DNF
May 18	Trans Am	Mi. Int'l Speedway, MI	Camaro	Roger Penske	2nd
May 30	USAC Indianapolis 500	Indianapolis, IN	Lola T152-Offy	Roger Penske	7th
June 8	Trans Am	Mid-Ohio, OH	Camaro	Roger Penske	7th
June 22	Trans Am	Bridgehampton, NY	Camaro	Roger Penske	2nd
July 6	Trans Am	Donnybrooke, MN	Camaro	Roger Penske	DNF
July 20	Trans Am	Bryar, NH	Camaro	Roger Penske	1st
July 27	USAC	Ind. Raceway Park, IN	Lola T150-Chevy	Roger Penske	DNS
Aug 3	Trans Am	St. Jovite, Canada	Camaro	Roger Penske	1st
Aug 10	Trans Am	Watkins Glen, NY	Camaro	Roger Penske	1st
Aug 17	Can Am	Mid-Ohio, OH	Lola T163-Chevy	Roger Penske	DNF
Aug 31	Trans Am	Laguna Seca, CA	Camaro	Roger Penske	1st
Sep 8	Trans Am	Kent, WA	Camaro	Roger Penske	DNF
Sep 14	USAC	Donnybrooke, MN	Lola T150-Chevy	Roger Penske	7th
Sep 14	USAC	Donnybrooke, MN	Lola T150-Chevy	Roger Penske	4th
Sep 21	Trans Am	Sears Point, CA	Camaro	Roger Penske	1st
Oct 5	Trans Am	Riverside, CA	Camaro	Roger Penske	1st
Oct 19	USAC	Kent, WA	Lola T150-Chevy	Roger Penske	16th
Dec 7	USAC	Riverside, CA	Lola T150-Chevy	Roger Penske	DNF
Dec 28	SCCA F-5000	Sebring, FL	Lola T190-Chevy	Roger Penske	DNF

1970

DATE	EVENT/SERIES	LOCATION	CAR	OWNER	RESULT
Feb 1	Daytona 24 Hours	Daytona, FL	AMC Javelin	Roger Penske	DNF
April 4	USAC	Sears Point, CA	Lola T150-Chevy	Roger Penske	25th
April 19	Trans Am	Laguna Seca	AMC Javelin	Roger Penske	2nd
May 9	Trans Am	Lime Rock, CT	AMC Javelin	Roger Penske	13th
May 30	USAC Indianapolis 500	Indianapolis, IN	Lola T152-Ford	Roger Penske	2nd
May 31	Trans Am	Bryar, NH	AMC Javelin	Roger Penske	3rd
June 7	Trans Am	Mid-Ohio, OH	AMC Javelin	Roger Penske	3rd
June 21	Trans Am	Bridgehampton, NY	AMC Javelin	Roger Penske	1st
July 5	Trans Am	Donnybrooke, MN	AMC Javelin	Roger Penske	19th
July 19	Trans Am	Elkhart Lake, WI	AMC Javelin	Roger Penske	1st
July 27	USAC	Ind. Raceway Park, IN	Lola T150-Chevy	Roger Penske	2nd
Aug 2	Trans Am	St. Jovite, Canada	AMC Javelin	Roger Penske	1st
Aug 9	Pro/AM	Ontario, CA	Porsche 914-6	OMS	4th
Aug 16	Trans Am	Watkins Glen, NY	AMC Javelin	Roger Penske	2nd
Sep 6	USAC	Ontario, CA	Lola T152-Ford	Roger Penske	30th
Sep 13	F5000	Mosport, Canada	Lola T192-Chevy	Roger Penske	1st
Sep 20	Trans Am	Kent, WA	AMC Javelin	Roger Penske	2nd
Sep 27	F5000	Mid-Ohio, OH	Lola T192-Chevy	Roger Penske	3rd

DATE	EVENT/SERIES	LOCATION	CAR	OWNER	RESULT
Oct 4	Trans Am	Riverside, CA	AMC Javelin	Roger Penske	3rd
Oct 25	F5000	Sebring, FL	LolaT192-Chevy	Roger Penske	1st

1971

DATE	EVENT/SERIES	LOCATION	CAR	OWNER	RESULT
Jan 31	Daytona 24 Hours	Daytona, FL	Ferrari 512M	Roger Penske	3rd
Mar 20	Sebring 12 Hours	Sebring, FL	Ferrari 512M	Roger Penske	6th
Mar 27	USAC Phoenix 150	Phoenix, AZ	Lola T152-Ford	Roger Penske	6th
Mar 28	F-1/F-5000 Questor GP	Ontario, CA	LolaT192-Chevy	Roger Penske	9th
Mar 28	F-1/F-5000 Questor GP	Ontario, CA	Lola T192-Chevy	Roger Penske	DNF
Apr 25	USAC Trenton	Trenton, NJ	Lola T152-Ford	Roger Penske	DNF
May 8	Trans-Am	Lime Rock, CT	AMC Javelin	Roger Penske	1st
May 29	USAC Indianapolis 500	Indianapolis, IN	McLaren M16-Offy	Roger Penske	DNF
May 31	Trans-Am	Bryar, NH	AMC Javelin	Roger Penske	DNF
June 6	Trans-Am	Mid-Ohio, OH	AMC Javelin	Roger Penske	2nd
Jun12-13	Le Mans 24 Hours	Le Mans, France	Ferrari 512M	Roger Penske	DNF
June 20	Trans-Am	Edmonton, Canada	Javelin	Roger Penske	1st
July 3	USAC Pocono 500	Pocono, PA	McLaren M16-Offy	Roger Penske	1st
July 4	Trans-Am	Donnybrooke, MN	AMC Javelin	Roger Penske	1st
July 17	Trans-Am	Elkhart Lake, WI	AMC Javelin	Roger Penske	1st
July 18	USAC Michigan 200	Mi. Int'l. Speedway, MI	McLaren M16-Offy	Roger Penske	1st
July 24	Watkins Glen 6 Hours	Watkins Glen, NY	Ferrari 512M	Roger Penske	DNF
July 25	Can Am	Watkins Glen, NY	Ferrari 512M	Roger Penske	DNF
Aug 1	Trans-Am	St. Jovite, Canada	AMC Javelin	Roger Penske	1st
Aug 15	Trans-Am	Watkins Glen, NY	AMC Javelin	Roger Penske	1st
Sep 5	USAC Ontario 500	Ontario, CA	McLaren M16-Offy	Roger Penske	DNF
Sep 6	Trans-Am	Mi. Int'l. Speedway, MI	AMC Javelin	Roger Penske	1st
Sep 19	F-1 Canadian GP	Mosport, Canada	McLaren M19A-Ford	Roger Penske	3rd
Oct 3	USAC Trenton 300	Trenton, NJ	McLaren M16-Offy	Roger Penske	6th
Oct 23	USAC Phoenix 150	Phoenix, AZ	McLaren M16-Offy	Roger Penske	DNF

1972

DATE	EVENT/SERIES	LOCATION	CAR	OWNER	RESULT
Jan 23	NASCAR	Riverside, CA	AMC Matador	Roger Penske	DNF
Feb 17	NASCAR Daytona 125	Daytona, FL	AMC Matador	Roger Penske	5th
Feb 20	NASCAR Daytona 500	Daytona, FL	AMC Matador	Roger Penske	DNF
Mar 5	NASCAR Ontario 500	Ontario, CA	AMC Matador	Roger Penske	DNF
Mar 18	USAC Phoenix 150	Phoenix, AZ	McLaren M16B-Offy	Roger Penske	DNF
Mar 26	NASCAR Atlanta 500	Atlanta, GA	AMC Matador	Roger Penske	15th
Apr 23	USAC Trentonian 200	Trenton, NJ	McLaren M16B-Offy	Roger Penske	DNF
May 27	USAC Indianapolis 500	Indianapolis, IN	McLaren M16B-Offy	Roger Penske	1st
June 4	USAC Rex Mays 150	Milwaukee, WI	McLaren M16B-Offy	Roger Penske	2nd

DATE	EVENT/SERIES	LOCATION	CAR	OWNER	RESULT
June 11	Can Am	Mosport, Canada	Porsche 917-10	Roger Penske	2nd
Sep 17	Can Am	Donnybrooke, MN	Porsche 917-10	Roger Penske	DNF
Sep 24	USAC Trenton 300	Trenton, NJ	McLaren M16B-Offy	Roger Penske	2nd
Oct 1	Can Am	Edmonton, Canada	Porsche 917-10	Roger Penske	1st
Oct 15	Can Am	Laguna Seca, CA	Porsche 917-10	Roger Penske	2nd
Oct 29	Can Am	Riverside, CA	Porsche 917-10	Roger Penske	3rd
Nov 4	USAC Phoenix 150	Phoenix, AZ	McLaren M16B-Offy	Roger Penske	DNF

1973

DATE	EVENT/SERIES	LOCATION	CAR	OWNER	RESULT
Jan 21	NASCAR	Riverside, CA	AMC Matador	Roger Penske	1st
Feb 2-3	Daytona 24 Hrs	Daytona, FL	Porsche 911RS	Roger Penske	DNF
Apr 1	NASCAR	Atlanta, GA	AMC Matador	Roger Penske	DNF
May 28	USAC Indianapolis 500	Indianapolis, IN	Eagle-Offy	Roger Penske	DNF
June 3	F-5000	Mid-Ohio, OH	Lola T330-AMC	Roger Penske	3rd
June 3	F-5000	Mid-Ohio, OH	Lola T330-AMC	Roger Penske	3rd
June 10	Can-Am	Mosport, Canada	Porsche 917-30	Roger Penske	7th
June 16	Trans-Am	Watkins Glen, NY	Porsche 911RS	Holbert's Porsche-Audi	8th
June 17	F-5000	Watkins Glen, NY	Lola T330-AMC	Roger Penske	2nd
June 17	F-5000	Watkins Glen, NY	Lola T330-AMC	Roger Penske	4th
July 1	USAC Pocono 500	Pocono, PA	Eagle-Offy	Roger Penske	DNF
July 7	Can-Am	Road Atlanta, GA	Porsche 917-30	Roger Penske	1st
July 8	Can-Am	Road Atlanta, GA	Porsche 917-30	Roger Penske	2nd
July 15	USAC	Mi. Int'l. Speedway, MI	AMC Matador	Roger Penske	DNF
July 21	Watkins Glen 6 Hours	Watkins Glen, NY	Porsche 911	Roger Penske	6th
July 22	Can-Am Heat 1	Watkins Glen, NY	Porsche 917-30	Roger Penske	1st
July 22	Can-Am Heat 2	Watkins Glen, NY	Porsche 917-30	Roger Penske	1st
July 28	F-5000	Elkhart Lake, WI	Lola T330-AMC	Roger Penske	6th
July 29	F-5000	Elkhart Lake, WI	Lola T330-AMC	Roger Penske	6th
Aug 8	Can-Am Heat 1	Mid-Ohio, OH	Porsche 917-30	Roger Penske	1st
Aug 8	Can-Am Heat 2	Mid-Ohio, OH	Porsche 917-30	Roger Penske	1st
Aug 19	F-5000	Road Atlanta, GA	Lola T330-AMC	Roger Penske	1st
Aug 19	F-5000	Road Atlanta, GA	Lola T330-AMC	Roger Penske	2nd
Aug 26	Can-Am	Elkhart Lake, WI	Porsche 917-30	Roger Penske	1st
Aug 26	Can-Am	Elkhart Lake, WI	Porsche 917-30	Roger Penske	1st
Sep 2	USAC Ontario 500	Ontario, CA	Eagle-Offy	Roger Penske	DNF
Sep 3	F-5000	Pocono, PA	Lola T330-AMC	Roger Penske	6th
Sep 15	Can-Am	Edmonton, Canada	Porsche 917-30	Roger Penske	1st
Sep 16	Can-Am	Edmonton, Canada	Porsche 917-30	Roger Penske	1st
Sep 30	F-5000	Kent, WA	Lola T330-AMC	Roger Penske	2nd
Sep 30	F-5000	Kent, WA	Lola T330-AMC	Roger Penske	2nd

DATE	EVENT/SERIES	LOCATION	CAR	OWNER	RESULT
Oct 14	Can-Am	Laguna Seca, CA	Porsche 917-30	Roger Penske	DNF
Oct 14	Can-Am	Laguna Seca, CA	Porsche 917-30	Roger Penske	1st
Oct 27	IROC	Riverside, CA	Porsche 911RSR	IROC	1st
Oct 27	IROC	Riverside, CA	Porsche 911RSR	IROC	DNF
Oct 28	IROC	Riverside, CA	Porsche 911RSR	IROC	1st
Oct 29	Can-Am	Riverside, CA	Porsche 917-30	Roger Penske	1st
Oct 29	Can-Am	Riverside, CA	Porsche 917-30	Roger Penske	1st

1974

DATE	EVENT/SERIES	LOCATION	CAR	OWNER	RESULT
Feb 15	IROC	Daytona, FL	Porsche 911RSR	IROC	1st
Sep 22	F-1 Canadian GP	Mosport, Canada	Penske PC1	Roger Penske	12th
Oct 6	F-1 U.S. GP	Watkins Glen	Penske PC1	Roger Penske	DNF

1975

DATE	EVENT/SERIES	LOCATION	CAR	OWNER	RESULT
Jan 12	F-1 Argentine GP	Buenos Aires	Penske PC1	Roger Penske	7th
Jan 26	F-1 Brazilian GP	San Paolo	Penske PC1	Roger Penske	DNF
Mar 1	F-1 South African GP	Kyalami	Penske PC1	Roger Penske	8th
Apr 5	F-1 Race of Champions	Brands Hatch, England	Penske PC1	Roger Penske	DNF
Apr 13	F-1 Daily Express Trophy	Silverstone	Penske PC1	Roger Penske	6th
Apr 27	F-1 Spanish GP	Montjuich Park	Penske PC1	Roger Penske	DNF
May 18	F-1 Monaco GP	Monte Carlo	Penske PC1	Roger Penske	DNF
May 25	F-1 Belgian GP	Zolder	Penske PC1	Roger Penske	11th
June 8	F-1 Swedish GP	Anderstorp	Penske PC1	Roger Penske	5th
June 22	F-1 Dutch GP	Zandvoort	Penske PC1	Roger Penske	8th
July 6	F-1 French GP	Paul Ricard	Penske PC1	Roger Penske	DNF
July 19	F-1 British GP	Silverstone	March 751	Roger Penske	5th
Aug 3	F-1 German GP	Nürburgring	March 751	Roger Penske	DNF
Aug 17	F-1 Austrian GP	Osterreichring	March 751	Roger Penske	DNS

Mark Donohue Career Race Results

Races   315

Starts	311
Finishes	237 (76%)
Wins	119 (38%)
Top 3	175 (56%)

Entrants (19)

Penske Racing	201
Mark N. Donohue (self)	55
Malcolm Starr	16
Yale Kneeland	9
Jack Griffith	7
R.M. Imports	6
Holman-Moody	4
IROC	4
Ken Brenn	3
John Mecom	2
Walt Hansgen	2
Shelby-American	1
TVR Cars Ltd	1
Renault Imports	1
Michael O'Hara	1
Herrymond Maurer	1
Holbert's Porsche-Audi	1
OMS	1
John Kalhoven	1

Circuits (57)

Watkins Glen	25
Marlboro	22
Vineland	21
Riverside	19
Daytona	16
Bridgehampton	15
Mid-Ohio	14
Lime Rock	14
Laguna Seca	11
Kent	10
Mosport	10
Elkhart Lake (Road America)	10
Sebring	10
Bryar	8
Nassau	7
Ontario	7
St. Jovite	7
Thompson	7
Donnybrooke (Brainerd)	6
Edmonton	5
Indianapolis Motor Speedway	5
Stardust Raceway (Las Vegas)	5
Trenton	5
Michigan Int'l. Speedway (MIS)	4
Phoenix	4
Road Atlanta	4
Le Mans	3

Pocono	3
Atlanta Motor Speedway	2
Connellsville	2
Continental Divide	2
Indianapolis Raceway Park	2
Meadowdale	2
Sears Point	2
Silverstone	2
Virginia International Raceway	2
Buenos Aires	1
Anderstorp	1
Brands Hatch	1
Bainbridge	1
Cumberland	1
Green Valley	1
Kyalami	1
Mexico City	1
Milwaukee	1
Modesto	1
Monte Carlo	1
Montgomery	1
Montjuich	1
Mount Fuji	1
Nürburgring	1
Paul Ricard	1
Roosevelt Raceway	1
San Paolo	1
War Bonnet	1
Zandvoort	1
Zolder	1

Cars (By model– excluding individual chassis)

AMC

1970 Javelin	13
1971 Javelin	9
Matador	8

Chevrolet

1967 Camaro	10
1968 Camaro	13
1969 Camaro	11

Cooper-Offy (Midget)	3
Daimler SP250	3

Eagle

Mk4-Chevy	3
7200-Offy	3

Elva

Courier	42
300 (F-Jr.)	9

Ferrari

250LM	1
512M	5

Ford

Cobra	7
Shelby GT-350R	17
GT Mk2	4
GT Mk4	1

Lola

T70-Ford	1
T70-Chevy	28
T70 Mk IIIB-Chevy	2
T150-Chevy	7
T152-Offy	1
T152-Ford	4
T163-Chevy	1
T190-Chevy	2
T192-Chevy	5
T330-AMC	11

Lotus

22 (F-Jr.)	1
20 (FC)	7

March 751	3

McLaren

M6A	9
M6B	7
M16A	6
M16B	6
M19A	1

MG

MGA	1
MGB	2

Penske PC1	13

Porsche

911RS	3
911RSR (IROC)	4
914-6	1
917-10	5
917-30	13

Renault 1093	1
TVR	7

Index

[Note: GP stands for Grand Prix; MD stands for Mark Donohue]

Walt Hansgen
His Life and the History of Post-War American Road Racing

Hardcover, 8 3/8" by 9", 400 pages
Photos: 140 black & white photos and 15 color photos
ISBN: 1-893618-54-4
$49.95

Walt Hansgen was a star in both sports cars and single-seaters, and his meteoric career carried him from the early days of amateur road racing to the very highest level of professional competition in America and Europe.

As the lead driver on Briggs Cunningham's dominant team, and later John Mecom's team, Walt evaluated and developed race cars working closely with Jaguar, Lister, Maserati, and Ford. At different points in his career he paired with Dan Gurney, Stirling Moss, John Fitch, Archie Scott Brown, and Augie Pabst on circuits as far-flung as Watkins Glen, Le Mans, Silverstone, Sebring, and Road America. Walt was a relentless competitor, but his sense of fairness and camaraderie made him respected by his peers and a leader in the sport. For many up-and-coming racers, including Mark Donohue, Walt was a crucial mentor.

The 1950s and 1960s were a time of tremendous change in racing. In this exciting, fast-paced biography author Michael Argetsinger shows how Walt's life encompassed the conflict between amateur and professional racing, the extraordinary advances in technology, and the joyful ambition of his era. The result is a vivid account of the remarkable history of post-war American road racing.

Argetsinger...has met [his] task superbly. Highly recommended —ROAD & TRACK

A worthy tribute to [Hansgen], and to a vanished era. —OCTANE

An incredibly in-depth and revealing picture of Hansgen's remarkable life —VINTAGE RACECAR

Kudos to David Bull for publishing this thumping 400-page hardback —MOTOR SPORT

A redlined ride. You'll love it —VINTAGE MOTORSPORT

A fascinating story of a man who very clearly left his mark —BRDC BULLETIN

Gold Medal winner and Best of Books —INTERNATIONAL AUTOMOTIVE MEDIA AWARDS